D1246934

*The Black Corps*

# The Black Corps

The Structure
and Power Struggles of the Nazi SS

Robert Lewis Koehl

The University of Wisconsin Press

Published 1983

The University of Wisconsin Press
114 North Murray Street
Madison, Wisconsin 53715

The University of Wisconsin Press, Ltd.
1 Gower Street
London WC1E 6HA, England

First printing

Printed in the United States of America

For LC CIP information see the colophon

ISBN 0-299-09190-2

*For my students*

# Contents

# Illustrations

# Preface

It is more than twenty years since I pored through the personnel records of SS officers in the Berlin Document Center. I was approaching forty as I spooled through endless reels of microfilmed SS records; now I am approaching sixty. Much of this study was completed in the years 1962–1968 and lay untouched except by a few of my graduate students. The encouragement to revise the manuscript and publish it at this time was supplied by Stanley G. Payne, my colleague and chairman of the University of Wisconsin-Madison History Department, 1979–1982. It is chiefly owing to him that the manuscript found its way to the University of Wisconsin Press and to the reading public. I wish to thank him, the readers, and the staff of the Press who have assisted me in making a difficult manuscript presentable. I wish also to thank the University of Nebraska and the Rockefeller Foundation for the assistance that made my travel to Berlin in 1960–1961 possible, and the librarians of the universities of Nebraska and Wisconsin for assistance in acquiring the myriad reels of microfilm needed for the research. To the Department of State and particularly to James S. Beddie, then Director of the Berlin Document Center, my special thanks for facilitating the all-important consultation of biographical records there. Thanks are due also to librarians at the Hoover Institution on War, Revolution and Peace at Stanford, the Wiener Library in London, the Institut für Zeitgeschichte in Munich, and the Center for Research Libraries in Chicago for their aid. In addition, I should like to express my appreciation to the Hoover Institution for supplying the photographs which appear in this book, and to the Cartographic Laboratory at the University of Wisconsin-Madison for preparing the maps. Last of all, I owe a debt of gratitude to the many people at National Archives who helped me get at the captured SS records in the 1950s before and during microfilming. Some must have wondered what happened to that young man in a hurry. Well, here he is, no longer in a hurry. A long bout with alcoholism, which is thankfully now over (a day at a time), has taught me to keep life simple. I hope this is a useful, substantial book. I have dedicated it to my students because they never lost faith in me.

# Introduction

The men in the black coats were, after all, men. Many but by no means all of them donned these coats as other men in other lands and other times might put on ritual masks and join in strange dances, to propitiate a threatening nature. They became "otherwise" and acted like men possessed. Such persons, both in their own consciousness and in that of their countrymen, acted for others in the German community who therefore did not have to participate directly in the ritual. Thus, they were permitted to torture and kill, to conquer and destroy, and to take part in a theatrical production of immense proportions. Yet this drama and its props remained exactly what it was for other ordinary men, both German and non-German: tinsel and cardboard.

Especially in the *Waffen-SS*,* in the field-gray of the front, SS men sought later to escape the curse of these same black coats, to become "just soldiers like the others" (*Soldaten wie die anderen auch*).† Indeed, in the field-gray uniform also, they were only men. But their SS past, the patterns of soldiering and of German society as well as national socialist power politics, thrust many of them into brave exploits, ruthless savagery, and thoughtless destruction. An SS unit of the *Wehrmacht* could never be just another military unit, although many of its officers and men were rather ordinary individuals. Tradition, that familiar concept in military annals, had its influence in the SS too and not always as desired by SS commanders — or by SS volunteers — forcing the man to become both more than himself, and a good deal less.

Adolf Hitler experienced this once in the uniform of the Bavarian Infantry. When the overlays of myth surrounding his military service have been removed, he too emerges as an ordinary man, whose Austrian accent was not erased by the uniform and who did not become a comrade or a hero yet nonetheless was stretched (and not merely inflated) into

---

*Waffen-SS* (Armed SS): This term was used after 1939 to refer to the former *Verfügungstruppen* (Special Duty troops), garrisoned military forces in contrast to the paramilitary and largely parade-ground General SS. The Waffen-SS became part of the Wehrmacht in 1939.

†*Soldaten wie die anderen auch* (just soldiers like the others): This is an expression attributed to Chancellor Konrad Adenauer (1953).

something new. This happened not merely for Hitler but for all the men who had grown up and lived in peacetime. The front generation of 1914–1918 was neither more nor less creative than its fathers. Its members made do with what they had, as all men do; and what they improvised out of their emptiness and their very partial fulfillment became their "messages" to the civilian world to which they were forced to return as arbitrarily as they were forced to leave it in 1914. None of the foregoing was unique to Germany; France, Britain, Italy, eastern Europe, and even Russia and the United States experienced the returned civilian-soldier as an alien if not an enemy, a confused and impatient reformer. Yet to the degree that each country, each environment, could replace what had been lost (or squeezed out) of the war veteran, that man gradually reintegrated himself into the civilian world. Individuals vary due to an infinite or almost infinite set of early influences, so that again in Germany as everywhere there were many exceptions. There was, after all, not much of a common denominator to "front experience." There was only a *potential* common denominator of a common uniform, to which the conditions of postwar Europe could then add content: defeat, disgrace, hopeless job conditions, political instability, and moral anarchy.

It is a commonplace today that national socialism was not Germany's inevitable fate any more than soviet communism was Russia's. The action and inaction of countless millions, by no means all of them in Germany or Russia, led to consequences of which they themselves were neither the masters nor choosers. But individuals *did* choose, *did* plan, *did* act; and these choices, plans, and acts had the consequences of communism and national socialism because of complex but not incomprehensible patterns of human behavior, especially *institutional* behavior. German institutions, and especially the processes of change in these institutions, provide the matrix in which individual goals, responses, improvisations, and concepts lead to predictable social and political consequences. Popular monarchy could become the Weimar presidency, ready for conversion into dictatorship; the Prussian army could evolve into the "school of the nation" with potential for becoming a people's army (*Volksheer*) or an elite cadre — or both. Germany evolved into national socialism without "choosing" it; individual Germans, faced with overwhelming changes in the framework of their lives, their expectations, their assumptions, their timetable of existence, *chose, planned,* and *acted* national socialism.

Nineteenth-century European states were the products of monarchical-aristocratic power compromises over recent centuries in which bourgeois elements had been grudgingly admitted out of necessity. Even in

Britain, France, Scandinavia, and the Low Countries, the remnants of monarchical-aristocratic power-monopoly were visible in the chief instruments of the state, the higher bureaucracy, the military, and the clergy. But what had happened first in these lands was increasingly characteristic of all the European states, especially those undergoing industrialization. Notably Germany but even Russia, Austria, Italy, the Iberian peninsula, and parts of the Balkans (perhaps even Turkey and Egypt) were experiencing a *pluralization* of power as opportunity had to be given—indeed was *taken*—by nonaristocratic, loosely identifiable as urban-bourgeois individuals, families, and groupings. Bismarckian Germany was a congeries of competing pressure groups, plastered over with a thin gloss of a novel patriotism and an untested commitment to a common national fate. The operation of its *new* political institutions depended heavily upon the skill of Bismarck himself, the product of that blend of urban bourgeoisie and country squiredom with which so many western European lands had prospered since 1700. Bismarck wisely used the older institutions of Prussia as long as he could to rule Germany and defend it, but inevitably he and the institutions of which his office was a part had to share the arena with the newly fledged *national* institutions and political formations of the Second Reich. After 1890 Germany, Russia, Austria-Hungary, and perhaps Italy and Ottoman Turkey struggled to modernize themselves as states before the centrifugal forces generated by economic and technological change rendered their old governmental and defense machinery totally inoperative. Germany was undoubtedly the most successful. Precisely because this measure of success rested heavily on Bismarck's Prussian legacy and on the energy and wealth of the post-1871 industrial revolution, most German and foreign observers alike failed to recognize the very sharp limits of German unity and national strength. It was natural that foreigners admired German military efficiency, the incorruptible civic authorities, the rational and humane systems of education and apprenticeship and penology, the imaginative and thorough business and professional man, the warmth and security of German family life, the loyalty and honesty of the German workman, etc.

To be sure, the shrewdest observers, often those with more than a little personal dissatisfaction with their own lives, could point to signs of social strain, cultural malaise, intractable dilemmas almost hidden in the rich variety of prewar German life. In reality, the problems which many Germans faced before 1914 were the same ones faced by numerous Britons, Frenchmen, Italians, and other Europeans. World war only exacerbated them and magnified them for all to see. These problems concerned the adaptation of the chief institutions of the society—the family, the community, the state, the church, the production unit, the military — to the satisfaction of newly felt and newly expressed demands for the wealth, the material and spiritual products of the system, for protection, status, and psychological security. The old narrow distribution of power was inconsistent with these demands, while even defense of the existing power bloc within the society as well as from outside the system required some sharing of power and rewards with the most effective challenges.

Something had to be done with the increasing excess rural, agricultural population no longer functional; the burgeoning population in metropolis and countryside had to be prepared in training and motivation to cope with a mechanized apparatus necessary to meet the demands of those capable of making their demands felt. Indeed, the regulation of human beings from cradle to grave, to prevent them from damaging the delicate and precious system, as well as the painstaking regulation of the interlocking parts of what no longer appeared to be a self-regulating economy and moral order, seemed to go beyond the powers of human intellect, courage, and decency. Moreover, all the certainties of religion and science were being swept away and with them the reliability of human experience, certainty of parental and authoritative preachments, and rightness of the social order. What a few thousand intellectuals worried over in little magazines and popular cafes before 1914 millions upon millions of autodidacts debated in the "movements" and beer halls of 1923. Before another decade had passed, few Europeans could ignore these challenges to the "eternal verities" of daily life; the Great Depression seemed to underline questions previously ignored. By 1945 the challenges and the "wrong answers" had spread far and wide beyond Europe, even after the experiments of national socialism had all failed.

While the *Kulturkritik** evolved, forming a body of doctrine from which later it would draw spiritual sustenance and fatal direction, the generation of middle-class Germans born after 1880 (those thirty-five or younger when war broke out in 1914) were raised in an atmosphere of pride in German achievements in every field. They were not to challenge the authority of "natural" *Obrigkeiten†* in the family, the school,

---

*Kulturkritik:* This term means literally "a critique of culture," but more specifically it refers to the literary and philosophical movement in German thought from the 1890s on which attacked the materialistic excrescences of the Wilhelmine era but also the assumptions of humanistic Kultur.

†*Obrigkeiten* (authorities): The German expression conveys a mystifying flavor absent from the English "authority" and is the subject of much German philosophizing. Similarly, the word "state" (*Staat*) conveyed the notion of a timeless entity quite different from our word "government." It occupied the sacred position once held by "the Crown."

the church, the military, and the state. Achievement was expected of
the young, and authority was held to be vested in those best able to
achieve and to inspire, compel, and teach achievement. In a system of
rewards and punishments that was merely a variation on a theme familiar in European bourgeois households for hundreds of years, the German youth was encouraged to turn all his energies to advantage, as
defined by his parents, teacher, clergyman, state officials, and heroic
figures of the past. Above all, young Germans learned to think of the
natural world around them as interesting and almost infinitely capable
of being studied — and what was more, turned to their advantage. The
scientific and technological bent of the prewar German was no accident
in spite of lags in schooling and survivals of preference for classical hu-
manism; to Germans, late-comers on the industrial scene, the more effective utilization of resources and tools was a necessity. The age-old
artisan values of German town life survived even in attenuation in the
tool-and-die maker; the quality requirements of the old guilds persisted
in the producers' associations, both in cooperatives and in cartels. In
spite of the wails of cultural despair from the critics, the German middle class was a good deal more communally minded than its British or
French counterparts. Dog-eat-dog competition was supposed to be al-
lowable only toward the outsider; Manchester liberalism was never
popular. Of course, in reality the small producer, the small community,
the small province *did* have to adopt every ruthless trick to survive competition with the larger units more efficient in using resources and tools.
The oldest short cut to success in the human repertoire was not underdeveloped among the German bourgeoisie: employing persons as tools.
Marx and Engels were Germans, after all, although they found their
best examples of human alienation in France, Belgium, and England.
By 1880 the German bourgeoisie was fighting a delaying action against
what threatens all scions of industrial society: treating *themselves* as
tools. The outsider, be he a newcomer from the countryside, a grimy
miner or ragged mill-hand, a Polish migratory laborer, or a Jewish ped-
dler, could more comfortably be treated as a tool; however, treating
fellow German *Bürger* as tools did not come easy. Yet this generation
found itself pressed inexorably up against the choice, "Either you use
*them* or you use *yourself,* but achieve you must!"

Under these conditions, rebellion was perhaps to be expected among
the young, but in Germany it was supposed to be channeled, as forcibly
as necessary, against *alien* tyranny, never against the home, church,
community, or state. Naturally, the reality was often otherwise. Some
middle-class youth did rebel against home, church, community, and
very marginally against the state, inspired in part by a few of their

elders, the *Schwarzseher** of the *fin de siècle*.† But most of the generation of the *Hohe Meissner*‡ were very patriotic and merely the pathfind-
ers of a greater German national unity. Like their brethren in other
lands, pre-1914 middle-class German youths went out to convert their
rural and proletarian age-mates** to the gospel of freedom, purity, service, and decency. That such gospels might be snares and delusions in
the German (or European) society of 1914 rarely dawned on this generation. It was slightly more likely that working-class youth or rural
members of the classes of '90–'99 might include in their revolt fathers
and clergymen, schoolmasters, and drill sergeants, the "Herr," and
*seine Majestät*. Many would be worn down and resigned by the end of
two years military service. The German social, economic, and political
system did not legitimize rebellion.

The rebelliousness of youth need not have become a problem in an expanding economy, indeed an expanding *society*, such as Germany, although it could threaten occasionally to join with protest from other
groups in the population during depression times in the 1880s and
1890s. Like youth everywhere in Europe, impatient young Germans assimilated the slogans, aspirations, and faiths of protest groups with
which they temporarily affiliated. These they carried forward into ma-
turity as nostalgic memories, unfulfilled dreams, and emotional re-
treats for the *Stammtisch*†† and the family reunion. Meanwhile they
thought they could rely on the security of Germany's political, social,
economic, and cultural institutions to stand like *rochers de bronze* in
the flood — to provide them and their offspring with strong, firm guidance, recognition, a livelihood, and a measure of happiness. In fact, the
German state, the Germany army, German business, the German social
elite (a blend of patricians, Junkers, and traditional aristocracy), and

---

*Schwarzseher* (literally "those who see black"): Another, somewhat derogatory term
for critics of Wilhelmine German, including the usual proportion of ordinary pessimists
about human morality, critics of urbanization, liberalism, socialism, etc.

†*fin de siècle:* Since *siècle* means both century and era, it was fashionable in the 1890s
throughout Europe to speak of the "end of an era" with overtones of "*Après moi, le
déluge!*"

‡*Hohe Meissner:* This is the location (a mountain in Hessen) of a famous meeting of
German youth groups on October 13, 1913, in protest against a militaristic celebration in
Leipzig of victory over Napoleon in 1813. They founded the so-called Free German Youth
movement.

**age-mates: This means persons born in the same year — not "classmates" because in
Europe members of different social classes went to different schools.

††*Stammtisch* (permanent table): In German coffee houses and beer taverns, a particular table was reserved for regular customers and their friends where they could feel perfectly "at home away from home."

the institutions that create and transmit cultural values — were changing very rapidly, with an increasing momentum. It was the *effective* adaptation by assimilation of the new and challenging elements in European life that made it possible for most Germans to take the solidity of their institutions for granted. The imagery of stability had often been combined with notions of "progress" in European thought, especially in the liberal era that was coming to an end in the prewar period. Precisely *because* change and adaptation was on the increase in Germany, the style of thought for individuals and groups already enjoying or expecting to enjoy the fruits of the society was insistently optimistic. Protests and demands for reform were referred to the future, just around the corner, while a rising standard of living, a more efficient distribution system, and the special advantages of Germany's entry into manufacturing just when she did gave credence to the promises.

Thus, even without the irreversibilities of the first world war, perhaps even more certainly than other national segments of the European middle class, the Germans were riding for a fall. As a "belated nation," the German bourgeoisie had postponed its reckoning with kings, bluebloods, cavaliers, princes of the church, and all their minions. After a long and rather exaggerated insistence on its impotence, German *Bürgertum* (bourgeoisie) was riding high by the last decades of the nineteenth century, proclaiming its prowess at home and abroad, with a blind eye to the social and constitutional chasms that lay between it and the power to determine its own destiny. In a tradition that was not solely German, numerous intellectuals actually supplied the invective and subtleties with which the relics of old classes created a mythological Reich in which *Pflicht und Gehorsam* (duty and obedience)* transcended class and caste, making social mobility unnecessary and even wrong. By comparison with this "golden ideal," the Wilhelmine reality was tawdry indeed. But in its infrequent encounters with the upper classes, the middle-class generation born after 1880 was inclined to be two-faced: obsequious and given to mimicry for official purposes while in private hostile and impatient to settle old scores.

It should not be surprising, therefore, if members of this generation of middle-class Germans should bring together after 1918 a *Weltanschauung*† composed in about equal parts of faith in idealized versions of the very institutions that had failed them by thrusting them unpre-

---

*Pflicht und Gehorsam* (duty and obedience): Always linked, these terms are clearly part of a military, in fact feudal, tradition. They are also Prussian.

†*Weltanschauung* (way of looking at the world): This term term originated with philosophers but had already become popularized by the 1920s among the semieducated younger generation. The Nazis especially cultivated it.

pared into a holocaust of defeat and destruction, and of determination to *succeed* the "next time" (in the not too distant future) by making up for the mistakes of the past. They conceived such mistakes as failure to carry out one or another of the "reforms" with which they as youths had been enamoured. The restoration of a "reformed" pre-1914 Germany was the common denominator which front veterans could share with their civilian brethren, both increasingly fed a diet of superpatriotism and mythology by the High Command. Since the "reforms" that had been advocated in German protest movements before 1914 reflected the imagery of various sub-classes and interest groups, with corresponding recipes for success, by 1919 there was a plethora of alternatives but no unity.

Pre-1914 Germany had been slowly bringing into existence a set of national institutions, with a corresponding national consciousness, out of a welter of divergent interest systems. It had already occurred to many intellectuals and ordinary thinking persons that this process had not gone far enough or fast enough. Perhaps, they felt, the war had been lost for this very reason! They wished to carry the process forward, speed it up, and get rid of roadblocks. Local loyalties, local bureaucracies, had to give way. Wider ties — religious, intellectual, economic — unity with something *all* Germans could not be loyal to had seemed threatening to national unity and the defense of German achievements and institutions long before 1914. With the help of the rich fantasy-life of the academic demimonde, the doctrines, myths, and misconceptions of pre-1914 chauvinism, anti-Semitism, and mystical imperialism were disseminated through the mass media. Stripped of a good deal of their refinement, these "explanations" became part of a cheap system of psychological defense and later weapons of attack for Germans in responsible positions in the institutions that had been found wanting. The Nazis only learned slowly to use these "stripped-down" fragments of ideology as tools; they were shown how by men of higher status and rank.

It was the *projective* potentiality of this "fashionable despair" which accounted for its popularity among a generation trained toward an unquestioning optimism and taught to channel hostilities away from home. The generation *could* have blamed itself, and many members did. They could have blamed their leaders. Some did this, but these leaders and their institutional underpinnings were only rocked and shaken by the events of 1914–1918, not swept away as so many thought at first. These leaders could and did fight back, with the weaponry of scapegoating, pointing out "alien, evil-doers" as the real cause of German suffering and failure. Instead of facing up to the conflicting loyalties and consciousnesses, indeed the conflicting *nature* of modern life, arch-Nazis — and many who just wore a pin or a uniform — projected outward onto Jews, Catholics, Marxists, and *Reaktion* the dangerous personal and national traits that supposedly led to 1918. Instead of realizing that German defeat was in part due to forces beyond German control, thus freeing German institutions and individuals from the *whole* burden of failure, the Nazis and their allies chose to preserve pre-1914 imagery of institutions as so many *rochers de bronze*. The institutions were superhuman; the guilt was all the fault of individuals, and unbearably so. Objectified and externalized in the "evil-doers" who profited from the defeat, eradication of the guilt by eradication of the "evil-doers" was the key to all the problems. But "eradication" itself threatens to add more guilt, and besides it is a dangerous measure when so much power is projected onto "evil-doers" that they can supposedly subvert superhuman institutions. So a *new* superhuman institution must be conceived to tackle the problem, in which "good" Germans can take shelter in preparation for the Armageddon, the "Movement" (*Bewegung*). By processes that do not require profound psychological insight to grasp, the accumulated destructiveness of numerous middle-class generations was concentrated in certain Nazi institutions — notably the SS. In a kind of societal "return of the repressed," the SS became the agent of German middle-class hostility.

Of course, the *Schutzstaffel* (guard squadron, the SS) did not spring in a trice from Hitler's forehead. It is remarkable enough how much of the SS did lie embryonically in the minds of Hitler's generation even before 1914. But the reality of the SS could only take shape gradually in the experience which the Nazis had in confronting the political exigencies of postwar Germany, with the naive imagery of pre-1914 youth. Membership in the bodyguard of any leader implies one's own importance: even the power of the strong man is incomplete without the guardsman. Since the academic soothsayers had created an elaborate modern justification for what so many men in different times and ages have craved, a messiah, Adolf Hitler could gradually *evolve himself* into a magical, quasi-religious *Führer*, the chief of a holy band of crusaders, the political soldiers of a "super pressure group." To be his bodyguard was to partake of his charisma, *to be important to him*. This sense of a special relationship to god-on-earth was a gift of grace Hitler knew very well how to foster among his alienated, *petit bourgeois* followers long before 1933; yet his "grace" was not limited to the SS. This special relationship was merely there, ready to be elaborated if the opportunity arose, by the right man. All the characteristics of the SS were not inevitable in national socialism. Himmler, R. W. Darré, and Reinhard Heydrich each made large contributions. Hitler himself started out with the "bodyguard" idea. Wilhelmine Germany spawned dozens of Teutonic secret societies; eugenic breeding schemes were not limited to prewar Germany, No one Nazi invented the SS, but much of its design reproduces the mental furniture of *Jahrgang '00** and postwar Munich.

Many Germans starting with the assumption that there had been a "natural order" in Germany before 1914 took the conditions of 1919 readily enough to be those of "a world turned upside down." If disorder was the result of revolution, then to reestablish "order" required another revolution, the conquest of power in the interests of all except the "evil-doers." Amid much groping, hundreds of groups in Germany decided that they were duty-bound to accept the responsibility of leading this revolution of restoration. Some wished to restore the Kaiser. Some preferred the Wittelsbach dynasty of Bavaria. Others thought of the Hindenburg-Ludendorff dictatorship of 1916–1918. Their common characteristics were a belief in violence, in conspiratorial technique, in whipping up the "masses" to follow *them* instead of the "evil-doers," and in the methods of German militarism. Power was something to be *conquered;* under conditions of extreme instability — politically, economically, socially, and psychologically — force and symbols of force were most appealing. If "pressure groups" dominated the political field, why not armed pressure? The armed reformer was the only reformer that seemed to matter in 1923. Amid the multiplicity of *Kampfgruppen,* † the *Stosstrupp Hitler*‡ did not stand out. In their field-gray, those Bavarian faces did not look different from those of opponents on the left and right, and their red swastika-armbands were not yet memorable. Yet their aggressive propaganda methods gave them a strategic advantage over many another group of armed reformers, although these methods too were hardly unique.

Out of just such elements, by accretion and trial-and-error, the Storm Troops evolved, through the disaster of November 1923 and many near-disasters after that until 1934 — with the *Schutzstaffel* merely another variety of themselves, a rather silly, even preposterous variety, exaggerating some of the romantic imagery of prewar and postwar Munich *petit bourgeois* youth. What might have been of no consequence except to the play-actors, with their black uniforms and death's heads, became

---

*\*Jahrgang '00* (Class of 1900): Heinrich Himmler's age-mates. This term refers to the birth cohort of a given year and is derived from military calculations. Comparable terms were used everywhere on the continent where conscript armies existed.

†*Kampfgruppen* (combat units): Strictly speaking, the armed units were "bands" (Verbände); "combat leagues" is also used to refer to the paramilitary units of 1921–1923.

‡*Stosstrupp Hitler* (Shock Troop Hitler) was the enlarged bodyguard of Hitler in 1923 that became the historical pattern after which the SS was modeled.

part of national socialism and thus part of Germany's struggle to adapt itself to the demands of an international machine age, the tremendous juggernaut of destruction for Jews, Poles, Yugoslavs, Russians, and Germans themselves. Even Himmler was quite incapable of choosing and planning for the SS to become all that it was in 1945. How much an SS leader could form and direct what he and his men would become depended on so many factors that at times even the hypnotic *Führerprinzip* (principle of leadership) failed the men in the top echelons, and they admitted that they had lost control. Theodore Eicke, Reinhard Heydrich, Otto Ohlendorf certainly formed and molded more in the SS than their own lives, while other SS officers, both named and nameless, created "refuges" in their corner of the SS bureaucracy for themselves and a few others. But for the majority of officers and men, the SS became a nemesis, a labyrinth in which at first they willingly lost themselves and later from which they could not escape back into humanity, even on furlough. Ironically and significantly, the front was their best camouflage. The Waffen SS remains even today the anonymous, if never wholly neutral, realm of the ex-members of the "Black Corps."*

Modern industrial societies — whether they have been defeated in war or not, whether they are prosperous or impoverished — must improvise new forms of action for their younger generations, must *grow* and expand in terms of their material output and distribution of that output as well as in terms of their use of resources, both human and inanimate. The NSDAP, the SA (brown shirts or Storm Troops), and the SS as well as numerous other Nazi institutions like the German Labor Front† and the *Reichsarbeitsdienst* (National Labor Service)‡ must be understood as cruel, wasteful, and wrong social efforts, partly conscious and partly unintentional, to do better what had already been done poorly or imperfectly by other processes in the society. Extreme measures of internal and external defense, the organization of other human beings as *tools* (rather than as co-workers), the gathering of information and the manipulation of information to control others — all these are the features of

---

*The "Black Corps" (*Das schwarze Korps*) was adopted as the name of the SS magazine in 1935 because the romantically inclined wished to make a parallel between the Schutzstaffel as a paramilitary unit in black uniforms and the similarly attired free corps volunteers of the 1813 War of Liberation. It has been chosen as the title because it conveys the theatrical, cheap romanticism of the SS.

†German Labor Front: This was a mandatory national union to which employees and employers had to belong and contribute. It enforced labor contracts and imposed settlements in disputes. It also sponsored productivity contests and after-hours recreation.

‡*Reichsarbeitsdienst* (National Labor Service): Compulsory nonmilitary service for both boys and girls of a year's duration, usually outdoor work including labor in agriculture.

most, if not all, modern societies in crisis. That the Germans produced in the dictatorship of 1933–1945 so foul and ghastly a combination of features should not tempt non-Germans to any spiritual pride; at best we can merely take warning from the misfortunes of a people. Like all of us, they did not choose their history, but they made many choices. It is to the dialectic of events, the consequences of past choices of specific men, that we must turn if we are to comprehend the SS.

# Abbreviations

| | | |
|---|---|---|
| **AHR** | *American Historical Review* | |
| **a.M.** | am Main | On the Main (River) |
| **AO** | Auslands-Organisation der NSDAP | Party organization for Germans living abroad |
| **AW** | Ausbildungswesen | Military training organization of the Storm Troops, 1933–1934 |
| **BDC** | Berlin Document Center | |
| **DAF** | Deutsche Arbeits-Front | German Labor Front |
| **DAL** | Dienstaltersliste der Schutzstaffel der NSDAP | Officers Rank List of the SS |
| **DAP** | Deutsche Arbeiter-Partei | Original German Labor Party from which the NSDAP sprang in 1920 |
| **DBFP** | *Documents on British Foreign Policy* | |
| **DF** | *Der Fuehrer* by Konrad Heiden | |

| | | |
|---|---|---|
| **DGFP** | *Documents on German Foreign Policy* | |
| **DNVP** | Deutsch-Nationale Volkspartei | German Nationalist Party |
| **FHA** | Führungshauptamt | SS Leadership Main Office |
| **FM** | Fördernde Mitglieder | Sponsoring or Supporting "Members" of the SS |
| **Gestapa** | Geheimes Staats-Polizei-Amt | Secret State Police Headquarters (in Berlin; origin of Gestapo) |
| **Gestapo** | Geheime Staats-Polizei | Secret State (political) Police |
| **GISASS** | General-Inspekteur der SA und SS | Combined SA and SS Inspector (1930–1932) |
| **GmbH** | Gesellschaft mit begrenzter Haftung | Limited Liability Company (Ltd.) |
| **GRUSA** | SA Grundbefehl | Fundamental SA Order |
| **HIGA** | Hilfsgrenzange-stellten | Auxiliary Border Employees |
| *Hitler* | *Adolf Hitler. Eine Biographie* by Konrad Heiden | |
| **HSSPF** | Höhere SS- und Polizei-Führer | Superior SS and Police Leaders |
| **I-A** | Political Police Office in Berlin (forerunner of Gestapa) | |

| | | |
|---|---|---|
| **I-C** | Intelligence Service or Intelligence Officer in German Army, Storm Troops or SS | |
| **IMT** | *Trial of the Major War Criminals before the International Tribunal at Nuremberg* | |
| **KL** | Konzentrations-Lager | Concentration camp |
| **KPD** | Kommunistische Partei Deutsch-land | German Communist Party |
| **KRIPO** | Kriminalpolizei | Criminal Investigation Division |
| **Lt. a. D.** | Leutnant ausser Dienst | Lieutenant, Retired |
| **MK** | *Mein Kampf* | |
| **MUL** | Mannschaftsunter-suchungsliste | Mustering Questionnaire |
| **NAPOLA** | National-Politische Lehranstalt | State Political High School |
| **NCO** | non-commissioned officer | |
| **NSBO** | National-sozialistische Betriebszellen-Organisation | National Socialist Factory Cell Organization |
| **NS** | *History of National Socialism* by Konrad Heiden | |

| NS-Dienst | Nationalsozialist- ischer Dienst | Camouflaged Storm Troops in the Sudetenland |
| NS-Mannschaft | National- sozialistische Mannschaft | Camouflaged SS in the Sudetenland |
| NSK | National- sozialistische Korresponenz | National Socialist Press Service |
| NSDAP | National- sozialistische Deutsche Arbeiter-Partei | National Socialist (Nazi) German Workers' Party |
| NSKK | National- sozialistische Kraftfahrer- Korps | National Socialist Automobile Corps |
| O.C. | Organisation Consul | Secret assassination (terrorist) band |
| OCS | officer candidate school | |
| OKH | Oberkommando des Heeres | Supreme Com- mand of the German Army |
| OKW | Oberkommando der Wehrmacht | Supreme Com- mand of the German Wehrmacht |
| Orgesch | Organisation Escherich | Underground group resisting compliance with Versailles |
| ORPO | Ordnungspolizei | "Order Police"; general purpose or regular police |
| OSAF | Oberster Sturm- Abteilung- Führer | Supreme Com- mander of the Storm Troops |

| | | |
|---|---|---|
| **O.T.** | Ordnertruppe | "Marshals" |
| **PI-Dienst** | Presse- und Informations-Dienst | Press and Public Relations Service |
| **PO** | Politische Organisation | "Political Organization"; cadre for mobilizing political activists (NSDAP) |
| **RAD** | Reichsarbeitsdienst | National Labor Service |
| **RGB** | Reichsgesetzblatt | Reich Law Gazette |
| **RKFDV** | Reichs-Kommissar für die Festigung Deutschen Volkstums | Reich Commissioner for the Strengthening of Germandom |
| **RMBliV** | Ministerialblatt des Reichs- und Preussischen Ministerium des Inneren | Ministerial Gazette of the Reich-and-Prussian Interior Ministry |
| **RSHA** | Reichssicherheits-hauptamt | Reich Security Main Office |
| **RuS** | Rasse und Siedlung | Race and Settlement |
| **RuSHa** | Rasse- und Siedlungs-Hauptamt | Race and Settlement Main Office of the SS |
| **SA** | Sturm Abteilung | Storm Troop(s) |
| **SABE** | Sturm Abteilung Befehl | Storm Troop Order (from the Supreme Commander of the SA) |
| **SD** | Sicherheitsdienst | Security Service (secret intelligence unit of the SS) |

| | | |
|---|---|---|
| **SGV** | Schriftgutverwalt-<br>ung des Persön-<br>lichen Stabes,<br>Reichsführer SS | Records Manage-<br>ment of the<br>Personal Staff,<br>Reich Führer of<br>the SS |
| **SIPO** | Sicherheitspolizei | "Security Police";<br>investigative po-<br>lice for criminal<br>and political<br>matters |
| **SS** | Schutzstaffel | Guard squadron(s) |
| **TV** | Totenkopf-<br>Verbände | Death's Head<br>Units |
| **TWC** | *Trials of War<br>Criminals before<br>the Nuernberg<br>Tribunals* | |
| **Uschla** | Untersuchungs-<br>und Schlicht-<br>ungs-Ausschuss | Investigation and<br>Conciliation<br>Committee (of<br>the NSDAP) |
| **VB** | *Völkischer<br>Beobachter* | |
| **VDA** | Verein für das<br>Volkstum in<br>Ausland | Society for<br>Germandom<br>Abroad |
| **VJHZ** | *Vierteljahrshefte<br>für Zeit-<br>geschichte* | |
| **VoMi** | Volksdeutsche<br>Mittelstelle | Liaison Office for<br>Ethnic Germans |
| **VT** | Verfügungstruppe | Special Duty<br>Troops (of the<br>SS) |
| **VVV** | Vereinigte<br>Vaterländische<br>Verbände | United Patriotic<br>Leagues (of<br>Bavaria) |

| | | |
|---|---|---|
| **VWHA** | Verwaltungs- und Wirtschafts-Hauptamt | Main Office for Administration and Economy (of the SS) |
| **WVHA** | Wirtschafts- und Verwaltungs-Hauptamt | Main Office for Economy and Administration (reorganization of VWHA) |
| **zbV** | zur besonderen Verwendung | On special assignment; temporary duty ("TDY") |

*The Black Corps*

# 1

## Prehistory 1919–1924
## The Wild Bands

When Hitler and his comrades of the Replacement Battalion of the Second Bavarian Infantry Regiment set about to plan a new kind of revolutionary party in the spring of 1919, they were acting like thousands of other German soldiers who since 1914 had become increasingly resentful at the civilian world. They did not wish to see themselves for what they were — civilians temporarily in uniform — because in civilian life they had been nonentities. Now that the civilian world lay in shambles, there was no excuse any longer to bow to its outer social or political forms. The new "party" should be, in brief, not a parliamentary fraction but a formation of political soldiers, intent on making good the error of the old army of being "unpolitical," of following incompetent civilians into defeat. They would bring order into the chaotic civilian world, for were not republicans and Marxists "merely civilians"? And was their thinking counter-revolutionary? Far from it — theirs was the true German revolution, the revolution of the trench soldiers.[1]

"Soldierly nationalism" in postwar Germany was to take a multitude of forms, many of them contradictory to one another. Before Hitler could become master of this powerful force, it had spawned numerous organizations, each of which became the matrix of a different type of political soldier. Many of these types were later to join together to form the Nazi Schutzstaffel. Though it did not come into existence until 1925, and scarcely counted three hundred members five years after that, the SS had its inception and acquired its basic ethos in the social and political maelstrom of the years 1919–1924. In these years many Germans experimented with new and revolutionary forms of political and social life; among them were the Nazis, who found meaning and personal fulfillment in their version of the ubiquitous political combat league (*politischer Kampfbund*) — the SA or Storm Troops, within which grew the future SS.

It is very likely that the stimulus for the formation of the rightist political combat leagues came with the formation of Soldiers' and Workers' Councils (*Soldaten- und Arbeiterräte*) and Red Guard (*Volkswehr*) units in the first days of the revolution in Germany. The negative image of these formations is regularly part of both Nazi and rightist literature devoted to the prehistory of national socialism, always alleging ruthlessness, cruelty, and bestial stupidity on the part of these units.[2] Why should not German soldier-patriots of the right turn the device around, against the Marxists, replacing "anarchy" with the orderliness of the great Prussian military tradition? This appears to be the intention of *Freikorps** leaders Maercker, von Epp, Reinhard, and some others when the Majority Socialists appealed for military assistance and gave Gustav Noske power to recruit volunteer units to guard the republic. But the very contradiction which was to haunt the relationship between the SA, the SS, and national socialism — the question of whether ultimately the tail would not wag the dog — crept in when the nominally Marxist republicans called back to arms the soldierly nationalists of the right to protect the regime against their revolutionary rivals.

The older exponents of the Prussian militarist tradition were themselves forced to call upon a generation of lieutenants, captains, and majors who were far more revolutionary than restorationist. In the guise of units for the restoration of order, junior officers like Ehrhardt, Rossbach, and Röhm constructed paramilitary forces — to enhance their own political prestige and power — against the old army clique which had lost the war.[3] Moreover, the trench soldiers such as Hitler, who were after all civilians in uniform, also found themselves in need of the counsel of the professional soldier class.

Thus, Hitler and the *Deutsche Arbeiter Partei* (German Workers Party) served as agencies of the Munich *Reichswehr*† headquarters in

---

*The *Freikorps* (free corps) were privately organized military and paramilitary units employed by the provisional regime in Germany in 1919 to fight the revolutionary left and Polish insurgents. The term harked back to similar units recruited to fight Napoleon in 1813.

†*Reichswehr* (Reich Defense): The so-called provisional Reichswehr was set up by the

1919. Hitler and his comrades were encouraged to enter the miniscule parties of the right and recruit likely candidates for paramilitary units like the *Einwohnerwehr* (Citizens' Militia) and the *Zeitfreiwilligen* (Temporary Volunteers).* The free corps leaders' purpose was always to remain essentially the same, though the aims of the Reichswehr leadership changed to the creation of a new model army to whose members soldiering for Germany was a way of life. The pattern for military manipulation of civilian life through patriotic parties had been set by the *Vaterlands-Partei*† of 1917. The north German *Stahlhelm*‡ and *Deutsch-Völkischer Schutz- und Trutzbund*** were products of the same striving to combine military preparedness with right-wing politics. It is true that the soldierly ideals of Ernst Röhm, the adjutant of Franz von Epp — the conqueror of the left-wing *Räte-Republik*†† — scarcely extended beyond counter-revolution and the reconstruction of a usable fighting force. In this Röhm had thousands of military counterparts. For such men any paramilitary organization of the right would do. However, the political movement which remained for men like Röhm merely a means

---

German National Assembly on March 6, 1919. It operated out of the General Commands of the old Imperial Army Corps.

*Einwohnerwehr* and *Zeitfreiwilligen* were local middle-class militias with a sprinkling of front soldier leadership. Their personnel usually slept at home and did not move far from their own communities. They functioned as guards and as auxiliaries for the free corps.

†*Vaterlands-Partei* (Fatherland Party): This organization was founded in 1917 by the German High Command to rally opinion behind a prolongation of the war for imperialist gains. It consisted of members of radical right groups like the Pan-Germans, Anti-Semites, and previously unorganized superpatriots.

‡*Stahlhelm* (Steel Helmet), also called *Bund der Frontkämpfer* (League of Front Soldiers): This veterans' organization was founded Christmas Day, 1918, retaining the imperial colors (black-white-red) as a symbol of its rejection of the republic and its black-red-gold flag. Stahlhelm members assisted in the *Grenzschutz Ost* (Border Defense East) paramilitary units defending Germany's eastern frontier against Polish irregulars.

**Deutsch-Völkischer Schutz- und Trutzbund* (German-Folkish Protection and Defiance League): Founded in 1919 with the explicit support of the Pan-German League, this anti-Semitic organization specialized in propaganda publication and rallies among the folkish movement in urban and small-town Germany. The "folkish" (populist) tradition dated back to the 1880s among the artisans and small business people overtaken by industrialization and urbanization. The system of regional *Gauleiter* of the *Schutz- und Trutzbund* was copied by the Nazis, and some Nazi gauleiters came over from the *Schutz- und Trutzbund* (Josef Grohé, Ludolf Haase, Martin Mutschmann).

††*Räte-Republik* (Soviet Republic) was the short-lived Communist dictatorship established in Bavaria April 7, 1919, to May 2, 1919. Largely confined to Munich, the badly organized and led "dictatorship" had a certain resemblance to the Paris Commune, including the execution of hostages. It was followed by a much bloodier "white terror" in the same parallel tradition.

to soldierly ends soon became for Hitler and his comrades much more
than a recruiting ground. Rechristened the National Socialist German
Workers Party (NSDAP), the former civilian conventicle became a soldiers' movement (*Bewegung*) into which Hitler and his friends poured
their dreams and their ambitions. Being civilians and thus by no means
as narrow as Röhm in their goals or methods, they absorbed the con-
tending tendencies of postwar Germany into their new party and improvised from them something remarkably successful within the cir-
cumscribed limits of the Bavaria of 1920–1923.[4]

Hitler seems to have realized very soon that the postwar parliamentary regimes rested on the masses as never before. The new age was to
be an age of propaganda. Much as the soldier in him detested persuasion, he grasped the dependence of modern states on it. Even before
1914 persuasion had ceased to be the reasonable, refined process of the
bourgeois press, the public lecture, or the formal debate. The war years
had exacerbated the lying style of a yellow press and irresponsible dem-
agogues. Press censorship, bribery, and strong-arm squads had made
their appearance along with the conspiratorial methods of infiltration,
spying, murder, and putsch used by bolsheviks and syndicalists. Without abandoning the elitist ideal of political soldiers as the core of their
movement, these civilian soldiers began immediately to consort with
quite unsoldierly types who were necessary for the capture of the masses
and for conspiracy. Thus, inevitably the first Nazis introduced into
their ranks the very contradictions of civilian society which they were
fighting, and which were in effect part of themselves. But they went
further and created a separate political soldierdom (*politisches Soldatentum*), resembling yet not the same as themselves (the SA, later the
SS) and never wholly subordinate to themselves. On the other hand, the
unsoldierly types with whom they had to work, and the civilian masses
whom they needed for the power the masses represented, seemed to
many far less admirable and indeed often despicable. The ambivalence
of German society in the early 1920s toward the soldier thus became a
permanent element in national socialism.[5]

This ambivalence is illustrated in the history of the strong-arm
squads of the infant NSDAP. The guards for the founding meeting of the
NSDAP on February 24, 1920, in the Hofbräuhaussaal am Platzl were a
squad of *Zeitfreiwilligen* (temporary volunteers) armed with pistols
and clad in the field-gray of the Munich Reichswehr to which they were
attached — perhaps as part of a mortar company. Supplied with the cooperation of Röhm and the rightist Minister of the Interior, Ernst Pöhner, they were composed of younger police officials and students.[6] Such

guardsmen might well be sympathetic, but there could be no thought of undying loyalty to the ridiculous little movement.

Certainly Röhm sent a number of the Bavarian Reichswehr division — perhaps also some of the *Einwohnerwehr* (citizen militia) and especially the young, temporary volunteers (*Zeitfreiwilligen*) — into the party itself. They were often avid nationalists, but their first loyalties lay elsewhere.[7] Hitler describes the very earliest party guards in October 1919 as some of his truest trench companions, probably as usual a more figurative than literal statement but an indication that he preferred his cronies' loyalty to Röhm's assignees.[8] Then in 1920 after the Kapp Putsch in March and the installation of the Gustav von Kahr regime in Munich, the field-gray had to disappear from the NSDAP. Hitler and his comrades had to accept discharges. Röhm found it advisable to disguise Reichswehr support of paramilitary and revolutionary activities.[9] The places of the soldier guards were taken by fifteen- to twenty-man *Ordnertrupps* (marshals) in civilian clothing with red armbands on which a swastika was displayed on a white disk. Possibly the use of the swastika symbol of the Ehrhardt-Brigade free corps on marshals' armbands indicates the role played by these veterans of the ill-fated Kapp Putsch as Nazi bouncers in the summer of 1920. In this thin disguise von Kahr and Pöhner permitted Röhm to keep a "force-in-being" for future use against the Republic.[10]

They were, however, unreliable and even mutinous bands, intrinsically less valuable to Röhm and the Nazis than the members of the well-organized Bavarian Einwohnerwehr system of Dr. Georg Escherich. Organized in towns ("banners"), counties, and regions (*Fahnen, Kreise und Gaue*), these farmers and white-collar workers formed an antitrade union, anti-Marxist militia, which extended west and north of Bavaria as the *Organisation Escherich (Orgesch)* and into Austria as the *Organisation Kanzler (Orka)*. These were counter-revolutionary bands loyal to Kahr, although they contained revanchist hotheads and conspirators.[11] Röhm tried for some time to capture this organization. He encouraged Hitler to copy the structure of Orgesch and enlist some of its radical membership in his strong-arm squads. Thus, toward the end of 1920 we find signs of a permanent and regular Nazi guard organization in Munich (*Saalschutz*, or hall-guard) grouped in hundreds (*Hundertschaften*) like the Orgesch. Indeed, they may have often been essentially Nazi "cells" within Orgesch hundreds strengthened with a few free corps men.[12] When Escherich unwisely tipped his hand by an armed anti-French rally during the 1920 *Oktoberfest* and Berlin passed a law requiring troops like the citizen militia to register and/or surrender their weapons, Röhm made preparations to abandon the Orgesch, branching out beyond the NSDAP in several directions to form in Munich not only a unit of the reactionary *Nationalverband Deutscher Offiziere* (National Union of German Officers) but accepting leadership of a Munich detachment of Captain Adolf Heiss's *Reichsflagge* free corps.[13]

While not exactly independent, Hitler began to improvise fighting forces out of his own immediate following, drawing upon other paramilitary groups for leaders and "stiffening." In January 1921 he felt strong enough as Nazi propaganda chief to threaten publicly in the large Kindl-Keller to break up "unpatriotic" meetings with them, and in February he was able to put some of them on "propaganda trucks" which roamed throughout Munich distributing leaflets and posting placards for the first mass meeting in the building of the Krone circus.[14] The success of these methods can be gauged by the continued growth in the size of the mass meetings. They paid off with Hitler's capture of the organizational structure of the NSDAP in July 1921, whereupon he strengthened and consolidated these "battle units" inside Munich and in the outlying towns of Upper Bavaria where Nazi groups had been founded.[15] However, owing to allied pressure during the summer, the strong-arm squads had to go through another metamorphosis: into *Turn- und Sportabteilungen* (Gymnastic and Sport Sections), which were really camouflaged party troops (*Schutz- und Propaganda-Truppe*) under the command of an Ehrhardt free corps officer and conspirator, Lieutenant Hans Ulrich Klintzsch.[16]

The dissolution of the Orgesch during the summer of 1921, due partly to the allied pressure and partly to internal dissension, weakened Kahr, so that he fell in September and was replaced by the moderate Lerchenfeld regime which favored cooperation with the Berlin government and the allies. Hitler and Röhm nearly parted company for the first time in the fall of 1921 (an episode to be repeated several more times until 1934), for Röhm now decided to back Escherich's successors, Dr. Otto Pittinger and Rudolf Kanzler, whose semimilitary and semiconspiratorial *Bund Bayern und Reich* toyed with a Danube federation and "temporary" dissolution of the Berlin tie. Röhm's motives were purely opportunistic; he saw no contradiction in simultaneously supporting the Nazis. Hitler, however, saw in Pittinger's group the Nazis' most dangerous rivals. Breaking up its meetings as well as those of the left became the chief function of the Sport-Abteilungen (SA).[17] In November 1921 Hitler adopted the term *Sturm-Abteilungen* (Storm Troops) and thus openly alluded to the elitist military ideal of the trenches. This suggested that the movement with military ideals should triumph over both bourgeois parliamentary parties and conspiratorial cabals. But could it also triumph against the irresponsible *Landsknechte** of the free corps on which it still depended?[18]

Throughout 1922 the Nazi movement continued to grow throughout Bavaria and penetrate northwards to middle Germany, and with it the Storm Troops, for they absorbed the semisecret *Arbeitsgemeinschaften* (work-groups) of the illegal free corps and feme† societies. Hitler's month of imprisonment in the summer of 1922 at the hands of the Lerchenfeld regime for the use of strong-arm methods against the Pittinger group did the Nazis no harm.[19] In August they displayed six SA "hundreds" among the 50,000-person *völkisch und vaterländisch‡* protest rally in Munich against the *Republikschutzgesetz*** and immediately attracted additional volunteers for more "hundreds." Under pressure from Röhm, Hitler tentatively made common cause with Pittinger in September 1922 in a putsch plot that failed to come off.[20] By October fourteen SA "hundreds" from Upper Bavaria were represented (about 700 men) in a demonstration-march to Coburg on the Thuringian frontier to join the Third Annual German Day of the Schutz- und Trutzbund. The latter organization was about to disappear due to the application of the Law for the Protection of the Reich, but its defiant invitation to the Nazis to join it in supposedly "red" Coburg led to Nazi intimidation of the town after pitched battles with democratic and left-wing groups.[21] In November 1922 Julius Streicher brought *völkisch* Franconia solidly into the Nazi sphere by merging his branch of the *Deutsch-Soziale Partei* with Hitler's, while in Munich the Nazis were pressed by Röhm into their first temporary alliance, the United Patriotic Societies (*Vereinigte Vaterländische Verbände*, VVV). In the north scattered bands of Nazis

---

*The original *Landsknechte* ("servants of the country") were mercenary soldiers of the sixteenth and seventeenth centuries who were romanticized by the German Youth movement before and after World War One, thus adding to the image of the Wars of Liberation (1813) that of the Peasant War and the Thirty Years War to blur the realities of the anti-bolshevik free corps.

†feme (German *Fehme*, or *Vehme*) was another resurrected historical institution, a popular lynch proceeding in the Middle Ages, applied in the 1920s against the political left and outspoken democratic liberals by secret clubs operating in a gangster mode. Probably the most infamous of these clubs was the O.C. (*Organisation Consul*).

‡*Völkisch und vaterländisch* (sometimes VV) stood for the folkish and conservative-patriotic movements, overlapping of course, in Bavaria and elsewhere which opposed the Republic and all it stood for (particularly the revolution).

**The *Republikschutzgesetz* was a Law for the Protection of the (German) Republic, passed after the assassination of Walther Rathenau on June 24, 1922, Rathenau having been a state official famous for the Rapallo agreement with Soviet Russia of April 1922. It made verbal or physical attacks on the regime high crimes.

opened up liaison with the new anti-Semitic *Deutsch-Völkische Frei-heitspartei* of Reinhold Wulle and Albrecht von Graefe.[22]

Behind this trend of consolidation lay the strivings of the whole German right and the hopes of the free corps — perhaps even of segments of the Reichwehr — for a German uprising against the demands for reparation. Now the NSDAP received unprecedented recognition by being forbidden by the state governments of Prussia, Saxony, Thuringia, and Hamburg. By January 1923 Hitler could summon to his first "national" Party Day several thousand SA men — a figure swollen by free corps members, of course. Their organization and outfitting had at this time been turned over to the air ace, Hermann Göring, a fellow student at the University of Munich with Rudolf Hess and Alfred Rosenberg. The first SA uniform of gray field jackets and ski caps was worn by the relatively well-to-do Munich student SA "hundred," led by Rudolf Hess.[23] But most of the SA wore whatever clothing they had, perhaps parts of their World War One uniform, sometimes a helmet with a swastika. Nor should we assume that these were organized "hundreds" neatly grouped in the four official "standards" (*Standarten*)* — Munich I, Munich II, Landshut, and Nuremberg. Everything was improvised, loose, changing from day to day. Records and rosters were not kept, and SA volunteers were not necessarily listed as NSDAP members either in *Ortsgruppen* (locals) or in the new, incomplete Munich party card file. Many of them were "members" of two or three *Wehrbünde* (defense leagues)† at the same time. Staunch "civilian" party members not in the SA were pressed into service for rallies and propaganda marches. Thus, most of the large figures for the early SA in Nazi sources, repeated by many later writers, are misleading.[24]

Misjudging the chances of success, the German right thought its hour had struck in January 1923 with the French occupation of the Ruhr. A state of undeclared war developed between Germany and France, in which the free corps groups again flourished openly and bourgeois par-

---

*The *Standarte* was literally a Roman "standard," consisting of a banner with a swastika reading "Germany Awake!" — an old folkish slogan — surmounted by the initials N.S.D.A.P. (in place of S.P.Q.R.!) and the eagle, also bearing the name of the community or unit below the scarlet banner. Like the *Fahne* (banner) of the Einwohnerwehr, the Standarte also denoted the unit itself. Choice of Standarte instead of Fahne probably indicates the influence of Italian fascism at this time.

†*Wehrbünde* (defense leagues) replaced the free corps to some extent by 1923, although they were often composed of free corps veterans and sometimes whole free corps units. Their membership was also drawn heavily from the former Einwohnerwehr and Zeitfreiwilligen. Of dubious legality, they were especially plentiful in Bavaria, which flouted the Republic and the entente.

liamentary procedures seemed more irrelevant than ever. Hitler himself was swept along with this tide, although not without misgivings. He detested alliances with rival groups, particularly with amateurs, patriotic businessmen, and republican politicians. He was afraid of being used by the Reichswehr and then cast aside. He had few illusions either about storming republican barricades or about the real intentions of colonels and generals of the old army. Nevertheless, he could not appear merely to want to go on propagandizing while patriotic Germans were *acting*.[25] Above all, his efforts to demonstrate his movement's strength in the Party Day planned for January 1923 in Munich forced him to reveal his dependence on Röhm and Röhm's military sponsors.

Under the influence of the lawless Nazi performance in Coburg and the Fascist takeover in Rome, Bavarian Interior Minister Franz Schweyer and Munich Police President Eduard Nortz forbade the Party Day and other Nazi demonstration-meetings as well. Hitler had to promise everybody not to try a putsch; ultimately it was von Epp and the top-ranking general in Bavaria, divisional commander Otto von Lossow, who arranged to let him have his rally. Six thousand volunteers were present from the various friendly combat leagues and the SA.[26] However, in return for saving face, Hitler had to let his "party troops" slip partly under the aegis of the Reichswehr. Röhm joined the SA with other combat leagues to form the *Vaterländische Kampfverbände Bayerns* under Lieutenant Colonel Hermann Kriebel, formerly of the Einwohnerwehr; Hitler could not even count on using his SA as he wished, for his men were turned over to Reichswehr officers for drill as an element of the secret reserve being formed throughout Germany as part of the Seeckt-Severing agreement to strengthen the hand of the Cuno regime in resisting the Ruhr occupation. The SA was organized more tightly and given a "general staff" of Reichswehr and free corps staff officers. Klintzsch served Göring for a time as head of this staff, withdrawing in the month of April, since a quarrel with Ehrhardt's *Wiking* free corps and O.C. (*Organisation Consul*) people in the SA was brewing, precipitated in part by Hitler's double-dealing with them and with the Reichswehr.[27]

At this time Hitler designated a squad of twelve bodyguards as a *Stabswache* (headquarters guard), composed of old comrades and persons personally dependent on himself. He had had a bodyguard or two before, and the idea of forming a headquarters guard out of it probably crystalized gradually in 1922. But now in the spring of 1923, his dangerous policy of double-dealing with the army and with the other combat leagues made him more fearful and therefore less willing to be dependent for his safety and that of his headquarters on just any "political soldiers." The Stabswache donned black ski caps with a skull and cross-bones.[28]

Hitler still did not really want to putsch. He did want to repeat the Coburg success by destroying the socialist May Day rally in Munich and demonstrate to his followers and his free corps allies that he still had control over the SA. He would not let Röhm stop him, nor indeed did Röhm dare, for the allegiance of the secret reserves seemed too tenuous. The call went out to the Vaterländische Kampfverbände Bayerns to assemble, and friendly members of the Reichswehr assisted them in taking weapons illegally from the Reichswehr barracks which they had already used from time to time on maneuvers with the Reichswehr. Hitler did not know whether to believe von Lossow's warnings that he would be fired upon by Reichswehr troops and therefore did not join his 6,000 volunteers in battle with the socialists on the morning of May 1; indeed confronted at noon with a token show of military force and abandoned by Röhm, he ordered the arms returned. Nobody was arested, but Hitler had lost important segments of his free corps and student volunteer allies (Zeitfreiwilligenkorps).[29]

In May Hitler authorized the formation of a crack military detachment, in part to replace the lost forces, in part to assure himself a fully reliable, mobile reserve separate from Röhm's larger undertaking. With the twelve-man bodyguard as cadre, Hitler created a hundred-man Stosstrupp (shock troop)* possibly out of the third Munich SA battalion (Abteilung)†, fully clad and accoutered as soldiers with a couple of trucks for special duty in support of propaganda marches, especially outside Munich and in workers' districts. In the fall the unit had acquired combat readiness for putsch employment by being divided into three platoons — an infantry platoon of four squads, a machine gun platoon, and a machine-pistol and mortar platoon. Here Hitler was improvising and characteristically tentative. The Stosstrupp was a relatively unpolitical military unit which could be used to support basically polit-

---

*Stosstrupp was a term like Sturm-Abteilung, carrying the elite ethos of the trenches. It referred to small "shock" or attack units. The term was employed in Germany after the war for strong-arm squads used by political groups; it was not unique to the Hitler movement. (However, the SA was.)

†Abteilung means both section and battalion. A Sport-Abteilung was the "Sport Section" of a party local; a Sturm-Abteilung, on the other hand, called to mind a "Storm Battalion" used to lead a trench attack or to hold an endangered sector. The SA Hundertschaft (hundred) became a battalion when it outgrew (during 1922) its numerical denomination. Each battalion was supposed to be composed of four companies, and four battalions made a Standarte (regiment). In reality 1923 Standarten were little more than battalions, and companies were temporary phenomena of the summer and fall of 1923. In fact, the whole Munich SA was grouped into SA Regiment München at the time of the putsch.

ical activity or for a putsch. Its formation can best be explained by Hitler's admiration for "pure soldiering," by his mounting fears of betrayal both by his free corps and Reichswehr allies, and by his grudging acceptance of the putschist mood of the summer and fall of 1923.

Although Himmler was not even in this Stosstrupp, and none of its members ever played a decisive part in the future Schutzstaffel, Nazi historians were to point to this diminutive and relatively unimportant formation as the origin of the SS. Nor was this a falsehood or an historical anomaly. The ambiguity of this improvisation of 1923 was transmitted through Hitler himself to the first small Schutzstaffel of 1925, from it to the insignificant group of Schutzstaffel throughout the movement between 1926 and 1929, and from 1929 on through the ambiguous Hitler-Himmler relationship to survive the death of Führer and Reichsführer in the pages of the Waffen-SS veterans' magazine, *Der Freiwillige*.[30]

It is incorrect to assume that the Nazis were badly hurt by the May Day fiasco. The Vaterländische Kampfverbände Bayerns continued in existence with extensive weekend "maneuvers" in the fields around Munich, Landshut, and Nuremberg. Party membership and participation in the SA grew to an unprecedented 55,000 and 10,000 respectively that fantastic summer of 1923. The chaotic inflation, the patriotic tension — often giving way to senseless internecine street squabbles and ambushes — the widespread expectation of communist revolution led many a right-wing *Spiessbürger* (philistine) into the ranks of the "wild and wooly" Nazis. The growth of the SA in 1923 must certainly be associated with its semi-respectability as part of the secret reserves under the auspices of the army. Lack of records makes it difficult to gauge the relative importance of "professional" free corps men and civilian part-time volunteers among the 10,000 recruits, but a perusal of numerous Nazi personnel records suggests the widespread presence of "floaters," individuals who were never in one free corps organization very long, who oscillated between civilian life and the combat leagues from 1919 until as late as 1932. Hitler had good reason to distrust the harvest of discontent which he and Röhm were reaping, but he nonetheless capitalized upon it. He authorized Göring to recruit paid officers with the requisite specialized talents to organize such supporting units for the SA as medical, motorcycle, cavalry, communications, light artillery, and technical battalions. At least temporarily both foreign and domestic monetary sources were available to pay for these right-wing mercenaries, who had little interest in Hitler or the Nazi Party per se.[31]

The Nazis certainly did not retire from their struggle for the center of the political arena that summer but used their SA for demonstrations,

propaganda marches, street brawling, and intimidation and for the
street-corner sale of the enlarged *Völkischer Beobachter*.[32] It is true that
there were severe limits upon their effectiveness. They could not rule
the streets of Munich unchallenged, let alone other comparable cities.
Nor could Hitler capture the Austrian Nazi Party at Salzburg that August, even with Göring's help in taking over the *Vaterländischer Schutz-
bund*, the former O.T. (Ordnertruppe) of Hermann Reschny, slated to
become the future Austrian SA.[33] But Berlin seemed to be playing into
Hitler's and Röhm's hands. The Cuno regime had fallen, and Stresemann had failed to win the north German radical right for a policy of
less than all-out resistance. Wulle and Graefe of the northern *Deutsch-
Völkische Freiheitspartei* courted Hitler; at the *Deutscher Tag* in Nuremberg on September 1–2, Ludendorff allowed himself to be made the
symbol of an all-German patriotic union (*Deutscher Kampfbund*). It
was a loose alliance, no better than the former VVV of 1922 and the
VKB of the spring. Hitler did not delude himself that he controlled this
ramshackle set up.[34] But there were many signs of a "revolutionary situation" in Germany in the fall of 1923. There was a total lack of confidence in the established order, into which even the Reichswehr was
swept for its failure to support continued and overt military resistance
against the French. Hitler and Röhm believed with some reason that
they could channel the forces of Bavarian separatism and hostility to
the renewal of a fulfillment policy in Berlin into a "March on Berlin"
modeled after the bloodless coup of Mussolini. They agreed on their use
of Ludendorff as a figurehead, the symbol of an undefeated and uncompromising Germany. Röhm, after being transferred out of Munich
by the Reichswehr, resigned his commission — apparently to cast his lot
finally with Hitler. This act undoubtedly impressed Hitler and many
others, in view of Röhm's uncertain behavior on the first of May.[35]

There was not a little desperation and a great deal of open rivalry in
the maneuvering behind the scenes. Many signs existed that the German right was considering a number of alternatives, none of them favorable to Hitler. A leading possibility was the formation of a "director-
ate" of big business, the landed interest, with representatives of the
Reichswehr, black-white-red Nationalists of the Stalhhelm sort, and the
Pöhner-Kahr axis in Bavaria. A less attractive arrangement was the formation of a number of German states independent of Berlin and supported by France, for example a Rhineland federation and a Danubian
federation. Stresemann and the moderates were considering a business
deal with Great Britain and the United States in connection with stabi-
lizing the mark. The more normal, more personally ambitious young
men of the combat leagues and the SA, especially the students and

white-collar workers, were thinking of taking jobs and getting married. When Wilhelm Brückner, commanding the SA-Regiment München, told Hitler this, it was already common knowledge. Ludendorff and the free corps leaders certainly knew it. Kahr, Ebert, and Seeckt knew it. There was a long risk involved in attempting to tip Kahr's hand, but the times might not be so ripe again.[36]

A number of "German Days" were sponsored by the Deutscher Kampfbund in Augsburg, Hof, and Bayreuth to whip up popular enthusiasm for a putsch. To each the Nazis sent their Stosstrupp Hitler, to reinforce their local SA and insure their speakers' prominence and to guard against "treason" from their comrades of völkisch and vaterländisch allied groups.[37]

When Stresemann announced the end of the Ruhr resistance September 24, Bavaria replied with the reinstitution of the von Kahr dictatorship and moved rapidly toward severing its connections with Berlin. Kahr was supported not only by Pittinger and Ehrhardt but one of the mainstays of Röhm's plans and of the abortive Deutscher Kampfbund, Captain Adolf Heiss's Reichsflagge, broke up over the issue of loyalty to Kahr. Röhm quickly reconstituted the south Bavarian contingents as the *Reichskriegsflagge* in which he placed his own trustworthy hangers-on such as young Heinrich Himmler.[38] Röhm — and even more so Hitler — was dependent on the willingness of Kahr and von Lossow, who had cast his lot with Kahr, to march on Berlin. When the Berlin regime took over the leftist Thuringian and Saxon administrations, which experimented with workers' militias, and the Rhineland separatist "movements" turned out to be flashes in the pan, Kahr and Lossow put off action, perhaps intending to bargain with both Paris and Berlin for greater autonomy. Hitler, Röhm, and Friedrich Weber, the leader of the Oberland combat league, decided to present Kahr and Lossow with a *fait accompli*, essentially out of desperation, for Hitler was doubtful from the beginning, and Röhm knew that the best he could hope for from Seeckt and the Reichswehr outside Bavaria was neutrality, as in the Kapp putsch.[39]

The Hitler putsch consisted of several improvised political demonstrations by persons in uniform, but as a military operation it was woefully inept. Too much reliance was placed on quick transfers of allegiance, theatrical shows of force, and symbolic gestures of coalition. Seizure of most Bavarian towns failed because SA, Bund Oberland, and Reichskriegsflagge units went to Munich. No serious effort to cooperate with putschists outside Munich occurred. Several hundred Munich SA surrounded the *Bürgerbräukeller*, and the Stosstrupp Hitler escorted the excited would-be revolutionary to the podium. For a while his bluff

worked; uncertainty as to the true conditions in the Reich and the mutual rivalries and distrust on which Hitler's movement had fed gave his
show of force an initial advantage. Röhm's Reichskriegsflagge and
Weber's Oberland combat league, however, contributed more effectively
to the atmosphere of a military coup than the bulk of the SA. Röhm used
the Reichskriegsflagge to surround army headquarters. The Stosstrupp
Hitler stormed the socialist *Münchener Post*. All the other putsch measures failed ludicrously. In the morning confusion reigned as to the future of the putsch, but before either army or police had fired a shot, a
few Stosstrupp members "arrested" the socialist mayor and the city
council. SA men "arrested" Jews and prominent socialists as hostages
and held them under guard in the Bürgerbräukeller. The Stosstrupp
half-heartedly tried to capture the downtown police headquarters but
gave it up without shooting. Toward noon about two thousand armed
men in parallel columns of four abreast — Stosstrupp Hitler on the left,
SA-Regiment München in the center, Oberland on the right — paraded
from the Bürgerbräukeller toward the bridge over the Isar which led to
the heart of Munich. They were greeted by cheering crowds, and they
overwhelmed undermanned police outposts at the bridge, crossing easily. Virtually surrounded now by excited onlookers and well-wishers,
they marched in the general direction of the surrounded army headquarters, through the narrow passageway to the right of the Feldherrnhalle. Here they were stopped by police with rifles held in crowd-control
position (horizontally or diagonally), but they pushed and jostled
through this cordon. They were now met by a second wave of police.
There is dispute about who opened fire, but certainly a brief fire-fight
ensued. There was some firing from the cover of buildings. Fourteen
putschists, one a Stosstrupp member, were killed. Another exchange of
bullets in front of army headquarters killed two members of Reichskriegsflagge before a surrender was arranged. Groups of Bund Oberland surrendered after a brief skirmish. Of the sixteen dead, none were
members of the SA. A few SA officers, one of them a Wiking (Ehrhardt)
free corps leader, even proved disloyal at the last minute.[40]

Hitler was forced to recognize that his "political soldiers" had been
worthless as revolutionaries and that alliances with free corps leaders,
party politicians, and Reichswehr officers were fragile in the extreme.
His trial early in 1924 was a twenty-four-day sensation which resulted
in much favorable publicity for those of his followers who remained
outside prison walls; and Hitler permitted himself in his closing speech
to extol the "wild bands" of "our growing army" which would one day
grow into regiments and divisions.[41] But he already had second
thoughts, and at Landsberg prison he took little interest or pleasure in

the electoral successes of the *Völkisch-Sozialer Block* (Folkish-Social Block) which had been formed as an electoral coalition of his followers with the northern Freedom Party, or in the growth to 30,000 of Röhm's *Frontbann* into which flowed his SA as well as many other free corps veterans. Hitler came to see how falsely conceived was the opportunism of Röhm and of some of his own followers, who imagined political soldiering to be merely gathering personnel and driving them forward to the attack as if politics were merely "going over the top" en masse as in 1916. He resigned the leadership of the *Hakenkreuzler* (men of the swastika) in July 1924, partly for superficial tactical reasons (to get out of jail), partly for deeper strategic reasons: he thereby hoped to avoid responsibility for the disintegration which he foresaw at a time when many of his followers still believed in early fulfillment of the glowing promises of his final plea.[42]

The year 1924 in Germany began radical and ended conservative. The armed bands were very much in evidence in the early part of the year, since unemployement was soaring and wages under the new *Rentenmark* had plunged to a new low after the ridiculous shopping bags full of near-worthless notes had come to an end. Political violence continued into the summer, and the May 1924 elections gave the Communists, the far right, and the Nazi-folkish coalition sizeable gains. Distrust of the moderate parties — including the Social Democrats — was correspondingly reflected in loss of seats in the Reichstag. Yet by the time Hitler temporarily withdrew from responsibility for his feuding supporters in July, German industry was hiring again, the merchants and bankers were confident enough to arrange future orders and mortgage loans, and the far right (*Deutsch-Nationale Volks-Partei*, German Nationalist People's Party) was swallowing the Dawes Plan to bail out Germany by an international gold loan so the country could resume reparation payments and get France out of the Ruhr. The fellow-travelers among the combat leagues gradually drifted off to get married or join the more respectable Stahlhelm, although the hard-core Landsknechte continued in a hundred different bands loyal to some charismatic captain or major. The business world no longer wanted them around; they were refused handouts, and shakedown attempts began to lead to jail sentences. By December another Reichstag election reduced the Nazi-folkish representation to twelve, the Communists lost their gains of May, and the moderates made a small comeback to join with the far right in ruling Germany until 1928. The political soldiers would have to take on the ballot box and show that the struggle could go on in that form too, as long as necessary until they had power to do away with it. The SS was conceived within this new context.

# 2

## The Early Years
## 1925–1929

Kerle aus besonderem Schrot und Korn[1]

The putsch resulted in the proscription of both the Nazi Party and the Storm Troops in most of the German *Länder* (states). As a consequence, northern national socialists joined up with Wulle and Graefe's *Deutsch-Völkische Freiheitspartei* (German Folkish Freedom Party), by early 1924 well established except in Munich, Nuremberg, and Bamberg. Even in Landshut, hometown of the Strasser brothers, Otto and Gregor, the DVFP spoke for the folkish movement and similarly in Bavarian Coburg and Hof, as well as across the frontier in Thuringia and western Saxony. True, the NSDAP was never proscribed in Thuringia, led there by the religious maverick Artur Dinter. But Julius Streicher, Max Amann — Hitler's old sergeant, now editor of the *Völkischer Beobachter* (renamed *Grossdeutsche Zeitung*) — and the party orator Hermann Esser as well as the party's philosopher and link with radical right conspirators, Alfred Rosenberg, founded a substitute organization, if not precisely a political party, the *Grossdeutsche Volksgemeinschaft* (Greater German Folk Community). Having collaborated electorally with the DVFP in the May 1924 elections as the *Völkisch-Sozialer Block* (Folkish-Social Block), the ultraloyal Hitlerites reversed themselves when Ludendorff seemed to threaten to replace Hitler in the leadership of the *National-Sozialistische Freiheitsbewegung* (National Socialist Freedom Movement) in the summer of 1924. This folkish unity

18

ploy failed because Hitler saw it headed for putschist adventures along with Röhm's Frontbann. Another initiative from the north was the *National-Sozialistische Arbeitsgemeinschaft* (National Socialist Work Community), formed of pro-Hitler locals who refused to join the Freedom Movement.[2] Each of these factions was associated with paramilitary bands, each professed loyalty to Hitler, and each would contribute divergent tendencies to the reconstructed NSDAP of 1925, causing suspicion and fear in the Munich leadership for which the future "ultraloyal" SS was supposed to be a remedy.

Hitler's loss of the field to Röhm and Ludendorff in the heyday of the *völkisch* (folkish) movement — the summer of 1924 — necessarily led to a loss of influence on the SA membership, which was compounded by the official illegality (even if only nominal) of the Storm Troops and the adhesion of many newcomers to the Hitler movement to the northern folkish wing with its parliamentary ambitions. Röhm's Frontbann was a loose confederation of disparate combat leagues which retained their individual identity throughout 1924 and into 1925. Organizations like the black-white-red Stahlhelm that Hitler hated were welcomed by the Frontbann as allies, and SA units camouflaged as sport and hiking societies often fraternized extensively with non-Nazi paramilitary "clubs" like the *Jungdeutscher Orden, Tannenbergbund,* and *Blücherbund.** Formal responsibility for the SA slipped from hand to hand, from Walter Buch, former commander of the *SA-Regiment Frankenland,* to Wilhelm Marschall von Bieberstein, free corps leader and commander of a Munich SA batallion, and thence to his adjutant, Emil Danzeisen, in the winter of 1924–1925. Röhm utilized Hitler's passivity to press SA men into the Frontbann, while Captain Gerd Rossbach and his young associate, Edmund Heines, sought to seize the SA from the faltering hands of quarreling and despondent party bosses and merge it with their brown-shirted *Rossbach-Organisation*† and *Schill-Jugend.*[3]

According to a secret handbook of the Frontbann, that organization was to be divided regionally into three types of units: Storm Troops (*Sturm-Abteilungen,* not necessarily the Nazi units of the same name);

---

*These groups were more or less conspiratorial, more or less armed, right-wing "clubs" which flourished in urban Germany among young men of bourgeois background, both of the front generation and younger. Their political goals were opposition to cooperation with the victors, opposition to the Republic, and hostility to Marxism. Not strictly combat leagues, they tended to be locally based, with local policies and interests.

†The *Rossbach-Organisation* was a combat league, while the *Schill-Jugend* was a youth contingent organized on a local basis by Heines. The two units were notorious for homosexuality and for their wearing brown shirts which had been prepared for German colonial troops, acquired from the old Imperial army stores.

Reserves (*Stamm-Abteilungen*), made up of inactive veterans willing to serve in emergencies and to drill once a month; and a Stosstrupp, a "police unit and model unit (of company strength) for the support of military propaganda, composed of the best personnel." The organization was divided nationally into three almost independent commands ("Groups"), *Gruppe Nord, Gruppe Mitte,* and *Gruppe Süd.* Theoretically, each Gruppe was divided into sectors (*Abschnitte*), and each sector had one of these Stosstrupps. In fact, except for staff units, most of this organization was on paper, but it was to leave its mark on the Nazi SA and SS.[4]

The Frontbann was well designed as the paramilitary ally of an authoritarian, rightist revolution from above in which the parliamentary National Socialist Freedom Party could have cooperated with the *Deutsch-Nationale Volks-Partei* (DNVP) and the Reichswehr. But the tide of revolution receded in the summer of 1924, and the demagogic withdrawal of the Freiheitspartei from a Reichstag which approved the Dawes plan with the aid of black-white-red votes was not the trumpet summoning the paramilitary forces to a popular revolution to free Hitler from prison or place Ludendorff in Berlin as dictator. In fact, the day of the folkish parties was waning fast. While the combat leagues remained and the formal framework of the Frontbann was to persist and thus complicate the task of reconstructing the SA, the rapid disintegration of the Freiheitspartei even before its defeat at the polls in December 1924 paved the way for the victory of the ridiculously parochial splinter "party" created by Streicher, Amann, and Esser in Munich, the Grossdeutsche Volksgemeinschaft as the unadulterated embodiment of Hitlerism.[5]

After a short delay, due to the putschist maneuverings in both northern and southern echelons of the Frontbann — squelched by a series of arrests including that of the SA leader Wilhelm Brückner in Munich — Hitler was released from Landsberg prison in time for Christmas, 1924. Hitler hastened to assure the Bavarian regime of his legalitarian change of heart; neither they nor many of his followers could quite believe it. Hitler did not know exactly how he was going to come to power — but he knew how he was *not* going to make it, which was a good deal more wisdom than that possessed by Röhm and most of the Frontbann leaders. Röhm tried to hold on to the Frontbann throughout the spring of 1925, although Ludendorff had already abandoned it as a lost cause (only to take up his wife's fanatical anticlericalism). Röhm and Hitler completely failed to understand one another. Hitler still hoped to subordinate Röhm and a future SA to the role of a *condottiere* of propaganda troops at the beck and call of party leaders who were political soldiers,

with the accent on political. Röhm still imagined that political soldiering was a good in itself and that he and his confederates should be on
even terms with "civilians"; they were political soldiers with the accent
on soldiers. Finally, in May 1925 it was Röhm's turn to vacate the field
to Hitler. He turned the Frontbann over to the commander of its
Central Group, Count Wolf von Helldorf* and, like Rossbach and Ehrhardt, withdrew into a semiprivate life to conduct intrigues as a part-
time amusement.[6]

Hitler succeeded in getting the rival Nazi factions to join him in refounding the National Socialist German Workers Party in February,
and slowly throughout 1925 the local political organizations reformed
and separated themselves from the folkish groups with whom they had
been merged or allied. Patiently the business manager, Philipp Bouhler,
repeated to local party officials that the question of the SA was not yet
settled. Organization, clothing, and leadership would be decided upon
soon. He urged them to make out as best they could in "self-defense"
with whatever personnel was available. There was no national SA, and
even in Munich, Nuremberg, and Landshut the SA was not clearly separate from the Frontbann and the other combat leagues. Legally the SA
was still forbidden throughout the Reich, where it did exist as a separate, distinctively Nazi organization; and in view of the number of persons under eighteen in such groups, it was often little more than a social
club of young roughnecks.[7]

Already in March 1925, in the course of the reestablishment of a party
headquarters soon to be located at Schellingstrasse number 50, Julius
Schreck, one of Hitler's drivers and a veteran of the earlier Stabswache,
reformed the headquarters guard detail with the other drivers, the personal bodyguards of Hitler, and a few of the Stosstrupp Hitler who had
been in prison with Hitler, numbering twelve in all. In April 1925 eight
of these men served as torchbearers in the funeral for Ernst Pöhner,
killed in an automobile accident. During the summer, when it became
clear that Röhm was not going to assist in the reforming of the SA, Hitler decided to recommend to local party leaders the formation of small
guard details on the model of the Stabswache. They were to be known
as *Schutzstaffeln* (guard squadrons) — a term entirely new, subject to no
old prohibitions, not identified with sports or free corps traditions, con-
noting if anything, a *garde mobile*, since Staffeln were widely identified with cavalry, motor and air squadrons. It was stipulated that they
should be about ten in number, selected from the most reliable of the

*Wolf von Helldorf would become a leading Storm Troop Commander in Berlin, then
the Police Chief of Berlin, and finally a conspirator against Hitler.

party members of an *Ortsgruppe* (party local). They were to wear black caps with a skull and crossbones, the insignia of the old Stosstrupp Hitler.[8]

The call for the formation of Schutzstaffeln was issued by driver Schreck September 21, 1925, "with reference to the approval . . . by Herr Hitler and the Party leadership," along with a set of guidelines for the men named as leaders of the new groups by gauleiters or the leaders of independent party locals. The names of the designated leaders, who must unreservedly subscribe to the guidelines, were to be submitted to the *Oberleitung der Schutzstaffel der NSDAP*\* (note the singular usage of Schutzstaffel here). In order to keep things tightly under control, membership cards could be obtained only from the *Oberleitung* (OL), which would supply application forms. Applicants had to secure the endorsement of two local party members — one of them prominent — be registered with the police in their locality for five years, be between twenty-three and thirty-five years of age, and be of powerful physique. Dues were to be one mark a month, and the items of the uniform cost altogether sixteen marks, all of which was to be sent to the OL. Furthermore, special cards were to be distributed for use in collecting donations for the Schutzstaffeln, but only one-fourth of such collections might be retained locally along with a fund to transport the unit to Munich and back. The units were to be employed as salesmen for the *Völkischer Beobachter*, both of subscriptions and advertisements for which prizes were to be offered for the highest sales. Members were to clip all references to the movement in other papers and magazines and send them in for the archives of the Oberleitung and were also to collect data on embezzlers, confidence men, and spies in the movement for the OL.[9] That this was no imaginary problem is indicated by the large number of such tricksters reported in 1925 by the outlying party headquarters and also a report by Schreck to Munich headquarters September 24 of a denunciation of Hermann Esser at a local meeting in Neubiberg, which Schreck thought should be looked into.[10]

The rush into the Schutzstaffeln was not overwhelming. Numerous local party chapters were getting along by using some combat league or other. Hamburg was using the adolescents from the conservative *Blücherbund*. Berlin was using the Frontbann with Hitler's blessing. Cuxhaven was using the right-wing Stahlhelm. The Ruhr had formed its own SA already in 1924 under free corps leader Franz Pfeffer von Salomon. Amid three-cornered rivalries such as existed in Saxony between

---

\**Oberleitung der Schutzstaffel der NSDAP: Oberleitung* means High Command. This military term did not stick. The term *Schutzstaffel of the NSDAP* would technically be preserved but rarely used.

Helldorf's Frontbann, *Organisation Rossbach/Schillbund*, and an SA that would not recognize the official *Gauleitung*, there was little personnel left over for a new guard unit.[11] Schreck complained to the Munich Party headquarters on November 27 when the *Völkischer Beobachter* innocently reported that day a ludicrous "founding" of a Schutzstaffel in Neuhausen at a family evening between musical and theatrical numbers, which was in fact merely the rechristening of some fifteen former SA men by a self-styled SS officer from Schwabing of whom Schreck had obviously never heard. Schreck also forwarded a complaint in November to the *Parteileitung im Hause** from a traveling party speaker against the SS leader in Silesia, who was in fact the business manager of the gau, for drunkenness, molesting women, small thefts, etc. Letters Schreck wrote to Viktor Lutze,† the SA leader in Elberfeld, requesting assistance in forming a Schutzstaffel remained unanswered. Nevertheless, on the second anniversary of the November putsch, the Schutzstaffel was officially proclaimed in Munich in a ceremony at the Feldherrnhalle and in the *Völkischer Beobachter*, so that in later years the SS traced its founding to this date and commemorated the occasion in a far more elaborate ceremony of oath-taking‡ at the Feldherrnhalle.[12]

In later years it would also be alleged that the Schutzstaffeln had been formed especially for use in Thuringia and Saxony because public meetings there, while supposedly legal for the NSDAP, were so threatened by "red" hecklers. There is some evidence of an early SS in Thuringia, where meetings were indeed legal; in Saxony where they were not, there were serious *Saalschlachten* (battles for the hall) that the Nazis lost in 1925, and one of the earliest Schutzstaffeln was founded in industrial Plauen. Nevertheless, the legend probably developed after the extensive Nazi electoral campaigns in these two states in 1926, in which SA were used fully as much as Schutzstaffeln, a curious relic of the early, and recurring, argument about the proper role of SS and SA. The SS claimed that it could and should guard party meetings, having been created for that purpose; the SA felt that this was its prerogative. In places where there had been no SA (Thuringia) or where the SA was in a disintegrated state (Saxony), the SS got a head start; but the Schutzstaffel was not created for these areas alone, nor as a permanent substitute

*Parteileitung im Hause:* Presumably Schreck then had a desk himself at Schellingstrasse #50, so he directed the complaint "to the Party Leadership in the building."

†Viktor Lutze would become Röhm's successor as chief of the SA. He never liked the SS.

‡oath-taking at the Feldherrnhalle: The German term *Verpflichtung* (from *Pflicht* or "duty") means, literally, swearing-in. The Feldherrnhalle was the monumental shrinelike museum honoring Bavaria's generals, before which fourteen of the Nazis were shot on November 9, 1923.

for the Storm Troops. Something of a temporary substitute while Hitler regained control of the SA, the early SS must have been big bruisers of the traditional storm trooper variety. However, from their initiation they were supposed to form local units for special tasks of security where a small number of men were sufficient and for intelligence purposes.[13]

Most of the seventy-five Schutzstaffeln in existence at the time of the Weimar Party Day in July 1926 were formed in the spring of 1926. Heinrich Himmler, the business manager of the *Gau Niederbayern*, was just getting Schutzstaffeln organized in April and May, and as late as July wrote urging the Munich party headquarters to order the "gentlemen of the Schutzstaffel" to hurry and send one hundred application forms, a characteristically overoptimistic number. Already in February 1926, however, the *Oberpräsident* of the Prussian province of Hanover sent out a notice to the *Regierungspräsidenten* (Prussian district chiefs) regarding the formation of Schutzstaffeln, which he correctly described as opposed to members carrying arms, maintaining weapons caches, or belonging to combat leagues. Even more, he identified the motives of the party leadership as separation from the folkish and *Wehr* (defense) organizations. In contrast to the secrecy of these other groups—especially the Frontbann—the Nazis probably welcomed this "revelation," especially since they were as yet far from achieving their purpose of freeing themselves from dependence on such groups for protection.[14]

The *SS-Oberleitung* was personally responsible for guarding the anniversary meeting of the party on February 25, 1926, in Munich, an indication that as yet the Munich Schutzstaffel and the Oberleitung were one and the same. The Munich Schutzstaffel had its baptism of fire alongside of SA in civilian clothes at an anticommunist meeting jammed with leftists on March 31. The "hall guards" of the NSDAP of Danzig-Zoppot in March consisted of the chairman, his brother, and two others; they applied for SS membership. The next month when a meeting was called to found an SA, forty-five Nazis who had just been expelled from the Danzig *Einwohnerwehr* (citizen's militia) for forming "cells" signed up. By July there were seventy-five SA men outfitted personally by the Danzig gauleiter, and twenty *Schutzstaffelleute* (SS people), led by the assistant gauleiter.[15]

The Oberleitung, though diminutive, was not without its intrigues that spring. A certain Ernst Wagner went with the assistant chief of the Schutzstaffel, Erhard Heiden, to Philipp Bouhler and F. X. Schwarz,*

---

*Philipp Bouhler was the general office manager of the Nazi headquarters. Franz Xaver Schwarz was the treasurer of the NSDAP.

and later to Hitler, to request that Joseph Berchtold, who had returned to take over the Munich SA—left leaderless by the refusal of Wilhelm Brückner to continue without Röhm—also take on the Schutzstaffel, heavily criticizing Schreck. While Bouhler and Schwarz resented this attack on Schreck, Hitler did in fact give the SS to the old commander of the Stosstrupp Hitler in April, who began by sacrificing the intriguer to Bouhler and Schwarz. Although Wagner had just returned from organizing trips to Heilbronn and Esslingen, he was excluded from the Oberleitung headquarters.[16]

Berchtold's greater initiative was responsible for a recruiting campaign for the SS in the *Völkischer Beobachter* and in local recruiting evenings set up by the gauleiters. He also rewrote the guidelines for the SS and founded an ancillary organization of SS sponsors (*Fördernde Mitglieder*)* to raise funds, all before the Party Day in July 1926. He stressed that the SS should be a collecting center for front veterans while insisting that it not be a combat league. He reduced the dues but made life and accident insurance† compulsory. He gave the local party chairmen the power of expulsion but reserved the right to hear appeals, and claimed the exclusive power to name Schutzstaffel leaders. He ordered that the Schutzstaffel must consist of at least ten men (never really observed until 1929) and that they meet twice a month as units. Monthly membership rosters must be submitted. Above all, he denied that the SS was subordinate to the SA.[17] In his early appeals in the form of personal letters to SS Sponsors (FM), he stressed the need for transportation costs to bring the scattered Schutzstaffeln together for effective service at the time of visits of major party speakers and at meetings of the party leaders, quite frequent in 1925–1926. He clearly did not want the Schutzstaffeln to degenerate into local bands to enforce the petty wishes of small-time party bosses. He fought bitterly with the gauleiter of Halle-Merseburg in June for disbanding an officially authorized Schutzstaffel because it did not agree with his political direction, apparently successfully, since the gauleiter soon left the NSDAP to form a more radical, leftist national socialist splinter party. Similarly, Berchtold wrote sharply to Viktor Lutze in Elberfeld in April scolding him for neglecting the SS.[18]

At the party congress in Weimar, Hitler rewarded Berchtold for his

---

*\*Fördernde Mitglieder* (FM): Literally, supporting members, these "sponsors" were not members of the SS, but they received numbered tiny silver SS pins for their lapels.

†life and accident insurance: "Bouncing" and street fighting were dangerous to life and limb. Uninsured SA and SS men's relatives sought to sue or otherwise collect from the party. Later a fund was devised to "insure" SA and SS personnel when insurance became too expensive or unobtainable.

energy by bestowing on him, as self-styled Reichsführer of the Schutz-staffel, the *Blutfahne* of November 9, 1923 — the flag stained with the blood of Andreas Bauriedel. Of the alleged "thousand" SS membership, only a fraction was present at the National-Theater for the ceremony. Probably the transportation funds were not sufficient. The SA is sup-posed to have sent 3,000 in their new brown shirts, purchased from Heines's mail order house, the *Sportversand Schill*. Heines soon re-placed Berchtold as SA commander in Munich, bringing into the SA the Bavarian *Rossbach-Organisation* and *Schill-Jugend*, the original "brown shirts."

Very likely many of the "SA" at Weimar were these very units, just as many of the SS present were Berchtold's old Munich companions of the Stosstrupp Hitler.[19] Though the break with the past was thus still not complete, Hitler had won major battles in the party organization over the insubordinate northern faction of Goebbels and Strasser. His charis-matic consecration of eight SA standards by simultaneously touching the Blutfahne and the new banners symbolized not only his own central position but also the clear intention to continue the SA as well as the SS. By September 1926 the police already had heard that Hitler had de-cided on Pfeffer von Salomon as Supreme SA Leader (*Oberster SA-Führer*), although Gregor Strasser had wanted the post.[20] This was to prove a fateful decision! Pfeffer, whose Ruhr SA had been a model of *Hitler-Treue* (Hitler loyalty), would become a lesser Röhm, while Stras-ser's new job as propaganda boss was to advance his assistant, Himmler, from the gau office in Landshut to the Munich headquarters as deputy propaganda chief. The SA, although nominally politicized, was handed back to the soldiers; and the future Reichsführer SS (from January 1929) began to make political contacts throughout the movement but espe-cially in Munich.[21]

Hitler's "good behavior," his repeated admonitions to SA and SS alike to stop playing soldiers, and the peaceful recovery of Germany that made putsches unthinkable disposed nationalistic bureaucrats to per-mit the Storm Troops to organize and march openly in the fall of 1926. Thus, the Schutzstaffeln were no longer so vital to the protection of public meetings and electioneering street-corner assemblies. Nor was the absolute loyalty of the SS to Munich and to Hitler so decisive after the Frontbann dissolved or swung behind Hitler and as Goebbels and then the Strassers gave up the effort to depose "the Munich Byzantines." Berchtold uneasily acknowledged the suzerainty of Pfeffer in the fall of 1926 and was "confirmed" as Reichsführer by Pfeffer on the anniversary of the formal founding of the SS, November 9, 1926. But Berchtold rap-idly lost interest and relinquished his office in March 1927 to Erhard

Heiden, the unimaginative second-in-command under both Schreck and Berchtold. The latter turned his talents to writing for the *Völkischer Beobachter* while maintaining a connection with the SA, believing perhaps that the Storm Troops held after all the promise of political soldiering which for a time the Schutzstaffeln had seemed to offer.[22]

In his fourth SA order (SABE, i.e., SA-*Befehl*) of November 4, 1926, Pfeffer stated that the Oberster SA-Führer had the power to name the Reichsführer of the SS, to designate which communities were to have Schutzstaffeln (only the larger ones), and to regulate temporary situations where well-organized Schutzstaffeln existed without a comparable SA structure. Normally the SA commander of an area was to be responsible for the commitment of the SS. Sabe 4 goes on to emphasize that the SS was to consist of men especially hardened to individual employment (*Einsatz*) in contact with opponents, in contrast to the SA — which could expect to be used *en masse*. Thus was preserved a sort of elitism, although no mention is made of a requirement that the members be party members as well.[23] It would be safe to say, however, that the local SS commanders in the period 1925–1929 were usually party officials such as the business manager of the local branch; they rarely appear as officers in the SS officers' lists of the 1930s. A dozen or so "founders" of local SS-Staffeln finally made it to *Sturmführer* (second lieutenant) in 1933 or 1934 as a retrospective recognition. Another sixteen men clearly have officer rank before 1929, including Berchtold and Heiden, but neither Berchtold nor Heiden were listed in the SS during the 1930s. Rudolf Hess, although he was never assigned an SS number, may certainly be regarded as an SS officer during this period, as revealed by many old photographs of him in SS attire.[24] Clearly, the status of SS officer (*Staffelführer*)* was uncertain and of variable importance as compared to positions in the party and even in the SA. To judge from the records of very early SS "privates," they only needed a party card and a good physique.

Preserved in a magazine called *Die Schutzstaffel*, of which only the second issue of the first year (December 1926) is known to the author, are accounts of joint propaganda activities by small SS and SA units in Saxony, Thuringia, and Danzig. The methods of the Salvation Army are enthusiastically recommended along with torchlight processions, bonfires, and wreath-laying. Combat "maneuvers" are also described,

---

*Staffelführer* (squadron leader): This is the only "SS officer's" rank until 1930 when the SS introduced *Stürme* and *Sturmbanne* (companies and battalions like the SA). Like the SA, the SS preferred the term "Führer" (leader), developed in the prewar German youth movement, to *Offizier*, a foreign loan word.

apparently without weapons and in very small proportions (squads). An atmosphere of boyish earnestness survives in the accounts. Police and newspaper records suggest more dangerous and bloody pastimes whenever the police were absent or passive. No differences between SS and SA are ever mentioned.[25] Pictures from the years 1926–1929 rarely show ten SS men together, although they are clearly distinguishable in their black hats and sometimes black riding breeches. They are intermingled with numerous Storm Troopers, though often in positions of prominence, obviously bodyguards for Hitler or some other party speaker.[26]

As early as November 13, 1926, Himmler, signing for the *Propaganda-Leitung*, sent out a warning to propaganda officials of the regional organizations based on secret intelligence information on Stahlhelm, Ehrhardt, and Rossbach activity sent in by gauleiter Hildebrandt of Mecklenburg to the Oberleitung of the SS. The SS was beginning to function as an intelligence unit in close collaboration with propaganda. It was not long before Himmler was made second-in-command of the SS in September 1927 under Heiden, a logical combination with the former's propaganda work. Himmler's own experience in raising and organizing the SS of Lower Bavaria gave him an added advantage. As deputy propaganda chief, he had the problem of arranging speakers for the gaus, which inevitably brought with it the question of "protecting" them from catcalls, broken-up meetings, and occasionally physical harm. The existence of a small Schutzstaffel guaranteed that protection — at least at a minimum — was available.[27]

Hitler was indeed pursuing an uncompromising path of legality. The work of the party was one of organizational consolidation under the absolute authority of the Munich headquarters while at the same time it entered every public debate as well as municipal and state elections and sought to reach the unpolitical masses by street-corner rallies, beer hall gatherings, meetings in the tenement backyards, and tens of thousands of leaflets as well as the *Völkischer Beobachter* and a slowly increasing number of other magazines and newspapers. While Hitler never repudiated violence as an aid to propaganda, and it was rarely absent from news of Nazi activities in the years 1926–1929, he did not expect to destroy his opponents by force—only to hold them at bay while the movement went about its missionary work with the German people. Hitler had no different intentions for SA and SS in this respect, although their employment might vary. In times of middle-class comfort and modest optimism, the Nazis could not afford excesses of rowdyism or the amoralism of the free corps. In May 1927 Heines, an unsavoury figure, was dismissed from the Munich SA leadership and Pfeffer strengthened the discipline and chain-of-command in the SA. As never before, the party organization became *petit bourgeois* through and through, and Heinrich Himmler, the deputy SS leader was a perfect example of the type.[28]

Himmler was well educated not only by Nazi standards but even in the context of postwar Germany: he was the graduate of a *Technische Hochschule* (Institute of Technology) with a diploma in agronomy. His father was a university-educated high school teacher who had tutored a scion of the Bavarian Wittelsbach dynasty for a time. In fact, Heinrich Himmler was named after the tutee. Young Himmler wanted to be a soldier but was twice cheated of real service — first in 1918, when he spent the year in officer candidate school without ever going near the war; and in September–October 1923, when he briefly belonged to a unit of the "Black Reichswehr" known as "Werner Company" organized to crush the leftist Saxon and Thuringian regimes. It was formed out of Captain Heiss's Reichsflagge combat league, which Himmler had joined with some of his friends from the Hochschule and from his job at a fertilizer factory. When "Werner Company" was dissolved by the Bavarian regime as unreliable (the Berlin government had liquidated the leftist regimes in Saxony and Thuringia), Röhm put Himmler and his friends into Reichskriegsflagge, where they camped around the Munich Reichswehr headquarters and Himmler got his picture taken with the unit flag. He was not even arrested. He joined Röhm's folkish officers' league (*Deutsch-Völkischer Offiziersbund;* Himmler was theoretically a second lieutenant, retired) and looked for a new job in desultory fashion. In July 1924 he became the secretary for Gregor Strasser in Landshut, then gauleiter of the Lower Bavarian National Socialist Freedom Movement. He bought a motorcycle and began speaking at local rallies. In May 1925 when Strasser joined the new NSDAP, Strasser was still gauleiter of Lower Bavaria, but he now designated the twenty-five-year-old Himmler as his deputy and business agent. It was in this capacity that Himmler organized the SS in Lower Bavaria. In September 1926 he moved with Strasser to the Munich party headquarters in the Propaganda Section. Now in 1927 he became engaged to a thirty-five-year-old nurse who had her own clinic in Berlin. They planned to buy a small farm in nearby Waldtrudering and raise chickens!

The effect of Himmler's firm hand and his taste for detail are revealed in SS Order No. 1 of September 13, 1927. While praising the Schutzstaffeln for having "passed the test" of the Nuremberg Party Day, in which they had functioned as honor- and bodyguards of the Führer, the author also orders a tightening of uniform regulations to avoid a repetition of the motley effect of *Lederhosen* (short leather pants), colored sports apparel, etc. Black sports breeches, black neckties, and black leather equipment must accompany the brown shirt and the black hat. The Schutzstaffeln were to have four activities every month: to attend the first discussion meeting of the party local in uniform *but not to engage in the discussion*, to hold two training meetings where drill and singing were practiced, to carry out a propaganda march or a meeting with a neighboring SS — in case the fourth occasion had not already been provided by "protection" duties at public meeting. The SS commanders were urged to make systematic intelligence reports on the following as the basis for the formation of an intelligence service: (1) unusual activity among opponents, (2) names of prominent Freemasons and Jewish leaders, (3) special events in the community, (4) secret orders of the opposition, and (5) press clippings about the movement. The commanders were reminded to stay out of intraparty politics but to report improper conditions to the Oberleitung of the SS, to have their Staffeln on a twelve-hour alert basis, and to get their dues, insurance premiums, and monthly rosters in on time. SS members with official positions in the SA and in the party were to be reported as well as those still incompletely outfitted.[29]

There were probably fewer than seventy-five active Schutzstaffeln between 1927 and 1929. Official membership seems to have fallen from 1,000 to 280. But it would be wrong to say that the SS was reabsorbed by the SA at this time or that it fell into inaction. The first and subsequent SS orders breathe a spirit of hard-bitten vigor and slow, if not steady, growth. If Aachen and Danzig are scolded by name for their inactivity, Frankfurt-am-Main is praised for its initiative in dyeing its uniforms and selling the most *Völkische Beobachter*. Plans are made for "motorization" of Staffeln by collecting information about drivers' licenses, access to vehicles, etc. Berchtold's clever scheme of SS Sponsors (FM) to supply the SS with funds above and beyond its dues was rigorously applied and perfected during these years.[30] Unlike the SA, which since the summer of 1926 was supported by a ten pfennig per member tax on the general NSDAP membership, the SS was without party subsidy; indeed its members sometimes paid the SA subsidy. The SS lived very frugally, without an expensive overhead or staff organization such as the SA soon developed. No one seems to have devoted himself full time to the SS, not even Heiden or Himmler, though Himmler accomplished more for the organization in time taken from his propaganda activities than Heiden — who seems to have become a fifth wheel, hanging around the offices of the *Beobachter* as a survival of an earlier free corps type, now more a hindrance than a help. Himmler must have found many SS officers less businesslike than he in view of the earnest scoldings issued for reports sent in on scraps of paper, false reports, clippings sent without identifying newspapers, recruits under age and size, failure to salute SA officers, disrespect of party bosses, and so on.[31]

Beside the reborn SA, the SS had other rivals. In Berlin, for example, Reinhold Muchow's reports to the Munich party headquarters tell of not only a *Zivil-Ordnungs-Dienst* (public order service) but also the formation of a *Freiheitsbund* (freedom league), three hundred strong, founded by the new gauleiter Goebbels to finance and staff a special duty combat unit, "the future noncommissioned officers of the new state." Kurt Daluege, the head of the old Berlin Frontbann, was serving as Goebbels's deputy as well as both SA and SS chief and leading a very vigorous — indeed vicious — around the clock attack on "reds."[32] The early SS officer (Kurt Wege) who was his subordinate could never be anything but an appendage; Daluege's position was the important one, and throughout the Reich there were a dozen Nazis like him, none of them SS men.

It was in the years 1927, 1928, and 1929 that so many of the colorful local Nazi leaders emerged from the brown mass of petit bourgeois *Vereinsmeier* (club enthusiasts). The men over forty, i.e., older than Hitler, were thanked for their services and thrust aside to make room for the "Front Generation," more ruthless, better organized, lacking the veneer of pre-1914 Germany. Men like Erich Koch in East Prussia, Karl Kaufmann in Hamburg, Fritz Sauckel in Thuringia, and Josef Bürckel in the Palatinate were in many respects the embodiment of Hitler's conception of the political soldier. They did not "play at soldiering," nor did they indulge in the "paper wars" (*Papierkriege*) of an older generation of *Stammtischhelden* (beer club patriots) and amateur parliamentarians. They set about the business of organizing propaganda on a modern mass scale in their communities, and they used whatever methods came to hand, including conspiracy and violence.[33] They often found that the SA members were initially more readily ordered about than the party "civilians," and so local party leaders used them for many tasks and so unremittingly that they protested. Although the average SA man in his twenties was himself a civilian, with increasingly less in common with the old free corps veterans, he prided himself on his soldierly obedience, his *Draufgängertum* (aggressiveness), and his *esprit de corps*, in contrast with party bigwigs (*Parteibonzen*) and callow fellow travelers (*Mitläufer*). Thus, the Storm Troops gradually developed a sense of superiority and resentment against the Political Organization (PO), while the rising generation of younger gauleiters demanded manageable cohorts, not "equals" who had to be consulted about policy.[34] It is not surprising that the SS men of these years are faceless nonentities who did not rise to prominence even later, since it was just such individuals who could be employed without any later kickback.[35] By 1929, faced with a contumacious SA, Munich would rediscover the SS and start it upon the road to independence of the SA and of the gauleiters also.

The year 1928 may well be regarded as a turning point in Nazi fortunes. A few electoral victories in 1926 and 1927, and the slow restoration and surpassing of the old membership figure of 55,000 in 1927 were crowned by their passing the 100,000 mark in membership and the acquisition of enough seats in the Reichstag (12) and in the Bavarian and Prussian *Landtage* (9 and 6 respectively) to raise the possibility of coalition politics. In the comfortable year of 1928, the Nazis were becoming a respectable part of the political right. Gregor Strasser had given up the propaganda leadership to Hitler personally before the spring elections and was paid off with the organizational leadership, which needed tightening. After the elections Hitler characteristically divided the authority for propaganda between Goebbels in Berlin and Fritz Reinhardt in Munich, with Himmler assisting Reinhardt.[36]

The PO was also divided in such a way that Strasser got control over the party and its affiliates — an apparatus for attacking the existing order (although he lacked control over the SA and the two propaganda centers), while a kind of general staff or "shadow cabinet" began to form around the former Reichswehr colonel Konstantin Hierl. This was more than a division of labor; Hitler was dividing his forces, not only to prevent being overwhelmed by a coalition against himself at the moment of a possible temporary coalition with others of the political right but also to make possible the courting of other groups like non-Marxist workers in Saxony and the farmers of Schleswig-Holstein.[37]

In view of party leaders' quarrels with the SA, what more obvious extension of this policy could there be than the expansion of the SS under its efficient deputy, Reichsführer Himmler? Amid charges in the Social Democratic press that Heiden was being sacked as a venal police spy, which Hitler denied, Himmler was made Reichsführer SS on January 20, 1929, retroactive to January 6, and charged with consolidating the scattered fragments (280 men, according to tradition) into a mobile police task force with its strength in the thousands. However, Himmler was not relieved of his major propaganda secretarial duties, and he was able only to make a few trips during 1929 to get things started, on time taken from speaking engagements. Only because he was a very energetic, indeed compulsively self-driving, young man of twenty-eight was he able to accomplish anything for the SS that busy year of the "battle against the Young Plan." Himmler increased the roster to about a thousand men in less than a hundred Staffeln.[38]

Pfeffer was willing to see the SS grow a little because by the spring of 1929 he was contemplating a massive SA, between the 100,000 in Hitler's mind (perhaps modeled on the Reichswehr) and 250,000. In reality, the twenty-five SA Standarten of early 1929 probably did not exceed 10,000 men. But the notion of the SA as cadre of a future *Volksheer* (people's army) certainly antedates Röhm's return at the end of 1930.[39] The SS was to be accorded its own "higher officers' corps" (until then there were simply SS-Führer and no noncommissioned officers, although the SA already had *Standartenführer* (Regimental Commanders, i.e., colonels), *Gauführer* (Regional Commanders), and *Oberführer* (Superior or Senior Colonels) as well as *Gruppenführer* (Squad Leaders) and (*Stoss-*) *Truppführer* (Platoon Leaders). Whereas each larger town or rural county was to have its SA-*Sturm-Abteilung*, made up of several SA-Stürme and corresponding to a battalion made up of companies, the SS retained temporarily the term Staffel for the local unit. The designation of the local SS commander as a Sturmführer, however, indicated the tendency to assimilate the SS to the SA structure, which was to become even stronger under Röhm in 1931–1932. The official use of the plural term Schutzstaffeln continued long after the local units became SS-Stürme. Although purely on paper in 1929, the SS was given a regimental (Standarten) level in some of the more active gaus (Franconia, and Upper and Lower Bavaria), and each gau was supposed to have a *Scharführer* (gau SS leader).* Hess, incidentally, was made Scharführer of Upper Bavaria, an indication that high party position rather than full-time SS service was demanded. This soon changed, however, when Sepp Dietrich† replaced him; in Franconia too Johan ("Jean") Beck, a long-time SS (and SA) veteran who somehow could get along with gauleiter Streicher, was appointed.[40]

But in fact there were not that many higher SS officers in 1929. Most of the SS growth took place as prescribed in the SA Basic Order VII of April 12, 1929: local SA commanders selected five or ten SA men to form a Schutzstaffel and often named the commander also. In Dessau the party district leader (*Bezirksleiter*) was also the local SA leader. When at the request of the SS-*Oberführer Ost* (regional commander) in Berlin

---

*\* *Scharführer* (gau SS leader): The term *Schar* was another romantic borrowing from the prewar youth movement, who took it from medieval literature. The SS also used Gauführer and even spoke of the *SS-Gauleitung*. Later the SS adopted the SA term "Gruppenführer" (Group Leader), but by then (1932) such commands were no longer congruent with the gaus.*

†Sepp Dietrich was a favorite of both Hitler and Himmler. In 1933 he was put in charge of yet another SS bodyguard, known as the *Leibstandarte Adolf Hitler* (literally, the body regiment of Adolf Hitler). He rose to become a five-star general of the Waffen-SS.

(Kurt Wege), the leader named seven men, they were subsequently rejected by Munich because it was discovered that the commander was *also* the gau business manager, and "the SS should be independent of the political organization." The gauleiter Wilhelm Loeper complained that all this was going on under his nose but without his being asked — the gau did not have that much personnel for so much decentralization.[41] Many of the early SS officers whose records were studied by the author also had held positions in the PO and the SA. They did tend to give up their SA and party positions in the course of 1930, however, though returns to the SA in 1931 were also common.

Hitler gave the SS their first ten *Sturmfahnen* (company banners) at the National Party Rally in Nuremberg on August 4, 1929. They had arrived with only one — the original Blutfahne borne by the Munich Staffel I. The diminutive size of the SS is revealed by their lack of Standarten — the SA had forty at Nuremberg — and the existence of only *ten* company-size units (Stürme) eligible for flags. When Heinrich Himmler took the salute alongside Hitler from a supposedly thousand-man-strong SS contingent bringing up the rear of the SA, he should have had the satisfaction of knowing that 95 percent of the SS had come to Nuremberg. They were only a fraction of the SA present that day, supposedly 30,000 strong (perhaps, really 10,000!). The true significance of the SS was to show up later, when on August 5, after the main program was over, the party, SA, and SS units had dispersed to roam the town and quench thirsts aroused by marching and shouting in the hot weather. Rowdies in SA and party uniform — perhaps assisted by a few imposters — began to pick fights, molest Jewish businesses, and generally upset the atmosphere of patriotic camaraderie in the town. Gradually the party and SA personnel were sent back to the local quarters with the help of the quickly assembled SS. Functioning as a kind of paramilitary police, they prevented the rally from ending in chaos. The violence and disturbance was still a nine-day sensation in the democratic and Marxist press, leading Pfeffer to issue a SABE (*SA-Befehl*) urging that the SS be built up to handle just such emergencies before they got so large. Ironically, one result of the Nuremberg rally was the dismissal of Himmler's first SS adjutant, Hans Hustert, another unsavory free corps veteran like Heiden. Retired for "health reasons," he was charged with no specific shortcoming. He was simply bad for the image of the new SS.[42]

The five years 1925–1929 had brought Germany a taste of prosperity, a modicum of international respectability, and a little practice in parliamentary give and take. By 1929 a severe agricultural depression beset the rural areas, and capitalist rationalization had already begun to drive small businessmen to the wall. Hitler and his henchmen had whipped the Nazi party into an entirely new shape as an electoral machine, which had begun to pay off in 1928, though not handsomely. The propaganda line had been shifted away from an urban "German socialist" appeal to nonunion workers (which had failed) to a call for nationalistic, *anticlass* folk solidarity, which made inroads on the frightened middle class. Hitler carefully disentangled support for unruly "anti-System"* farmers in Schleswig-Holstein and Lower Saxony from revolutionary National Bolshevik† firebrands. Through it all the paramilitary bands, though shrunken, had never disappeared. The SA retained contact with them, and by 1929 could march with the more respectable versions (no maneuvers!) and even the "reactionary" Stahlhelm could be seen at party rallies. Pfeffer hoped to expand his SA from these sources. Hitler kept his eye on Pfeffer, but Hitler also dreamed of absorbing the German right as the world depression approached. The SS would have a special appeal to the "respectable" right—businessmen, medical men, and the university community.

---

*System (the same word in German): A term of opprobrium in use during the Weimar Republic. It referred especially to the (1) parliamentary system, (2) the capitalist system, and (3) the system of reparations.

†National Bolshevism first appeared in 1923 during the Ruhr occupation. Free corps types like Leo Schlageter combined chauvinist and militarist convictions with an essentially non-Marxist liking for Lenin-like revolutionary organization and slogans. The second wave appeared in the agricultural north and among the Reichswehr. Some later joined the German Communist Party.

# 3

## Formative Years 1930–1932

Die Kampfzeit war die beste Zeit.[1]

Already in the year 1929, when the miniature SS tripled and quadrupled in size, there was a sense of uneasiness in Germany, as if the good times were already over. However, the coming years provided a much clearer argument for Nazi radicalism.[2] The SS grew in 1930–1932 within the matrix of a rapidly expanding SA and party membership. The SS engaged in rigorous combat in the streets with socialists (*Reichsbanner*), communists (*Roter Frontkämpferbund*), nationalists (*Stahlhelm*), and in numerous party headquarters with rivals and opportunists. To experience rapid growth while fighting on a double front was not without its disadvantages — many members joined and left[3] — but it provided for a process of "natural selection" from which arose some of the best cadre of the future officers' corps.

Whereas SS growth in 1929 was still part of the need to expand the effectiveness of the party's propaganda instrument which the SA itself had represented since 1926 — and the type of recruits were accordingly merely the bolder, most determined, and perhaps more intelligent SA men[4] — by 1930 the increasing possibility of political coalition and political responsibility required a greater discipline in the party as a whole and in its political soldiers in particular. A military elitist, Pfeffer desired this discipline as much for the purged SA as Himmler desired it for the SS. However, Pfeffer had not only to work with the kind of ram-

bunctious men available but depended on their organized independence for the realization of his own ambitions vis-à-vis those of other SA
"top brass" like Walter Stennes.[5] Himmler, on the other hand, having
little to begin with and certainly no powerful local SS leaders, could
select a new type of officer, no less bold, determined, or intelligent than
the seasoned veterans of countless SA and SS propaganda missions but
more interested in discipline, self-education, the social virtues, and
ideas. Himmler could and did recruit SA officers and men for the SS,
but he was never restricted to the SA.

As the SA expanded by leaps and bounds in the hard winter of 1929–
1930 and the spring of the new year, it tended to grow out of the hands
of Pfeffer and even of Hitler. Pfeffer in 1927–1928 had set up an elaborate system of regional staffs (*Brigaden- und Oberführer-Bereiche*) to
control the old centrifugal tendencies of the regional combat leagues,
yet already in 1929 these staffs themselves became the subject of much
bitterness and altercation with the gauleiters and the Munich PO headquarters. Hitler had purposely reduced the size of the party gau, even
dividing some into subgaus (*Untergaue*) to correspond with electoral
districts; thus no gauleiters would become independent enough to challenge Hitler as Strasser's northwest alliance of 1925–1926 had done.
However, Pfeffer had insisted on creating seven large SA regions
(*Oberführer-Bereiche*): north, east, south, center, west, Ruhr, and
Austria — headed by former officers of the world war.[6] In 1929 he made
five of these men his deputies (*OSAF-Stellvertreter*, Deputies of the Supreme SA Commander) downgrading the party-oriented Lutze in the
Ruhr and Reschny in Austria. These intermediate SA staffs concentrated SA talents and syphoned off SA income from lower levels, leaving
units dependent on the good will of district and local party leaders. In
1929–1930 as the old SA units expanded and new units were formed —
often by the remains of some older combat league coming over as a unit
— the need for funds for clothing and equipment brought bitter recriminations from unemployed SA men against the still comfortable *Spiessbürger* ("squares") of the NSDAP, whom they accused of niggardliness.
Occasionally they also blamed Munich "corruption" — but only rarely
their own top-heavy staffs.[7] Pfeffer himself complained about "civilian
interference" and did his best to support the regional staffs' requests
for ever more funds for their expanding local units, so that a local SA
usually felt more loyal to its own higher headquarters than to its
party local. Furthermore, all of the regional SA leaders and many regimental commanders were ex-free corps officers and practitioners of
charismatic leadership composed of camaraderie, paternalism, and
self-dramatization.[8] Such was Walter Stennes, whose revolt against

Goebbels first threw the SS into the limelight in Berlin on August 30, 1930.

Walter Stennes had served as a battalion commander of the Black *Reichswehr** major Ernst Buchrucker and had played a part in the abortive north German putsch† of September 1923.[9] Already in August 1928 he is supposed to have "gone on strike" against the Munich party headquarters to obtain funds in his eastern SA region, including Brandenburg, Mecklenburg, Pomerania, Danzig, East Prussia, and Silesia. Supported by Pfeffer, he had got what he wanted, and the local Berlin SA were his most loyal adherents.[10] In July 1930 funds were short again, but there were other grievances. Lawlessness was increasing, and so was the appeal of communism or at least of anticapitalist radicalism. In this setting the breach between Otto Strasser's *Kampfverlag*‡ and Munich over the right of Saxon workers to strike gave rise to the well-founded suspicion among unemployed Berlin SA men that the party, which had joined hands with the press tycoon Hugenberg** in the referendum campaign against the Young Plan†† and was courting the rival Stahlhelm, was abandoning them.[11] This impression seemed confirmed when Hitler refused Stennes and several eastern SA leaders places on the Nazi list for the Reichstag elections at a time when it looked as if anyone on the Nazi list in Berlin could win. Paramilitary leaders of Reichsbanner (Social Democrat), Stahlhelm (Nationalist), and Storm Troops

---

*Black *Reichwehr*: This term refers to units like the one Heinrich Himmler belonged to briefly in September–October 1923. They were assembled illegally by the Reichswehr to help resist French, Polish, or other incursions at the time of the Ruhr occupation, to quell Communist risings, and to put down various secession schemes. They were disavowed in the course of 1924, but many of them continued in existence as combat leagues, especially within the Frontbann.

†abortive North German putsch of September 1923: After trying to seize the government quarter of Berlin with two hundred men on September 29, Buchrucker and his men were quietly sent home to Küstrin by the military authorities. There another attempt to seize the military fortifications failed also. Slight disturbances at Spandau fortress and elsewhere among Black Reichswehr were also easily crushed.

‡Otto Strasser's *Kampfverlag*: Otto Strasser was more doctrinaire than his brother Gregor. By 1930 Otto was advocating alliance with the Communists and with the USSR. His newspapers were successful rivals of the *Völkischer Beobachter* in north Germany. Hitler expelled him from the Nazi party.

**Hugenberg: Alfred Hugenberg controlled a large newspaper chain since the early twenties; he came to dominate the DNVP (German National People's Party) in late 1929. He was power-hungry, ruthless, and reactionary.

††referendum campaign against the Young Plan: Originally the brain child of the Hugenberg press, Hitler committed the Nazis to it in the fall of 1929 with considerable success in winning new voters in the Nazi cause, probably from the DNVP! The referendum itself lost.

all sought Reichstag seats in order to get unlimited railroad passes (and salaries) to enhance their organizing capacity, and probably in the case of the Storm Troops to "take over" the "gossip-club" (*Schwatzbude*) by spectacular theatrics. Pfeffer was not averse to intimidating the party people and even forcing Hitler's hand. But Hitler refused Stennes's demands, and his delegation of Berlin SA men were refused a hearing in Munich on August 23. Stennes's staff resigned on the spot. Pfeffer temporized with Stennes's clique even after about thirty SA men raided the Berlin gau headquarters and beat up the NSDAP business agent on August 28. Two days later Stennes called a "peace" meeting at the headquarters, but the discovery of an SS "spy" at the meeting led to the forcible removal of seven SS guards from the building, two of whom received head injuries. Goebbels flew off to Munich and on September 1 brought Hitler immediately to Berlin, which was in a complete uproar. A police riot squad arrested the rebels, releasing them when Goebbels refused to press charges. Hitler had to brave hisses and catcalls at the SA taverns and clubs (SA-Heime), but his charisma was still effective. The Führer rallied the mutinous bands of SA men with promises of more paid SA posts, more funds for the units, and better relations with the PO. He did not remove Stennes or the SA gau leaders who had joined him, but on his return to Munich he removed Pfeffer. He even placed a few SA officers on the Nazi ballots, though none from Stennes's group. Not all of them were elected, but Heinrich Himmler, Reichsführer SS, was.[12]

Pfeffer had made efforts to bring the SA under stricter control in 1930. In June he had created a general inspectorate under the retired Lieutenant Colonel Kurt von Ulrich, formerly SA Commander West, whose new job was to inspect and regulate local SA and SS units. Pfeffer had also brought in as *Stabschef* (executive officer) Otto Wagener, once a captain in the German General Staff and now a disciple of Gottfried Feder.* Wagener hoped to develop a classless social and economic order of "professional estates" (*Stände*) within and through the SA. Nor were Pfeffer's military ambitions putschist in character — they were merely preparatory to forming a people's army after a legal victory.[13] Finally, Hitler did not yet know whether Röhm, who had returned from Bolivia, would accept the SA leadership on Hitler's terms. In fact, Pfeffer had actually offered his resignation to Hitler as early as August 12, following Hitler's refusal of the Reichstag seats for the SA. Hitler an-

---

*Gottfried Feder had been one of the original German Workers Party members when Hitler joined in 1919. He contributed some of the planks to the Nazi platform, notably those against "interest-slavery." Largely utopian petit bourgeois fantasies of free business loans and currency manipulation in the interest of small business, his views were no longer important to the Nazi world view, though still of propaganda use during the depression.

nounced it on September 2. Pfeffer's offer to manage affairs temporarily was not accepted. Instead, Hitler made himself Supreme SA Commander, keeping Wagener on temporarily as *Stabschef* (executive officer or chief of staff) to manage affairs. Thus did Hitler prevent a wholesale desertion of SA officers before the national election, a move indirectly threatened by Pfeffer in his formal letter of resignation of August 29. The remarkable electoral victory of September 14, 1930,* to which SA and SS propaganda teams contributed much, helped to convince Röhm that the Nazis were indeed on the road to victory. Heinrich Himmler had also done his part to bring Röhm back with a steady flow of correspondence to his old Reichskriegsflagge commander. The SS would not be neglected if Röhm did return. Indeed, Röhm had promised Himmler money for the SS "if he ever had any."[14]

With about one hundred fifty numbered SS-Stürme brought into existence by the end of 1930, overhead costs were bound to mount even if little or nothing was paid to several hundred "full-time" officers and NCOs. Like their SA counterparts, the SS units as yet usually paid no rent for their meeting places, utilizing a back room in a local public house owned by a party member or sympathizer. They paid their rent with their purchase of beer "after duty." SS men were expected to pay for their own outfitting, black cap, pants, tie, belt and shoulder strap, brown shirt, etc. If a "paper Sturm" was ever to advance much beyond its original Staffel character of seven to fifteen men, at least one man had to be freed from the burden of full-time employment elsewhere to devote himself to the unit, or at the very least he could not be expected to pay for printing handbills, licenses, telephone bills, and gasoline for his motorcycle. The pride with which a Sturm of twenty-five to thirty men was reported in 1930 indicates that few even reached this weak "company strength." Although officially commanded to do so, not all SA commanders bothered about setting up SS units, and few cared to part with the best ten SA men in a community, much less devoting time and money to seeing that, once created, a Sturm went on existing. Nonetheless, nineteen of the thirty-five SS officers of 1930 were from the SA.[15]

It was fortunate that Himmler was able to locate a number of reason-

---

*Electoral victory of September 14, 1930: The Nazis won 107 seats as compared to 12 in 1928. Even with the DNVP, which had lost seats due to the breakup of the party under Hugenberg's influence, the Nazis could still not have formed a majority cabinet, but they did not want such a coalition (which they did accept in January 1933). The chancellor, Heinrich Brüning, would continue to govern with a minority cabinet, tolerated by all parties except Nazis, Nationalists, and Communists. Even when voting together, these three parties did not have enough votes to dismiss the cabinet.

ably competent Gau-SS-Führer in the course of 1930, and even to set up three *Oberführer-Bereiche* (east, west, south) on the model of the more numerous SA areas of the same name. The system of Standarten — two or three per gau — was filled out somewhat on paper by designating two or three Stürme as a Standarte, numbered from I to XXX, but the SS could not really afford the luxury of so many staff levels. At the gau level, soon to be designated as SS-*Brigaden,* there was usually an adjutant-and-business manager (*Geschäftsführer*) and a treasurer (*Geldverwalter*); often the former had some accounting experience and the latter was a small businessman. To replace Hustert, Himmler acquired as an adjutant (later *Stabsleiter*) Josias von Waldeck und Pyrmont, a nobleman with some university education; Himmler picked up a business manager and a treasurer as well. The local business managers handled the rosters, reports, and correspondence while the treasurers looked after the collection of dues and contributions from supporting members and "active members" and also made disbursements. Often in the absence of a treasurer, the "adjutant" was supposed to do everything, and the books often were in slovenly condition or nonexistent.[16]

The 1930 revolt of Stennes and his SA cohorts in north and east Germany ushered in a period of SA-SS jostling for position and favor in Munich and in local communities. If the seven "unknown SS men" in Berlin had accomplished little else in August 1930, they had underscored the value of SS units independent of SA dominance. While Hitler did not dare displace Stennes and the SA commanders in Pomerania, Silesia, etc., he very much needed "objective" reports on local conditions; that is, reports written from the point of view of the movement as seen with eyes loyal to Munich, not from the local party headquarters. It was hoped that the SS could begin to collect this information. Naturally — especially in Berlin, Mecklenburg, Pomerania, East Prussia, and Silesia — the Storm Troops would have nothing to do with the SS, regarding any new local units as "wild and unauthorized." It is perhaps not accidental that we have no record of Gau-SS-Führer at this time for Mecklenburg, Pomerania, and East Prussia. In Silesia the blueblooded Udo von Woyrsch took over this function in open opposition to the SA. Above all, Himmler, now one of the 107 Nazis with an unlimited railroad pass, was finally relieved of his propaganda duties to devote himself full time to setting up the SS as "fully independent of the SA."[17]

In a circular letter to the OSAF-Deputies, now including Lutze, Stabschef Wagener on October 3 described the SS as a police unit inside the movement, with the duty to guard against infringements of government regulations. He stressed the need of the SS to be independent of the SA, especially in recruitment, according to special standards which had been given to the Reichsführer SS. He gave the SS a quota of 10 percent of the SA strength, a figure often repeated thereafter, but stated that an SS unit should not be formed until an SA company (Sturm) in the area had reached fifty members. The SS was not to recruit among SA members. These regulations were regularly disregarded, though they were given lip service for several years. The SA was to turn away from propaganda, guard duty, and the solicitation of funds to prepare for its role as the future reservoir of the national army, while the SS would presumably take over these duties and serve as the personal guard of the leader, analogous to Royal Guards.[18] A belief in the imminence of the National Socialist accession to state authority is likewise reflected in an order (SABE) of OSAF Deputy August Schneidhuber of Munich in November. He stressed military training, the formation of motorized and medical SA units, the combing out of opportunists, the geographical analysis of recruiting to fill up gaps, and the creation of a regimental (Standarte) staff level. In an earlier memorandum of September, Schneidhuber had called for equality between the Gau-SA-Führer and the gauleiter as well as the use of SA corps commanders with tactical and not merely administrative authority over the Gau-SA-Führer. Thus, before the reappearance of Röhm on the scene, the SA showed many signs of empire-building as a preliminary to taking over the state in addition to ominous claims to independence of the political organization. It even decided to create its own SA headquarters guards (Stabskompanien) to provide security, a move which would free them from reliance on the SS.[19]

Some of Schneidhuber's organizational proposals were indeed carried out by Röhm in 1931 and were copied by the SS; but the SA did not gain independence of the PO, and therefore the SS did not gain independence of the SA. Himmler's announcement on December 1, 1930, that the SS's final separation from the SA had occurred was followed six weeks later on January 14, 1931, by the order of Hitler clearly subordinating the SS to the SA. Röhm's new position as Stabschef was carried through a meeting of SA leaders at Munich on November 30 only with considerable difficulty and by Hitler's will.[20] Both before and after November 30, Stennes and his SA leaders in the north and east resisted party efforts to reduce them to submission; Stennes seemed to try to enlist Röhm on his side. Röhm cleverly steered a middle course that favored SS strength but bound the SS to the SA, insisting, for example, that SA cadres continue to be furnished for the formation of new SS units. That this winter (1930–1931) saw a serious struggle for power is shown by the appearance of Göring, already a potential rival of Röhm, as an "official mediator" between SA, SS, and the gauleiters.[21]

Conditions for the recruitment of several thousand relatively competent "political soldiers" for the SS improved steadily as unemployment
mounted to four million that winter and early spring. Soup-lines and
lines for unemployment pay (*Stempelstellen*) attracted Communist and
Nazi recruiters. The political atmosphere darkened; and revolutionary
tendencies, banished since 1923, reappeared. The police increasingly
failed to protect life and property. Street battles, political brawling in
public places, "raids" on "enemy" headquarters, and murder by political thugs enhanced the desire of the more educated activists of the right
to join "protection units" such as the SS represented. Still very much
"strong-arm squads," SS units tended to be better prepared for each
confrontation, better disciplined vis-à-vis the police, and subject to
control. While it is doubtful that all the 4,000 numbered identity passes
of the SS were really in the possession of that many active SS men by December 1930, it is clear from SS personnel and organizational records
that the six months following the great electoral victory did see a wave
of SS recruitment at the higher (officer) ranks as well as rapid promotions to officer from within existing units, in order to staff the newly
created SS units of late 1930.[22]

Under Röhm the SA also grew very rapidly, attaining sometime in
1931 its first one hundred thousand men. The forty SA-Standarten became several hundred; Röhm reorganized the SA regionally into ten
"Groups" (the corps recommended by Schneidhuber), each composed
of several subgroups, the former *Gaustürme*. While the powerful
OSAF-Deputyships were done away with, a vast staff network was created, whereby brigades of several Standarten were formed to manage
the auxiliary formations being set up, and the term "*Sturmbann*" (battalion) was improvised to take the place of the old Sturm-Abteilung
designation for a local tactical unit. Many a German petit bourgeois,
frightened by the return of all the violence of 1919–1923, was led to don
a uniform and assume a military rank which permitted him to dream of
a future position of honor and respect in a restored national army reserve. Hitler helped out by publicly reissuing orders to SA and SS units
alike against carrying military weapons or creating weapons depots.
Citizens need not fear involvement in a putsch.[23]

Many of the "straight" bourgeoisie took offense, however, at the
rough and blatant disregard of their morality in the ranks of the Storm
Troops, especially as a number of old free corps veterans and even adventurers were attracted back to the SA with Röhm's return. Hitler saw
fit to issue an impatient warning, not to the malefactors but to their ac-
cusers, pointing out that the SA was no "school for girls" and promising
expulsion for disloyalty for tongue-wagging, letter-writing party mem-

bers. While there was no dearth of roughnecks in the SS at this time, certain traces of prudish, middle-class morality began to appear in 1931, which may reflect a cultivated sense of superiority on this issue in terms of discipline. The SS never recruited groups of the old combat leagues; Röhm did so precisely at this time, partly to offset the Stennes faction in the north and east.[24] Röhm and Hitler could wink at homosexuality, pimping, petty thievery, and heavy drinking, but they would not tolerate insubordination. Pfeffer's institution of the general inspectorate (*Generalinspekteur der SA und SS*, GISASS) was retained and widened to include regional inspectorships. One of the major duties was the removal of controversies between SA and SS units, to save Röhm's organization from internal interference by the PO and especially by Hitler's "official mediator," Göring.[25]

Early in 1931 the SS was kept busy changing and rechanging its unit designations to keep up with the elaborate tables of organization constructed by Röhm and his staff. The SS-Stürme had scarcely been given arabic numbers when the arabic numbers — locally often the same ones — had to be reassigned to Standarten. Weak SS companies thereby became even weaker SS regiments; thirty weak SS regiments formerly designated with roman numerals became SS brigades. This forced–draft cadre system taken over from the SA, which of course was aping old familiar military procedures and practicing for the rapid buildup of a citizen army, both helped the SS to expand more rapidly than many local SS leaders would have preferred and also challenged the ingenuity and constructive ability of many new SS men recruited for command purposes. The brigade system (five regiments) was soon abandoned again, for the SS really was not large enough for as many levels as the SA; and light, purely administrative units known as *Oberführer-Abschnitte* (sectors) were interposed between about forty Standarten and the Reichsführung SS. As in the SA, however, the effect was to destroy the special position of the SS-Oberführer as favored "Deputies of the Reichsführer SS," although the term lingered on in 1931, and Sepp Dietrich and Kurt Daluege may have exercised this function even later.[26]

Sepp Dietrich was already termed the commander of the SS in the south by a police report of December 1930. While Himmler was in Berlin at the Reichstag, it was certainly the hearty charisma of the ex-truck driver rather than the new SS bureaucracy of the Brown House* which

---

*the new SS bureaucracy of the Brown House: The Brown House was a palatial residence on the broad Königsplatz of Munich, which the NSDAP bought in December 1930 and occupied early in 1931. The SS bureaucrats included Josias, Prince of Waldeck-Pyrmont, Himmler's deputy; Georg Aumeier, the SS business manager; Josef Weber, the SS

helped the SS grow in Bavaria.[27] Kurt Daluege in Berlin had been displaced earlier by Stennes as SA leader; Hitler set Daluege to watch his rival by having Himmler make him Oberführer Ost in place of the less effective SS veteran Kurt Wege. Daluege set up his SS headquarters at the corner of Lützow-Strasse and Potsdamer Strasse near the Sportpalast, across from Stennes's SA offices. This "intelligence center" utilized links between SS and SA as well as with government workers and businessmen to keep Hitler and Himmler abreast of the political currents of seething Berlin. Daluege was also instrumental in the spring of 1931 in setting up fledgling SS units in the traditional SA territories of Brandenburg, Pomerania, and Mecklenburg. Thus, the northern SS leader and his cohorts were able to alert party and state police authorities against Stennes when Hitler was ready to goad him into a second fruitless "revolt."[28] Foreshadowing the plot against Röhm, Hitler's tactics with Stennes included an intensive wooing to catch him off guard, an effort to divide his followers among themselves and from him, a sudden maneuver to place him in the wrong, and afterwards a vilification campaign. Just as in the previous August, only a few SS personnel seem to have been involved in the preliminaries, but the subsequent removal of virtually all the ranking SA leaders in the northeast by resignation and expulsion put the SS at least temporarily in the position of "protecting the movement," so that a legend could be created out of the "Stennes-Putsch" of Easter Sunday, April 1, 1931.

Hitler began by offering Stennes the Ministry of the Interior in the state of Brunswick, opened to the Nazis by their September electoral victory and collaboration with the Nationalists. When Stennes refused, Hitler began to remove Stennes's appointees as Gau-SA-Führer. Stennes did not remain inactive, stirring up his SA against gauleiters and the Brown House for their showy inefficiency. But Stennes's plotting only united his enemies, inside and outside the party, without being decisive.[29] Hitler precipitated the "revolt" on March 31 at a party meeting at Weimar called to patch up the differences with the Nationalists in Thuringia; repeating his orders to observe the strictest legality, he announced that Stennes, a thorn in the side of the right, would be transferred to Munich as Röhm's chief executive officer — not an unworthy move but disruptive of Stennes's connections. Stennes had not been consulted, but five SS men were warned by telephone during the night of March 31 of the move, which then appeared in the morning papers.

---

treasurer; Heinrich Höflich, the local SS brigade commander; Dr. Hans Deuschl, the head of the SS medics; and a certain Freiherr von Thüngen for recruitment. Only the prince had a significant SS career, though a checkered one.

Stennes's gau SA leaders wired Hitler in protest, Stennes wired his refusal to come to Weimar to parlay with Hitler at Hitler's request, and
Berlin SA forces took over the party headquarters and the *Angriff*
(Goebbels's paper) as a kind of public protest. It was an act of despair,
for the SS had alerted party personnel of Hitler's intentions to observe
strict legality. The police cleared away the stubborn SA minority in the
next days amid charges and counter-charges of betrayal.[30]

Daluege and his men had acted in the interests of Röhm as well as
Hitler, but Röhm put another ex-free corps officer, Paul Schulz, in
charge of what was left of the northeast SA. Friedrich Wilhelm Krüger,
the SS lieutenant who had been Daluege's courier to Röhm, became SA
Staff Leader for the region. When later Schulz himself turned against
Röhm, the Staff Leader replaced him, leaving the SS and ultimately rising to a high staff position close to Röhm. (Nevertheless, he was to return successfully to the SS in 1935 as an Obergruppenführer.) Daluege
subsequently issued a card of thanks in Hitler's name to the SS of the
Berlin Abschnitt III bearing the inscription, "*SS-Mann, Deine Ehre
heisst Treue*" ("SS man, Your honor is your loyalty"). Changed to, "My
honor is my loyalty," Himmler would adopt it as the inscription for the
SS belt buckle in the tradition of the "*Gott mit uns*" ("May God be with
us") on the buckles of German World War One uniforms.[31]

The summer of 1931 in Germany with its bank collapse was trau-
matic for the German middle class. All illusions about the previous
year's supposed "bottoming out" were swept away as more and more
white collar men joined the bread lines.[32] For the Nazis the chaos was
the confirmation of their world view. Although many of their membership had supposed they would already be in power by that time, the
Nazi leadership experienced the impasse in the parliamentary system as a
confirmation and justification of the party's doctrine. These men carried
on their bombardment of the public with rallies, propaganda marches,
handbills, new party newspapers, undaunted—indeed stimulated—by
ineffectual police measures against them.[33] The SS emerges at this time
in the speeches and orders of its leaders remarkably full blown; though
it would be long years before they could realize their ambitions for the
SS, its ideal contours appear remarkably complete by the summer of
1931. While the reasons for this emergence remain obscure, it is likely
that by then all the conditions which had given rise to national socialism had had time to express themselves fully, and the potential role of
the SS as political soldiers of this movement was now clear, at least to an
inner core of Hitler's followers. That this role was in fact permanently
bifurcated—intrinsically so, due to the contradiction between soldiering and politics—was much less clear then than it now appears to the
historian's eyes.

No less a person than Hitler himself that summer defined the SS in its dual aspect as: 1) *Polizeidienst* (police service), and 2) *Elitetruppe* (elite troops). Neither Hitler nor Himmler, then or later, regarded these as mutually exclusive or even opposing functions. The police task is described in the speeches and orders of the summer of 1931 as *Sicherungsdienst* (security service) and *Ordnungsdienst* (regulative service), concepts borrowed from German police practice. The former consisted of *Abwehr und Gegnerforschung* (counter-intelligence) and *Schutzdienst* (protective service). The regulative functions were carefully distinguished from the more inclusive SA-*Saalschutz* (protection of meetings).[34]

The SS responsibility was to prevent party and SA personnel from threatening public order — a counter-revolutionary, or perhaps more accurately a regulative, role of preventing the revolutionaries from going off half-cocked and thus jeopardizing the long-term revolutionary ambitions of the leadership. The commonest concrete example of this function was searching SA men for concealed firearms, not surprisingly a source of great bitterness. Counter-intelligence activities were of course not as yet limited to the SS, but the anti-Stennes operations in the north and east were undoubtedly a strong argument and incentive for investing the SS with this role. Its smaller size and selective character offered more possibility of secrecy and protection against spies and agents provocateurs. Reinhard Heydrich, who joined the SS in 1931, did not have to introduce the idea of a *Sicherheitsdienst* (security service). SS regiments and even battalions and companies had "I-C officers"* by 1931, as of course did many SA units, by analogy with the intelligence staff officer system of the German army. The protective functions of the SS were distinguished from those of the SA by this time: the *personal* defense of the Führer, all speakers, functionaries, and invited guests as well as protecting special gatherings of party leaders. Last of all, there was a general category of "special tasks" which was kept purposely vague. Emphasis was placed upon the absolute reliability of the individual SS men involved, including commitment of murder.[35]

The concept of the SS as a mobile unit, a storm battalion for employment at a point where it would throw the balance to the side of national socialism, was as prominent a theme as the police duties. Whereas the Storm Troops were to be foot soldiers, whose early motorized formations had been detached to form the independent National Socialist Motor Corps (NS-*Kraftfahrerkorps*, NSKK), the SS was encouraged to create its own motorized companies. Molding together the tradition of

---

*I-C Officers: In the German staff system, the positions were designated by a Roman numeral followed by a letter. The troop commander's staff was designated with I and the letter C stood for intelligence. The United States parallel would be G-2.

the Stosstrupp Hitler and the November "martyrs" by way of the Blutfahne, Hitler had already conferred on the SS the status of a Garde. It
was Himmler, however, who insisted in the summer of 1931 and ever afterwards on transcending police traditions and copying the traditions of
the guardsmen of the old army. "We are not wiser than the men of two
thousand years ago," said Himmler at a meeting of the SS leaders in
Berlin in June. "Persians, Greeks, Romans and Prussians all had their
guards. The guards of the new Germany will be the SS." The use of
members of elite guard units as personal bodyguards for heads of state
was of course traditional; the SS's role as Hitler's bodyguard was reinforced as Sepp Dietrich and a few hand-picked aides accompanied him
everywhere.[36]

The SS was described ideally in 1931 as the *Kerntruppe der Bewegung* (the core troops of the movement) and "the most active fighters
of the party,"[37] reflecting the initial conception of 1925–1926; but SS
speeches and orders made amply clear that the PO was something
apart, just as appeals to be "good comrades to the SA" *while setting
them an example* suggest a similar sense of separation. In fact, the SS
was supposed to become the very best paramilitary troop in Germany,
so it would attract by its very nature the best of the front veterans, replacing the Stahlhelm in the public eye. The future guardsman of the
future national army should be recognizable anywhere in civilian clothing; his bearing, build, outlook–indeed his biological heritage–would
show his SS membership. There were to be no Slavic or Mongoloid faces
in the SS, said Himmler. The SS was to become a blood community
(*Blutgemeinschaft*), the bearers of the blood of the Nordic race. The future SS officer should have his family and background thoroughly investigated, for it was supposed that when the fatal decisions must be
made, only the purest of the pure could act without hesitations, "on
principle." Recognizable here are the values of the old officer caste
translated into Nazi racism.[38]

Himmler did not stop with this, however. The task of the SS did not
lie primarily on the battlefield but in the homeland. In war it must be
the instrument which at the most difficult moment decides the battle —
the last reserves. The year 1918 — that terrible trauma — should never be
repeated. Instead of faint-hearted or mutinous rear-echelon protectors
of the home front, mobile storm battalions would be at the state's command to crush bolshevism, to close a gap in the defenses, to thrust home
the victory. "We are called to lay the foundations upon which the next
generation will make history," said Himmler. He foresaw in the summer
of 1931 a future ring of two hundred million Nordic farmers around
Germany, an impregnable wall against bolshevism, the enemy of the

Nordic race and thereby of civilization. Thus, the shadow of Richard Walter Darré, author of *Das Bauerntum als Lebensquell der Nordischen Rasse* (*Farming as the Life Source of the Nordic Race*), was cast on the SS that summer, soon to dominate its ethos if not its ultimate purposes.[39]

Himmler, Sepp Dietrich, and Kurt Daluege clearly visualized a future SS officers corps at this time, perhaps by contrasting their current difficulties with SA and PO leaders, especially with the Stennes clique. Absolute obedience to Hitler, modeled on the supposedly traditional soldier's unquestioning loyalty to the Prussian king, was to be combined with the "Prussian" or perhaps "Germanic" conception of voluntary self-subordination of independent personalities to constituted superiors in the interest of a higher good. To maintain the authority of the party against the interests and will of dissident minorities, to handle mob situations independently and responsibly, and to stamp their personality upon their followers, SS officers were to have implanted within them an indestructible esprit de corps. They were to be welded together as one body of interchangeable units and yet capable of replacement from below by men of merit. The future corps would be made up of thoroughly trained men in all branches of SS discipline; there were to be no mere specialists nor professional branches to engage in service rivalries. Himmler did not want any SS bookkeepers or SS doctors: all were to be political soldiers. Parade-ground drill, dressy uniforms, and marching bands were to be better in the SS than in the SA or PO but only to impress SS superiority on the public and on SS men themselves — never an end in themselves. The SS officer must be the type to understand this and not love the show for its own sake, just as he must want his men to understand their training and purpose rather than desire their ignorance and consequent subordination and inferiority to himself. He must know his men as individuals, their jobs and their family conditions. The SS officer was to be a practitioner of the bourgeois virtues — again not for themselves but for their influence upon the German community. The future SS officers corps was to become the treasury of the "best human material" (*Menschenmaterial*) in Germany left over after the supposed terrible "decline in human heredity" during the past century.[40]

The summer of 1931 ended with a new outbreak of Nazi violence in Berlin against the Jews on the occasion of the Jewish holidays, but it was becoming increasingly clear to the German right that Hitler was in control of his strong-arm squads and that he really intended to come to power legally. Hitler's problem was to make this conviction stick, without being forced to come into a government on terms other than his own. The Harzburg meeting,* the demonstrations in the Reichstag, the SA and SS rally of one hundred thousand at Brunswick,† all in October 1931, were designed to hold this balance between reassurance and intimidation. It was no longer merely or mainly a problem of agitating the populace; the economic catastrophe was now apparent. The inflow of members was also becoming a matter of course. Rather the problem was to maintain control *in fact* of local and regional Nazi activists, and to prevent the invasion of the controllable membership by such masses of new "human material" that agents provocateurs (real and fancied) could destroy Hitler's bargaining power.

The Storm Troops were still the most vulnerable area in this respect, although the PO was not altogether impregnable. A temporary coalition of Otto Strasser and Walter Stennes, involving Erhardt and some "National Bolsheviks," plus the specter of infiltration from the KPD (due probably more to self-styled "communists" who turned Nazi, and vice versa, than to genuine Communist Party efforts to bore from within) created a spy scare among the Nazis which produced numerous "intelligence bureaus" in the SA, SS, and PO. That the SS's intelligence operations were more trusted by Hitler than the others' and ultimately were more successful is doubtlessly due to Reinhard Heydrich; yet if the SS had not had an "edge" with Hitler in late 1931, it is doubtful if the opportunistic ex-naval officer would have bothered to insinuate himself into Himmler's good graces. Himmler may also have been looking for someone for the Munich office, to offset the threat of Daluege's intelligence center in Berlin. He is supposed to have set Heydrich up as the SS-*PI-Dienst (Presse- und Informationsdienst)* that fall in a Munich apartment with Himmler's card files on individuals and newspaper clippings assembled over the years in the Propaganda-Abteilung with the aid of his correspondents at gau levels. It was to be some time, actually only in 1933 and 1934, before Heydrich was able to assert clear authority over

---

*Harzburg meeting: This was a huge rally of all the rightist groups in Germany on October 11, 1931. It was staged by Hugenberg in Bad Harzburg, a resort in the Harz mountains of Brunswick (Braunschweig), a small German state in central Germany which had a Nationalist-Nazi coalition cabinet. Hitler and the Storm Troops appeared together with the Stahlhelm and other rightist combat leagues, big businessmen, royalty, etc. The expression "Harzburg Front" was coined to describe this atmosphere, but no real coalition or agreement was achieved.

†Brunswick (Braunschweig): This was a separate all Nazi rally in the *city* of Braunschweig a week after the Harzburg rally. It was essentially an SA and SS demonstration of their mobilizing capacity (in the event of a civil war or invasion). There was a Reichswehr observer present at the suggestion of Kurt von Schleicher, the intriguing liaison officer with the Weimar parties. Later all participants were awarded a medal, a replication of the medal for having gone on the "march to Coburg."

the "I-C personnel" in SS regional and local headquarters, not to mention Daluege's apparatus. However, in early 1932 with the official formation of the *Sicherheitsdienst des Reichsführers SS*, Heydrich made a beginning by designating some new SS members from professional and academic circles as his local agents, who were to remain outside the regular SS formations.[41]

The PO and SA were beginning to resent the SS for its still vague pretensions of superiority, more and more enhanced by the predilection of the better-educated and the bluebloods to its ranks. Probably for this very reason Hitler allowed Himmler to develop his own connections in the business and professional world at this time and also to develop a special SS ideology to distinguish his units even further from SA and PO. This ideology was furnished by Richard Walter Darré, whose first connections with the NSDAP dated back only to 1930. Darré's educational background in agronomy was similar to Himmler's. Darré had begun in the party by helping Konstantin Hierl organize a farmers' wing of the NSDAP but was not satisfied or comfortable as a rabble-rousing political organizer. He was attracted by the elitism of the SS, which he proceeded to give ideological footing by tying Himmler's vague racism with Darré's own theory of a Nordic race of aristocratic farmers. The SS was to restore a mystical golden age of rural splendor by rigorous self-selection, mate selection, and retraining its members as future aristocrats of the soil. This romanticism was tinged with right-wing reformism which opposed the "impersonal cash nexus of the market" with a familistic, personalistic corporativism. The idealized East Elbian Junker was contrasted with the absentee Jewish landlord. The old Junkers could not be restored, but the SS aristocrats would take their place. In the meantime Darré was a drawing card in the SS not only to landed and formerly landed bluebloods but to a good many businessmen and bank clerks who had dreamed of owning a little farm some day. He also drew to the SS the leaders of his Farm Policy Apparatus (*Agrarpolitischer Apparat*) — the well-to-do farmers of north Germany who were not so much Nazis or racists as rebels against low prices and high interest rates. Late in 1931 Himmler made Darré head of a new Racial Office within the SS and put him in charge of approving the marriages of SS men. The already married were not, however, subject to review.[42]

Both Himmler and Röhm turned more and more to the professional classes at this time, forming not only a medical branch, cavalry, and flying corps but also signal and engineer units — a complete paramilitary infrastructure. Himmler's units were somewhat more homogeneous, both within themselves and in relation to the larger body of which they

were a part. The SS had always been largely white collar, petit bourgeois in character, while SA doctors, directors, lawyers, and college students too often found themselves rubbing shoulders with SA bricklay-
ers, farm laborers, headwaiters, and newsboys. It became increasingly
necessary in the Storm Troops to make rank distinctions above and beyond functional and command distinctions — and the practice spread
immediately to the SS. All the old army ranks reappeared, and persons
with education and social standing began higher and rose faster. Noblemen were given commands. In the ten thousand-man SS of December
1931, the original two or three hundred had been bypassed. Even the
"founders" of 1929 were being swamped. Formalities expressed by stress
on proper uniforms, numerous printed forms, colored stamps, elaborate filing systems, forms of address, precedence at public functions,
clearance for publication, and so on were irritating SS and SA men alike
that dismal winter of 1931–1932; but they divided the SS less than the
SA, uniting it with the SA top brass and both with the German bourgeoisie outside the Nazi movement.[43]

"What is Hitler waiting for?" was repeatedly asked in German circles
— especially within the SA, where putschist sentiment for a march on
Berlin was heightened by the suffering of their own families, and
within circles of conservatives expecting Hitler to come to them with an
offer. The existence of an increasingly better-disciplined SS scheduled to
grow to 22,000 by spring of 1932 helped to keep Hitler's hand steady in
dealing with firebrands in SA and PO and with impatient negotiators
from the right. Stennes and Otto Strasser, ex-free corps commanders
Buchrucker and F. W. Heinz, Himmler's former adjutant Hustert, and
eastern regional SA commanders Tietjens, Lustig, and Kremser formed
the *National-Sozialistische Kampfbewegung* (National Socialist Combat Movement) with contacts to National Bolsheviks like Ernst
Niekisch. They managed to subvert hundreds of SA men in the northern
half of Germany. Not merely to combat this internal "plague" but to
stiffen the resistance to it of the national SA leadership was the role of
the now favored SS. Doubtless some white-collar unemployed chose the
SS unit in their community to avoid contamination by "red" SA units.[44]

In a sense, Hitler was not waiting at all. He was forming his cadres
for the administration of the Third Reich within the party, the Storm
Troops, and the SS. He was fanning the fires of political revolution in
Germany, thereby building up social pressures which he hoped to thrust
him and his party into power. He was training his cadres in the art of
graduated terror and counter-revolutionary repression while he cultivated reckless violence in the streets and seemed to permit his followers
to prepare for a putsch. The leak of just such a putsch plan occurred in

Hesse in November 1931, the so-called Boxheim Plot. But Hitler had the Italian Fascist example of 1922 clearly in mind: he would not putsch. He was waiting to be invited. He would make himself and his movement acceptable — even attractive — to businessmen, military leaders, and conservative state officials, he would not beg. In another sense, Hitler did not know what he was waiting for — what conditions he would find acceptable.[45] From the electoral victory of September 1930 through the Harzburg Front era of late 1931 to the presidential campaigns of March and April 1932 and beyond, he was improvising, trying to build up popular pressures behind his cause, for he did not know just how he would come to power.

For this reason, he fostered every imaginable sort of political, social, and economic affiliation; he allowed all sorts of professional and ideological groupings to develop as part of the "movement," with fantastic and self-contradictory promises and programs.[46] The SS in 1932 was at once (1) an odd grouping of white-collar reformers; (2) a collecting center for professional men, business leaders, and landowners; (3) a surveillance and control group to channel useful tendencies in the Nazi movement toward the Munich leadership and harmful tendencies away from the center of the political arena. Thus, a year before Nazis came to power, the SS took on most of the organization and the attributes of their subsequent history.

With 350 officers and 10,000 enlisted SS men as cadre, Himmler and his top-ranking lieutenants rapidly expanded the SS in the early spring of 1932 to a figure of 432 officers and 25,000 enlisted men in April at the time of the official dissolution of SA and SS by the regime. When the effort at dissolution was cancelled as a failure in mid-June, there were 466 officers and 41,000 men.[47] This four-fold expansion could take place without an extensive officers corps because the original staff organization had been built up in 1931 in the form of approximately forty regimental staffs, consisting of a regimental commander and an executive officer and two or three similar pairs for the battalions in each regiment. Companies were regularly entrusted to noncommissioned officers, sometimes even to brand-new SS men on trial. Some thirty SS officers with the rank of colonel or better staffed the eight regional commands, the newly created *SS-Oberstab* (top staff), and the oldest and strongest regiments. Most regiments were commanded by newly created SS majors and even captains, many of whom were transferred in from the SA, while the battalions often had to get along with new SS lieutenants lacking even SA experience, although many had had free corps careers. The growth took place by the filling out of the "paper" or "skeleton" units created in 1931, the further breaking up of battalions to form new ones, and the formation finally of a dozen new SS regiments in virtually undeveloped areas: Mecklenburg, Pomerania, Danzig, East Prussia, Silesia, Austria, Württemberg, and the Mosel valley.[48] The practice of transferring SS officers to new regions to organize a fresh unit or reinspire a somnolescent one was begun at this time. Rapid growth continued to take place in the SS, and with it the expectation that the Nazis would soon come to power. Even before the period of illegality, which interfered with record keeping, the Munich headquarters had fallen far behind in the registration and acknowledgement of new SS members. This breakdown in record keeping would continue into 1933.[49]

A real SS headquarters had begun to take shape in 1931, after several years in which Himmler had tried to operate almost without staff due to hatred for bureaucracy, lack of funds, and a naive estimate of his own ability to do everything. In 1932 under the influence of a proliferation of SA bureaucracy, more funds, the expectation of many new tasks associated with early Nazi victory, and the availability of men with the technical skills, Himmler began his Oberstab. It was to be constructed along German staff lines, with five sections numbered I–V, each made up of a half-dozen *Referate* ("desks") staffed by *Referenten* (specialists), lettered a-b-c-d-e-f-g, etc. Modifications of course occurred to serve the political soldier's goals, such as Darré's Section V (Race). Technical experts rather than the seasoned SS commanders were recruited. Daluege, with whose Berlin office Himmler came increasingly in contact due to his Reichstag post, supplied several candidates for Section I, *Führung* (Leadership), already also know as the *Führungsstab* (leadership staff). There was, however, nothing permanent about this Oberstab.[50] Himmler seems never to have accustomed himself to bureaucratic institutions, though he ultimately was responsible for a great many of the worst sort. Although service on Himmler's staff was soon much sought after, for much the same reasons as in other military organizations (nearness to power, rapidity of promotion, future prestige), already in 1932 it became a riskier venture than setting up a new unit or cementing ties with a jealous gauleiter. Himmler was most difficult to satisfy, since his ideals were not only both vivid and yet vague but his concrete requirements were both highly specific and also unreasonable. Of the early Oberstab, only Heydrich really kept Himmler's confidence; Darré kept it for several years; most of the lesser figures disappeared within a year or two. Himmler reserved most of his confidence for SS officers whom he kept or who remained by choice in field commands: Sepp Dietrich, Fritz Weitzel, perhaps Kurt Daluege (although he and Himmler were virtual rivals), and a dozen or more younger officers. Even after 1939, when Himmler had found a number of congenial and capable staff officers, he did not succeed in retaining them; he usually drove them away albeit inadvertently. He was a far cry from the charismatic Röhm or indeed Hitler himself, both of whom he admired. He could be pleasant and he could be harsh, but if there were such a thing as negative charisma, Himmler possessed it.[51]

In the year 1932, however, the political, social, and economic chaos drove able and aggressive men toward all the Nazi formations in a mood symbolized by the phrase, "We have tried everything else." Less known and therefore less stereotyped in the public mind, the SS appealed to many middle-class persons as a relatively unstructured elite in which they could effectuate their own reformist notions. Its tight discipline, its relative reserve in relation to the public, its incipient quasi-mythical undertones could only recommend the SS to a generation sick of disorder, noisy demonstrations, and false sentiments. At a time when both the Storm Troops and the Nazi Party appeared to pass beyond the original elitist dreams of their founders to become mass-movements, the SS seemed to retain and embody the ideal of selectivity now enhanced by the elaborate rigamarole of "racial" qualifications for admission and for marriage partners of the members. For all these reasons Himmler did not require positive charisma, which is not to say that local commanders could do without it. The SS of 1932 did possess some charismatic leaders, though perhaps fewer than the SA; at the staff and technical levels, the SS tended to have rather colorless personalities. But like the party itself, the much larger Storm Troops had more poor local leaders and more stuffed-shirt bureaucrats at intermediate levels than the SS.[52]

In the elaborate power game which Hitler played, it was both necessary and very dangerous that the Storm Troops under Röhm should court the Reichswehr, that the National Socialist Factory Cell Organization (*National-Sozialistische Betriebszellen-Organisation*, NSBO)* should court the workers, that Darré should court both the small and the large farmers, that Frick, Ley, and Göring† should court bankers and business leaders. Himmler's SS provided a device for checking up on each of these "partnerships" on the inside and also a potential checkmate against disloyalty. Yet the SS was not so strong as to be itself a serious

---

*National Socialist Factory Cell Organization: This was a pseudo-union begun in 1929 in Berlin by Reinhold Muchow. It was essentially an antiunion "cell" for Nazis in factories. Goebbels espoused the NSBO in January 1932 as a device for vote-getting among workers in preparation for the presidential election in March.

†Frick, Ley, and Göring: Wilhelm Frick was a former Bavarian police official who had served as a Nazi in the Reichstag in the lean years 1924–1930 and looked and acted the type of the solid civil servant. Robert Ley was a chemist who worked for a big chemical concern on the Rhine, and Göring had ties with the aristocratic set who dabbled in business.

challenge to SA, party, or Hitler. Himmler's undoubted personal loyalty to Hitler entirely coincided with the interests of the SS, which could easily have been destroyed in 1932 by either the party or the SA. Indeed the increased contacts between Himmler, Göring, and big business interests in 1932 suggest that Himmler was both insuring a flow of funds to the SS independent of Röhm and F. X. Schwarz, the party treasurer, and aiding Hitler to move in the political direction which he wanted against the wishes of a very large segment of his own party. The role of adjunct to Göring — though perhaps distasteful — was profoundly wise, since it enabled Himmler to outmaneuver Daluege, virtually independent in Berlin.[53]

Röhm sought to subordinate the SS to the SA and partially succeeded in 1932, in that the major preoccupation of all the paramilitary units in Germany was street combat and preparation for civil war, necessitating at least minimal cooperation between allied units. Röhm's — and probably Hitler's — ambition to win a partnership with the Reichswehr in a future people's army (*Volksheer*) also held out valuable compensation for many ex-soldiers among SS officers in the form of a reestablished military career.[54] Thus, in 1932 the SS held the same kind of weekend maneuvers as the SA, often jointly with them. Street and beer hall battles were common tactical operations often planned in detail by SA and SS officers. Propaganda marches of SA were in turn "guarded" by carloads of SS in advance and at the rear of the columns as well as on motorcycles and along the line of march. Indeed, many of the quarrels that year turned on how much protection the SA needed; leaders complained of getting none at all or else of being guarded too ostentatiously.[55] The SS in turn resented the "luxurious" *SA-Heime* (combination clubhouse and headquarters) which increasingly appeared throughout the more Nazi sections of the country, while the SS usually still had to hold their weekly *Appell* (roll call) at a tavern. However, both kinds of units were guilty of gangsterlike "shakedowns" to obtain money. For example, the FM (Sponsors) records of the Munich SS Standarte I for the spring of 1932 include the names Hirschmann, Goldschmidt, Levi, Rosenzvet, and Rosenberg.[56]

For world war veterans in the SS and SA, the year 1932 began to look more and more like 1918: battle after battle, victory after victory, but the final battle still unfought. Victory, momentarily expected, remained elusive. The nervousness of the "holding on tactics" (*Durchhaltetaktik*) of the trenches permeated the whole Nazi movement, but the action-oriented Storm Troops took the successive false alarms of 1932 the hardest. They had been placed on an alarm footing in March before the first presidential elections; special detachments (*Alarm-Bereitschaften*) were assigned the task of preventing a Reichswehr coup against them.* Even those not directly involved either in planning or operations at this level had great expectations. Hitler's acceptance of the SA-SS prohibition† without a coup was hardest for the newest storm troopers, but even the *alte Kämpfer* were perplexed when their triumphs over Groener in May and June, leading to the electoral victory of July 31, ran off into the sand. The *Alarm-Zustand* ("condition red alert") of the first weeks in August‡ was virtually a repetition of their experience in March; Berlin was encircled; SS and SA units in every community made ready to secure railroad stations, ammunition depots, police headquarters. Then came two weeks leave, followed by orders to prepare for new propaganda marches, new Reichstag elections, and another *Hungerwinter*. Small wonder that Communist agitators began to disrupt SA-Appelle and ex-SA men multiplied on the platforms of SPD and KPD rallies.[57] Röhm had again reorganized the SA, reducing the geographic scope of the *Gruppen* (SA divisions) and increasing their number to eighteen, and returning to five *Obergruppenbereiche* (SA corps areas). What he had begun as a response to tremendous growth and increased optimism only added to the confusion and resentment in the months of uncertainty ahead. The publication of new, more complicated and restrictive SA service regulations in October seemed to mock SA impotence.[58]

---

*A Reichswehr coup against the SA: In spite of a certain courtship of the NSDAP by von Schleicher since the fall of 1931, some top Reichswehr officers tended to agree with Prussian Interior Minister Severing and the Bavarian regime that the Storm Troops (and SS) were becoming a revolutionary apparatus. Thus the alarm footing of the SA in March during the election was essentially two-pronged — defensive if need be, offensive should Hitler win the presidency or nearly win it.

†The SA-SS prohibition occurred on April 13, 1932, and lasted until June 14. Reich Interior Minister Groener and Reich Chancellor Brüning were tricked into believing that von Schleicher and Hindenburg would support them in this prohibition, while in reality the Nazis were kept informed of deep divisions in the regime, which in fact led to the fall first of Groener and then Brüning himself at Schleicher's behest. Thus, Hitler could keep the units invisible and inactive with the certainty that the prohibition was shortly to be lifted. The von Papen cabinet did so with face-saving regulations for all uniformed paramilitary units.

‡The August alert was in great part preparation for a seizure of power (*Machtergreifung*) accompanying Hitler's being named to the chancellorship, but it was also intended as a "clean-up" of the Communists and the Social Democratic Reichsbanner. Thus, it was also two-pronged, like the March manuevers, yet not totally offensive. SS units were primed to march on Berlin, and Himmler even delegated a Stuttgart *SS-Kommando* under the later SS killer Dirlewanger to seize an armored train there. In fact, civil war conditions reigned until Hitler demobilized SA and SS, aware that he could not putsch his way to power.

Even the SS began to show signs of losing its momentum in the fall of 1932. The recruitment was slowed down by efforts to establish the identity of all new candidates. The eight SS-*Abschnitte* (sectors) had proliferated into eighteen to correspond with the SA divisional Gruppen and was topped by five SS-*Gruppenkommandos* (division headquarters): North, South, West, East, and Southeast. SS men also began to feel remote from higher headquarters. Certain units, requested to help the SA collect money to keep their soup kitchens in operation, rebelled or collected the money for themselves. Other SS units took part in "mutinies" against gauleiters, "against Goebbels" or "Munich." In Halle SS men joined SA in jeering at Hitler when he asked for their continued loyalty. However, other SS men descended on the rebels, SS and SA alike, beating them with truncheons and brass knuckles.[59] Sustained from the ranks of the unemployed, the SA did not collapse in the lean winter months. Moreover, accessions of unemployed white-collar workers to the SS stiffened the loyalty of the Black Corps to the bourgeois party leadership when men like Ley, Streicher, Frick, Goebbels, and Göring were attacked by more Nazi "renegades" like Stennes and even Gregor Strasser.* Unlike many of the SA, the average SS officer had no sympathy with rebels, working men, or the down-and-out.[60]

Himmler's appearance with Hitler in the home of the banker Kurt von Schroeder on January 4, 1933, along with Wilhelm Keppler† and Rudolf Hess seems to have been primarily symbolic. Himmler and the SS were not yet so important to Hitler that they should have been granted a voice in the counsels of the mighty. Himmler stood, however, for the absent Röhm in a double sense, both as a reminder of the armed masses who stood behind the demagogue Hitler and as an alternative. Hess too represented the party, as a reminder of the absent Strasser whom he had defeated and also of Röhm, his less palatable rival. It is

---

*Gregor Strasser: When the Nazis' vote actually declined in the balloting for another Reichstag in November 1932, Gregor Strasser began to negotiate behind Hitler's back with von Schleicher. His resignation from the NSDAP early in December was the culmination of a growing realization on the part of many anticapitalist Nazis that Hitler intended to make major concessions to the big business interests in order to come to power legally. Strasser did not succeed in dislodging a major segment of the party from Hitler's influence, but many temporarily quarreled and fell away, especially in the SA.

†Wilhelm Keppler: A Bavarian industrial chemist and manufacturer (born in 1882) who joined the party in 1927, Keppler organized a circle of business leaders and bankers in the course of 1931–1932 known as the *Freundeskreis Adolf Hitlers* (Circle of Hitler's friends), who hoped to advise Hitler in economic matters but whom he merely tapped for campaign funds. Himmler, Göring, and Ribbentrop all dabbled in this circle for financial and prestige reasons. Himmler captured Keppler for the SS in March 1933 and ultimately the whole Freundeskreis with its finances and economic influence.

not unlikely that Himmler and Hess were also there to watch each other and to help Hitler reassure his followers later that he had not "sold out." In any case, this portentous promotion of Himmler had been well earned, or if it had not yet, soon would be.[61]

The world depression, much more than the treaty of Versailles, withered the tender seedling of German democracy. Republicans-of-the-head (*Vernunftrepublikaner*) outnumbered republicans-of-the-heart in Germany for most of the time since 1919. It no longer seemed rational to favor a parliamentary system that was powerless to cope with the suffering, the mindless violence, and the political division of families and communities. The Catholic Center Party and the Social Democratic Party had sought to save the pieces; the core of their support was still intact when the German right, heavy industry and banking, the Reichswehr leadership, and the conspiratorial politicians around Hindenburg began to "tame" the Nazi wolves by introducing them into the sheepfold. The Communist cadres too were intact, with their masses of supporters in German cities ready to engage in a civil war on orders from Moscow. Hitler needed the threat of the Storm Troops to force the right to the bargaining table and later to convince it that he could handle the Communists. He needed the Storm Troops to engulf the police and intimidate the supporters of the Center and SPD, while he carried out the "revolution from above" which the German right had preached since 1920. But he also needed the SS, to absorb the right, destroy its positions of influence and impregnability, and channel the constructive and destructive potential of the "Conservative Revolution" so long heralded in Germany. And ultimately he needed the SS to watch the SA, that kaleidoscopic and centrifugal mass of political soldiers swollen with the poor and the hungry, the greedy and the psychopaths, the Landsknechte and the crooks. The next eighteen months would see the total transformation of Germany but also of the Storm Troops — and the SS.

# 4

## The Age of Opportunity
## 1933

Die Zeit der grossen Chancen[1]

Torch-bearing SS units marched under the Brandenburg Gate the night of January 30, 1933, indistinguishable in the dark from their more numerous SA comrades.[2] In the moment of victory, rivalries and organizational differences were forgotten. National Socialists of every branch — PO, SA, SS, NSKK, HJ, alte Kämpfer and newcomers of last summer — were united in the determination to make a revolution. After so many disappointments and false starts, they were determined to seize and hold power. The spirit of a unifying, national renaissance which permeated the ranks of many a non-Nazi organization in the coming months, and penetrated even to foreign observers, did not becloud the purpose of the political soldiers, whether Party *Reichsleiter* (National Party Officer) SS-Standartenführer, or SA-Mann: to wrest the whole power from their conservative allies and to crush any counter-revolution, from the bourgeois right as well as from the Marxist left. No one knew how, where, or when this challenge would be faced; opinions differed as to method and timing. But within the movement there was a deep reservoir of faith and confidence replenished by victory, upon which Hitler and his lieutenants could draw.[3]

In spite of the quarrels and the partial differentiation of tasks among party, SA, and SS since 1929, the years of combat side by side, the steady hammering out of a propaganda line, the common denominators of class, education, region, and above all world war and free corps memories gave nearly all those who were Nazis in January 1933 a functional similarity which is best expressed in the term "political soldier." Out of the amorphous and romantic *ressentiment* of 1918 had come in practice a functioning reality: *a political instrument.* Just as the actual soldier — be he private or general — must possess will and intelligence in order to be a good instrument, thereby opening up the possibility of insubordination and error, so the political soldiers of national socialism were not automatons. Their disagreements and quarrels, like those of the Communists but unlike those of most other political factions, concerned *means* exclusively, not ends. They agreed in their image of themselves as instruments. The rise of the SS, particularly in this period but also later, at the expense of SA and party can be explained by its more rapid and efficient adaptation to the Nazi ideas of political soldiering. The party and the SA did not wish any less to be political soldiers; indeed they were, each in their way, quite successful. But their size, structure, and composition ultimately militated against "perfection." Of course, the SS never became a perfect instrument, and the party was to be at least partially rehabilitated years later by Bormann's skill.

Hitler had evolved his revolutionary methods in the practical, day-to-day political conflicts of the past decade. His political soldiers of every branch were (1) tools of conquest, (2) cadre, (3) control apparatus, and (4) devices for exercising pressure. For Hitler conquest meant the seizure of power, from below in the streets, from above in parliaments, cabinets, executive offices and bureaus. Cadre meant a reservoir of indoctrinated, reliable personnel. Control apparatus meant a two-way communications network, directed outwards toward the opponents, toward state authorities and foreign countries, and toward potential allies and members as well as inwards toward lower ranks and different branches of the movement. Pressure devices meant instruments of propaganda and terror for the purpose of holding and using power, which were directed against the masses, counter-revolutionary opponents, allied groups, foreign countries, and various branches of the movement. While differentiation among PO, SA, and SS began at this level, all three were equipped in all the above areas.

While the exercise of force was in some respects left to SA and SS, the emphasis on legality and persuasion in the movement meant that all three branches had developed as propaganda organizations. The SA and the SS were accustomed to holding forth as rabble-rousers and expected to join in the conquest of parliaments, cabinets, executive posts, and bureaus. The party stalwarts were in the SA and the SS; they had personally dealt out violence and terror, and filled the streets with their membership for elections and alarms throughout 1932.[4] Except in the military area, there was little to distinguish the SA and SS from the party in aspiration toward responsible positions in the state and the economy. All three branches were attractive to the ambitious on the Nazi lower rungs of professional success. There was a multitude of intelligence services, and every branch sought to infiltrate the state, the economy, and the other branches with confidential agents.[5] Since the exercise of pressure had been the chief means for conquering power before January 30, all parts of the Nazi movement were equally conscious of their importance as pressure groups in holding and exercising power thereafter.

Where, then, did the seeds of future antagonisms lie? Not — as might too readily be surmised — in the powerful ambitions of the SS officers corps. Of the three branches, the SS was the least hungry for a monopoly of power. The difficulty lay with the nature of the victory of January 1933 and with the subsequent revolution of that year. Hitler had only barely won power. The door had been opened to him because he was noisy and dangerous, but he had not captured the power as yet. While not intact, the powers of the German state, the army, the economy, and the social institutions were immense. If these institutions, their flanks once turned, could have been seized by direct frontal assault, it is unlikely that the SS would have been elaborated *jenseits von Partei und Staat* (beyond Party and State) — although an SA-Staat formed from the most revolutionary elements of the NSDAP, the SA, and the SS is quite conceivable.[6] Hitler, Göring, Goebbels, Hess, and Himmler as well as many gauleiters gradually discovered that to conquer a whole modern society requires time and technical ability. Amazing as the extent of their subsequent victory was in the struggle for hegemony in Germany, the Nazis were not prepared for frontal assaults upon all the entrenched power of political, military, economic, and social institutions. They feared absorption by the conservative inertia of a professional army, a skillful bureaucracy, a tough capitalistic elite, and the German masses.[7] To have cast their lot with the radicals, a far from insignificant minority in their own ranks and throughout Germany in 1933–1934, *might* have brought an earlier success; but the shadow of November 9, 1923, and even more of November 1918 — when internal factionalism weakened Germany in the face of her enemies — thrust them all almost against their will into the solution found after June 30, 1934; a silent revolution in permanence.[8] For this revolution the SS was best equipped, or could become so earlier than the other factions.

It is erroneous, however, to carry back to early 1933 the deep antipathies (SA-SS and ultimately party-SS) of later years. Even the party-SA polarity, prominent in the Stennes case and as late as May 1933 in Pomerania, emphasized differences among flamboyant personalities and quarrels over money rather than ideological principles.[9] The party in 1933 was not well disciplined, and it was not conservative. Röhm held the SA remarkably well in hand right until his demise; its atrocities were more or less intentional. Hitler was in the habit of using both SA and PO as power-political instruments as a kind of one-two punch, whereby it was wholly incidental which fist flew first. Both were to expand rapidly in 1933 (as indeed the SS did too), far too rapidly. But whereas the party's newcomers were civilians who admired the success of political soldiering, the SA's growth came from the Stahlhelm, who were ex-soldiers. Furthermore, the structural weaknesses of the NSDAP hierarchy, marked by localistic gauleiters and the wound left by the Strassers, were greater than those of the SA due to Stennes and other Landsknecht-figures, for Röhm had built a formidable command structure. Thus, the party was more quickly overrun by opportunists than the SA, more easily persuaded to adjust to a long-drawn-out conflict with existing institutions, and ultimately ready to accept the substitution of the smaller, better disciplined, and apparently more subordinate SS for the SA as its instrument of force and violence.[10] But before all this could occur, the SA was to gather unto itself all the prerequisites of a state-within-a-state, to foreshadow the SS-Staat to come, indeed to form the matrix in which the SS ripened.

No small part of the SA's power came from the survival of the notion in nationalist, militarist, and conservative circles that the SA contained "good human material" which could be exploited in rearming Germany. Coupled with the loose thinking of men like Schleicher and Papen that the Nazis could be tamed and harnessed was the plan to use the SA domestically against the Marxists without involving the "unpolitical" Reichswehr.[11] There was thus just enough acceptance by Hitler's Nationalist partners of both a domestic terror role and a share in defense responsibilities for the SA to permit Röhm to penetrate rapidly in 1933 not only into police and defense activities but the operations of numerous administrative bureaus at national and regional levels. While party personnel proceeded to enter state positions of all kinds with equal rapidity, the SA tended to set up a kind of secondary governmental framework *beside the state authority (Nebenregierungen)*.[12] In all these operations, Himmler and the SS played a supporting role. The SS had few if any unique activities in the *Machtergreifung* (seizure of power) and the *Gleichschaltung* (coordination); everything it did, SA units did too. Yet by the winter of 1933–1934, older differentiating tendencies — particularly with regard to police activities — combined with reawakened antipathies and new political alliances had thrust the

SS into the front ranks of the defenders of the National Socialist edifice, while Röhm's power system, of which the SS was still a part, threatened to secede. Not the act of secession (the nonexistent *Putsch*) but the credibility of SA secession and belief in the seriousness of the consequences, due to the extent of the SA-Staat, led Hitler to strike on June 30. The top leadership of the SS was to contribute to the notion of the danger — out of motives of ambition, loyalty to Hitler, and a conviction that the SS was better equipped to fullfil the tasks Röhm had set for the SA — anticapitalist, anticlerical, above all, anti-Semitic — which they held to be as vital to national socialism as did the men the SS killed.

The peculiar blend of random lawlessness and calculated political crime found in the SS murders of June 30–July 3, 1934, can be discovered in the performance of the *Hilfspolizei* (auxiliary police) as early as February 1933. Indeed, the strange pedigree of the June 1934 *Nacht der langen Messer* (night of the long knives) traces back to the feme-murders of 1921–1923. There too a bloody amateurism was combined with cool, ruthless Realpolitik. There was nothing peculiarly SS in the Hilfspolizei arrangements; yet from this short-lived institution grew two of the most characteristic SS organizations, the *Totenkopfverbände* and the *Verfügungstruppen* (special duty troops).

The Nazis' main concern in February was the elimination of the maximum number of their rivals in the coming election. They wished to come as close as possible to a monopoly of influence over public opinion before March 5. In a sense, all they needed to do was to expand their 1932 techniques of electioneering propaganda and terror. Often in 1932 the police had failed to do them either much harm or much good; the Nazis' real concern was the paramilitary organizations of the Social Democratic and the Communist left (Reichsbanner and *Roter Frontkämpfer-Bund*).* Most of the "martyrs" of SA and SS died in brawls or ambushes at the hands of their opponents, not from the police, who were forbidden to use firearms.[13] After January 30 it was certainly not the police who accounted for the many deaths and injuries among SA and SS, beginning with Hans Maikowski in Berlin returning from the torch procession. The Nazi effort to capture the police, seen first in Prussia on February 11 with the creation of a *Höherer Polizeiführer West* (Superior Police Leader West)† by Göring as Prussian commissarial Interior Min-

---

*Roter Frontkämpferbund:* The *Rot-Front*, as the Red Front Soldiers' League was called from its battle cry, had been founded to compete among veterans with the Social Democratic Reichsbanner and the Nationalist Stahlhelm. Officially illegal since 1930, the Red Front was as much a part of urban Germany in the depression as the SA. Its slogan was "Schlag die Faschisten tot!" (Kill the fascists!).

†*Höherer Polizeiführer West:* This post was created for the police Major Stieler von

ister, was not defensive but offensive—to procure tools of repression. Furthermore, it was tactically important to moderate the civil war atmosphere which pure SA and SS repression would have created, not only in behalf of the elections but to lull Social Democrats and other future victims into a postponement of serious resistance until it was too late. The designation of only specified SA and SS units as auxiliary police, with special armbands, had a triple advantage: (1) the reluctance of some veteran police officials to use violence against the left could thereby be bypassed, (2) the authority of the police was maintained for future use, and (3) the revolutionary radicalism of some units could be controlled. It is not surprising that the first auxiliary police were in effect a kind of SA and SS military police (*Streifendienst*) created February 15. Individuals and groups of SA and SS men had to be prevented from molesting innocent persons and alerting the leftist parties by uncoordinated raids on their headquarters.[14] On February 17 Göring ordered the Prussian police to use their firearms freely, and a week later on February 22 he issued orders for the creation of an auxiliary police force of 50,000, a doubling of the existing Prussian police force of 54,712. They were to carry firearms and to remain in intact units of SA, SS, and Stahlhelm in the proportion of 5:3:1 (25,000, 15,000, and 10,000), wherein the SS was greatly overrepresented and the Stahlhelm underrepresented. Their actual employment was reserved for the Interior Ministry of Prussia and its subordinate police officials, who only gradually and incompletely were replaced by SA, SS, and party personnel by March 5. Their commanders were to be police officials. The first official auxiliary police in Berlin were a direct forerunner of the garrisoned SS-*Verfügungstruppe* (Special Duty Troops). On February 24 two hundred hand-picked SS men were especially armed and garrisoned under Wolf von Helldorf, commander of SA-*Gruppe Berlin-Brandenburg*. The remainder of the subsequent Hilfspolizei in Berlin were SA volunteers, operating in detachments from their regiments and battalions. They were supposed to work with the regular precinct stations of the police.[15]

Auxiliary police appeared in February in such National Socialist strongholds as Brunswick and Thuringia, but detailed negotiations

---

Heydekamp and extended over the Prussian provinces of Westphalia and Rhine. A comparable post was invented for the detached East Prussian area (*Höherer Polizeiführer Ost*) March 14; it was located at Königsberg. Göring conceived the positions as part of a police general staff in the expected civil disturbances to be caused by the Communists. Although the positions were abolished June 10, they may have suggested the later position of *Höherer SS- und Polizeiführer* (1937–on), which had a general staff role in preparation for wartime crises on the home front.

were still necessary in Brunswick on February 25 to win approval of a specific action desired by an SS commander. The men were not permitted to wear their uniforms, and authority was withdrawn again after a specific action. In several Länder (Hessen and Saxony), there were no auxiliary police, due to socialist interior ministries. Nevertheless, even before the excuse of the Reichstag fire and the *Notverordnung* (Emergency Decree) of February 28, auxiliary police units of SA and SS were engaged in terroristic acts. Especially in the Rhineland and Ruhr areas with their intense "class war" atmosphere, SA and SS auxiliary police rounded up workers and labor leaders as alleged Communists and beat them in the police prisons. While in Hanover province — still briefly presided over by Gustav Noske* — the police retained the upper hand, Göring's purge of the police system in the Ruhr and Rhineland led to the overrunning of the regular police headquarters by "auxiliaries" who were without central direction and control.[16]

The emergency decrees of February 28, 1933, created the conditions necessary for the future SS state to flourish, yet it appears highly improbable that the SS had anything to do with starting the fire in the Reichstag. While it is less certain that the SA can be as definitely excluded, it now seems that if young Marinus van der Lubbe did receive some help, this came from the Berlin SA with or without Göring's knowledge and not as part of a Hitler conspiracy among Göring, Goebbels, Röhm, and Himmler — as is still sometimes alleged. Röhm and Himmler were in Munich, as was Heydrich although not Daluege. Daluege and Helldorf rapidly mobilized SS- and SA-Hilfspolizei to aid hand-picked, regular police units in their arrests before morning on February 28. There is no question that all units worked from lists prepared long in advance, yet neither their alacrity nor their thoroughness are proof of a plot to burn the Reichstag but rather of a plot against civil liberties which was already suspected by astute political observers.[17] On the basis of Frick and Gürtner's *Verordnung zum Schutz von Volk und Staat* (Decree for the Protection of People and State) of February 28, the auxiliary police when acting "on orders of the *Reichsregierung*" (national government) were empowered to arrest persons; stop public meetings; raid homes, businesses, and meeting places; seize property and printed matter; and intercept mail, telegrams, and telephone calls. Their influence was no longer confined to Prussia and Nazi strongholds

---

*Gustav Noske had been the Social Democratic "bloodhound" who had helped set up the free corps against the far left revolutionaries. As provincial Oberpräsident, he survived the Papen coup in Prussia of July 20, 1932, but arranged with Göring personally to go on leave until his pension began in October 1933. His police apparatus lasted long enough to "keep the lid on."

but could be applied anywhere in the Reich by the Hitler regime. A wave of arrests, beatings, and even killings followed in which former Communists and suspected Communists were included with card-carrying ones. SA, SS, and Stahlhelm units were rushed into service as guards at public buildings, power plants, and frontier outposts. An atmosphere of public emergency was created for the election day, aided by Göring's pronouncement that he would fight communism not with the state police but "with those down below there" — the SA and the SS. Intimidation extended well beyond the ranks of the Communists through the SPD to the Center and even against the erstwhile Nazi allies, the DNVP.[18]

Nevertheless, in spite of true stories of SA and SS "supervision" of the voting on March 5, the election must be recorded as the last German one in which secret ballots and genuine alternatives could not be successfully counteracted by implied or actual threats of retaliation. The Nazis received exactly 43.9 percent of the votes despite all their repressive tactics. They still needed the votes of the Papen-Hugenberg bloc to govern legitimately. Clearly, the revolution had not gone far enough. The street terror techniques of 1932 had proved insufficient, and the capture of the state apparatuses had scarcely begun. Instead of having won, the Nazis had their biggest battles still ahead of them. But now they had regained their own momentum, while their opponents were rapidly to lose theirs. The task of the coming months was obviously to create chaos and then to "liberate" the German people from it while simultaneously reorganizing the society along the lines desired by the "order-bringers." This general conception was shared by widely divergent supporters of the new regime: conservative revolutionaries in Papen's circle; business and military leaders of the right like Schacht and Blomberg; party theorists such as Hess, Goebbels, and Rosenberg; the practical politicians Hitler and Göring; and Röhm's SA leadership just as definitely as by Himmler's SS officers.[19]

As early as March 5 and 6, groups of SA and SS men entered public buildings and raised swastika banners on the flagpoles. They were not always Hilfspolizisten with white armbands, nor were they always successful at first. When they met resistance, they called for reinforcements and sometimes ended by destroying property, notably records and furniture. "A revolution is, after all, a revolution, even when it comes to power legally," wrote Goebbels in his diary. This was a revolution by command (*Revolution auf Befehl*). A show of violence was needed to help topple bureaucracies and vestiges of local autonomy. Thus, on the one hand, the auxiliary police now made their appearance everywhere, symbol of the revolutionary people's justice, while on the other hand, *Rollkommandos* (mobile details) of "unauthorized" SA and SS perpetrated acts of savagery and license. In Liegnitz the press building of the SPD *Volkszeitung* had been under guard by SS-Hilfspolizei. On March 10 it was "seized" by SA-Hilfspolizei under the leadership of the police; during the following night an SA squad from Breslau led by an Oberführer (Colonel) broke in and destroyed or stole much of the equipment. Here and elsewhere the blame was put on Communists in SA uniform — just like the accomplices of van der Lubbe, according to Göring.[20]

One of the chief Nazi concerns was the possible development of centers of armed resistance in Hamburg, Saxony, Hessen, Bavaria, Württemberg, and Baden. The SA and the SS played a vital role in the skillful coups d'etat in these areas. Formations of SA and SS gathered in front of government buildings, demanding the raising of swastika flags and the formation of Nazi regimes. Local police, not wishing bloodshed and possible retribution, refrained from dispersing them; the Reichswehr refused to intervene. Thereupon Frick, acting on the basis of paragraph two of the February 28 emergency decree, appointed Reich Police Commissars "to maintain peace and order." Intimidation of local regimes, who resigned out of fear of bloodshed and civil war involving an overestimated Communist threat, was thus combined with actual bloodshed and violence which justified the intervention of Berlin against the autonomy of the Länder, more or less in the spirit of the Nationalist Right's ideal of Reichsreform. No Reich Police Commissar was an SS officer. Dietrich von Jagow in Württemberg and Manfred von Killinger in Saxony were SA-Gruppenführer and former free corps leaders; some Police Commissioners were party leaders like Robert Wagner in Baden, discharged from the Reichswehr for his support of the 1923 putsch. In Bavaria the free corps general Ritter von Epp, a strong exponent of the Nazis since 1923, assumed this role and assigned Himmler the post of Munich's Commissarial Police President. These Reich Police Commissars gave way quickly to so-called Reich Commissars (occasionally, as with Epp, the same person), who created commissarial cabinets to replace the collapsed regimes. Thus, irrespective of the majorities in local parliaments, the Nazis were able to form majority cabinets in which the interior ministries controlling the police always fell to them. This made the use of auxiliary police a matter of course. It also opened the way to replace police officials outside Prussia with SA and SS officers. Moreover, these Reich Police Commissars and Reich Commissars were authorized to commandeer the party and its formations in case of serious armed resistance. This resistance never came, and the post of Reich Commissar was eliminated. Instead, in a matter of weeks Hitler had named eleven leading Nazis, mostly gauleiters, as *Reichsstatthalter* (Viceroys of the Realm) with Hindenburg's approval. They were in effect local dictators.[21]

There was little difference in the employment of the SS and the SA in the months of March and April. Since there were far more SA than SS members, the latter were perhaps already slightly more dependable as executors of official policy in contrast with the SA's more numerous private vendettas and general hell-raising. This might account for the relatively greater employment of SS as auxiliaries, as much as any pre-1933 plan to use the SS primarily as police while the SA developed as a people's militia. Indeed, it was the SA rather than the SS which laid claim to the offices of police president and police director. SA and SS men alike were frustrated by their failure to capture the local police apparatuses wholesale in March; they formed their own *Sturmbanne zur besonderen Verwendung* (battalions for special purposes) at this time, whose headquarters rapidly became jails and torture chambers — the so-called *Bunker.** While the Berlin variety were notorious, they appeared elsewhere and simultaneously with the first concentration camps, located in deserted barracks, factories, wharves, etc. The purpose of both Bunker and *Konzentrationslager* (KZ or KL, Ka-Tset or Ka-El) was dual: to have a place for enemies other than the jails controlled by conservative officials, and to have *secret* dens where prisoners could not be found by the police or by their friends. There was nothing uniquely SS about either phenomenon; at all times there were also SA and SS auxiliaries as guards in official jails. Significantly, however, SA and SS men seem to have been always separately assigned and not mixed in jails, bunkers, and camps.[22] Not yet a result of antipathy in most cases, this was rather an expression of the difficulty of asserting authority over the groups except through their own personal leaders. In fact, it is likely that Röhm and Himmler in Munich were temporarily in a poor state of communication with their regional commanders, who behaved like local despots alone or in collaboration with the party leaders who had become commissarial ministers. In Brunswick an anti-Semitic and anti-Stahlhelm terror exploded prematurely in March on the authority of Minister President Dietrich Klagges and the leadership of SS battalion and regimental commanders. Yet Klagges and the SS could actually be restrained better than many gauleiters and SA-Gruppenführer; this terror was "cancelled."[23]

Kurt Daluege beat Himmler to access to state police authority by be-

*Bunker:* In World War One this was an underground sleeping room in the trench system. Under civil war conditions, a Bunker was a more or less fortified hideout. The Nazis assumed a civil war stance in 1933; in some communities this may have been justified for a short time but the psychological value must have been more important.

coming Prussian *Staatskommissar zur besonderen Verwendung* (Special Commissar) in Göring's Ministry of the Interior on February 6. Göring's political sense, like that of his master, told him not to concentrate all the police power in one man's or one agency's hands. He used the select battalions of Nazi police Major Wecke in Berlin for his personal security. He made Rudolf Diels Chief of the Political Police (IA-*Chef*)* under a Police President (Admiral Levetzow) who was neither an SA nor SS officer; and he placed Daluege as a watchdog in the police section of the ministry while he selected as Permanent Secretary (*Staatssekretär*) a business-oriented, practical bureaucrat, Ludwig Grauert, to replace the monarchist Herbert von Bismarck. Helldorf, the dashing SA-Gruppenführer, he kept at arm's length, with only the police presidium in Potsdam for a prize. Daluege was of course Göring's liaison with the SS, and to some extent with Himmler. However, Daluege and Himmler, though *Duz-Freunde* (privileged to use "Du"), were nearly open rivals in the spring months of 1933. Daluege seems to have understood his function in the Prussian police primarily in terms of his old intelligence role in the Potsdamer Strasse. He expanded his liaison "bureau" into a clean-up detail and was rewarded by being put in charge of the police section of the ministry while he went on collecting incriminating information from IA-files, from denunciations, from SS commanders, and by watching the intrigues of party, state, and business leaders in Berlin. He preferred to court the SA, Göring, businessmen, and state officials rather than Himmler, his nominal superior.[24]

Himmler was just as interested in securing a state position, however minor, as a foothold. He was swept into office along with Röhm and the alte Garde of Munich. In the critical weeks before and after election day, Röhm and Himmler, the Bavarian SA and SS, were assigned the special task of checkmating any efforts at a Bavarian secession with possible international repercussions. Probably this chimera was born of the 1919–1923 era, like the much-feared but largely illusory Communist uprisings in Berlin and the Ruhr. However, it must be emphasized that just as Röhm did not even receive an executive position, having to return to the old staff relationship with Epp of 1919, so Himmler became the subordinate of gauleiter Adolf Wagner, commissarial Bavarian interior

---

*Chief of the Political Police (*IA-Chef*): The practice of maintaining a sub rosa political police in Weimar Prussia goes back to 1919. The Berlin police established a special "office IA," which effectively became a clearing house for political intelligence inside the Prussian police system. It had also been used against the Nazis. There was little concealment of this operation in the 1930s, and von Papen's seizure of the Prussian state apparatus on July 20, 1932, had enhanced its authority. Diels's formal position as Chief of the Political Police *was* new.

*Courtesy Hoover Institution*

Himmler standing in front of a door marked "Polizei Präsident," early 1933.

minister. Heydrich modestly entered state employment as chief of the political bureau of the Munich police. Himmler's promotion to the newly created post of *Politischer Polizeikommandeur Bayerns* on April 2 did not change his subordinate status, though it widened considerably the area of his and Heydrich's legal influence over the police apparatus. Himmler and Heydrich created a 152-person office out of 133 transfers from other police posts (including some of the most notorious old undercover cops like Heinrich Müller, Franz Josef Huber, and Friedrich Panzinger). Some 19 temporary appointments were probably SS personnel, possibly I-C (SD) in some cases. Himmler was forced, however, to give up his post as Munich police chief to August Schneidhuber, the SA-Obergruppenführer (General). Röhm was collecting offices for the SA, becoming a Staatssekretär in the Bavarian government in charge of the so-called "Security Police" (*Sicherheitspolizei*) — actually just the auxiliary police (SA, SS, and Stahlhelm). He also commanded the various SA-Kommissare in local communities, as he did in Prussia and elsewhere. Yet Daluege's shift to the command of the Prussian *Landespolizei* (state police) — a comparable move — would turn out to be of more lasting import for Daluege and the SS. Röhm did not move to consolidate SA power over the state apparatus as did Himmler, Heydrich, and Daluege. The apparent strength of the SA "beyond party and state" led Röhm astray.[25]

The differentiation between the SA and the SS that set in with the fall of 1933 had its origins in the spring. When the membership of the two organizations were turned loose on the German population after the elections, Hitler expected "abuses," "injustice," and "excesses." These he regarded with a cynical relativism as valuable lessons to his enemies and even his friends. He expected to "correct" some of them, but in the majority of such cases in the past, he had merely made a show of punishment — or if he were personally irritated, had made an example of one or two luckless devils. From the very beginning he carried on an ambiguous, on-again, off-again policy of restraints on the SA to confuse his allies on the right. Over a period of many months, he succeeded in this; he also succeeded in confusing the SA. The ultimate failure of the SA to resist its own emasculation in June 1934 was an important result of the very same process that led a significant proportion of officers and men in the Storm Troops to lose faith in Hitler, in the revolutionary slogans and promises of the *Kampfzeit*, and in the ideal of politisches Soldatentum. Their confusion as to what was expected of them was perhaps no greater than many in the SS, but Himmler weaned the SS away from the spontaneous radicalism and violence of the resentful declassés and gave it leaders who understood how to mold it into an instrument of revolutionary terror and control that did not become confused by tactical shifts in state policy. The SA was not intrinsically incapable of discipline and training. Had it been a smaller organization and therefore forced to restrict its ambitions — as was the SS, for example — to the police or to absorbing the Reichswehr, Röhm and his top leaders could not have been tempted to try so many avenues to power and fail in all of them.[26]

The theatrical character of the "legal revolution" which appears in the Potsdam Day ceremony, the passage of the Enabling Act by the Reichstag, the "quiet and bloodless" pogrom of the *Judenboykott* of April 1, and the celebration of May Day as a Day of National Unity conceals from modern day observers the violence, confusion, and spontaneous radicalism of the Nazi *Machtergreifung*. Few persons living in the Reich in March and April 1933 could cherish the illusion that soon all would be as before. The contrary illusion, that soon everything would be different and much better, was in the atmosphere. It was felt that the violence and the terror *must* be short-lived and quickly restricted to enemies of the state. Genuine efforts to restore order on the part of countless members of the right in the old state apparatuses, and even among the new officials such as Rudolf Diels in his newly created Berlin *Geheimes Staats-Polizeiamt* (Gestapa) in the Prinz Albrechtsstrasse, lulled Germans into accepting Nazi theatrics as a New Order — even while the Storm Troops and Schutzstaffel poured out the *ressentiment* of two frustrated generations upon the defenseless bodies of their victims at Dachau and the *Columbia Haus*, Kemna, Dürrgoy, and Oranienburg.[27]

Not the least significant phase of Nazi radicalism in March and April 1933 was the onslaught against the business world, industrial and commercial. While SA and SS often formed the vanguard of "committees" and "flying squads," party rank-and-file of distinctly bourgeois origin made up a goodly proportion of the scarcely veiled shakedown and blackmail enterprises which intimidated and infuriated businessmen and managers. Numerous cases occurred where boycott actions against chain and department stores leading to violence and plundering were initiated by functionaries of the NSBO (*National-Sozialistische Betriebszellen-Organisation*) and Adrian von Renteln's *Kampfbund des gewerblichen Mittelstandes* — and then executed by SA and SS. However, the SS were themselves initiators though not the exclusive executors of programs to recruit paying supporters or sponsors among both "Aryan" and "non-Aryan" managers of large firms, the enforced "contributions" of automobiles, motorcycles, and trucks to the SS, and the forcible requisitioning of Masonic and Jewish community buildings as SS-Heime. The SA was of course not inferior to the SS in these exploits. Its specialty was the naming of Kommissare and even *directors* to local firms, who were obliged to pay them a salary for the privilege of not being interfered with.[28] The highly arranged boycott of Jewish businesses on April 1 may be understood as a technique of Goebbels and Hitler to concentrate the attention of foreign observers and native Germans on the Jewish issue, to divert them and perhaps minimally even the Nazi radicals from the unrestrained expression of Nazi envy and hatred against all the propertied class. The success of this maneuver, at least domestically, demonstrated the superior advantages of disciplined units, whether of SA or SS, over self-constituted "committees" in which SA or SS men fulfilled the function of executors of random mob violence. During the coming year the SS was more effectively subjugated to this ideal than the SA, though never completely.[29]

We have seen that Goebbels and Hitler's conception of a dramatic use of staged events made excellent use of the SA and the SS as symbols of Revolution *and* Order. For several years already uniformed platoons of SA and SS men had paraded into the churches, to underscore the Nazi appeal to Germans who were both pious and nationalistic. These demonstrations reached their height in 1933 during the struggle for a National Church. Similarly, on March 21 the Potsdam square was lined on one side with Reichswehr and on the other with SA and SS in shiny new uniforms, all in perfect order. Again, on March 23 the outside of the Kroll Opera was surrounded with SS *in formation*, while the inside was lined with SA, arms akimbo, against the walls of the corridors and in the chamber around the benches of the SPD and the *Zentrum*.[30] Already in the Kampfjahre the pictures show a change from a scattering of black-capped SS in a confused crowd of civilians and brown shirts surrounding the speakers to a rigidly aligned platform squad of six or eight SS men in black caps and breeches, with the SA stationed at entrances and in rows at the back and sides of the audience. Intimidation was becoming massive and shifting to a demonstration of potential terror rather than outright violence.[31] In the boycott action of April 1 and again in the seizure of the union headquarters on May 2, SA and SS were employed essentially to *prevent* random violence and destruction by enthusiastic and venal participants from the NSBO and the Kampfbund. That individuals and units of both SA and SS in April and May 1933 too readily joined in gratuitous abuse of persons whom Goebbels, Göring, Ley, or Frick would have spared, or stole properties belonging to national-minded individuals or to the German people, was indeed a *Schönheitsfehler*, a temporary inadequacy — which Hitler and the rest were prepared to overlook, provided Himmler and Röhm could bring their men into line when it seemed absolutely necessary. In fact, Röhm never lost the ability to do so, even if Himmler did outshine him in this matter of commanding discipline. The ultimate crime of the SA was not radicalism and indiscipline but too much overt ambition. Himmler and the SS leadership learned better to keep silent and to wait.[32]

After the passage of the Enabling Act on March 23, the essential task of party, SA, and SS became the piecemeal conquest of the remaining centers of resistance. The maintenance of disorder as a technique for dissolving old obligations and loyalties had to be balanced by the ability to cut off disorder at any time and place that demanded and was ripe for *Gleichschaltung* (co-ordination). Gleichschaltung was accomplished in two or more stages — never at one dramatic swoop. First came infiltration, often based on a few persons already in a bureau; meanwhile Nazi agitation for massive changes and even noncompliance with the bureau's measures could go on. Next there arrived one or more Kommissare, often SA, occasionally party officials or an SS man, to supervise the top leadership. With semiofficial status, these Kommissare collected "information" with the help of the other Nazis in the agency, interfered with operations they thought deleterious to the revolution, and arranged for the employment of friends and relatives and members of their SA, SS, or party formation. Later, in most cases by the summer of 1933, the office or agency would receive a Nazi chief, a Nazi majority — or minimally, as in the cases of the Reichswehr, the Foreign Office, or big business firms, a collaborating leadership. At this time open resistance to the agency's acts had to cease, although undercover acts of disobedience and policy twisting might continue where "non-National Socialist" survivals still had to be tolerated. Here the older conflicts within the Nazi system resumed their force: party, SA, and SS struggled for priority and "leverage." Furthermore, since the tougher resistance to Gleichschaltung came from their rightist partners rather than from the supposedly dangerous Marxist and liberal "November criminals" in the state apparatus, the task of the Nazis remained that of dissolving the old authoritarian structures without destroying the instruments of control and conquest which they wished to conquer. It was no mean accomplishment of Hitler and his lieutenants to have preserved the Reichswehr, the Foreign Office, and the conglomerates and banks from the onslaught of his radicals and the rivalries of gauleiters without succumbing wholly to the inner purposes of these institutions. Naturally, their powers of resistance — enough to preserve them from total destruction or subjugation for many years — were nonetheless limited by short-sighted estimates by their leaders of such factors as communism, world opinion, and above all of Hitler and his chief lieutenants, including Röhm and Himmler.[33]

Hitler's concept of the SA as *political* soldiers and Röhm's concept of political *soldiers* were not diametrically opposed, but the potential differences between the two possibilities became exaggerated during 1933, so that after a year of "plastering over the cracks," Hitler destroyed the SA's chances for either alternative. The SS then occupied the former role, only to develop the same alternative emphasis on soldiering in the Waffen-SS of 1940–1945. Thus, the path of development taken by the SS was laid down for it by Hitler and Röhm and to some extent by the Reichswehr leadership. It was the shortsighted decision of the Reichswehr leaders in 1934 to drive the devil (Röhm) out with Beelzebub that placed Himmler's SS squarely in the path of the conservative generals between 1938 and 1944.[34]

Confronted almost immediately by Hitler's policy of cooperation with the Reichswehr, Röhm developed an octopus-strategy of seizing a maximum number of power positions for the SA in the new regime. He sought to develop a monopoly of force outside the Reichswehr and to outmaneuver "the old codgers" for whom he had a free corps captain's contempt. We have seen that the SA had made steady progress in the capture of the police systems in the Länder, even in Göring's bailiwick. Similarly, through the device of *Kommissare z.b.V.* (Commissars for Special Duties) responsible to himself and scattered throughout all levels of administration, Röhm secured leverage and listening posts.[35] His most important coup, however, was the piecemeal absorption of the Stahlhelm between April and September 1933. He accomplished this with Hitler's help, for indeed it was in the Nazi interest to deny to its allies of the right an independent paramilitary arm. However, Röhm was also denying the Reichswehr a valuable ally, he believed, forcing them to come to him for the "good material" with which to build a great army. Starting in June with the transfer to Röhm's authority of the *Jungstahlhelm* — the "replacements" from post-front generations — as well as their youth groups to the *Hitler-Jugend*, the Stahlhelm was further hollowed out in July by the transfer of all men under thirty-five (*Wehrstahlhelm*) as a separate formation to Röhm's command. On October 31, 1933, the separate formation was done away with inside the SA, adding 500,000 men to the SA regulars. On December 1 the remaining Kernstahlhelm was split into a 450,000-man unit known as the SA-Reserve I (men between thirty-five and forty, mostly veterans) and another larger group of 1.5 million known as SA-Reserve II. Ultimately this spectacular SA victory not only drove the generals into the arms of Himmler and Heydrich but weakened the SA by watering down its revolutionary character. The SA of July 1934 that took its own emasculation lying down might be said to have been destroyed by the very "bourgeois rot" which Röhm had preached against so long.[36]

Yet this was not the picture Röhm, Hitler, or the Reichswehr had of the SA at the Bad Reichenhall conference (near Berchtesgaden) July 1–3. The army had just completed its three-month pilot project (*Kurzausbildung* — "short course") in SA training and was ready to undertake a full-scale training program as well as the systematic integration of the SA into the *Grenzschutz* (border defense) and *Zollschutz* (customs defense) systems as part of an overall militia-defense network. Röhm intended to and partially did create an SA elite of 250,000, the *Ausbildungswesen* (AW), or "training system," under the former (and future) SS officer F. W. Krüger, to tap the talents of the Reichswehr while he prepared to lay down the cadre of a future German People's Army in the SA units assigned to the Grenzschutz. Blomberg and Reichenau had given up on the Stahlhelm and Seldte; in fact they now hoped to woo "the best part of the SA" away from the party while quickly building up a strong militia to protect Germany from a preventative war. Although they feared the radicalism of the SA, they admired its vitality; they hoped to bring it under constant surveillance and ultimately military discipline. Hitler made it perfectly clear that the Reichswehr and the SA were of equal status: "This army of the political soldiers of the German Revolution has no wish to take the place of our army or to enter into competition with it. . . . The relation of the SA to the Army must be the same as that of the political leadership to the Army." Hitler's ambiguity of language paralleled the regulations for the AW, which gave them a Reich budget beyond the reach of the Reichswehr but prohibited their acquisition of weapons outside Reichswehr channels. In F. W. Krüger's file notes for July 1933 lie the elements of the SA of 1935, a veterans' organization and preservice training unit for high school and college youths; yet these same notes reveal an ambitious SA program of penetrating the Reichswehr with its ideologically selected trainees from the high schools and universities. Indeed, the men close to Röhm in the summer of 1933 were moving toward a conception of the SA as a future military elite with its members in all-important parts of the social and political system, a people's Junkerdom with its own inner elite in the form of an officer corps composed of free corps commanders, former Reichswehr officers, political soldier-statemen, administrative wizards, revolutionary intellectuals and artists, and university students as cadets. There was no special status of any kind for the SS.[37]

To realize this conception, it was necessary to avoid unnecessary clashes with potential allies. The revolutionaries of yesterday had to become outwardly respectable. Although serious efforts along these lines were made by Röhm and throughout the SA — many of them ridiculous, some of them fairly successful — generally the speed and complete success of the initial Machtergreifung had given the average SA man, or SS man for that matter, little time to prepare himself psychologically for the slower upward pull to respectability. Accustomed to self-help and a goodly portion of eye-winking at their foibles by superiors, the massmen still engaged in brawling with a vengeance. The result was a wave of protests from Reichswehr, SS, party, and citizens, with some efforts at repression. Expulsions from the SA and the SS became the order of the day. With the summer a gradual selection process began to take form in both the SA and the SS whereby those persons who could not conform to regulations and take out their violence on official victims were gradually removed from positions of prominence and increasingly disciplined.[38]

In this context the struggle for a separate SA jurisdiction and the creation of a special *SA-Feldpolizei*, or internal SA police force, represent a self-correcting mechanism as well as an escape from the control of lingering survivals of the *Rechtsstaat* (rule of law). As early as April 28, 1933, a law was passed creating a *Dienststrafgewalt* (disciplinary authority for the services) in SA and SS whereby unit commanders received state authority to punish crimes committed by their subordinates. The reintroduction of the 1898 code of military justice in the Reichswehr on May 12, 1933, gave rise to SA efforts to achieve the same complete severance from civilian authority. On July 31 Röhm cautioned SA members that nonservice connected acts of violence against opponents were not yet covered by SA justice and could be prosecuted by the police. Kerrl, the Prussian Minister of Justice, ordered his Feldgendarmerie not to prosecute SA and SS members unless caught *in flagrante delicto* without first getting the approval of their commanding officers. Röhm decreed in October that arrests of SA members be made only by the newly created *Feldjägerkorps*, accompanied by ordinary police. The law of December 1, 1933, for the securing of the unity of party and state expressly confirmed the principle of separate SA justice where derelictions of duty were involved, while the Dienststrafordnung (Service discipline order) of December 12, 1933, limited the authority of the commanders to service-connected acts.[39]

The SA-Feldpolizei were formed by Göring out of the toughest SA personnel of the Hedemannstrasse and General-Pape Strasse Bunker in Berlin. Actually dating only from the summer of 1933 and restricted to the Berlin-Brandenburg SA district, they were soon replaced by the Prussia-wide Feldjägerkorps, whose cadre they became as of October 7. The latter were formed in groups of 65–100 known as *Bereitschaften*, or *Hundertschaften* (police terms also adopted by SS units set up at this time for riots and other emergencies), to cooperate with Rudolf Diels's Gestapa. Subsidized by private sources, these SA police troops spread throughout the Reich before their dissolution in 1936. Göring did not trust the Feldjäger, however. He sponsored the development of his own armed police regiment under Major Walter Wecke, the *Landespolizeigruppe Hermann Göring*, which played a significant role in the purge of June 30, 1934, and also survived until 1936, the date of Himmler's complete police monopoly.[40]

We have insisted that the SS in its make-up in 1933 was not intrinsically more disciplined or respectable than the SA. Nevertheless, from Himmler's closing of membership in April 1933 to the introduction of the SS's special oath to Adolf Hitler on November 9, 1933, it developed bases for reliability beyond the power of the SA. Moreover, its smaller scope, limited potential, and Himmler's concentration on the police power gave it relative freedom from powerful enemies such as the Reichswehr, the party, and the business world. Above all, Hitler and Göring did not need to fear Himmler, as they did fear Röhm not only as a rival but as a blunderer who could upset the Nazi apple cart.[41]

Both the SS and the SA doubled their membership between January 30, 1933, and May 1933, the SS going from 50,000 to over 100,000, the SA from 300,000 to about 500,000 before the addition of Stahlhelm units. However, where Röhm proceeded to incorporate a million more men from the Stahlhelm into his gigantic edifice, Himmler stopped all but a trickle of actual additions, to allow his processing procedures to catch up. The fifty Standarten were urged to develop three *Sturmbanne* (battalions), each of four *Stürme* (companies), and to fill these out to one hundred each, but the formation of additional units was strictly forbidden. The temporary closing of SS membership, a technique already employed in October 1932, was borrowed from the party, which resorted to the same tactic in May. Thus, the SS not only strengthened its elite appearance but identified itself effectively with the party at a time when the SA seemed intent on accepting everybody and anybody.[42]

Probably a more decisive factor in the long run, however, was the creation of specialized SS units at first within and later alongside the general membership. That this was not an exclusive SS procedure is shown by the formation of the separately garrisoned auxiliary police units of SA men as early as February and the parallel development of the so-called *Gruppenkommandos z.b.V.*, special duty units for terror purposes attached to the *SA-Gruppe* (divisional) headquarters. The SA-Feldpolizei is another case in point. Above all, the creation of the AW (training) system in July was a step toward the formation of an SA elite.

The first distinctive SS formation of 1933 was the *Sonderkommando Berlin* (Special Detail for Berlin) begun by Sepp Dietrich in Berlin in March with 120 selected SS men as a headquarters guard (*Stabswache*) for Hitler's chancellery. From the beginning this unit was armed and designed as a self-contained combat force. It is referred to as a regiment (*Standarte Adolf Hitler*) as early as September 1933, with the feudal-sounding *Leibstandarte* (literally body-regiment, *viz.* the personal regiment) added a few months later. Sepp Dietrich had made it his business to remain as a personal bodyguard of Hitler throughout 1932, thereby consolidating the prior claim of the SS to be the traditional Führer guard. The right to arm openly and to be detached from the main body of political soldiers created the basis for its participation in the purge of June 30, 1934, as well as its role thereafter as the nucleus of a future field SS (Waffen-SS). It is improbable that this latter development was the intention of Sepp Dietrich or Heinrich Himmler at the time, but the idea of protecting the Führer from an SA mutiny was certainly real enough. Hitler's choice of an armed SS unit for this protective purpose is also interesting: he did not choose a Reichswehr unit or a unit of Major Wecke's (Göring's) Prussian police. Thus, the SS came in handy again, as in 1925 and 1930–1931.[43]

Besides the Leibstandarte Adolf Hitler, the future Waffen-SS had other *Sonderkommandos* (special units) as indirect antecedents in 1933. These too had obvious SA parallels. Corresponding to the Gruppen-kommandos z.b.V. (variously, *Gruppenstäbe z.b.V.;* special divisional staffs) of the SA, several of the SS divisions (Gruppen) set up in the spring of 1933 *kasernierte Hundertschaften* (garrisoned hundreds) or *Politische Bereitschaften* (political ready-reserves) as police reserves, who were not given regular police duties but trained for riot duty and used for terror raids. These units became the future special duty SS troops or Verfügungstruppen.[44] Secondly, SS-Sonderkommandos were despatched by Standarten and Abschnitte to set up and operate concentration camps such as Papenburg and Dachau, much as SA-Standarten operated their own quasi-legal prison camps by means of detachments of unemployed SA men. The difference was that the SA never created a separate type of organization for this purpose, while the SS *Wachver-bände* (guard units) became the dreaded *Totenkopfstandarten* (Death's Head Regiments), later a part of the Waffen-SS. Both Politische Bereit-schaften and the *Wachverbände* played a part in the purge of the SA in 1934 along with the Leibstandarte.[45] These measures were not exclusively their province, however. Not only were the top regional SS commanders and their staffs vitally important in the preparation and execution of the coup, but the planning and leadership came from the oldest separate SS organization, Heydrich's *Sicherheitsdienst.*

Consisting first of Heydrich and three assistants, the SD had grown in 1932 to between twenty and thirty paid agents scattered throughout the Reich and the Nazi apparatus by January 30, 1933. About two hundred "volunteers" in the world of business, government, and education supplemented Heydrich's information-gathering system. These persons were not synonymous with the I-C personnel of the SS, although some of the latter joined the SD later, even after 1934. Heydrich certainly did not break contact with his embryo apparatus when "reassigned" to Himmler's personal staff January 27, 1933, and sent to Geneva as an SS representative along with Friedrich Wilhelm Krüger for the SA. Heydrich's actions there (unauthorized display of a large swastika-banner) seem almost extracurricular. Heydrich continued "on special duty" (*zur besonderen Verwendung*) when put in charge of the political police section of the Munich Police Presidium on and after March 9. The young twenty-nine-year-old, who could not even get in to see the self-important *Kommissar z.b.V.* (Commissar for Special Duties) Daluege in the Prussian Interior Ministry on March 15, rapidly set about weaving a net of SD men in and around Prussia by commissioning often very young lawyers and academicians to act in Himmler's interests within the newly formed political police of neighboring states such as Württemberg, Baden, Saxony, and Thuringia as well as in Hessen-Darmstadt, Lübeck, Hamburg, Bremen, and Mecklenburg. Indeed, Heydrich opened an SD office in Berlin's West End (Eichen-Allee 2) in a small villa, where he installed twenty-six-year-old Hermann Behrends, one of his earliest admirers, as his personal representative.[46]

During the next few years, Heydrich's major rival for influence with Heinrich Himmler was Richard Walter Darré, the chief of the SS-*Rassenamt* (Racial Office), soon to become, on June 28, 1933, Reich Minister of Food and Agriculture. With its name changed to fit its ever-widening duties (*Rasse- und Siedlungs-Amt;* Race and Settlement Office), his still-diminutive organization began in 1933 a growth which carried it past the SD in size if not in influence. In 1935 it became, alongside the *SD-Amt* and the *SS-Amt* (administrative headquarters), one of three Main Offices (*Hauptämter*). The Rassenamt assumed a significance out of proportion to its couple of desks in the Munich SS headquarters for two reasons: Darré supplied Himmler with a pseudo-scientific "intellectual" rationale for his elite corps, and Darré proceeded to form a branch of the SS out of his own independent political apparatus, the network of agricultural advisors (*Landwirtschaftliche Fachberater*) to the *Gau-* and *Kreisleiter* (County Leaders) of the NSDAP. This *Agrarpolitischer Apparat* (Farm Policy Apparatus), headed by the *Amt für Agrarpolitik* (Office for Farm Policy), dated back to 1930 and played a decisive role in many Nazi election upsets in farm areas. It was composed of fairly well-educated middle- and upper-class farmers with a community following. Though like the SD it included a number of young men beginning their careers, it also attracted a good many older persons with political experience. Some of these younger men joined the SS in 1931 and 1932, copying Darré, while the majority merely joined the party at this time but the SS only in 1933 and 1934. The latter rarely came through the SA.[47]

In 1932 the SS Racial Office had a staff or advisory function in connection with the approval of new engagements and marriages of SS members, the approval of new applicants for the SS — especially upper ranks — and in granting officers' commissions. It should be remembered that in the depression new engagements and marriages were few and far between, especially in the lower middle class from which the SS drew its membership; nevertheless there is evidence that not all of these were formally approved in advance in 1932 and 1933. Rather, the approval of the SS man's superior, usually the company or battalion commander, was forwarded to the Munich SS headquarters, often after the fact. Photographs, locks of hair, very occasionally a medical "bill of health" on doctors' stationery, appear for 1933. The role of the Racial Office seems to have been largely limited to correspondence, advising and admonishing the commanders regarding criteria.[48]

Himmler's reminiscences before the Wehrmacht officers in 1937 of examining 150–200 photographs a year of SS candidates probably dated not from 1929–1930 as he implied but from 1931–1932. Since there is no evidence for the use of photographs at the earlier date, and since photographs were required for officer-candidates in the later period, it appears likely that what he recalled was the last step in the processing of promotions to officer-status or original acceptances of new SS personnel at officer rank. The Racial Office's part in these procedures consisted of drawing up the regulations to be promulgated by the Leadership Staff (*Führungsstab*) or the SS Administrative Office (SS-Amt), a new examination report-form for the SS physicians (*Mannschafts-Untersuchungs-Liste*, MUL), and correspondence with commanders and physicians.[49]

During the period of mass recruiting in 1932 and 1933, there were a number of changes in the physical specifications for SS membership, notably age and height, representing a gradual tightening up for which the Racial Office was probably responsible. However, even the MUL had little or no racial criteria as such to follow, and the Racial Office staff was utterly incapable of checking on the mass of new candidates' records, not to mention those which never reached Munich or reached the headquarters without the data filled in. Darré could have devoted only very little time to this office during the hectic campaigning of 1932 and the first half of 1933, when he carried on the fight against Hugenberg in the agricultural pressure groups. When he moved to Berlin as minister, the office was moved there as well, but he was busier than ever. Nonetheless, the new SS branch actually began life at this time.[50]

The real architects of the Race and Settlement Office (renamed in 1933) were Dr. Bruno K. Schultz and Dr. Horst Rechenbach, respectively an academic anthropologist-publicist and an army teacher of veterinary medicine. Their collaboration with Darré dated back to 1930, but their direct part in the SS began only in late 1932; in fact their full time activity did not begin until 1934. Nevertheless, these two provided Darré and thus Himmler with the concept of the racial examiner, the white-coated technician with calipers and measuring tape employing standardized and scientific-looking ruled worksheets and number-letter combinations as symbols of human worth. Like the lawyers and academicians of the SD, these chosen few of the Racial Office helped the SS to appear "scientific," thus helping to distinguish the SS officer corps from the SA by giving them a sense of being on the inside track, of being winners, of being correct.[51]

The press to join the SS in 1933 gave the Race and Settlement Office a double opportunity. First of all, it acquired a chance to acquire medically or academically trained agents and collaborators in the Standarten and regional staffs among the numerous physicians, professors, and lawyers who clamored for the opportunity to join an "exclusive" Nazi unit. Secondly, it could begin to enforce a genuine screening at the time of admission, since commanders could no longer claim the necessity of a broad acceptance policy. The *Rassereferent* (race expert) at regional headquarters and the *Musterung* (a kind of army "physical") of new recruits by him date from the late 1933 and early 1934. An especially important aspect of this new SS branch was its educational function, symbolized by the formation of a *Schulungsabteilung* (training division) and the naming of education officers in all units, responsible for the general indoctrination of the men but especially for their training in "racial eugenics," particularly racial anti-Semitism.[52]

The idea of combining the settlement of SS men on farms and in suburban garden homes came from Darré himself. It was almost fully developed in his 1930 book, *New Aristocracy of Blood and Soil*, but nothing could be done to apply it to the SS until he was in power. With the formation of the *Reichsnährstand* (Reich Food Estate) on July 15, 1933, Darré had the mechanism for controlling agricultural production and to some extent the transfer of farm land. The RNS was in fact the Agrarpolitischer Apparat invested with state powers. Although it is probably untrue, as alleged, that the Nazi *Erbhof* (hereditary estate) and production control laws were first written in the Munich and Berlin offices of the SS-Rasse- und Siedlungsamt, the authors were Werner Willikens, Herbert Backe, Hermann Reischle, and Wilhelm Meinberg, all except Willikens in the SS since 1932 (Willikens joined May 1933).[53] Reischle and Meinberg started the *Siedlungsamt* (Settlement Office) and joined Rechenbach and Schultz to become pillars of the SS Race and Settlement Office. While these gentlemen were far too busy in 1933 reorganizing German agriculture to plan in detail for SS settlement, junior academicians and lawyers with time on their hands were not hard to find in the SS. Before long there were elaborate plans for SS suburban housing developments, no end of financing schemes for the purchase of homes and farms, and training programs for new farmers. The Rasse-referenten became *Rasse- und Siedlungsreferenten* (specialists on race and settlement). Above all, they were recruited increasingly from the *Kreisbauernführer* (county farm leaders) and *Landesbauernführer* (state farm leaders) of the Food Estate, the old-line personnel of Darré's apparatus who were increasingly strategic individuals in the country-side.[54]

Thus, by the fall of 1933, there was in embryo the SS-state-within-a-state. It was largely obscured by the whole revolutionary process and more especially by the visibility of the "SA-State." Nonetheless, the major parts of Himmler's apparatus for the conquest of state power were in existence, like the miniature hands and feet and nose and ears of a human foetus. Still delicate and quite underdeveloped, each of the SS offices and the command structure, the special units, and the General SS — with its corps and divisional staffs, technicians, and sponsoring auxiliary — all were ready to be strengthened, to expand and to *operate*. Many of the leading lights of the period 1934–1939 and some of the "brass" of 1940–1945 were in place or at least approaching the starting mark.

# 5

## The Betrayal
## Winter 1933–June 30, 1934

Die Kugel kam geflogen, gilt es mir oder gilt es dir?[1]

The brown-shirted Storm Troops were the hallmark of the National Revolution (*Nationale Erhebung*) in 1933. The SS—the men in the black coats—were somehow different, but they were merely one of many Nazi variants for Germans and foreign observers that year. Only a few who were "in the know" grasped their potential and their special threat.

As early as June and July 1933, perceptive and perhaps wishfully thinking observers thought they recognized signs of stabilization in the Nazi revolution—even a counter-revolutionary tendency. In actuality the struggle was shifting in Germany away from the conquest of power from the Weimar executors to a struggle to control the institutions of national defense—the army, the police, the ministries, and the bureaucracy. The need to gird Germany for battle, including the need to restore its productivity, was felt throughout the length and breadth of the land, without reference to Nazi affiliation. Only the methods were at issue—and also who might be allowed to lead or even participate in the reconstruction. Yet the fall and winter brought more disorder, and the radical elements not merely of the SA and SS but also of the party and its affiliates like the Factory Cell Organization and the Small Business Employees Organization (*NS Hago*) carried out attacks on chain stores, Jewish firms, and unloved employers. The conservative right also showed its teeth and even pressed for a restoration of the monarchy. Yet what was needed to signal the "end of the revolution" simply could not be identified. Ultimately the bloodletting of June 30, 1934, required no civil war, no vast measures of repression but only a resolute action by a small, reliable force. But neither the army nor the Storm Troop leaders could make up their minds to provide that intervention, though even Röhm and his deputies recognized the need for action. The army was not ready to destroy its potential allies on the political right; Röhm and his top colleagues were unwilling to destroy the revolutionary forces which had brought them into power. Both sought for a year to temporize, aided by Hitler's own indecision.[2]

Röhm's method was to preach the permanent revolution while reorganizing his leviathan SA into numerous specialized segments, with emphasis upon military tasks. In July he restructured the Obergruppen (SA corps) along the lines of the army's seven *Wehrkreise* (defense zones),* reemphasizing liaison facilities with the Reichswehr.[3] In August in Berlin and again in September at the Nuremberg Party Day, he marshalled vast brown-shirt armies decked out as much as possible like soldiers. He strove to integrate the ablest ex-officers and ex-NCOs of the former Stahlhelm with his own hand-picked SA front veterans in the five succeeding classes of the AW military training program beginning in October. He set up recruiting and training units (*Hochschulämter*) at every university to skim off the cream of the nationalistic student corps.[4] He encouraged his units to toughen themselves and vie with each other in sports and combat maneuvers. By setting up press offices for every SA region, he saw to it that the local populace read what served SA interests. He expanded SA ranks once again to make promotions easier, and he awarded honorary SA rank to party bigwigs and business tycoons whom he despised, hoping to gain their support by appealing to the widespread love of martial splendor. He even wooed Heinrich Himmler with the privilege of being addressed as "Mein Reichsführer," instead of the less exclusive "Herr Obergruppenführer." An enormous increase in the use of color in SA uniforms gave SA gatherings the gaudy aura of a circus or a cage of tropical birds. Meanwhile Röhm made speech after

---

*Wehrkreise* (defense zones): The Reichswehr had maintained a modified version of the old imperial system of draft and recruitment zones throughout the Weimar period, using the cover term "defense zones." Each Wehrkreis was composed of two *Wehrbezirke* (defense districts); thus a Reichswehr division was responsible for an old army corps area, and a regiment was responsible for an old divisional area. Röhm's SA corps (Obergruppe) was composed of two or more Gruppen (divisions — formerly *Brigaden*), fitted neatly into the Wehrkreis-Wehrbezirk system. He even went as far as styling his Standarten (two or more Standarten formed a Gruppe) with the old imperial regimental numbers.

speech warning the conservatives that the revolution was far from over, seeking thereby to keep alive the forces he hoped would thrust him (and Hitler) into the saddle still firmly occupied by the old German military and economic elites.[5]

The army's method was to keep "hands off" the Nazi movement, to encourage its nationalism and elan, to use its volunteers in the quasi-secret *Grenzschutz* (border defense), to resist all efforts to combine the SA with the Reichswehr, and to press Hitler for economic and political stabilization and an end to revolutionary terror while insisting that he carry out his own house-cleaning. By refusing to participate directly in the restoration of law and order, army leaders thrust authority into the hands of Himmler and Heydrich. When on June 30 SS units were assembled and armed in Reichswehr barracks, the army was putting the stamp of approval on a measure which it neither initiated nor controlled.[6]

For the time being Himmler avoided reorganizing the SS regionally along military lines as the SA had done. While the masses of the Stahlhelm and even small groups of the Reichsbanner and the Roter Frontkämpferbund entered the SA, Himmler opened and closed the membership of the SS selectively, on a regional and an organizational basis.[7] He also made revolutionary speeches supporting Röhm, and the SS vied with the SA in military precision at Berlin in August and at Nuremberg in September. But Himmler did not seek to penetrate into the AW training system. The differentiation and the separateness of the SS began to be emphasized. Indeed, the SA took issue with a newspaper article appearing that September in Hamburg which contrasted the SS as elite with the SA as mass.[8] The SS began to compete with the SA for the students, the business leaders, and professional people in a community and above all for the party bigwigs. A race began in the summer and fall to see which could attract more gauleiters, Munich Reichsleiter, and party heroes. Gauleiters who quarreled with the SA—Goebbels and Mutschmann, to mention only two—favored the SS and employed SS men as bodyguards and private detectives even when they resisted SS membership.[9]

More important, however, was Himmler and Heydrich's exploitation of the traditional SS police and intelligence function to seize the German police apparatus. Although the Storm Troops actually had a head start in their auxiliary police role and their control of all the largest urban police headquarters (as police presidents) outside Munich, their great disadvantage lay in the need to repress the excesses of their own members, only partially met by the Feldpolizei. In August Göring in Prussia and Frick outside Prussia had sought to tame the SA by abolishing the auxiliary police and resisting further SA encroachments on po-

lice prerogatives. The SA responded with the formation of armed and
motorized special duty units and headquarters guards.[10]

SA defiance of the police in nonpolitical crimes, SA complaints of police brutality and "old-style" police bureaucracy, and court sentences
for SA men engaged in rioting and looting filled the press. Amazing
cases of "Wild-West" gunplay and private feuding among Nazi officials
occurred that fall.[11] Naturally, the SS was not aloof from all this, nor
was it much better disciplined. However, the SS had several advantages: (1) it had fewer members — the troublemakers therefore represented a smaller percentage of the total problem; (2) national-minded
police officials were more willing to join the SS than the SA because the
SS already had a superior social status due to its appeal to business and
professional men in previous years; (3) Heydrich's SD provided a coordinative national network lacking in the SA, a device permitting plain
clothes if not conspiratorial secrecy and party backing for claims to control at least the political police in a community.[12]

With the assistance of Reich Interior Minister Frick, between October 1933 and January 1934 Himmler had himself made political police
commissar in all the German states except Prussia. The political police
were either already opened to Himmler through a few (usually
younger) policemen who joined the SS (and/or SD) in 1932 or even as
late as 1933 — or I-C personnel from the local SS were hired by the police following the erection of a special local bureau in Himmler's name.
There was amazingly little bureaucratic opposition to this move, owing
perhaps to the massive confusion of the times, dislike of the SA commissars, the youth of the SS and SD personnel making them seem "harmless," or the assimilation of more trusted older criminal police (KRIPO)
officers into the SS and SD. The erection of an SD headquarters in
Stuttgart is a good example. The young Hessian Nazi police official
Werner Best made a name for himself there as both efficient and diplomatic. Naturally, the SA police officialdom recognized and resented
Himmler and Heyrich's tactics, but Röhm and the SA seem to have
isolated themselves both from the local party headquarters and police
officialdom, so that they had no allies except in the streets — exactly the
spirits which needed to be exorcised.[13]

In Prussia Daluege held the key to SS police power. He fought for his
independence from Himmler under Göring's aegis and with the aid of
the Nazi criminal investigator Arthur Nebe. Probably due to a recognition of his limitations and those of Gestapa chief Rudolf Diels regarding SA commander Karl Ernst *and* Reinhard Heydrich, Daluege as a
Prussian Landespolizei general conspired first with the Berlin SA to
"get" Diels, and when unsuccessful turned to Heydrich. Heydrich's

characteristically indirect methods are shown by Diels's appearance in September in the SS promotion lists as a Standartenführer. Diels represents the type of revolutionary conservative with whom the army should have been allied; however, as revealed in his memoirs, the generals continually underestimated their Nazi partners. Diels was a clever man, cleverer than Daluege although not a match for Heydrich. Allied with Göring, Diels was still a far more powerful man than was Heydrich allied with Himmler. Daluege had to separate Diels from Göring — in which he almost succeeded despite his clumsiness, due to Göring's lack of principle — but the rebellious SA were the wrong allies to use with Göring. In the fall Daluege tried again, again clumsily and again failing; yet this time SS organization succeeded in intimidating both Diels and Göring, so that a bridge of cooperation could be built between the SD and the Gestapo while Daluege fell rapidly into line as a loyal SS officer.[14]

In the course of the intrigue, Himmler relieved Daluege of the command over the relatively weak, ultracritical SS-Gruppe Ost with its headquarters in Berlin. He replaced him with Sepp Dietrich, whose embryonic Leibstandarte had been installed by Göring in the Lichterfelde police barracks of Major Wecke's special police detachments — which Göring used as his personal paramilitary unit. Thus, Dietrich had ample resources for controlling SS-Gruppe Ost, an area rich in the traditions of the SA *fronde* since 1930. Even before Diels's final defeat in April 1934 when Himmler and Heydrich occupied the Gestapa at Prinz Albrechtstrasse 8, Daluege, Heydrich, and Himmler had used Göring's fears of the SA to penetrate what had been one of the strongest conservative bastions, the Prussian police system. Far from resisting SS-SD penetration into the Prussian police, Göring actually encouraged it in the winter of 1933. Himmler and Heydrich aided the penetration by stressing their interest in law and order, the collection of incriminating evidence against SA terror, and absolute loyalty to Göring's master, Adolf Hitler.[15]

During the Munich ceremonies on November 8–9, 1933, commemorating the triumphant tenth anniversary of the beer hall putsch, Himmler submitted the SS men gathered before the Feldherrnhalle to an oath to Adolf Hitler:

Wir schwören dir Adolf Hitler Treue und Tapferkeit. Wir geloben dir und den von dir bestimmten Vorgesetzten Gehorsam bis in den Tod. So wahr uns Gott helfe.

(We pledge to you, Adolf Hitler, loyalty and bravery. We swear obedience to you and the superiors appointed by you, even unto death, as God is our witness.)

*Courtesy Hoover Institution*

The SS lining the streets to control the crowd when Hitler, Hess, and Himmler marched in Munich, November 9, 1934.

Foreshadowing, if not serving as a model for the momentous oath of the Wehrmacht of August 2, 1934, this personal SS pledge of loyalty came to hold far more significance than Röhm's earlier SA oath of October 1932. SS men were thus provided with a visible focus of loyalty modeled after the old army's loyalty to the sovereign. The SA failure to follow up and consolidate their lead in this respect was symptomatic: loyalty to Hitler was irrelevant to them. In this they were in error.[16]

The award of a ministerial seat to Röhm along with one to Hess on December 1, 1933, has seemed to many observers a mere "plastering over the cracks" by Hitler preparatory to his breach with Röhm in good time. In view of his earlier treatment of Stennes, Hitler's move might well be taken as an effort to deceive and mollify Röhm. Without destroying this dimension of Hitler's tactics, it may still be possible that Hitler thus gave Röhm a new arena of activity, parallel with Hess, in which he hoped the former would develop his SA into a viable training institution — not merely for pre- and postmilitary exercises but to train Germans in political struggle with Jews, Catholics, reactionaries, etc. Nor did Röhm leave his appointment in the realm of a gesture; he capitalized mightily on the potential of a state apparatus that he could wield in the power struggle. In the *Ministeramt* (Ministerial Office, handling his cabinet duties) and the *Politisches Amt* (Political Office, handling his relationships at state and local levels), Röhm was copying Schleicher's tactics and developing control facilities which were formidable powers to reckon with.[17] For personnel he drew upon the *Verbindungsstab* (Liaison Staff), a joint SA-SS-party Berlin installation of March 1933 which had already played a vital role in channeling and sifting information passing between the ministries and party agencies. The overlapping of the work and personnel of Röhm's new Ämter with the Verbindungsstab in the early months of 1934 suggests that he was not as yet descending in power. SS officers sought positions in his new apparatus, and high-ranking SS men who met with his disfavor had to be consigned to limbo by Himmler. Röhm, not Himmler, recommended all SS appointments of field grade to Hitler, even and especially those of honorary ranks.[18] Röhm was in a position to stifle the SS, and only his dogged determination to challenge Hitler and the Reichswehr delivered the Storm Troop leader and his mighty SA-state into Himmler and Heydrich's hands.

During the winter months of 1933–1934, Himmler cautiously began the reorganization of the SS structure, partially to bring it more in line with the SA reforms of the previous summer and fall, partially to strengthen it for a possible struggle for power with the SA. It was at this time that the SS-*Oberabschnitte* (Main Sectors) make their appearance in place of the old Gruppen. The SS Main Sectors were organized, like the SA-Obergruppen, to conform to the army's seven Wehrkreise. Tactical military training was secretly ordered in January 1934 in rifle practice, extended order drill, light machine gun, and patrols in preparation for training in AW-*Sportlager* (Sport Camps). A combat officers' school was announced to be opened later at Bad Tölz. SS membership rapidly doubled, going from 100,000 to more than 200,000, as tens of thousands who had applied during the *Sperre* (closure) of April to November 1933 were admitted under the new, stringent standards of the SS-Amt and the Rassenamt. The number of Standarten rose from fifty to one hundred, with Sturmbanne in every town of consequence. Rapid promotions were the rule, and most of the men who had joined in 1930, 1931, and 1932 were given opportunities to try their hand at commanding. More systematic evaluation of each officer was now demanded, however, and also more careful methods of reporting unit strength.[19] Both the field and headquarters structure of the SS in the spring of 1934 began to assume the form that it would keep until wartime. About 2,000 officers formed the basis for a future SS officers corps which could grow and differentiate itself but would retain until 1939 its basic character.

The pioneers of 1930–1932 who attained officer rank at this time were to form the backbone of the SS; the second wave of "March casualties" (*Märzgefallene*, a term of not-so-good-humored contempt for the opportunists of March 1933) formed the Nachwuchs, or "replacements," long regarded as second best, until the war began. In 1934 special emphasis was placed on the recruitment of personnel for the military support organizations, engineers, communications, motor, and cavalry units. Standards were kept low for these recruits, who might otherwise go to the SA. In the case of the SS cavalry, there was a distinct snobbery involved as whole rural riding clubs were assimilated in a body. Here too there was a direct challenge to SA ambitions for an SA cavalry.[20] The SS had very few paid positions to offer as compared to the SA, which went on the Reich Interior Ministry payroll in October, 1933, to the tune of 2.6 million RM per month. Yet quite a few of the new SS were unemployed petits bourgeois hopeful of winning state or private business positions through "connections" with the large number of regularly employed civil servants and professional people being wooed by the SS for prestige as well as penetration into their social milieux. Academic people, for example, were sought after, first for the SS and then for the SD. Often secret "supporting members" from the business and professional community revealed their interest after a little urging and joined the SS without joining the party. Thus, the atmosphere of being socially "a little better" was reinforced after 1933. For example, the Berlin SS gave a "spring concert," featuring a chorus of the Leibstandarte singing "songs of the black hundreds of 1813 around the campfire." It supplied honor guards for the wife of the Shah of Persia on tour in Germany and protested with feeling against "roughneck" treatment of foreign guests by a minor rival, the Berlin Watch and Ward Society (*Wach- und Schliessgesellschaft*).[21]

The winter of 1933–1934 was harder on the SA than the previous one, which had been bad enough with its mutinies and desertions. To the simple SA man, Röhm's high politics meant little. Jobless, this man was supposed to content himself with party handouts from the Winter Help campaign. If he had got a small position, often conferred on him by labor office officials and Nazi employers as a huge favor, he had to see his SA unit filled with better-heeled ex-Stahlhelmers and with perhaps a few of his former foes, the *Bananen* (the Nazis called the Reichsbanner people "bananas") and "reds" who argued openly that the time was ripe to hold Hitler to his promises.[22] The local SA leaders discharged some of the pent-up frustration in protest marches against exclusive social clubs, unfriendly factory managers, and reactionary communal authorities. Much was made of decorations and awards for the alte Garde of SA, SS, Bund Oberland, and Reichskriegsflagge. Plans for summer vacations for adults and camps for children were announced. Housing developments for SA and SS men were started. But Röhm was forced to take cognizance of *Miesmacher* (chronic complainers) who protested against the deluge of opportunists, increased deductions from their pay envelope, repetitive drill and derogating tone of the Reichswehr drillmasters, neglect of units by the commanders, etc. A secret order of SA-Gruppe Berlin-Brandenburg warned against drunken battles with the police and with opponents in the taverns. Noisy talk about a "second revolution" could be heard in SA circles by early spring. On the other hand, Röhm seems to have made serious efforts to rid the SA of its dead weight and its worst troublemakers.[23]

While Röhm's foreign press conferences and meetings with the foreign diplomatic corps and military attachés do not quite deserve the suspicions Hitler lavished upon them — since they really seem designed to reassure other countries, especially France, about the nonaggressive character of the SA — the conduct of Röhm as Reich minister was to say the least aggressive.[24] From January on a definite polarization between him and Hitler set in, which Göring and Himmler were quick to capitalize upon. Both set to work to collect as much information about SA excesses as possible. Yet mutual suspicions kept them working against each other as well. When Gisevius was forcibly taken to the Lichterfelde barracks in mid-February, Sepp Dietrich wanted information about Diels's Gestapo as well as Karl Ernst's SA. As late as March Diels descended on the new SS concentration camp on the *Vulkanwerft* in Stettin and with Göring's support cleaned it out. This was the last straw, however; in the inevitable *Aussprache* ("talking it out"), Göring agreed to install Himmler as his "deputy" in the Gestapo. Heydrich installed Werner Best, the young Hessian Nazi, as *his* deputy in the Bavarian Political Police and moved up to Berlin, where he split his time between Prinz Albrechtstrasse 8 and the new SD offices at Wilhelmstrasse 112 nearby. Diels's appointees were rusticated in the provinces, replaced by SD people from Munich, many of them old Munich KRIPO officials (Criminal Police) like Heinrich Müller. On the other hand, the Berlin circle of Arthur Nebe went directly into the SS, though Nebe himself remained in the SA until 1936.[25]

Himmler thus acquired the whole Prussian political police apparatus, while Daluege won control of the rest of the police throughout the Reich. The regional offices of the Gestapo had been rendered independent of the regular police channels on March 14; now a systematic assignment or appointment of an SD official to each Stapostelle occurred in every Prussian *Regierungsbezirk* (section of a province). There were about 300 Gestapo officials throughout Prussia, and about 250 more in Berlin when Heydrich took over. Only a few of them were in the SS; most were nationalist police officers from before 1933. The Gestapo consisted of three main offices: (1) administration, (2) investigation and prevention, and (3) espionage and treason. Heydrich took personal charge of the second, placing Heinrich Müller, neither a Nazi nor an SS man but a hard-bitten Bavarian rightist from the Munich criminal police, in charge of "fighting Marxism" and of all political arrests (*Schutzhaft* in concentration camps). Another Bavarian policeman named Reinhard Flesch, with an SS-and-Nazi past, was set to watch Müller for a time (he resigned in 1935); and Müller's friend Friedrich Panzinger was put in charge of the Berlin *Stapostelle* (he finally joined the SS in 1939!). Franz Josef Huber, who had prosecuted Nazis in Bavaria before 1933, came to the Berlin Gestapa and joined the SD to fight "reaction, the Church, and Austria." Josef Meisinger, also from the Bavarian Political Police, was literally put in charge of investigations of the NSDAP, SA, SS, *and* homosexuality! SS and SD membership for them came after the fact of their employment by Heydrich, either in Munich or Berlin. Exceptions with a Nazi-and-SS past included the Bavarian career policeman Hans Rattenhuber, who was charged with setting up Hitler's personal security guards; Anton Dunckern, who went to the Berlin Stapostelle; and Walter Potzelt, SS since 1930 and SD since 1932, who became chief-adjutant of the Gestapa. Heydrich brought his personal adjutant and factotum, SS-Sturmführer Alfred Naujocks, up from Munich. Holdovers from Diels's staff included the non-SS-Oberregierungsrat Bode, the local Berlin expert on Marxism and trade unions; Reinhold Heller, who did not join the SS until 1938; Günther Patchowsky, SD member from 1932 and now in charge of the main office for espionage; Karl Hasselbacher, specialist for Masons, sects, and Jews (joined SS and SD December 1934); Ernst Damzog; Kurt Riedel; and Walter Kubitsky, who worked with Patchowsky in espionage.[26]

Heydrich was a shrewd and effective organizer. He did not merge the SD with the Gestapo and only slowly brought the secret state police of the other Länder into line with the excellent Prussian apparatus that Diels had left him. The SD was to remain an SS installation *par excellence*, and in fact a *Heydrich* installation! At the SD headquarters (*Sicherheitsamt*), he set up five sections: administration, archives, political police, counter-intelligence-inland, and counter-intelligence-foreign. Müller of the Gestapo he put in charge of all political police operations; Best, still operating the political police for the time being in Munich, he gave the internal security section and the administration, retaining foreign intelligence for himself. The archives went to a capable thirty-one-year-old SS captain, a doctor of law. The SD recruited many young lawyers in the spring of 1934 as well as businessmen, judges, state councillors, mayors, and police officials in the middle or lower ranks. Many of them seem to have functioned with the SD for months or even years before acquiring SS membership and rank. Some served in the SS without rank in 1934.[27] Certainly the SD was too embryonic in June 1934 to be capable of running the whole German police, let alone the SS. At best it could serve as a transmission belt. Its potentialities in these directions were shown, however, by Hess's order of June 9 forbidding other party agencies to maintain intelligence nets. Unfortunately for the SA, it lacked a unified intelligence system to warn it of the impending denouement. Army intelligence even soaked up false reports about the SA planted by the SD.[28]

Understandably, the Reichswehr had been loath to give up on the SA. Even in the fall of 1933, confronted by hostility from high-ranking SA leaders like von Jagow in Stuttgart and von Obernitz in Frankfurt-am-Main and by "strikes" and mutinies among companies assigned as border guards in Pomerania, Silesia, Frankfurt-an-der-Oder, and Saxony, the Reichswehr went ahead with AW training in *SA-Geländesport-schulen* (field sport schools) and on its own training grounds, putting five SA classes through one-month basic training until March.[29] The fear that the eastern units of the SA would prove useless against a Polish invasion was less troubling after the signing of the nonaggression pact with Poland January 26, 1934, but SA efforts to maintain control over Reichswehr weapons depots during the spring months helped to harden the resistance of the army. Army inability to dislodge F. W. Krüger by naming a regular army officer as AW executive officer in January also may have contributed to the army's decision to withdraw training officers from the SA in March. Actually the 13,000-man AW was the friendliest segment of the SA, and Krüger himself was disliked by many of the SA officers corps and party leaders like Baldur von Schirach of the *Reichsjugendführung* (National Youth Leadership), who suspected him of playing a double game and building up a personal following through control over the chief route to Reichswehr appointment. Krüger, an ex-SS officer, seems to have tried to serve all his masters. His extensive plans for a great network of SA "sport" schools were later realized when the AW no longer existed and he had returned to the SS. The army was disappointed, however, in the low military quality of the SA both as officers and as troops. Fritsch's ascendancy over Reichenau may also have helped prepare the Reichswehr leadership to believe the worst about the SA.[30]

Whereas in mid-1933 Hitler and Röhm had been thinking of a 300,000-man militia with one-year service, utilizing a smaller permanent corps of officers, NCOs, technicians, and training personnel, by February Hitler had moved to a more professional soldier's view of universal conscription, under the influence of French intransigeance toward any and all of Röhm's blandishments. Hitler now shifted to Ribbentrop's "British" line, making rather amazing offers to reduce the SA by two-thirds and to allow international inspections to verify the nonmilitary character of the SA, and rejecting wholeheartedly Röhm's conception of a people's army headed by Röhm himself. He met Röhm's mid-February cabinet proposals that he should head a new Defense Ministry by forcing Röhm into an abortive agreement with the Reichswehr which he could not or would not keep.[31]

As Röhm found himself blocked by Hitler and the Reichswehr from February on, he permitted himself numerous incautious outbursts and stressed to SA and non-SA alike that the SA was to remain the revolutionary mainspring of the movement. Through the spring he permitted his commanders to channel the unrest of their men into marching demonstrations, which were clearly unsafe for public order. He did nothing to prevent the arming of SA headquarters guard detachments, Grenzschutz units, and even *Hilfswerklager* (work camps) housing unemployed SA men, including refugees from Austria. Nevertheless, there is no evidence that he planned a putsch, though he kept up a steady system of contacts with his SA leaders as well as with top SS officers and leading figures in German and international life. This system of contacts was doubtless his device for heading off surprises both from within the SA — for he must have been aware of the readiness of some of his highest-ranking officers to putsch — and also from Berlin, Munich, or abroad. Its failure to aid him implies that there was neither a clear and firm putsch plan among his own officers nor among his opponents at the time when the July SA furlough was announced — as early as April 1934. Even his May 16 order to SA units to collect files on critics of the SA must have been largely intended as intimidation for noisy spokesmen of party and right-wing circles, for it was rather late to start intelligence operations in earnest and especially with a public announcement.[32]

Röhm probably had to give his SA their long-promised furlough, and he may have welcomed their temporary removal from the social scene as a means of quieting down negative public sentiment. He doubtless reckoned on a fall or winter crisis brought on either by continued unemployment and/or von Hindenburg's demise, at which time Hitler would be more willing to make concessions to the guarantors of the revolution. Nevertheless, Röhm must be held largely responsible for the easy destruction of his edifice by a tiny minority on June 30; no more telling condemnation can be made of a military commander than that of total ignorance of an impending attack. Röhm's isolation from party leaders, military commanders, and his own SA system in spite of his "contacts" — perhaps involved in some way with his homosexuality — was a death blow to an organization erected, after all, on charisma and the Führerprinzip. Röhm remained an amateur to the last: the amateur leader of an amateur army. Himmler also was an amateur, but many of his lieutenants were not. Indeed, he developed his professional side as a policeman (with their help) at this very time.[33]

The army had begun to collect data on the arming of the SA *Stabswachen* (headquarters guards) and on arms transports in April; and Captain Patzig, head of the army *Abwehr* (intelligence), had his agents in the AW even earlier. Von Reichenau is alleged to have gone over to Himmler after a partnership with Röhm failed, but the evidence for this is slim. (Such contacts seem provable only in the last two critical weeks of June.)[34] May was a month of intensive staff meetings, tours of inspection, and speeches. Not only was the army consulting, so were the SA and the SS, the party and the reactionaries. Röhm and Himmler both were checking on their new regional structures; Hitler, Goebbels, Hess, Bormann, and Buch feverishly harangued and intrigued to bring their enemies out in the open, while the monarchists and conservatives plotted and speculated on the death of von Hindenburg. There was much less anxiety in the SA camp than around Papen, in army, right-wing, and party circles. A civil war seemed in the offing with two clear-cut sides, a strong radical protest in which the non-Nazi left might be expected to join and a hard-bitten reactionary core of army, big business, the Catholic Church, and royalty. The middle class and many Nazis saw themselves caught between the fronts. Uncertain even of Hitler's choice, they fed the atmosphere of deterioration which drove him to act. Characteristically, he struck at both fronts.[35]

The earliest signs of an SS alert appeared in Munich at the outset of June. The Bavarian Political Police and the SD, under the command of Werner Best, received orders to prepare for suppressing a revolt. Theodor Eicke, commander of the special SS troops at the multipurpose Dachau installation (a concentration camp with a quartermaster unit, an embryonic Politische Bereitschaft, and an Austrian SS refugee camp) began practicing seizure of positions in the Greater Munich area, including Bad Wiessee. The regular SS-Standarten in Munich received sealed mobilization orders to be opened on the code signal, "*Versammlung.*" No comparable SS alerts for the other regions occurred until the last week in June.[36]

Already noticeable since April, the atmosphere of crisis worsened in June. Hindenburg retired, seriously ill, to Neudeck in East Prussia; Röhm went publicly on sick leave; and everybody made speeches. Papen's speech of June 17 at Marburg was thus part of a general wave of criticism and counter-criticism.[37] Hitler's choice of this time to pay a visit to Mussolini was classic Hitlerian tactics: he withdrew from the battlefield, hoping perhaps to come back with a triumph; at least he might throw many people off the scent. (Hitler was probably aware of Austrian Nazi putsch plans at this time—if indeed he did not instigate them through Theo Habicht, the NSDAP *Landesleiter.*) His interview with Mussolini was inconsequential, but the opportunity to pay a visit to von Hindenburg on June 21 to "report" and check up on the old man's state of mind and health may have steeled Hitler's nerve to proceed with his coup.[38] That the decision may have come about at the time of the Italian trip or right after the Papen speech is suggested by the fact that Himmler on June 19 broke a more than two-week delay when he forbade higher SS officers to go on a northern cruise with Röhm in August, after temporizing since the June 1 invitations went out. On August 20 Himmler claimed to have been shot at by an SA ambush. By August 23 the rumors of a forthcoming putsch were widespread. The SD representative in Breslau conveyed to the local Stapostelle secret orders to collect data on fifteen SA leaders, including Heines. As early as June 22,

Himmler told the SS commander in Dresden that an SA putsch was expected and to alarm his units and contact the army Wehrkreis commander for aid. Heines the following day got wind of *army* preparations in Breslau and alarmed Göring with talk of a Fritsch-led army revolt, while on June 24 Fritsch notified von Kleist in Breslau to expect an SA putsch there! Von Reichenau and Himmler were definitely now in contact, discussing the sharing of weapons and the use of army barracks and transport vehicles.[39]

A summons to congregate in Berlin on June 25 went out to all SS regional commanders, and for two days Himmler held conferences with them, giving them sealed orders to be opened on the above code word and ordering them to make lists of suspected persons for automatic arrest. They were convinced of the reality of an SA plot by Himmler's manner. He described Silesia as the hotbed of the revolt. The regional commanders were impressed with the need for absolute security; only SS-Abschnitt commanders and the Standarten commanders in Silesia were to be informed ahead of time. In Berlin Daluege and Sepp Dietrich did their part to alarm high Reichswehr officials with what appear to have been faked SA documents, including execution lists. Again Heines intervened on June 28, warning von Kleist that Himmler and Heydrich were pushing things to a head; von Kleist actually flew to Berlin, where von Reichenau told him that "it was too late to turn back."[40] Hitler made a phone call to Röhm that evening to put him off guard, announcing his own presence at a previously scheduled SA staff conference at Bad Wiessee for the morning of June 30. At this time Sepp Dietrich had completed plans to move two companies of the Leibstandarte (*SS-Wachbataillon*) by rail and army truck to Bad Wiessee for the same morning, on Hitler's orders. Clearly, Berlin was being left for Göring's measures and his units. No general SA alarm occurred, but it was not surprising that with all the rumors flying about a Munich putsch, the SA there became alarmed on the evening of June 29. Heines arrived, having sent only half his armed personnel on leave; yet he failed to arouse Röhm to serious defensive measures. That evening noisy SA rallies were held on the Oberwiesenfeld, and some troop commanders did tell their men that Hitler had joined the Reichswehr against them; but lacking Röhm's support, no council of war was held, and by 1:00 A.M. Munich was quiet. Efforts to trace rumors reaching the SA, probably spread by agents provocateurs, led SA Gruppenführer Schneidhuber and Schmid to visit gauleiter Adolf Wagner that evening. Wagner was probably an accomplice of Himmler, for he reassured the two, only to arrest them a few hours later.[41]

The purge operations were far from uniform. They were most intense in Munich, Berlin, and Silesia. In most of the other areas, the SS operations did not extend beyond routine arrests of top SA leaders. In Pomerania, East Prussia, and Saxony, SS leaders protected their SA comrades by refusing to send them to Berlin. Himmler and Heydrich stayed in Berlin, leaving Best and later Sepp Dietrich to carry out actions ordered by Hitler and gauleiter Wagner. Hitler was accompanied to Wiessee by his oldest cronies, Christian Weber, Emil Maurice, and Walter Buch. In Berlin Göring was in command, although he may have received proscription lists from the SS leaders. Arrests were carried out by all kinds of units, including plainclothes SD personnel. In Breslau the alert came from the Berlin SD; and the regional SS commander, Udo von Woyrsch, personally supervised the roundup of SA and the attack on an armed SA work camp, which resisted briefly. Wild and irresponsible SS measures occurred in several parts of Silesia involving Jews. Most of the actual security measures in Munich and Berlin were carried out by Reichswehr and Prussian State Police. The secret SS orders, opened on an SD signal, sent the SS units to Reichswehr barracks to draw weapons and await orders. Most of them stood guard duty in their communities, and many never left the barracks. On the other hand, the individual killings in Berlin and Munich were almost universally ascribed to the SS, especially since so many black uniforms were identified. Few if any of these murders were ever subjected to court investigation. At Wiessee Hitler's cronies did the first killings. In Munich the executions at Stadelheim prison were carried out by units of the Leibstandarte under Sepp Dietrich and units of Eicke's Dachau SS. Eicke and Michael Lippert, Eicke's aide, killed Röhm. In Berlin executions were carried out in the Lichterfelde barracks after a mixed court martial consisting at various times of Himmler, Daluege, Waldeck, Heydrich, Buch, and Göring. The executioners appear to have been drawn from remaining units of the Leibstandarte. The Feldjäger and Major Wecke's Landespolizeigruppe General Göring were also closely involved. In Breslau the executions insisted upon by Heydrich were carried out by a small detail of regular SS after buck-passing because few wished to kill SA comrades. Here too Feldjäger and Prussian Landespolizei units participated in the arrests, if not the killings.[42]

Of about two hundred people who lost their lives during the terror of June 30–July 3, over half were non-SA. SS men doubtless killed nearly all of them; the actual number of SS killers remains quite small, perhaps several dozen, and the number of SS officers who participated in the plot beforehand—even including those who seriously believed in a Röhm revolt—would not exceed fifty. SD network personnel might account for another fifty. The majority of the SS personnel employed on June 30 and thereafter knew little of what was happening and performed security functions no different from the army and police units alongside which they served. Nevertheless, Hitler chose to bestow and Himmler to accept massive credit for the purge. The willingness to kill and to take credit for the killings was to mark the Black Corps forever afterwards, though as stated only a few were responsible.[43]

The peculiar service which Heydrich and Himmler rendered Hitler was the murder of persons whom Hitler did not wish to *order* killed. This certainly included Gregor Strasser and Father Stempfle, and probably several others. Heydrich's often-discussed regrets that he could not kill more highlight the prime fact that actually very few SA officers were killed. That the SA should have been so effectively maimed by the loss of these few regional commanders and staff officers indicates either their outstanding role in the organization or the SA's general inefficacy, or a little of both. Lutze seems to have regretted his part in the betrayal of his comrades and voiced the view that even many of them had been killed "unnecessarily." Perhaps he had been led to believe that only Röhm and five or six others were to be eliminated.[44] On the other hand, the intimidation of the rightist politicians was just as complete. The Reichswehr harbored a grudge against the SS for its brutality in the deaths of General and Mrs. von Schleicher and General von Bredow, but they still later conceded the SS a division's worth of armaments. The party gained new respect for the SS — largely out of fear — while a rivalry set in with the various branches of the police, who saw the SS as their major critics and possible replacements.[45]

The independence the SS gained from the SA by Hitler's order of July 20, 1934, did not require an immediate reorganization. Rather, it was followed by a thorough house-cleaning, leading to the expulsion of as many as 60,000 of the newer members. The SA of course was thoroughly screened also, but its losses were proportionally no heavier than the SS. The AW continued on as an independent unit under Hitler through the fall but was liquidated the following January. Krüger took many of the AW officers with him into the SS.[46]

Himmler was to profit throughout the 1930s from many of Röhm's organizational innovations of 1933–1934, above all the structural *Gleichschaltung* (coordination) with the Reichswehr districts but also from the idea of penetration into the university community, the development of an independent press agency, the emphasis on the sport achievements associated with the SA Sport Insignia, and finally the notion of a military elite for the Leibstandarte Adolf Hitler and the Verfügungstruppe realized the ideal of the AW. Yet Himmler knew better than to let the SS proliferate visibly in the Third Reich. The contrast of 1934 between the noisy SA demonstrations and the quiet work of the SS was never entirely forgotten, even in the war years.

# 6

## Years of Growth
## 1934–1939

"So sind wir angetreten und marschieren nach unabänderlichen Gesetzen als ein
nationalsozialistischer soldatischer Orden nordisch-bestimmter Männer und als
eine geschworene Gemeinschaft ihrer Sippen den Weg in eine ferne Zukunft und
wünschen und glauben, wir möchten nicht nur sein die Enkel, die es besser aus-
fochten, sondern darüber hinaus die Ahnen späterer, für das ewige Leben des
deutschen germanischen Volkes notwendiger Geschlechter."[1]

### Consolidation

In the aftermath of the Röhm purge, the position of the SS was far
from a settled matter. An atmosphere of tension, mutual suspicion, and
open recrimination colored the relations of the SS with the Reichswehr
and with state and party officialdom. In August at the time of Hindenburg's death, an SS unit was employed to control access to his estate,
much to the chagrin of Reichswehr and nationalist figures who had
hoped to find an anti-Nazi will. On the other hand, the SS (and SA)
sought in vain to worm information from the Reichswehr about its
plans for expansion. Fritsch complained that SS personnel in the
Reichswehr spied on their commanding officers.[2] Tension reached a
maximum in December 1934 with rumors of a showdown between two
evenly matched adversaries of about 300,000 men each, the Reichswehr
and SS, some favoring the idea of an SS putsch-initiative, others of a
counter-revolutionary army maneuver. On January 3, 1935, Hitler held
a meeting in the Kroll Opera for party and Reichswehr leaders, where
he warned the party against encroachments on the army and called the
Reichswehr "the sole bearer of arms." British papers at this time noted
that the SS was to be reduced, but references were made to more heavily armed SS "riot units" in the process of formation — the future Verfü-

gungstruppe. Then at a conciliatory *Bierabend* sponsored by Blomberg, Himmler on January 10 had the bad taste to accuse Fritsch of meddling in party matters by inviting Professor Carl Schmitt to address select Reichswehr officers on the justice of putsches. At another Bierabend matters were apparently patched up enough for Himmler to be invited to address Hamburg Reichswehr officers in February about the need for his "riot squads," one of which was in the process of formation in their district (SS-Standarte Germania).[3] Characteristically, Himmler dwelt on the 1918 experience, the "stab-in-the-back" and the need to free the front soldiers of the worry and responsibility about the home front in time of war. Of course, the cause of this tension and jockeying was the imminent proclamation of *Wehrhoheit* (defense sovereignty) and the part an armed SS might play as units in a new Wehrmacht. Although Hausser errs in claiming that Hitler announced to the Reichstag that an SS division would be included in the thirty-six proclaimed on March 16, he reflects Himmler's expectation that the special, armed SS regiments being formed in Munich, Hamburg, and Berlin would become a regular army division in time of war. Hitler does not seem to have ever made that clear-cut a promise.[4]

One of the chief reasons for army leaders' resistance to SS ambition may have been their doubts about the discipline and counter-revolutionary reliability of Himmler's units. This same doubt was rife among state authorities, both in late 1934 and well into 1935. One of the worst areas of SS offense was Silesia, where in August 1934 the regional SS commander, von Woyrsch, gave the provincial attorney general an ultimatum to release SS personnel accused of illegal actions in the purges — and in September SS men accused of wanton murders on and after June 30 were given light sentences while the Gestapo persecuted state officials who sought to bring them to justice. The regular police were distressed by SS officers who not only appeared in public in a drunken condition but beat up people with whom they disagreed in public places and generally challenged the forces of law and order much as had the SA (and the SS) before June 30. While Hitler and men like Göring, Goebbels, and Himmler clearly desired to perpetuate ambiguities regarding the purpose of the purge for the purpose of intimidation, they also had to control the perception of lawlessness abroad in the land. Individual SS commanders could not be left free to determine whom they would frighten.[5]

The manner in which Himmler mastered this problem, insofar as he did master it, by rationalization and bureaucratization deeply affected the kind of leadership corps ultimately evolved by the SS; but in a sense the direction had already been taken within the SA. The antibureaucratic tendencies of the free corps tradition, indeed of the free lance street fighter leadership, had already been subjected to an organizational straitjacket even within the SA of Röhm and especially in Himmler's units. However, just as Röhm's SA had threatened toward the last to institutionalize dissent in its very bureaucracy (e.g., *Politisches Amt, Ausbildungswesen*), so ultimately the SS, having reined in its untamed rowdies and free spirits of the streets, was to pose a far greater threat to rival German institutions as the embodiment of political soldiering in the interests of permanent revolution. In the short run, however, the SS faced the problem of indiscipline left over from its SA heritage. Rapid growth and congruence with the SA structure had made its central administration, although modified repeatedly, disjointed and overlapping — while its regional structure was essentially a continuation of that of the party from the *Kampfjahre* (years of struggle), with the SS leaders embedded for better or worse in sticky conflicts or bosom friendships with old party comrades.

Austria, where the SS was embarrassingly involved in the putsch fiasco of July 25, 1934, less than a month after the supposed Röhm putsch, is a good illustration of Himmler's problem of SS reorganization. The Austrian SS, *Abschnitt* VIII, was characterized both by its noisy vigor and its unruly character. One of the oldest Abschnitte — with strength in nearly all the Austrian Länder — the Austrian SS, like the Austrian Nazis as a whole, was little inclined to subordinate itself to Munich and even less to Berlin. The despatch by Himmler in 1932 of a commander in the form of a Berlin *Oberführer* (senior colonel) and intelligence agent (Dr. Walter Graeschke) had not helped matters any.[6] The tangled network of intrigue characteristic of the Dollfuss dictatorship enveloped the Austrian SA and SS in 1933, so that control became even harder for Himmler and Röhm than might have been expected from the international aspect. When Dollfuss drove the SA and SS underground in June 1933 due to the widespread participation of their membership in overt violence, he began a process of splitting the Austrian Nazis between those who remained to fight and those who fled to Germany. The SA and the SS who fled were to form the nucleus of a faction willing to subordinate themselves to the Nazi and Reich German purposes and timetable, while those who remained became increasingly restless and activist, anxious to use Hitler Germany rather than be used by it. The former group were headquartered in Munich, with many refugee camps — primarily of young men — located in Bavaria near the frontier. The latter group remaining in Austria were very loosely organized, with an estimated SS strength by January 1934 of about 5,000 (less than 1,000 of whom had been recognized by Munich) in five Standarten.[7]

Utilizing the cross connections of the Austrian Nazis with the fascist *Steyrischer Heimatschutz* (Styrian Home Defense) and the nationalist *Heimwehr* (Home Army), Himmler appears to have conducted his own version of foreign policy in league with Theo Habicht.* In October 1933 Himmler arranged for Schuschnigg to visit Hess secretly in Munich, probably as an agent for Dollfuss. In January 1934 Himmler sent Prince Waldeck-Pyrmont to Vienna to attempt a further rapprochement between the Austrian Nazi party and the Heimwehr. When a leak developed and the home of the Austrian party chief was raided, the SS officer had to be recalled.[8] A temporary wave of caution swept over Hitler and Himmler at this time, associated with the growing division of policy between Hitler and Röhm. Alfred Rosenberg warned Röhm in February 1934 that rumors of a putsch instigated by SA from Bavaria were circulating in Vienna. In Bavaria both the SA and the SS were gathering young Austrian male refugees into military units on the frontier, known collectively as the Austrian Legion. Efforts to remove them from the immediate proximity of the border resulted in rioting. The tension between Austrian legionnaires and German SA broke out in clashes that April in Vilshofen, near Passau. SS units were even used as border guards to prevent raids across the frontier from the German side.[9]

Meanwhile in Austria intrigues continued. Theo Habicht continued to seek accommodation both with the supporters of Dollfuss and with Starhemberg of the Heimwehr. Habicht worked with high Austrian SS and SA leaders, probably with Himmler's and Röhm's knowledge, but the rivalry between the two formations led to separate negotiations. Probably Hitler and some members of the German Foreign Office were informed although incompletely, especially as the idea developed of a "faked" putsch in which elements of the Austrian SA and SS were to capture Dollfuss and proclaim a new pro-German government with the cooperation of the Austrian police and army. The mutual suspicions, perhaps the underlying intent of the several groups involved to trick each other, led to serious leaks resulting on July 25 in the fiasco of the murder of Dollfuss, the isolation of the participating units of the 89th SS-Standarte, and the official repudiation by Hitler of the revolutionaries.[10]

The failure of the Austria SA to assist in the plot may be traced in part to the Röhm purge three weeks previous in which SS elements of the Austrian Legion stationed at Dachau concentration camp had played a

*Theo Habicht was the Party Reichsinspekteur for the Austrian NSDAP. A Reich German, Habicht had been a gauleiter in Wiesbaden before being sent to Vienna in 1931. Himmler knew him from the time when Himmler arranged for party speakers.

part. The Austrian SA was later accused of leaking critical information
to the Austrian authorities in regard to the putsch plans, but there could
have been other sources for these leaks. The Austrian episode suggests
that the SS was not yet wholly a reliable instrument of Hitler, for
Himmler was most certainly acquainted with the intentions of the plotters, though he may have been carried along by the enthusiasm and
vigor of his Austrian subordinates and by Habicht's ill-informed optimism. It is not impossible that Hitler was kept partially informed and
that he hoped to mask the Röhm purge by a cheap diplomatic victory in
Austria, but the ineptitude of the entire plot and the dangers it involved
are inconsistent with Hitler's careful preparation of the Röhm purge. It
would seem more likely that both Hitler and Himmler were the victims
of overconfident and uncontrolled subordinates.[11]

The consequences for the SS were increased bitterness between it and
the SA; renewed suspicion on the part of governmental and military figures among conservatives toward the SS as a reliable political tool; loss
of its organization in Austria through imprisonment, flight, and withdrawals from activity (partially recouped after 1936); and a heritage of
difficulty with the Austrian SS forever afterwards. On the other hand,
individual Austrian SS men who fled to the Reich swelled the corps of
competent SS officers, and the SS portion of the Austrian Legion became a battalion of the future Verfügungstruppe (2nd battalion, *Standarte Deutschland*). In 1938 a plaque was erected on the Austrian
chancellery commemorating the seven men of the 89th SS-Standarte
who were executed for their part in the putsch.[12]

Although the fall and winter of 1934–1935 remained a period of ambiguity for the SA and even the SS as to size, structure, scope, and
purpose — marked by contradictory utterances and tendencies — both
units showed a steady tightening up, the SS first, the SA more slowly. A
distinction was made between special courts of honor and disciplinary
powers within the SS and SA and claims of both units to be independent
of the state courts, the SA claim being disallowed. The SS finally set up
its own system of disciplinary courts, separate from the SA and headed
by Paul Scherfe, a sixty-year-old ex-police major directly subordinate to
Himmler. On the other hand, the authority of the Feldjägerkorps over
SS personnel was reasserted. Persons who did not really intend to serve
in SA or SS units because they were full-time civil servants, students,
business people, or were in the Voluntary Labor Service, were put in reserves or even forced to resign. Earlier regulations which had gone un-
enforced were taken up, such as requiring gun permits; collecting dues;
getting marriage, health, and ancestry certification; making sure all
had taken the oath to the Führer; punishing clandestine clients of de-

partment stores and Jewish merchants and professional men; forbidding attendance at church functions in uniform; and removal from the SS (on honorable terms) of all ministers of religion.[13]

The process of differentiation within the SS according to specialties had been very irregular up to the time of the Röhm purge. Physicians, flyers, motorcyclists, cavalry, engineers, and radiomen—both active and reserve—could either regard themselves as in special formations or not, depending on local conditions. Only the Sicherheitsdienst had really been cut off organizationally from the SS unit structure. However, by December 1934 a decisive distinction had developed between the so-called General SS (*Allgemeine SS*)—actually the bulk of the membership both paid and unpaid, both active and reserve—and certain special units. A secret order by Himmler does not mention the Sicherheitsdienst among these special units; it does mention: (1) Verfügungstruppe—the former Politische Bereitschaften including the Leibstandarte Adolf Hitler, and (2) *Wachverbände* (guard units)—the former Sonderkommandos, organized in guard battalions and guard companies (*Wachsturmbanne* and *Wachstürme*).[14] In each case, the initiative had come from regional Oberabschnittsführer, who had created from their subordinate Standarten special riot or guard units (aktive Hundertschaften or Sonderkommandos) subordinate to themselves in 1933. As early as July 4, 1934, Himmler, probably on Hitler's suggestion, had made Theodor Eicke—since June 1933 commander of the SS concentration camp at Dachau—inspector of state concentration camps and chief of the SS guard troops. These camps and the guard units in them were then systematically removed from local police authority because Himmler was both head of the regional political police and the SS superior of the regional SS commanders who had detailed the Wachverbände in the first place.[15]

In November 1934 Himmler also appointed Generalleutnant a.D. Paul Hausser to head up SS officer candidate schools for the future Verfügungstruppe, but he did not create the parallel inspectorate of the Verfügungstruppe until October 1936.[16] The date of October 10, 1934, may be taken, however, as the official beginning of the Verfügungstruppe, since it was selected later by the *Oberkommando der Wehrmacht* (OKW) as the date for reckoning seniority in the Verfügungstruppe. Probably before this date the Politische Bereitschaften had been solely financed by the SS-Oberabschnitte, while thereafter the Reich Ministry of the Interior or the Länder were at least partly responsible financially. In the case of the Wachverbände, the Länder became financially responsible in the latter part of 1934.[17]

Thus, after an initial stage where ordinary SS personnel were "de-

SS leader corps in Braunschweig, 1935.

tailed" for special duty as Hilfspolizei (auxiliary police) on an individual basis, or occasionally on a unit basis, the SS began to make the transition to quasi-state status for some of its formations. During 1933 and 1934 this relationship was somewhat irregular, as symbolized by one-year contracts drawn up between individuals involved and their commanders. They "enlisted" for one year. It is probable that for the most part neither they nor their commanders made a clear distinction between party service and state service. In July 1935, however, a regular enlistment procedure was worked out whereby the Reich Ministry of the Interior granted Himmler the power to administer oaths, which he then reassigned to the unit commanders of the Verfügungstruppe. Regular enlistment documents in the name of the Reich Ministry of the Interior were drawn up in 1935 but predated at some time in 1934 (some earlier than October 10, 1934). The *Oberabschnitte* (Main Sectors), however, retained control over the Verfügungstruppe formations throughout 1935 and most of 1936.[18] In the case of the Wachverbände, there was greater but not uncontested autonomy vis-à-vis the SS regional commanders in 1934 and 1935, probably due to the concentration camps' tie to the Gestapo. By 1936 Eicke was strong enough to earn the simpler title of Commander of the Death's Head Troops (Totenkopfverbände) and complete independence of the regional authorities both of the state and the local SS.[19] On the other hand, tendencies toward autonomy in the auxiliary units such as cavalry, motors, engineers, and communications were sharply checked, first in 1934 by placing their commanders on the staffs of the regional chiefs of the General SS and later by reductions in size (1935) and the destruction of higher level staffs (1936). After having allowed these units to grow out of proportion to their usefulness in an effort to attract skilled personnel, it was obviously necessary to restrict them to the really competent. In spite of their obvious relevance to the mobilization potential of the SS, these units were not made part of the state paid troops. Nevertheless, by 1936 it became necessary to create state paid medical units outside the General SS structure.[20]

### New Staff Offices

The first significantly new top-level structure in the SS after the Röhm purge was the *SS-Hauptamt* (SS Main Office), created January 20, 1935. While Darré's Rasse- und Siedlungs-Amt and Heydrich's Sicherheitsamt were both promoted to Hauptamt status as well at this juncture, their autonomy was already of long standing. On the other hand, the coordinative tasks of the new SS Main Office were more than an extension of the duties of the old SS-Amt and less than the all-encompassing conception of the defunct Oberstab of the Kampfjahre. Himmler had experimented in 1932 with Prince Waldeck-Pyrmont as personal adjutant and simultaneous executive officer, or Stabsführer; and in 1933–1934 with Siegfried Seidel-Dittmarsch, a former Prussian officer who was a super liaison man called *Chef des Führungsstabs* (Chief of the Leadership Staff), no longer Himmler's adjutant but also detached from narrow administrative duties. When Seidel-Dittmarsch died, Himmler abolished the Führungsstab and turned to the idea of strengthening the administrative prerogatives of the old SS-Amt, which had been overshadowed by the Führungsstab. Himmler found for the position Curt Wittje, another retired army officer with business connections, whose energy as *Oberabschnittsführer* (Main Sector Commander) in unfriendly Hamburg had recommended him. After a few months of getting accustomed, Himmler asked him to coordinate such SS tasks as the concentration camps, the Gruppenstab z.b.V. (an SS liaison office at Berlin working with Reichswehr, Foreign Ministry, etc., disbanded in July 1935), the Politische Bereitschaften (garrisoned SS units under arms) as well as supervise training, weapons, inspections, personnel, judiciary, budget and maintenance, and medical services. The SS Main Office under his charge was divided into Offices (Ämter), Main Sections (*Hauptabteilungen*), and Sections (*Abteilungen*), the heads of which met monthly as a group.[21] Transfer of the SS-Hauptamt from Munich to Berlin, a process which had been begun but not completed in 1933 and 1934 under the Führungsstab, took place in the first half of 1935, delaying somewhat the centralization process in the SS. In May 1935 Himmler suddenly removed the recently named Main Office chief because of charges of homosexuality during his army career (perhaps revealed to Himmler by the Wehrmacht), replacing him with August Heissmeier, a younger man with an academic background. In spite of ambition and vigor, the latter never succeeded in mastering the drawbacks in his position, so that he left the SS Main Office in 1939 no stronger within the ramified SS system than it had been in 1935. He did, however, make an elaborate bureaucracy out of the rudimentary staff system on which his predecessor had only just begun to build.[22]

Just as in 1932 and 1933 the staff positions in the old Oberstab had tended to become independent offices (Sicherheitsamt and Rassenamt), so ultimately several SS-Hauptamt offices also broke off and were set up independently. The Administrative Office (*Verwaltungsamt*) even in 1932 tended to be a separate operation, with its own training, uniforms, promotions, and procedures — based on the so-called *Geldverwalter* (treasurers) in the units who managed the *Fördernde Mitglieder* program. Renamed *Verwaltungsführer*, they still retained a certain separateness. When Oswald Pohl, a dynamic ex-naval officer, took over the Administrative Section of the supposedly strengthened SS-Amt early in 1934, he worked steadily to become "Chief of Administration" (*Verwaltungschef*) directly under Himmler responsible for administration in the Security Service, Race and Settlement System, Special Duty Troops, and Concentration Camps. By 1939 he was head of *two* overlapping main offices, the SS Administrative and Economic Main Office (*Verwaltungs- und Wirtschaftshauptamt*, VWHA) and the Police Main Office for Budget and Construction (*Hauptamt Haushalt und Bauten*). While the former was financed from the party funds controlled by F. X. Schwarz, the latter tapped the resources of the Reich for the future combat SS (Waffen-SS) and the concentration camps.[23]

A similar process, complicated by many changes in the top personnel, occurred with the Leadership Office (*Führungsamt*). Its first chief had been an ex-Reichswehr major who had taken it over as the Munich Führungsabteilung (Leadership Section) when it was still overshadowed by the Berlin Führungsstab. He never succeeded in becoming more than an office manager; he was replaced temporarily in 1935 by Leo Petri, a fifty-eight-year-old ex-lieutenant colonel of police with World War One occupation experience in Poland, China, and Africa. When the latter was given a new post as head of a special Security Office to combat assassination of Nazi leaders, Himmler experimented with having the chief of the SS Main Office run the Leadership Office personally but soon gave it up. The Leadership Office then gravitated into the orbit of the future combat SS and was headed for a time in 1936 by Paul Hausser until he was named Inspector of the Special Duty Troops; but it was largely run by Hermann Cummerow, also an ex-Reichswehr colonel.[24]

An elaborate bureaucracy within the rest of the SS Main Office developed for much the same reasons. In 1935 sections for SS welfare, recruitment, security, population policy, and the press were added along with a big chancellery. In 1936 three new inspectorates were added to that for the concentration camps (now changed to a regular command over the Death's Head Troops as well): Special Duty Troops, Border and Guard Troops, and Officer Candidate Schools. But the press section soon had a press *chief* and in June 1937 had to give way to an independent agency known as the Press Office of the SS and Police (*Pressestelle SS und Polizei*), reflecting an amalgamation process of SS and police which had produced the two overlapping Administrative Main Offices referred to earlier. 1937 did not reduce the number of departments in the Main Office, however, for with Himmler's approval its bureaucratic chief added offices for calisthenics, communications, archives, and procurement. In 1938 Himmler split the recruitment office in two, to separate the record keeping and statistical functions from the active, policy forming operations. This fragmentation did nothing to strengthen the influence of the SS Main Office due to delays as well as shifts in emphasis and personnel, even though a kind of bureaucratic imperialism within the agency had produced the office.[25] Its ambitious members had to leave it to achieve power and prestige — led by Heissmeier, its chief who as early as 1936 began to diversify his interests by becoming Inspector of the National Political Training Schools (*Napolas*), not an SS operation. By 1939 Himmler was willing to create for him another Main Office, designated simply by his own name, so that Heissmeier could pursue his schoolmasterly interests with the prestige of the SS but without laying full claim to the Napolas. Whatever advantages this interest of his gave Himmler and the SS in influence on German youth, it reduced proportionately Heissmeier's attention to the SS Main Office, which found itself bypassed time and again by the other

Main Offices, by regional SS and police commanders, and especially by Himmler himself. Himmler's own lack of sustained interest in a unified staff system was a serious contributing factor, although not the only reason for the problem. Changing conditions and functions within the SS also created difficulties.

The year 1936 is in many ways the key one in the evolution of the SS system, for it was in mid-1936 that Himmler was able to achieve the unification of the German police under himself, thus creating the basis for the steady amalgamation of SS and police in the following years. In 1935 the SS was still picking up pieces from the period of topsy-turvy growth, the revolutionary upset, and the Röhm purge. Expulsions, consolidation, and differentiation were the main themes. A basic, long-overdue reorganization in the ranks of the General SS took place in January 1936 to reduce the variety of special honorary ranks. Henceforth there were merely paid, full-time SS and unpaid, part-time "honorary" ranks.[26] After 1936 the SS appeared to have found its direction and stride — perhaps also its limits, although these would not remain permanent — so that a kind of watershed is formed by the acquisition by Himmler on June 17, 1936, of the title of *Reichsführer SS und Chef der deutschen Polizei* (RFSSuChddPol!). This change is reflected indirectly in the revision of the relationship of the regional SS commanders (Oberabschnittsführer) to the Main Offices by Himmler on November 9, 1936. Formerly these commanders had been subject only to Himmler and to the SS Main Office. Now they were also made subject to the Security Main Office and the Race and Settlement Main Office, and also in a sense to two additionally created Main Offices, Himmler's Personal Staff Main Office (*Hauptamt Persönlicher Stab*) and a Main Office designated simply with Daluege's name but identical with the Main Office Order Police (*Ordnungspolizei*). This basic change meant that the SS regional commanders received nominal influence over the police operations in their regions as well as over the activities of the Race and Settlement system, which at this time included ideological SS training, SS family welfare, SS urban and rural settlement and housing, and liaison with the *Reichsnährstand* (Food Estate) system in agriculture.[27]

Even at this point, however, it is necessary to note an ambiguity, for the creation of the three new inspectorates in 1936 — including Special Duty Troops, Border and Guard Troops, and Officer Candidate Schools — plus the independence of the Concentration Camps and Death's Head Troops took away with the left hand at least part of what Himmler had given with the right. The regional SS commanders were not to receive orders from the inspectors or from Eicke; thus the special SS units were in turn cut off from regional influence, a step in the separation of a professional military SS from the ranks of the traditional political soldiers. As we have seen and shall see even more clearly, the effort to amalgamate the SS and police was a quite separate process, slow and uneven, and never more than partially successful. Similarly, the complete isolation of the professional SS soldier was certainly not openly striven for and was even opposed by Himmler himself on occasion in favor of a three-way amalgamation of political soldier (*Allgemeine SS*), police, and professional soldier. Some leading SS officers managed this synthesis, but by far the majority combined only two of these features in their career and outlook; many remained only political soldiers, policemen, or professional soldiers. Some of the latter rose to very high rank, as did SS officers who could better be characterized in other terms than any of these, such as technicians and professional men.

### Persönlicher Stab

Perhaps due to Himmler's split personality, which encouraged the bureaucratization of the SS-Hauptamt but then sought to circumvent his own bureaucracy, the new and powerful Main Office known as the *Persönlicher Stab, Reichsführer* SS (Personal Staff, RF-SS), began in 1936 to collect and create responsibilities growing out of adjutants' duties. Formerly known as the *Chef-Adjutantur*, it had been headed since 1934 by Karl Wolff, a shrewd "operator" who succeeded as Himmler's first adjutant where two or three previous men had failed because he was cleverer, more flexible and imaginative, and willing to take Himmler's abuse. His reward was to remain in Himmler's close confidence and to manage all aspects of his relationships with SS, party, and state agencies and personnel—a role for which the SS-Hauptamt seemed to have been originally designed.[28]

The Chef-Adjutantur had moved up to Berlin with five or six low-ranking SS officers and NCOs in 1935 as still primarily a letter-answering service. Its membership was young, willing, and eager to please not only Himmler but all SS, party, and state authorities. In return, SS officers and other officials were grateful for little services rendered them in gaining a hearing or recognition from the Reichsführer SS, so that soon a tone of mutual accommodation and even intimacy entered the correspondence of the office. By November 1936 when Himmler erected it into the equivalent of a Main Office, ensconced in the Prinz Albrechtstrasse, the Personal Staff had basically three functions: (1) liaison, (2) financial, and (3) cultural. Out of the letter-answering function developed an extensive forwarding mechanism, so that personal letters to Himmler could be passed on to one of his many subordinate agencies. At the same time as more and more high-ranking persons inside and outside the SS sought to gain Himmler's ear outside regular channels, the Personal Staff became the focus of influence in the SS. Himmler increasingly employed it for delicate negotiations where "channels" had to be avoided. Matters properly dealt with by the Personnel Office, uniforms, decorations, even promotions became the stock-in-trade of junior officers in the Personal Staff office, while the most sought-after honorary SS position after 1936 was Stab, Reichsführer SS because it opened official channels to the center of influence.[29]

The second aspect of the Persönlicher Stab was economic, for Himmler ultimately controlled the sources of financial perquisites. SS salaries were low, and it soon became apparent that it was dangerous for Himmler to allow his officer corps to become dependent on state offices controlled by Göring, Frick, or Gürtner or on positions in private industry. Special allowances for expenses in addition to grants-in-aid to get out of debt and loans, became available by 1936, from funds obtained by Himmler by private negotiation with the Party Treasurer as well as from the circle of industrialists (*Freundeskreis*) founded in 1932. These funds were placed in special account R (*Sonderkonto* R) under the control of the Section "Economic Aid" (*Wirtschaftliche Hilfe*). The SS Chief of Administration, Pohl, transferred one of his better officers, Bruno Galke, to Himmler for this purpose in 1936. Furthermore, starting in November 1935 with one of his Basic Decrees, Himmler had founded a kind of compulsory SS credit union to which all had to contribute one mark a month. The management of these funds rested with the Personal Staff, who might use them also for the support of SS widows and orphans. No interest was paid, however, and there was no real insurance principle for survivors. In other words, Himmler and his adjutants gained an additional lever to insure "enthusiasm" among the SS and their dependents. In fact these funds were largely invested in business enterprises in which the Personal Staff owned more than 50 percent of the stock. The first of these was founded as early as December 1934 — the *Nordland Verlag*, a publishing house set up in Magdeburg to further Himmler's Nordic ideas. The second was the Allach Porcelain Works, privately founded at Himmler's request in 1933 and then taken over by the Personal Staff as an SS enterprise to manufacture Dresden-like figures and "Nordic" cult objects such as birthday candle holders (*Lebensleuchter*). Other business enterprises founded in the mid-1930s by the Persönlicher Stab included a photographic firm, a bicycle reflector company, a mineral water bottling works, and several urban real estate companies to provide housing for SS officers in model suburban developments or in new villas in the best neighborhoods.

In the later 1930s the Personal Staff expanded its economic activities to include support of non-SS inventors (some of them unsavory characters who ended up in concentration camps after embezzling Reich and party funds), the development of raw material supplies for the SS in conjunction with Göring's Four Year Plan Office, the search for manpower for German agriculture, and the finding of jobs in industry for retiring full-time SS officers. Inevitably they came into conflict with Pohl's equally ambitious SS administrative branch and were forced to part with many of their enterprises and activities by 1939. The war soon brought them plenty of new opportunities for regrowth.[30]

The third function of the Personal Staff was related to Himmler's cultural pretensions, already somewhat involved in the development of the porcelain works to "purify" German *objects d'art*. Here too the involvement took the form of foundation, in 1935, of the *Forschungs- und Lehrgemeinschaft Ahnenerbe (Ahnenerbe-Stiftung)*, or the Research and Teaching Society "Ancestral Heritage" (Ancestral Heritage Foundation), and in 1936 of *Die Gesellschaft zur Förderung und Pflege Deutscher Kulturdenkmäler*, the Society for the Advancement and Preservation of German Cultural Monuments. In each case the societies were governed as sections of the Personal Staff with SS officers at their head. Funds were solicited and collected from interested German individuals and firms for excavations and restorations of real and supposed Germanic cultural relics — including medieval cathedrals. Expeditions were launched to South America and Tibet, and expensive publications were undertaken in the archaeological and artistic fields. Again the Personal Staff was able to acquire extensive contacts in the intellectual and scientific field as well as in the highest circles of German philanthropy and finance. Many persons who might otherwise have had no reason to associate with Himmler or the SS became thereby involved and often even joined the ranks as honorary members. Through the Personal Staff Himmler acquired a very broad range of "respectable" friends and supporters whom he could draw upon for assistance, financial and technical, both for the furtherance of the SS and to help it perform more and more functions for the Reich. However, the second- and third-rate minds of the "scientists" which the Ahnenerbe, for example, sponsored tended to make SS "research" the laughingstock of the universities Himmler wished to penetrate. This did not of course prevent even scoffers from capitalizing on Himmler's naiveté or the SD from recruiting the scoffers for intelligence work.[31]

## RuSHa

Another SS Main Office which tended to grow out of shape and fragment as it expanded in connection with ever-increasing involvement in government, party, and business activities was Darré's Race and Settlement Main Office. While its original line of development came from the power to grant or withhold approval for marriage among SS men, Darré's affiliation with the Food and Agriculture Ministry and the Food Estate inevitably carried RuSHa into extensive economic activity in competition or in cooperation with party, state, and private interests. We have already noted that it was this same Main Office which received in 1933 the main educational responsibilities within the SS, enabling it to penetrate the local units organizationally. Thus, by the time it became a Main Office in January 1935, it had acquired four duties: (1) ideological training, (2) racial selection, (3) liaison with German agriculture, and (4) family welfare within the SS. For each of these duties, there was a section or office staffed by one or two paid SS officers and headed by an "honorary" chief who was usually one of Darré's officials in the Ministry and Food Estate. Furthermore, every *Oberabschnitt* (Main Sector) had a *Rassereferent* (Racial Advisor), who was really a salaried officer of RuSHa, and a *Bauernreferent* (Farm Advisor), who was usually the *Landesbauernführer* (State Farm Leader) in the Food Estate system and an honorary SS officer. At lower levels there was a Training Officer (or NCO) who was also part of RuSHa, all the way down to company level. The latter were unpaid. Attached to units at every level was also a regional farm leader (normally an actual farmer) of the Food Estate with RuSHa (SS) rank, also a part-time volunteer. It should be noted that these Training Officers or NCOs and Farm Advisors were still just being taken into the SS at the time (1934 and 1935) and were thus neither well known to RuSHa nor the local units. Their party background and professional competence were usually stressed.[32]

While the sections of the Race and Settlement Main Office worked out policy in their respective fields of competence and passed upon doubtful cases (primarily having to do with admission and marriage), the Advisors and Training Officers were the executives of policies within their units. They were to help SS commanders and their men carry out the routines ordered by RuSHa. For their instruction RuSHa held a number of short courses at a special school in the Grünewald suburb of Berlin as well as other professional gatherings. They were to subscribe to the Food Estate's *Deutsche Zeitung*, which "expressed the views of the Race and Settlement Office." In July 1935 this was replaced by the official monthly magazine of the *RuS-Schulungsamt* (Training Office), the *SS-Leithefte*. Nevertheless, it appears that the whole network of Training Officers and Farm Advisors was very slowly filled and often changed. An endless flow of forms to be completed by commanders and their men originated with RuSHa as early as 1934, combined with extensive training materials. Unit RuS representatives could rarely have had the time, education, enthusiasm, and unit support for so much routine activity. Thus, it is not surprising that RuSHa seems gradually to have grown away from the units to become its own executive in many fields. As usual, the turning point is approximately 1936, when Darré appointed a kind of field representative to regain contact with the RuS "branch units."[33]

Whereas the 1935 structure of the Main Office for Race and Settlement was based on the use of a large number of honorary SS officers whose chief focus of attention lay in Darré's state and party apparatus, with a small number of low-ranking officers and NCOs to tend the shop, changes initiated in 1936 and continued in 1937 produced a professional Main Office which attracted former General SS commanders and staff personnel to Berlin.[34] One of the most marked examples of this was the Settlement Office, which was transferred in 1936 from Herbert Backe of the Agriculture Ministry to Curt von Gottberg, a minor aristocrat from East Elbia cultivated by Darré. Von Gottberg dabbled in Agricultural Settlement Companies, a form of real estate speculation associated with the conversion of East Elbian estates to small farms. He brought to RuSHa the scheme of working through these companies to aid in the settlement of SS men on the soil (also in suburban units). Under his leadership an old company (*Deutsche Ansiedlungsgesellschaft*) was reorganized with an SS majority (private stock purchase) on the board of directors for purposes of rural development, and a new company (*Gemeinnützige Wohnungs- und Heimstätten G.m.b.H.*) was organized to build and operate SS suburban settlements. He forced the coordination of all SS housing projects by local and regional units under his control. He persuaded Darré and Himmler that he should have an architectural and planning section under him which could be consulted even by the German police in barracks construction. By 1939 he had built up his office to twenty paid employees; there were at least seven settlement areas in the Reich administered by his office and numerous "SS Settlement Companies" in which Himmler had a controlling interest, through private stock purchases made by Backe and other SS officers working with him. There were difficulties ahead, however, because Oswald Pohl, the Chief of the SS Administration, sought increasingly to bring all economic activities of the SS under his control. Furthermore, in 1938 Darré was to quarrel with Himmler and thus remove some of the Settlement Office's backing, though not all.[35]

The other RuSHa office which developed far beyond its original scope was that known as the *Sippenamt* (Office for Family Affairs, sometimes translated as Genealogical Office). Whereas the original

Rassenamt continued to function after 1936 as a "scientific" or policy advisory unit for Himmler and especially for liaison with state and party bureaus, the Sippenamt took over the approval of admissions and marriages and in 1936 launched an ambitious program of *Sippenpflegestellen* (Family Welfare Offices) in the SS units at regimental level. The background of this program lies not so much in an ambitious SS officer, although one soon turned up, but in Himmler's own personal interest. In November 1935 the Reichsführer SS determined that the SS should care for its own — specifically that the well-known reluctance of men who had just come through the depression to marry and have children could only be overcome by a sort of guarantee that the SS as a kind of *Sippengemeinschaft* (family community) would care for widows and orphans. Thus, the basic decree concerning widows and orphans laid the foundation for a network of Family Welfare Offices, formally headed by the regimental commanders but actually staffed by one or more unit officers taken into the Sippenamt for this purpose. Their functions overlapped those of the Training Officers, who were often given this position. In 1937 RuSHa received state funds for the upkeep of these offices on the grounds that they served the racial and eugenics program of the Reich. By 1939 there were between two and three hundred paid employees in the Office for Family Affairs, many of them attached to the SS units spread throughout Germany, although it is certain that some of the funds were employed to erect a sizable processing staff in Berlin for the great backlog of genealogies and racial-eugenics investigations they accumulated in the admissions and marriage approval operation.[36]

This was not all the Sippenamt accomplished, however, backed as it was by Himmler's strong enthusiasm. In December 1935 it founded one of the most publicized and controversial of SS installations, the Well of Life Society (*Lebensborn*, e.V.). With marriage such a risky economic matter, large numbers of SS members were found to be fathering children outside of marriage. While many of them were contributing to the support of these illegitimate children, some were getting into trouble for their efforts at abortion, which the Nazi regime was engaged in suppressing. Thus, Himmler conceived of an agency to aid unwed mothers to have their children in comfortable seclusion in a well-run hospital and sanatorium. The organization was founded as a registered society (*eingeschriebener Verein*, e.V.) with the Reichsführer SS as chairman. Although the SS did not appear in its official title, the administration of Lebensborn was placed under the Sippenamt as "Section IV." Its business manager was the staff officer of the Sippenamt, Guntram Pflaum, a career SS officer in his thirties intent on making a name for himself. The medical aspects, and indeed the official leadership, Himmler gave to his family physician, Dr. Gregor Ebner, an old SS associate and fraternity brother. In 1936 they set up the first maternity home not far from Munich and began urging SS men to join the Society by arranging for monthly payroll deductions. It was not long before all the higher-ranking full-time officers were compelled to contribute on a scale which taxed bachelors and rewarded men with large families. The demand for the services of the home was immediately high, and three more homes were planned in 1937 and opened in 1938 in Brandenburg, Pomerania, and the Harz Mountains. The homes were available to SS wives and young women referred to the SS by party and state agencies. Arrangements were made to place the children for adoption with SS families if the mothers wished, but efforts were also made to smooth the way for marriage or at least force the father to provide child support. The liaison operations naturally fell to the Family Welfare Offices, while the administration was taken away from the Office for Family Affairs and placed in the Reichsführer SS' Personal Staff early in 1938.[37]

This move of Himmler's seems to have been the first sign of a decline in the fortunes of the Main Office for Race and Settlement, reflecting underlying disagreements with Darré. While Himmler's real reason for quarreling with the Minister of Food and Agriculture may have been Darré's independent position — possibly even strengthened by ties with Göring's growing economic empire — the SS reasons had to do with SS training. Not only had there been considerable turn-over in the leadership of the Schulungsamt, with none of the office chiefs a decisive personality, but the influx of academically oriented persons into this branch of activity had produced a plethora of abstruse and fantastic training materials quite unusable by the Training Officers. At the same time that Himmler was himself indulging in the sponsorship of pseudo-scientific investigations outside of RuSHa, he demanded that it limit itself to practical matters.[38] The result was Darré's refusal in February 1938 to carry on the training role assigned to RuSHa; Himmler transferred the Schulungsamt to the SS Main Office, although he retained its chief, Dr. Joachim Caesar — an SS colonel whom he had previously castigated for academic tendencies — and the office remained in the Hedemannstrasse complex with RuSHa. Clearly, Himmler's real object was to drive Darré out entirely, which he accomplished in the summer, while keeping that from the public. Günther Pancke, the new RuSHa chief, was a practical administrator, an SS-Altkämpfer and Freikorps veteran, most recently *Stabsführer* (business manager) of one of the SS Main Sectors (*Oberabschnitte*). It was to be his melancholy duty to preside at the dismemberment and shelving of RuSHa, though not before one last flurry of activity by the Settlement Office.[39]

Pressed by the SS Administrative Main Office to surrender his control over SS-sponsored settlements, the head of the Settlement Office looked for new worlds to conquer in Austria and Czechoslovakia. Thus, in the spring of 1938 while Himmler was forbidding the formation of "wildcat" SS Settlements, Curt von Gottberg quietly arranged the formation of the Viennese version of his *Gemeinnützige Wohnungs- und Heimstätten G.m.b.H.* and entered into the Aryanization proceedings conducted by the Gestapo against Jewish real estate, "in the interests of the SS," although with private funds. His *Deutsche Ansiedlungsgesellschaft* also soon appeared in the Sudetenland as trustee for confiscated Czech farmland, administered by SS personnel recruited by the Siedlungsamt from the Standarten of the General SS as early as August 1938. Von Gottberg's real coup was achieved when Himmler named him, on Heydrich's advice, as chief of the former Czech Land Registry (*Bodenamt Prag*). Here he was heading straight for a fall, although as was so often the case in Nazi power politics, the immediate source of his success was Himmler's refusal to take sides against him; actually Himmler and Heydrich were obviously not averse to letting von Gottberg show them the technique of outfoxing their new rival, the Reich Minister of Food and Agriculture.[40]

The Settlement Office had submitted a proposal to the new chief of RuSHa — who sent it on to Heydrich — for a Reich Settlement Commission, possibly modeled on the Prussian Settlement Commission of 1886, to coordinate all German "internal colonization" and beginning with a plan to settle SS families in Bohemia and Moravia. The eviction of Czechs and Jews "dangerous to state security" would provide a base for property acquisition. Speed was of the essence, however, for the Food and Agriculture Ministry was already active in the former Czech Land Registry attaching former German properties taken in the Czech land reform. In cooperation with Wilhelm Stuckart of the Interior Ministry, a Himmler confidante and SS-Brigadier-General (in the SD), von Gottberg was ensconced with a team of SS officials from the Settlement Office at Prague in June. They proceeded to grab properties so ruthlessly, without careful investigation of the consequences and in such a strange mixture of private and public looting, that it was only a matter of months before even Himmler was forced to suspend von Gottberg and several of his henchmen. The subsequent investigation led back into Austria with such devastating revelations of venality and improprieties that Himmler sent several SS officers to concentration camps, although Heydrich managed to aid von Gottberg's rehabilitation in the course of the war. The latter's forthright brutality appealed to Heydrich, although it does not appear that the perenially indebted nobleman actually took anything for himself. The direction of SS settlement, however, left his hands for good, and the RuSHa Settlement Office declined accordingly.[41]

## Police

Darré and Heydrich were both relative newcomers to the top hierarchy of the SS, while Daluege was one of the true Altkämpfer. Although Heydrich outstripped both of them in the erection of a personal empire, Daluege turned out to be more effective than Darré in combining his state position with SS power. The very narrowness of Himmler's concerns prevented him from following Darré too far into the bypaths of settlement projects; he preferred his police role, which meant that Daluege, and of course Heydrich, would have the advantage in their fields of ambition. In June 1936 when the latter two were made formal equals by each receiving a police Hauptamt in the Ministry of Interior, Daluege was consolidating a position he had in effect already as coordinator of the state police in Germany (now renamed *Ordnungspolizei*, ORPO). Heydrich, on the other hand, was entering a new position created for him by Himmler against the wishes of Frick as the Minister, Nebe as the chief of the criminal police, and countless other police officials in the SS. Each man accomplished much in bringing about a national integration of the police, but neither was entirely successful, losing interest in the course of the war and turning to the problem of assimilating the Protectorate of Bohemia-Moravia, where both ultimately were to lose their lives.[42]

We may recall that Daluege entered police activity in the service of the Prussian state, moving from Kommissar z.b.V. in the Prussian Ministry of the Interior to a generalship in the Prussian State Police (*Landespolizei*). When the two interior ministries were combined on November, 1, 1934, Daluege took over the police section (Abteilung III) of the united ministry. Thereafter he was often, though incorrectly, referred to as the Commander of the German Police. Technically the state police of the Länder still existed with their own budgets, locally subordinate to the interior ministry of their state and thence to the Reich governor (*Reichsstatthalter*), and only subordinate to the Reich Ministry of the Interior for technical instructions. What Daluege had done in Prussia before November 1934, he now sought to do throughout the Reich: to "clean out" the ranks of the police officers corps by speeding up the retirement of so-called Marxists, liberals, and "political Catholics" (former Center Party). He of course also removed many commissarial SA personnel after June 30, 1934. Serious efforts to locate SS officers in non-Gestapo police positions began in the summer of 1935, from the SS

Main Office rather than from Daluege, which was understandable. Police directorships and presidencies were too often assigned to active SS commanders, with the result that one or the other position was neglected and often a transfer required by one service was inimical to the other. An unsystematic pursuit of paying jobs in the police bureaucracy was continued in the SS, much as it had existed in the SA in 1933, until the basic coordination of the whole system began with the appointment of Himmler as *Reichsführer SS und Chef der Deutschen Polizei* as of June 17, 1936.[43]

The conception of a unified German police under the control of Frick went back to 1933 and appeared as late as the second half of 1935 in the form of a draft decree and memorandum stressing the loss of the garrisoned state police (Landespolizei) to the Wehrmacht and the need for a national police in their place, the more so because only police were still allowed in the "demilitarized" Rhineland. While its author is not known, the draft decree and the memorandum sound enough like Daluege to suggest that it was at least written to meet his approval. With the military occupation of the Rhineland in March 1936, the need to include the Rhineland police formations in some national police force disappeared, or rather was met in a different way by the SS-Verfügungstruppe. We find therefore a modification in the proposal of the Reich and Prussian Ministry of the Interior — again not strictly identifiable with Daluege, though certainly in his interest. An Inspector of the German Police was to be named in the ministry, probably originally meant to be Daluege; in fact he was proposed as the permanent deputy (*ständiger Vertreter*) *of Himmler* in this post. This proposal was rejected by Himmler through Heydrich, who represented him in the negotiations. Instead Himmler wanted to be appointed as Reichsführer SS and Chief of the German Police. This he achieved, although Frick attached the words, "in the Ministry of the Interior" to the title. Nothing was said in the decree about Daluege being his deputy, although a press notice of June 18 stated that he would represent Himmler in the latter's absence, a quite different matter. Daluege's actual post was created June 26 by Himmler on his own authority along with Heydrich's. There had never been *Hauptämter* (Main Offices) in the Ministry of Interior; the two police offices were obviously copied from Heydrich's *SS-Sicherheitshauptamt*, which soon came to be called the *SD-Hauptamt* to differentiate it from Heydrich's new police headquarters.[44]

While Heydrich truly had two offices with largely (but not wholly) separate personnel, Daluege's SS-Hauptamt Daluege was exactly the same as the Hauptamt Ordnungspolizei, unless we count a police major who served Himmler as an adjutant and signed the SS orders of the

Hauptamt Daluege. Furthermore, Daluege also lost from his field of influence the Kriminalpolizei. He had gained of course a vast apparatus of uniformed policemen, which was especially large in a Germany where not only fire departments but numerous regulatory bodies were part of the "administrative police." Yet not until March 19, 1937, did he gain, through Himmler, direct power of appointment and budget determination for the police of the Länder, and even then until March 28, 1940, certain state administrative police organizations eluded him. Nevertheless, after 1937 Daluege had a solid enough base to deal with Himmler and Heydrich for advantages for "his" police within the SS and to open up lower ranges of police activity to qualified SS applicants — motorized gendarmerie and protective police (*Schutzpolizei* or *Schupo*) in the cities. In 1938 Schupo were permitted to wear SS runes on their uniform — perhaps to enhance their authority — and many of the higher ranks in the Ordnungspolizei were taken into the SS with equivalent SS rank and a minimum of questions asked.[45] The creation of the post of Inspector of the Order Police as early as 1936, a position to be occupied by a police colonel in each province of Prussia and at each Reich governor's seat, formed the basis of SS-and-police union, for eventually these positions had to be filled with SS officers of comparable rank. Few if any were to come from the old SS ranks; however, inducted into the SS for this purpose, these career policemen would form a cadre for the Superior SS and Police Leaders of the war years and for the general staff which Daluege was reforming in his Hauptamt, at once both an SS and a state agency. There too his "General-Inspectors" were not taken into the SS until the "peaceful" invasion of Austria in March 1938, when SS status had begun to include quasi-military privileges.[46]

On the other hand, Heydrich was nibbling away at the middle ranks of Daluege's apparatus, the twenty-eight police directors and fifty-six police presidents, by placing some in the SD as early as 1936 and more after 1938. While a certain number of these persons were indeed the "old reliable" SS fighters who had been placed in these positions in 1933, the great majority were not even in the SS but went directly into the SD. Thus, Heydrich as well as Daluege carried out a union of the SS and police largely by naming new SS officers via Himmler, not always through the personnel office and often with small regard to the formal admission requirements of RuSHa. In the Sicherheitsdienst, however, Heydrich possessed a better apparatus for SS penetration into the police, for its top echelons were more SS-oriented than Daluege's right-wing higher police officers, and its intelligence function suited it to destroy its opponents by turning in damaging information about them to superiors. A police director or police president would often join the SD in self-defense against some junior officer. All these persons held unpaid positions in the SD, attached to the field apparatus of the SD run by a small professional cadre.[47]

In the 1935 pamphlet *Wandlungen unseres Kampfes (Changes in Our Struggle)*, Heydrich managed to verbalize what both Hitler and Himmler had been trying to express for so long — that political soldiering had to combine ideological defense with some kind of inner loyalty so strong that police operations, military operations, and propaganda operations would all be merely varieties of one reality. The old SA-free corps spirit was not enough, and *Kadavergehorsam* (the corpselike obedience of the drill ground) was insufficient; the ethos of a sworn elite had to be created and preserved. It was for this purpose the SD existed. Heydrich was a true believer, whose cynicism was reserved for the faint of heart and hand. Perhaps a disbeliever in this or that Himmlerian dogma about race, runes, and natural religion, Heydrich was a consistent practitioner of the strenuous life, the imaginative innovation, and the thorough solution. In the professional SD he sought out the most ruthless, the most consistent, the most unprincipled. With relatively low ranks and small opportunity of promotion and public visibility, he dissuaded the grandstander and the venal. Persons who liked to wield power without responsibility, to weigh and judge their superiors, to torture and to kill coldly at a distance — these were the men Heydrich gathered about himself in the Sicherheitsamt in the Wilhelmstrasse and in the professional SD field structure of 1935 and 1936. Some were SS-Altkämpfer; some were from the SA; many of them had been unpolitical. With a few prominent exceptions, they remained unheard of in 1945, providing deadly mechanisms for the use of the more colorful SS and police leaders from the ranks of the career SS, the free corps, and the SA. The criminality of the latter was plain for all to see, while clerks of the SD remained largely anonymous.[48]

When we said earlier that Heydrich — unlike Daluege — achieved two separate headquarters, we were merely continuing an observation made in a previous chapter, where it was remarked that Heydrich cleverly did not attempt to merge the state Gestapa and the SS Sicherheitsamt. Serving as bridges between the two offices were Heydrich himself; Heinrich Müller, an epitome of ruthlessness from the Bavarian Political Police without SS loyalties but very much Himmler's man; and Werner Best, who came up from Munich January 1, 1935. Best was less ruthless than Müller and possessed some of the intellectual's complexities of personality. With more loyalty to SS ideas and ideals than even the pragmatic Heydrich, he served as a link to the party as well as the professional and academic world within and beyond the General SS. In the Gestapa on Prinz Albrechtstrasse, he served as Heydrich's executive officer (I-AO) in 1935–1936 and then deputized for him as its chief until the total reorganization of September 1939 placing the Gestapa under Müller within the larger structure of the so-called *Reichssicherheits-hauptamt* (RSHA).[49] It was Best's legal skill and ingenuity which threw the Gestapa into the breach in February 1936, when the absence of a Reich police just before the reoccupation of the Rhineland seemed to threaten loss of regional control in a national emergency. The Prussian Gestapa by the law of February 2, 1936, was transformed into a Reich agency for the political police, months before Daluege and Frick reached agreement with Heydrich and Himmler about the Order Police. The mechanism which made this possible was Best's control position in the SS Sicherheitsamt (later Sicherheitshauptamt) at Wilhelms-strasse 102. Its five sections he reduced to three offices in 1935 to parallel the Gestapa, taking over the first, Organization and Administration, which included the appointment and promotion of both professional and unpaid ("honorary") SD personnel.[50]

During 1935 and 1936 some more of the political police, both in the Prussian Stapostellen and in the Länder, were added to the SS and SD above and beyond the original spies and agents of Heydrich from before April 1934. Aside from a hard core of old SS men in this group taken into the SD essentially as administrative measure, many of these new SD people were young lawyers beginning careers as police officials. Through the SS and especially the SD, Best and Heydrich played on their ambitions and intellect, so that they became willing tools. Through the SD system the larger Gestapo, recruited from older career officials and often from the criminal-investigation forces, could be directed and controlled. In the Gestapo fear of the SD and ambition for advancement, which might depend upon SD cooperation, were sufficient to gain compliance with Berlin directives no matter how unpalatable. In August and September 1936, the Prussian system of Stapostellen was extended to the entire Reich on a systematic basis under the direct control of the Berlin Gestapa sections. Needless to say, Best had seen to it that the key personnel of the Gestapa were primarily loyal to Himmler rather than to Göring or Frick, with the result that a considerable shuffling had occurred and continued to occur with the headquarters and between it and the provinces. Since those loyal to Himmler were either SS officers already or were placed in the SS and SD, the result of this shuffling was the rapid promotion of this segment of the SS officers corps to catch up with the General SS (and later the Order Police), so that by 1938–1939 the SS-Dienstalterslisten had a markedly different complexion from those of 1934–1936.[51]

With the formation of the *Hauptamt Sicherheitspolizei* June 26,

1936, the Gestapa was joined (on paper) to the former Prussian Criminal Police Headquarters under Arthur Nebe — which now in turn was erected into a Reich police office in charge of a network of Kripostellen in the major cities. Increasingly the younger officials and later even the older ones in these offices succumbed to the advantages of SS and SD membership. Nebe, its opportunistic chief who was well aware of the risks involved, himself finally joined the SS as a major on December 2, 1936, perhaps partly as a "cover" for his rather modest oppositional role. Heydrich's control over the criminal branch of the Security Police (SIPO) was initially scarcely more effective than his influence via the SD over the Police Directors and Police Presidents of the ORPO, although the official lines of his command were extended even down to the criminal investigators at county and town police headquarters.[52] It required his SD structure and the concept of SS membership to weld enough of this ramified apparatus into a responsive whole by 1939 so that a series of extra-legal orders and assignments could be silently accepted and carried out by middle-class German officials. The institution of Inspectors of the Security Police, parallel to the Inspectors of the Order Police but with fewer ties to the regional police apparatus, also provided tighter central control, since these posts were normally filled with the cream of the professional SD. However, the regional SD chiefs who held this position were not permitted to use the title publicly until 1939.[53]

It was not until 1936 that the Berlin SD headquarters (SS-Sicherheitshauptamt) began its expansion into a true intelligence clearing house, with the SD field network increasingly devoted to depth reporting and special studies rather than the pursuit of specific enemies of the state. Its three-fold organization was to survive its assimilation along with the Gestapa into the Reichssicherheitshauptamt at the outbreak of war. Indeed, many of its NCOs and junior officers of these mid-1930s were to become commanders of the death squads in Russia and managers of the Jewish Holocaust. Otto Ohlendorf, head of *Einsatzgruppe D* which in 1941 killed Jews and communists in the South Ukraine, began here as a minor subsection leader; and Eichmann started out as an assistant in the subsection on freemasons. On the other hand, some of its chief officials of the 1930s were to sink into oblivion or withdraw or be sent away from the centers of power. Its chancellery, for instance, was headed from 1935 to 1937 by an old Berlin SS comrade of Daluege, Siegfried Taubert, who had become the chief staff officer of Sepp Dietrich as regional commander of the SS eastern region. "Opi" (grampa) was in his later fifties and a favorite of Heydrich "because he could play the piano," having once been a piano salesman. His connections were obviously of value in the transition years, but in 1938 he was "promoted" to being in charge of the SS castle-school of Wewelsburg, near Paderborn. His departure signaled the end of the need for amateurs in the top SD leadership.[54]

While Best had been originally designated to head the "inland service," Heydrich soon discovered that the cloak-and-dagger fame of the composer of the Boxheim documents was perhaps exaggerated. Heydrich also preferred him as a bureaucrat, in charge of administration. He was assisted by Dr. Herbert Mehlhorn, an early SD member who had helped subordinate the Saxon political police to the control of Himmler and Heydrich, and by Walter Schellenberg, who replaced Taubert at the chancellery. Heydrich did ultimately make Best his second in command in the Sicherheitshauptamt, and Wilhelm Albert replaced Best as head of Amt I, Administration. Albert had operated the SD Main Sector West in Frankfurt and was also an early SD man.

*Amt Inland* (Amt II) went to Hermann Behrends, Heydrich's "agent" in Berlin since late 1933. This was the basic information gathering and evaluating branch, with small teams of "experts" on Marxism, Catholicism, the Protestant churches and sects, freemasonry, the Jews, the business and academic world, the press, radio, film, and the arts. Elaborately subdivided into sub-subdivisions in Kafkaesque style, the *Judenreferat* was II/112 — with II/1121 for assimilated Jews, II/1122 for Orthodox, and II/1123 for Zionists! These subdepartments and even sub-subdepartments were run by very junior SS NCOs and junior officers with modest educations. Thus, better educated men like Franz Alfred Six, Reinhard Höhn, and Otto Ohlendorf were able by 1936 to insert themselves at higher rungs in the maze, and to climb through the professional policemen and political soldiers of the General SS to positions of policy and prominence. Six and Ohlendorf were to overtake Behrends, who ultimately came to specialize in ethnic German intelligence affairs, Six managing the coordination of the numerous departments of Amt Inland while Ohlendorf became its head and policy maker. Höhn invented the idea of running a permanent opinion-gathering system within the *Lebensgebiete* of German society (the regions and sectors of ordinary life), which produced confidential reports on German political, economic, and cultural opinion by 1936.[55]

*Amt Ausland* (Amt III) was nominally run by Heinz Jost, the slippery, unsavory chief of the former SD-*Rollkommando* (hit squad). In actuality Heydrich himself meddled in the operation of the division. For instance, Wilhelm Albert, mentioned above, functioned in collaboration with Heydrich as a specialist on counterespionage toward France both while in Frankfurt and later while officially in Amt I. Amt III maintained liaison with and surveillance over the Wehrmacht and developed the technical services necessary for espionage and counterespionage. Several of the most colorful adventurers in SS uniform served in this branch. Owing partly to the necessity for caution vis-à-vis the military, both the formal and the true head of this bureau did not fully emerge from their obscurity in the 1930s; and Walter Schellenberg, the future chief of this branch whose whole career and advanced education had taken place in the Nazi era, did not begin here but as an assistant to Best — first replacing Taubert, the old SS officer, and later Best himself as Heydrich's main advisor. Much like Darré, Best proved to be too impractical as an executive. Vain and sensitive, he came to detest Heydrich, the cutter of Gordian knots.[56]

The process of forming more specialized varieties of political soldiers as illustrated in the SD and in the police generally, whereby new talent was added to a leavening of "old fighters," contributed to the downgrading of the regional SS structure in favor of the various specialized central headquarters. Thus, whereas the SD field system went on being organized in the same Main Sectors and Sectors (Oberabschnitte, Unterabschnitte) as the General SS — the regional SD chief even called "SD-Chef in Oberabschnitt . . ." — between 1936 and 1939 the reality of the specialization process made it increasingly unlikely that an SD chief or his professional staff would be recruited from the SS region, which was still occasionally the case as late as 1936 in spite of Heydrich's interest in separating his SD system from the General SS. The parallel structure of SD and General SS, which survived until the reorganization of September 1939, made it easy to treat the lower units of the General SS as recruiting grounds for the unpaid SD (SD des Reichsführers SS) — occasionally even for new professionals though in declining numbers — and also as "cold storage" for less able persons who had been tried and found wanting. Many of the latter, including many old fighters with intellectual and character defects, could be placed in the Stamm-Einheiten, "retired units" originally designed for those over forty-five, a kind of inactive reserve in contrast to the active SS reserve units for those between thirty-five and forty-five abandoned in 1936. Thereafter only persons under forty-five and active in the SS (though not necessarily in paid posts) were considered as a "ready reserve" to be heavily drawn upon in emergencies, such as mobilization (im Mob-Fall). Naturally, persons over forty-five in paid positions were not in Stamm-Einheiten. After 1936 the General SS at Standarte level and below tended to grow out of touch with the daily problems of the police and questions of military mobilization, and to become the pool of less specialized, less able, less mobile, and even less committed SS members at both officer and enlisted ranks. To remedy this and to enhance the ties between this "ready reserve" and police and Verfügungstruppe, the institution of the regional Superior SS and Police Leaders was initiated in 1936.[57]

Two steps in the conversion of the SS regional commanders into the Superior SS and Police Leaders (*Höhere SS- und Polizeiführer*, HSSPF) have already been noted. Himmler's order A 2/36 of November 9, 1936, placing the SS-Oberabschnittsführer under RuSHa and the Security Main Office gave them nominal authority over the SD chief in their Main Sector. The creation of both ORPO and SIPO Inspectors in the cities where regional SS commands were located brought police officials into parallel with the SS system. Since this move might seem to reassert the primacy of the police channels, and in fact did often result in bypassing the SS regional commanders, Himmler began in 1937 to have draft schemes drawn up for institutional unification at regional levels of the SS and police. Yet Himmler had to proceed with great caution and some camouflage, for not only did he still have to reckon with resistance from the state police bureaucracy but party circles were less than enthusiastic about SS capture of so vital a regional citadel. Moreover, the SS and the SD were afraid of being absorbed into the state system. That the successful plans were drawn up by an Order Police colonel (von Bomhard) who was not even in the SS until March 1938 suggests Himmler's skill in balancing forces within his own field of competence. He did not let either the General SS leadership or Heydrich's minions have the prestige and advantages of authorship.[58] Daluege's ORPO was successfully "hooked" by involvement in the design for a wartime system of home front controls. It was hardly accidental that the first formulation of the concept of this office of Superior SS and Police Leader placed it within the concept of war mobilization: the need for a common leader for planning and execution of joint actions by ORPO, SIPO, and SS-*Verbände* (a term referring specifically to concentration camp guards and special duty troops) within each army corps area. There is little doubt that the initial removal of the wraps around the new SS and police structure, revealing parallelism with the army corps area system rather than the Gau and Land system of party and state bureaucracy, underlined the preoccupation of Himmler with "battle theater inner Germany"—the suppression of a future Dolchstoss in wartime. The move could have been known only to the initiated, for it was in an unpublished decree of the Interior Ministry, and its implementation was delayed and spasmodic enough to allow for considerable ambiguity and uncertainty in military and party circles. The HSSPFs were not announced publicly until mid-1938 and then not all at the same time; Daluege ordered them to issue a generalized press release saying nothing about the army corps area connection; ceremonial measures and the security of party and state personages were pushed into the foreground while the actual command over both ORPO and SIPO in the event of an emergency was concealed in all public documents. On the other hand, the subordination of the HSSPFs to the *Reichstatthalter* (viceroys of the realm) was stressed — a matter of great importance to the gauleiter who held this position. Precisely this relationship was abandoned at the outset of the war.[59]

## Concentration Camps

Next to the SD, the SS institution which earlier obtained its autonomy from party and state, and indeed in part from other branches of the SS, was the concentration camp system. Like the SA concentration camps, those of the SS had begun as "wild camps" outside the authority of the state, sometimes in close cooperation with party leaders and sometimes not. The SS camp at Papenburg, which gave so much trouble to Diels and Göring in 1933, was such a local camp with purely SS connections — while the Stettin camp had been operated by the SS in collaboration with the local gauleiter. Dachau, near Munich, and Columbia-Haus in Berlin-Tempelhof were early SS concentration camps affiliated with the SS-Gruppen (later *Oberabschnitte*) *Süd* and *Ost*. Theoretically, during 1933 and early 1934 each SS region (and SA region) had a camp at its disposal, staffed by regional personnel on detached service. Such personnel was often of poor quality by SS standards, and there are indications that even at this early date assignment to this service was regarded as a chance to prove oneself after failure of one kind or another. On the other hand, at first the camps were also used to carry out service punishments, and extensive numbers of uniformed SS and SA personnel turned up in camps in the spring of 1934. Right-wing Nazi efforts to regularize the punitive measures of the new regime in the winter of 1933–1934 gradually led to the closure of many small camps, the transfer of others to state authority, and after the Röhm purge replacement of SA by SS guards as well as subordination of all camps to Gestapa control, specifically Gestapa section II-D. SS concentration camp personnel played an important part in the SA purge (notably from Dachau and Columbia-Haus); and the newly acquired concentration camp at Lichtenburg, near Torgau, served the SS as a sorting center for arrested SA personnel. Air Force General Erhard Milch was shown SA personnel in Dachau from the purge in the spring of 1935.[60]

*Courtesy Hoover Institution*

SS parade in Dachau, 1936.

Even before the purge but definitely after it, SS troops guarding concentration camps were enlisted for terms of one, four, and later twelve
years as state officials or employees. With the transfer of a camp to state
authority, the pay for the SS guards came from the interior or police
budget of the Land in which the camp was located, but Gestapa regulation effectively removed the control from local gauleiter. Moreover,
Dachau remained a purely SS installation of several interlocking parts:
the concentration camp, the General SS training camp (*Übungslager*),
the supply camp (*Ausrüstungslager*), the headquarters of the Politische
Bereitschaft for the Munich area, and lastly an "assembly point" (*Sammelstelle*) for male Austrian refugees (Austrian Legion). The battalion-
strength guard unit at Dachau was separately distinguished from other
detached personnel of the Oberabschnitt as early as March 1934, as was
the Saxon unit (*Sonderkommando Sachsen*). The generic term "*Wachverbände*" first appears in November 1934, a month before Eicke was
named as Inspector of Concentration Camps, though his position as
commander of *all* Wachverbände was uncertain until 1936. Technically
the commander of the guard unit in each camp was still subordinate to
the regional SS commander. However, Eicke is referred to as inspector
of concentration camps *and* guard units in a memorandum of September 1935 setting up a unified finance administration for both concentration camps and guard troops. From November 1935 on SS guard personnel are officially listed as assigned to the *Inspekteur der Wachverbände*
rather than *Inspekteur der Konzentrationslager*. During 1935 five Wachverbände, each with five companies, make their appearance — first as
Wachtruppen, then Wachsturmbanne, and last as Wachverbände:
Oberbayern (Dachau), Sachsen (Sachsenburg), Elbe (Lichtenburg);
Ostfriesland (Esterwegen), and Brandenburg (Columbia-Oranienburg-
Sachsenhausen).[61]

During 1935 a distinction begins between the SS administrative personnel of the camp proper, responsible for handling the prisoners, and
the guard units stationed in the watch towers and in control of work details. The latter were recruited from the very young volunteers while
the former were more often the old SS veterans. Separate commands for
the two groups, separate barracks, and separate regulations established
foundation for the formation of the Death's Head units of 1936, no
longer so much prison guards as a special police force capable of quell-
ing both prison riots and civilian disorder by the same ruthless measures. In April 1936 Eicke received the designation of Commander of the
Death's Head Troops, whereupon the small number of personnel under
his command increased from 2,876 to 3,222. The newly designated
units were given a place in the Reich budget and the right to recruit

directly from the Hitler Youth instead of depending on what personnel the regional SS commanders allowed them. Although Himmler became Chief of the German Police in June 1936, the concentration camps and the Death's Head Troops did not become a part of the German police system, but they were now also under the Ministry of the Interior. Eicke's post remained where it had been placed in 1934 — under the SS Main Office. Gestapa control in the camps continued to be exercised in a small delegation of SIPO-Hauptamt officials known as the "Political Section," whose authority extended over the prisoners rather than the camp proper but who also might "watch the watchers" to prevent corruption and collusion, an ever-present danger. At this time the term "concentration camp" was rigorously limited to a half-dozen official camps; and plans were made to abandon some of these (e.g., Columbia-Haus) and build newer, more economically advantageous installations, notably at Buchenwald (Ettersberg), near Weimar.[62]

A large reshuffling of commanders and personnel also took place in 1936 after a renewal of conflicts and complaints involving regional SS commanders, all branches of the police, and the Ministry of Justice. The core of the problem was the continued irresponsibility of the camp personnel, made up as it was of "deserving" old SS men with very low SS numbers lacking most of the skills necessary to succeed in other SS enterprises and of rural youths in their late teens totally lacking insight even into National Socialist principles. An ideological training officer was assigned to them from RuSHa for the first time in May 1936, but there is little evidence of extensive RuSHA penetration into the Death's Head units. Ideological training seems to have been intensified largely in Eicke's own hands, whose simplified charismatic preachments did not place any intellectual strain on his charges and often stressed the apartness of his units and their task. Intense rather than measured punishment for offenses against discipline became the fashion in the guard units, along with increased military training for the new recruits. A system of three-week basic training followed by one week of guard duty was instituted, concentrating contact with inmates upon whom the guards could wreak vengeance for the previous three weeks' indignities. If anything, the reforms of 1936 made the lot of concentration camp prisoners worse by removing some of the corruption and laxity of their keepers. No basic change in administrative personnel in the camps occurred. Indeed, most of the infamous commanders of the new camps in the war years came up through the ranks of administration in Dachau, Lichtenburg, Sachsenhausen (opened in 1936), Esterwegen (transferred back to the SA for the second time in 1937), and Sachsenburg (closed in 1937).[63]

On the other hand, a top-level administrative hierarchy began to develop at Oranienburg with the formation of a two-fold staff, one for the
camps' economy and the other for the Death's Head troops. The former
were really part of the ever-increasing administrative empire of Oswald
Pohl, the SS-Verwaltungschef, while the latter were successful unit
commanders from the General SS and the ranks of the Special Duty
troops, from the Officers Candidate Schools, and from the Death's
Head units themselves. While SS experience in the Kampfjahre still predominated in this new hierarchy, the men in it were neither the misfits
who preponderated in the concentration camps themselves nor the
driving fighters and ideologues who rose as regional SS commanders to
become the wartime Superior SS and Police Leaders. As a managerial
bureaucracy, they were ruthless enough where the interests of the inmates were concerned but tended to be the colorless counterparts of the
organization men in the SD system.[64]

None of the Nazis' complaints really concerned humanity or justice
anyway — the issue was control, predictability, and the meshing of the
concentration camp system with other aspects of the SS and Nazi empire. Himmler was by no means interested in completely subordinating
the camps to anyone's supervision except his own, resisting their take-
over even by Heydrich as late as 1942.[65] Thus, the system evolved auton-
omously by somewhat reducing friction with other agencies of the SS
and police (even here only in part) and by becoming more rational, not
in terms of punishment or reeducation but in terms of economic exploitation of the inmates.

From the outset at Dachau, and soon introduced into other camps,
there had been an interlocking system of workshops to aid the equipment of the Special Duty troops. Pohl, the head of the SS Administrative Office, had been hired in late 1933 to help with the equipping of an
SS military force; and well before 1936 concentration camp inmates
had been employed on construction details on behalf of housing the
Special Duty troops. With the intensification of military-economic
planning (Wehrwirtschaft) in Germany associated with Göring's appointment as head of the Four Year Plan (October 1936), the concentration camp system focused more systematically on economic goals. After
the Olympic Games of 1936, roundups of potential slave labor for camp
workshops began among the so-called "work-shy," "asocial elements,"
professional criminals, and pacifists and religious sectarians.[66] At this
same time Himmler announced to the Wehrmacht that he planned to
expand his 3,500-strong Death's Head battalions to 25,000 in thirty
units built on cadre formed by the twenty-five guard companies (Hundertschaften). While the army was reassured that these forces were

there to relieve them of concern for the home front in time of war, the increased military training of the Death's Head units, the exchange of personnel with the Special Duty troops, and the evolution of a common supply system based on the concentration camp workshops foreshadowed by 1937 the wartime striving of the Waffen-SS for *Gleichberechtigung* (equal rights) with the Wehrmacht. Only the diminutive size of the two units combined (18,000 in January 1938) was reassuring. With the construction of the "modern concentration camp" at Buchenwald in the summer of 1937, Eicke realigned the Death's Head troops into three regiments exactly like the Special Duty troops, each at its own headquarters (*Standort*): *Oberbayern* at Dachau, *Brandenburg* at Sachsenhausen, and *Thüringen* at Buchenwald. In May 1937 Himmler had begun a program of training 1,250 recruits for six months in special companies within each battalion, preliminary to the setting up of regular Death's Head Reinforcement Battalions.[67]

### Verfügungstruppe

The parallelism of 1937 between the Death's Head Formations and the Special Duty Troops is expressed not only in numerous orders in which they are lumped together (*VT und TV . . .* i.e., *Verfügungstruppe und Totenkopfverbände*) but also in a common term, *Sicherungsverbände*, Security Formations. This parallelism may be said to have its roots in the tentative separation in 1933 of armed or garrisoned units (*bewaffnete SS, kasernierte SS*) for special purposes (*Sonderkommandos zur besonderen Verfügung*), made definite after the Röhm purge by the contrary category of *Allgemeine SS* (General SS) and completed in January 1940 by the common term Waffen-SS (Armed SS). The line of development is, nevertheless, not so direct. While there is an initial period of least differentiation in 1933, when for example Sonderkommando Sachsen probably served both as concentration camp guards and an armed reserve to suppress an insurrection in "Red Saxony," the creation of Wachtruppen at the concentration camps quite separate from the Politische Bereitschaften — and unlike them *included in the category of General SS* (still true as late as 1937) — meant that the Verfügungstruppe, as they were known after December 1934, appeared to be a unique military unit without parallel in Germany.[68] Indeed, Sepp Dietrich on October 12, 1933, described the Adolf Hitler Standarte as "solely and uniquely a special unit alongside the Army" (*"einzig und allein eine besondere Truppe neben dem Reichsheer"*). The future Leibstandarte was unique in that its commander was at the same time the General SS Main Sector Commander (*Oberabschnittsführer*), and it

was set up in two battalions, or six companies. However, the new kasernierte Hundertschaften were set up like the grüne Polizei, or garrison
police, of the Weimar Republic (still in existence as Landespolizei and
shortly to be absorbed by the new *Wehrmacht*) in smaller units known
as "hundreds" to form a Politische Bereitschaft (Political Emergency
Unit) commanded by an SS major or lieutenant colonel who was responsible to the SS Main Sector Commander, an SS General. Furthermore, while Prussia paid for the Leibstandarte out of its police budget
(1934–1936) and Württemberg, Bavaria, Saxony, and Hamburg did the
same for their garrisoned SS hundreds, the Reich Ministry of the Interior compensated only Prussia. Already before the Röhm purge, however, the SS-Amt on May 5, 1934, ordered markings for the Politische
Bereitschaften, which though distinct from the Leibstandarte now provided for three Standarten (regiments) numbered 1–3 and assigned to
the Main Sectors South, West, and Center (*Mitte*) — each consisting of
three Sturmbanne (battalions) of four Stürme (companies) each. In
June 1934 Himmler ordered the Leibstandarte to abandon its too-
military sounding *Kompanien und Batallione* for the *Sturmbanne und
Stürme* of political soldiering. On the other hand, the concentration
camp guards retained the Hundertschaft system until 1937.[69]

Of the Political Emergency Units, only the first of the three Standarten listed in the May 1934 order developed as planned, and that only
in part by December 1934 when the Verfügungstruppen were announced. The Politische Bereitschaft at Munich had been formed from
volunteers out of the 1st and 34th General SS regiments along with the
initial *Streifendienst* (auxiliary police). A second battalion was formed
by December 1934 from the Austrian legionnaires at the so-called
Dachau Collecting Point (*Sammelstelle*) attached to the *Hilfswerklager*
Dachau (Refugee Aid Camp). At first it was unclear whether the Austrians should be regarded as part of the VT, and for many years they
were treated by the other units as undependable foreigners. This SS-
Standarte 1 (as distinguished from 1. SS-Standarte of the Allgemeine SS)
was headquartered at the same location as the notorious Dachau concentration camp, for a time sharing facilities and personnel with the
Wachtruppe which was to become the Death's Head Unit 1 — Upper
Bavaria.[70]

The Württemberg Politische Bereitschaft had been intended for
Standarte 2 and was so designated briefly; but the interruption of the
purge and the limitations on an armed SS imposed by a jealous Reichswehr and a cautious Hitler led to the reduction of the Ellwangen contingent to less than a battalion, which was carried as the third battalion
of SS 1. The balance of III/SS 1 was made up of additional Austrians at

the Sammelstelle Dachau. Numerous young Württembergers who volunteered for the SS as well as Hanoverians who enlisted for the stillborn SS 3 (Mitte) were assigned as concentration camp guards instead, where they distinguished themselves by their humane decency even to the point of being put behind barbed wire for it (perhaps out of pique at not becoming soldiers). Instead of the planned second and third regiments, three separate battalions were set up as Standarte 2, battalion one at Hamburg-Veddel; battalion two at Arolsen, Waldeck; and battalion three at Wolterdingen, near Soltau in Hanover. Judging by the dates when company and battalion commanders were appointed in both Standarten (spring 1935), the units were a long time in "shaking down," probably with little if any professional military leadership and inadequate weapons. On the other hand, the Leibstandarte enjoyed extensive military training at army camps before the Röhm purge, and a secret order of March 1935 provided for training SS personnel by army units. Yet in July 1935 VT training regulations written by Himmler were still only promised for September. VT officers and NCOs were provided specialized training beginning in September 1935 at Döberitz, Wünsdorf, and Halle (Army Communications School).[71]

We may recall that Paul Hausser had been signed up in the SS in November 1934 to supervise the erection of Officer Candidate Schools, for it was Himmler's intention to make himself as independent as possible of army training. The model for the schools, however, was the pre-1914 Kadettenanstalt. Actually the first OCS at Bad Tölz (Bavaria) was begun with cadre recruited from various General SS regiments in Upper Bavaria starting in April 1934, along with preparations for the General SS training camp (*Übungslager*) at Dachau. Its first commander, Paul Lettow, was a professional soldier who returned to the army in 1935. The first class at Tölz was conducted under the former commander and in early 1935 was under observation by the cadre of the second OCS assembled by Hausser (Braunschweig). The first 60 graduates of Tölz became second lieutenants April 20, 1935, 2 of them remaining as cadre at Tölz and 3 going to Braunschweig. Eighteen went to Standarte 1, 16 to Standarte 2, and 4 to Leibstandarte; however, a year later SS 1 had retained only 9, SS 2 only 8, and the Leibstandarte 1. The biggest magnet for the young officers was the SD-Hauptamt (13), with another 7 going to RuSHa and 7 to the staff of the Reichsführer SS. Two went to the Death's Head Battalion "Upper Bavaria." Twenty-seven of the 60 were already first lieutenants by November 1936. A second class was conducted at each school, 62 graduating from Tölz and 142 men graduating from Braunschweig April 1936. Thereafter there were annual classes until wartime. An increasing participation in the OCS from the

Death's Head units may be noted, with a continued heavy withdrawal of young officers for the Berlin Main Offices (more than half). Indeed, the Special Duty Troops could have gotten only about 200 junior officers from the two OCS by the outbreak of war; theoretically the whole output of more than 600 by April 1939 was available as reserves. Himmler conceived the idea in 1937 of assigning the graduates to successive two-year tours of duty with General SS, Sicherheitspolizei, and Special Duty or Death's Head Troops. Although he did not repeat the experiment with further classes, the bulk of the 1937 personnel only returned to the combat units in wartime.[72]

After first being appointed as commander of the Braunschweig OCS, Hausser exercised direct control over the OCS as Inspector of SS Officer Candidate Schools from August 1935 until his appointment as Inspector of the Special Duty Troops October 1, 1936. During the period when Hausser also functioned as chief of the SS Leadership Office in the SS-Hauptamt (May 1936–1937), the commanders of the schools were subordinate to that office. Tölz was commanded by a retired police colonel for three years and then until the outbreak of the war by a temporarily "retired" Wehrmacht colonel. Braunschweig was also turned over to a sixty-five-year-old Reichswehr colonel who had retired in 1924. In 1937 Himmler turned the inspectorate of the OCS (redesignated as *Junkerschulen*) over to Walter Schmitt, the head of the SS Personnel Office who also had in his charge the General SS Officers School (the former Übungslager at Dachau) as well as Drivers' and Cavalry Schools for both General and Armed SS. This was no doubt an effort on Himmler's part to further the integration of the SS officers corps as a whole. Another reason may have been a considerable turn-over in the large training cadre of the schools. Both the schools and their products tended to give rise to complaints until well into the war years.[73]

When Standarte 2 reached the approximate strength of Leibstandarte and Standarte 1 (2,500) in the fall of 1935, the three units were held there for a full year. An exchange of officers also occurred between the regiments, even with a reduction in their absolute number as some went into the army or were sent to the General SS. A Standarte had to get along with less than 100 officers, less than half of whom had had front experience, although the majority were seasoned Altkämpfer who had joined the SS before 1933. The NCOs, who were usually also men with very low SS numbers, played a heavy part in the training and command structure. On the other hand, the recruits were largely new SS, not from the General SS at all but young men of between seventeen and twenty-three often without even a Hitler Youth background. In a period of continued wide unemployment, a four-year enlistment in what promised to be an elite troop with possibilities of promotion well beyond the traditional limits of the German army was not a serious barrier. Selection commissions stressed size and brawn rather than education and ideology. Training programs dwelt heavily on basic training of the soldier with rifle and bayonet, much like the AW training of 1933–1934 the officers and NCOs knew by heart and which in fact their new battalion and regimental commanders had themselves conducted in Reichswehr and SA. Indeed, the majority of the VT commanders came out of the most suspect circles of SA and Reichswehr, those who had believed all along in the possibility of a "new model army" and who rejected the idealization of the old German army yet also rejected party hegemony over military matters.[74]

In 1936, during which elements of the new Wehrmacht entered the demilitarized zone without French retaliation and Himmler tightened his hold on the defenses of "battlefield inner-Germany," Special Duty Troops and the new Death's Head Battalions could be referred to together in SS orders as markedly different from the General SS. Plans for their increase might still arouse concern in the more jealous and conservative military quarters; but by now it was clear that, like the SA before it, the General SS was rapidly losing any claim to *Wehrhaftigkeit* (combat preparedness). The Wehrmacht seemed to be master in its own house as never before, and armed SS units with machine guns and mortars but without armor and artillery could be safely expanded to relieve *Wehrkreis* (regional defense district) commanders of the need of holding army troops in their areas for security in wartime.[75] The restructuring of the Wehrkreis and army corps area system following the inclusion of the Rhineland in the defense network led to modifications in the General SS Main Sectors, the SD Main Sectors, and the relocation and expansion of Special Duty troop installations. The SS Main Sectors were thus in the process of becoming the replacement districts of the Special Duty Troops and Death's Head Battalions and their commanders—the future Superior SS and Police Leaders—coordinators of security and emergency measures in their district. Step by step against weakening Wehrmacht resistance, Special Duty Troops and to a lesser extent Death's Head Battalions in 1937 won rights comparable to those of the Wehrmacht—reduced travel rates, postal privileges, pensions, and emergency weapon use. But the pensions took years to be implemented; the right to employ weapons in home front emergencies was still subject theoretically to conventional German court adjudication until the war years.[76]

*Courtesy Hoover Institution*

Traditional defensive formation of SS soldiers guarding the speakers' tribune, Parteitag, 1936. Hitler, Hess, and Himmler.

The Verfügungstruppen of the mid-1930s were organized in a modi-fied three-fold system of three regiments of three battalions, with four companies each, but there are signs that a four-fold system was contem-plated. For example, SS 1, renamed *SS-Standarte Deutschland*, ac-quired a fourth battalion at Ellwangen in 1937; and a fourth regiment, formed from elements of the battalion known as "N" (for Nuremberg, though actually at Dachau) existed in 1936. Although there is a 1938 reference to "SS VT Nürnberg," the fourth regiment seems to have been postponed until the *Anschluss* and the forming of *SS-Standarte Der Führer* in Austria. Supporting units for a division in the form of a Signal Battalion stationed first at Berlin-Adlershof and after 1937 at Unna in Westphalia, an Engineers Battalion at Leisnig and after 1937 at Dres-den, and medical teams (*Staffen*) at battalion level freed the VT both from the General SS organizations with the same functions and from the corresponding army branches. An OCS for medical officers for both VT and TV was begun in October 1936.[77]

Above all, a coordinating system for the VT was begun in 1936, first in the spring with the formation of the *Führungsstab der SS-Verfügungstruppen* constructed significantly of the same administrative personnel who were managing the concentration camps' economy, and secondarily in October with the development of a kind of general staff of the Inspector of the Special Duty Troops, soon replacing the Führungsstab. After a few years in the administrative branch of the inspector's staff, the former group gravitated back toward the concentration camp orbit in the war years, while the more strictly military figures from the SS Main Office and the office of inspector formed the nucleus of the Führungshauptamt of the Waffen-SS. Technically, all personnel and Hausser himself, as Chief of the Leadership Office, were still part of the SS Main Office; but instead of a gain in centralized control (which may have been intended) the failure of the SS Main Office head (August Heissmeier) to comprehend the military side of SS operations any better than he had the administrative empire of the SS-Verwaltungschef led to the disintegration of the SS-Hauptamt already noted above. When in October 1937 Hausser gave up the post of Leadership Office chief to a purely General SS veteran, the position reduced itself to housekeeping responsibilities for the General SS. By this time the Office of Inspector of Special Duty troops amounted to more than fifty officers, the nucleus of a general staff. In 1938 with the restructuring of the Recruitment Office of the SS Main Office under Gottlob Berger, one of the most competent and ruthless of the old AW personnel fated to become one of Himmler's leading wartime lieutenants, another quasi-independent staff agency was formed which would aid the future Waffen-SS. Thus, little by little and camouflaged against a General SS and Police background, an armed SS "crystallized out" as a separate entity. Aided by its small size (12,000 in January 1938) and its divided nature—successfully bridged in the person of Heinrich Himmler—the combat branch of the SS was soon capable of effective employment in whole or in part and, above all, of massive growth in the interests of SS aggrandizement when Hitler's imperial designs had ripened.[78]

## Austria

The SS played an important part in the preparation and execution of every German conquest, and Austria was no exception. In fact, Himmler's Austrian SS played a decisive role in carrying out the pressure tactics of Hitler and even initiated a few parts of the scheme. The SS had been prominent in July 1934 also, we may recall; however, at that time serious doubts existed about whether it was truly carrying out Hitler's orders. Nor was the Austrian SS immune to the disarray after the failure of the putsch in National Socialist ranks. Many prominent SS leaders there were arrested and sentenced to long prison terms or fled to Germany in 1935. However, the tightening discipline of the German SS, the close tie between SS and SD, Himmler's early foothold in the Bavarian Secret Police with old ties to Austria, and Himmler's control over the German-Austrian frontier not only through the HIGA (*Hilfsgrenzangestellten*) but also through the Border Police all combined to thrust the few loyal SS officers in each Austrian Land into the center of the inevitable Nazi conspiracy.[79]

While Hitler disavowed connection with the Austrian Nazis and genuinely disapproved of continued insurgent tactics, he heartily approved of the "iceberg" approach developed in Carinthia whereby an official group of moderate Nazis sought accommodation with the authoritarian Schuschnigg regime while an illegal network was perpetuated under the strictest discipline, primarily for communications purposes. Respectable, middle-class persons could be won for SD work, first in Carinthia and later in Vienna and elsewhere, while some of the most adventurous Carinthians and Styrians of free corps days were drawn to the SS, if they were not there already. Quite a few transferred from the SA, which in these regions unlike Vienna and Linz had exposed itself in the putsch. By 1936 Himmler had enough control over the Austrian SS to guarantee that its members would not act up disobediently, a perennial problem with the Austrian party leaders. The agreement with Schuschnigg of July 11, 1936, not only created a dual system of financial aids — legal and illegal — for hard-pressed Austrian Nazis; it also set up a mixed commission under the chairmanship of Wilhelm Keppler, a businessman who was Göring's chief liaison with Himmler and now also became Hitler's secret mouthpiece to the Austrian Nazis. Since the control of funds for Austria rested to a considerable extent with SS personnel, either in the Hilfswerk-system or through Keppler — who ranked as an SS General — the disobedient party faction could be brought to heel, not at once but in a matter of months. With the communications system between the Nazis and the Reich in SS-SD hands, it was also impossible for the dissident group to get a hearing from Hitler or Göring. On the other hand, the idea of bringing Schuschnigg to Berchtesgaden to be intimidated, the ferreting out of his plebiscite plans in time to intervene against them, and even the initiative in capturing power the night of March 11 in Vienna and the Länder capitals can be traced to the SS. In

fact, these can be traced to a single venturesome SS man, Odilo Globocnik, on whom Himmler bestowed a colonelcy the next day.[80]

While it is certainly true that Hitler had no blueprint for the annexa-
tion of Austria and lacked even conventional military plans for an occupation, the SS provided him with a precision instrument of subversion
under the cover of legality, if it did not actually show him the way and
lead him step by step to success. Göring and Himmler, working through
Heydrich, had collaborated closely on the "framing" of Blomberg and
Fritsch at the outset of 1938, meeting Hitler's desires as they had in June
1934. The Austrian *Anschluss* originated with them too, capturing opportunities presented by Hitler's search for a "cover" for his purge of
Wehrmacht and the Foreign Office and Schuschnigg's desperately
staged appeal to the victors of 1918 to defend their own creation. The
smoothness with which the Germans improvised the integration of
army units, the motorized Leibstandarte, 40,000 Ordnungspolizei, the
Death's Head Regiment Upper Bavaria, and elements of both "Deutschland" and "Germania" regiments between March 7 and March 15 all be-
lie the notion that the very real interservice rivalries were strong enough
to disturb cooperation in a real emergency. Indeed, staff work and drills
of some kind must have preceded the first real test, even though no large
scale practice alert or mobilization scheme seems to have existed.
Himmler *may* have been surprised by Hitler's exact decision to intervene urged on by Göring, but he was well prepared for the intervention, and his intelligence provided the circumstances for it. Within Austria some 7,200 SS (called *NS-Dienst*) members under the command of
Ernst Kaltenbrunner—a ruthless lawyer with a low SS number—went
into action about 9 P.M. on March 11 to seize public buildings in the
various state capitals along with even larger SA contingents (*NS-
Mannschaft*) already—though still illegally—designated as auxiliary
police. By midnight Kaltenbrunner had become Police Minister, and at
2 A.M. when Himmler arrived and removed the non-Nazi Minister of
State Security, this future Superior SS and Police Leader of Austria
(later "Danube") had become the first of the many SS proconsuls of a
Nazi empire.[81]

After a very brief transition as a single SS main district, the Ostmark,
or Eastern March, was split into two Oberabschnitte, corresponding to
the gaus, themselves following the old Land boundaries. The gauleiters
uniformly became high SS officers, by no means a regular procedure in
the past but here indicating the increased importance of remaining
within negotiating range of the Reichsführer SS. Indeed, Globocnik—
the new SS colonel who had done so much to assist the Anschluss—
became for awhile the gauleiter of the Vienna region until his involve-

ment in flagrant "Aryanization" abuses along with hundreds of other Austrian SS officers forced his removal. The SS had to suffer a minor setback in the course of 1938 in Austria as Hitler placed control in the hands of a German Reich Commissar for Reunification, Josef Bürckel, who was a party stalwart and former gauleiter. Although since November 1937 he had accepted the rank of SS General, this party man quickly disassociated himself from the SS and police system, intimately associated as it was with the apparatus of the local Austrian Nazi leadership; and he quarreled with Keppler, the other SS general who was Göring's (and Hitler's) emissary. After he had managed to embarrass quite a number of SS higher-ups in shady dealings with Jews and receivers of Jewish property, Bürckel himself was ultimately deposed, having made some serious foreign policy mistakes during the Czechoslovak crisis. In this way the SS could reemerge in Austria in 1940 virtually unscathed, in fact much strengthened. Instead of three General SS-Standarten, Austria could boast of seven Standarten with 17,000 men. More important, Himmler had set about immediately in April 1938 to form a three-battalion Verfügungstruppe (*Der Führer*) with elements in every Land out of cadre from units sent in for the parade and occupation. A third Officer Candidate School was opened at Klagenfurt. Furthermore, a fourth Death's Head regiment (*Ostmark*) was also formed at the former Austrian concentration camp Mauthausen, near Linz, soon to become one of the deadliest of its kind. After a flurry of conflict over the relative powers of the new offices of Inspectors of Order Police and Security Police vis-à-vis the Superior SS and Police Leader, the system of treating the former as the very highest subordinates of the latter worked its way into practice, so that Austria almost never enjoyed the luxury of Nazi cross-purposes in police matters. The Austrian police were often Nazis of long standing, especially in Vienna and Graz; many of these quickly became SS colonels and even generals. No very extensive housecleaning of the police was necessary in Austria, and the SS assimilation of the police officer corps in the Reich proceeded without marked exception in the former Austrian gaus.[82]

Well before the seizure of Austria, the Sicherheitshauptamt had made extensive studies of Austrian Jewry, since it was well known that Hitler's own anti-Semitism had arisen there. Thus, it was not really surprising that Adolf Eichmann should be sent to Vienna to pursue his specialized studies of how best to eliminate Jews from the German Lebensraum. What was notable of course was Eichmann's transition to executive powers in the Central Office for Jewish Emigration which he set up in Vienna, August 26, 1938, on specific orders of the Reich Commissar for Reunification. Eichmann was clearly not acting on his own initiative, nor was he carrying out a specifically SS policy, for the same Reich Commissar was making things difficult for the SS due to the latter's Aryanization proceedings against the same Jews. When Göring (not Himmler) ordered the formation of a Reich Central Office for Jewish Emigration on January 24, 1939, as a multiministry agency, however, it was entrusted to Heydrich — who delegated his powers to Heinrich Müller, head of the Gestapo. Eichmann's Austrian bureau then became merely a branch office, although again a cooperative effort by bureaucrats of numerous agencies. The Gestapo chairmanship in this arrangement was to become the accepted form for other wartime state bureaus of immigration and deportation in which worked many officials both in and out of SS uniform.[83]

### Czechoslovakia

Because the public appearance of the SS alongside the Police and the Wehrmacht in Austria had given rise to considerable speculation about the future role of the SS, especially in wartime, Hitler signed on August 17, 1938, what was intended to be the decisive ruling about the relations between it, police, and Wehrmacht. The fact that it did not represent anything final at all, merely pointing in the direction in which Hitler wished the SS to develop, does not reduce its importance. Although its authorship is uncertain, we know that Himmler saw it and made some changes before Hitler signed it. The draft was drawn up as early as June 3 and was seen by the SS-Hauptamt in July prior to Hitler's signing it. The document was marked "Top Secret" (*Geheime Kommandosache*) and certainly was not widely known, though referred to officially.[84] After a brief introduction discussing the close connection between the SS and Police created by the June 17, 1936, decree, the order divides itself into four parts of unequal length: (1) General (one page), (2) The Armed Units of the SS (more than seven pages), (3) The General SS (one page), (4) Executive regulations (one page). The SS in its entirety is described as a political organization of the party and without need of arms; however, for special internal tasks of the Reichsführer SS and Chief of the German Police and for mobile use with the army in wartime, certain enumerated SS units were excepted from that characterization. These units were the Special Duty Troops, the Officer Candidate Schools, the Death's Head units, and the Police Reinforcements of the latter (not yet in existence). In peacetime Himmler had the sole authority over them, although he had to purchase his military equipment from the Wehrmacht. Of the Special Duty Troops, it was written that they formed neither a part of the Wehrmacht nor the police but were part of the NSDAP for Hitler's exclusive use. They were budgeted in the Interior Ministry subject to approval of the Oberkommando der Wehrmacht. An enumeration of the elements followed, with Himmler's handwritten additions on the original decree, showing that he wanted to maximize motorization. Certain special units were to be added for internal employment (e.g., an armored car platoon), and in wartime the whole Verfügungstruppe was to be organized as a Wehrmacht division. In case of mobilization, replacement units used in peacetime for training the so-called Police Reinforcements of the Death's Head units would produce replacements for the Verfügungstruppe division. In case of mobilization, Hitler would determine when and how to turn the VT over to the army (in which case he stipulated that they would still remain party troops), or he could still assign them to Himmler for internal emergencies. The only distinction Hitler made in the description of the Death's Head units was a lack of reference to their being solely for his personal use. They too are characterized as an element (*Gliederung*) of the party, neither of the police nor the Wehrmacht. Their purpose is said to be the solution of special problems of a police nature assigned by him. Duty with them did *not* fulfill military service requirements. After mobilization they would form the cadre of the Police Reinforcements to be trained beforehand in the new replacement units with funds obtained by the Interior Ministry from the OKW. The concentration camp guard duty would then be performed not by the Police Reinforcements (who were intended for occupation purposes) but by members of the General SS over age thirty-five. The Police Reinforcements *were* to be counted as police troops. In wartime members of the General SS were mobilizeable in the armed services just like anyone else, except that the Main Office staffs as well as the Main Sector and Sector staffs were to be deferred "for duties of a police character." Executive regulations for police matters and internal commitment could be issued by Himmler, while the OKW was to issue such orders for all other mobilization conditions affecting VT and TV.[85]

While SS expansion along purely military lines had seemingly been quite firmly limited again by Hitler in this order, Himmler had been developing a quite different alternative for increasing SS power and influence in the Germanic empire of the future. Taking advantage of Ribbentrop's need for a collaborative relation with the SS to advance his bureau in the aristocratic Foreign Ministry, Himmler had managed to appoint quite a few of Ribbentrop's personnel to SS rank and to have Werner Lorenz, an old SS fighter, made their formal superior for SS purposes. Lorenz was possessed of an East Elbian background, education in a Kadettenanstalt, and an entree to international society that made him seem suitable for appointment in January 1937 both by Hess for the party and Ribbentrop for his Foreign Ministry bureau as head of the so-called *Volksdeutsche Mittelstelle*, the Liaison Office for Ethnic Germans. This was a typical "iceberg" operation with nominal power to manage interstate friendship associations and actual funds to aid German-speaking citizens of other nations to maintain their German-ness, to support German schools, and in effect to influence so-called ethnic German groups to support Nazi ideals. Furthermore, from the start VoMi — as Lorenz's organization soon came to be called — became a vehicle for SD penetration into German folk groups abroad, and indeed it was not long before the second in command at VoMi was Hermann Behrends of the SD. At no time was VoMi actually a branch of the SS, although later many, although not all, of its officials wore SS and police uniforms. Its chief advantage to Himmler was to provide him with a substitute for what he had had naturally in the Austrian SS and police — access to a controllable German apparatus. Himmler and the SS actually rode into influence and power in Czechoslovakia, Poland, and the Balkans on the backs of agents of the party and the Foreign Ministry, assisted of course by the clever assignment of SD personnel as soon as possible. While there was no official SS connection with VoMi until the naming of Himmler as Reich Commissar for the Strengthening of Germandom in October 1939, to perform the task of resettling ethnic Germans originally given by Hitler to VoMi, in plain truth Himmler sought from the very beginning of 1937 to penetrate the east European ethnic German groups via SS recruiters in order to expand SS influence into what he already regarded as settlement territory.[86]

Next to the Austrians, the easiest folk group for the Nazis to penetrate were the Sudeten Germans. While Hitler was to go to war ostensibly in the interests of the ethnic Germans of Poland, the party and the SS did not do half so well there before 1939 as they did in the second home of national socialism, Czechoslovakia. A German National Socialist Workers Party was founded there November 15, 1918. As in Austria, the homegrown variety of Sudeten Nazi was hard to control from Berlin. However, in comparison with the ethnic Germans of Poland, divided in their traditions by the Polish partition, by religion, and more recently by numerous party rivalries, the Sudeten Germans were a powerful, united front against Prague and Czechdom, eminently worth subverting to Hitler's cause. SD and Abwehr activity in the Sudetenland preceded January 30, 1933, as did Reich-Nazi activity in the form of a secret *Bereitschaft* (Alarm Squad) within an Austro-Fascist *Kameradschaftsbund*. The rise of Konrad Henlein's *Sudetendeutsche Heimatfront* was aided with funds from the Nazi-dominated League for Germandom Abroad (*Verein für das Deutschtum im Ausland*, VDA) before VoMi took over in 1937. By that time SD influence in Henlein's immediate circle provided Heydrich and Himmler with information and control — if not over Henlein himself, over his deputy, Karl Hermann Frank, the future Superior SS and Police Leader in Prague. There was both an illegal SA and SS, the former masked as a sport or gymnastic society, the latter in various student associations. There can be little doubt that Henlein, who exercised a tight control over the vast majority of ethnic Germans in Czechoslovakia through a network of organizations besides his Sudeten German Party, was taking orders from VoMi by November 1937.[87]

When Hitler decided to turn the heat on Czechoslovakia immediately after the Anschluss, VoMi was in on the conspiracy at every step. A *Sudetendeutscher Schutzdienst* was formed openly from the secret SA formations under Reich SA guidance, with the advice of a former SA and AW officer now in the SS — Hans Jüttner, the future chief of Himmler's military general staff, the *Führungshauptamt*. Plans were made for a military seizure by the Wehrmacht accompanied by risings of the Schutzdienst after the abortive Czech mobilization of May 20, and there is evidence that these plans extended to Bohemia and Moravia. During the hectic summer months of 1938, while all Europe hoped for peace while preparing for war, the SIPO-SD headquarters laid out the police procedures for the seizure of specific properties and personages in the vanguard of the Wehrmacht. Thus, the first *Einsatzkommandos* were called into existence. These police teams were to make contact with SS personnel and SD agents in the Sudetenland, who were secretly organized to take over police duties even before the arrival of the Wehrmacht. Liaison between Wehrmacht and SS, VoMi and the Foreign Office, SIPO-SD and Abwehr was far better than at the time of the Anschluss. Indeed, the atmosphere of common purpose and essential agreement — enhanced by the conferring of numerous honorary SS ranks in the Foreign Office and other state bureaus — the acceptance by the Wehrmacht of young SS-Junker and officers for temporary duty with their units, and the sharing of espionage secrets between Canaris and Heydrich brought the SS closer to *Salonfähigkeit* (respectability) than ever before. Rivalry and jostling for first place there still was, but it was subdued; the joint formulation by SS and Wehrmacht of the Hitler decree of August 17, 1938 illustrates some degree of give-and-take on both sides under the impetus of the oncoming crisis.[88]

Immediately after the August 17 decree, the OKW ordered the call-up of the Police Reinforcements specified in the decree from lists supplied by the SS Main Sectors; but due to resistance and overtaxed staffs, the army corps areas refused to do the SS's work for it. Therefore, the new Recruitment Office of the SS (*Ergänzungsamt*) under Gottlob Berger and the SS Main Sectors had to improvise their own procedures in September. A total of 12,000 General SS members were mobilized by October 1 above and beyond the 15,000-strong Special Duty troops and the 8,000-man Death's Head battalions. It was on September 17 that Henlein's deputy, K. H. Frank, persuaded Hitler to approve the arming of the Sudetendeutscher Schutzdienst, waves of which had fled temporarily over the borders to Silesia, Saxony, Bavaria, and Austria. The resulting *Sudetendeutsche Freikorps* consisted of between 10,000 and 15,000 men in four Gruppen (brigades, the old SA unit) of four *Abschnitte* (sectors, the current SA and SS unit formed of several Standarten). A strengthening of SA officers, SA uniforms, and SA camping equipment was rapidly improvised — with confiscated Austrian arms, VoMi, SD, and Abwehr advisors. General directions for these fifth column troops came from Henlein's headquarters at Schloss Donndorf near Bayreuth, with advice from Hans Jüttner of the VT Inspection (Replacements), Canaris of the Abwehr, and Gottlob Berger as the new head of the SS Recruiting Office.[89]

Incursions across the international frontier even involving German SA elements occurred on September 22, and by September 25 the town of Asch had been seized and transferred to two Death's Head battalions from Dachau. Next day Himmler announced that *all* elements of the Freikorps would come under the SS in the event of invasion, and although this ran counter to army orders, it was never countermanded. In fact, while VT and TV units were mixed in with Wehrmacht divisions, the Freikorps was committed on and after September 30 as independent operational units under Order Police authority. Before their dissolution on October 15, a rapid scramble for their commanders as new SS officers poisoned relations between the two future Main Office chiefs, Jüttner and Berger. Both had come out of the SA/AW experience and both were empire-builders oriented to expanding the armed SS. Jüttner would temporarily have to accept subordination to the brusk SS recruiter during the formation of the *SS-Führungshauptamt* in 1939–1940. Jüttner's vendetta with Berger in the SS Main Office was to last throughout the war, long after the SA and the Sudetenland had ceased to be important. Henlein and K. H. Frank both accepted SS generals' oak leaves; the former Schutzdienst commander became the Sudetenland Abschnitt commander of the SS. There was no wholesale transfer of the Freikorps to the SS, however, and many joined the SA.[90]

Except in the case of the *Ascher Zipfel*, SS forces entered Czechoslovakia on or after October 1 either in the form of VT or TV regiments;

regular military units incorporated in Wehrmacht divisions; or as mixed teams of Order Police, Gestapo, and SD (two Einsatzstäbe, each consisting of five Einsatzkommandos). The latter did the "dirty work" of arresting (or killing) suspects and enemies in the name of troop security. Some SS men under thirty-five with previous military training served as ordinary Wehrmacht members, although there was no general mobilization. There was no military occupation; transfer to civilian control on October 10 meant that the German divisions departed and with them the VT and TV regiments. SS and Police power was assured by the setting up of Order Police, Criminal Police, and SD and Gestapo headquarters by the Einsatzkommandos according to plan. The Grenzpolizei (Border Police) — a part of the Gestapo since the previous year — played a central role in the staffing of detachments for the Gestapo offices, and unpaid SD officials from the Reich (largely SS of long standing) and among the Sudeten Germans (new SS, mostly) provided much of the new SD-Abschnitt personnel. The Einsatzstäbe as such were disbanded after it became clear that Hitler was not yet ready to proceed with the total liquidation of Czechoslovakia. SD efforts to assert its leadership over the teams' operations, expressed in its supplying the team commanders, were not entirely successful vis-à-vis the Gestapo; an Interior Ministry decree of November 11 sought to supply state sanctions for SD activities to improve cooperation by state agencies with the SD. Its agents did not thereby become state officials; the inclusion of the SD within the *Reichssicherheitshauptamt* (Reich Main Security Office, RSHA) a year later showed that the November 1938 measure was insufficient. The team approach for the "hit squads" had proved itself, however, and even the same commanders were used again in Poland and Russia, albeit not under SD authority.[91]

Amt III, SD-Ausland was at the height of its influence that busy fall and winter in cooperation with Abwehr, Foreign Office, and VoMi in creating the conditions for Hitler's next move. No one knew, least of all Hitler, which of the many German folk groups in eastern Europe he would have need of next. In order to keep all options open, tighter controls and better knowledge of local conditions were necessary. Academic specialists, businessmen, state officials, and the ethnic Germans themselves were recruited for the SD — and incidentally for the SS — in increasing numbers. Along with VoMi and SD went representatives of the SS Recruitment Office (*Ergänzungsamt*), for the Sudeten Freikorps had proved a model for combining fifth column work with future SS recruitment, not merely for General SS expansion but for the armed SS legions otherwise so seriously limited by the August 17 decree. SS-SD penetration into the Baltic states, Poland, and Rumania made good progress; But Hitler succumbed to the temptation to capitalize on the Czechoslovakian disorganization and the need to meet the disappointment of the remaining German minority there as well as to Slovak pressure for support. Hitler possibly lost a chance to effect a Bismarckian settlement in Europe after Munich in part due to the ambitions of the SS — Himmler, Heydrich, and some of the high SS officers corps — to engage in foreign policy intrigue and carve out a settlement area in central Europe. They were of course fulfilling Hitler's own un-Bismarckian imperial conceptions.[92]

Himmler's entry into foreign policy matters in the Austrian case had strengthened SS ties not only to Ribbentrop's apparatus in the Foreign Office but also to Göring's operatives in the world of finance. Now both of these gentlemen had a vested interest in dominating Hitler's foreign policy moves after Munich, where he demonstrated more independence than suited either his Foreign Minister or his *Luftwaffe* commander. Thus, each for his own reasons was willing to assist Himmler, and the latter was glad to penetrate more deeply into foreign affairs and high finance in the interests of SS expansion. Through VoMi Himmler began to play a more direct role in discussions of foreign policy problems, while VoMi's second-in-command, Hermann Behrends, developed a network of information and influence beyond the folk groups themselves to the corresponding native governments and parties of their regions. Heydrich also engaged quite personally in foreign intrigue now, laying the foundations for German domination of fascist movements in Lithuania, the Ukraine, Slovakia, Hungary, Rumania, and Bohemia. Heydrich's SD-Amt III agents had the advantage of cooperation with Göring's people and vice versa, since economic penetration into eastern Europe via antiwestern, anticapitalist fascist conspirators undercut official German connections handily. Thus, VoMi Folk Group connections and SD fascist connections might also run together at either end, in Berlin and the field.

On the coattails of both VoMi and SD, often in the form of a senior SS officer, the SS-Ergänzungsamt rode into foreign capitals in search of Menschenmaterial (human material). The lure of the Reich was never so great as in late 1938 and early 1939 for young ethnic Germans. Four years service in Himmler's elite guard seemed to many not too high a price to pay for a future of prominence and influence, especially as an alternative to being drafted into one's native army as a member of a minority not universally admired. Last but not least, the SS Race and Settlement Main Office — freed at last from the burden of Himmler's long quarrel with its founder, Darré, over SS ideological training — looked for new worlds to conquer for SS settlement, long stymied in the Reich

by Wehrmacht land purchases and the needs of "the battle of production." The fertile soil of Bohemia-Moravia attracted the eye of the Settlement Office Chief, von Gottberg, who called Heydrich's attention to
settlement possibilities there. SD agents made a careful inventory of
both urban and rural properties in the hands of "enemies of Germandom" before March 15, 1939. A scheme for expelling the whole Slavic
population of Bohemia to make room for German settlers found its way
into SD files.[93]

So neatly did Heydrich's and Göring's agents work, with the cooperation of Ribbentrop's Foreign Office, that Hitler's own indecisive nature
did not have a chance to manifest itself. His natural instinct to abuse a
fallen foe was all that was necessary to prevent him from grasping the
opportunity to pacify France and Britain by cultivating Czechoslovakia. Aided by tendentious reports of Czech perfidy and anti-German
plans supplied through Foreign Office, SD, and VoMi, Hitler went
every step of the way with the conspirators without making a firm decision for himself until the last minute—probably some time on March
12, 1939. On that day while Wilhelm Keppler negotiated in Hitler's
name with the Slovak separatists in Bratislava, a week *after* the delivery
of explosives by SD-Amt III agents, VoMi organized demonstrations in
Prague and Brno using SS students; and SS commandos arrived from
the Reich in both Bohemia and Slovakia to carry out acts of terror and
provocation. Special agents within the Folk Group who carried out
tasks under SD orders were taken into the SS in the next few days.[94]

The Czech army was involved in skirmishes against two different
Slovak paramilitary formations and a German *Freiwillige Schutzstaffel*
by March 13, all under orders from VoMi, SD, and Abwehr sources; so
that Hitler's talk of "pacification" in Czechoslovakia with forces of the
Wehrmacht seems infinitely cynical. His invitation to Horthy to send
Hungarian troops into Slovakia and Ruthenia on that date appears
equally Machiavellian, unless indeed he was still really in the dark
about the extent of the plot. In the early hours of March 15 before leaving for Prague with Himmler, he told Czech President Hacha that "a
few weeks ago he had really not known a thing about the whole matter.
It came as a surprise to him." Perhaps this was close to the truth. But he
must have known that the mechanized Leibstandarte had already entered Mährisch-Ostrau "according to plan," as Göring remarked, to
keep the Poles out.[95]

Three truckloads of SS officers seized the police headquarters in
Prague early on March 15 and began immediately to work with Sudeten-
German volunteer police and Czech collaborators. Himmler was quite
impressed with the "high quality" of many of the Czech police. Gestapo

and SD headquarters were opened like magic in the chief towns, and arrests from prearranged lists began. In Bratislava a surprised Tiso was confronted by the German Folk Group Leader and VoMi spokesman accompanied by a mysterious stranger—the VoMi Deputy Chief and SD veteran—and ordered to sign a "protection agreement" in the best gangster fashion. Wehrmacht forces entered Slovakia as well as Bohemia and Moravia, but civil government began immediately in all areas. There was no military government to interfere with the SS. The partially mechanized Special Duty regiments of the SS had functioned well as part of Wehrmacht armored divisions for the first time. By mid-April only Germania was left on occupation duty along with one Death's Head Battalion. The rest were already feverishly training for the Polish campaign; most of the Death's Head Battalions were busy training new recruits from Germany, Austria, and the Folk Group volunteers. Order Police, Gestapo, and SD remained, reinforced with thousands of Sudeten German SS coordinated after May 5 by a new Superior SS and Police Leader, K. H. Frank, Henlein's former deputy and now the real dictator of Prague. The figurehead protector of Bohemia-Moravia whom he represented was no more significant than Henlein, relegated to provincial Reichenberg. Gone also were many of the Vienna Party clique who had schemed with Heydrich and Keppler; but the Prague Land Office (*Bodenamt*), a RuSHa installation, remained as a symbol of SS imperial plans. To it flocked Reich SS members by the dozens, as they earlier flocked to Vienna, drawn by easy money and a chance to "Aryanize" properties left behind by clients of Eichmann's new Emigration Office in Prague located at Gestapo headquarters. Less-coveted Slovakia had no Superior SS and Police Leader—merely a Police Attache, a SIPO-SD agent who coordinated arrests, deportations, and seizures in Himmler and the Reich's interest. But the Freiwillige Schutzstaffel remained, an unforgotten reservoir for the future Waffen-SS.[96]

### Northeast

A "side show" involving the General SS of East Prussia, the SD, VoMi, and another barely camouflaged ethnic German SS—the *Memelländischer Ordnungsdienst*—was ended March 22, 1939, when the Memel territory was "peacefully" annexed to East Prussia after Lithuania had been forced to agree to it by an ultimatum. The East Prussian SS managed the seizure and occupation without recourse to military forces, having long functioned as liaison with the Ordnungsdienst, which was so completely under Berlin that the unusual step of transferring it as a body into the East Prussian Main Sector could occur that same day.[97]

The Danzig SS was one of the oldest units in Germany, dating from 1926. It was unnecessary to camouflage it, even before the Nazi regime began in the Free City in 1933. Indeed, from 1937 on the SS there completely controlled the police and managed liaison with Heydrich and Daluege so completely that Danzig was virtually a part of the SS and Police system. Athough gauleiter Albert Forster had been one of the original SS of 1925, he was not sympathetic to Himmler's ideas and ambitions. Yet his second-in-command, Arthur Greiser — the future gauleiter of the annexed Polish territories around Poznań — was quite positive toward the SS. Working with Himmler in an attempt to shore up his own position vis-à-vis Forster, the Senate President was in a good position to aid the introduction of secret SS reinforcements for the Free City in May and June 1939, and to set up a 4,000-man *Danziger Heimwehr* with Death's Head cadre. The East Prussian Main Sector was also directly involved in Wehrmacht plans for the seizure of Danzig as early as April 1939. Forster could not directly resist Himmler's encroachments in his gau, but making use of his own channels of influence which flowed through the Göring-Ribbentrop agents Hitler used to prepare each of his territorial seizures, Forster succeeded in bypassing his pro-SS deputy and rival at the very last minute (August 23, 1939). However, since SS lines ran through these agents as well, Himmler was merely inconvenienced by having to use conspiratorial and ancillary channels of control during the critical months ahead. Both SS and SA units figured in the step-by-step destruction of the few barriers that still separated Danzig from the Reich by August 25.[98]

Himmler had had just about a year to convert an essentially peacetime General SS, with adjuncts for domestic emergencies (Death's Head and Special Duty troops), to a wartime footing. From the time of the August 17, 1938, Führerbefehl until the actual mobilization for the war in Poland, feverish activity in the Berlin Main Offices and at the Main Sector headquarters presided over by the Superior SS and Police Leaders had shifted the emphasis from the General SS to its armed units and the police. Men of the General SS between age twenty-five and thirty-five were called up under a Göring emergency service order of October 15, 1938, and trained by Death's Head cadres in Westphalia and Silesia as Death's Head Reinforcements. Those over thirty-five were also *notdienstverpflichtet* (drafted for emergency service as civilians) for concentration camp guard duty in wartime, already serving trial periods in 1939.[99] Where General SS men were found unable to serve in these capacities for health or business reasons, Himmler ordered them discharged from the General SS, and even men over forty-five were to be discharged if they were recent transfers from other branches like SA and grumbled about their assignments. Not many of the latter were actually "drafted," but they often had more work to do because the younger full-time SS personnel were called up. About 10 percent, or 30,000 men, were thus available from the General SS for occupation duty over and above the existing armed formations, which amounted to 25,000 in September 1939. The formation under Gottlob Berger of a unified recruiting system for General SS, Armed SS, and Police in the spring of 1939 produced an overall increase in all three services of 15,000 youths for the calendar year, most of whom went to the new recruit training battalions of the Verfügungstruppe (*Ersatzbatallione*) formed after the outbreak of the war. Several thousand came from Folk Groups abroad, the majority from Hitler Youth formations as volunteers. Efforts to enlarge the Death's Head Battalions proper bogged down over the twelve-year enlistment, nonrecognition of this service as military service, and noncooperation of the Wehrmacht in recruiting drives among two-year servicemen about to return to civilian life. In the short run this experience led to the expansion of the Death's Head Reinforcement Battalions using the original battalions as cadre; in the long run the entire tie-up of concentration camp guards and the Death's Head units was dissolved. The experiment had essentially failed.[100]

In the last week of August 1939, as the Special Duty regiments joined their assigned Wehrmacht divisions according to the mobilization plan and the Death's Head Reinforcements reported at the Breslau camp to be formed into the new *Totenkopfstandarten*, the Einsatzkommandos of the SIPO-SD began their rendezvous with other attack formations and the sabotage and provocation teams of the Abwehr and Sicherheitsdienst took up their places on the Polish border and signalled their ethnic German allies. Meanwhile Himmler remained at Hitler's side ready for a rapid change in plans, a new emergency, or a new assignment. His stock and that of the SS had never been higher with the Führer, but it was scheduled to rise even farther in the years ahead, bringing with it vaster projects and untold suffering for millions.[101]

Five short years had elapsed since the Röhm purge. During them the SS had made itself indispensible to the Führer-dictatorship. Outwardly still show-figures in their black parade uniforms, the General SS must have held the popular spotlight. But the reality of Himmler's Order for those "in the know" must have seemed to lie in the police apparatus — Gestapo, KRIPO, and SD. Few would as yet have grasped the potential of the concentration camps as economic resources to free the SS of dependence on party and state — the camps seemed to be part of the terror system. Few could have imagined the Armed SS as a fourth arm of the Wehrmacht — least of all could the High Command itself. Whether because of their low opinion of SS military prowess or faith in their skill in starving the SS of young manpower, German army leaders did not fear the Armed SS — only the police sneaks and the party intriguers with Hitler. But another aspect of the SS must have been apparent to many Germans by 1939; what Albert Speer in his last book called "infiltration."[102]

By 1939 Himmler had created a veritable second SS of honorary personnel. Perhaps to some observers he had overdone it. The wholesale award of SS Generals' ranks to the party brass could have watered down the value of the rank. The broad scale of SS colonelcies in the government bureaucracy certainly indicated some claim upon the time and attention of office chiefs and policy makers; the business world seemed to revel in SS majorities and colonelcies. Perhaps many were merely pleased to have an impressive uniform and a little "clout" — maybe even a little protection. Realistically, no one — not even the Reichsführer SS — knew exactly how loyal the honorary membership rendered an otherwise powerful figure of party, state, or the economy. Rapid promotion in the SS must have been observed by the watchful — but was it an indication of the man's importance to the SS in his chosen field, or of services performed? Today it is still difficult to say. Yet the impression of widespread *infiltration* and influence by the SS in countless walks of life could easily be gained by 1939. It served to impress, whether it was actually a genuine power or not. Whereas in 1934 the SS had merely begun to claim a special position in German society and in the state, by 1939 it appeared to have arrived — or if not quite arrived, to be at the point of arrival. Of course, the ability to continue to draw unto itself cadres of skill and competence from all walks of German life rested in part on its own intrinsic claims as "a sworn community of blood," as a community of families (*Sippengemeinschaft*); but the war would bring to the SS an external motivation — the desire on the part of the able and the ambitious to enter what appeared to be *the* system of power and decision in Germany. To win the war and to shape the future required membership in the SS.

# 7

## Years of Tragic Fulfillment 1939–1945

"... die Bewegnung soll schaffen ein germanisches Reich deutscher Nation. Die Partei mag dann in Trümmer gehen."

... Uns war gesagt worden, es handele sich um unsere Sicherheit und um solche Personen, von denen man annahm, dass sie die Sicherheit gefährden und als solche bezeichnet würden . . .[1]

Seven short years had passed since Germany, torn by civil strife, had succumbed to Hitler. In those years the SS had changed from a street-fighting militia into crack military and police formations. In such a short time, much had been accomplished; yet inevitably when war came, that state of emergency (*Ausnahmezustand*) for which the SS was peculiarly designed, nearly everything had to be remodelled. During the years in between the old Kampfjahre and the new, the SS had been prepared for war after a fashion, along with most other Nazi institutions. But the imagery of 1932 and 1918 bound Himmler and his officers within a circle that was narrower than the war they had to wage. The experiences of 1932 and 1918 were still fresh enough between 1939 and 1945 to mislead men steeped in Nazi ideology to the conviction that the chief dangers in wartime would come from inveterate enemies at home rather than on the battlefield. Rendering traitors harmless (*unschädlich machen*) had been the chief purpose and glory of the SS. Designed for the inner-German theater of operations (*Kriegsschauplatz Inneres-Deutschland*), Himmler's SS found it hard to transcend the role of po-liceman, turnkey, and hangman. Indeed, the destruction of the Jews represents an insistence on the necessity of there being an inner enemy large enough to justify the Nazi Weltanschauung. Furthermore, the role of the SS as security forces in the occupied areas of Europe preserved among these troops the narrow, punitive, and suspicious outlook of 1932 and 1918.[2] Even Hitler had not rendered the Germans quite friendless in Europe in 1939; it was the fate of the SS, due to Himmler's and Hitler's efforts to prevent subject peoples from "repeating the Dolchstoss of 1918," to breed hatred of Germany everywhere in Europe.

Yet, as Himmler liked to say, the SS had its "constructive" side. Out of the settlement romanticism of Blood and Soil, Darré's contribution to the infant SS of the years of struggle, Himmler was to improvise an instrument of German imperialism, an SS agency for the resettlement of Germans on newly conquered soil as farmers and tradesmen — the Reich Commission for the Strengthening of Germandom (RKFDV).[3] The expulsion of the former residents, carried out with characteristic SS ruthlessness and brutality, was to sharpen the problems of the occupying German forces wherever Himmler located his colonies, giving rise to a partisan movement and increasing the need for retaliatory police measures of an ever-more-military character. Thus, a kind of self-fulfilling prophecy was at work within the Nazi imperialism as practiced by the SS: believing that they lived in a Hobbesian world of enemies, they raised up opponents where there were none. Ultimately all the SS administrators and policemen had to become soldiers of the Waffen-SS, as an embattled Germany had to defend herself against enemies from every direction. And in the Waffen-SS another old Nazi theme was to be preserved and revived, the SA's ambition to outdo and replace the Wehrmacht as a people's army (*Volksheer*). The soldiers' plot of July 20, 1944, not only seemed to confirm the stab-in-the-back imagery of 1918, its failure appearing to augur a different outcome for Germany under Nazi leadership than in 1918; it also gave the SS under Himmler a chance to make good the supposed errors of 1934. However, the Waffen-SS had become by then both much more and much less than the dream of the free corps veterans. Between 1939 and 1945 the few regiments of hand-picked volunteers had swelled to many divisions — first of young Germans without SS background, soon of ethnic Germans from eastern and southern Europe, then of northern Europeans, later of allied peoples from southern and eastern Europe, and ultimately no longer of volunteers.[4] The dream of a new community of political soldiers, European volunteers for a postwar settlement program stretching to the Caucasus and building a Greater Germanic Reich for Adolf Hitler, went down piecemeal in the midst of a chaotic power struggle among the Nazi leaders in which Himmler too sought to extricate himself and his apparatus from the defeat by intrigue and unprincipled bargaining.[5]

The wartime SS endured nearly six years, almost exactly as long as the *Aufbaujahre* (years of construction) from July 1934 to August 1939.

During these later years the SS changed more than it had since the Röhm purge and the Machtergreifung. Just as the pre-1933 street-fighting SS stamped its image on the SS of 1933–1934, so during 1939–1941 up to the attack on Soviet Russia, the SS retained the impress of 1938. Lines of development which had enabled Hitler to accomplish the Anschluss and the absorption of the Sudetenland with minimal distur-bance of the German scene could be continued. Many new features of SS activity, such as RKFDV, could emerge from the assumptions of 1938 with little relevance to the life-and-death struggle that national social-ism itself had begun.

By July 1941, however, the SS entered a new terrible phase of blood-letting—in which Himmler's dictum that the SS man does not fear to shed his own or others' blood for his cause was realized in the decima-tion of ranks of the original political soldiers and in the destruction of Jews and communists on a scale so vast that the SS itself was not capable of mastering it, turning over part of the bloody work to Wehrmacht units and subject peoples. By the spring of 1943, the illusions involved in the earlier planning of the SS imperialists had given way to a grim de-termination to convert everything and everyone in their system to total war. For the men who could remember 1932 and 1918, the latter years of the war seemed a confirmation of the truth of their worst fears and deepest convictions. Conditions of total emergency seemed to justify an altering of values in which new institutions, new loyalties, and new men must be born. At this time the SS came as near being a counter-state, beyond the party and beyond the German Reich, as it ever came. But in truth the SS never reached this transvaluation, though some indi-viduals probably did. It was too much a part of the whole fabric of the German war effort, too much a part of the German state for that. Ef-forts to penetrate into and capture the citadels of the German social and economic system also failed at this time, although they appeared nearer to success than ever before. In many respects the war years presented opportunities for the SS to fulfill its most cherished purposes, and the evils which it perpetrated were indeed a tragic fulfillment of Himmler's oldest ambitions. Yet in another sense the war years exposed the rather young and untested Nazi institutions to a withering blast, and they did not stand up well—even before defeat wiped them off the face of the earth.

## The SS and Police System

In September 1939 the SS and the Police were still two very separate entities. Only 3,000 Gestapo officials out of 20,000 had SS rank; the proportion of the SS in the Kriminalpolizei and the Ordnungspolizei

was even less, though sizeable in absolute figures. To qualify for SS
runes, a police officer had to have joined the NSDAP in 1933 (or earlier)
— hardly a strong basis for devotion to Himmler's Order. Other qualifications included withdrawal from church affiliation, an "orderly marriage" (divorce and remarriage was on the borderline), and more than
one child. The sixteen Inspectors of the Order Police had long police
careers behind them, rendering their high SS ranks secondary; they
were officially loyal to Daluege and the Order Police apparatus in contradistinction to the Interior Ministry system of the administrative bureaucracy. Ambitious individuals among them still could on occasion
choose either to work closely with the gauleiter as Reichsstatthalter or
with the SS. While the sixteen Inspectors of the Security Police and SD
implied in their very titles a firmer union of SS and Police, and included
several old and convinced SS officers from 1931–1932 days, the bulk of
the Security Police were professional police officials who had risen
through cooperation with Heydrich. They exemplified the traits of con-
scientious bureaucrats willing to serve the Nazi cause rather than of devoted SS men.[6]

## Superior SS and Police Leaders

The real focus of SS and Police fusion was the Superior SS and Police
Leader, in every case an old SS fighter, who was the SS Main Sector
commander, and after mobilization in emergencies the tactical superior
of both branches of the police via the Inspectors. But here too there was
ambiguity. Not only did the formal Interior Ministry system of administration remain even after mobilization as long as a special declaration
of emergency was withheld but there was uncertainty about the nature
and degree of subordination of the Superior SS and Police Leaders to
the gauleiters as Reich Defense Commissars and as Reichsstatthalter.
Himmler ordered them to report for duty to the latter (or in some cases
to the Prussian Oberpräsidenten) on August 25. An order issued by Daluege in Himmler's name on September 11 transferred authority to the
gauleiters in their capacity as the newly created Reich Defense Commissars, but Himmler cancelled it October 16, returning to the strictly
Interior Ministry chain of command. Thus, a party bid to enhance the
role of the gauleiters was turned aside, incidentally weakening Daluege's role as an independent channel of command and negotiating
partner. This kept the Superior SS and Police Leaders within the administrative bureaucracy of the state. In fact, Himmler in his October 16
decree even used the term "subordinate," missing in the August 25 orders. The Reich Defense Commissars might merely make use of Superior SS and Police Leaders from time to time (*sich lediglich bedienen*).

Himmler's caution kept these high-ranking SS officers from becoming part of party satrapies until he took over the Interior Ministry himself in 1943.[7]

All in all, the lot of these old SS fighters was not a comfortable one, but as Himmler might say that was not what they were there for. They were to represent the Reichsführer SS and Chief of the German Police in the fullest sense of the word. In coming years they could assert the unity of SS and Police in a number of ways. A unified SS and Police court system was on the drafting boards, to be implemented in a matter of months, making Superior SS and Police Leaders chief magistrates for their Main Sectors and for *all* SS and Police units within them. As commanders of the SS Main Sectors, they had charge of admissions and promotions within the SS — of interest to ambitious policemen — and also of ideological training within the SS and by the SS for the police. Through the latter channel they could strengthen mutual understanding and comradeship.[8]

*Formation of the RSHA*

Himmler's caution is also demonstrated by what he did *not* do either before or after the outbreak of war. Although the creation of a super SS- *und Polizei-Hauptamt* had been proposed by Daluege's ORPO-Hauptamt in November 1938, Himmler rejected it and did not even include the latter main office in a consolidated Gestapo and SD headquarters for coordinating all wartime security activities. As Chief of the German Police, Himmler did not wish to have a large, ostentatious office, so he operated simultaneously out of Unter den Linden 74, Daluege's headquarters, and of course from Prinz Albrechtsstrasse 8 — which on September 27, 1939, became the headquarters of the new *Reichssicherheitshauptamt* (RSHA). This controversial agency had been under discussion most of 1939.[9] It certainly represented a step forward in the integration of SS and Police, inasmuch as the longstanding separation of the SD-Main Office and the Security Main Office (KRIPO and Gestapo) was finally surmounted. On the other hand, the question whether the RSHA was a state agency was never resolved; and the Ministry of the Interior went on characterizing Heydrich, RSHA's new chief and architect, as Chief of the SIPO (Security Police) and SD — a designation he actually accepted in his letterheads for external correspondence. The Reichssicherheitshauptamt headings were reserved for internal and SS communications. When one realizes that even the geographic separation of the SD offices at Wilhelmstrasse 102 was retained, one may too readily jump to the conclusion that this dreaded new agency was merely a paper tiger.[10]

In the discussions of 1939, one of the chief features was the problem of what to do with the SD. The evolution of the Gestapo system into an exclusive executive with the removal of all investigative as well as arrest powers from SD agents by 1937 had put the SD network and the SD-Hauptamt into the shade as a truly important service. Furthermore, in spite of ambition to serve as a kind of international German secret service, Heydrich's coterie was relegated to a very secondary place by the more professional army Abwehr. Thus, the SD was left to cloak-and-dagger work of the oldest and meanest variety, such as the faked Polish attack on the Gleiwitz radio transmitter; to vaporous speculations and second-hand gossip about enemy and friendly countries no better than what Rosenberg's Aussenpolitisches Amt turned out; to situation reports about internal German conditions; and to the study and penetration of the ethnic German communities of eastern Europe. Without giving up the former preoccupations, Heydrich seems to have decided to push the latter two. The first organizational chart of RSHA, for which Werner Best was still responsible, had an Amt III, Inland-Abwehr and an Amt VI, Ausland-Abwehr. While each of these virtually reproduced the old SD-Abteilungen II and III, the real change occurred in the merging of the SD-Abteilung I with the former administrative elements of the SIPO-Hauptamt in the Prinz Albrechtsstrasse. This consolidation, though not in its permanent form due in part to an imminent quarrel between Best and Heydrich, was necessitated by the large new tasks thrust upon the RSHA by the war. It must have been a trick of Heydrich's to carry out a reorganization while key personnel were absent on temporary duty in Poland, where ever-changing conditions demanded their presence. Heydrich saw to many of the new tasks himself, bypassing Best and relaying many of Himmler's decisions directly to the special SIPO-SD units in the field.[11]

We have seen that already in the summer of 1938, in preparation for the conflict with Czechoslovakia, the conception of special SIPO-SD teams as tactical units was developed. In the form of teams attached to the invading regiments — both SS and *Wehrmacht* — the so-called Einsatzkommandos, of mixed composition but essentially SD-led, ferreted out the centers of opposition to the Nazi take-over in the Sudetenland and later in Bohemia-Moravia. Mobility and independence were their chief virtues. These organs had no permanent structure, quickly giving way to regular ORPO, KRIPO, Gestapo, and SS structures in the course of months. Here was an executive function for the SD, which really demanded as central headquarters an executive-type office. Thus, the RSHA owed its existence in part to the need for a coordinating — indeed directing — center for the much more elaborate SS and Police invasion of Poland.[12]

### SS *Occupation Forces*

Since March 1939 elements of the SS, especially Verfügungstruppe and Totenkopfstandarten, had been employed as occupation forces in Bohemia-Moravia alongside Wehrmacht units and to some extent replacing them. The scheme for the handling of Poland, in whole or in part, once captured, was to turn over police duties to improvised SS (Death's Head) regiments made up of training cadre from the replacement units of the Verfügungstruppe and the original Totenkopfstandarten, to which were added General SS personnel called up for the emergency. These groups would be spearheaded by Einsatzkommandos, whose task was to form so-called Ethnic German Self-Defense units led by SS officers and NCOs supplied and directed by the Recruitment Office of the SS Main Office. Thus, a very intricate liaison system was evolved through SS institutions, involving the following: the SS Main Office, whose chief, Heissmeier, became for the following year "Inspector General of the Death's Head Police Reinforcements"; Totenkopfstandarten (*Polizeiverstärkung*); the SS Recruitment Office, whose blustery chief, Berger, was destined to become the new head of the SS Main Office for his efficient handling of recruitment and the Self-Defense units; the ORPO-Hauptamt; and the RSHA, working through the SD network in contact with Volksdeutsche Mittelstelle (VoMi).[13]

We know that the Einsatzkommandos were organized and ready to fall upon Poland in August 1939 from the correspondence of one of them with the SD-Hauptamt regarding Jewish policy. By September 19–21 Heydrich was laying plans and sending out instructions to these units already in Poland for the concentration of Polish Jews in communities over five hundred in size, the arrest of Polish intellectuals, and the clearing of residential housing (apartments) in Gdynia and Poznań to make room for the first Baltic Germans being registered by VoMi for "repatriation" from Latvia and Estonia. There were at least a half-dozen of these teams in operation in Bydgoszcz, Poznań, Radom, Łódź, Cracow, and Katowice as soon as each city fell. By quickly involving ethnic German males in the Self-Defense units, they reduced the burden of the Wehrmacht units and even freed their own specialists for the deadly work of rounding up known and suspected opponents of Nazi Germany. On their heels came a battalion each of Death's Head Police Reinforcements for every district capital, equipped with trucks and small arms. These battalions had been pulled out of relatively recently formed Death's Head regiments, often with inexperienced officers and NCOs and sometimes with General SS personnel having no background except the memory of street fights and crude ideological training programs.

It was from this early wave of Einsatzkommandos, Self-Defense units, and Death's Head Battalions that the SS occupation tradition took its beginning in wanton cruelty, sadism, and senseless death. The Wehrmacht protested without effect on Hitler; most soldiers and officers were glad to be withdrawn from occupation duty in late October and early November to be replaced by thousands more of the Death's Head Police Reinforcements, a regiment of them in each district.[14] Order Police battalions also made their appearance along with the SS units, performing the same tasks. Their personnel were drawn from regular Reich police garrisons, replaced at home by over-age "police reserves," often General SS. With the appointment of a Superior SS and Police Leader "East" on October 4, 1939 — none other than F. W. Krüger, the old AW-Chief of the SA and more recently commander of the SS Border Guards and SS Cavalry — the permanent police structure in Poland began to take shape.[15]

With the creation of another separate political entity beyond the Reich like the "Protectorate of Bohemia-Moravia," to be known as the *General-Gouvernement Polen* (the General Government of Poland), Krüger found himself SS and Police commander of a colonial no man's land, a dumping ground for unwanted Poles and Jews from the Polish territories contiguous to the Reich and from the Reich itself. Lopping off Polish territories on the 1937 Reich frontiers, some of which had belonged to Germany before 1919, Hitler expanded older provinces like East Prussia and Upper and Lower Silesia. The northern portion of the Polish corridor he reconstituted as "Danzig-West Prussia" while to the south he recreated the pre-World War One Posen district, soon expanded to include the industrial district of Łódź, renamed Litzmannstadt. While these last two gaus, as they were to be called, also acquired new Superior SS and Police Leaders, the former regions fell under the command of Superior SS and Police Leaders in Königsberg and Breslau. A separate gau of Upper Silesia and a Superior SS and Police Leader in Katowice (Kattowitz) came later, in January 1941. The Superior SS and Police Leader "East" found himself confronting the ambitious Hans Frank, the so-called Governor-General. Instead of Inspectors of Order and Security Police, Himmler installed *Befehlshaber* (Commanding Officers) for each service, an independent commander (Führer) of the Self-Defense units, and commanders (*Kommandeure*) of the district police at Warsaw, Radom, and Cracow (later also at Lublin). Frank regarded these police officials as strictly answerable to himself, continuing the struggle opened earlier in the Reich between the gauleiters and Superior SS and Police Leaders and their Inspectors.[16]

In the other former Polish territories annexed to the Reich, there were merely the two Inspectors of Order and Security Police, but since the new gauleiters and Reichsstatthalter did not have experienced administrative bureaucracies as yet — only party adventurers and a certain number of Reich officials transferred to them "for good riddance" — the Superior SS and Police Leaders and the Inspectors rapidly became as decisive as the gauleiters. In Danzig-West Prussia, gauleiter Albert Forster opposed Himmler wherever he could, and Himmler prodded his representatives to ignore the gauleiter as much as possible. In Posen (later Wartheland), the gauleiter agreed with Himmler and was cleverer in maintaining some of his independence. Superior SS and Police Leaders sought in all the former Polish territories to maximize their powers on the grounds of emergency conditions, which certainly prevailed at the time of establishing civilian governments composed largely of "carpet-baggers" from the old Reich and with tiny German minorities facing sullen, hungry Polish majorities.[17]

The resettlement operation was in full swing by November and December, adding to the chaos. The Death's Head Police Reinforcements were used extensively in the expulsion of families from their homes to make way for Germans not only from the Baltic and eastern Polish territories ceded to the U.S.S.R. but also from the Reich, who streamed in now as managers of real estate, business agents, and party organizers. The brutality of these SS units was no different against the innocent Polish families they expelled than against Polish patriots who had opposed Germany before September 1939 or against local and deported Jews they browbeat in forced labor battalions. Having been born out of replacement cadres for the original Death's Head regiments who guarded the concentration camps — where many an unteachable roughneck had been sent because he was hard to get along with in his original unit — these SS occupation forces of 1939 and 1940 were the last degenerate vestige of the old street-fighting élan, with some of the bestiality of the concentration camps thrown in. In fact, there was considerable overlap and interchange between the Death's Head Reinforcement Regiments' administration and the concentration camp system in the winter and spring of 1940. Neither aspect of the SS had yet the look of cold bureaucracy as in the mass-murders of 1942–1943. While some of the Death's Head Police Reinforcements went on to this "more exacting work," the majority were doomed to death as ordinary soldiers of the Waffen-SS or in antipartisan police duty. The sixteen Death's Head regiments did not survive as occupation troops beyond 1940, although several were briefly employed in Norway, Denmark, and Holland.[18]

### Concentration Camps

The three original Totenkopfstandarten were only withdrawn from the concentration camp guard duty for which they were set up when sufficient replacements had been called up from the General SS. Approximately 6,000 SS men between twenty-seven and forty were drafted (*notdienstverpflichtet*) for concentration camp guard duty during the winter of 1939–1940 in *SS-Totenkopf-(Wach-) Sturmbanne (KL Verstärkung)*. The latter units, at battalion strength and with cadre from men left behind from the departing Totenkopfstandarten, took over the concentration camps at Dachau, Sachsenhausen, Buchenwald, Mauthausen, Ravensbrück, and Flossenbürg by early spring of 1940, directly subordinate to the Inspector of Concentration Camps, now Richard Glücks. The original Totenkopfstandarten in turn formed the Death's Head *Division* of the new Waffen-SS under their old commander, "Papa" Eicke, ceasing to have anything further to do with the concentration camps.[19]

The departure of Eicke from the Oranienburg headquarters of the Inspector of Concentration Camps merely removed a source of irrational interference and flamboyant ideology from the administration. Glücks, his former deputy and successor, governed the several hundred SS-Altkämpfer on the concentration camp staffs with the same strict, uncomprehending rigidity, aiming neither at rehabilitation nor economic exploitation of the inmates. Little effort was made to educate the new recruits. There was not much ambition shown within the older SS of the concentration camp system. The striking growth of the war years was thrust upon them by Hitler's and Himmler's suspicious and punitive outlook and by the discovery made by Oswald Pohl, the clever and very aggressive *SS-Verwaltungschef*, that the concentration camps could be made to pay many of the SS's expenses. This notion had come first to some of the intelligent administrative personnel at Oranienburg on loan from the *SS-Verwaltungs- und Wirtschaftshauptamt* (Main Office for Administration and Economy); it took several years before it was the preponderant factor in planning concentration camps.[20]

The first new concentration camps were quasi-illegal improvisations in the newly conquered Polish territories or contiguous German rear areas. The Superior SS and Police Leaders or their deputies, the inspectors or SIPO-SD commanders, set up collecting camps for persons they rounded up and arranged for guards from General SS or Death's Head Police Reinforcements. In December 1939 Himmler got around to in-

quiring about potential new concentration camp capacities and ordering the official transfer of these "wild" camps into the regular system
under the Inspector of Concentration Camps. Auschwitz had its beginning at this time, as did Stutthof and the Lublin complex of camps later
used for the wholesale destruction of Jews. The "euthanasia" experiment at Kulmhof (Chełmno) also fits into this early, quasi-unofficial
stage of concentration camp development. So does Camp Hinzert, an
*SS-Sonderlager* (special camp).[21]

The wartime innovators and operators were not regular personnel of
the old KL system but a fresh wave of General SS officers and NCOs
faced by a totally new, unfamiliar environment and determined to
"smash their way through" in the old tradition of civil war *Drauf-*
*gängertum* (aggressive spirit). When Himmler ordered the integration
of the two camp systems, the Oranienburg administrators sent some of
the old Reich personnel out to the new camps. More of the old concentration camp staff were drawn off in 1940 and 1941 to set up additional
concentration camps in the Reich on Himmler's orders: Natzweiler,
Neuengamme, and Gross Rosen. These camps also began to show the
rationalizing influence of the SS Main Office for Administration and
Economy in their plans, as did Auschwitz.[22]

The process of transferring older, more experienced concentration
camp administrators and establishing ever-larger camps tended to create an atmosphere in all camps of frustration and incompetence, which
was taken out on the inmates. Even without an official policy of killing
prisoners or working them to death, the raw newness of the camps or
their personnel — or of the tasks set before them — joined with the dislo-
cations of war and recent occupation to make all the Nazi concentration
camps equally horrible, defeating Himmler's own wish that the camps
be graded in terror and implication. The policy of regular transfers of
staff personnel, designed at least in part to reduce corruption and maintain a high degree of discipline, spread the worst features of the old type
of SS bully and increasingly the frontier ruthlessness of Lublin and
Auschwitz. Thus, a kind of common denominator did develop in the
war years among a few hundred officers and men who stayed in the
camp administration; since preference for remaining implied disinter-
est in the front, there was an additional ingredient of ruthlessness in the
determination to become indispensable in the productive efforts of the
camps.

However, among the 35,000 who ultimately saw service as concentration camp *guards*, at least 10,000 were not SS members at any time.
Furthermore, Waffen-SS units detached personnel on temporary duty
to the camps as early as 1940, and wounded Waffen-SS personnel served

as guards toward the end of the war. During the years 1940–1945, there was certainly no single type of concentration camp guard, although the early SS staff personnel succeeded in putting its stamp on many of them. An additional irony which confuses matters further is the policy begun in 1940 of inducting the camp administrators, and later the guard personnel, into the Waffen-SS to keep them from being drafted for the Wehrmacht. While some of these persons certainly saw service at the front, it was not possible for Himmler to pursue his policy of wholesale rotations of even top officers through all branches of SS activity. Once absorbed into the rapidly growing system, the concentration camp SS tended to remain there, while correspondingly only a fraction of the Waffen-SS had any official contact with the concentration camps.[23]

Thus, the phrase "concentration camp SS" may be justified as expressing a common tendency even in the war years more distinct than, say, "General SS" in the prewar period, or even "Waffen-SS" after 1941. Nevertheless, organizational and functional differences persisted among: (1) the economically oriented personnel from the VWHA; (2) the two waves of camp administrators which merged with a third wave involved in the "death factories" after 1941; and (3) the guards, ranging from older General SS men, young Waffen-SS recruits — including ethnic Germans and other eastern Europeans — SA and party people hiding from the front or being disciplined, and ordinary German soldiers. Within the rapidly expanding SS officers corps of the later war years (1941–1945), the first group occupies the most prominent place in terms of rank and importance, if not in numbers. Even the second group is remarkable for its small size as far as officers are concerned; but among its captains and majors it included a very high proportion of the early pioneers of 1930–1931 whose limited capacities and vices had suited them to be accomplices in evil and nothing more, although that was enough for Himmler's purpose. In spite of its relatively large size, the third group, the guard personnel of 1939–1945, had very few officers, and those were of low ranks (first and second lieutenants), often of post-1933 vintage. Largely lacking even the ideology of the administrators — certainly without the education and skills of the economists — the guards were untrained policemen confronted with tasks beyond them even on SS terms. Many of their crimes were due to ignorance, fear, corruption, and the bad example set by the camp administrators.[24]

The prewar camp personnel had been well adapted to the punitive, revenge-seeking purposes of the Nazis in erecting the camps in the first place, but increasingly after 1939 two quite different and powerful pressures were put upon them: the effort to capitalize upon the labor power of the inmates, and the drive to destroy Jews and after them other categories of humanity. Both features were known to the earlier personnel, but both had been incidental. The work before the war was often ridiculous; if practical, it was limited to camp advantages. Killing was frequently accidental or at least the random result of individuals' whims. Now SS organizations outside the concentration camp system, the *Verwaltungs- und Wirtschaftshauptamt* (VWHA) and the *Reichssicherheitshauptamt* (RSHA), began to demand of the concentration camp SS — deprived of their charismatic leader, Eicke, and most of his professional guard troops — feats of production and of human destruction that were almost intrinsically self-contradictory. It is not surprising that chaos and degradation ensued beyond anything previously imaginable. Yet the relative efficiency of concentration camp production in the later years, coupled with the absolute efficiency of the killing operations, implied a cooperative achievement and a flexibility of the varied personnel that is horrible to contemplate.

The imagination and engineering skill of the "top brass" supplemented the literal-minded and undaunted *Menschenschinder* (human butchers). Indeed, the arrival of the latter among the former in 1943 and 1944 (Hoess and Eichmann) signaled the completion of a process of merging and identification of SS types more effective than the SD and Gestapo or Superior SS and Police Generals and Waffen-SS generals. However, before this occurred numerous sharply differentiated apparatuses came into existence for handling, sorting, and transporting human beings as if they were so many pieces of goods. That the depersonalization of others had a backlash on its practitioners is symbolized in transfering the practice of tatooing prisoners' numbers on their arms to tatooing armpits of the Waffen-SS with their blood types. But here too there was differentiation; it is not recorded that higher SS officers, even in the Waffen-SS, had to submit to this indignity.[25]

The managerial bureaucracy of Oranienburg, interested in economic exploitation of concentration camp labor for construction purposes — especially of endless *Kasernen* (barracks) and of apartment houses and farmhouses — saw to it that Flossenbürg, Mauthausen, and later Natzweiler and Gross-Rosen concentration camps were built in or near stone quarries, the original idea behind Dachau. Already prodigal in the creation of quasi-state companies, financed with party and SS funds and by borrowing from private lenders (the great D-banks), the SS economists created additional companies (*Deutsche Erd- und Steinwerke* and *Deutsche Ausrüstungswerke*) for producing building stones and bricks and for producing and distributing food, clothing, and furniture for the SS, police, and new settlers. The boards of directors of these companies were none other than higher SS officers of the Main Office for Administration and Economy, who were even permitted to bring in some of their own capital, part of which they had already made through other SS enterprises, especially land sales.[26]

These men can neither be described as ideologically motivated nor as misfits of the depression but simply as very ruthless entrepreneurs who, quite clear-eyed, saw opportunities for profit in the exploitation of concentration camp labor and were forced to share these opportunities with the SS. They began well before the war and were going strong in 1938–1939 but really didn't become tycoons of vast enterprises until the conquests of 1940–1942 gave them millions of human lives to play with and a patriotic justification for expanding the SS concentration camp system to squeeze the utmost from Germany's victims, beginning with the Jews. With the erection of countless "branch camps" wherever Jews were concentrated in ghettos, and wherever "enemy" economic enterprise could be put into operation for the war effort with concentration camp or even war prisoners (first Poles, later Russians, and to some extent French prisoners of war), the men of the Verwaltungs- und Wirtschaftshauptamt (VWHA) compelled the Inspector of Concentration Camps to develop new administrations and guard units.[27]

Small wonder that Eicke's old chief of staff, Richard Glücks — unimaginative, lacking in energy if not lazy, even unperceptive compared to a man like Hoess — should find these men meddling in "his affairs," regulating the new camps which had never been properly integrated into the old system anyway. But Heydrich bristled far more than Glücks at the SS-Verwaltungschef's minions' interference when it was a matter of state security. Yet even in 1940 after the formation of the RSHA, Himmler would not place the concentration camp system under it, preferring rather to transfer the Inspectorate of Concentration Camps and Guard Troops to the newly fashioned Leadership Main Office of the Waffen-SS! Since the latter organ clearly did *not* care to interfere in this domain, the real effect was to force Heydrich to battle it out with Oswald Pohl, the Verwaltungschef and no mean opponent, in an area now doubly consecrated to national defense. After inconclusive skirmishes as early as 1939, the battle lines were drawn in 1940 in terms of prosecutions of peculating SS-*Wirtschafter* (Economic Managers) in Austria, Sudetenland, and Bohemia-Moravia. Before the clash reached many of the higher offices, a working compromise based on a balance of power had emerged in 1941. German conquests brought enormous possibilities for confiscation of productive properties, especially those in Jewish or enemy hands.[28]

The Reichssicherheitshauptamt was the appropriate agency for seizing this wealth but not to administer it. Heydrich was thus in a position to reward his friends with pieces of property and to punish his enemies by taking away their ill-gotten gains, but only with the cooperation of the SS-Verwaltungs- und Wirtschaftshauptamt. Together they could protect the interests of the SS and the Reich (always alleged to coincide) against greedy and dishonest individuals and firms. The formation in July 1940 of an SS holding company, *Deutsche Wirtschaftsbetriebe*, to capitalize and supervise the daughter companies represents the shift to businesslike management demanded by Heydrich, though in effect the small abuses and private dishonesties of individual SS officers and men were thereby erected into a state-sanctioned system of pillage and enslavement.[29]

By late 1940 the RSHA was pressing the concentration camp administration to take ever more inmates, including Jews, and was working hand-in-glove with the VWHA to enlarge the camps and secure raw materials to be worked on therein. It is true that within the system there were still disagreements: the Jewish Desk (*Judenreferat*) did not like the sorting system which preserved Jews for labor; security regulations prevented the use of able political prisoners as foremen, so that inefficient and corrupt criminals had to be used; endless reports and investigations demanded by the RSHA absorbed time which might otherwise have gone into productive labor. Nevertheless, the concentration camps had attained by 1941 a level of productivity such that with businesslike management and additional investment of scarce materials, reasonably capable SS personnel, and food for the rising number of inmates, they might be regarded as sinews of the Nazi war effort. Thus, it was rumored that Fritz Sauckel, as Plenipotentiary for Labor Mobilization, might lay claim to the productive capacity of the concentration camps early in 1942; and to head this off Himmler finally integrated the concentration camp system into the new, consolidated Reich-and-SS Main Office, the renamed and reconstituted Wirtschafts- und Verwaltungshauptamt.[30]

Whereas the 1939 formulation of the Verwaltungschef's powers had still conceived of two spheres—a state sphere for the police and the armed SS (*Hauptamt Haushalt und Bauten*), and an SS-and-party sphere (*Verwaltungs- und Wirtschaftshauptamt*)—the reorganization of February 1, 1942, clearly combined the two and placed the concentration camps as *Amtsgruppe D* within one unified economic administration for Police, Waffen-SS, and General SS. In this way the camp system was brought wholly into even more direct relationship with the business managers and supply personnel of all three systems. A goal of self-sufficiency for these three interlocking systems could now be set up as a bargaining counter with the rest of the Nazi state and party, and especially the Wehrmacht — all glad to have a larger share in what Police and SS could produce with scarce resources. Needless to say, this future SS economic independence (it was never really attained) could become a dangerous weapon in the hands of men disloyal to Hitler, yet given Himmler's loyalty (until April 1945), it was a valuable aid to Hitler vis-à-vis the army, German business, and even the state bureaucracy.

Thus, it was that Hitler refused to let Sauckel tamper with the concentration camps' production potential, so that they remained purely SS installations until the end. On the other hand, the needs of German industry for manpower were increasingly met by setting up detached elements of existing concentration camps near factories and exchanging concentration camp labor for a sharply negotiated share of the production for SS and Police purposes. General SS membership and contributions through Himmler's *Freundeskreis* enhanced an entrepreneur's chances to get this labor, but some of the best bargains were driven by businessmen outside Himmler's influence. If the SS did not become economically self-sufficient even in 1943 and 1944 despite even larger investments in the camp system financed from German banks, it was not due to Hitler's opposition but to bottlenecks of others' making, partly even of a strictly technical character. Doubtless the formal survival of the punitive and destructive purposes within the concentration camp system, in addition to the informal institutional rigidities described by Hoess (chicanery, stupidity, sadism), played a very large part in keeping the SS and Police dependent to the last upon the Wehrmacht, government agencies, Party Treasurer Franz Xavier Schwarz, and German big business. Killing the Jews, starving the Russian prisoners of war, and "working to death" persons convicted of *lèse majesté* was a luxury the SS could ill afford. Yet the view that all three of these operations could be made to pay direct dividends to the war effort was not restricted to the SS.[31]

### The Final Solution*

The destruction of the European Jewish communities and their members had been a money-making operation from its inception in Germany in 1933. While the SS neither initiated the "Final Solution" of the "Jewish Question" nor was its chief beneficiary, the SS in all its branches

---

*"The Final Solution of the Jewish Question" (*Die Endlösung der Judenfrage*): There is no satisfactory history of this ghastly euphemism. Perhaps it dates back to the anti-Semitic movement of the 1880s with various intended outcomes. Hitler had "prophesied" that world Jewry would not emerge from a world war which he accused "them" of fomenting in 1939. Göring ordered Heydrich to "solve the Jewish question finally" in 1941. The term became widespread after the attack on the USSR.

took a conscious hand in the process and sought to enrich itself collectively and individually thereby. It was impossible to keep a monopoly in Germany of so popular and rewarding an activity as stealing from the Jews. However, as Himmler pointed out, the rest of Germany and even most of the party were glad to leave the killing to the SS. Although they engaged in all the forms of official and unofficial thievery invented by others, it remained for the SS to steal their victims' shoes and underwear, hair and gold fillings. The fact that even the latter had to be shared with the Reich Finance Ministry underlines the deep involvements of non-SS sectors of German public life in the ultimate meanness of the *Endlösung*.[32]

While it may properly be said that the physical destruction of Jewry was implicit in Hitler's whole Weltanschauung, killing the Jews of Germany and Europe was not an explicit goal of the SS leadership (or of the Nazi Party) until the war years. Of course, the murder of individual Jews was a heritage from the Kampfzeit, concentrated in the SA and passed on to the SS glorified as politisches Soldatentum — unflinching willingness to commit crimes, even when recognized as such, on the command of higher authority. From 1933, when they aided in "keeping order" in the boycott of April 1, to November 8, 1938, when they were mobilized to keep the pogrom started by others within bounds and make it pay by imprisoning well-off Jews for ransom, the SS learned to expect to do the dirty work of the Nazi leadership. As it became bureaucratized and differentiated, the SS assigned its anti-Semitism to specialists, and as is usually the case with specialists, they were volunteers. Far more important in this regard than Adolf Eichmann, Reinhard Heydrich — combining personal psychological reasons with shrewd ambition — accepted if he did not volunteer for the responsibility of solving the Jewish question *so oder so* (one way or the other). Thus, the Chief of the Security Police and the Security Service (*SIPO und SD*), in particular the Gestapo as Amt IV of the RSHA under Müller, became the competent agency for Jewish matters even before July 1941, the official date of Heydrich's assignment from Göring "to solve the Jewish Question." While Heydrich and later Eichmann seized the initiative in organizing the resettlement and killing of the Jews, they were continuously abetted and even rivaled by other government and party agencies. Not the least of the motives involved in this initiative was the seizure of Jewish wealth.[33]

Austria, Sudetenland, Bohemia-Moravia, and Poland were successively subjected to organized and unorganized rapine, with Jews the first and most defenseless victims. Each step of the way saw Heydrich and "Gestapo Müller" tightening the controls which prevented "wild

Aryanizations" even by SS men and channeling the process of seizures according to prearranged divisions of the spoils. By the time the Germans reached France and the Low Countries, the plundering of Jews and their deportation had become a fine art, although here and there was a sense of tentativeness and experiment due to the Nazi illusion of an imminent peace treaty with France and England. The real shift to mass death comes with the decision to destroy the Jews of the Soviet Union in the process of the invasion, a certainty by the winter of 1940–1941. Now the experience with Einsatzgruppen in Poland; with Eichmann's emigration centers in Vienna, Prague, and Berlin; with killing operations at Chełmno; and with the rapid expansion of concentration camps for the exploitation of slave labor could all be combined under RSHA Amt IV leadership. Hitler's verbal approval seems certain at this time, but we should not conceive of one mastermind or master-plan, even Heydrich's and least of all Eichmann's. The task was chiefly one of coordinating initiatives of many SS and non-SS agencies and on occasion supplying initiative where reluctance was involved.[34]

Reluctance had of course a moral component, especially where brutality and death were involved. Thus, it was regularly advised that Germans not do the killing, although Germans were expected to transmit orders and, naturally, to arrange matters. Here the creation of the complex and ramified SS system, from RSHA and Superior SS and Police Leaders down to the military framework of squad and platoon in both the old General SS and the new Waffen SS, made possible the expectation that even criminal orders would be flawlessly transmitted and if not enthusiastically and imaginatively carried out, at least not sabotaged consciously or unconsciously by men in desperate turmoil of conscience. But even the Order Police, so thinly penetrated numerically by the SS, had been effectively captured and coordinated (*gleichgeschaltet*) by the ambitious in top ranks to the degree that they too could be used interchangeably with SS units for the grisly purpose of dragging old people, women, and children to their execution by "foreigners" equipped and uniformed as policemen. Even the Wehrmacht, grown callous watching Death's Head and SIPO-SD brutalities in Poland, gave up protesting and knowingly turned over Jews and commissars as well as partisans to the SS for destruction.[35]

Of course, a great deal of the reluctance had nothing to do with conscience. Himmler's intervention in the fall of 1941 against the resistance of the mayor of Litzmannstadt (Łódz) to taking more Jews into his ghetto "temporarily" was necessitated by a purely administrative situation. Heydrich had hoped to shift the area of concentration for the Jews from the annexed Polish territories to the "Jewish Reservation" in the

Lublin district belatedly added to the General-Gouvernement in exchange for Lithuania. However, Hans Frank successfully ended the unlimited "dumping" of Jews there begun in October 1939. So it became
necessary, after all, to cram an additional 20,000 Jews into 2,000 buildings, already the dwelling places of 144,000 persons. Quite aside from
the high death rate under such conditions, Heydrich meant their so-
journ to be temporary, for he had set about converting the experimental
"euthanasia" operation conducted at Chełmno and elsewhere in the
Reich (Hadamar, Gräfeneck, etc.) into mass-killing camps, not only in
the Lublin district but also at Auschwitz and in occupied Russia (Riga
and Minsk). Yet strangely enough the Litzmannstadt ghetto slowly became popular with its German administrators, just as later Jewish labor
centers in Upper Silesia and Minsk found their German "protectors."
The reason is not hard to find: profits for everyone except the Jews, including the SS.[36]

It had been Adolf Eichmann who had forced the additional Jews into
Litzmannstadt, and it was he in 1943 who kept insisting on the liquidation of the ghetto there against the wishes of the army, businessmen,
party officials, and even branches of the SS. Its survival until 1944, like
that of other profitable SS enterprises employing Jews, reveals efficiency rather than inefficiency in the SS. The desire of particular SS
agencies to spare "their Jews" indefinitely did not prevent the rapid liquidation of all the rest of the Jews; and ultimately Himmler's and
Hitler's backing for the indomitable Eichmann resulted in the withdrawal of these last remnants, usually after replacements from other
slave-labor reserves had been found or the raw materials and fuel had
disappeared which alone had made their labor profitable. Thus, a tangled web of guilt and responsibility was woven right within the SS itself
in regard to the destruction of the European Jews, hardly different from
that enmeshing countless officials of the government and industry.
Hundreds of thousands knowingly exploited the desperate fight for life
of other human beings in order to reap profits, resisting Adolf Eichmann's importunities to the last with an easy conscience. Many SS
members had their Jewish protectees, as did other Germans — and perhaps some who were not even profitable, except in terms of assuaging
consciences. However, the SS system made these practices "harmless,"
since over the long run the vast majority of these Jews would surely
die.[37]

The "death factories" were basically the same at Chełmno (a "small
operation"), Auschwitz-Brzezinka (the largest), and at the network of
camps at Belzec, Maidanek, Sobibor, and Treblinka in the General
Government. Common features were an "assembly line" procedure, a

sorting operation which saved for a time the able-bodied of both sexes
to do the actual work of destruction, and a salvage operation (*Aktion
Reinhardt*) to get the last usable bit of clothing, combs, false teeth, hair,
and gold fillings from the victims. This coordination was superimposed
on very different establishments even run by different parts of the SS
and certainly by SS officers of varied background; it was made possible
by the planners and administrators of the SS-Wirtschafts- und Verwaltungshauptamt. The skills involved were those of accountants and economists. While such persons had to oversee the operation step by step,
they could leave the enforcement and dirty work to officers and men of
Amtsgruppe D.[38] Many of these people also might be regarded as "specialists" at solving on-the-spot problems of killing, with the typical
craftsmen's rivalry about alternative methods (carbon monoxide versus
hydrogen cyanide).

Yet they too had a most varied background. Discernible are (1) Altkämpfer, (2) young intellectuals, (3) strict technicians — from police and
business backgrounds, and (4) underworld characters. Inasmuch as service in this exclusive group (no more than one hundred officers can be
identified) was in some degree a kind of sentence as well as a trial, it is
not surprising that so many of them ended on the gallows themselves.
The SS and Police courts thus provided a kind of alibi for "decent" SS officers even during the Nazi era by destroying the destroyers, though not
of course for their chief crimes but for *stealing*.

There were naturally more SS officers and men involved in guarding
the death factories than in their operation, and indeed many of the
worst excesses were performed by just such guards. They were in fact
precisely the same kind of excesses that had occurred in concentration
camps since 1933, although few if any of these guards were the Altkämpfer of 1933. It was not the kind of SS men which was decisive; it
was the situation SS bureaucrats had created in the camps which made
these excesses possible. Indeed, the excesses were more "normal" than
the *fact* of the death factories itself.[39]

Eichmann's team of "emigration specialists" of RSHA Amt IV-B-4
traveled about Europe in 1942, 1943, and 1944 enlisting the support of
high and low officials of the SS and Police system in tracking down the
Jews of France, Holland, Belgium, Italy, Greece, Slovakia, and Hungary, and then shipping them off to the death factories. Only because of
this extensive network of cooperating officialdom could a dozen men
arrange for the destruction of one million persons. Yet it is vital to an
understanding of the SS system to realize that Eichmann's teams were
not necessary for the destruction of the Jews of Yugoslavia, Rumania,
and the Soviet Union, who never saw the inside of a death-factory run

by the Wirtschafts- und Verwaltungshauptamt. These Jews died at the hands of the SD-Einsatzgruppen whose organization and management lay in quite other hands, though the line of authority traces back to the Reichssicherheitshauptamt (RSHA) and Reinhard Heydrich.[40]

The model for the "mobile killing operations" of the murder battalions attached to the German Wehrmacht in Russia lay in the ad hoc teams used in the Sudetenland, Bohemia-Moravia, and Polish invasions. Temporary duty and a mixture of elements from Gestapo, SD, Order Police, KRIPO, and Waffen-SS characterized the teams of battalion strength put together for Operation Barbarossa. At the top levels, in command positions, men were placed who were to prove their absolute loyalty and dependability to Himmler and Heydrich. Many of them were academic and professional people with an "idealistic" interest in SS ideology, bolshevism, the "Jewish question", and Russia. Above them, in charge of planning and liaison with the Wehrmacht, were the officials of the Reichssicherheitshauptamt (IV-A-1). The lower officers were usually ordinary policemen. There is no evidence that they were especially selected; the great likelihood is that these men too were simply gotten rid of by their superiors. Thus, it is not surprising that an atmosphere of devil-may-care, of determination to prove just how ruthless and inhuman they could be, permeated these groups. While the killing was *played down* in the death-factory system, partly to make it easier, the butchers of the Einsatzgruppen "showed off," creating problems for German army commanders who wished to remain in ignorance and keep their troops "innocent." It was not long before the Einsatzgruppen were ordered to employ non-Germans as killers, a procedure extensively used in Yugoslavia and Rumania.[41]

### The SS Occupation Bureaucracy

What made it possible for relatively few inhuman killers like Hoess and human bloodhounds like Eichmann to mesh with another brand of butcher in the Einsatzgruppen to destroy efficiently without upsetting the very system in which they were nourished? In part the answer lies in the evolution of the SS-and-Police framework that supplied them with directives and shielded them from conflict and prying eyes of the rest of the bureaucracy. The lack of a central SS-and-Police Hauptamt made itself felt in failures of coordination, but the fact that Himmler, a kind of universal spider, sat at the center of all the systems equipped with an efficient team of busybodies in his Personal Staff offset the intrinsic rivalry of the RSHA and the ORPO-Hauptamt. Himmler was clever enough to permit Daluege to handle an increasing amount of the organizational growth of the SS and Police system in 1939 and 1940, so that even Heydrich did not have control over everything. After the move of Heydrich to Prague in September 1941, the two offices were better able to work together on a routine basis, a procedure enhanced by the development of a couple dozen police generals as *truly* SS-and-Police generals at both staff and field command levels.[42]

The spread of occupation responsibilities in 1940 and even more so in 1941, until large stretches of Europe were subjugated to SS-and-Police rule — embodied in SS-and-Police Generals as *Höhere SS- und Polizeiführer* (HSSPFs) — actually created the opportunity Himmler and the SS had worked for since before 1933. *One* universal net or web of influence and control was to be set up in which police responsibilities and SS growth could take place surmounted by the position of Superior SS and Police Leader, the highest and most honorable field command in both systems — the prize to be sought by Altkämpfer and police newcomer alike. The position had from its inception within the Reich in 1938–1939 been tied to the notion of emergency conditions (*Ausnahmezustand*); and its evolution outside the Reich, where normal standards of government, security, and individual rights were in abeyance, was both rapid and fruitful.[43]

If the Superior SS and Police Leaders in the newly annexed Polish territories had more powers than their brethren in the old Reich, the position of the Superior SS and Police Leader in the Protectorate of Bohemia-Moravia and in the General Government was vastly more influential still. It was enhanced in the latter case by the creation in 1940 of SS- und Polizeiführer out of the Police Commanders at the Distrikt level, for which there was no comparable, fully integrated position in the Reich. But it was to be in the occupied countries, especially Russia, that the system could flourish with the least competition from Reich officialdom and in closest coordination with the defensive and settlement functions of the SS as envisaged by Himmler and Darré in 1932. It was in Russia that some of the oldest SS officers became SS and Police Generals responsible for: the military defense of their regions, not only against partisans but even incursions of the Soviet armed forces; resettlement and expulsions from their regions to create settlement areas for Germandom; the setting up of SS organization and recruiting; and last but not least the order and productivity of the occupied territory and the subject populace. Truly satraps out of ancient times combined with the notion of politisches Soldatentum from the Nazi struggle for power, this segment of the higher SS officer corps most fully represents the ideal toward which Himmler and his closest advisors had been striving. More rounded and actively engaged than the bureau-generals or the pure soldiers of the Waffen-SS, they bear the largest burden of guilt for the total implementation of Nazi purposes in wartime Europe.[44]

It is scarcely an accident that the fullest development of the mature SS officer corps occurred in the imperialist venture of 1941–1942 *in the east*, parallel with the military phase and with the extermination of the Jews, resting upon but essentially different from both. SS political soldiering in Russia in that period really entailed a fundamental *Landnahme* (land seizure), in the language of Carl Schmitt, followed by a pacification of the *imperium* and a reconstruction in the spirit of the conquerors. Furthermore, the higher SS officer corps assigned to Russia did not come there as the agents of the German government merely as hangmen and policemen for other decision-making agencies. They themselves were supposed to be the bearers of the forming culture, the rivals and opponents of erroneous conceptions of administration and colonization. The story of the German occupation of Russia is thus not only entwined with SS brutality and atrocities but with the running battle fought from top to bottom of the SS and Police hierarchy with Rosenberg's Ministry of the East and with other Reich agencies. It was of utmost importance that the SS was responsible for the policing of occupied territories, yet a "mere" police agency within the German government could not have succeeded in acting so independently in so many areas. Far better coordinated than its rivals, the system was nonetheless too new, too ambitious, too steeped in illusions to succeed in building half so well as it destroyed. However, as a system for exploiting the land and labor resources of conquered areas, while seizing those resources for itself and its collaborators, the SS and Police of 1941–1942 had advanced far beyond the SA amateurs of 1933–1934. Perhaps it had advanced not quite far enough, for the aberrations of *hybris* and *furor* so characteristic of the SA pursued some of the most prominent of the Altkämpfer SS Generals.[45]

The SS-and-Police had been kept in its place, *in the background*, among the occupation policies of Germany in Norway, Denmark, Holland, Belgium, and France. The evil reputation that followed the Death's Head Reinforcements and the SIPO-SD-Einsatzkommandos from the east made army, foreign office, and party officials chary of granting Himmler a free hand in 1940. Moreover, while Hitler reiterated his own stand against SS military proliferation, emphasizing precisely the police role of the postwar SS, Himmler had begun to implement his old dream of a Germanic aristocracy of blood and soil drawn from soldier volunteers of northern Europe. Consequently, Himmler himself did not wish to unloose the Death's Head units on Norway, Denmark, and Holland. Temporarily stationed there, a few battalions were readied for regular combat duty and kept off the backs of the populace. SIPO-SD-Einsatzkommandos made a brief appearance in Norway and then disappeared. Denmark and Holland went over immediately to regular police administration, while Belgium and northern France under military government virtually excluded the SIPO-SD system at least for a time. Although Superior SS and Police Leaders were indeed appointed for Norway and Holland, their hands were tied by powerful party-oriented Reichskommissars and Hitler's policy of courtship of the Nordic countries with which Himmler could hardly disagree. Separate treatment for Alsace and Lorraine also dictated that Superior SS and Police Leaders in Strassbourg and Metz (also responsible for the Saar) made their appearance, but both were overshadowed by the Old Reich gauleiters who were given authority over the French provinces in addition to their former gaus.[46]

Himmler was all the more resolved, with Hitler's full approval, to apply the most ruthless repressive measures in the initial stages of occupation of the Soviet territories. In *Mein Kampf* Hitler had sketched just the combination of depopulation and resettlement for Russia which Himmler contemplated. In March 1941 Himmler could gather at a meeting a preselected group of SS colonels and generals at Wewelsburg — the "SS castle" at Paderborn in Westfalia used as a council hall for the future knights of blood and soil — and initiate them to their future duties as Superior SS and Police Leaders or those of their subordinate SS and Police Leaders (on the model of the General Government). One of their number, Bach-Zelewski, has testified that Himmler spoke of eliminating millions of Slavs and Jews to make room for Germanic settlements. In April 1941 Hitler appointed all Superior SS and Police Leaders within the Reich and outside as Generals of the SS *and also* as Generals of Police, with police epaulettes and field-grey uniforms.[47]

Thus, a powerful institution had come of age, and the way was prepared to coordinate and protect the most daring and reprehensible actions in the east from intervention and sabotage by other parts of the German state and society. Through their hands were to run all the threads, both of information and control, of Himmler's web dealing with the most delicate and political matters, including relations with the party — especially the gauleiters — the army, the state bureaucracy, and leading figures of Germany's business and professional world. Through their position as *Oberabschnittsführer* (Main Sector Commander) *of the General SS*, which retained its character and significance as an SS community both within the Nazi party community and well beyond it in the general civilian sector until 1943 or 1944, they had access to channels of influence and information of strategic importance to the SS. Through their control of countless auxiliary forces — such as *Technische Nothilfe* and the airraid wardens, beside all armed SS units not transferred to OKW authority (replacement and training battalions) — they had emergency strength independent of party controls. Moreover, their virtual command over all police forces via the SIPO and ORPO Inspectors (SIPO and ORPO Commanders outside the Reich) gave them a reasonable chance even against Wehrmacht power in a political showdown.[48]

Within the Reich their importance lay chiefly in supplying alternative power centers and channels of command for Hitler beside the gauleiters and corps area military commanders. In a sense, they even became *intendants* of the state system, superimposed upon the rest of the old bureaucracy and the new party men. They were gradually to bypass much of the state bureaucracy, while their relations with the party group depended heavily upon the personality of the gauleiter and on their own natures. Quite a few quickly became embedded in the party fabric of mutual favors and antipathies and were removed by Himmler. Unlike the gauleiters, *whom Hitler could remove but not move about,* the Superior SS and Police Leaders — like the army corps commanders after which they were copied — were at least ideally and theoretically available for many different kinds of assignments. Only rarely did their power and influence rest on local ties, and when it did Himmler usually saw to it that they were weaned away from their home grounds, even if new assignments were thoroughly uncongenial.[49]

Nomination by Himmler to one of the higher SS and Police posts outside the Reich represents an accolade for dynamism and ruthlessness. Only six or seven Altkämpfer of the original Reich HSSPF's remained at their posts throughout the war, the rest being "promoted" to imperial proconsulates in Russia, the Balkans, or the west. Those who remained behind (one was killed in an air raid) were either too dynamic and restless to get along with the Wehrmacht or a bit stodgy and unimaginative. Another nine or ten assigned to inner-Reich higher SS and Police commands were of the younger generation of pre-1933 SS officers, largely on the way up after more or less distinguished apprenticeships; a few were "put on ice" after some fiasco. Three police generals figured in the wartime ranks of the home front Höhere SS- und Polizeiführer, one-sixth of the total.[50]

A great deal of the power on the home front, however, rested with the professional policemen, for the ranks of the inspectors of security police and order police were also raided of their SS-Altkämpfer for assignments abroad and replaced by a new generation of jurists, Kriminalräte, and police bureaucrats with nominal SS rank, rising through Gestapo and SD regional commands. The latter positions too, filled during the war with men of assimilated SS ranks from captain to lieutenant colonel, became more and more the key positions in a unified SS-and-

Police administrative hierarchy calling less for aggressiveness (Drauf-gängertum) and ruthlessness than for systematic hard work and *Finger-spitzengefühl* (sensitivity). Although these men, in their thirties and forties, had not fought in the brawls of the Kampfzeit or attended the endless *Appelle* (roll-calls) of the General SS after the Machtergreifung, the SS was still their ticket to success because its expansion during the war called their superiors to the far-flung battlefronts and offered them a dream of power as well. Many did indeed go off before 1945 to occu-pation assignments, and more fell in battle as Waffen-SS officers. Re-pression, torture, all the evils of the police-state were in their power; taught by their Altkämpfer superiors to regard themselves as soldiers in a permanent civil war with an implacable enemy, they found justifica-tion in the real battles in Russia and their own likely commitment. They lacked the self-justification in their own past, however, which played such a large role in the men of Himmler's generation. What they shared with their mentors were large ambitions and a willingness to satisfy these upon the bodies of the weak and defenseless. Partly because the war ended before many of them reached high positions, and partly be-cause they were indeed not Nazis by conviction, this generation had no progeny. The younger survivors of the Waffen-SS, while perhaps also reviled and shunned in postwar Germany, are nevertheless able to iden-tify with the SS traditions in a way that the police segment never could. Yet politisches Soldatentum was far more fully embodied in the SS-and-Police officer than in the "pure soldier" of the later Waffen-SS.[51]

Himmler and Heydrich had to fight their way into Russia as much against other Nazis as against the Russians, but this time the Wehr-macht was on their side and for much the same reasons that it had con-spired with them in 1934 — the soldiers did not want to be soiled with the blood of civilians. The Wehrmacht had enough to do just in con-quering the Soviets; there would be no troops left over for the tasks of repression. SS fighting units were even welcomed; the spurned and hated police units from Poland and Bohemia were good enough to hold a rebellious Russian countryside in check. It still took hard negotiations by Himmler to keep the murder commandos in the forefront of the bat-tle area in order to catch the commissars and Jews before they vanished, but ultimately Wehrmacht commanders realized they thus spared men for battle and stayed out of a messy business. The Russians could then reserve their hatred for the SS. Rosenberg, and behind him Bormann, Göring, and Goebbels — and sometimes even Hitler — were to be the real obstacles to absolute SS power in the east.[52]

Nowhere is Hitler's policy of "divide and conquer" within his own ranks more apparent as a force for evil for all concerned than in Russia.

While it is too much to say that Hitler defeated himself in Russia, since Stalin, the Red Army, and the Russian people surely made a big difference, nevertheless Hitler's determination not to let any one part of his power system have its way greatly weakened the German conquest of the east. Freedom to kill Russians the SS won easily; but even if the SS had had the skill and organization to control and exploit the vast reservoir of manpower and resources of occupied Russia, it would have had to devote half its skill and energy fighting other Germans for its share. As it was, the SS proved far from ready for the scope of the operation, so that skilled personnel had to be stretched very thin — until the old Reich was drained of its SS and Police cadres even before the climax of the military phase in 1943–1945 when so much of the SS went into army and Waffen-SS uniform.[53]

In the short run, however, especially in 1942–1943, the SS was able to take advantage of Hitler's predilection for disorganization. Already in occupied Yugoslavia and Greece in 1941, it seized additional police powers because authority there was so widely diffused by excessive partition, military and civilian rivalries, and above all a general lack of fixed ideas about such new and distant lands starting with Hitler and including many Nazis. Although Hitler and Rosenberg certainly had fixed ideas about Russia, Hitler's scheme of assigning wide authority to Rosenberg's nominal subordinates — the Reichskommissars — and the army's insistence on controlling the forward areas for logistical reasons meant that the conspiratorial schemers in the SS from Himmler down past Heydrich to the Verwaltungschef (Pohl) and head of the SS-Hauptamt (Berger) found ample opportunities to worm their way into very strategic offices. This occurred despite chiefs of those offices actually opposing SS expansion and its ruthless philosophy of a subhuman east. Boring from within, SS policy makers broke down the opposition to wanton acts of Superior SS and Police Leaders in the pursuit of an SS empire. Almost every year there was an additional breakthrough. In 1941, after months of careful effort to limit Himmler's power in Russia to the level he had elsewhere, Hitler cut the Gordian knot on July 16 by giving the SS authority to act "on its own responsibility" for the maintenance of order there. In August 1942 Hitler authorized the SS to conduct military operations in the rear areas, especially against partisans. By the summer of 1943, Gottlob Berger, the agile head of the SS-Hauptamt, had persuaded Rosenberg to place him in charge of political operations in the Eastern Ministry, where he could sabotage any remaining resistance to SS exploitation of the countryside and its human burden. In September 1944, after the July 20 coup and in the expectation of reconquest, Himmler sponsored Vlassow's Russian Liberation

Army and a whole series of puppet exile-governments for a *cordon sanitaire* from Estonia to the Ukraine. The SS was making foreign policy right and left, but of course it was too late.[54]

Russia was the grave of between 200,000–300,000 SS officers and men. Most of these died, weapon in hand, as soldiers of the Waffen-SS or the army. A much smaller group of SS officers and men constituted the repressive forces who did so much to make the Germans hated in the hamlets and cities of the Soviet Union. Ten thousand, even including the Einsatzgruppen, is an ample figure to include the antipartisan SS units; the concentration camp administrations at Riga, Kaunas, and Minsk; the network of Order police and SIPO-SD officials; the SS administrators of farms, mines, and factories; and the staffs of the Superior SS and Police Leaders and their regional subordinates. Less than 2,000 SS officers were involved, even if we include those commanding non-SS units of police, both German and foreign—and a great many of these officers would have to be termed "nominal SS" members. Truly, a few hundred officers at the rank of major and above were the deadly means by which so much havoc was wrought. From the grisly mass-murders of 1941 to the routine execution of hostages and prisoners of war, from the liquidation of all living inhabitants of "partisan" villages to kidnapping hundreds of thousands of slave laborers, from the systematic looting of Soviet art treasures and museums to the brutal destruction of every productive facility and living thing before it cleared out— the gestating SS officer corps let itself be represented by a fraction of its membership. But that fraction was damned by its training, its selection, and the condition of unrelenting warfare to be devils incarnate.[55]

Initially an elaborate differentiation marked the SS occupation policies. Heydrich himself sought to steer a different course vis-à-vis the Czechs from that toward the Poles. The Serbs were repressed without mercy while the Ukrainians of Galicia were "liberated" by the SS administrators at Lemberg (Lwów). Beside the underlying distinction between western and eastern peoples, which gave even Frenchmen rights before SS and Police authorities, the Nordic lands like Holland, Denmark, and Norway were especially to be favored. There was of course also the distinction between allied peoples like the Slovaks, Magyars, Croats, Finns, Italians, Rumanians, and Bulgarians and conquered groups like the Greeks, Albanians, Estonians, Letts, Lithuanians, and Turkic peoples from inner Russia. Racial theories and evolving recruiting practices for the Waffen-SS conflicted; the consequence was a familiar one with the Nazis: without modifying the theories but simply by ignoring them, the regulations were stretched to make room for more foreign recruits, and with them came relaxation in the negative differentiation for their relatives and even their home communities. At the same time, however, spasmodic exhibitions of resistance multiplied in favored western areas. The *Nacht und Nebel* (Night and Fog) decree with its ultrapunitive response to any attacks on Germans in occupied areas helped to reduce the level of the treatment of western and northern Europeans by SS and Police officials to a common denominator with eastern peoples.[56]

Naturally, a vicious circle of retaliation by resistance groups set in, so that by late 1942 the number of Superior SS and Police Leaders equipped with tyrannical powers was on the increase, not only in the west but in the Balkans. Himmler had also increased the number in the former Austrian areas, to which former Yugoslav (Slovene) territories had been joined. A cautious system of partial concealment in nominally independent areas led to the withholding of the actual HSSPF title in Albania, Greece, Slovakia, Croatia, Hungary, and Belgium until as late as 1944. Although designated as plenipotentiaries of the Reichsführer SS and Chief of the German Police, leading SS and Police Generals were very obviously powerful channels of German influence. They facilitated the implementation of the Final Solution of Eichmann in these areas.[57] There were two examples of an even higher SS and Police rank created in 1944: Supreme (*Höchste*) SS and Police Leader. In the first case, the position was assigned to Hans Prützmann, one of the oldest and most deadly serious of the younger Altkämpfer, who was placed in charge of all South Russia during the scorched earth phase of the evacuations there. The second time the title was used was in Italy, during the successful resistance to allied invaders and the formation of the Republic of Saló. The post went to Himmler's own personal staff commander, Karl Wolff, an indication that it was a *political* rather than a military appointment.[58]

The subordinate position of SS- und Polizeiführer was introduced into France and Norway in 1944, showing that Himmler had finally determined to consolidate the two arms even at the risk of disturbing relations further with the Wehrmacht and the subject populace. These posts went largely to products of the police *Laufbahn* (career); the era when deserving SS-Altkämpfer could be "rewarded" with important police posts was long past. Indeed, as the war years passed, the sequence of crises had offered so many challenges and screenings of SS and Police personnel that even the selection process of the growth years after 1934 had become irrelevant. The Altkämpfer who had risen through the 1930s to police ranks of prominence were few by 1939; they were certainly reinforced by the addition of a sizeable number from the General SS in the course of the war, selected for abilities demonstrated during the 1930s.

But the preponderance of the officialdom responsible for the police activities of the SS during the war, and especially the rising generation of new talent under forty, were *not* the products of the General SS and its vicissitudes.[59] Numbers of course do not tell the whole story. The leavening of General SS veterans, and especially of a few thousand fanatical and competent pre-1933 fighters and killers, was indeed decisive in warping and constraining hundreds of thousands more who passed through the police system. The influence of formal indoctrination in the form of training programs and published materials like *Der Untermensch* (*The Sub-Human*) surely must take second place to the power of a totalitarian system to create a milieu of terror and disregard for human life in which even the moderately healthy adjust themselves to injustice as a matter of course, and the neurotic and asocial are in their element.[60]

## The RKFDV System

A particularly telling example of adjustment and rationalization occurred in the case of the several thousand SS officers and NCOs who constituted the staff of the government agencies known collectively as the *Reichskommissariat für die Festigung Deutschen Volkstums* (RKFDV). Himmler had invented for himself the grandiose title as Reich Commissioner (or Commissar) for the Strengthening of Germandom in October 1939, when he won from Hitler the authority to supervise and implement resettlement of ethnic Germans "rescued from Bolshevism" in the Baltic states and eastern Poland. Himmler liked to say that he had his good side and his bad side, and that if the police duties were his bad side, then the creation of new German Lebensraum in the east was his good side. Thus, Himmler himself created for those SS officers and men whom he employed for this purpose a very special alibi — a defensive interpretation of their activities, essentially police in nature, which extended even to the removal of less fortunate peoples from their homes and farms, the rejection of "racially inferior" stocks for the future settlement areas, and the kidnapping of "racially superior" children from their parents.[61]

Hitler had begun by giving the resettlement task to the Party-Foreign Office bastard agency, the *Volksdeutsche Mittelstelle* (VoMi), the Liaison Office for Ethnic Germans; but Himmler rather easily seized the reins from Werner Lorenz, the SS colonel in charge, the more readily because of the penetration into VoMi of Heydrich's SD agents. Himmler's ploy with Hitler was precisely the need for police supervision, and he inserted Heydrich decisively into the operations in the newly occupied Polish territories to make way for the new settlers. VoMi retained the subordinate organizing responsibilities for "bringing them back alive" and for their care and feeding in camps while awaiting settlement. Before 1939 the Liaison Office's network of officials and employees abroad wherever ethnic Germans were to be found was only lightly sprinkled with SS, usually doing double duty as SD agents. However, already in the case of the Sudeten crisis, the value of more extensive SS contacts to start the fledgling SS in motion in the new area was made apparent. VoMi therefore developed an SS and a non-SS wing in 1939, but more and more of the employees and officials joined the SS.

The arrival into the Reich proper (*Altreich*) of many ethnic German refugees from Poland, even before the outbreak of the war, gave rise to the organizational innovation of Liaison Office branches in each party gau responsible for the necessary camps. Naturally, the closest cooperation with regional SIPO-SD headquarters became *de rigeur*, so that the gau VoMi offices needed SS officers to handle their business more expeditiously, and preferably SD officers. The Volksdeutsche Mittelstelle developed teams to go into newly conquered areas (Yugoslavia, Russia) to evaluate and earmark ethnic Germans and Nordic types, including children of partisans, for resettlement. Naturally, they needed or at least wanted field-gray uniforms, either of the police or the Waffen-SS. Consequently, VoMi came to form a constituent of the RKFDV system after mid-1941, and the SS part of VoMi was organized as an SS Main Office (Hauptamt VoMi). The SD component gradually became less important as better intelligence channels opened up for SD-Ausland (RSHA Amt VI), although VoMi remained an important pipeline for Himmler and later Kaltenbrunner, Heydrich's successor, to and from party and Foreign Office branches. Rightly or wrongly, VoMi personnel were regarded as "the SS" and as tale-bearing fanatics.[62]

In the reorganization of the Sicherheitsdienst accompanying the formation of the Reichssicherheitshauptamt (RSHA), a Main Section III-ES (*Eindeutschung-Siedlung*) was formed in Amt III (SD-*Inland*), headed by Hans Ehlich, an SS colonel who specialized in nationality problems. His office thereupon received the assignment from Heydrich to supervise the processing of the potential settlers in elaborate "immigration centers" (*Einwanderungs-Zentralstellen*, EWZ). The first of these was located at Gdynia (or Gotenhafen), moving to Poznań (Posen) in November 1939; yet the most active was situated at Łódz (or Litzmannstadt) with branches at Berlin, Stettin, Cracow, and later also at Paris. The staff of the centers were chiefly non-SS and largely not even police but instead governmental clerks and bureaucrats representing relevant ministries such as Interior, Transport, Food and Agriculture, Labor, Finance, Economics and Health. They were, however, all

under the RSHA in their immediate duties along with a registration bureau of the Order Police, a Race and Settlement Main Office team
charged with racial examinations of the settler families, General SS (later Waffen-SS) physicians, and Waffen-SS recruiters. The managers of
the centers were officers of the SIPO-SD system whose job was to keep
smooth the flow of resettlers; inevitably a degree of intervention in the
decision-making process resulted from their powerful connections vis-à-
vis the non-SS personnel and even RuSHa examiners.[63]

An even more direct integration of RKFDV activities into the SIPO-
SD system occurred in the *Umwanderungszentralstellen*, (UWZ, Resettlement Centers) set up in the spring of 1940 expressly for the processing
of evicted Polish families. Although here too there were problems of
sorting out persons for "Germanization" and ultimate Reich citizenship
by the use of racial examinations and other checks, the operation was
conducted almost entirely by Security and Order Police, with RuSHa
teams called in rather than being assigned. All involvement of non-SS
agencies was avoided until the few Re-Germanizeables (*Wiederein-
deutschungsfähigen*) arrived back in the Reich, where the Security Police still was responsible for pushing their cases through the relevant
agencies, including VoMi and RKFDV representatives. The heads of the
UWZ were of course SIPO-SD officers, reporting *directly* to the Inspectors of their regions but in closest liaison with VoMi camp administrators and RKFDV representatives in their gaus. As the war reduced the
number of RuSHa officers and men available for racial selection, the
UWZ even carried out the crude separation of expellees for eventual Re-
Germanization, slave-labor in Germany, or shipment to the General
Government. In other words, the very same type of procedures used in
Eichmann's operations crept into the handling of Slavs, and in fact the
EWZ and UWZ administrators landed quite regularly in the Einsatzgruppen and in Eichmann's Sonderkommandos. The RKFDV opera-
tions were no more hermetically sealed off as Himmler's "good side"
than was the Waffen-SS from Himmler's genocidal activities.[64]

On the other hand, it was possible for RuSHa personnel to blame
Heydrich and later Kaltenbrunner for the executions and other suffering resulting from their negative verdicts on people, since the former
were merely making a "scientific" evaluation of some Pole accused of
sexual intercourse with a German woman, or of some Jew who had
smuggled himself along with a transport of Ukrainian metal workers to
the Reich. While they used and were aware of the true meaning of the
term *Sonderbehandlung* (special treatment: death) in certain cases of
"racial inferiority," RuSHa examiners were largely spared the grisly
context of their activities. Indeed, wartime RuSHa devoted only a small

part of its time to such work, though of course the absolute amount increased considerably. The absolute growth of RuSHa officers did not
keep pace with the enormous increase in the SS due to the expansion of
military and police branches, all of which required racial examinations
for admission to the SS. Hundreds of General SS officers and NCOs had
to be recruited for RuSHa posts in 1940–1941 and given rather short, inadequate "anthropological" training. Crass ideology, simplified biol-
ogy, and pseudo-genetics were crammed into six weeks basic training —
with the result that later positive *and* negative verdicts were likely to be
reached under the impulse of some extraneous factor, like the need for
more Waffen-SS recruits or the desire of the Security Police to be rid of a
case. Most of the examiners were men of relatively low rank compared
to Waffen-SS and SIPO-SD officers in whose bailiwicks racial examinations were merely an added complication.[65]

Many high-ranking, older RuSHa officers had little to do with this
routine matter, whether "bad" (condemnation to death as subhuman)
or "good" (admission to the Waffen-SS — for many also a condemnation
to death). The task of the RuSHa colonels, and of many clever younger
officers also, was to devise schemes for a RuSHa comeback to prominence as a settlement agency in Russia after a period of eclipse owing to
Himmler's quarrel with Darré — caused in part because Himmler
thought RuSHa's ideological training for the SS was too "intellectual
and impractical." Thus, RuSHa was instrumental in the development
of settlement plans for Russia, entailing the acquisition of large collective farms to be established as training farms for wounded Waffen-SS
veterans with farming backgrounds. RuSHa also won for itself the right
to select and supervise the assignment of all SS men to agricultural management positions under the WVHA-Economic Managers (*Wirtschafter*), even when they remained in the Waffen-SS and were also
subordinate to Pohl, the jealous Verwaltungschef. Ultimately in the
winter of 1942–1943, a complete breakdown in the rate of racial examinations resulted from overtaxing an already thinned-out system. New
recruits and thousands of settlers could not be processed while RuSHa
bigwigs and junior officers drove around Russia inspecting settlement
sites. Himmler lost his temper and fired the acting head of the Race and
Settlement Main Office, Hofmann — the third man to fill the post since
1938. Richard Hildebrandt, one of his most trusted and ruthless Superior SS and Police Leaders, was given the post with a top SIPO-SD officer as his deputy. They were to reduce red tape, stop the empire-
building, and hold the line till the war ended.[66]

A new large task gradually devolved on RuSHa, or rather on the
Main Sector RuS-officers: caring for the families of the Waffen-SS casu-

alties. There were a number of reasons why Himmler picked RuSHa for this duty. RuSHa had traditionally a responsibility toward the SS-*Sippen* (clans) reflected in the Sippenamt. While there was a separate *SS-Versorgungs- und Fürsorgeamt* (Maintenance and Welfare Office) and of course the Well of Life Society (*Lebensborn*), both soon became technical bureaucracies that needed a regional channel to the SS home front via the still existing, skeletonized General SS-Standarten (regiments). For this purpose the SS-*Pflegestellen* (Care Centers) were set up at each General SS headquarters under a wounded Waffen-SS man responsible to the Main Sector RuS-officer. Through these miniature welfare bureaus passed the major and minor tragedies of SS widows and orphans, wounded SS men seeking a pension and farm in the east, a mother whose fourth son had been called up, and unmarried girls with babies due.

Procedural directives from Lebensborn, the Versorgungs- und Fürsorgeamt, and other SS Main Offices were channeled through RuSHa to the Pflegestellen along with the regulations of Reich ministries, and the implementation was left to the young Waffen-SS junior officer in charge, with perhaps assistance from some overage General SS personnel and, in delicate cases, the regimental commander. Himmler was forced to insist a number of times that the latter *must personally* notify parents and wives of sons' and husbands' deaths. Inevitably the tragedies and incongruities of war led to mistaken and unsuitable treatment by the inexperienced and untrained "welfare" personnel, but mingled with complaining recriminations the correspondence of these offices contained many letters of heartfelt gratitude and simple faith. At a time when some SS men were killing the innocent, others were succoring and giving solace. Certainly these home front positions were not matters of personal choice, although an element of preference seems to be associated with the type of man who insisted on returning to his comrades on the front. With the increase in allied bombing of German cities in 1942 and 1943, there was not much hope of safety and a great deal more horror at home. On the other hand, the close collaboration of RuSHa and the Pflegestellen with the SD, and probably also the Gestapo, sheds an eerie light even on this "decent" SS role. SD procedures were primarily informational in character, but the Gestapo "warning" was a regular method of pressure during the later war years if widows and parents complained too loudly of mistreatment. The concentration camps were never very far away from any SS bureau.[67]

Threats of punishment for rumor-mongering had to be increasingly backed up as the war progressed, among them the persistent story of the SS "breeding homes" associated with half-knowledge about the Well of

Life Society. A girl who wrote to Himmler to learn about them in 1944 was ordered committed to a concentration camp, yet there is not a shred of evidence that there ever were such places. We have seen that Lebensborn expanded its system of lying-in homes greatly after 1937, and Gestapo seizures of Jewish properties in Austria were the basis of Lebensborn expansion there. Similarly, Lebensborn entered Poland with the Einsatzkommandos to help the ethnic Germans and incidentally to seize whole warehouses of supplies. The multiplication of such homes in far-flung places like Norway and Holland, the General Government and Russia may have been an indirect encouragement to SS men to sexual indulgence with the local population, but the homes were strictly for pregnant women. Admission to them involved an elaborate health and police check, with racial evaluation formally included if not always done by an "expert," so that the SS did not sponsor just any liaison. The staffs in the homes outside the Reich were not all officially part of the Lebensborn society, and the Munich headquarters of that organization was not really capable of keeping a check on every place that bore its name. These homes too, being run by the Nazi party, may have winked at illegitimate pregnancies in cases where the SS might have frowned — but they were not brothels.[68]

Aside from the operation of a dozen or more official lying-in homes, Lebensborn grew into a large-scale adoption agency. Starting with the placement of illegitimate children born to German girls and women, largely in SS officers' families, Lebensborn soon branched out to combing orphanages in occupied Poland and other lands for "Germanic" children under seven. Secrecy used to protect the unmarried mothers was readily adapted through SS ties with the police authorities to name-changing and record alteration which concealed the whereabouts of these children from relatives. The children were well treated even though many of them had to be taught German. In 1943 legal changes were brought about to equip the SS, acting through Lebensborn, to act as guardian for the children during a period of adaptation until final adoption; and authority was vested in the SS-Pflegestellen to function as Youth Protection Offices (*Jugendämter*) instead of the regular state offices. Thus, the SS could exclude the state from all inquiries into dubious cases at all stages of the proceedings. The Lebensborn headquarters was even given a kind of fictitious status as a branch of the Ministry of the Interior (Amt L), so that the *personalia* of the children could be legally falsified without interference.[69]

Lebensborn became a huge financial operation as well, taxing all full-time SS officers inversely in proportion to their progeny and conducting its own health and death benefit insurance for its charges.

When Himmler extended Lebensborn responsibilities to the care of selected children of partisans, even those who had been shot or committed to concentration camps, he burdened its personnel with tasks too far removed from their original assignment to succeed. The children from Slovenia, the Ukraine, and Bohemia (e.g., Lidice) were often much older than seven; they were aware of what had happened and miserable. SS families did not want them. In this way an added Lebensborn responsibility evolved: supervision and even operation of children's homes or boarding schools into which unwanted and unplaced "valuable" children were placed. Here, as in so much of Lebensborn activity, the major roles were women's, although SS officers held formal responsibility. The functions of Lebensborn were certainly caritative from beginning to end, although its chief personnel were quite clear that they were cooperating with other SS personnel who had in fact kidnapped many of the children and even killed their parents. Lebensborn officers sought to increase their "empire" and fought the splintering of the original procedures into non-SS hands, so their pleas of utter innocence and disgust with the taking of older "non-German" children "by mistake" and through "excessive administrative zeal" rings hollow. Since they were business managers and lawyers rather than social workers, the children were probably incidental.[70]

Strictly speaking, none of the foregoing groups of SS and Police personnel had duties limited to the RKFDV. At the core of the imperialist project but by no means always "in" on the whole scheme as Himmler evolved it was the staff of the *Dienststelle* (office) on the Kurfürstendamm set up by Ulrich Greifelt, an SS colonel whom Himmler had used as a liaison man with Göring's Four Year Plan Office. This headquarters, known from June 1941 as the Staff Main Office to give it equality with other SS Main Offices, was a Supreme Reich Authority as well as an SS Main Office. Its personnel were a judicious blend of professional SS officers (though by no means Altkämpfer) experienced in SS administration since 1933, including lawyers and economists lacking previous SS ties. The latter were soon "assimilated" to SS rank without significant duties beyond RKFDV, while the former soon acquired high *police* ranks. Beginning rather weak vis-à-vis the Superior SS and Police Leaders and the police main offices, the RKFDV-Dienststelle rose to prominence in the heyday of settlement fervor and enthusiasm in 1942, thrusting aside such ancient SS citadels as RuSHa and challenging SIPO-SD planners for hegemony.[71] Its strength rested on the control over landed property in the east, in collaboration with Göring's installations, and on a network of executive personnel in the settlement areas who were assigned by Berlin and able to offer Superior SS and Police

Leaders additional power over their rural areas in exchange for police support in the evacuations and settlement stage. Most fully developed in the "settlement gaus" of Danzig-West Prussia, Wartheland, East Prussia, and Upper Silesia, they penetrated successfully into the Slovene borderlands but were ineffective in the General Government, the Baltic states, the Ukraine, and Alsace-Lorraine — where powerful Superior SS and Police Leaders and gauleiters acted without consulting the "planners." Neither Himmler nor even Heydrich was ever capable of drawing up a blueprint or master-plan of imperialist settlements or of vesting central authority in one SS Main Office, least of all in this ad hoc creation of 1939.[72]

Improvisation was often the chief strength of the middle-level SS officer-bureaucrat, and the RKFDV officers had to be good improvisors. Ideological trimmings of "blood and soil" were less important than simple faith in ethnic German abilities, in Germany's winning the war, in Hitler, and in the SS as a team. After that technical know-how, imagination, and energy made RKFDV junior officers in the field a kind of Nazi Peace Corps. Naive concentration on helping new settlers establish homes and put down roots could obscure for many the intimate tie with the genocidal expulsion of Jews and Poles. The men in the field had to see the connections more vividly, but they also had the compensation of direct knowledge of their own "good" efforts. The higher-ups in the desk jobs could be blissfully unseeing when it came to the disposal of the wastage of human lives, even ethnic German lives, caught up as those officials were in working out a big picture of a *Gross-Germanisches Reich deutscher Nation* (Greater Germanic Reich of the German Nation).[73]

## The Waffen SS

One of the most vigorous planning agencies of the SS in this last regard was not part of the RKFDV at all: the Germanic Guidance Office (*Germanische Leitstelle*) founded in March 1941 by the former chief recruiting officer for the Waffen-SS and wartime chief of the SS Main Office, Gottlob Berger. It was not merely his energy, which was bottomless, that gave the Germanische Leitstelle its importance and prestige. This forty-man organization, nominally within the SS Main Office, became the apple of Himmler's eye because it combined his Nordic preoccupations with a primary purpose of finding new recruits for the Waffen-SS.[74] Far from having things his own way, Himmler had a long struggle with the Wehrmacht to get sufficient recruits for more than one SS combat division in wartime. The person who achieved a final breakthrough in the winter and spring of 1941–1942 was Berger, the new chief of the SS Main Office since August 1940. The former SS Main Office chief, August Heissmeier—after an unimpressive year in charge of the Death's Head Reinforcements over which he had little real control and interest—was made Superior SS and Police Leader of the Berlin area, and the "new broom" of the vigorous SS chief recruiter soon swept out many of the place-holders of the 1930s from the SS Main Office. His bombast and fits of temperament turned the SS Main Office's quiet bureaucracy inside out. Ineffective negotiations that had rumbled on for months or even years with Wehrmacht offices were stepped up, and amid a great deal of noise and smoke, the Waffen-SS got more recruits as Operation Barbarossa took shape in the fall of 1940.[75]

Initially weakened by the loss to combat command of their chief, Paul Hausser, the old Inspectorate of the Special Duty Troops at Oranienburg gravitated back to the SS Main Office at Berlin, as the *Kommando (Kommando-Amt) der Waffen-SS*. But the skills and specialties of the staff officers of the former Inspectorate threatened to be dissipated under the crude and reckless hand of Berger at the Recruitment Office, so Himmler—never one to allow one SS office to become too strong—raised up Hans Jüttner, the chief of the Kommando-Amt, to be head of the independent Leadership Main Office (*Führungshauptamt*, FHA) in August 1940, practically an SS general staff for military training and operations. Thus, by 1941 the revitalized SS Main Office was freed, much against the will of its ambitious new chief, of the all-consuming responsibilities of immediate military policy making and the training of replacements. Instead, the Main Office could turn to making the SS a truly Germanic and European Order by *finding* the replacements—first among the youthful Jahrgänge of rural Germany; secondly among the ethnic Germans "returning" from areas ceded by Hitler to the Communists and from other German folk groups in the Balkans and eastern Europe; and lastly, though equally vital, among the Dutch, Belgians, Norwegians, Danes, and Finns.[76]

We have seen that even before the outbreak of the war, Himmler tied up recruitment procedures for the Armed SS with penetration into the ethnic German groups. By 1939 the future Main Office chief was pulling in ethnic Germans from Estonia, North Schleswig, Rumania, and Slovakia. His daughter's marriage to Andreas Schmidt, a Nazi Party chieftain in Rumania, made easier a haul of more than one thousand ethnic German volunteers from Transylvania in February 1940.[77] After the outbreak of the war, his network of ethnic German Self-Defense units located able young volunteers for formal military training in the Reich as soon as local situations stabilized. A main disadvantage, however, was the lack of regular recruiting organs and special replacement training units for personnel with specific linguistic and other cultural differences from Reich Germans. The new Main Office chief had to battle not only the foreign governments loath to part with cannon fodder and jealous party and even VoMi officials who did not like to see their best young men spirited off, but even Waffen-SS training officers and the new Führungshauptamt general staff, who disliked making special arrangements for ethnic German recruits. Since the Wehrmacht dragged its feet in cooperating with Himmler to get Reich Germans, the SS would have to get along with ethnic Germans as Menschenmaterial.[78] The conquest of the Low Countries, Denmark, and Norway was what really opened up the possibility of a Germanic-European combat community (*Kampfgemeinschaft*) which would justify special organizations and special training for the non-Germans. Even so, it was not until Barbarossa loomed up large before the top military planners both inside and outside the SS that the Germanische Leitstelle was authorized.

While Himmler had talked proudly of twenty Germanic volunteers in the Special Duty troops at an SS Generals' Conference on November 8, 1938, and the figure had reached one hundred before the 1940 campaign in the west, this trickle of enthusiasts was unimportant compared with the larger recruitment problem of the Armed SS.[79] Since the summer of 1938, Himmler had been determined to break through the one-division limit on his forces, if only to be prepared for the double duty of policing the home front and handling occupation responsibilities as foreseen in the Hitler directive of August 17, 1938. His tactics and those of his chief recruiter had been ones of conspirators. By creating as many different kinds of unit as possible, they could tap different sources of personnel and also conceal the growth ratio of the whole force. Thus, the SS retained the distinction between the motorized *Leibstandarte Adolf Hitler* (LSAH) and the Verfügungstruppe after the latter too became motorized in 1939; the former kept its special height requirements and its right to be committed integrally when the VT was made into a division in the winter of 1939–1940. The LSAH could be committed in the west as a reinforced regiment, while the Verfügungsdivision would be cannibalized to form another SS division, the Fifth or Wiking Division.[80]

Himmler converted the original three Death's Head regiments into the Death's Head Division during the fall and winter of 1939–1940 and furthermore pieced together a Police Division from 150,000 of his younger Order Police officers and NCOs. Moreover, in the Death's Head *Reinforcements*, which he organized into twelve regiments during the Polish campaign — swelling their numbers to 50,000 or 60,000 by June 1940 — he had a force of General SS led by Altkämpfer officers from the original Totenkopf units, supposedly occupation police but as draftees subject to transfer to the Waffen-SS.[81] He now introduced ethnic Germans, noncitizens and thus not yet subject to a German draft law, as a sixth ingredient.

Clearly, Himmler's problem in 1940 was that while he succeeded sneaking in more Armed SS volunteers under Hitler and von Brauchitsch's noses, he risked destroying what unity had evolved in the SS before 1939. The term "Waffen-SS," which he himself coined that winter of 1939–1940, represents more than an obvious subterfuge in dealing with an OKH jealous of every attempt to increase the Special Duty troops. It encompassed in its 75,000 men the Special Duty troops, the Death's Head troops — both twelve-year enlistments in the Totenkopf division — and emergency service men drafted for the duration in the police reinforcements. But its charisma, harking back to the oldest theme the SS shared with the Nazi movement — the *Frontgemeinschaft* (the front soldiers' community) — succeeded in bridging the gulf between young and old, Reich German and ethnic German, fanatic Nazi and ordinary patriot, and ultimately among the soldiers Himmler enlisted from Norway and Holland, Rumania and Croatia, Estonia and Turkestan.[82]

Heavy losses by the SS units active in the Polish campaign were no secret. This did not make the SS campaign for youthful volunteers or older party volunteers any easier, but Himmler managed to convert the spilt blood into a badge of honor for the widely proclaimed Waffen-SS. The right merely to draft his own General SS for the duration as "police reinforcements" could now be combined with a claim on ever-so-small a fraction of German boys of eighteen to twenty-two and sealed with the charisma of blood. The OKH reluctantly approved in principle the right of the Waffen-SS to have replacement battalions (*Ersatz-Bataillone*) just like the German army; this meant that if Himmler and the SS Main Office chief could find the men, they could channel them wherever they wished. The sharp separation between Death's Head units for nonmilitary duty and Special Duty troops for the front was chipped away in 1940 even before the organizational lines were destroyed. Thus, the OKH gave the Waffen-SS a share of the precious right to be a part of the Wehrmacht, retaining merely formal qualifications excluding the *Death's Head units* per se. Himmler would go on drafting his "police reinforcements" among the General SS, even retaining the Death's Head designation throughout most of 1940; but the draftees went along with the volunteers to the new replacement battalions and from there to new units of the Waffen-SS.[83]

Once the conception of the Waffen-SS had taken root in Hitler's mind, and the recruitment and replacement channels were laid down, Himmler could proceed to the formation of foreign volunteer units. Although he had assured von Brauchitsch on April 6, 1940, that no additional *units* would be formed, Himmler wrote Hitler ten days later that volunteer units from the Germanic countries would be recruited. On April 20 he secured Hitler's approval for a *VT-Standarte Nordland* made up of Danish and Norwegian volunteers; by May 25 Hitler had approved a *Standarte Westland*. A fifth Waffen-SS division (*Wiking*) might be carved out of the Verfügungsdivision; by channeling more Reich German and ethnic German recruits into the replacement cadres of the Verfügungsdivision the way was paved to get the third regiment for Wiking.[84] However, the German offensive in the west, like the Polish campaign, decimated Waffen-SS ranks, especially among the officers. The units had generally made a favorable impression on their Wehrmacht superiors, so that there would be less resistance to replacements, but replacements were needed thick and fast if the SS was to fulfill its ambition to become 10 percent of the peacetime Wehrmacht, as it once had been of the SA. With a peacetime Wehrmacht strength of sixty-two divisions, this meant six divisions, or about 125,000 combat soldiers. Heavy weapons and vehicles were also far below strength, even including the booty of Czechoslovakia and Poland to which the SS had privileged access.[85]

An additional anxiety in high SS circles proved groundless: that Hitler would demobilize, removing at one blow the 60,000 General SS men drafted for the duration. There actually was some demobilization on an individual basis of men over thirty-five, and three of the Death's Head Police Reinforcement Regiments were really deactivated as a consequence. But Barbarossa was sufficiently prominent at the top echelons of SS and Wehrmacht by August to shift the balance once more to cooperation, ending a phase of subterfuge on both sides in which the SS clearly had been the more successful.[86] Hitler's remarks of August 6, 1940, circulated by the OKH in 1941, define the new balance: a Waffen-SS *in wartime* amounting to "five to ten percent" of the peacetime strength of the Wehrmacht, to become the future Staatstruppenpolizei of the Greater German Reich, relieving the Wehrmacht of the onerous duty of protecting internal security. Incidentally, he also designated the Leibstandarte to become a brigade (it was soon made into a division).

There is no reason to suppose that these remarks represent other than Himmler's own views of the future of his political soldiers.[87] Even if Hitler did not give sufficient prominence to the occupation duties of the Staatstruppenpolizei, Himmler himself did so in a speech at Metz in

September 1940. Stressing the harm inherent in organizational snobbery within the SS, he pointedly referred to the SS actions in Poland — expulsions, killing, the settlement of ethnic Germans from abroad, guarding Jewish labor camps — as no less important than the exploits of the Leibstandarte. It was portrayed as a privilege for the SS man to serve as a soldier at the front, and the SS needed to spill its blood in order to earn the right to carry out the unspeakable yet necessary police tasks which most Germans shunned.[88] Symbolic of this mantle of righteousness which the Waffen-SS could wrap around SS crimes was the formal inclusion of all parts of the concentration camp system within the Waffen-SS. In reality, the dissolution of the special inspection of the Death's Head Reinforcements at the time of the formation of the Führungshauptamt (August 1940) along with the transfer of the Inspectorate of Concentration Camps to the latter meant very little more than the acknowledgement that the distinction between VT and TV troops had finally ended.[89]

The Germanische Leitstelle had a very modest prelude in the setting up in late 1940 of a special training camp at Sennheim in occupied Alsace, to provide ideological and physical conditioning for non-German SS recruits. By this means Gottlob Berger, the SS Main Office chief, hoped to get around the already familiar objections of military commanders that the East European ethnic Germans, Danes, Norwegians, Dutchmen, and Flemings were simply not ready for inclusion in regular German units. Particularly poor experience with the Nordland and Westland regiments seems to have motivated Himmler to approve this special treatment; and an increased flow of SS volunteers from southeast Europe after the arrival of German forces in Hungary and Rumania made it all the more necessary to prepare these volunteers physically and psychologically to share the lot of the Reich German SS. Over the protests of VoMi, the new Main Office boss was able to construct an elaborate network of specialized branch offices to look after the families of the volunteers, oversee the Folk Groups to guarantee the recruiting, and mold the recruits along lines different from those laid down by VoMi in agreement with their local leaders.[90]

To coordinate the activities of the Sennheim-Lager with those of field personnel in the Balkans and in the Nordic countries, Himmler authorized the creation of a new "Office Six" within the reorganized SS Main Office early in 1941. It proliferated in the next few months before the attack on the Soviet Union to three Main Sections: Ethnic-Germanic Leadership, Ethnic-Germanic Recruitment, and Ethnic-Germanic Education (Volksgermanische Führung, Volksgermanische Ergänzung, and Volksgermanische Erziehung). Its official title was the Germanic Volunteers' Guidance Office (Germanisch-Freiwillige Leitstelle), but the shortened form of Germanic Guidance Office became current almost immediately. The office's six regional subsections included the east, southeast, and south of Europe. While some of the paper plans envisaging "overseas branches" must be taken with a grain of salt, there is good evidence that Himmler supported his ambitious subordinate in his schemes to penetrate even into power structures of the party and Foreign Office such as VoMi and the *Auslands-Organisation* (AO), where the SS already had its supporters.

Like Hitler, Himmler was a thorough conspirator, who profoundly believed that power struggles even in his own ranks could be productive as long as he knew about them. The VoMi and AO chiefs had not proved sufficiently enterprising, yet he did not try to remove them or destroy them. He let his new Main Office chief, Berger, bypass them, as Berger had bypassed his former superior, Heissmeyer — the previous, ineffective chief of the SS Main Office. Himmler thus created a rival even to the RKFDV leadership, for ethnic German policy was so intimately tied to manpower problems that too much success in recruiting for the Waffen-SS could actually undermine the settlement efforts. This is exactly what happened, but of course winning the war in 1943 and 1944 was far more critical than RKFDV goals.[91]

In 1941, however, the need for soldiers for the Waffen-SS created new opportunities for empire-building in the SS instead of reducing them. In at least partial competition with the recruitment of replacements for the Nordland and Westland Waffen-SS regiments, national legions were started in Denmark, Norway, Holland, and Flanders.* While the former were recruited through straightforward SS channels and were henceforth treated as Waffen-SS (they did *not* automatically become General SS members), the latter merely had SS commanders and SS NCOs, at least some of whom were their own nationals. Recruitment took place through native Nazi parties. It was inevitable that friction should develop even within the SS structure itself, for the Germanic Guidance Office quickly "went underground," so to speak, so that not only local populations but also Superior SS and Police Leaders were in the dark about the source of funds, informants, and the purposes of complicated intrigues. Himmler intervened sporadically and just enough to contain the bitterness of some of the oldest and most loyal SS generals in the regional commands. Clearly, he was playing for high stakes — the chance to help make German foreign policy.

Heydrich's personnel of course kept very close tabs on the native poli-

---

*Flanders: There was no national legion for Belgium *per se* because the Nazis wished to encourage only the Flemish speakers. Later, however, the French speakers (Walloons) would also secure their own legion.

ticians used by the Germanische Leitstelle, but Berger's operatives kept their work very well concealed. The RSHA system certainly had no partiality for the new empire-builder and his charges, yet Heydrich's own foreign ambitions and his basic support of Himmler's strategy dictated a cautious pattern of weakening or removing highly placed individuals who exposed themselves, even SS officers, while permitting the empire itself to grow. The ruthless vigor of Himmler's chief recruiter was to pay off in the critical years of 1943 and 1944, when many hundred thousand SS soldiers flowed through the channels he had created in 1941. The short-term advantages, as measured in soldiers, were more modest.[92]

### The Russian Campaign

Waffen-SS strength on June 22, 1941, was 160,405, with a combat force of 95,868. Ninety percent of these men were Germans, still largely from the Reich proper. Ethnic Germans were considerably better represented in the replacement units and field formations not under the army but under the *Kommandostab Reichsführer* SS in the new *Führungshauptamt*. During the period of maximum commitment and before heavy losses were reported (September 1941), Waffen-SS strength rose to 172,000, with the additional forces nearly all engaged. They were still Reich German units sprinkled liberally with ethnic Germans: the First and Second SS Infantry Brigades, the SS Cavalry Brigade, the Combat Group (Kampfgruppe) Nord, and the old Ninth Death's Head regiment that had served in Norway in 1940. In fact, this whole new combat element was formed from a thin Death's Head cadre, the younger Police Reinforcements, and ethnic Germans. The foreign legions did not join in combat until November 1941, mostly in the Second SS Infantry Brigade at Leningrad.[93]

In discussing the shortcomings of these units, Himmler later was to observe that the "officer-cover" (*Führerdecke*) for many of them, and indeed for the whole combat SS, was thin. Yet the summer and fall of 1941 saw the SS officer corps in its best condition. An influx of new blood from the police, Wehrmacht officers, party and state officials, and able young doctors, lawyers, and youth leaders as well as the rapid promotion of thousands of young SS men from ranks of the General SS had raised the total of SS officers to nearly 20,000 — of which some 5,000 held Waffen-SS commissions. In many ways, the latter were the cream of the crop along with the other elite of the Reichssicherheitshauptamt (RSHA) apparatus (perhaps 5,000). Soon the blood-letting in Russia would destroy this cream, whose replacements would increase the officer corps and the whole SS far beyond the size of 1941 until both bore scarcely a token resemblance to the prewar body.

Three times as many SS officer dossiers (61,438) survived the war as there were SS officers in 1941. The great bulk of the remainder were not General SS expellees of the 1930s or early turnover from pre-1933 but *wartime commissions in the Waffen-SS granted between 1942 and 1945.* Tens of thousands of officers were thus added to the potential corps, whose ties to the prewar SS were tenuous or nonexistent; indeed party membership was also significantly lower in this group than in the first 20,000. Within the group of approximately 5,000 Waffen-SS officers of mid-1941 were not only the products of the SS-Junkerschulen since 1934 but the self-selected elite of the professional SS officers of the 1930s — VT, TV, and the battalion and regimental commanders of the General SS units who had volunteered for Police Reinforcement duty in 1938. Decimation had been their lot already in Poland; proportionately lighter losses in France and the Balkan campaign had added nevertheless to the absolute loss of experienced and committed SS leaders.[94]

Himmler's prodigal squandering of his officer corps in Russia after the lessons of the previous campaigns must be traced to his own convictions about the tremendous advantage which would accrue to the survivors for having shared in the blood-letting as a new "front generation," and also his desire to impress Hitler vis-à-vis the officer corps of the army and the party's Führerkorps. In view of Hitler's own character and that of the two rival leadership elites, Himmler's policy was not irrational; the risks involved were part of the SS charisma. It was essential, however, that enough of the leaven of the officer corps of the 1930s survive to produce a postwar crop with qualities similar to those of the front generation which had built the SS. Still quite possible in 1942, this necessary process became more and more attenuated in 1943 and 1944; even the police and concentration camp systems were inundated with officers from outside the SS, although this leadership preserved itself better while giving up much of the ideology of political soldiering for an empty bureaucratic *Pflichtbewusstsein* (consciousness of duty).

In the Waffen-SS the Germanic idea merged in 1942 with a pan-European concept of antibolshevism which survived the war, largely through the medium of the Waffen-SS-*Frontgemeinschaft* (front community). But the bearers of this concept had little in common with the administrative bureaucracy of the SS that predominated in the police, in the RKFDV system, and in the Main Offices, including the Führungshauptamt which supposedly ran the Waffen-SS. Indeed, because the Germanische Leitstelle preserved a good deal more of the amateur spirit of the prewar and even pre-1933 SS, it was still able to innovate and grow with the tasks of the war, thus bridging the gulf between the politisches Soldatentum of the SA from whose ranks its founder came and the European Landsknecht of 1945 and after.[95]

Success in breaking down the resistance of Hitler and the OKH to enlarging the Waffen-SS in the winter of 1941–1942, due in part to its demonstrated *Draufgängertum* (aggressiveness), meant that a battle royal broke out between the SS-Hauptamt and the Führungshauptamt over the management of the huge increment. While the doughty chief of the SS-Hauptamt claimed the whole credit for the breakthrough, there was little question that the growth in 1941 of a real SS general staff made up of military professionals for whom the organization of new units, their training, management, and staffing was routine reassured the Wehrmacht professionals — and perhaps Hitler too. The SA background of this headquarters, from its chief on down, seemed ample guarantee that it was not reactionary. But the old dilemma of the SA was to be repeated in the internal quarrels of top Waffen-SS leaders; a revolutionary elan was hard to keep consonant with military efficiency, and close aping of traditional military structures too easily vitiated the special virtues of an elite guard. These quarrels reverberated into the combat officer corps in terms of titles, saluting, uniform, decorations, and — far more important — noncooperation with other branches of the SS such as the Superior SS and Police Leaders.[96]

The Führungshauptamt (FHA) captured the General SS, strange as it might seem — since the chief functions of the skeleton structure remaining by 1942 were pre- and postservice military training and the care of dependents.[97] Outside the Reich, however, the Germanische Leitstelle maintained its lead in the care and development of the new SS and captured strategic positions originally held by the Leadership Main Office, such as the Censorship Bureau of the SS military postal system (*Feldpostprüfstelle*), through which it could build up a strong case against any practice which seemed inimical to recruiting success in non-German areas. Himmler and Hitler showed an avid interest in this intelligence operation, which was kept entirely separate from the RSHA.[98]

Yet the Leadership Main Office (FHA) managed to develop a pattern of Waffen-SS command-posts (*Standortkommandanturen*) within the Reich and Waffen-SS commandants (*Befehlshaber der Waffen-SS*) abroad, nominally subordinate to the Superior SS and Police Leaders — actually their close collaborators and aides — who often could "freeze out" a delegate of the SS Main Office chief (Berger) bent on increasing the role of the Germanic Guidance Office. The creation in 1942 of a separate Waffen-SS Welfare and Maintenance system independent of both the state system and the old General SS network signaled another attempt of the SS to operate *jenseits von Partei und Staat,* but it was equally a result of internal rivalries within the SS system itself. It was not long before this potentially strategic sluice-gate of favors and rewards was detached from the SS Main Office and reassigned to the Race and Settlement Main Office, where it was removed from the control of both jealous chiefs.[99]

When Himmler toyed in 1942 with the penetration of Rosenberg's dilapidated empire by sending the inventor of the Germanische Leitstelle to be Rosenberg's lieutenant, he considered giving the Main Office to Richard Hildebrandt, another aggressive SS general and Superior SS and Police Leader; but instead he kept the SS Main Office chief at his old post and used the other SS general as a trouble-shooter in the tangled affairs of South Russia, where Erich Koch was outdoing the SS in ruthless barbarity. It was not accidental, then, that Hildebrandt became the new RuSHa chief as well, since RuSHa had been made responsible for the postwar settlement of SS veterans and already had begun to set up large SS-run collective farms to train personnel and supply food for the troops. This whole operation fell outside both the SS Main Office and the SS Leadership Office, just as did the antipartisan operations.[100]

### SS Antipartisan Campaigns

While Himmler had underestimated the extent and toughness of the partisan movements, he had provided initially for their control by the Death's Head Police Reinforcements. When these units had proved ineffective in Poland and Norway, he substituted an extensive system of police formations drawn first from Reich police reserves and later from Baltic and Balkan volunteers not yet considered eligible for the SS. He supplemented these police battalions (later police regiments) with *Waffen-SS-Ausbildungs- und Ersatz-Bataillone* (training and replacement battalions) under FHA control after 1940. However, by 1942 it was clear that in Russia and Yugoslavia use of these types of unit by Superior SS and Police Leaders was not sufficient to check the growth of partisan-controlled areas. Cooperation among HSSPFs, the Führungshauptamt, and the Order Police headquarters was weak.[101]

So Himmler created yet another elaborate command system under one of the oldest SS generals, Erich von dem Bach-Zelewski, a former Superior SS and Police Leader both in the Reich and later in Russia. This time Himmler arranged — perhaps out of necessity — that the Plenipotentiary for Anti-partisan Warfare had no permanent troops but drew Waffen-SS troops and police formations on an ad hoc basis. Operationally, however, this new command was free even of Wehrmacht control. A series of campaigns in 1942 and 1943 were conducted so brutally and ruthlessly that nothing living was left in vital communications zones.

As in the case of Waffen-SS and police units temporarily assigned to SIPO-SD-Einsatzgruppen, criminal acts were demanded of the personnel, and these acts occurred as a matter of course; yet the troop units assigned had not been designed for this purpose, and few of the personnel intended such acts to be part of their service. It would be exceedingly difficult if not impossible to establish participation in specific acts by specific units, since the turn-over of these units was probably even greater than was intended, due to military exigencies. Himmler clearly preferred to keep such operations from resting on the conscience of his crack troops or coming to the knowledge of the German population; still, while rotation was regular practice, it had limits. Sadly enough, it appears that it was often easy for many Germans within the SS and outside — in the Wehrmacht, the state, and party sectors — to see and look away, thankful that *they* were not called upon. An increasingly large number of SS officers and units did, however, need to become involved with the failure of these "pacification drives," so that in 1944 the division between antipartisan measures (*Bandenbekämpfung*) and other assignments broke down. Wehrmacht units were increasingly involved from 1943 on, and thus the special status of FHA units outside the OKH sphere disappeared.[102]

### Evolution of the Waffen-SS Divisions

The Russians mauled the Waffen-SS so badly during the winter months of 1941–1942 that a total rebuilding of all outfits was necessary. In preparation for the "final" summer offensive of 1942, Himmler and his Leadership Main Office (FHA) pumped men into *eight* field divisions, four of which received tank battalions so as to become armored infantry. The Leibstandarte Adolf Hitler finally attained division strength as *1. SS-Panzergrenadiere* (First Armored Infantry Division), but its exclusive 1.72 meter height requirement had to be abandoned. Sepp Dietrich, its dashing commander, and a sprinkling of pre-1939 officers were left to carry on the "aristocratic" *Tradition*. Of course, not all the rest were dead — some had been taken out as early as 1941 to supply officer cadre for other units, especially those formed from Death's Head Reinforcements.[103] *Das Reich*, formed out of the *Deutschland* regiment and *Der Führer* of the old *Verfügungsdivision*, had already added a regiment of Death's Head Reinforcements in 1941 (the Eleventh Totenkopfstandarte, renamed simply the Eleventh SS infantry regiment). Now the Second SS Armored Infantry Division, *Das Reich*, acquired Georg Keppler as its commander by New Year's Day 1942, Paul

Hausser having been pulled back to the Führungshauptamt for staff duties. Keppler perpetuated what Hausser had made a firm tradition among the officer corps from the Verfügungstruppe of the 1930s — a strong orientation to the Reichswehr tradition and antiparty *ressentiment*.[104]

On the other hand, the Death's Head Division with Eicke, its intrepid Nazi commander who hated brass hats, still consisted in June 1941 of its three original regiments created in 1937, though without the regional designations. Its devil-may-care spirit and versatile military prowess contrasted favorably with army divisions, according to non-SS military specialists. An original disfavor associated with its concentration camp origins, reflected in a dearth of decorations after the western campaign, was reversed in 1941–1942, so that the divisional officer corps had an enviable record of decorations but also of losses. Himmler had to write very sharply to Eicke, who would not part with his old regimental commanders in exchange for VT "brass hats"; and the second regiment had to be cannibalized to preserve the other two regiments as early as July 1941. Attached to it during the gruelling *Winterschlacht* in the far north were the *Freikorps Danmark*, a Danish legion under Waffen-SS officers, and the Ninth Reinforced Totenkopfstandarte, renamed "Thule" for its valorous role in northern Finland.[105]

The Fourth or Police Division — unofficially a Waffen-SS division since April 1941, officially in February 1942, and publicly in September 1942 — languished in comparative obscurity with its old-fashioned horsedrawn vehicles and artillery and it strictly police replacement system (contrary to Himmler's own stated policy). It had the distinction of being the first SS division to have its commander, Arthur Mülverstedt, one of the crop of 1938 police generals, killed in action. Due to its character, it could only be used for besieging Leningrad, not conducive to the winning of Ritterkreuze by its police officer corps.[106]

The Viking Division and its commander, Felix Steiner, was the special favorite of the Germanische Leitstelle and its chief for the obvious reason that the bulk, although not all, of the Germanic volunteers were in the division's regiments Westland and Nordland. Its third regiment had been part of the original Verfügungstruppe: SS-Standarte 2, *Germania*. With the strongly profiled character of the division commander, who had transferred *out* of the Wehrmacht into the old AW in December 1933 and risen through the VT from its inception, the "Germanic division" acquired a marked spirit of soldierly independence and even insubordination which gave Himmler many attacks of stomach cramps and provoked his most choleric outbursts. After all, here was an officer corps of political soldiers par excellence — and in their officers' casinos "not even the Reichsführer SS was spared."

Since in 1941 a stark contrast existed between the lower-middle-class officer and NCO personnel of the German cadres and the upper-middle-class enlisted men from the Scandinavian and Lowland countries, Nordic dissatisfaction made it obvious that the officer replacements for this division should come from within rather than by transfer from other German units. Himmler was very reluctant to accept this separateness, as was the Leadership Main Office (FHA), while Steiner and Berger — with the latter's Germanic connections — pressed for field commissions and officer candidate school appointments. Himmler only succumbed in the winter of 1942–1943 after desertions and public unrest in the volunteers' homelands made clear the danger of treating this elite as second-class soldiers. But by then the volunteers were going into national legions, and the Viking Division drew its replacements from wherever they were available, Reichsdeutsche and Volksdeutsche included.[107]

The Sixth, or Northern (Nord) Division, got off to a bad start. Begun in the fall of 1940 as a motorized mountain combat group from the Sixth and Seventh Death's Head regiments of Police Reinforcements, these troops were placed under army command in Norway as early as November 4, 1940, where they got little training and plenty of guard duty. The soldier personnel were almost all General SS who had been called up under the 1938 emergency service law; officers and NCOs were personnel combed out of the original Death's Head regiments preparatory to the constitution of the combat division and from the Special Duty troops. Thrust into battle after marching six hundred miles across Lapland, the battle group collapsed; its company and battalion commanders lost control of their units, and the two regimental commanders, both former police officers, also had to be relieved. Karl Demelhuber, the combat group commander who only assumed command a few days before the battle, was a VT veteran who later demonstrated great military competence; but he too had to be pulled back to the Leadership Main Office.

In August 1941 Himmler persuaded the army group commander to reassemble the remains of the unit, which had been distributed in battalions; and with an all-new officer corps from VT veterans robbed from other units, the *Gebirgs-Division Nord* was created. Initially it was given as a backbone a third regiment, the better-trained and outfitted Ninth Death's Head regiment from Kirkenes. The new division, especially the latter regiment, gave a good account of itself in Finland. When the ninth regiment was removed to join the Death's Head Division as *Standarte Thule*, the Sixth SS "Mountain Division" became a fast, light (*Jäger*) unit with a reputation for being northern specialists.[108]

The formation of the Seventh Volunteer Mountain Division "Prince Eugene" sheds additional light on the improvising, not to say conspiratorial, tactics of Himmler and his recruiters. Immediately after the occupation of Yugoslavia, in the military government district of Serbia the ethnic Germans who were concentrated in the area called the *Banat* were directed to form the familiar Self-Defense units which had become the hallmark of SS and more especially SS-Main Office penetration. After a combing out of genuine volunteers for the Waffen-SS by Recruiting Commissions (*Annahme-Kommissionen*), Himmler simply ordered that ethnic Germans in Serbia be subjected to compulsory military service. Since the Serbian Banat had once been part of the Austro-Hungarian Empire, Himmler hit upon the ridiculous subterfuge that they were still subject to "the Tyrolese *Landsturm* ordinance of 1782." In spite of serious objections from the Ethnic German Liaison Office (VoMi) and the Foreign Office, the Self-Defense units were made the cadre of a new mountain division to be made up entirely of ethnic Germans. Its purpose was antipartisan warfare, and its theater was to be the Balkans, as revealed by its name and its first commander Arthur Phleps, a K.u.K. and Rumanian army veteran. Recruited and committed as it was, it is not surprising that the division gained a horrible reputation for cruelty.[109]

Himmler's Eighth Division, "Florian Geyer," a cavalry unit, began as two Death's Head cavalry regiments of Police Reinforcements set up in Poland early in 1940. As the SS Cavalry Brigade, they were thrown into Russia in the dead of winter; what was left over by the spring of 1942 became the cadre of the new division. Ethnic Germans increasingly replaced the Reich German General SS personnel from the fashionable Reiterstandarten. Ethnic Germans, especially from Hungary and Rumania, also preponderated as replacements in the two SS infantry brigades formed out of Death's Head Reinforcement regiments. Himmler and his recruiters resorted to the meanest kinds of trickery in these nominally independent lands, against the advice of the Foreign Office and the protests of VoMi and the FHA. Men were told they were going to the Reich for brief sport training or were being hired as laborers; those who caught on and hid had their homes destroyed by gangs of the party-led Folk Group. The Hungarian government also retaliated by denaturalizing the "volunteers" and their families.[110] It is little wonder that their Reich German officers tried to get seventeen- and eighteen-year-olds fresh from the Hitler Youth instead. Their initial experience with the small foreign legions in the Second Brigade (Norway, Netherlands, and Flanders) was also unimpressive; unlike the western volunteers for the Waffen-SS, these legionnaires were younger members of the fascist parties whose eyes were constantly turned back to their homelands, where vicious and deadly power struggles went on among the collaborating factions.[111]

The Waffen-SS had a strength of 222,000 men at the opening of the summer 1942 campaigns, of whom approximately 90,000 were recruited in 1941 or later. Between 30,000 and 40,000 of the new recruits were ethnic Germans; there were some 10,000 additional western volunteers. All the rest were German boys born between 1921 and 1924 channeled to the Waffen-SS through the Hitler Youth. They were still volunteers, many with extensive political indoctrination; but after February 1942 their parents' approval was no longer needed, opening up the possibility of intense pressure on seventeen-year-olds (class of 1925). The appeal of joining a first-rate military formation especially approved by the party and the Führer had to be balanced against the grim knowledge of SS losses. The SD reported that from the winter of 1941–1942 on, the German population also regarded the Waffen-SS as capable of being used against other German formations or in other capacities (antipartisan warfare). Parents' refusals were of critical importance, since the SS was still trying to recruit the boys before they could be drafted by the Wehrmacht. Some of these boys had been recruited while still in the *Reichsarbeitsdienst* (Labor Service), away from home and without a chance to be influenced by parents or clergymen. Later this tactic was to become a favorite method of SS recruiters. In the spring of 1942, however, Hitler still exercised a moderating influence, as can be seen in his table remarks about the necessity of keeping the Waffen-SS an elite guard by limiting recruiting. He explicitly alluded to the heavy losses as a badge of honor, as if to counteract implications of incompetent leadership.[112]

A larger incompetence, that of Hitler and his military professional advisors, soon overshadowed any question of the SS's technical competence. With scarcely enough time to rest from gruelling defensive operations for which the *schnelle Divisionen* of the SS were not especially suited, they were thrown into the July 1942 offensive under-strength and without operational training in any unit larger than a company. After brief triumphs, due in part to a shift in Soviet tactics from sacrificing large units in initial holding actions to extensive withdrawals to the Volga and the Caucasus, the SS divisions began to bleed to death in fruitless attacks along with the rest of the German army.[113]

But the SS losses had not even begun to show up before Himmler began to cash in on them and on Hitler's faith in the SS. It was only July 15, 1942, when the Waffen-SS examiners already began to apply the lower Wehrmacht standards to new "volunteers." Largely in deference to Hitler and because he alone could force a change on the Wehrmacht, Reich German youths still had to volunteer for the SS for another year. Especially for officer replacements and specialists, the struggle for volunteers continued hot and heavy.[114]

The General SS superstructure in 1942 was still largely intact, and even expanded to include not only annexed territories (Main Sectors Vistula, Warthe and Westmark) but occupied countries as well (Main Sectors North and Northwest for Norway and Netherlands, Ostland and Ukraine for the Soviet Union). This superstructure, minus the intermediate or Abschnitt level, continued to play an important role in recruitment through liaison and propaganda in premilitary training camps, farm and labor service units, and Hitler Youth security patrols. It could also be tapped directly for older personnel until eventually it became so hollow in 1944–1945 that it no longer functioned.[115]

*SS Armor and an SS Army Corps*

In the fall of 1942 in the midst of the heavy fighting that led up to the battle of Stalingrad, Hitler gave Himmler permission to make the First, Second, Third, and Fifth SS Divisions *panzer* (armored) divisions, and to motorize the Fourth or Police Division. He also approved the formation of an SS panzer corps superstructure. He does not appear to have authorized the formation of any more SS divisions, still clinging to the elite concept with which the panzer formations were quite consistent. The SS panzer corps was a tribute to SS loyalty; the time had passed when the army and Hitler himself would fear to concentrate so much fire power and elan under one SS commander. A powerful combine in the hands of a competent commander, the SS panzer corps of the Leibstandarte, Das Reich, and Totenkopf was constructed in the heat of combat around Kharkov in January and February 1943. Light on personnel and panzers, it nevertheless proved the advantage of larger operational SS units and made the last successful German counter-offensive on the eastern front at Kharkov an SS triumph. Yet the Fifth or Wiking Division did not get its tanks until another year had passed, and the Police Division only became armored infantry in 1944.[116]

The explanation for this is not far to seek: the SS triumph at Kharkov supplied Himmler with the justification he needed to compel the Wehrmacht to let him create more SS divisions. Three *more* armored SS divisions were called into existence in the spring of 1943, the Ninth SS or *Hohenstaufen*, the Tenth SS or *Frundsberg*, and the Twelfth SS-*Hitlerjugend*. Actually the Tenth SS was formed from the remnants of the First SS Brigade, while the first of several new *Panzergrenadier* divisions was made out of the Second SS Brigade (11.SS). The Ninth SS and

Twelfth SS, however, were brand-new constructions, with an SS-Führerkorps exclusively from the younger generation of the Junkerschulen. The fresh personnel of all these new divisions were Reich German volunteers between seventeen and nineteen, products of the Nazi educational system par excellence (they had reached puberty between 1936 and 1938). The SS recruiters found them ideal for panzer troops. Often more patriotic and healthy than well educated, and usually without any earlier contact with the General SS, they were as different a breed as the ethnic Germans or the Germanic volunteers.[117]

Speaking in October 1943 at Poznań, Himmler claimed that as early as December 1942 Hitler had ordered him to put together two additional SS divisions in France by mid-February 1943 in order to cope with an allied invasion. Up to 27,000 of the class of 1925 in the Reichsarbeitsdienst camps were promised, although only 15,000 had become Waffen-SS by February. The notion of armor was born even later, of course, made feasible through a loosening up of SS weapons procurement in 1943 in return for increased use of concentration camp labor for war production. It is typical of this latter-day SS growth that it preserved an elite character of sorts (armor), was improvised from the external necessity of Hitler and the Wehrmacht (fears of allied invasion), was carried beyond the original authorization (from two infantry divisions to three armored and one armored infantry, or *Panzergrenadiere*), and was given a "new look" which added further to the bewildering multiplicity of the SS. Every one of these units became crack divisions, respected by their Wehrmacht comrades-in-arms and by the enemy. There was no sense yet of "scraping the bottom of the barrel." On the other hand, efforts to turn these young people into political soldiers were necessarily minimal.[118]

*Four More SS Panzer Corps*

An additional factor in the forming of these units was the new military doctrine, absorbed by Hitler and Himmler from unit commanders, of the value and even necessity of panzer corps as relatively independent operational units. The First and Second Panzer Corps, under Sepp Dietrich and Paul Hausser, were set up as pairs of panzer divisions. The Third Panzer Corps was designed to realize the ambition of Wiking's commander to command a Germanic corps, albeit with only one armored division, Wiking itself. The new Panzergrenadier Division Eleven, *Nordland*, consisting of Danish, Norwegian, Flemish, and Walloon legions, the refurbished Nordland regiment, and the SS-*Freiwillige Panzergrenadierbrigade Nederland*, provided motorized infantry. Himmler even looked forward in October 1943 to two more additional armored corps! The new Ninth and Tenth Armored Divisions had not even received all their armor yet, but he was planning to match each with a new armored infantry division in January 1944, *Reichsführer SS* and *Götz von Berlichingen* (SS Nos. 16 and 17).[119]

For this purpose, Himmler was counting on the Reich German class of 1926, part of which was already *drafted* that same month. The sole survival of SS criteria in this case was a height requirement: 166 centimeters for those under twenty. This reduction in SS height requirements from 168 centimeters had applied since January 1943, on the grounds that the boys had not reached their full growth. The drafting of youths for the Waffen-SS had begun without fanfare in the spring of 1943, the final breakthrough occuring at Wehrkreis levels responsible for the call-up procedure. Such personnel, as indeed the vast majority of the ethnic Germans and volunteers from eastern countries discussed below were, strictly speaking, "nominal SS." They had special SS numbers or none at all, while General SS personnel — including eighteen-year-olds who volunteered and Germanic members who were not even in the Waffen-SS — continued to receive SS identity cards in the #400,000 series on into 1945.[120]

Thus, although the SS "victory" over the Wehrmacht was pretty hollow at this juncture, since the new recruits were scarcely elite in any sense, the General SS as a future potential elite still loomed large in Germany's future in the event of a negotiated peace or a German victory. In fact, Himmler envisaged twenty to thirty SS divisions in arms at the time of the peace or armistice, and from then on he would draft annual classes for Waffen-SS service on the military frontier, an SS preserve. In this way, the General SS would always be the product of survival of the fittest and always have a "front tradition." In the meantime the SS got an even wider range of choice for its future elite; they had access to the whole class of 1926 instead of merely those addressed by SS recruiters.[121]

*A European SS?*

The term "European SS" occurs for the first time in Himmler's conversations with his masseur, Felix Kersten, on March 6, 1943 — although the term "European volunteers" occurs earlier, especially in 1942. The shift in emphasis from a Germanic SS — for the two concepts had continued side by side since 1941 — corresponds to the development in 1943 of Waffen-SS units which were definitely not claimed to be Nordic. When we recall the gradual evolution of the Germanische Leitstelle and with it the notion of a *Waffengemeinschaft* (community of arms) as the basis for a political union after the war, it is clear how the racial theme and even the General SS as *the* vehicle of unity could be eclipsed, though not eliminated, from the minds of Heinrich Himmler and his close associates.

Himmler even alluded at Poznań in October 1943 to the formation of a fifth and sixth SS army corps, neither of them armored—composed in the first case of the old Seventh SS Mountain Division (all ethnic Germans) and a Bosnian mountain division, and in the second of a Latvian brigade (already in existence) and a future Latvian division. In the background of these units already lay more than a year of bitter SS factionalism and indecision on Himmler's part.[122]

*Himmler and His "Generals"*

Himmler had always needed practical advisors with realistic plans because of his tendency to substitute his wishes for present realities and his grasshopper mind, which conceived a thousand schemes only to forget them. He seems to have lost Heydrich even before Heydrich died in June 1942, out of mutual suspicion and rivalry; three or four less able men took Heydrich's place, so that never again did Himmler have the certainty that comes from a single planner at the helm. Since late in 1942 Himmler kept having disappointing encounters with his Gruppenführer. In plain terms, Himmler "could dish it out"—meaning harsh truths—"but he could not take it." The result was the pursuit of unrealizable and even inconsistent goals rather than give up any avenue of power. Paths of least resistance were chosen without his conscious awareness because men who survived as his advisors succeeded in tricking him simply in order to enhance their own power and to "show results." Individually these men, chiefs of the SS Main Office, the Leadership Main Office, the Reich Security Main Office, and the Economics and Administrative Main Office, were tough and shrewd. But pitted against one another, their practicality was used up enhancing the viability of their own sectors, often only in the short run.[123] The foreign SS legions were a typical product of "hard-headed SS realism" gone berserk. Not all were unsuccessful in military terms, but they cost the SS a very high price.[124]

Inroads on the Nazi-SS gospel of genetic purity came from several directions, but in the last analysis the force of necessity lay behind all the breaches. As early as 1939 the Czech police were utilized in the "Protectorate" of Bohemia-Moravia as one aspect of indirect rule, clearly with the approval of Himmler and Heydrich if not on their initiative. In Poland "direct rule" was believed necessary, through the use of Death's Head Police Reinforcements and German police battalions. The horrible consequences led even Hitler and Himmler to moderate this policy in the Scandinavian and the western occupied regions, through exten-

Heydrich funeral; SS soldier carrying Heydrich's decorations on a velvet pillow.

SS officers saluting Heydrich's grave.

sive use of native police.[125] Initial plans for Russia, however, suggest the intention to follow the Polish pattern except to emphasize German po- lice units and rear-echelon Waffen-SS troops instead of the nearly worthless Death's Head Reinforcements. Yet in practice Russia was the theater where the most extensive use of native police units took place. The second such theater was the Balkans. In both cases, the manpower problem in juxtaposition to technical difficulties of controlling vast partisan-filled territories with second-line German troops led both Himmler and the Wehrmacht to employ native forces. The SS actually lagged behind the Wehrmacht in 1941–1942 in the willingness to use such personnel, and it was partly because of competition with the Wehrmacht for power in these regions and for prestige with Hitler that Himmler had to bow to improvising suggestions among his own SS staff and grudgingly permit police units of Ukrainians, Russians, Lithuani- ans, etc.[126]

When we recall the ideal of a future Staatsschutzkorps of SS and Po- lice, it is not very difficult to see the dangers of admitting the camel's nose under the tent. However, the rationalization employed by Hey- drich and Himmler with regard to the Czechs was applied first to the northern Baltic peoples, Finns, Ests, and Latvians—that a winnowing process involving service, or being put to a test (*Bewährung*), might eventually make a certain portion of these peoples worthy of assimila- tion. With a thin underpinning of racial theory and history—and an element of willingness to collaborate on the part of certain segments of these populations—the analogy of elite formation from SS practice in Germany and subsequently in Scandinavian and western countries helped SS planners in 1943 and 1944 convince Himmler, Hitler, and themselves that they were still operating consistently. Only when their inconsistency became visible to everybody else late in 1944 did they ac- cept the fact that they themselves had wiped out the SS elite concept in the process—the SS becoming in the minds of Germans and non- Germans merely another part of the German forces, and for many an evil part.[127]

### Foreign SS Legions

Thus, the SS Main Office moved imperceptibly from the creation and use of police and special antipartisan units separate from the Waffen-SS to the creation of Waffen-SS units for special use in partisan-filled areas (the Bosnian unit, later SS Division 13, "Handschar").[128] The notion of converting a police unit after Bewährung into Waffen-SS was already present in the development of the Fourth or Police Division. Similarly, the assignment of "nominal" Waffen-SS status to police formations guarding the concentration camps (increasingly ethnic German and even non-German) for the convenience of pay, welfare, rationing, and privacy from Wehrmacht prying had made a precedent ready to hand for units like the Bosnians, which by no stretch of the imagination could be considered Germanic. The technique of using Waffen-SS cadre (*Rahmenpersonal*) had been perfected by the Leadership Main Office (FHA) not only for the handling of the young German recruits but also for the ethnic Germans after 1940.[129] Thus, ready at hand were many of the forms and patterns out of which Himmler's technicians, far more than he personally, improvised division after division for him to "present" to Hitler. He did not even dare to tell Hitler in 1945 just who all the thirty-eight-odd SS divisions were, not to mention Bulgarian and Rumanian battalions, Indian, Turkoman, and Transcaucasian legions, and three Cossack cavalry formations.[130]

In order to have a Waffen-SS-*Ist-Stärke* (actual strength) of 330,000 men in 1943, the SS Main Office had had to add as many men as comprised the whole Waffen-SS in September 1941 (172,000) — estimating losses during the winter of 1942–1943 conservatively at around 60,000. Thus, a swamping of the Reich German personnel had to occur in 1943. Ethnic Germans from Hungary and the Balkans as well as the resettlers of 1939–1941 taken from their new Polish farms and VoMi camps amounted to over 40,000; western volunteers, largely from Holland and Belgium, amounted to another 40,000 or more; Letts, Estonians, and Bosnians already under arms in Waffen-SS units must have totalled at least 40,000 — all compared to new Reich German additions of some 50,000.[131]

*A New SS Officer Corps?*

The Waffen-SS officer corps available to train and lead this motley array consisted almost entirely of Reich German personnel, 10,702 as of July 1, 1943. Of these, only 4,145 were designated as career or professional officers, about 1,000 of whom held ranks above the rank of captain. The latter were in effect the military elite of the SS. A year later a quarter of the officers had fallen, with losses of professional and field grade officers at a not appreciably lower rate than reserve and company officers. Thus, a figure of 5,102 professional Waffen-SS officers on July 1, 1944, meant an addition of some 2,000 new officers including field grades. The "military elite" commanding the European SS of 1944 was, then, far from congruent with the SS officers corps of the later 1930s. Former Wehrmacht and police officers stood shoulder to shoulder at high officers' conferences with the younger generation from the VT and TV of the 1930s, NCO's then at best, who had passed through the

Junkerschulen or had no special training at all. Neither their exploits nor their crimes as perpetrated through their units can be traced directly to the Kampfzeit.[132]

Indeed, more of the General SS officers corps of the 1930s were in the Wehrmacht than in the Waffen-SS, and most of the latter were reserve officers. It is probably true that their training duties and command responsibilities toward rear-echelon replacement units were the real vehicle for transmitting values and techniques of the Kampfzeit to thousands of Waffen-SS recruits. Political soldiering, in terms of the old values, survived in the boot camp and the garrison, the replacement depots and infamous special duty units like the *SS-Bataillone z.b.V. der Waffen-SS*, the Kaminski Brigade, and the Dirlewanger Brigade.[133] The newer officers corps either had a conception of the political soldier associated with the imagery of a Germanic or European comradeship in arms, or had none at all. In fact, the *Nur-Soldaten* (only-soldiers) preponderated in the Waffen-SS. Himmler's betrayal of Röhm's SA avenged itself upon the SS by the AW "refugees" of 1935 becoming the worst offenders in shedding the political. Could it have been otherwise? This was the would-be officer-elite of the SA; when Himmler let the SS become "a department store where anything and everything could be found" — like the SA of 1934 — the Nur-Soldaten recognized a familiar milieu and acted accordingly. They retreated into the "inner emigration" of the front.[134]

By the fall and winter of 1943, "the front," now in Italy as well as in Russia and the Balkans, extended far behind the *Hauptkampflinie* (HKL, chief line of battle). Partisans and infiltrators made "rear echelon" an almost meaningless term. The conditions of the Kampfzeit, of civil war, returned, for which the Nur-Soldaten were ill-equipped. The inner emigration was hard to practice for an extended length of time; nevertheless the determined SS officer could now get to the front much more easily than before, since it was harder for Himmler or the Main Office chiefs to hold such a man back due to the burning necessities of the battlefield. Sooner or later such men were struck down, eliminating selectively a vital part of the Waffen-SS. The officer records for the whole year of 1944 are mute and tragic evidence of the disappearance of "only-soldiers" and the survival of *political* soldiers. Naturally, the deepening front took its toll of Draufgänger in rear-echelon special units, police formations, and antipartisan defense operations closer to home in the General Government and the Slovene marches.[135] Still, even with heavy allied bombing creating *Kriegsschauplatz Inneres Deutschland* (battlefield inner Germany) for which, after all, the SS had been developed, the home front was still safer and more rewarding in promotions in 1943 and 1944.

Thus, the nature of the SS and of its incipient officers corps was contradictory to the very end; there was an increasing alienation of its combat forces from the goals of its political-soldier leaders. Its mass armies of foreign mercenaries and Landsknechte had more in common with the Nur-Soldaten who led them than with Main Office chiefs and the Reich German honorary SS whose profits and prestige were increasingly tied to a victory for Himmler's empire. The task on the home front of staving off popular revolution and foiling putsches called for very different sorts of men; by their very nature these men were better equipped to survive even defeat.[136]

Even on paper Himmler's acquisition of the title Reich Minister of the Interior in August 1943 and Commanding General of the Home or Reserve Army after the July 20, 1944, fiasco contributed remarkably little to the long-dreamed-of fusion of party and state, SS and Police, into a political soldierdom — the Staatsschutzkorps (state security corps).[137] The curse of the SA of 1933 and 1934 pursued the SS of ten years later. Overloaded with opportunists, top-heavy with staff positions, dependent on and therefore afraid of its combat forces, and above all lacking the self-discipline which sets limits to ambition and commitment, the SS of 1943 through 1945 failed to "shake down" as a functioning institution. In spite of last-minute abortive efforts on the part of individuals, even Himmler himself, the SS failed to consolidate. Efforts to transcend its own past, the shortcomings of the state and party to which it was bound almost against its will, and the grim realities of unconditional defeat simply tore the SS apart.[138]

## Denouement

At the time of the allied invasion in the west, the *Gesamt-SS* (entire SS) had reached its maximum size — 800,000 men, not counting strictly police units of all kinds and subsidiary foreign mercenaries like the Cossack divisions. At least 100,000 SS men had already fallen as Waffen-SS; more than that many of the General SS were serving with the Wehrmacht; and no separate record was kept of SS casualties in army, navy, or air units. Some effort to maintain contact with General SS personnel in the Wehrmacht continued in 1944 by means of newsletters from the Berlin offices and regional commanders; and, as has been noted, notification and care of the spiritual and physical needs of survivors was supposed to be extended to General SS casualties in the Wehrmacht. However, these duties were being neglected already in 1942; in later years when the bombings destroyed the Berlin offices, scattering records and personnel widely over Germany, and local and regional staffs were reduced to the bone, the casualties of the General SS went unnoticed unless some wounded soldier made his appearance on furlough. Such individuals were quickly caught up by frantic home front administrators, the soldiers' old General SS status giving one or another agency connected with the SS and Police first claim on them. Often they were added to the Waffen-SS precisely to keep them on the home front instead of returning to their Wehrmacht unit.[139]

The General SS itself was partly run by such severely wounded men as well as by those temporarily returned to active General SS duties from *Stamm-Einheiten* (SS reserves of over age forty-five). The 64,000 General SS men *not* in the Wehrmacht, Organisation Todt, Technische Nothilfe, Reichssicherheitshauptamt, or other organizations for which one could be drafted (*notdienstverpflichtet*) were in fact largely members of the overage SS reserves, a kind of vestige of Altkämpfertum. That Himmler was quite interested in preserving this remnant and was far from abandoning the concept of a General SS is shown by the plethora of his orders in 1943, 1944, and even 1945 solely for the purpose of defining some feature of it or making changes surely meaningless in a dying structure. It is hard to avoid the conclusion that the General SS was headed for political oblivion along with the SA, and for the same reasons.[140]

Himmler did not relish the truth that all of his real power apparatus lay, after all, within the state sector: the Police, RKFDV, and Waffen-SS. The General SS had been a vehicle to carry him *into* and not out of the state apparatus. What remained of that vehicle was a mere esprit de corps, *der SS-Geist*, transmitted from the Altkämpfer to the Waffen-SS and the younger administrators of the Hauptämter. Perhaps still viable in the Germanic conception — with its claim to transcend the German state system — as the esprit de corps of a European SS, Himmler's realm was now little more than a comradeship of arms, unsophisticated anti-bolshevism, and a Landsknecht-elan which fought to avoid dying.[141]

Scattered about the Reich and its shrunken empire lay the fragments of the future Staatsschutzkorps in the form of many hundreds of separate Waffen-SS units ranging in size and complexity from armored corps to temporary *Marschkompanien* (companies in transit); Security and Order Police headquarters as well as police regiments, battalions, and hundreds; Superior SS and Police installations with RKFDV, SD, and Waffen-SS rear-echelon command posts; and the dozen or more SS Main Offices, each already split between Berlin and countryside locations.[142] The coordination of this hydra's many heads should have occurred in the personal staff of the Reichsführer SS and Chief of the German Police. However, what coordination occurred was largely the work of the adjutants of the Main Offices and of Rudolf Brandt, the *deputy* chief of the *Persönlicher Stab*. Karl Wolff, the actual chief of that organization—no match for the "rival satraps" vying for Himmler's ear—had not unwillingly taken his leave of "Byzantine" Berlin to become the Supreme SS and Police Leader of Italy in 1943. His deputy, Brandt, was an affable nonentity with a talent for getting along with everybody and especially with other adjutants whose horizons were no wider than their file-drawers. To this latter-day breed of SS bureaucrats posterity owes the *Schriftgutverwaltung* (Records Administration), which preserved the "Himmler files" so rich with trivia for the years 1943–1945.[143]

Coordination in the form of *Gremium*, or advisory council of Main Office chiefs, Superior SS and Police Leaders, top military commanders, and the like hovered in the plans and projects of the men around Himmler; but the Reichsführer SS himself could only talk of an Arthurian Round Table "after the war" and gather together one hundred and fifty or more Gruppenführer to digest his rambling *pronunciamentos* instead of talking back. Modeling himself after Hitler, Heinrich Himmler denied the SS a chance to depose him and thus also a chance to coalesce sufficiently at the top to avoid being broken apart by the successive blows Hitler's Reich experienced.[144]

As it broke, the SS and its officers corps fragmented along lines of class and regional cleavage that had never quite been sealed over: SS soldiers went with non-SS soldiers, SS bureaucrats with non-SS bureaucrats, SS fanatics with non-SS fanatics, and SS opportunists with non-SS opportunists. The political soldiers of the SS who still were alive in 1944–1945 did not have enough in common to transcend these fractures, especially since they lacked a leader.[145] Himmler allowed himself to be caught up in the state apparatus, first via the Police and the Interior Ministry, reforming German justice out of existence; then in the military arena, playing at generalship without regard for the military potential of his troops—thinking only of 1918 and determined to slaughter hundreds of thousands rather than yield territory. The high quality of many SS divisions and the SS armored corps did much to prolong the war which was to have been fought till "five minutes after twelve," in Goebbels's classic phrase. But Goebbels and Himmler lacked the willpower to depose Hitler and join what was left of their respective power systems to preserve Germany within the frontiers of 1939, the goal of the vast majority of German fighting men and of the Resistance itself.[146]

Even if this goal was not achievable, neither the allies nor the Germans in 1944 doubted the capacity of the Reich to stave off defeat for a year or two, inflicting terrible casualties on both sides. Thus, Himmler

had something to bargain with as he picked up the threads of the Abwehr and Resistance ties to the allies, only to stampede the plotters into
precipitate action on July 20 due to arrests made necessary by their ineptitude. The SS had been founded to prevent just such a counter-
revolution against Hitler and the party; the imagery of 1918 had often
played its part in strengthening Himmler's hand over the police and the
Waffen-SS. Yet when the long-feared Dolchstoss occurred, its main effect was to interrupt Himmler's own feeble efforts to cast the SS itself in
the role of a counter-revolutionary junta! The RSHA was barely efficient enough to prevent other elements of the SS from collaborating
with the Resistance and with foreign intelligence — including Himmler
and his former chief adjutant; it did not figure in preventing Hitler's
death.[147]

In the aftermath of the plot — which resembled the atmosphere of the
summer and fall of 1934 when SA and SS purged their comrades in ner-
vous anxiety that they should not be next — the SS leadership assisted in
the purge of business, bureaucracy, and military comrades with mixed
emotions, even heavy hearts, believing that the victors this time were
Goebbels and Bormann. Instead of reaffirmations of SS unity that fall
and winter, the purges brought new splits in the Main Offices. Rather
than sticking together, the Staatsschutzkorps broke up into rival intrigues, with Himmler heading the pack.[148]

While some SS military leaders, bureaucrats, and policemen contributed to the bestiality of the German efforts to keep Finland, Hungary,
Slovakia, and Rumania in the war,[149] others with Himmler in the lead
sought to trade Jewish lives and other "expendable material" for trucks,
food, passports, time, and good consciences.[150] Himmler meddled in
foreign policy far too long, yet there was no uniform SS foreign policy in
Italy, the Balkans, Scandinavia, or the west.[151] Eichmann complained
that he got better cooperation from the Foreign Office than from the
Superior SS and Police Leaders. They in turn waged their own wars
with the Foreign Office, High Command, and with SS Main Offices increasingly manned by SS lieutenants and captains — the adjutants determined to go down with the ship. Few Superior SS and Police Leaders
died with their boots on, preferring to save their skins by collaborating
with the invaders.[152] However, Waffen-SS officers were prominent in
the kangaroo courts hanging army deserters and shooting civilians who
talked of surrender.[153]

Needless to say, there was nothing cohesive about the last waves of
the Waffen-SS. With a paper strength of nearly 500,000 in spite of losses
totalling 300,000 the rag-tag units of grounded Luftwaffe and sailors;
the sallow, starchy complexioned boys of sixteen and seventeen; the

confused and frightened eastern Europeans with only a dozen words of halting German; the grimy, tired Kampfgruppen of thirty or forty veterans of too many winter campaigns — this Waffen-SS was no longer an elite corps of political soldiers.[154] Bravery and self-sacrifice grew apace in some units, under commanders who had learned how to lead — some in the Kampfjahre, others in the Junkerschulen, and far more on the battlefield. Cruelty and sadism, useless destruction and pillage multiplied in other units whose leaders as often as not were on Himmler's blacklist for drunkenness, neglect of duty, corruption, and cowardice. Both kinds of SS officers had their counterparts many times over in the Wehrmacht; it was merely that "when they were good, they were very very good; when they were bad, they were horrid."[155] The Sixth SS Panzer Army in the Ardennes offensive was merely a moderately well-equipped German military formation; and even the trick formations of Skorzeny's American-speaking jeep drivers only preserved the elan of their fathers in the free corps. These were not political-soldiers.[156] The much-feared Alpine Redoubt, with its intrepid SS divisions, was a better trick, which Himmler and Goebbels perpetrated with Göring's help. But in the end the hardest fighting SS units were chewed up in Budapest, the Baltic states, and Berlin, so that Himmler knew better than to migrate south to a defenseless land of pretty scenery.[157] In strange contrast to the corps anthem, "Wenn alle untreu werden" ("If everyone became disloyal"), Himmler, his Supreme SS and Police Leader in Italy, several army corps commanders and assorted division commanders, numerous Superior SS and Police Leaders, and countless SIPO-SD officials dickered with the allies for a negotiated peace — not for Germany but for their own immediate entourage. The SS had ceased to exist.[158]

SS insignia at Heydrich's funeral.

# 8

# Conclusion:
# Behind the Mask of Possession

Scholars and nonscholars alike have had a field day assessing the Nazi SS. For more than a generation now, the men in the black coats have been weighed in the balance and been found wanting. The ineradicable fact that their most decisive activity was the death-machinery that destroyed many millions of helpless and harmless Jewish men, women, and children has led to monolithic condemnation and sweeping generalization about "the SS." This book's Conclusion cannot and must not reverse that condemnation of the system and the men who ran it. Yet it seems that our last remarks should be devoted to a deeper understanding of the forces and mechanisms that made possible the "tragic fulfillment" of Hitler's and Himmler's theatrical fantasies. Considered in that attempt is a need for differentiation among those men in the black coats, a return to the German and European social and economic context referred to in the Introduction, and some insight into our own times with their own dreams and illusions.

It should not be forgotten that the history of the SS is fundamentally a part of the history of the national socialist movement and that this movement only lasted twenty-seven years. On the one hand, then, both the SS and the Nazis went through very rapid development, changing and growing so fast that generalizations for periods shorter even than a decade are often inadequate. On the other hand, the whole evolution was truncated by total disintegration caused by massive military defeat, partition of their geographical base, and systematic proscription of all national socialist writing or political activity. Processes of change, whether of adaptation or internal decay, were thereby cut off, absolutely. The whole trajectory of SS experience, of SS thought, and of SS plans can be followed for less than a quarter century, which even for a human lifetime is not very long. In our kaleidescopic century the twenty-one years, 1925–1945, of the Schutzstaffel risk being taken out of context, isolated and reified as some sort of epic — albeit of evil, for most observers — and *incorrectly* used as a lesson. Lessons there undoubtedly are in the history of the SS, but we should take care that we learn them from stubborn reality, not from images and theater.

"The SS" was anything but a monolith. Though sometimes presented as such, during its lifetime, and excessively thereafter, the SS was more often manipulated to appear to be different things to different viewers. The mask of possession was merely one of these manipulations, though it rested on some features of the Order. But the substance of the SS did change — so much that it is tempting to say that it was never one specific phenomenon at all. Still, at least from the early 1930s, in the mind and at the hands of Heinrich Himmler the SS developed continuity. Some of this continuity came from the vision he shared with Hitler and with countless Germans: the wish that in 1918 there had been strong men with authority who could have struck down the rebellious soldiers and sailors and their civilian supporters, rallied the German armed forces, and fought until "five minutes past twelve" — thereby securing a peace more consonant with Germany's posture in Europe, especially eastern Europe. The illusion of 1914 that victory could be *willed*, and that German institutions had the inner resilience to withstand anything their combined enemies could direct against them, was a dogma of the nationalist right. But the idea of creating more popularly based German institutions and a band of political soldiers to defend those institutions was Hitler's own contribution, even if it was the Storm Troops and not the SS that Hitler had originally conceived for this role.

Another part of the continuity came from the intrinsic need in a pugnacious and violent movement to have not merely a "headquarters guard" (Stabswache) but even more to have a body of committed roughnecks who could be asked to do quite literally "anything." This also was Hitler's own conception, for he had no use for the liberal utopia of John Stuart Mill in which truth and good judgement can battle it out, using words and logic alone. The war, the revolutions, and the postwar European political milieu all gave the lie to expectations of a return to pre-1914 conditions. Hitler had recognized the falsity and superficiality of the genteel and intellectual tradition in German politics in any case. Again, the original version of these roughnecks had been the SA, who were to guard the meetings, protect the speakers, beat up opponents — and very literally commit any imaginable crime on orders of the Führer. Hitler, not Himmler, had already singled out a Stabswache and then a Stosstrupp in 1923; and in 1925 the Schutzstaffel was called into being not so much as a replacement for the SA but *as special duty units*, again antedating Himmler.

Yet Heinrich Himmler definitely put the impress of his own enthusiasms on the "permanent SS" in two regards: the role of snoopers within the party and in German life, high and low; and the task of being a future gene pool for the German people. Here we find Hitler in the background. While he authorized Himmler's detective proclivities, it went against Hitler's grain to give any Nazi a monopoly of anything — Himmler built up a mere police potentiality into so deadly an instrument that nearly all rivals were intimidated out of existence. Goebbels and Bormann did keep systems of their own but did not quarrel openly with the SS; Hitler parried Himmler's investigative power by enlisting Ernst Kaltenbrunner of the Reichssicherheitshauptamt (RSHA) to watch Himmler. It is doubtful if Hitler ever took the SS gene pool seriously. Nevertheless, the general Nazi support for eugenics, "race purity," and biological viewpoints ("Blood and Soil," body-building, nature religion) helped make the peculiarly SS version of racism seem very appropriate.

The SS, then, reflected Adolf Hitler's world view, not merely by being his sworn liege men in a feudal sense but by evolving under Himmler's hand into a Staatsschutzkorps — a corps of state guardians willing and able to carry out any task, abominable or disgusting, on orders from its leader. The SS was made by Himmler into a network of influentials, of spies, and of lodge-brothers (in spite of the alleged SS hatred of all lodges), each of which overlapped the others. This aspect of the SS did not reflect Hitler; it reflected Himmler — and, more than Himmler, the unmodern bourgeoisie of postworld war Germany. In its world view the failure of Germany to win World War One, the mishandling of the German revolution, the depression, and SS members' own checkered careers *must* imply a fundamental faultiness in the twentieth century. To such men, as to Himmler, the "rottenness" was everywhere; they imagined conspiracy and enemies of Germany, of its ways and ideas, in each social class. They had been taught that obedience and diligence was everything, but they had learned in war and business, in politics and human relations that more was needed. That "more" was perceived as a blend of volunteer spirit and personalized loyalty, of ruthless self-seeking and the harshest self-abasement. In the fantasy of a future biological community of *Sippen* (clans), Himmler and his generation indulged in a reversal of their fears of being inadequate and degenerate. As a "sworn community of superior men," SS volunteers imagined that they had been co-opted by Adolf Hitler's truest henchmen into becoming the ancestors of *the better Germany* they projected into the future. The unreachable, just, and moral society which had failed to emerge after 1918 — or even after 1933 — could be something they carried in their loins! The destructive urges and hatreds born of their frustrated lives were channeled outward away from those near and dear to them toward the foreigner, the alien, and those symbols of awakening self-doubt — the Jews and the Catholic clergy. Anticlericalism was almost as strong in the SS as racism, but this trend also was only partly Hitlerian. The SS was kept tethered vis-à-vis the church, though only up to a point.

The mental furniture of Himmler and his intellectual cohorts was the warmed-over folkish world view that well-educated Germans regarded as slightly ludicrous. National socialism itself was not a set of ideas at all but a set of attitudes and aspirations, covering what political scientists like to call primordial feelings — such as fear, resentment, envy, and rage. In its earlier versions (1919–1923), national socialism was relatively naive and honest — and hopelessly crude. Its political soldiers *were* soldiers, or if not they were young men who thought soldiering was breaking heads and politics was shouting and booing. After its refounding, national socialism slowly took on the trappings of bourgeois sophistication in the form of a Goebbels, the Strassers, or even a Hermann Rauschning. Yet clever slogans, cartoons, posters, and handbills were only means to a single end, the ballot box and electoral majority. In this respect, the Nazis were in their element, for their ultimate goals and their fundamental world view was well concealed by this resort to the enemy's weapons. It was in this double game that the SS began — hardly more than local Stosstrupps but with the difference that as picked men from the party, they could be stamped with the pseudo-superiority of the "Master Race." The best of the Nazis must thus be racially superior — if not wholly by external hallmarks at least by behavior, *Haltung* (bearing), and *attitude*. It was virtually inevitable that such a group would find its Himmler, a devotee of human breeding and Nordic archaeology, an amateur detective and would-be officer. He was a good bureaucrat, at least for many years — though ultimately the very antithesis of orderliness and routine. Himmler had the skills to organize the primitive SS units into a unified system of party security in a no-nonsense fashion admired by Hitler and many other bigwigs; yet he was, or seemed to be, relatively harmless as a man or a thinker. His predilection for a certain amount of racial hocus pocus, cephalic indexes and marriage approval for his charges, did not seem to matter much.

Weimar Germany may have had more than its share of cranks and windbags, of head-breakers and conspirators. Societies undergoing fairly rapid change are likely to exhibit such phenomena. In our century fascism seems to be symptomatic of a badly blocked society trying to shake itself loose of the blockages by massive reverberations. Fascists are part of the reverberation mechanism, cast up by the force of the social jerkings and tremors, but their own purpose is to use the reverberations to seize control over the society. Once in command, they seek to control the thrusts and vortexes in the rapidly changing system, yet in so doing they free some of the blockages while choking off adaptive mechanisms in the subsystems of their society. Weimar Germany spewed up the Nazis in its agony, just as it spewed up the Stalinist KPD with its, "Heil Moskau!" and all the other forgotten "remedies" for a sick society. The German people, like all of us, deserved better of their institutions than they received. Few of us are wise enough to invent new institutions; the Germans tried, and their copying was very well meant. The breakdown of their electoral system took some time to register, and as it broke the tremors benefited the Nazis. The Nazi strategy was itself clumsy and contributed to the general chaos without necessarily furthering the Nazi goal of a *Machtergreifung* (seizure of power) because they did not know where to turn for support at the polls. Gradually they put together a reasonably strong coalition of voters from the country, the small towns, the comfortable (yet frightened) suburbs, and among the unorganized unemployed; but they were stymied by the toughness of the political institutions so recently erected, notably the presidency and the chancellorship. End-running these institutions, occupied by none-too-intelligent human beings, the Nazis succeeded in frightening the business and financial world with exaggerated images of a Götterdämmerung of private property during a bloody civil war with the communists. Thus, the nationalist right was persuaded by its financial supporters to let the Nazis *pretend* they had made a Machtergreifung, the famous "taming" maneuver, which gave the Nazis a chance to seize actual power in stages from within. For this strategy the Nazis were quite well prepared, but here too the crudity and indiscipline of the movement threatened to give away the game before the victory. It was to be the SS that kept the game alive when Röhm and the SA became impatient.

It was not so much that German institutions were all that fragile in 1933, but that too many Germans had temporarily ceased to trust in them. In a press agentry of theatrics and bombast, the Nazis taught followers to put their trust in a kind of *renovatio imperii* (renewal of empire) constructed of a popularized and simplified version of the conservative revolution (e.g., the Third Reich). Appeals to technocratic tastes were joined to pseudo-religious themes linking Hitler with Luther and even with Jesus Christ. "German Socialism" in the form of a paternalistic welfare system was linked to a militarized shop-floor with the boss a junior Führer. Of course, not all Germans swallowed this bait, but German society had gone too long without charisma, having had to put up with too much cynicism and too many threadbare appeals to the lesser of two evils. The opportunity of 1933 was skillfully exploited by thousands of Goebbels; and in spite of *Schönheitsfehler* (beauty marks) of wanton violence and cruelty, the public mood by late 1933 and early 1934 was one of acceptance of Nazi leadership in a restored and stabilized conservative Reich symbolized by the ancient Hindenburg and the "loyal" Reichswehr. The restoration of faith in what were to prove to be badly eroded institutions — notably the army, courts, police and state bureaucracy — was a Nazi trick. In the long run everyone was hurt by this trick, even the Nazis themselves, although the party and the SS would gain immense power by pulling wires from within the empty shells.

The SS that took part in the conspiracy to destroy Röhm and his top brass already had some of the features of the Staatsschutzkorps towards which Himmler had been heading his unified Stosstrupps since the early 1930s. From being merely local groups to protect speakers and spy on party goings-on, the SS was made into striking forces in 1931 and 1932 which could aid and stiffen Storm Troop expeditions and street warfare, and which it was thought might combat a communist coup or carry out a Nazi Machtergreifung after some landslide victory. Its units were often simply slightly more respectable (and more dependable) Storm Troops. Some of their number misbehaved according to Nazi standards, but others could be used to "clean out" pockets of "Stennes SA" in 1931. In the actual Machtergreifung, the SS role was absorptive: to sponge up the business and professional classes, the bureaucrats and the academics, the police and the jurists turned off by Storm Troop hooliganism yet still anxious to jump on the most likely bandwagon. This sponging-up had begun at least two years earlier and was part of the NSDAP strategy of creating their version of the leftist "front organization," known by the Nazis as "auxiliaries." In 1933 this process gave the SS access to money, influence, and power — without confrontation and bad blood. In this respect, it resembled the party itself, which also absorbed many times its weight within preexisting organizations; but un-

like the party, at least for the peacetime years, the SS did not swell up
with fellow-travelers. The SA, on the other hand, had already swelled
rapidly in 1932, if not earlier, and in 1933 became a monstrosity by adding the Stahlhelm. Yet its leadership preferred the confrontation style,
defiance and contumely. If SS men regularly joined with SA men in
headbreaking, housebreaking, and drunken escapades, the former did
not boast — did not make speeches for the press or challenge editors to
fisticuffs. They were kept silent, and a few were punished.

Above all, Himmler had systematically created a state apparatus for
himself in the secret police units of the Länder, capping the edifice with
the Prussian Gestapo. This network was in principle detached from the
authority of local administrations and was united only in Himmler's
person. Thus, the feudal features of the Führerstaat (which would be
reproduced and ramified from 1933 to 1945) appeared very early with
respect to the secret police. It may also be noted that here the SS — and
especially the SD — were essentially growth points, organizing centers,
pressure groups, or entry facilitators. The police units did not *become*
SS, nor did the SS become the secret police. However, control over the
Gestapo and other secret political police made rivalry with the SA for
influence over the rest of the police at least an equal match for Himmler.

The Röhm purge cannot be divorced from the intimidation of the
German right at the same time, and in this respect the usability of the
SS against *all designated enemies* must be emphasized. The SS may
have seemed for a time to be a refuge and rallying point of the upper
classes, *Bildung und Besitz* (Culture and Property), and even a potential *fronde* — there is evidence that the right-wing resistance still
thought so in 1943! They were in deadly error, and this was already true
in 1934. Here the name of Heydrich must figure, for while we now
know he was always loyal to Himmler and certainly did not push him
around then or later, Heydrich had the brains and imagination that
were lacking in the majority of the SS officers of 1933. Specifically, he
helped Himmler to "frame" Röhm and other SA leaders, which was
highly necessary in view of Hitler's ambivalence about striking them
down. Again, the police apparatus available to Himmler to strike at the
SA was partly the work of Heydrich. Here, though, we must mention
both Kurt Daluege and Sepp Dietrich as well. Daluege was the conduit
through which Himmler developed his connections with Hermann Göring, all-important in gaining the Gestapo in Prussia — although without
Heydrich, Himmler might have been outmaneuvered by Daluege, who
was there first. Göring was Himmler's co-conspirator against Röhm; indeed without Göring, a Himmler initiative against Röhm even supported by Heydrich was unthinkable in 1934. Thus, Daluege was the tie

that bound Göring and Himmler together. On the other hand, it was Sepp Dietrich to whom Himmler entrusted the Stosstrupp functions at Bad Wiessee—using the embryonic Leibstandarte to do the very dirty work of the "long knives." The three men, Heydrich, Daluege, and Dietrich, were movers and shakers in a corps that prided itself on *Draufgängertum* (the *gung ho* spirit). But none of them contributed any ideas to the SS.

It was Richard Walter Darré who enriched the SS beyond Himmler's own brand of blood-and-soil agrarian mysticism. Not Darré alone but his coterie of young and middle-aged *Agrarromantiker* (agricultural romantics), with their biological racism and confidence in human breeding, provided the SS from 1931 on—and especially after 1933—with a pseudo-scientific rationale for SS exclusivism, elitist ambitions, and penetration into the field of real estate. Although Darré himself would become more and more preoccupied with short-run policies designed to prepare Germany for war, his personnel, his friends, and his disciples would continue to give the SS the patina of *Wissenschaft* (science) at least for the ordinary German, including party members. Even the Ahnenerbe with its separate academic ties and its own ambitious strivers and schemers could never replace or erase the decisive impact Darré had had through the Rasse- und Siedlungs-(Haupt-)Amt. While the formal focus of the Ahnenerbe on ancestors could have suggested a fructifying historical enrichment of SS, Nazi, and German ideology, Walter Wüst and Wolfram Sievers chose to chase down Himmler's will-o'-the-wisps and to toady for Himmler in the field of military medicine (the experiments on concentration camp inmates). Nor was the work of Günther d'Alquen at the editor's desk of *Das Schwarze Korps* of any substance. That journal remained a shadow of the Reichsführer SS, in spite of apparent efforts to express the aspirations of a younger intellectual generation. Perhaps the ideas of Otto Ohlendorf and his friends concerning a centralized, planned economic system to replace the allegedly planless and selfish capitalism of German big business deserve to be classed as both theoretically interesting and of possible importance had the SS survived the war in a Nazi state. The trouble was that Himmler was a little too powerful, both in the SS and in the Nazi state: his crotchets and his judgement acted to stymie development of a systematic and consistent intellectual agenda for the SS. Ohlendorf was tried and executed for having commanded a killing unit in the USSR—one of his sidelines.

It is often remarked that totalitarian systems, no matter how inefficient and clumsy they are in areas related to caring for human needs, are quite effective at repression and war. In these latter areas, the name of Theodor Eicke stands out for his contributions to SS "achievement." For Eicke made the SS concentration camps the horror that they were, reducing opportunities for inmate self-protection and designing a system of brutalization for guards that totalitarian communism has never surpassed. Balkan, Latin American, Chinese, and Japanese prison camps, not to mention North American "chain-gangs" and other dehumanizing improvisations, all have demonstrated that human systems of torture and the destruction of personality are world-wide. Still, the SS was forever imprinted through Eicke with a style of dehumanization involving the perpetrators as well as the victims. This style was carried over into the wartime Totenkopf-Standarten; and through the so-called *Polizeiverstärkung* (police reinforcements) which they trained as replacements for regular divisions, it was carried into the field. It would of course be wrong to "blame it all on Eicke." Yet it was specifically Eicke who earned the sobriquet "Papa Eicke" which carried over into his Death's Head Division until his death in 1943. Why was this? Perhaps because his unique brand of primitive appeal to the emotions, his eyeball-to-eyeball violence, and his apparent lack of discrimination in punishments and rewards (resembling the stereotypic German *streng aber gerecht* father-figure) was congruent with the immaturity of the kind of volunteers drawn to the SS. This is not an argument for a special kind of German personality but rather a commentary on the apparatus that national socialist seizure of power had made possible, for which the SS supplied the raw material. Like so many other Waffen-SS generals, Eicke was long on courage and aggressiveness; he "looked after" his unit when it came to stealing from other units (even SS) and refusing to give up personnel to them, but he sacrificed his men wantonly to the Moloch of battle. He became in death a Waffen-SS legend that survived the war and in which his concentration camp feats were, it would seem, forgotten.

Oswald Pohl also contributed to the reality of the SS in the slave-labor empire of the wartime concentration camps. Albert Speer insists that the whole enterprise was a terribly inefficient operation, yet even in his last work, Speer makes it clear that Germany needed and used those wretched, starving men and women for its war production.[1] Like Eicke, Pohl was not a man of broad mental horizons. But, again like Eicke, he was entrepreneurial. In fact, his staff — partly from the camp administrators, partly from the General SS business managers and administrative officers — knew how to make personal fortunes out of their SS economic activities, and that quite legally and above board by prevailing standards. Their theft of human labor for their own advantage was combined with the theft (exploitation) of labor for SS advantage above and beyond that of the Reich. "Aryanization" was hardly an SS and Police monoply and, when privately practiced to excess, was sometimes punished; nevertheless the profitability of the Final Solution — both for individual personnel and for the SS in general — is important for understanding the intimate relationship between the SS willingness to "do anything for the Führer" and the probability of pay-off. Indeed, the whole integration of the concentration camps with the world of industry and finance, the cooperation of so many branches of the non-SS bureaucracy with the destruction of European Jews, brings us close to one of the secrets of SS success. Even before the seizure of power in Germany, the SS gave itself out as somehow near the seat of power, in fact as wielders of that power "on orders." Once the Nazis had power in plenty, the SS became identified with enforcement. Its manner of silent reserve was the direct opposite of the Storm Troops' noisy clamor for a share in the spoils. But yet the SS did get its share, and it let the business and professional world know that cooperation with the Reichsführer SS was minimally a token of safety from harassment and potentially a connection worth money. The judicious use of the carrot and the stick did the rest. It would be too simple to say that the SS was a Mafia or even a conspiracy to muscle in on the spoils of the German economy by sharing them with the more cooperative members of the economic ruling class. The SS took a good while to develop its blackmail methods, and perhaps if Ohlendorf and the younger generation of SS economists had ever risen to the top of the SS empire, their second Machtergreifung might have resembled Stalin's methods of destroying potential opponents. National socialism was a truncated episode in which the total war economy was of very short duration. It is a mistake to single out any one trend or phase in that kaleidescope as determining.

We have observed that Himmler liked to say he had both a good and a bad side. Ulrich Greifelt of the RKFDV (Reich Commission for the Strengthening of Germandom) and Adolf Eichmann of the RSHA (Reich Security Main Office) — each stands for the banality of a side of Himmler and the technocratic social engineers who served him. Neither Greifelt nor Eichmann molded the SS. Rather, they were molded by their experience and the opportunity it gave them to solve technical problems in which human beings were a matter of numbers. But the problems and the solutions became different from those encountered in the exploitation of prison camp labor or even in Aryanization, each of which found their ecological niche in the rapacious Nazi economy. The effort to collect, "evaluate," and resettle many hundred thousand "valuable" Germans in time of war — locating them in homes and shops and on farms of displaced Poles and Frenchmen — plus the commandeering of scarce transportation to cart off Jews to death camps while ammunition and replacements were waiting for trains entailed the use of SS-and-Police methods that flew in the face of the war effort, often went against party and surely military intentions, and cost the SS money and personnel. In Greifelt's case, the man coordinated a vast network of underlings and equals without much personal ego or effort at self-aggrandizement. In the case of Eichmann, another man was swelled with pride although only an *Obersturmbannführer* (lieutenant colonel) due to his ability to "get things done" in the face of all obstacles. Both were social engineers. Each is conceivable outside the SS — even outside of Germany, for instance, since Vietnam in the United States — but the SS created for them, and for thousands like Greifelt and Eichmann, a field of operations in which power was available in quantities not ordinarily accessible to such limited personalities.

The role of Wölfchen, Karl Wolff, in molding the SS is quite a different matter. The chief of the Personal Staff of the Reichsführer SS illustrates the Byzantine aspect of the whole national socialist edifice. More than any of the chiefs of the SS-Hauptamt — with the exception of Gottlob Berger — whose role was never determined by that post — Karl Wolff *managed* the SS. He did not do this by decrees or organizational changes. He did it through communications, or the interruption of communications. Fundamentally, Himmler, like Hitler and most of the leaders of national socialism, realized that regular bureaucratic structures were strait jackets. Therefore, they practiced "authoritarian anarchy" in exercising the privileges of spontaneity available to the powerful. But Himmler had evolved from a highly bureaucratic individual, so it was as he was approaching age forty and had already created quite systematic repressive agencies as well as top-down chains of command in the police and military SS (Leibstandarte and Verfügungstruppe) that he gradually relied on the Personal Staff to sift and winnow SS problems for him. Thus, matters that should have gone to the Personnel Office, the SS Main Office, or even the Race and Settlement Main Office found their way to Karl Wolff, who became a sort of "SS post office" — routing and rerouting inquiries and suggestions, complaints and gossip. Wolff posed as the "friend of all," and indeed he was not malicious, though certainly self-aggrandizing and dishonest. By wartime, persons outside the SS knew of his critical role and also knew that Himmler himself consulted Wolff frequently, with the result that the latter became much more than a "post office;" he was a sort of *eminence grise*, a mellow and occasionally sardonic critic of the foibles and insufficiencies of the great and near-great. He seemed to many "their friend in court" — and to many a dangerous enemy. It is not so easy to describe what he did to the SS; he helped to make it even less a rational system of command and policy than Himmler's basic design — yet in fact he did essentially what Himmler wanted. He smoothed and softened the rougher edges of the Reichsführer's moods and reactions, thus tending to encourage higher ranks to think they could "get away" with whatever they wanted to do. Of course, he humored Himmler and went to great trouble helping him carry out many of his fantastic schemes and whims.

The creation of the Waffen-SS cannot of course be credited to any single man. Bernd Wegner has argued that Himmler himself planned from 1934 on to create an alternative to the Reichswehr tradition of Nur Soldaten in the form of a cadre for a future national socialist army.[2] While persuasive, Wegner's thesis rests on circumstantial evidence. The formation of a highly creditable trio and then quartet of crack regiments by 1939 was accomplished by Sepp Dietrich, Paul Hausser, Hans Jüttner, and several dozen other officers, of whom many joined the SS after 1933, often with prewar or Weimar experience in the German army. The work of the staffs of the Junkerschulen before 1940 should also be mentioned as forming a type of military officer respected and valued beyond ranks of the Waffen-SS. While Waffen-SS boot camp was perhaps akin to that of the U.S. Marines, the ignominy and dehumanization characteristic of the Wachsturmbanne and Totenkopf-Standarten should not be attributed to these commanders. There is little doubt, however, that Waffen SS units were designed and trained for use against "traitors" — as in the case of June 30, 1934 — and against a German insurrection, whether from the left or right. Thus, the principle of absolute obedience and perfect loyalty, though not yet further perverted by being employed against helpless prisoners, was prepared ideologically and morally. Recognition of what Sepp Dietrich had expected his men to do at the time of the Röhm purge could not have been omitted from VT education. Still, this ruthlessness seems to be of a different order from that of the camps, and we should be careful as historians to keep the intentions and practices of 1934–1937 from all blending together as indeed they did after 1939. That they did so may be readily attributed to Himmler, to the "nature of the SS," to national socialism, or to the demands of war; all are partly to blame. It is less certain that something called "the SS mentality" should be added, made up of the determination not to let anyone stand in the way of the Führer or of a German victory, steady indoctrination with the importance of obedience, and local unit pride. Himmler gradually merged the Death's Head units, the Police Reinforcements trained by them, and the crack VT (Verfügungstruppe) regiments not systematically, as if by policy, but instead by improvisation. It would seem that the Waffen-SS was never born but, like Topsy in *Uncle Tom's Cabin*, just grew.

The "Almighty Gottlob" — Gottlob Berger, sometime SS recruiter, chief of the Germanic Guidance Office, last head of the SS Main Office — certainly would not agree that the Waffen-SS "just grew." For Berger the care and feeding of the infant institution was a twenty-four-hour job. He did not really enter the scene until 1938, at a time when the probability of war with the likelihood of severe casualties had become pressing for Himmler. It was also a highly delicate time for the Armed SS because mobilization spelled dominance by the Wehrmacht; in fact SS units were to come under the army's disposition in time of war. Berger was not only instrumental in developing and coordinating the Ethnic German Self-Defense units in Czechoslovakia and Poland (which fell outside the Armed SS proper and also were not subject to army control), but the chief recruiter laid the foundation for a "Nordic SS" *before* the Nazis had conquered any territory in western Europe. Thus, Berger unquestionably shaped the future of the wartime SS, both in the use of noncitizens as recruits as well as in the conception of a European SS. Berger was the chief agitator for a multiethnic SS from 1942 on; no other SS leader came near him in responsibility for this feature of the later Waffen-SS.

Here again we come to the knotty issue of the immanence of a European SS within the ideology and make-up of the "Order." National socialism had a hate-love relationship with everything foreign, perhaps an exaggeration of a form of insecurity not limited to Germans. The foreign admirer of the Nazis was much appreciated but was usually discounted. The Italian Fascist, though theoretically a "brother-in-arms," was often ridiculed. True admiration seems to have existed for the "Nordic specimens" among the Scandinavians and for certain of the English aristocracy. There is little in the evolution of the Schutzstaffel to prepare us for the European SS; it appears to have been the improvisation it has usually been painted. And yet . . . there was the intrinsic appeal of a racial elite, the fundamental doctrine of "good blood" scattered throughout Europe, and the SS as an antibolshevik, "classless" lodge. It would seem that in the national socialist dream of an "Order" — certainly not an invention of Himmler — there lay half-concealed, half-revealed, the potential of a pan-European rather than merely pan-German (or pan-Germanic) rallying point for the old elitist strivings of so many ethnic traditions. From such a vantage point we might be inclined to ask not how Berger and Himmler could come upon the European SS ideal but rather what features of the German SS got in its way.

The answer is that most of all the institution was itself unripe. The burden of assimilating ethnic Germans into the Reich as a whole, not to mention into the party and the SS, required time. Of course, the heat of war did something toward amalgamation, but the reverse was also true: the war generated suspicions and jealousies which all-too-easily could be discharged against the less than 100 percent German human being. SS training and spirit were not particularly well designed for assimilation, even though "strict orders" required it. The case of the Nordic recruits seems to have been doubly complicated by language difficulties and their expectations of autonomy. Unlike the ethnic Germans, the Nordics "got their way" after a fashion, or at least caused the uncompromising SS to compromise. After experimenting with a dual system of regular (German-led) units *and* foreign legions, the Waffen-SS developed the German-led but linguistically and culturally homogeneous division, which by 1943 could be applied to other than Nordic groups. Much of this experimenting and adaptation was engineered by Gottlieb Berger, who shared with Himmler the dishonesty and intrigue necessary to suck these men up from other employment in the Reich, from their homelands, or from the Wehrmacht.

Berger's and Himmler's expansion of the Waffen-SS, more especially by its internationalization, was certainly opportunistic insofar as they created a nonelite military system. It could only be justified within SS tradition as an extension of the elite, racial idea to all European societies. Probably the idea of a western European comradeship in arms with or without the antibolshevik crusade can be seen as consistent with the pacification of that region concomitantly with the expected armistice with Britain. Here there is no necessary contradiction with the picture of a future national socialist army being groomed to replace the Nur-Soldaten who did most of the fighting. The racial-ideological reinforcements from western Europe might have been allies in this ambition. However, the fateful attack on the USSR, more improvisation than inevitable fulfillment of Adolf Hitler's fantasy, doomed the SS as it doomed national socialism. It is probably a mistake to look for some profound or Machiavellian reason for Himmler's turning to quantity more and more between 1939 and 1942: he was a "true believer" in his Führer. While Hitler had not needed the numbers Himmler provided him before 1941, that was not known ahead of time. In 1941 those numbers were not enough, so Himmler with the help of Berger got more — many more — even at the temporary cost to the "SS idea" of consistency. After all, the Waffen-SS uniform did not supplant the membership card from Munich. Or, we may ask, did it? Certainly not in Himmler's mind — even in 1944!

It was left for the thousands of Waffen-SS officers of 1941–1945 to

shape the military aspect of the corps.[3] Largely men between thirty
and fifty, they were often but not always Nazis, some but not all veterans of the street fighting of 1930–1932, and a great many doing what
they had always wanted to do—command men in a war "for Germany."
Common denominators other than these are few and far between.
Many were impatient with Himmler, whom they regarded as "unmili-
tary," and they had little use for the racial or historical education the
SS-Hauptamt still supplied as late as 1944. They gave the Waffen-SS the
reputation as a "fire brigade" for threatened sectors of the front, they
had less than their "share" of cowards and turncoats in adversity, and
they worked very well with non-SS units and officers. They also included more than their share of "last-ditchers" who led their men to useless death and executed civilians who flew white flags.

In analyzing what the SS "was" and what it became, it is critically
important, then, to specify time periods and viewpoints. Viewing the
SS from the inside first, and from the center outwards, so to speak—
Himmler's conception of the SS certainly evolved between 1929 and
1945. In the Kampfzeit (before 1933), its small size and pick of relative
quality among party stalwarts—who were after all themselves volunteers under conditions of a wide range of political choice—made the SS
for Himmler like a personal troop. This troop he hoped to pound,
squeeze, and hone to an instrument of power for Hitler, for the party,
and for his own ideas—especially as an embodiment of his dream of a
future racial elite. Gradually from 1933 on state power lured him into
becoming the Reich's policeman but not before he had used the SS to
construct that state office and in such a way as to retain in branches of
the SS various reserve strengths—even striking power—and, equally
important, refuges from the exercise of state power against him in the
form of the concentration camps, the Gestapo, the SD, and even the
General SS. It is doubtful that any or all of these could really have secured him against Hitler had the Führer turned upon him; in fact they
might not have even protected the Führer against a determined military coup, as was shown in 1944. However, neither eventuality dis-
turbed the peacetime evolution of the edifice, so that by 1938 Himmler's
view of the SS-and-Police structure increasingly appears to be that new
national socialist breed of institution, *jenseits von Partei und Staat*, a
Führer-Institution. However, he continued to nourish and develop the
SS as a community of families, still with the gene pool in mind—
although it is clear that in view of the numbers involved, he tended to
think in terms of his officer corps, more especially the higher officers
(*Standartenführer*, colonels and above).

As the war years came and multiplied, Himmler was increasingly dejected about his conception of the SS, for although the war had seemingly brought wonderful opportunities for international expansion and the "blooding" that he felt necessary to justify the existence of a troop with such elite claims, he felt the SS slipping out from his control. He often spoke with satisfaction of the instrument he wielded against the internal enemies of the "movement" and was proud that in the SS-and-Police he truly did have an institution capable of doing the dirty work despised by everyone else in Germany—killing the Jews. Yet he was always fearful that "1918" would come again and the SS would not be quite united enough or selfless enough. Through the SD system, indeed through the whole network of contacts he had in business—the Wehrmacht, academia, and the media—already in 1942 he had become all-too aware how much depended on the Führer, the armed forces, the SS-and-Police to stave off an inner collapse. He complained that the Waffen-SS, which he had allowed to overshadow everything else except the police in his system, was going its own way; its officer corps were becoming Nur-Soldaten.[4] Still, he was bewitched by power potential, and he followed out every lead in international politics—now using the SS ploy, now the police, and inevitably the Waffen-SS. As Minister of the Interior, and even more as Commander of the Home Army and Army Corps, Himmler showed that he had wandered beyond his own design for the SS and beyond his own ingenuity in adapting it and his new positions to the Führer-constitution. But by this juncture (1943 and 1944), that half-myth and half-aspiration was itself showing signs of cracking under the burden of defeat. Strangely enough, Himmler in 1945 thought his police powers would be most appealing to the western victors, although no doubt he still imagined that an antibolshevik crusade "five minutes after twelve" would find use for what was left of his "European" SS. He may even have had the conspiratorial experience of the first SS up his sleeve for postwar years. His suicide remains enigmatic; the same uncertainty and ambiguity which apparently lay behind his stomach cramps dogged him in the last hour of his captivity. He chose to disguise himself as a member of the military police (a category liable to be detained), then voluntarily identified himself as Himmler and only bit the cyanide capsule when he was sure he was going to lose it.

Among the Altkämpfer (those who had joined before 1933), the view of the SS changed with their degree of adjustment to its changing demands.[5] For the many "losers" who had to be consoled with becoming unpaid SS lieutenants in 1933 or 1934, and retired by 1935 with the job of a factory night watchman or meter reader, the SS had become another part of the uncaring *Bonzenherrschaft* (rule of the bigwigs). For some who found a good civilian job and "connections" through the SS after 1934, the SS remained essentially a lodge, which sometimes took too much time and made inconvenient demands such as leaving one's church. Many of these became reserve officers or NCOs in the Wehrmacht and had little or nothing more to do with the SS. But others climbed from rung to rung of business and SS rank, of state office or party hierarchy and adjusted their official and unofficial views of the SS accordingly. There was a wide spectrum of loyalty to the Himmlerian ideal; minimal official loyalty meant responding positively to requests from SS headquarters, not just from Himmler personally — paying the numerous exactions required (which kept going up) and being "active." The latter meant more than attending a monthly meeting: it meant wearing the uniform, making appropriate appearances and speeches, getting one's family and relatives out of the church, and *getting married and having children.* Unofficial views of the successful Altkämpfer who did not make their living as SS officers range from deep personal commitment to Himmler, to the "Idea," and to the SS as shown by unstinting voluntary activity and dangerous service at home and at the front, to callous use of SS friendships, the uniform, position, and ideology for crass personal aggrandizement. As the war came, more and more SS members experienced the moment of truth, when talk of sacrifice and parallels with the Kampfzeit became very real and immediate. In 1943 and 1944 Gottlob Berger was still routing out of comfortable rear-echelon posts some of these types; he and others were still preserving others at home for the sake of SS power and influence in 1945.

At the very core of the SS between 1933 and 1945, there were a few thousand Altkämpfer with paid positions.[6] Already by 1939 their numbers were diluted by paid personnel who had joined in 1933 or later, especially in the military and police fields. As the war years continued, more and more of the paid positions went to men who had been in the SA or to those not even in the party before 1933. But it is this first group of Altkämpfer which should have been the leaven that gave the SS of 1937, 1940, and 1942 unity; and several hundred, perhaps even five hundred, of them did. Yet they were not enough; the other paid Altkämpfer succumbed to the "evil" which Himmler identified as breaking up the SS into soldiers, police, doctors, lawyers, business managers, and worst of all "SS bureaucrats." It is doubtful if even the possible five hundred shared the whole dream of the SS, but they showed by their evolution that they comprehended that it must become an SS-and-Police to withstand the fate of the SA and perhaps the party as well — becoming an adjunct to a reconstituted Wilhelmine state. They did not treat the police as an apparatus of the state *only* but as fighters for national socialist measures, no matter what those might be. Similarly, as soldiers they did not recognize the rights of civilians, of prisoners of war, of neutrals, or of the clergy. Victory at any price, the virtual rejection of a calculus of costs in blood and material — these were the attitudes of the minority of Altkämpfer commanders. Again, as policy makers and regional managers, this type of Altkämpfer thought of the SS first, last, and always in comparison to the self-interests of the civilians, the party, or the state bureaucracy. Such men were a thorn in the side of many other Nazis, and in their ruthlessness often seemed and sometimes were less interested in German interests (meaning those of the German people) than in SS interests. However, there were three or four times as many top SS leaders with SS numbers below #200,000 who did not fit these terrible — nay, damning — charcteristics. And of course the joiners of 1933, 1934, and later did include men with many of these ruthless traits, although rarely in the breadth and depth necessary to bridge the orientations of police, soldiers, administrators, doctors, lawyers, and so on.

So to summarize the view of the SS from within among the top brass who were *not* Himmler's ideal: Between 1929 and 1933 the SS was a "cause" that paid and promised to pay even better. Its doctrines and methods were all intended to be taken literally and internalized like a catechism. As fellows SS members were mostly a good sort, better than those of the SA, much better than the so-called party comrades . . . thus went the litany. In the early years after the seizure of power, the Altkämpfer in paid posts groused about the newcomers who got better positions in the SS while the newcomers groused at the incompetence of the "dead wood." There was nevertheless a lot of hope for expansion and for just rewards of hard work and devotion to the SS rather than one's family, a job in private industry, or a civil service post. This brand of SS staff person could always be trusted to flaunt his uniform, fight for his "rights" and "honor" on every conceivable occasion, and after some complaining pick up and move his family to a new city when ordered to in the interests of SS geographic coverage.

The years 1936 to 1938 truly did bring good jobs and prestige to these SS officers (and brought some newcomers into officer ranks as well, though not as many as had come in earlier or as came in after the outbreak of the war).[7] They now began to become quite differentiated one from another, specialists of many kinds — although as we have seen, they tended to think like soldiers, policemen, business managers, administrators, doctors, lawyers, etc. Their promotions began to be more closely related to their expertise as well as relationships within their own bailiwicks, whether topical or regional. The SS "began to look like a department store." There appeared the first signs of rivalry of one subgroup with another. Intrigue, always present, began to be a full-time occupation for some. It looked as if intrigue was necessary to get things done with some superiors — perhaps with Heinrich Himmler. As the signs of war began to multiply and some paid personnel began to desert the ship, jobs opened up even better for the rest. Some began to think in terms of empires abroad and of using international connections to lay the foundation for greater things to come. Himmler favored such activity.

Lastly, this group experienced the blood-letting of the war, at first in a proportion to be borne. Later the losses at the front, in occupied Europe, and in bombed-out German cities began to make being an SS officer a very exposed role. These men did not desert the SS. As police, as soldiers, as administrators, they killed, they tortured, they seized and operated, they designed and built, they inspected, and they investigated. Many were quite selfless, but many were very venal. They simply kept their noses to the grindstone of war and devastation, without too much thinking except to survive, get a furlough, a promotion and a raise, and to live a little. They were rarely wrestling with the future of the SS — as was Himmler — and they rarely wondered if the SS had gotten lost somewhere before the war — as did some of the Altkämpfer who stayed true believers. They were critical of Himmler for taking on too much; they were critical of much more than Himmler — of the party, the Wehrmacht, the other branches of the SS — but not of the Führer. (Naturally, paper records would only show this of someone who was later in disgrace. I do not doubt that Altkämpfer could privately doubt the Führer — we know others at their level did.) The essential thing about them is their lack of a *leitmotiv* at any time other than doing the job they saw before them without much imagination. It is doubtful if they can be said to have had an overall view of the SS during the war years; if so, it would have been heavily colored by their own interests and that of their branch of the service.

What, then, can we say about views of the SS and its importance from outside its own ranks? Here also we need to distinguish among friends, enemies, victims, and the disinterested observers. In the years of struggle, Hitler and the Munich party leadership had had a soft place in their hearts for Himmler and his minions. They found the SS to their liking for its manageability. But they saw it as merely one among many party organizations. Himmler did not get his way especially often — not nearly so often as SA commanders. Regional and local party chiefs had closer ties, more intense relationships of like and dislike, most of them personal. Many but not all preferred the SS to the SA, again because the

SS was disposable. The SS before 1933 certainly was neither feared nor treated with kid gloves. It was in the radical SA that SS men were detested as stool pigeons and spies. Yet many in the SA merely regarded the SS as another branch of their own service, to be roundly cursed, envied, and perhaps fought with on occasion but not especially respected — or hated. The German left sneered at the SS for its petit bourgeois pretensions, its (greatly exaggerated) capitalist supporters and wire-pullers, and the absence of "real workers" from its ranks. Unlike the SA — which the Communists wooed and even the SPD acknowledged contained workers — the SS was regarded as monolithically middle class. This was a mistake, but the class-conscious worker was indeed totally out of place in the SS, which could not be said of the pre-1933 SA. The workers and other victims of the SS before 1933 hardly distinguished it from the SA; except for the "Stennes SA," their victims in the movement rarely could single them out from other spies and intriguers of the party. Disinterested observers (ourselves) would have to add that the SS was largely under-appreciated and under-feared before 1933. Its impact was small upon German life, certainly compared to the party propagandists and the mass mayhem of the SA. Yet inside the movement and as an attraction for the potentially useful doctors, lawyers, civil servants, writers, academicians, and police, the fledgling SS of 1929–1932 provided reserves of strength against dissidence and disorganization. Still, had the party foundered as it threatened to do, the SS could neither have saved it nor could it have survived its demise. At best it could have offered a shipwrecked Hitler a nucleus with which to start over.

Slowly, in fits and starts, Hitler came to see Himmler with his SS as pieces useful in checkmating Röhm; but Hitler allowed nature to take its course with indirection. Göring seems to have given Himmler the strength to take risks about Hitler's intentions, but in truth Hitler clearly chose to happen what did happen at the hands of the SS. Thereafter, the rest of the party leadership and its regional staffs regarded the SS with awe and respect, though the loathing widespread in the SA must also have existed in the party as well. The SD, Heydrich, and the state apparatus (Gestapo and concentration camps, *as seen from the party side*) were powerful arguments with party leaders who did not like Himmler or the SS. The SS could become a bogeyman to frighten others with. The civil servants, judges, academicians, and writers hesitated to criticize SS lawlessness, although some did resist "legally" for some time (in some cases years). Now the victims knew their tormentors, and it is from this era (1935–1939) that the monolithic image of the black-coated fiends arose. Actually, the SS was still largely confused with the Gestapo, and antifascists generally regarded the SS-and-Police system as fully unified and integrated with the national socialist one-party state long before it was. In our judgement, the period 1933–1936 should be regarded as extremely tentative for the SS, a period of trial and error; its impact on the Nazi movement was to strengthen Hitler one more time against the grass-root forces which had made his rise to power possible. As for the impact on Germany, the SS power system gradually fastened itself by 1936 on the political and social order to such an extent that few processes could occur without SS surveillance and intervention. Since these effects were largely negative, the impact was cramping and warping toward outward compliance; but for that period it would be a mistake to magnify or reify a totalitarian Big Brother in place of the essentially unimaginative and repressive police mentality which was the SS-and-Police reality after 1936. There was room for intelligent and creative resistance, yet the mood of the German people did not promise much support for such resistance — and the SS had only a modicum to do with that mood.

As Germany prepared for war from 1937 on, Hitler and the Nazis valued the SS as security against a recurrence of internal resistance. Hitler cautiously gave Himmler the means to set up striking forces for internal security as well as for mopping up after a seizure of territory. The Staatsschutzkorps idea seemed to recommend itself in the face of a reluctant army leadership; and, as in 1934, Hitler arranged to be surprised by revelations concerning von Blomberg and von Fritsch supplied by Heydrich. By now the army leaders might fear and detest the SS — much as had their erstwhile enemies, the SA leaders of 1934 — though some anti-Hitler conspirators imagined the SS as an ally against the party. The victims of the Staatsschutzkorps in Austria, the Sudetenland, and Bohemia encountered a smooth and Machiavellian instrument which from their viewpoint was an agency of the Reich — and Hitler — and so it was. That it was also feathering its own nest by seizing properties and laying the foundation for an imperial rule of its own was rarely perceived. But we observers can record that now the SS was functioning on all cylinders, genuinely preparing the Reich for imperial conquest, giving Hitler that margin of assurance of domestic security he needed to make the Stalin Pact and to start what was known to be an unpopular war. The SS of 1939 was doing just what it was set up to do — and a little more, with regard to its own imperial ambitions arising from its plethora of technicians and dreamers.

Hitler was slow to realize the military usefulness of the Waffen-SS, and the army was even slower. The army was upset by SS behavior in occupied Poland and to a lesser extent in the Balkans. Hitler, on the

other hand, entirely approved and "understood" the reasons for SS terror. There is every reason to believe that he ordered it. Similarly, he
gave Himmler carte blanche in the rear echelons of Barbarossa; he
wanted the Staatsschutzkorps to kill and torture. With respect to the
Final Solution, there is only a shadow of doubt; it is probable that Göring arranged matters with Heydrich as he had both in 1934 and 1938, so
that the Führer could by indirection alone secure his ends with "clean
hands." The slow improvisation of the killing operations and the intri-
cacies of collaboration give the lie to an internal conspiracy within the
SS, of a segmented evil within an evil. Rather, it was a task thrust on the
men in the black coats, wholly consistent with their cultivated image at
least since 1933 within the party and German society. The mask of evil
which the SS donned at this time was desired for them by all who were
in the know. Individuals themselves may not have felt or acted as ones
possessed, but the attribution of total perversion to the perpetrators —
incorrect as it was then or now — reveals how much the onlookers always have to distance themselves from such behavior. The whole SS did
not do the killings, but the whole SS knew of them, and few could stand
aside when called to participate. Aside from the murder of the Jews, the
German people as a whole knew the SS as the deadly executioners of
eastern Europe and the guardians of law and order in western Europe.
Its members were inevitably seen as "different from ourselves." This
was despite the reality that few showed such differences. The SS for the
victims of 1941–1945 were all that the word "fiend" conveys, undiffer-
entiated and unforgivable. For the Russian soldier "SS" meant no quarter on either side. During the Battle of the Bulge, American interroga-
tors of prisoners of war had to go to the company command post for SS
prisoners because GIs beat them so badly they were worthless. The prisoners were greatly feared, being readily (and incorrectly) identified
with spies and infiltrators. Some of them were shot. Waffen-SS soldiers
in 1944 and 1945 had the reputation of committing outrages against
civilians on all fronts. And some of them had, although the majority
had not.

Thus, the SS of wartime became an alibi of a nation. The real SS
was more multiform — though always subject to the total power of a
dictatorship — in special ways not equally and usually applicable to
men of the Wehrmacht, civil servants, or ordinary Germans. SS members were pledged to obey; they were organized in handy units which
everyone expected to be ruthless and terrible. The impact of the wartime SS was at times as terrible as its reputation: certainly for the Holocaust the SS deserves all the blame it has gotten, if not the *exclusive*
blame sometimes bestowed. The Waffen-SS undoubtedly prolonged the

war; it bought the Nazis time they did not know how to use—perhaps the time bought by so many deaths would have been wasted in any case, for nothing could have bought the Nazis *enough* time. This was not then something men of the SS could decide. It was their tragedy that they had previously surrendered these choices to such masters as Hitler and Himmler. As sorcerers' apprentices, they found themselves in the ruins of the sorcerers' workshop—Germany.

Should we regard fascism, with its excrescences like the SS, as historically and geographically bound to Germany in the 1920s, 1930s, and 1940s? The black uniform, the jackboots, and the skull and crossbones are highly idiosyncratic, just as are the United States' burning crosses and sheeted Ku Klux Klan. Nor is the modernized Klan "America's SS." Fascism, either as a "generic" abstraction distilled from those decades or as a larger-than-life imagery extrapolated from all the fiendish displays of the twentieth century, is misleading as the warning to be drawn from the Nazi experience.[8] We need to understand that massive social transformations such as those now occurring in the United States may shake loose and propel into prominence, and into power, groups with mystical-magical and even supernatural claims to leadership. As was the case in Germany, their strength at the grass roots will be proportionate to the incapacity of our institutions to survive disbelief and rejection in times of peril and deprivation. The specifically American forms of repression and intimidation, of religious and personal renewal, of political activism and social pressure will never resemble the Nazi SS. We must look deeper if we are to detect the traits—perhaps one might label them "fascistoid"—which naturally lurk in any modern society like dormant infections. In fact, this very analogy of treating a huge complexity of events and experience as a unit—and an organic one at that, capable of being "sick"—is just such a trait. Yet the desire to comprehend opaque and uncontrolled reality through simple metaphors does not make people killers, at least not most people. By itself it is at worst dangerously misleading, at best occasionally perhaps a stab in the right direction. Another "fascistoid" tendency is our American presidency— that which has given us a very creative and dynamic two hundred years and also brought us closer than we like to admit to dictatorship and popular rebellion. Our military-industrial complex, with its advertising arm and its computerized surveillance system, is a powerful tool of rationalistic elites who compete for popular approval in the marketplace and at the ballot box; in the hands of a God- or goods-intoxicated minority of the greedy or righteous, this instrument is every bit as dangerous as the SS and without its visibility. Lastly, the American myth that we are all freedom-loving individualists, especially in the form of a belief that people do not need to be organized in interest groups — or that if they are so organized, they ought to serve the "public good" — has much to recommend it. Yet in the face of the frustrations and insufficiencies of an increasingly technocratic world, there is a growing likelihood that Americans will "drop out" of the ordinary struggle for power and status and will leave the arena to the more determined: the "saviors" of America. Perhaps the "Moral Majority" movement is our national socialism — its charisma is already being demonstrated. Its striking forces have just begun to surface and are much less visible than the men in the black suits but may be as dedicated — or as venal. Probably the strength of American institutional life will cause their absorption into the ordinary politics of communities at state and local levels or even into the national parties, where they will be tamed.

Or will they? Let us hope and work for international understanding, since international conflict, nuclear and "anticommunist," might bring their moment of conquest. And then, whatever the color of their coats, we may ourselves share in the deadly masquerade that results when power is beyond public scrutiny and control.

*Reference Matter*

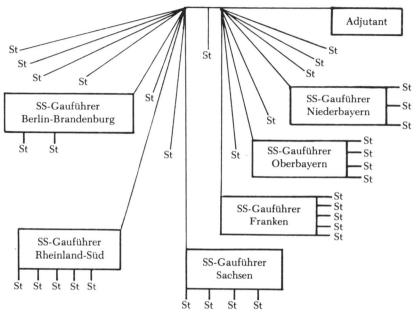

SS-Oberleitung München
Reichsführer-SS

Adjutant

St
St
St
St

St

St
St
St

St

St

SS-Gauführer
Berlin-Brandenburg

St

St

SS-Gauführer
Niederbayern

St
St
St

St    St

St

St

SS-Gauführer
Oberbayern

St
St
St
St

SS-Gauführer
Rheinland-Süd

St   St   St   St   St

SS-Gauführer
Franken

St
St
St
St
St

SS-Gauführer
Sachsen

St   St   St   St

St: Staffel

While in theory each party Gau should have had an SS-Gauführer, only a few can be identified. Many Staffeln dealt exclusively with the Oberleitung in Munich.

Chart 1. SS Structure, 1926–1928.

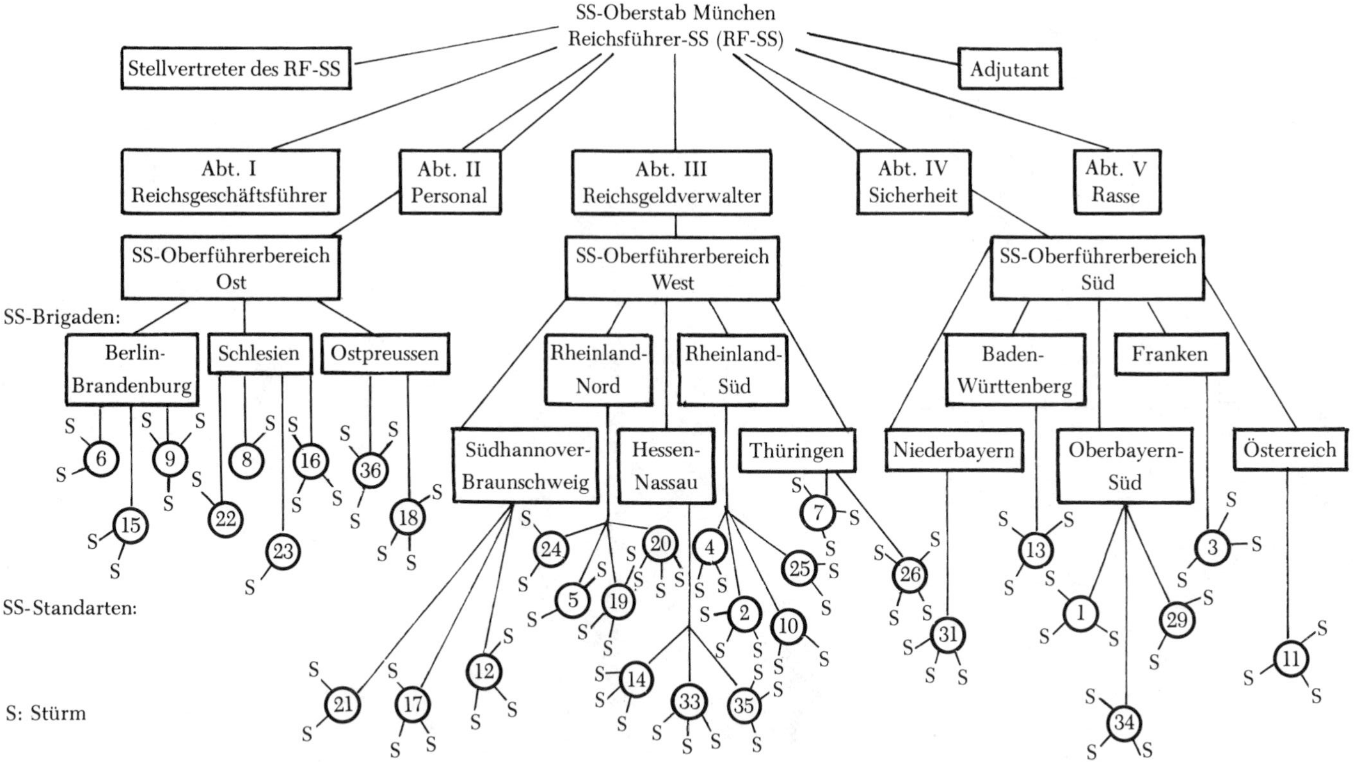

Chart 2. SS Structure, 1929–1930.

There were supposed to be 30 Brigaden corresponding to the Gaue. Each Brigade was supposed to comprise several Standarten, in turn made up of 3 to 6 Stürme.

S: Stürm.

252

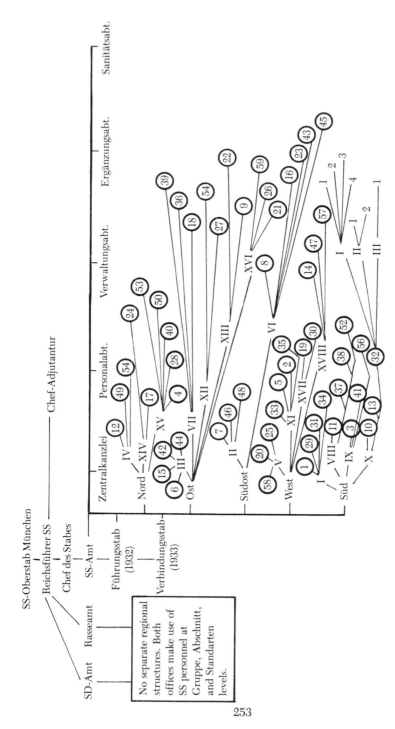

Chart 3. SS Structure, 1931–1933.

The breakdown of only one of the Standarten (32) is shown here. The regional names are the Gruppen; the set of roman numerals farthest left are the Abschnitte; circled arabic numerals are Standarten; the second set of roman numerals are Sturmbanne; uncircled arabic numerals are Stürme.

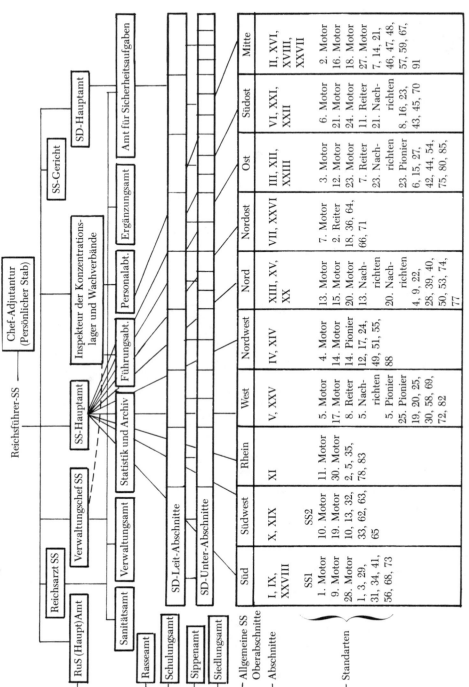

Chart 4. SS Structure, 1934–1939.

254

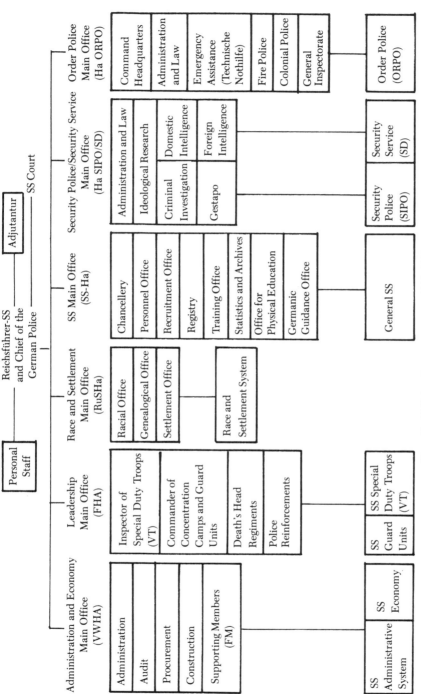

Chart 5. SS-Police Power Structure, 1938–1939.

Map 1. Location of SS-Staffeln, 1925–1926, and 1929.

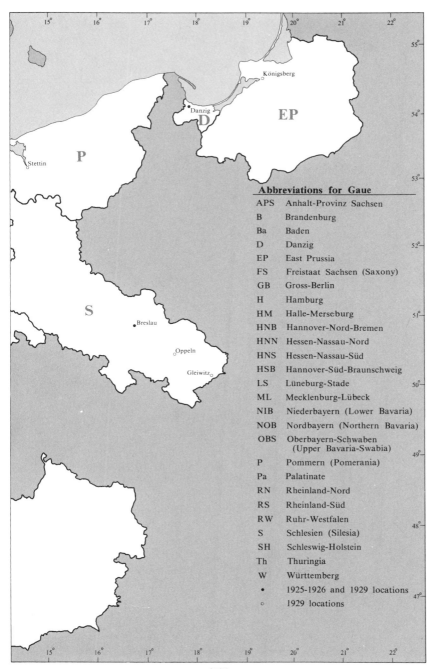

**Abbreviations for Gaue**

| | |
|---|---|
| APS | Anhalt-Provinz Sachsen |
| B | Brandenburg |
| Ba | Baden |
| D | Danzig |
| EP | East Prussia |
| FS | Freistaat Sachsen (Saxony) |
| GB | Gross-Berlin |
| H | Hamburg |
| HM | Halle-Merseburg |
| HNB | Hannover-Nord-Bremen |
| HNN | Hessen-Nassau-Nord |
| HNS | Hessen-Nassau-Süd |
| HSB | Hannover-Süd-Braunschweig |
| LS | Lüneburg-Stade |
| ML | Mecklenburg-Lübeck |
| NIB | Niederbayern (Lower Bavaria) |
| NOB | Nordbayern (Northern Bavaria) |
| OBS | Oberbayern-Schwaben (Upper Bavaria-Swabia) |
| P | Pommern (Pomerania) |
| Pa | Palatinate |
| RN | Rheinland-Nord |
| RS | Rheinland-Süd |
| RW | Ruhr-Westfalen |
| S | Schlesien (Silesia) |
| SH | Schleswig-Holstein |
| Th | Thuringia |
| W | Württemberg |
| ● | 1925-1926 and 1929 locations |
| ○ | 1929 locations |

257

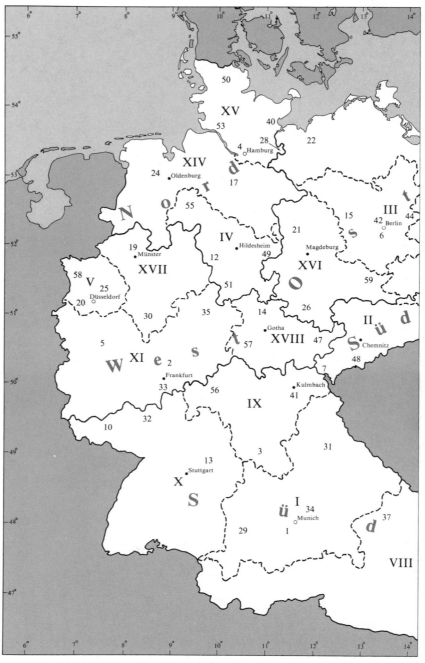

Map 2. Gruppen, Abschnitte, and Standarten of the SS in 1932.

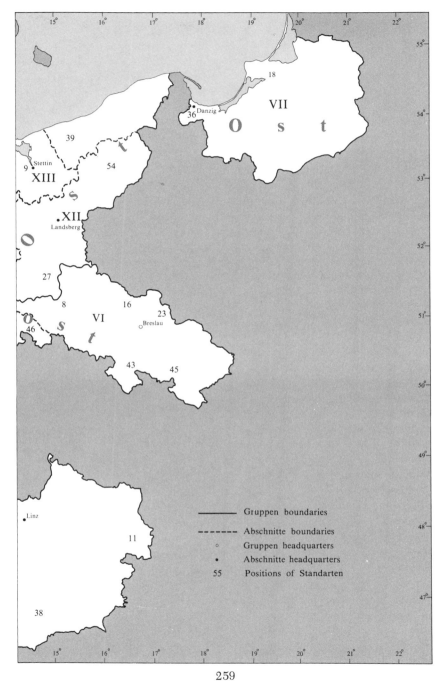

55°

54°

18

VII

36 Danzig

O s t

39

t

Stettin

9

XIII

54

53°

s

.XII

Landsberg

52°

O

27

8

16

23

51°

VI

o Breslau

46

s

43

45

50°

t

49°

Linz

Gruppen boundaries

———— Abschnitte boundaries

48°

o    Gruppen headquarters

11

•    Abschnitte headquarters

55    Positions of Standarten

47°

38

259

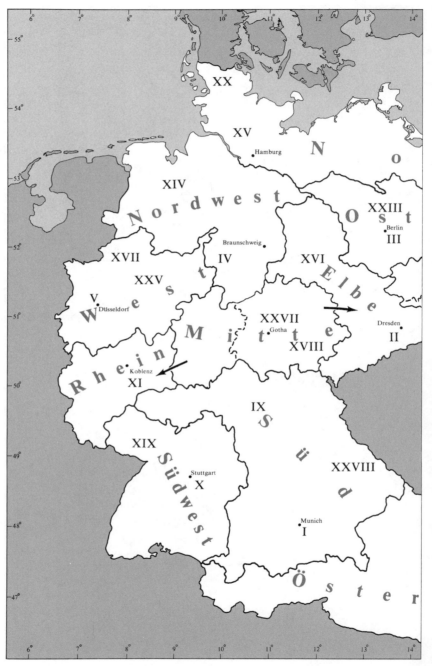

Map 3. Oberabschnitte and Abschnitte of the SS, 1933–1934.

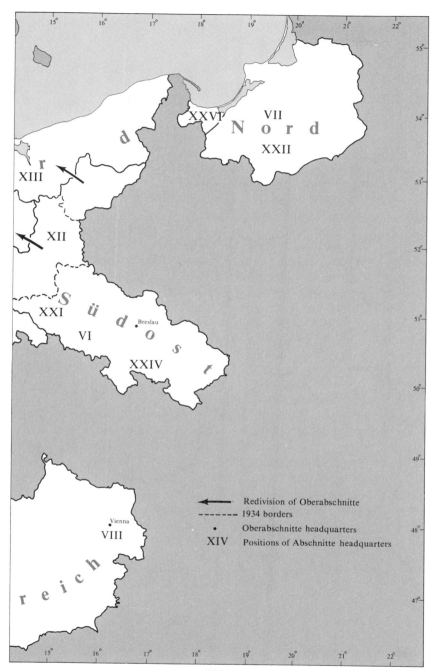

XXVI

VII

**N o r d**

XXII

d

r

XIII

XII

**S ü d**

XXI

Breslau

VI

**o s t**

XXIV

Vienna

VIII

**r e i c h**

⟵ Redivision of Oberabschnitte
-------- 1934 borders
• Oberabschnitte headquarters
XIV Positions of Abschnitte headquarters

261

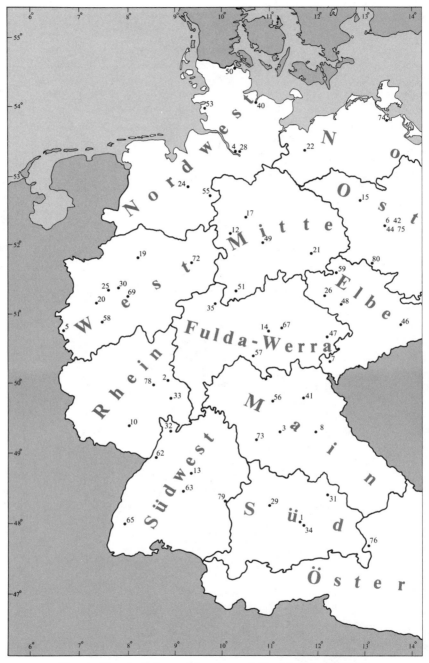

Map 4. Oberabschnitte and Standarten 1–80 of the SS, 1937–1938.

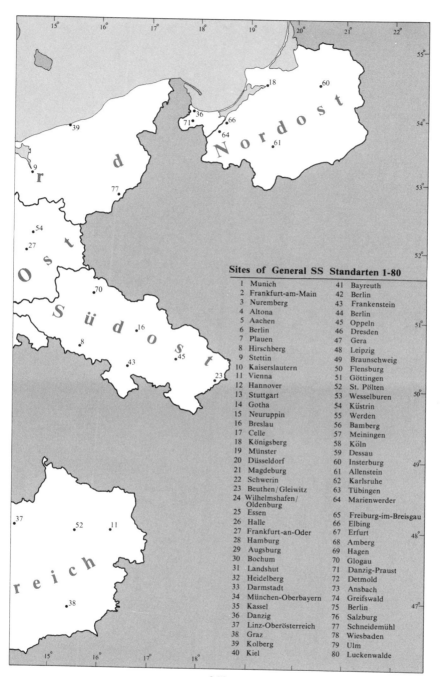

**Sites of General SS Standarten 1-80**

| | | | |
|---|---|---|---|
| 1 | Munich | 41 | Bayreuth |
| 2 | Frankfurt-am-Main | 42 | Berlin |
| 3 | Nuremberg | 43 | Frankenstein |
| 4 | Altona | 44 | Berlin |
| 5 | Aachen | 45 | Oppeln |
| 6 | Berlin | 46 | Dresden |
| 7 | Plauen | 47 | Gera |
| 8 | Hirschberg | 48 | Leipzig |
| 9 | Stettin | 49 | Braunschweig |
| 10 | Kaiserslautern | 50 | Flensburg |
| 11 | Vienna | 51 | Göttingen |
| 12 | Hannover | 52 | St. Pölten |
| 13 | Stuttgart | 53 | Wesselburen |
| 14 | Gotha | 54 | Küstrin |
| 15 | Neuruppin | 55 | Werden |
| 16 | Breslau | 56 | Bamberg |
| 17 | Celle | 57 | Meiningen |
| 18 | Königsberg | 58 | Köln |
| 19 | Münster | 59 | Dessau |
| 20 | Düsseldorf | 60 | Insterburg |
| 21 | Magdeburg | 61 | Allenstein |
| 22 | Schwerin | 62 | Karlsruhe |
| 23 | Beuthen/Gleiwitz | 63 | Tübingen |
| 24 | Wilhelmshafen/ Oldenburg | 64 | Marienwerder |
| 25 | Essen | 65 | Freiburg-im-Breisgau |
| 26 | Halle | 66 | Elbing |
| 27 | Frankfurt-an-Oder | 67 | Erfurt |
| 28 | Hamburg | 68 | Amberg |
| 29 | Augsburg | 69 | Hagen |
| 30 | Bochum | 70 | Glogau |
| 31 | Landshut | 71 | Danzig-Praust |
| 32 | Heidelberg | 72 | Detmold |
| 33 | Darmstadt | 73 | Ansbach |
| 34 | München-Oberbayern | 74 | Greifswald |
| 35 | Kassel | 75 | Berlin |
| 36 | Danzig | 76 | Salzburg |
| 37 | Linz-Oberösterreich | 77 | Schneidemühl |
| 38 | Graz | 78 | Wiesbaden |
| 39 | Kolberg | 79 | Ulm |
| 40 | Kiel | 80 | Luckenwalde |

Map 5.  Standarten 81–125 in 1941.

Sites of General SS Standarten 81-125

| | | | | | |
|---|---|---|---|---|---|
| 81 | Würzburg | 101 | Saaz | 121 | Strasburg |
| 82 | Bielefeld | 102 | Jägerndorf | 122 | Strassburg |
| 83 | Giessen | 103 | Aussig | 123 | Kolmar |
| 84 | Chemnitz | 104 | Troppau | 124 | Kattowitz |
| 85 | Saarbrücken | 105 | Memel | 125 | Metz |
| 86 | Offenburg | 106 | Augsburg | | |
| 87 | Innsbruck | 107 | Brünn | | |
| 88 | Bremen | 108 | Prag | | |
| 89 | Wien | 109 | Posen | | |
| 90 | Klagenfurt | 110 | Hohensalza | | |
| 91 | Wittenberg | 111 | Kolmar | | |
| 92 | Ingolstadt | 112 | Litzmannstadt | | |
| 93 | Koblenz | 113 | Kalisch | | |
| 94 | Leoben | 114 | Lesslau | | |
| 95 | Trautenau | 115 | Zichenau | | |
| 96 | Brüx | 116 | Bromberg | | |
| 97 | Eger | 117 | Konitz | | |
| 98 | Mährisch-Schönberg | 118 | Preussisch-Stargard | | |
| 99 | Znaim | 119 | Graudenz | | |
| 100 | Reichenberg | 120 | Kulm | | |

Map 6. Major German concentration camps.

Stutthof

Treblinka

Maidanek

Auschwitz

267

Map 7. Oberabschnitte, Wehrkreise, and SS headquarters in 1941.

Map 8. Hitler's Europe, 1941–1942.

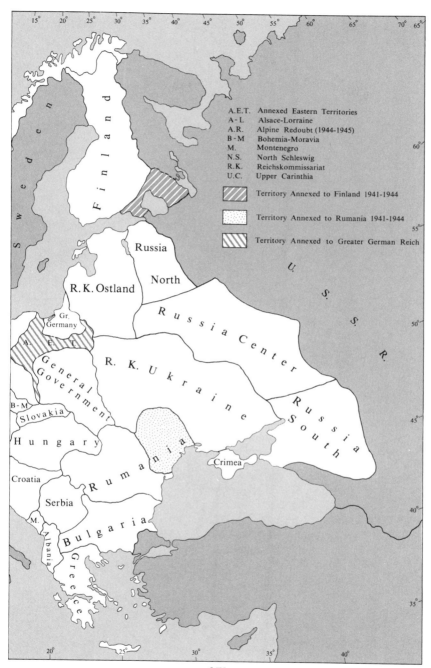

A.E.T.  Annexed Eastern Territories
A - L  Alsace-Lorraine
A.R.  Alpine Redoubt (1944-1945)
B - M  Bohemia-Moravia
M.  Montenegro
N.S.  North Schleswig
R.K.  Reichskommissariat
U.C.  Upper Carinthia

Territory Annexed to Finland 1941-1944

Territory Annexed to Rumania 1941-1944

Territory Annexed to Greater German Reich

# A Note on the Primary Sources

Six basic categories of records figure in the notes of this study. Biographical records of all SS officers of the rank of *Oberführer* and above were examined systematically at the Berlin Document Center, along with selected records of officers at ranks of *Sturmbannführer* through *Standartenführer*, and one hundred randomly chosen names from the 1936 *Dienstaltersliste*. References to these sources are anonymous, as was promised by the author in 1961. Extensive use has been made of the so-called Schumacher Collection (*Schumacher Sammlung*) insofar as it pertains to the SS and SA. Originally housed at the Berlin Document Center where it was assembled, this collection has now been transferred to the *Bundesarchiv* in Coblenz. The largest part of this collection, and the part most extensively used here, was filmed as "Schumacher Material" by the American Historical Association as National Archives Microfilm T-580. Some folders omitted from T-580 were filmed by the author for the University of Nebraska as T-611, and are also cited here. Finally there are stray items from the Collection that have not been filmed, which were seen at the BDC in 1960–1961. The third category is the *Schriftgutverwaltung, Reichsführer SS*, better known as the "Himmler Files" as they were designated by the Hoover Institution Library. This mammoth collection of the records of the *Persönlicher Stab, Reichsführer SS* made up Record Group 1010 of the Captured German Records of the National Archives, until they were returned to the *Bundesarchiv*. The Hoover Institution Library made photocopies of this collection. On the back of each photocopy was a lower case letter and a number. Each file in the original collection was designated by a number in colored crayon on each page. Subsequently, groups of these file folders were assigned an *Einheitsaktenplan* (EAP) code number (e.g., 161-b-10/5) along with a SIPO-SD (Security Police) collection from a different provenance. Finally, all the records of the Reichsführer SS and Chief of the German Police were filmed by the AHA as National Archives Microfilm T-175. Thus, in this study *Schriftgutverwaltung* records appear in a number of guises. Most often their form is that of the microfilm, with frame designations. However, the first research on this book was done at Stanford on the photocopies of the "Himmler Files"; furthermore, the Berlin Document Center also had some of these photocopies with their lower case letter and number on the back. It would have been impossible to locate all of these on T-175. Similarly, there are some citations to EAP code numbers without a reference to T-175, and some to T-175 roll numbers without frame numbers. In the first case the references are to documents seen at Alexandria in 1958 and 1959, which have not been subsequently located on the film. In the second case the references are to reconstructed notes for chapter seven, for which the original notes were destroyed through a janitor's carelessness.

The fourth category consists of a variety of SS records, some in the Berlin Document Center (some of which were filmed on T-611), and some on National Archives Microfilms T-74 (Records of the *Reichskommissar für die Festigung Deutschen Volkstums*) and T-354 (Miscellaneous SS Records: *Einwandererzentralstelle, Waffen-SS* and *SS-Oberabschnitte*).

The fifth category is a catch-all, consisting of Storm Troop, High Command, and Party records. Except for the Storm Troop records at the BDC and the *Grauert Akten* from the Berlin-Dahlem *Hauptarchiv*, all the rest are on microfilm: Headquarters, High Command, National Archives Microcopy T-78; NSDAP, National Archives Microcopy T-81; *Hauptarchiv der NSDAP*, Hoover Institution Library Microfilm.

The last category is the documentation and testimony at Nuremberg, both of the International Military Tribunal and the subsequent U.S. Military Tribunal Trials. Wherever possible, citation is made to published versions of the various trials. However, especially in the case of the trials of the concentration camp administrators, the *Einsatzgruppen* officers, the RKFDV personnel, and the ministries (Darré, Berger, etc.), the published versions are far too incomplete. In all such cases reference is made to the trial documentation of the Center for Research Libraries in Chicago, including the use of separate documents of the NO and NG series. Indictments and judgements of several German courts involving SS defendants (Sepp Dietrich, Udo von Woyrsch, et al.) have been used through the courtesy of the Munich Institut für Zeitgeschichte.

Contemporary newspaper and periodical references, though not strictly primary, are largely those used through the courtesy of the Wiener Library in London. The author subscribed to the Waffen SS veterans' magazine, *Der Freiwillige/ Wikingruf*, for many years. In a way, the latter is a primary source of a very special kind.

# Notes

## Chapter 1: Prehistory

1 Adolf Hitler, *Mein Kampf* (Munich, 1939) (hereafter cited as MK), pp. 226 ff., 391 ff., and ch. 9, esp. p. 596. Ernst Jünger, *Werke* (Stuttgart, 1960), vol. 1 (*Tagebücher: Der erste Weltkrieg*), esp. pp. 463–67, and vol. 5 (*Essays: Betrachtungen zur Zeit*), esp. pp. 45–47. See Wilhelm Hoegner, *Die verratene Republik* (Munich, 1958), pp. 120–21. Hanfstaengl observes: "When he [Hitler] talked of National Socialism, what he really meant was military socialism, socialism within a framework of military discipline or, in civilian terms, police socialism." Ernst F. S. Hanfstaengl, *Hitler. The Missing Years* (London, 1957), p. 174. Werner Maser, *Sturm auf die Republik. Frühgechichte der NSDAP* (Stuttgart, 1973), pp. 174–75; Konrad Heiden, *Adolf Hitler. Eine Biographie* (Zurich, 1936) (hereafter *Hitler*) vol. 1, pp. 57–61; Ernst Deuerlein, "Hitlers Eintritt in die Politik und die Reichswehr," *Vierteljahrshefte für Zeitgeschichte* (hereafter VJHZ) 7 (1959): 182, 204, 207, 208, 213, 215–16, 226. Hans Buchheim, *Glaubenskrise im Dritten Reich* (Stuttgart, 1953), p. 34, argues that Hitler and his comrades were *not* soldiers per se, not a *Kampfgemeinschaft* (fighting community), but a *Notgemeinschaft* (community of necessity).

2 MK, pp. 226–27, 585. Heiden sees a workers' militarism in the pre-Hitler Drexler party: Konrad Heiden, *A History of National Socialism* (New York, 1935) (hereafter cited as NS), p. 5. See also the Hitlerian idea of the SPD as disciplined through the prewar German army with the trade unionists as NCOs and Jewish intellectuals as officers and thus superior to the "parliamentary anarchy" of the bourgeois parties: ibid., pp. 509–10. Rudolf Kanzler, *Bayerns Kampf gegen den Bolschewismus. Geschichte der bayerischen Einwohnerwehr* (Munich, 1931), pp. 4 ff.; Ernst von Salomon, *Der Fragebogen* (Hamburg, 1951), pp. 187, 385–86; Georg Witzmann, *Thüringen von 1918–33. Erinnerungen eines Politikers* (Meisenheim am Glan, 1958), p. 115; Ernst Röhm, *Die Geschichte eines Hochverräters* (Munich, 1928), pp. 75–86; Hans Kallenbach, *Mit Adolf Hitler auf Festung Landsberg* (Munich, 1939), p. 115.

3 Röhm, pp. 95 ff. Manfred von Killinger is most eloquent: *Die SA in Wort und Bild* (Leipzig, 1933), pp. 8–16, 29–31. Gerhard Rossbach, *Mein Weg durch die Zeit. Erinnerungen und Bekenntnisse* (Weilburg-Lahn, 1950), pp. 53–78; Robert G. L. Waite, *Vanguard of Nazism. The Free Corps Movement in Postwar Germany 1918–1923* (Cambridge, Mass., 1952), pp. 33–57.

4  Röhm's first contact with Hitler may have been in 1919 in the *Eiserne Faust*, a rowdy officers' club. Hitler first attended meetings of the German Workers' Party (DAP) on orders of Captain Karl Mayr and probably heard there that Röhm also had contacts with the party. Hitler is also said to have hung about the stationery store of *Lt.a.D.* (lieutenant, retired) Berchtold, also of the Eiserne Faust and the DAP. Berchtold may have been the friend whom Röhm mentions as having introduced him (Röhm) to the DAP. Berchtold later became the first chief of the Stosstrupp Hitler: Konrad Heiden, *Der Fuehrer* (Boston, 1944) (hereafter DF), pp. 90, 101. Heiden, *Hitler*, vol. 1, pp. 91–93, 100; Röhm, pp. 114 ff., 123–24; Hoegner, *Verratene Republik*, pp. 87, 118; Georg Franz-Willing, *Ursprung der Hitlerbewegung 1919–1922* (Preussich Oldendorf, 1974), pp. 90–109 *et seq.*; Reginald Phelps, "Hitler and the *Deutsche Arbeiterpartei*," *American Historical Review* (hereafter AHR) 68 (1963): 974–86; Reginald Phelps, "Anton Drexler, der Gründer der NSDAP," *Deutsche Rundschau* 87 (1963): 1134–43, and "Dokumente aus der Kampfzeit der NSDAP — 1923," vol. 84 (1958): 459–68, 1034–44.

5  Hitler does not seem a particularly "soldierly" man. By contrast with Eckhart, Feder, Drexler, Harrer, Esser, and Rosenberg, however, he comes off pretty well. Berchtold, Amann, and Hess were relatively soldierly; Streicher was a nature enthusiast but no soldier. Heiden, *Hitler*, pp. 98–104, 129; Kurt Ludecke, *I Knew Hitler* (New York, 1938), pp. 8–9; "Politisches Soldatentum," in J. K. von Engelbrechten's *Eine braune Armee entsteht* (Munich-Berlin, 1937), pp. 23–24; Wilhelm Hoegner, *Der schwierige Aussenseiter* (Munich, 1959), pp. 18–21. See also Hoegner, *Die verratene Republik*, pp. 120–34. Oron Hale, "Gottfried Feder Calls Hitler to Order," *Journal of Modern History* 30 (1958): 358–62; Sterling Fishman, "The Rise of Hitler as a Beer Hall Orator," *The Review of Politics* 26 (1964): 244–56.

6  Heiden, DF, p. 92, and *Hitler*, p. 137. Letter of Ernst Wagner to Hitler, May 20, 1926, National Archives microcopy T-580 (hereafter, briefly, T-580), roll 87/folder 425. On Wagner see Franz-Willing, p. 179. Erich Czech-Jochberg, *Hitler. Eine deutsche Bewegung* (Oldenburg, 1930), p. 80; Röhm, p. 155.

7  Röhm, pp. 123–24. Hoegner, in *Verratene Republik*, says Röhm also got members of the Bavarian *Landespolizei* into the party (pp. 131–32).

8  MK, pp. 391–93, 405. These persons probably included several of the founders of the Schutzstaffel. Ludecke, pp. 79, 82, 272; cf. Maser, pp. 134–35, 172, 176, 192–93, 203. Franz-Willing, pp. 205–11.

9  Ernst Deuerlein, "Hitlers Eintritt in die Politik und die Reichswehr," VJHZ 7 (1959): 181–82, 191, 201 ff.; Reginald Phelps, "Hitler and the *Deutsche Arbeiterpartei*," AHR 68 (1963): 980.

10  Heiden, DF, pp. 142–43 ("The real nucleus of the SA"). See also Waite, pp. 81, 207. Franz-Willing, pp. 122–24, shows that the swastika was a racist, anti-Semitic symbol in the prewar Reichshammerbund and in Austria, so that the Ehrhardt Brigade swastika merely reinforced tendencies from Sebottendorf's Thule Society and the Austrian National Socialists. See Rudolf von Sebottendorf, *Bevor Hitler Kam* (Munich, 1933), pp. 61 ff., and illus-

trations, pp. 201 ff.; Maser, pp. 146–50. See also Andrew Whiteside, *Austrian National Socialism before 1918* (Hague, 1962), p. 87–122.

11  Kanzler, pp. 79 ff.; Röhm, pp. 114–15, 120; Hoegner, *Verratene Republik*, pp. 84, 102, 105; Hanns Hubert Hofmann, *Der Hitlerputsch* (Munich, 1961), pp. 42–43.

12  It was palpably impossible to use the Reichswehr or the Einwohnerwehr for the aggressive role in politics which Hitler envisioned — so the free corps men came in very handy in 1920–21; but it is also probable that the more aggressively inclined Einwohnerwehr personnel were happy to play the role of Nazi bouncers too. MK, pp. 541, 546–51; Franz-Willing, pp. 57–62; Heinrich Bennecke, *Hitler und die SA* (Munich, 1962), pp. 27–34.

13  Hofmann, p. 50; Hoegner, *Verratene Republik*, pp. 107–8; Röhm, pp. 125–26, 129.

14  Heiden, NS, p. 36, and *Hitler*, vol. 1, pp. 142–43; MK, p. 559.

15  Heiden, *Hitler*, vol. 1, pp. 146–48, and NS, p. 35. Heiden points out that these early groups also functioned as a kind of propaganda-claque in the meetings, hooting down opponents and noisily agreeing with the speaker. See Hofmann, pp. 55–57; and Franz-Willing, pp. 171–72. For the structural evolution of the DAP and NSDAP, see Dietrich Orlow, *The History of the Nazi Party, 1919–1933* (Pittsburgh, 1969), pp. 11–45.

16  The question may be raised as to how much Klintzsch was able to accomplish in view of the fact that he was in jail on suspicion of the Erzberger murder shortly thereafter, and Ehrhard's Marine Brigade, from which he was on leave, had become Bavarian and separatist, which was anathema to Hitler. Heiden, *Hitler*, vol. 1, pp. 151–52; Hoegner, *Verratene Republik*, p. 111; Franz-Willing, pp. 210–14. See also Ludecke, pp. 101 ff. A picture of Klintzsch in a black hat can be found in Heinrich Hoffmann, *Das braune Heer. 100 Bilddokumente: Leben, Kampf, und Sieg der SA und SS* (Berlin, 1933), p. 9.

17  Röhm, pp. 134–36; Hans Volz, *Daten der Geschichte der NSDAP* (Berlin-Leipzig, 1943), pp. 8–9; Heiden, NS, p. 36; Hoegner, *Verratene Republik*, pp. 105–10. Heiden suggests that Röhm's disagreement with Hitler stemmed, already in 1921, from Hitler's desire to make the SA an organization of *purely political* soldiers: NS, p. 84. The abbreviation of SA goes back to the *Sportabteilungen:* Hans Frank, *Im Angesicht des Galgens* (Munich, 1953), p. 103, citing Hitler's testimony at the Schweidnitz trial in 1930.

18  A note on semantics: Our terms "Storm Troops" and "Storm Trooper," while not literal translations, are admirably suited to emphasize the romantic image which hovered in the minds of the young men who volunteered as Hitler-guards in 1921. By the time Hitler bestowed *Sturmabteilung* as an honorary title (November), it must have been in use for some time, perhaps even antedating *Sportabteilung* (August). *Ordnertruppe* and *Saalschutz* (Order-Troop and Hall Guard) were bourgeois, parliamentary party expressions in postwar Germany, although even they obviously had military if not militant overtones. Hitler stresses the youth of his first Ordnertruppe in contrast to the greybeards of the other parties. In the recruiting call for the

sports units, the stress is on the military idea, a boundless desire for action, loyalty among comrades, and joyful obedience to the leader. MK, pp. 549–50; Heiden, DF, p. 107; Volz, p. 93. Alan Bullock dates the usage of *Sturmabteilung* from October 5: *Hitler. A Study in Tyranny* (New York, 1952), p. 66. For a perhaps fanciful description of the "birth of the Storm Troops" see MK, 562–67; and Czech-Jochberg, pp. 95–101.

19 For the growth of the Nazi movement during 1922, see MK, p. 613; Röhm, pp. 138–39; Heiden, *Hitler*, vol. 1, pp. 152–53; Orlow, *History, 1919–1933*, pp. 36–38; Maser, pp. 328–38. On the Arbeitsgemeinschaften, see Waite, pp. 189–96; Walter Kaufmann, *Monarchism in the Weimar Republic* (New York, 1953), pp. 98–110; Hoegner, *Verratene Republik*, pp. 111–12. In January 1922, Hitler was sentenced to three months in prison for the SA raid of September 1921 on the meeting held by the engineer O. Ballerstedt, one of Pittinger's spokesmen: Heiden, NS, pp. 36–37; Volz, p. 9.

20 On the August rally, see MK, pp. 613–14. Ludecke, pp. 11–15; Franz-Willing, p. 328. For the putsch plot: Röhm, pp. 147–51; Ludecke, pp. 54–58; Hoegner, *Verratene Republik*, pp. 113–14. See also Maser, pp. 353–54.

21 MK, pp. 614–18; Czech-Jochberg, pp. 105–10; Ludecke, pp. 81–90; Josef Berchtold, "Koburg, Symbol unseres Sieges," *Der SA-Mann* October 15, 1932, *Jahrgang* I, *Folge* 27. Many years later medals were awarded to all participants (the "Coburg medal"). The "march" tactic was repeated on a smaller scale in December 1922 when Hitler visited a newly formed party local in Traunstein accompanied by a 140-man SA contingent. The following May, Traunstein set up its own twenty-man SA *Bereitschaft* (ready squad): Neumayr diary, T-580/roll 24/folder 206. (A *Bereitschaft* is a *police* term, later used by the SS in 1933 for the *Politische Bereitschaften*, nucleus of the *Verfügungstruppe*.)

22 On Streicher, see Hoegner, *Verratene Republik*, p. 122; Ludecke, p. 99. For the VVV, see Röhm, p. 152; Volz, p. 10; Kaufmann, pp. 104–5 (citing Emil J. Gumbel, *Verschwörer* [Vienna, 1924], pp. 136–37, which is a more revealing analysis). On Wulle and Graefe: Kaufmann, pp. 111–12. Ludecke's autobiography illustrates a connection with Count Ernst zu Reventlow: pp. 9–11. See also Gumbel, pp. 97–100, who stresses Rossbach's role as a go-between (partially confirmed in Gerhard Rossbach's *Mein Weg durch die Zeit. Erinnerungen und Bekenntnisse*, pp. 79–81).

23 Erich Eyck, *Geschichte der Weimarer Republik* (Zurich, 1954–56), vol. 1, pp. 299–300, 307; Gerd Rühle, *Das Dritte Reich* (Berlin, 1934), vol. 1, p. 77; Heinrich Hoffmann, *Hitler Was My Friend* (London, 1955), pp. 52, 64; Röhm, p. 173; Heiden, DF, pp. 109–10; Volz, pp. 93–94; Engelbrechten, p. 31.

24 Hitler in 1936: "If today you saw one of our squads from the year 1932 marching by, you would ask, 'What workhouse have they escaped from?'" William L. Shirer, *The Rise and Fall of the Third Reich* (New York, 1960), p. 77. For pictures of the SA of 1923, see Hoffman, *Braune Heer*, p. 33; Rühle, pp. 379–81; Hoegner, *Verratene Republik*, p. 160. On SA organization: Volz, p. 94; Rühle, p. 78; Ludecke, p. 101; Heinz Lohmann, *SA räumt*

*auf!* (Hamburg, 1935), pp. 22 ff. The SA of the Ruhr in 1923 was made up of camouflaged youth groups, Rossbach units, sport and fencing clubs, and various other groups: Friedrich Alfred Beck, *Kampf und Sieg. Geschichte der NSDAP im Gau Westfalen-Süd* (Dortmund, 1938), pp. 104, 108, 109, 112, 114–15. Nazi tradition tended to assign the same relatively large, round number estimates to all rallies held about the same time; later, these round numbers often had a zero added! Another tendency was to confuse the total number of combat league participants at a rally with the number of SA present: Waite, p. 237; Bullock, p. 83.

25  MK, pp. 618–20; Röhm, pp. 162–63; Eyck, vol. 1, p. 313; Harold J. Gordon, *Hitler and the Beer Hall Putsch* (Princeton, 1972), pp. 185–89.

26  Röhm, pp. 164–65; Ludecke, pp. 110–11; Hoegner, *Verratene Republik*, pp. 134–35; Gordon, pp. 189–91.

27  Hoegner, *Verratene Republik*, p. 144; Gordon, *Hitler and the Beer Hall Putsch*, pp. 191–94; Waite, pp. 239–47; Kaufmann, pp. 98–100; Röhm, pp. 170–94. From this time forward, until 1926, the Standarten became SA (later Frontbann) regiments, a more military-sounding term. Cf. Volz, p. 11; and Beck, p. 110. On Göring and the Ehrhardt people, see Hanfstaengl, pp. 75, 79–81, 98. Nevertheless, a few Ehrhardt officers assisted Göring until the putsch: Röhm, p. 173; Ludecke, p. 182; Bennecke, *Hitler und die SA*, pp. 53–55.

28  On the *Stabswache:* Volz, p. 94. *SS-Leitheft*, *Folge* 1b, 7 (1941), 10. See also Adolf Hitler, *Secret Conversations* (New York, 1953), p. 138. A picture of a twelve-man *Stabswache* may be found in *Illustrierte Beobachter*, 1936, Nr. 21, p. 806.

29  Hanfstaengl describes an abortive putsch of April 15 in connection with "maneuvers" on the Frottmäniger Heath (p. 80). See Gumbel, pp. 182–83. On the May Day fiasco, see Hoegner, *Verratene Republik*, pp. 138–42; Röhm, pp. 194–99; Gordon, *Hitler and the Beer Hall Putsch*, pp. 194–206. Letter of Ernst Wagner to Hitler, May 20, 1926, T-580/roll 87/folder 425.

30  A major source on the *Stosstrupp* is Hans Kallenbach, *Mit Adolf Hitler auf Festung Landsberg* (Munich, 1939); the author was one of the platoon commanders. Kurt Ludecke takes credit for the idea, claiming to have set up a hundred-man unit in the fall of 1922, from which thirty men were later taken to form the *Stosstrupp Hitler* (pp. 100 ff.). Himmler "recalled" the number as 120 (*Führerbesprechung*, April 13, 1931, T-580/roll 87/folder 425), but the 1924 indictment of forty *Stosstrupp* members speaks of eighty to one hundred, and my researches have turned up only seventy-two names. (Cf. T-580/roll 85/folder 320.)

31  Bodo Uhse, *Söldner und Soldat. Roman* (Paris, 1935), p. 95; Volz, p. 13 (55, 787 *eingeschriebene Mitglieder*). The figure of 10,000 is my own estimate and is certainly a maximal one, based on the following figures: *Regiment München*, 2,000; *Regiment Franken*, 3,000; *Sturmbrigade Landshut*, 1,500; supporting units and "independent companies," (e.g. Ingolstadt), 3,000. Walter Görlitz and Herbert A. Quint, in *Adolf Hitler* (Stuttgart, 1952), p. 192, speak of a weak infantry division (10,000 men?) as SA strength

in the fall of 1923. See also ibid., pp. 176–77; and Gumbel, pp. 184–86. On sources of funds see Fritz Thyssen, *I Paid Hitler* (New York, 1941), p. 82; Ludecke, pp. 107–8, 150; Hanfstaengl, pp. 57–58; Gumbel, p. 192. See also Maser, pp. 396–410.

32  The Nazis played a significant part in the nationalistic Schlageter commemoration in June and the gymnastic festival in July: Volz, p. 11; Hanfstaengl, pp. 85–87. On the other hand, notices to SA leaders sent out by Göring in July suggest an atmostphere of confusion and internecine struggle: *Münchener Post*, August 20 and 23, 1923, quoted in Waite, p. 256, and Gumbel, pp. 190–91, 195. See also Eyck's excellent analysis of the confused summer of 1923 in Bavaria: vol. 1, pp. 335–37.

33  Volz, p. 94; Ludecke, pp. 126–29. Heiden, NS, pp. 27–28; Maser, pp. 416–17.

34  Röhm, pp. 209–10; Hoegner, *Verratene Republik*, pp. 146–47; Maser, pp. 419–21. See also the extensive account in the fifteenth anniversary edition of the *Westdeutscher Beobachter*, September 11, 1938.

35  There was considerable basis for the Nazi expectation of October 1923 that a Mussolini-like march on Berlin could succeed, which was partly confirmed by the consolidation of the German Right in the spring of 1924 in the new Reichstag and the formation of the *National-Sozialistische Freiheitsbewegung*. Hoegner (*Die Verratene Republik*) describes negotiations with Ludendorff in the fall which diverged widely from the direction of a Hitler-led regime, but which would have involved the Nazis as tools. Plotters in the north included Heinrich Class of the Pan-German League, Albrecht von Graefe of the Deutsch-Völkische Freiheitspartei, Theodor Duesterberg, leader of the Stahlhelm, Hugo Stinnes and various Krupp directors, representatives of the Landbund, etc. (pp. 155–56). See Röhm, pp. 206–16; and Hanfstaengl, pp. 91–94. Waite stresses a *lack* of cooperation with the northern free corps groups: pp. 261–62. Ernst Deuerlein, ed., *Der Hitlerputsch* (Stuttgart, 1962), pp. 67–99, and documents, pp. 166–307.

36  Brückner's warning: Gordon, *Hitler and the Beer Hall Putsch*, pp. 243–44. The end of the inflation would terminate the extraordinary value of foreign currency subventions, important for the SA officers' salaries: Heiden, NS, p. 103. See also Hanfstaengl, p. 131. On the shift in the attitude of business and conservative circles, see Eyck, vol. 1, pp. 347–49; and George W. F. Hallgarten, *Hitler, Reichswehr und Industrie* (Frankfurt am Main, 1955), pp. 30–32. Gumbel cites a warning issued by Göring to SA leaders not to play into the hands of Reichswehr commanders (*Schwäbische Tagwacht*, September 5, 1923): pp. 186–87.

37  Hauptsturmführer Rehm, "Geschichte der SA," *Der SA-Mann, Sonderdruck* 4, June 1941, Jahrgang 10, p. 10 (T-580/roll 85/folder 403); Waite, p. 257; Gordon, *Hitler and the Beer Hall Putsch*, pp. 212–16.

38  Eyck, vol. 1, pp. 349–50; Hoegner, *Verratene Republik*, p. 147; Gordon, *Hitler and the Beer Hall Putsch*, pp. 221–22. On Reichsflagge and Reichskriegsflagge, see Röhm, pp. 216–24; Hanfstaengl, pp. 123–24. As early as July 1922, Strasser's Landshut SA was one of the strongest detachments outside Munich: T-580/roll 19/folder 199 (Gau records: Niederbayern).

39  Röhm, pp. 224–31; Eyck, vol. 1, pp. 356–64; Hoegner, *Verratene Republik*,
    pp. 148–60; Hallgarten, pp. 33–40; Gordon, *Hitler and the Beer Hall
    Putsch*, pp. 246–64.
40  Harold Gordon's *Hitler and the Beer Hall Putsch* is the best treatment, by
    far. See his chapters, "Night of Confusion," pp. 270–312; "Day of Decision,"
    pp. 313–65; "The Putsch outside München," pp. 367–88; and "The Putsch
    in the Balance," pp. 389–409. On the traitorous SA officers, see Hanf-
    staengl, p. 98. See also Kallenbach, pp. 23–29.
41  Said Hitler in the closing speech of his trial: "Die Armee die wir herange-
    bildet haben, die wächst von Tag zu Tag, von Stunde zu Stunde schneller.
    Gerade in diesen Tagen habe ich die stolze Hoffnung, dass einmal die
    Stunde kommt, dass diese wilden Scharen zu Bataillonen, die Bataillonen
    zu Regimentern, die Regimenter zu Divisionen werden, dass die alte Ko-
    karde aus dem Schmutz herausgeholt wird, dass die alten Fahnen wieder
    voranflattern . . ." (Eyck, vol. 1, pp. 394–95.) "The army that we have
    built up is growing faster day by day, hour by hour. In these very days I
    proudly hope that one day the hour will strike, when these wild bands will
    become battalions, the battalions regiments, the regiments divisions; that
    the old cockade will be raised up out of the dust, that the old banners will
    flap in front of us again . . ." (author's translation). For a complete English
    version of the trial, see *The Hitler Trial before the People's Court in Mu-
    nich*, H. Francis Freniere, Lucie Karcic, Philip Fandek, trans., 3 vols., (Ar-
    lington, Va., 1976).
42  Röhm, pp. 310–25; Hanfstaengl, pp. 122–24; Ludecke, pp. 237–38, 260;
    Orlow, *History, 1919–1933*, pp. 46–52; Gordon, *Hitler and the Beer Hall
    Putsch*, pp. 555–72.

## Chapter 2:  The Early Years

1  Walter Buch, referring to existing conditions when he took over the Party
   Committee for Investigation and Arbitration (*Untersuchungs- und Schlicht-
   ungsausschuss: Uschla*) in 1927, observed, "All those that came at that time
   were very special fellows, rough-hewn, with their own wills. Everybody
   came *from* somewhere; everybody brought with them something that got in
   the way of the common effort in spite of all their glowing purpose." *Völkischer Beobachter* (hereafter VB), November 11, 1942.
2  Orlow, *History, 1919*–1933, pp. 46–53; Rainer Hambrecht, *Der Aufstieg
   der NSDAP in Mittel- und Oberfranken (1925–1933)* (Nuremberg, 1976),
   pp. 55–84; Geoffrey Pridham, *Hitler's Rise to Power. The Nazi Movement
   in Bavaria 1923–1933* (New York, 1973), pp. 22–32; Wolfgang Horn,
   *Führerideologie und Parteiorganisation in der NSDAP (1919–1933)* (Düsseldorf, 1972), pp. 154–97; Jeremy Noakes, *The Nazi Party in Lower Saxony,
   1921–1933* (New York, 1971), pp. 41–55.
3  Röhm, pp. 326–37; Volz, p. 95; Ludecke, pp. 244–48; Erich Ludendorff,
   *Vom Feldherrn zum Weltrevolutionär und Wegbereiter deutscher Volks-
   schöpfung, meine Lebenserinnerungen von 1919 bis 1925* (Munich, 1940),
   pp. 337–40, 343–45; Karl Koch, *Männer im Braunhemd* (Berlin, 1936), p.

44; Arnolt Bronnen, *Rossbach* (Berlin, 1930), pp. 170–74; Engelbrechten, p. 33. For the Charlottenburg SA as the *NS-Kameradschaftsbund*, see VB, "Aus anderen völkischen Verbänden," March 24, 1924.

4   *Dienstvorschrift des Frontbanns*, T-580/roll 19/folder 199a (Gau records: Berlin). See also a Prussian Secret Police (IA) report of October 22, 1924, ibid. Cf. Engelbrechten, pp. 34–35. The best treatment of the *Frontbann* is in a Johns Hopkins dissertation of 1969: Robert Henry Frank, "Hitler and the National-Socialist Coalition 1924–1932" (University Microfilms 72-16845), pp. 209–60.

5   Hoegner, *Verratene Republik*, pp. 178–86; Rühle, pp. 110–13; Ludendorff, pp. 368–96; *Abteilungsbefehl Nr. 2*, *Frontbann Nord*, Stettin, November 17, 1925, T-580/roll 24/folder 207 (Gau records: Pommern); Eyck, vol. 1, pp. 398–99, 421–22. See also Ernst Reventlow, *Der Weg zum neuen Deutschland* (Essen, [1933]), pp. 241–50.

6   Hanfstaengl, pp. 132–33; Röhm, pp. 337–46; Engelbrechten, p. 36; Bennecke, *Hitler und die SA*, pp. 109–12, 116–18.

7   T-580/roll 19/folder 199a (Gau records: Berlin); T-580/roll 21/folder 201 (Gau records: Hamburg, Hannover-Nord, Hannover-Süd); T-580/roll 24/folder 207 (Gau records: Pommern); Engelbrechten, pp. 38–42.

8   Gunter D'Alquen, *Die SS. Geschichte, Aufgabe, Organisation. Schriften der Hochschule für Politik*, Heft 33 (Berlin, 1939), pp. 6–7; Volz, p. 96; Rühle, p. 128; SS-Hauptamt, SS-Leitheft 7:1–b (1941):10; Hans Buchheim, "Die SS in der Verfassung des Dritten Reiches," VJHZ 3 (1955): 129, citing VB, April 18, September 23, and December 9, 1925; Hitler, *Secret Conversations*, p. 138. See also Hans Buchheim, "Die Rolle der SS in der Entwicklung der nationalsozialistischen Herrschaft," *Colloquium* 11:3 (1957): 14. The Pöhner funeral procession is depicted in Koch, *Männer im Braunhemd*, opposite p. 49.

9   *Rundschreiben Nr. 1* (September 21, 1925) and *Richtlinien* (version 1), T-580/roll 87/folder 425. For various tidbits (such as the name of the tavern where the veterans of the *Stosstrupp* could be recruited) see Heinz Höhne, *Der Orden unter dem Totenkopf. Die Geschichte der SS* (Gütersloh, 1967), p. 27, available in English as *The Order of the Death's Head* (London, 1969).

10  T-580/roll 87/folder 425.

11  T-580/roll 21/folder 201 (Gau records: Hamburg); T-580/roll 20/folder 201 (Gau records: Halle-Merseburg); Beck, pp. 99 ff.; Albert Krebs, *Tendenzen und Gestalten der NSDAP* (Stuttgart, 1959), pp. 42–43.

12  T-580/roll 87/folder 425; Koch, *Männer im Braunhemd*, p. 53.

13  See D'Alquen, p. 6. Volz distinguishes between Saxony and Thuringia (p. 21). For the electoral campaigns in these Länder in 1926, see Volz, p. 23. See the correspondence regarding Hitler's speech in Zwickau and the disturbances in Chemnitz and Leipzig of 1925 in T-580/roll 21/folder 201 (Gau records: Hamburg). See also *Tagebuch von Joseph Goebbels, 1925/26* (Stuttgart, 1960), pp. 42–43. On the early SS in Saxony and Thuringia: *Die Schutzstaffel* 1:2 (December 1926): 7–8, T-580/roll 87/folder 425. Ludecke's

assertion (p. 335) that "the main function of the SS was to constitute, in every district of the Reich, a block that would be unswervingly loyal to Hitler, upholding his rule as against any other Nazi who might become too popular or dare to jeopardize the leadership principle embodied in him alone" contains more than a grain of truth, but is also anachronistic. In 1925–1926, the SS had no hope of transcending local conditions.

14 Koch, *Männer im Braunhemd*, p. 53; T-580/roll 19/folder 199 (Gau records: Niederbayern); T-580/roll 21/folder 202/I (Gau records: Hannover-Ost). On *Frontbann* secrecy: Engelbrechten, pp. 36–38. In Saxony, the Nazis even refused to aid in *Grenzschutz* (border guard) exercises. Thilo Vogelsang, *Reichswehr, Staat und NSDAP* (Stuttgart, 1962), p. 59.

15 T-580/roll 87/folder 425; Koch, *Männer im Braunhemd*, pp. 53–54; T-580/roll 20/folder 200 (Gau records: Danzig).

16 T-580/roll 87/folder 425; Volz, p. 96; Goebbels's *Tagebuch*, p. 95, note 1; Röhm, p. 344.

17 *Rundschreiben Nr. 1* (April 14, 1926) and *Richtlinien* (version 2), T-580/roll 87/folder 425.

18 T-580/roll 87/folder 425; T-580/roll 20/folder 201 (Gau records: Halle-Merseburg).

19 Koch, *Männer im Braunhemd*, p. 55; Rühle, p. 130. See also Frank dissertation, p. 282. *Dienstvorschrift für die SA der NSDAP (SADV)* (Diessen vor München: J. C. Huber, May 30, 1931), T-580/roll 85/folder 403; *Lagebericht* (situation report) of the political police, September 22, 1926, T-580/roll 87/folder 425; Rossbach, pp. 89–90.

20 Hitler's victory is well mirrored in Goebbels's *Tagebuch*, January–July 1926, pp. 55–94. Strasser's desire for the SA: ibid., pp. 132, 135. See also Joseph Nyomarkay, *Charisma and Factionalism in the Nazi Party* (Minneapolis, 1967), pp. 77–89. Eight SA-Standarten at Weimar: Hambrecht, p. 117.

21 The Gau records of Lower Bavaria for 1925 and thereafter the Gau records of nearly every gau until 1930 depict the rise in party significance of the young Himmler. During the summer of 1925 he handles gau affairs because Strasser is ill; he comes to Munich occasionally on gau matters, quite unknown, but refuses to deal with Amann because of some insult. He becomes a *Referent* (specialist) on setting up SA and SS units in 1926, ordering his Party *Hitlerhemd* (shirt) and *Schutzstaffelmütze* (SS cap) from Heines's *Schillversand* (mail order house) after the Weimar Party Day: T-175/roll 99/frame 2620147. His earliest recorded action as deputy propaganda chief falls in November 1926: T-580/roll 19/folder 199 and roll 23/folder 205 (Gau records: Mecklenburg).

22 Hoegner, *Verratene Republik*, pp. 194–96; Engelbrechten, p. 45; D'Alquen, pp. 6–7; Hans Buchheim, "Die SS in der Verfassung des Dritten Reichs," VJHZ 3 (1955): 130: "trotz Berchtolds heftiger Gegenwehr" (against Berchtold's strong opposition). See Heiden, DF, p. 305, and *Hitler*, p. 232. Berchtold's confirmation: E. J. Cassel, "Geist, Kampf und Aufgabe der SS," *NSK Wahlsonderdienst*, 5 April 1938, Folge 13, p. 5, T-580/roll 87/folder 425. According to the entry for Berchtold in *Der Grossdeutsche*

*Reichstag 1938* (Berlin, n.d.) he became an editor for *Völkischer Beobachter* as early as January 1, 1927; in 1928 he became editor of the new *SA-Mann* and rejoined Pfeffer's staff.

23  T-580/roll 85/folder 403.

24  Hess was reported by the police to be an SS regional leader (*Scharführer*) in 1929. Early pictures of Hess at the 1927 Nuremberg Party Day in Hoffman, *Braune Heer*, p. 23; at the 1929 Party Day, in Koch, *Männer im Braunhemd*, opposite p. 128.

25  *Die Schutzstaffel* 1:2 (December 1926), T-580/roll 87/folder 425. See also police situation report for Upper Bavaria, September 22, 1926, ibid.; and a Berlin police report of April 19, 1926, T-580/roll 19/folder 199a; also the retrospective gory accounts for 1926–1927 in the *Westdeutscher Beobachter* of November 7 and 28, 1936.

26  Hoffmann, *Braune Heer*, p. 25; Koch, *Männer im Braunhemd*, opposite p. 52; Walter M. Espe, *Das Buch der N.S.D.A.P.* (Berlin, 1933), item 70; Georg Usadel, *Zeitgeschichte in Wort und Bild*, 2. Auflage (Oldenburg, 1942), vol. 3, p. 137; Joseph Goebbels, *Kampf um Berlin* (Munich, 1934), p. 193.

27  T-580/roll 23/folder 205 (Gau records: Mecklenburg); T-580/rolls 19–22/folders 199, 200, 201, 202 (I–II–III), 203, 204 (Gau records for Niederbayern, Halle-Merseburg, Hannover-Ost, -Süd, -Nord, Magdeburg-Anhalt, etc.).

28  Orlow, *History, 1919–1933*, pp. 101–21; Engelbrechten, pp. 62–65; Frank dissertation, pp. 323–27; Wolfgang Schäfer, *NSDAP. Entwicklung und Struktur der Staatspartei des Dritten Reichs* (Hannover-Frankfurt am Main, 1957), pp. 8–12. See also Daniel Lerner, *The Nazi Elite* (Stanford, 1951), pp. 34–52. Basic SA orders of Pfeffer (SABE's 1–15; GRUSA's I–IV): T-580/roll 85/folder 403. Also T-580/roll 25/folder 208 (Gau records: Saxony). SA clean-up: BDC Biographical Records (*Oberstes Parteigericht*). On Himmler, see Bradley F. Smith, *Heinrich Himmler. A Nazi in the Making 1900–1926* (Stanford, 1971), esp. pp. 154–72.

29  T-580/roll 87/folder 425. In May 1933 Himmler's adjutant wrote the *Münchener Neueste Nachrichten* that the SS had had between three and four hundred men at Nuremberg in 1927: T-175/roll 99/frame 2621099.

30  The thousand figure is from Höhne, p. 28, citing NSDAP-*Hauptarchiv*, roll 17. *SS-Befehl* Nr. 2, November 4, 1927; *Zusatz zu Befehl* Nr. 1, November 23, 1927; *SS-Befehl* Nr. 5, March 15, 1928 (all T-580/roll 87/folder 425). SA-tax: letter of F. X. Schwarz to gau Hannover-Süd, August, 9, 1926, T-580/roll 21/folder 202; still in existence according to a letter of gauleiter Loeper to Schwarz, January 3, 1929, T-580/roll 23/folder 204 (Gau records: Magdeburg-Anhalt). Nazi students at Cologne University were urged to join an SS unit as early as July 23, 1928: Robert Max Kempner, *Blueprint for the Nazi Underground as Revealed in Confidential German Police Reports* (Lansdowne, Pa., 1943), p. 165.

31  T-580/roll 87/folder 425. See the characterizations of SS fighter-types ("enforcers") in Peter Merkl, *Political Violence under the Swastika: 581 Early*

*Nazis* (Princeton, 1975), pp. 661–66, and *The Making of a Storm Trooper* (Princeton, 1980), pp. 263–82.

32 Martin Broszat, "Die Anfänge der Berliner NSDAP 1926/27," VJHZ 8 (1960): 93, 104, 108, 114–15. "Dokumente," Goebbels's *Tagebuch*, No. 1, pp. 113–14, No. 4, p. 117–19, No. 5, pp. 120–22; Goebbels, *Kampf um Berlin*, p. 50. See also Engelbrechten, pp. 52–59.

33 Older gauleiters thrust aside: Theodor Vahlen and Richard Corswant (Pomerania); Heinrich Haake (South Rhineland); Axel Ripke (North Rhineland); Josef Klant (Hamburg); Ernst Schlange (Berlin). New gauleiters: see Adolf Hitler, *Tischgespräche im Führerhauptquartier 1914–42*, ed. Henry Picker (Bonn, 1951), pp. 251–52. On Koch, see Hermann Rauschning, *Man of Chaos* (New York, 1942), pp. 87–93. On Kaufmann: Goebbels's *Tagebuch*, pp. 51 ff.; Krebs, pp. 113–14. On Sauckel, see his testimony at Nuremberg, IMT, vol. 14, pp. 602–6, and that of Max Timm, IMT, vol. 15, p. 208. On Bürckel, see Görlitz and Quint, pp. 448–49.

34 The problems and attitudes of the SA are thus characterized by *SA-Oberführer Süd* Schneidhuber (one of the victims of June 30, 1934) in a memorandum he circulated in September 1930: T-580/roll 85/folder 403. See also in folder 403 Basic Order I (GRUSA I), May 30, 1927, countersigned by Hitler, which reveals the difficulty Hitler was having as early as 1927 in keeping peace. (For example, Thuringian gauleiter Arthur Dinter thought Pfeffer had insulted him. Letter of April 6, 1927, ibid.)

35 See Heiden, DF ("chosen average men . . . not great individuals but 'good material' . . .": p. 308). In a sense, as Heiden implies, this desire for faceless "material" prevailed throughout the history of the SS, and the few notable exceptions of leading SS men with very low SS numbers which I deal with in chapter three, seem to be precisely "chosen average men in positions of mastery." Just 241 men who entered the SS before 1929 ultimately became SS officers, 179 of them pro forma and honorifically after January 1933 (*Dienstalterslisten 1934, 1935, 1936;* SS numbers 2–1299).

36 Erich Matthias and Rudolf Morsey, eds., *Das Ende der Parteien* (Düsseldorf, 1960), pp. 544–49. Karl Dietrich Bracher, in *Die Auflösung der weimarer Republik*, 2d ed. (Villingen/Schwarzwald, 1960), pp. 108–27, stresses 1929 as a clearer turning point. Cf. Krebs, pp. 21–26; Friederich Christian zu Schaumburg-Lippe, *Zwischen Krone und Kerker* (Wiesbaden, 1952), pp. 86 ff. Himmler correspondence with Bürckel (Palatinate) and Kube (Kurmark-Ostmark), 1928–1929: T-580/rolls 23–24/folders 205, 207 (Gau records: Palatinate and Kurmark-Ostmark).

37 Vogelsang, *Reichswehr, Staat und NSDAP*, p. 81; Herbert Erb and Hans-Henning von Grote, *Konstantin Hierl. Der Mann und sein Werk* (Munich, 1939), pp. 45–55. Hans Buchheim lists the following specialized professional groups formed at this time: *Bund Nationalsozialistischer Deutscher Juristen, NS-Schülerbund, NS-Lehrerbund,* and *NS-Ärztebund (Glaubenskrise,* p. 63). Otto Strasser, *Hitler and I* (Boston, 1940), pp. 90–92, 99–100; Rudolf Heberle, *Landbevölkerung und Nationalsozialismus* (Stuttgart, 1963), pp. 160–64. See also Noakes, pp. 105–7, 121 ff.

38  In December 1928 Sauckel was complaining *to Himmler* of Storm Troop
    violence in Weimar, and Himmler relayed this to Pfeffer in a Propaganda
    Section memorandum of December 19, 1928. T-580/roll 87/folder 425.
    Himmler correspondence with Koch, T-580/roll 24/folder 207 (Gau rec-
    ords: Ostpreussen); Himmler correspondence with Robert Wagner and
    Wilhelm Kube, T-580/roll 19/folder 199 (Gau records: Baden) and T-580/
    roll 23/folder 205 (Gau records: Kurmark-Ostmark). A police situation re-
    port of May 7, 1929, credits the SS with precisely 1,402 members: T-580/
    roll 87/folder 425. Since less than 100 communities can be identified with
    SS units in 1930, and few communities had more than one Staffel in 1929,
    it appears likely that in 1929 the SS merely filled out and extended slightly
    its "paper" 75 Staffeln of 1926. Only 218 of the new SS men of 1929 ever be-
    came officers — seven in 1929, ten in 1930, sixteen in 1931, ten in 1932, sev-
    enteen in 1933, and 158 in 1934 or later (retrospective honors); *Dienstal-
    terslisten* for 1934, 1935, and 1936 (SS numbers 1300–2000). For a picture
    of Himmler as a snooper, see Krebs, p. 210. (He had snooped on his broth-
    er's girlfriend as early as 1924: Bradley Smith, pp. 148–52.)
39  On Pfeffer, see Krebs, pp. 218–20. One hundred thousand SA (*Hunderttau-
    sendmanngarde*): Standartenführer Carl Gebhardt and Obersturmführer
    Rudhardt, "Die SA, ihre Entwicklung und Gliederung" (1935), p. 33,
    T-580/roll 85/folder 402. Two hundred-fifty thousand SA: Görlitz and
    Quint, p. 262. *Volksheer:* see item 22 of the party platform, Kempner, *Blue-
    print for the Nazi Underground*, p. 159. Cf. SABE 15, February 19, 1927,
    T-580/roll 85/folder 403.
40  SABE's 6–7, *Gliederung;* SABE's 13–14, *Gaubereiche, Aufbau einer Bri-
    gade;* GRUSA IV, June 4, 1927; all in T-580/roll 85/folder 403. Gebhardt
    and Rudhardt, pp. 33–34; GRUSA VII, April 12, 1929, T-580/roll 85/folder
    425. A parallel to the survival of the Staffeln is the continued use of Grup-
    pen of 20–30 in the SA: Engelbrechten, p. 73. For a time in 1929–1930,
    Staffeln in neighboring towns were theoretically united into a Sturm, e.g.,
    Zwickau, Werdau, and Chemnitz in Saxony; biographical records in Berlin
    Document Center (hereafter BDC). Police situation report of May 7, 1929,
    T-580/roll 87/folder 425; letter of the Scharführer of Franconia, June 22,
    1929, ibid. See also Hambrecht, pp. 118–19.
41  GRUSA VII, April 12, 1929, T-580/roll 87/folder 425; T-580/roll 23/folder
    204 (Gau records: Magdeburg-Anhalt). Himmler still depended on the
    good will of gauleiters like Hans Schemm in Bayreuth and Erich Koch in
    Königsberg to help set up a local SS: T-580/roll 19/folder 199 (Gau records:
    Oberfranken); T-580/roll 24/folder 206 (Gau records: Ostpreussen).
42  *SS-Befehl, Parteitag*, II. Teil T-580/roll 87/folder 425. Forty SA-
    *Standarten:* SADV 1931, T-580/roll 85/folder 403. SABE of August 20,
    1929, *Die Marxistische Angriffstaktik in Nürnberg*, ibid.

## Chapter 3: Formative Years

1  "The fighting days were the best" — an often repeated saying of Nazis in the
    period 1933–1945, usually referring to the years just before 1933. See Fritz

Stelzner, *Schicksal SA* (Munich, 1936), pp. 186–93. Numerous other examples in SS personnel records, BDC Biographical Records.

2  May Day shootings in Berlin: Eyck, vol. 2, pp. 219–20; 2.6 million unemployed in the winter months of 1928–1929: ibid., p. 252; fiscal and financial instability: ibid., pp. 255–56, 286–94. See also Karl D. Bracher, *Die Auflösung der weimarer Republik*, pp. 206–28; and Heinrich Bennecke, *Wirtschaftliche Depression und politischer Radikalismus 1918–1938* (Munich, 1970), pp. 67–143.

3  The SS grew from 1,000 in January 1930 to 52,000 by January 1933, from an officer corps of twenty to 800: *Dienstaltersliste der Schutzstaffel der NSDAP*, Bearbeitet von der Personalabteilung des Reichsführers-SS, Stand vom 1. Oktober 1935 (Munich, 1935) (hereafter *DAL 1935*), p. 152. Turnover can be established indirectly from the officer lists, since Himmler made the first 3,000 holders of numbered SS-*Ausweise* (identity cards) still in the SS on April 20, 1934, second lieutenants if they were not already officers: T-611/roll 6/folder 432, "SS-Sachgebiete: Beförderung." These were presumably those who joined before the first great electoral victory of September 1930. By this date there were thirty-five SS officers, fifteen of whom had been commissioned in 1930 and seven in 1929. During 1931 the SS passed the 10,000 mark, and had more than 200 officers by October 1931. Then while SS *numbers* multiplied five times in 1932, officers quadrupled. SA strength at the outset of 1930 was about 40,000, reaching 60,000 by the fall and winter of 1930 (Frank dissertation, pp. 419–20), 170,000 by September 1931, and possibly 290,000 by early 1932. In late summer of 1932 the SA reached 470,000: Merkl, *Making of a Storm Trooper*, p. 179.

4  SS functions in 1929, as noted in GRUSA VIII, April 12, 1929, include especially difficult propaganda marches, guarding speakers, rear guard for propaganda marches, and security-and-order tasks requiring individual persons rather than group action. T-580/roll 87/folder 425. SS recruits in 1929: Munich Police Report of May 7, 1929, ibid. On the possibilities of coalition, see Ludecke, pp. 338–41. See also Hermann Pünder, *Politik in der Reichskanzlei* (Stuttgart, 1961), p. 65; and Sigmund Neumann, *Die deutschen Parteien* (Berlin, 1932), pp. 85–86, who stresses the value and problems of "legality" in winning bourgeois collaborators.

5  Pfeffer's principles are well expressed in an early letter to the gauleiters of November 1, 1926. T-580/roll 85/folder 403. On the discipline problem in the party and SA: Peter Hüttenberger, *Die Gauleiter. Studien zum Wandel des Machtgefüges in der NSDAP* (Stuttgart, 1969), pp. 38, 42 (Berlin), 50 (Ruhr), 52 (Rheinland-Süd), 54 (Mecklenburg). Bennecke, *Hitler und die SA*, pp. 141 ff. On Pfeffer and Stennes, see Frank dissertation, pp. 328–43. The SS role in the sale of *Völkischer Beobachter* subscriptions continued: letter of February 27, 1930, of the SS-*Reichsgeschäftsführer*, T-580/roll 87/folder 425. SS police duty within the party: a Munich Police Report of December 4, 1930, ibid. A nonspecific order of Himmler stressing SS discipline and obedience: December 1, 1930, ibid.

6  On the SA reorganization of 1927–1929: Hauptsturmführer Rehm, "Geschichte der SA," *Der SA-Mann*, Sonderdruck 4, June 1941, Jahrgang 10,

pp. 30–34, T-580/roll 85/folder 403; also GRUSA III, June 3, 1927, ibid.; GRUSA IV of June 4 and GRUSA V of June 5 in Engelbrechten, pp. 64–65. Complaints of March 1 and March 14, 1927 by a *Bezirksleiter* (Bergisch-Land) about SA regionalism are a thinly disguised effort to nominate the local SA commander. T-580/roll 19/folder 199b (Gau records: Düsseldorf); Kempner, *Blueprint for the Nazi Underground*, p. 24.

7  "Festzug der SA Nürnberg, Sonntag den 4. August 1929" lists five OSAF-Stellvertreter and Lutze as Oberführer Ruhr: T-580/roll 85/folder 403. These deputyships are alleged to have been modeled after the prewar German Army inspection districts: Kempner, p. 171. SA feeling against the party is portrayed in a memorandum of the Munich SA leader, August Schneidhuber: *Stellungnahme zur vorgesehenen Umorganisation der SA-Führung*, September 19, 1930. T-580/roll 85/folder 403.

8  Robert G. L. Waite's list in *Vanguard of Nazism* contains twenty-seven SA officers and fifteen SS officers (pp. 285–96): see esp. Karl Ernst, Werner von Fichte, Hans Hayn, Edmund Heines, Hans Georg Hofmann, Dietrich von Jagow, Manfred von Killinger, Fritz Ritter von Krausser, Otto Lancelle, Viktor Lutze, and Otto Wagener. On Manfred von Killinger in Dresden, see Ernst von Salomon, *Der Fragebogen*, p. 115.

9  Charles Drage, *The Amiable Prussian* (London, 1958), pp. 56–61.

10  Drage, pp. 67–74. See also "Stennes Aktion," T-580/roll 51/folder 278. Engelbrechten is silent, although he reports a reorganization of both the gau and the SA on October 1 (p. 84).

11  Strasser, pp. 99–120; Michael Stern and Otto Strasser, *Flight from Terror* (New York, 1943), pp. 144–54. See also Strasser material from July 1930, T-580/roll 50/folder 278.

12  Drage, pp. 74–76; *Münchener Post*, September 2, 1930, and *Münchener Neueste Nachrichten*, September 2, 1930, T-580/roll 85/folder 403; Munich Police Report, October 24, 1930, T-580/roll 87/folder 425; Frank dissertation, pp. 361–84; Bennecke, *Hitler und die SA*, pp. 147–49; Julius Lippert, *Im Strom der Zeit. Erlebnisse und Eindrücke* (Berlin, 1942), pp. 173–75, 178–80.

13  On von Ulrich and his post as "GISASS" (*General-Inspektor SA-SS*), see SABE of June 4, 1930, T-580/roll 85/folder 403. See also Kempner, *Blueprint for the Nazi Underground*, p. 162. On Otto Wagener, stressing his role as SA quartermaster, see Görlitz and Quint, p. 278; also Richard Scheringer, *Das grosse Los* (Hamburg, 1960), p. 194. A SABE of July 12, 1930, issued by Wagener refers to an inspection tour by Pfeffer himself, in which he was to be accompanied by Himmler and Wagener. Among those visited was Viktor Lutze, newly promoted to OSAF-Deputy. This probably indicates a belated effort to tighten control. T-580/roll 85/folder 403.

14  Hitler was reported to be considering von Ulrich as Pfeffer's successor: Munich Police Report of October 29, 1930, T-580/roll 87/folder 425. Pfeffer's resignation: SABE of September 3, 1930, T-580/roll 85/folder 403. For Röhm's thinking and his very interesting correspondence with Himmler beginning October 1929, see T-580/roll 36/folder 238/I. See also Bennecke, *Hitler und die SA*, pp. 147–49.

15 One hundred fifty SS-*Stürme*: BDC Biographical Records show the formation of Stürme in August to December of 1930 with numbers in the 140s out
of much older *Staffeln* (Aue, Werdau, Ludwigshafen). SA and SS *Lokale*:
Hauptsturmführer Rehm, "Geschichte der SA," *Der SA-Mann*, June 1941,
p. 37, T-580/roll 85/folder 403. SS-*Sturm* rosters: Beck, pp. 313 (Hagen in
Westfalen), 366 (Lippstadt i.W.). SS financing: Himmler speech to Reichswehr officers, January 1937, 1992(A)-PS, IMT, vol. 29, p. 209. SA responsibilities toward SS unfulfilled: *SS-Führerbesprechung*, June 13–14, 1931, p.
9, T-580/roll 87/folder 425. A city the size of Bayreuth (35,000 in 1925) is
reported to have had 125 SA men in September 1930; it obviously could not
support a large SS! Memorandum of A. Schneidhuber, T-580/roll 85/folder
403. The SA leader in Pomerania claimed 3,000 SA members in November
1930; at this time there was no Pomeranian SS. Meeting of *Gau SA-Führer*,
November 30, 1930, ibid. The Munich police estimated the Greater Munich
SA at only 600, the SS at 200 in October 1930: Bennecke, *Hitler und die SA*,
p. 154.

16 In theory, both SA and SS were to get financial help from the PO; in fact the
SA got little and the SS nothing. Munich Police Report of May 7, 1929,
T-580/roll 87/folder 425. Himmler wrote a wheedling letter to Streicher in
November 1930 urging him to at least help SS men with legal aid, but relin-
quishing any claim to the party "war chest" (*Kampfschatz*) or SA credits
(*Umlage*): T-580/roll 87/folder 425. In December 1930 the SA and SS-
Gauführer of Niederbayern were urged to report their size to the party so
that it could check on SA contributions and credits: T-580/roll 19/folder
199. There were twenty SS officers on January 1, 1930, twenty-three on
April 1, thirty-five on July 1, and forty-seven on October 1; there were
seventy-one on January 1, 1931: *DAL 1935*, p. 152. About sixteen Gau SS-
Führer can be identified for 1930, of whom nearly a dozen acquired very
high SS rank (Gruppen- or Obergruppenführer) in the late thirties, and of
whom five or six were truly prominent in the Black Corps: BDC Biographical Records. On the thirty Standarten and the Oberführerbereiche, the
Reich and gau level Geschäftsführer and Geldverwalter, see letters of September 2, 1929, February 27, 1930, and July 23, 1930, in T-580/roll 87/
folder 425. Hitler reaffirmed the SS's right to collect dues from "supporting
members" (*Fördernde Mitglieder*) on March 15, 1929: printed in the FM
membership book, IMT, vol. 42, doc. SS 43, pp. 491–93. The FM membership was kept secret even from the party. The Munich SS headquarters was
supposed to get 85 percent of the "take"! Munich Police Report of May 7,
1929, T-580/roll 87/folder 425.

17 The SA-SS rivalry is especially well revealed in BDC Biographical Records.
See also: Bennecke, *Hitler und die SA*, p. 205; Munich Police Report of De-
cember 4, 1930, T-580/roll 87/folder 425. On Stennes, see *Bericht. Aussprache
der SAF mit Herrn Reichsschatzmeister Schwarz über Finanzierung der
SA*, T-580/roll 85/folder 403; *Landgericht Osnabrück. Schwurgerichtsan-
klage, gegen U. von Woyrsch et al., Ermittlungen (Institut für Zeitgeschichte)*.
Himmler: "Material für die Schriftleitungen zum 6. Januar 1939: Heinrich
Himmler. Zehn Jahre Reichsführer SS," p. 1, T-580/roll 87/folder 425.

18  Wagener's circular letter of October 3, 1930, T-580/roll 85/folder 403.

19  Munich Police Report of February 26, 1931, T-580/roll 87/folder 425.

20  A basic order separating the SS and SA was in preparation according to a Hitler memorandum of November 7, 1930: T-580/roll 87/folder 425. Himmler's announcement: SS-Befehl Nr. 20, T-580/roll 87/folder 425. Hitler's order and Röhm's implementation: SA-Befehl Nr. 1, ibid. For the November 30 meeting: calls of October 25 and November 13, 1930, T-580/roll 87/folder 425; call of November 27, 1930, T-580/roll 85/folder 402; records of the meeting, ibid.; and Munich Police Report of December 4, 1930, T-580/roll 87/folder 425.

21  Stennes's and Röhm's courses are revealed in BDC Biographical Records, as well as in Gebhardt and Rudhardt, p. 38. Röhm forbade all public discussion of SA politics. SA-Befehl Nr. 5, February 27, 1931, T-580/roll 85/folder 403. SA cadres for SS: SA-Befehl Nr. 1, January 16, 1930, T-580/roll 87/folder 425. See also Heiden, DF, pp. 370–72; Bennecke, Hitler und die SA, p. 164. On Göring's role: Hitler's order as Oberster SA-Führer, November 13, 1930, T-580/roll 85/folder 402; BDC Biographical Records.

22  Political and economic conditions: Eyck, vol. 2, pp. 348–74; Karl Dietrich Bracher, Wolfgang Sauer, and Gerhard Schulz, Die nationalsozialistische Machtergreifung, (Köln u. Oplade, 1960) (hereafter Machtergreifung), pp. 170–73, 367–70, 388–406. Unemployment: Statistisches Jahrbuch für das Deutsche Reich (Berlin, 1932), vol. 51, p. 291. Lawlessness: Görlitz and Quint, pp. 313–16. SS recruitment: DAL, Stand vom 1. Oktober 1934 (Munich, 1934) (hereafter DAL 1934.) A Munich Police Report of December 4, 1930, estimated the SS in south Germany at 1,640: T-580/roll 87/folder 425. Himmler promoted the first 3,000 SS men to lieutenant (only 521 remained who were still enlisted SS men) in April 1933. T-611/roll 6/folder 432.

23  Dienstvorschrift für die SA der NSDAP (SADV), Teil I (Diessen vor München, May 30, 1931). Röhm's military reorganization of the SA: Gebhardt and Rudhardt, p. 34. Munich Police Report, April 20, 1931, T-580/roll 87/folder 425; Otto Strasser, "Der Staat seid Ihr," Deutsche Revolution 1:7, Berlin, April 13, 1931, T-580/roll 51/folder 425. See Engelbrechten, pp. 159–64. The formation of both SA and SS "cavalry units" was very popular among business people and well-to-do country families: Munich Police Report, January 27, 1932, T-580/roll 87/folder 425. A system of SA and SS doctors was also inaugurated at this time: Munich Police Report, December 4, 1930, ibid. Hitler's antiweapon strictures are approvingly noted in the Munich Police Report of February 26, 1931 (ibid.).

24  Hitler's warning: Der Oberste SA-Führer, vol. 1, Nr. 12/31, February 3, 1931, included in Munich Police Report of February 26, 1931, T-580/roll 87/folder 425. SS "moral superiority": SS-Oberführer Befehl Nr. 8, April 1, 1931, ibid.; SS-Führerbesprechung, June 13–14, 1931, ibid. SS absorption of old combat leagues: interviews of Robert Frank with Walter Stennes, Kurt Kremsier, Hans Lustig, and Otto Strasser (personal communication to the author). Of course, a large percentage of the early SS officers also had combat league experience; in all cases studied these men made the transfer

as individuals and not with a unit, however small. BDC Biographical Records.

25  See background correspondence of 1929–1932 on and by Röhm in T-580/roll 85/folder 403. Reorganization of GISASS system, ordered by Hitler, February 10, 1931: included in Munich Police Report of February 26, 1931, T-580/roll 87/folder 425. Hitler told an SA-Appell in Munich in March that some SA units had to be dissolved as a result of infiltration by "spies": Munich Police Report of April 20, 1931. T-580/roll 87/folder 425.

26  The initial changes were ordered on February 20, 1931. Cassel, p. 6, T-580/roll 87/folder 425. Five-regiment brigades: *SS-Befehl* Nr. 22, in Berlin Police Report of April 1, 1931, ibid.; and BDC Biographical Records. The first seven *Abschnitte* covered the entire Reich, and the eighth was for Austria. The ninth and succeeding *Abschnitte* made their appearance in 1932, as did *Standarten* with numbers in the upper forties. BDC Biographical Records. Hitler told the March SA conclave in Munich that in a year's time he expected the SA and the SS to grow threefold. Munich Police Report, April 20, 1931, T-580/roll 87/folder 425. Organizational changes in the SA for Gau Westfalen-Süd can be traced in detail in Beck, pp. 99–148. For general SA organization in 1931 see *Nationalsozialistisches Jahrbuch 1932* (Munich, 1932), pp. 155–56.

27  Sepp Dietrich came from a humble background, was an ex-sergeant-major with experience in a shock battalion and with armored vehicles, had fought in Upper Silesia after the war, and came to the SS in 1926 from the *Bund Oberland* free corps. *Landgericht München I. Schwurgerichtsanklage gegen J. Dietrich et al., Ermittlungen (Institut für Zeitgeschichte)*. According to his eighth order as *Oberführer Süd*, dated April 1, 1931, Sepp Dietrich had under his command seven regiments (two in Munich, one each in Nuremberg, Landshut, Stuttgart, Kaiserslautern, and Heidelberg), a battalion in Augsburg, and companies in Kempten and Memmingen: T-580/roll 87/folder 425. The SS barracks at the Brown House held a battalion, but since no special unit can be identified, it was probably a rotated affair. Sefton Delmer, *Trail Sinister* (London, 1961), p. 112.

28  *SS-Abschnittsbefehl (Abschnitt III)* Nr. 4, March 21, 1931, T-580/roll 87/folder 425. See also a three-page untitled, undated typescript memorandum on Daluege's *Nachrichtenzentrale*, ibid. Formation of SS units in Brandenburg, Pomerania, and Mecklenburg: BDC Biographical Records. See opening remarks of Himmler at the *SS-Führerbesprechung* (offiers' discussion) in Berlin, June 13, 1931, ibid.

29  Drage, pp. 77–83. The intrigues are revealed in correspondence of February–March 1931 in Berlin Gau records; "Stennes Putsch," Hoover Institution Library; and a Berlin Police Report of May 1, 1931, T-580/roll 51/folder 278. See Delmer, pp. 107–10; and Frank dissertation, pp. 480–95.

30  Drage, pp. 83–84; Munich Police Report of April 20, 1931, T-580/roll 87/folder 425. See opening remarks of Daluege at *SS-Führerbesprechung*, June 13, 1931, ibid. See also two Stennes handbills and *Der Angriff*, April 4, 1931, "Stennes Putsch," Hoover Institution Library.

31 BDC Biographical Records; Walter Luetgebrune, *Ein Kampf um Röhm* (Diessen vor München, 1933), p. 9, T-580/roll 85/folder 403; Cassel, p. 5, T-580/roll 87/folder 425. "Just like in the old army": Himmler, June 13, 1931, *Führerbesprechung*, ibid.

32 Edward W. Bennett, *Germany and the Diplomacy of the Financial Crisis, 1931* (Cambridge, 1962), pp. 116–22, 142–48, 218–43; Golo Mann, *Deutsche Geschichte des 19. und 20. Jahrhunderts* (Frankfurt am Main, 1958), pp. 750–56.

33 Numerous colorful descriptions of SA and SS "armed propaganda" in: Beck, pp. 202–3, 245, 250–53, 319, 340, 370, 407; Koch, *Männer im Braunhemd*, pp. 110–31.

34 Hitler is quoted in the Munich Police Report of April 20, 1931, T-580/roll 87/folder 425. *Dienstvorschrift für die SA der NSDAP* (SADV), Teil I (Diessen vor München, 1931), T-580/roll 85/folder 403. *Vorläufige Dienstordnung für die Arbeit der SS*, June 1931, ibid. See Robert M. W. Kempner's report, drawn up in 1931, where he calls the SS "a kind of secret police, an elite group of the NSDAP, whose positions of leadership were to be held by former officers, if possible" (*Blueprint for the Nazi Underground*, pp. 176–77).

35 *SS-Oberführer Süd (Abschnitt I) Befehl* Nr. 8, April 1, 1931, T-580/roll 87/folder 425; *Besondere Anordnung Nr. 2: Saalordnungsdienst*, Hamburg, August 1, 1931, BDC Biographical Records. On Stennes: Drage, pp. 84–89; Goebbels, *Vom Kaiserhof zur Reichskanzlei* (Munich, 1934), pp. 25, 35. On the background of the SD: Himmler's 1937 speech to Wehrmacht officers, 1992 (A)-PS, IMT, vol. 29, p. 222. See also D'Alquen, pp. 21–22; and an excerpt from RF 1540, read into the transcript of the IMT, August 2, 1946 (a letter from Bruno Streckenbach referring to early illegal activities of the SD), vol. 20, p. 250. Himmler warned against provocateurs in SS uniforms on June 6, 1931: *SS-Befehl* A-Nr. 27, T-580/roll 87/folder 425.

36 Remarks of Himmler and Daluege at *SS-Führerbesprechung*, June 1931, pp. 13–14, T-580/roll 87/folder 425. *SA-SS-Gruppenführerbesprechung*, August 28, 1931, T-580/roll 85/folder 403. NSKK (as part of the SA, April–December 1930; thereafter, like the SS, quasi independent under Adolf Hühnlein): Engelbrechten, p. 170; Volz, p. 97. Sepp Dietrich accompanying Hitler: Hanfstaengl, pp. 185, 197. The SS served at Goebbels's home as personal guards, and an SS man whipped a journalist for having insulted Frau Goebbels. *Kaiserhof*, pp. 85, 88, 178.

37 *SS-Führerbesprechung*, June 1931, T-580/roll 87/folder 425; *SS-Oberführer Befehl* Nr. 8, April 1, 1931, ibid. In 1930, of fifteen Nazis killed in political conflicts, only one was an SS man. In 1931, of forty-two killed, six were SS; in 1932, of seventy deaths only nine fell from the SS, reflecting the approximate strength ratio of the units, but no extraordinary SS exertions. *Halbmast. Das Heldenbuch der SA und SS*, vol. 1 (Berlin, 1932); and *Mitteilungsblätter für die weltanschauliche Schulung der ORPO*, Gruppe B, Folge 27, February 2, 1943.

38 Himmler's remarks at Berlin: *SS-Führerbesprechung*, June 13, 1931, T-580/

roll 87/folder 425. Himmler claimed retrospectively to have studied the photographs of all SS candidates in the early years. The requirement to submit at least pass-photographs, going back to 1929, was not at all unusual in Germany, and must have been only partially observed if Himmler remembered only 100 to 200 a year: 1992(A)-PS, IMT, vol. 29, p. 210.

39 Richard Walther Darré, *Das Bauerntum als Lebensquell der nordischen Rasse* (Munich, 1929); *SS-Führerbesprechung*, June 13–14, 1931, T-580/roll 87/folder 425.

40 Himmler and Daluege: *SS-Führerbesprechung*, June 13–14, 1931, T-580/roll 87/folder 425. Sepp Dietrich: *Oberführer Befehl* Nr. 8, ibid. A three-page untitled and undated memorandum eulogizing Daluege's activities in 1930–1932 embodies many of the SS officer-ideals (ibid.). For Himmler's mentor Darré's views about the decline in heredity, see "Entnordung durch Kriege und Artprägung durch Bauerntum," *Die Sonne*, January 1930, reprinted in R. W. Darré, *Erkenntnisse und Werden* (Goslar, 1940), pp. 132–46.

41 Berlin Police Report of February 1932 dealing with an *SA-Führerbesprechung* of September 15–16, 1931, and referring to anti-Semitic demonstrations on the Kurfürstendamm, an SA strength of 170,000 in 500 Standarten, and a spy mania. T-580/roll 85/folder 403. On Otto Strasser and his allies, see his *Hitler and I*, pp. 120–33. Himmler renewed his warning against spies and provocateurs in *SS-Befehl* Nr. 53, October 10, 1931, T-580/roll 87/folder 425. On the SD and Reinhard Heydrich, see Shlomo Aronson, *Reinhard Heydrich und die Frühgeschichte von Gestapo und SD* (Stuttgart, 1971), pp. 37–62. See also Gunther Deschner, *Reinhard Heydrich. Statthalter der totalen Macht* (Esslingen, 1977), pp. 42–65; and Rolf Hoeppner's testimony, IMT, vol. 20, pp. 188–89. Heydrich's promotions: Lieutenant, August 10, 1931; Captain, December 1, 1931; Major, December 25, 1931; Colonel, July 29, 1932. *DAL 1934*, pp. 2–3.

42 SS connections with the business and professional world: Willi Frischauer, *Himmler, the Evil Genius of the Third Reich* (London, 1953), pp. 32–40; T-580/roll 23/folder 205 (Gau records: Ostmark). Even in 1931 Himmler's ties ran through Göring's business associates like Paul Körner: U.S. Nuremberg doc. NID 13607. Hermann Reischle, *Reichsbauernführer Darré* (Berlin, 1935), pp. 11–44. Other Darré personnel records: U.S. Nuremberg doc. NID 12213, NID 12497, NID 12975; R. Walther Darré, *Neuadel aus Blut und Boden* (Munich, 1930). The basis of Darré's activity was the famous "marriage order," *SS-Befehl* A-Nr. 65, December 31, 1931, reprinted in D'Alquen, *Die SS*, pp. 9–10; and *SS-Befehl* A-Nr. 67 of the same date, setting up an *SS-Rasseamt*. BDC Schumacher Collection, folder 427-R. A letter of Darré of January 16, 1932, describes a six-man bureau "to be set up next week": ibid. Besides Darré, only one, a young nobleman of twenty-three, had been in the SS previously. A supplementary order requiring SS approval of *engagements (Verlobungsbefehl)* may have been issued January 8, 1932. Cassel, p. 6, T-580/roll 85/folder 403.

43 Although separately set up, the SA and SS physicians were temporarily re-

united as *Sanitätsdienst* in October 1931, perhaps due to the units' failure to make use of personnel of the other service, *SA-Verordnungsblatt* 1:4, October 12, 1931, pp. 4–5, T-580/roll 89/folder 449. SA and SS bands also played together, and the SS cavalry put on a riding exhibition in Munich: Munich Police Report, December 29, 1931, T-580/roll 87/folder 425. Formation of SS signal units: ibid. Formation of SS air (flying) units: *SS-Befehl* D-Nr. 1, D-Nr. 3, January 14, 1932, March 18, 1932, ibid. In late 1931 and early 1932 the following printed SS forms appear: *Aufnahme- und Verpflichtungs-schein* ("Ich verpflichte mich für die Idee Adolf Hitlers mich einzusetzen, strengste Parteidisziplin zu wahren, und die Anordnungen der Schutzstaffeln und der Parteiführung gewissenhaft auszuführen. Ich bin Deutscher, bin arischer Abstammung, gehöre keiner Freimaurerloge und keinem Geheim-bunde an, und verspreche die Bewegung mit allen Kräften zu fördern") ("I swear to fight for the cause of Adolf Hitler, to maintain the strictest party discipline and to carry out the orders of the SS and the party leadership conscientiously. I am a German, of Aryan descent, belong to no masonic lodge or secret society and promise to advance the movement with all my powers") (BDC Biographical Records); *Mannschafts-Untersuchungsliste* (MUL), a nonracial physical and psychological examination report (see *SS-Befehl* Nr. 1, January 24, 1932, T-580/roll 87/folder 425); and an *SS-Haft-schein*, providing that members would give up their insignia upon leaving the SS. (BDC Biographical Records). New protocol: *SS-Befehl* Nr. 63, December 21, 1931, creating the rank of SS Captain retroactive to December 1 (T-580/roll 87/folder 425); Hitler's *OSAF-Erlass*, November 28, 1931, dividing the SA and SS officer corps into: (1) Lower (noncommissioned), (2) Middle (lieutenant through major), and (3) Upper (NSDAP *Hauptarchiv* folder 306, BDC). Deschner says noblemen formed "10 % of the SS battalion (*Abschnitt*) commanders and majors (*Sturmbannführer*)" at the time (pp. 43–44).

44 Goebbels, *Kaiserhof*, pp. 17, 35; Ludecke, p. 445. On the loose National Bolshevik tie-up with Otto Strasser, see the Communist periodical *Der Vorkämpfer* (Krefeld), September 1931, T-580/roll 50/folder 278. The planned 22,000 SS is mentioned in Hitler's OSAF order I, Nr. 7407/31, December 2, 1931, NSDAP *Hauptarchiv*, folder 306, BDC. Hitler announced on the tenth anniversary of the founding of the SA (November 4, 1931) that the SA had reached 200,000. T-580/roll 85/folder 402.

45 On Hitler's uncertainty, see Krebs, p. 152. Hitler's adoption of an improvising stance is well portrayed in the record of his remarks to the *SA-SS-Führerbesprechung* of September 15–16, 1931, found in the Berlin Police Report of February 1932, T-580/roll 85/folder 403. On cadres, see Munich Police Report of December 29, 1931, T-580/roll 87/folder 425. On Hitler's courtship of the *Reichswehr:* Kempner, *Blueprint for the Nazi Underground*, pp. 153–57, 191–92. See also K. H. Abshagen, *Schuld und Verhängnis* (Stuttgart, 1961), pp. 183–86; Görlitz and Quint, pp. 325–31; John W. Wheeler-Bennett, *The Nemesis of Power* (New York, 1954), pp. 210–12. The Boxheim documents present a possible version of an SA revolution (or

counter-revolution). *Schulthess' europäischer Geschichtskalender, 1931,* n.s. (Munich, 1931), vol. 47, pp. 262–63.

46  Bracher, *Auflösung,* pp. 121–27. See doc. 047-PS, a letter of Hitler to Rosenberg of August 24, 1931, IMT, vol. 25, p. 99.

47  SS Officers Corps: *DAL 1938,* p. 526. SS strength: 10,000, OSAF order I, Nr. 7407/31, NSDAP-*Hauptarchiv,* Folder 306, BDC; 25,000 and 41,000, *Statistisches Jahrbuch der SS der NSDAP, 1937,* p. 4. These figures correspond roughly to the assigned SS (pass) numbers of persons admitted in 1931 and 1932, but there was probably (a) a lag between the time persons began to serve in the SS and their official acceptance; and (b) a large number of unassigned SS members. An accurate official count might have been much lower (BDC Biographical Records).

48  BDC Biographical Records. Although Himmler spoke of fifty *Standarten* as early as June 1931, most of the *Standarten* in the forties and some with lower numbers were only created in late 1931 and in 1932. See SS-*Führerbesprechung,* June 13–14, 1931, T-580/roll 87/folder 425.

49  BDC Biographical Records. Local commanders accepted people and gave them subordinate commands, even creating new units without Munich approval, and Himmler *never* gave up the practice of promoting people on the spot without informing his personnel office.

50  The direct model for the SS-*Oberstab* was the six-section *SA-Oberstab* created by Pfeffer and Wagener in July, 1930. Its components were: (I) *Führung* (leadership); (II) *Personal* (personnel); (III) *Sanität* (medics); (IV) *Wirtschaft* (economy); (V) *Jura* (law); (VI) *Propaganda.* T-580/roll 85/folder 403. The SS-*Oberstab* seems originally, in late 1931, to have been subdivided thus: (I) *Führung;* (II) *Personal;* (III) *Verwaltung* (administration); (IV) *Sicherheit* (security); (V) *Rasse* (race). BDC Biographical Records. By mid-1932 there is already a tendency to speak of SS-*Ämter* (offices): Darré's *Rassenamt,* Heydrich's *Sicherheits- (dienst) Amt,* a *Verwaltungsamt,* and SS-*Amt* (personnel), the latter containing its own *Führungsstab* (executive staff). The designation *Oberstab* was dropped January 1, 1933: SS-*Befehlsblatt* 1:2, item 7, T-611/roll 4/folder 429. SS headquarters was moved to the Arcisstrasse at the same time: ibid., item 21. In February 1933 the chief of the *Führungsstab* became independent of the SS-*Amt:* T-580/roll 89/folder 449. His office was moved to the Alsenstrasse in Berlin. T-175/roll 99/frame 2621175.

51  Many a high-ranking SS officer has left behind a bitter characterization of Himmler. BDC Biographical Records. Except for the increasing guilt symptoms of the war years, the picture of him drawn by Felix Kersten applies equally well for the early 1930s — a strangely rigid and nongrowing personality, overburdened with crotchets — a near-sighted visionary. *Totenkopf und Treue* (Hamburg, [1952]), pp. 389–95, 400–407. Cf. Krebs, pp. 209–10.

52  For a strikingly plebian version of the SA man in an official text, see Koch, pp. 220–21. For SS appeal, see a quasi intellectual recruiting handbill which begins, "Don't be fooled. There is a rumor that SS membership is closed. Join now!" *Meldebogen für SS-Anwärter,* T-580/roll 87/folder 425.

Among the "charismatic" SS leaders in 1932 were von Woyrsch, Eicke, Lorenz, and Bach-Zelewski. Efficient but colorless types included Jeckeln, Prützmann, and Rediess. All these men rose to high posts; but the majority of the 400 to 500 SS officers of 1932 did not. One of the SS "martyrs" of 1932, for whom a Hamburg *SS-Sturm* was named by Hitler in March of that year, was discovered in 1936 to have been merely a quarrelsome bully who was shot while resisting arrest. Himmler File, folder 332, Hoover Institution Library.

53  In a sense the SS was already "free to starve," for numerous documents attest to the impossibility of squeezing anything for the SS from SA or PO. See for example a letter from the 27th and 54th SS-Standarten of August 6, 1932, complaining that while the SA got funds from a Hitler visit, the SS was out of pocket for guarding it: Miscellaneous SS Records, BDC. The SS even had to make a 60-pfennig contribution per nose to the local party by order of F. X. Schwarz, September 23, 1932: T-580/roll 89/folder 449. Karl Wolff's claim that every *Sturm* got ten to twenty Reichsmarks per month from Munich is open to dispute: U.S. Nuremberg doc. NI 6047F. Himmler and big business: Keppler affidavit, U.S. Nuremberg doc. NI 903. On Göring and big business, see a tribute from Erich Koch cited by Schultz in Bracher, *Machtergriefung*, p. 664. Himmler and Göring: Bracher, *Auflösung*, pp. 689–90, 692, 707–8.

54  Röhm arranged to have about ninety-five SS men attend the SA Officer's School in Munich in February 1932, the so-called "eighth class." This effort to bring the two units back together, though successful for the individuals involved, was never repeated. BDC Biographical Records. Buchheim's description of the SS of 1933 as "eine etwas feinere Variante der SA" ("a somewhat finer version of the SA") undoubtedly reflects Röhm's goal, and the thought of many SS opportunists. VJHZ 3 (1955): 130. A memorandum of August 17, 1932, penned by F. W. Kruger, the former SS lieutenant and courier of Daluege, warned Röhm, however, not to put too much trust in the Reichswehr. Röhm persisted, and his advisor survived him to become a leading SS general. BDC Biographical Records. Bracher names Himmler as well as Helldorf and Röhm as contact men to Schleicher (*Auflösung*, p. 498).

55  Letter of the 27th and 54th SS-Standarten to SS-Gruppe Ost, Berlin, August 6, 1932, Miscellaneous SS Records, BDC; reports of units of the 5th and 58th SS-Standarten for 1932, T-175/roll 15/frames 2518745–48; "Neumayr Tagebuch," T-580/roll 24/folder 206; *Der SA-Mann* 1:27 (October 15, 1932); Beck, pp. 493–94, 501–2, 513.

56  BDC Biographical Records. In his postwar affidavit, Karl Wolff distinguished between "individual contributions from the propertied classes" and "contributing members" (*Fördernde Mitglieder*) organized into an administrative body. Some of the latter's contributions went to Munich, while the former funds fell entirely under the control of local and regional commanders: U.S. Nuremberg doc. NI 6047F. Weekly Sturm-Appelle of the Munich SS were still being held in taverns in August 1932, and the monthly Sturm-

bannappelle were held at the Bürgerbräuhaus: *SS-Befehlsblatt* 1:2, December 20, 1932, item 6, T-611/roll 4/folder 429. *SA-Heime:* Beck, pp. 208, 279. SA crime: Heiden, DF, p. 517.

57  Röhm draws a parallel between 1918 and 1932 in his *Neujahrsbefehl*, December 27, 1932: T-580/roll 85/folder 403. Goebbels, *Kaiserhof*, pp. 74, 123, 131–32, 140–46. From BDC Biographical Records it is apparent that the SS and SA had made plans in 1932 for a seizure of power in towns throughout the Reich to accompany the *legal* accession of Hitler as president or chancellor. Some of these plans involved possible conflict with the Reichswehr. See Gebhardt and Rudhardt, p. 43, T-580/roll 85/folder 402. The Prussian government collected a mass of incriminating evidence during the presidential campaign: protocol of a hearing before the Staatsgerichtshof, T-580/roll 19/folder 199 (Gau records: Berlin). SA dissidence: SA reports from Hamburg of January 27, August 4, 6, 10, 1932, T-580/roll 50/folder 278; October 13, 1932, BDC Schumacher Collection, folder 330. Former SA men in KPD and SPD meetings: T-580/roll 34/folder 232 ("Gegner der NSDAP").

58  SA reorganization: *Dienstvorschrift für die SA der NSDAP (SADV)* (Diessen vor München, October 1, 1932), T-580/roll 85/folder 403. See also: "Leitung zum NS-Jahrbuch 1933," ibid. See also Volz, pp. 98–99. Plans for this reorganization, originally into twenty-five groups, go back to September 1931. Berlin Police Report of October 5, 1931, T-580/roll 19/folder 199a (Gau records: Berlin). Josef Berchtold, former *Stosstrupp* commander, writing in *Der SA-Mann* (October 15, 1932, *Jahrgang* 1, *Folge* 27), claimed 490,000 as the combined total for the SA and SS, but credited the latter with only 30,000 members. The same issue tells of setting up the SA Reserve in separate Standarten for less active members. Himmler warned the SS to obey the police but to note the names and faces of police officers arresting SS personnel. October 22, 1932, T-580/roll 89/folder 449.

59  The official SS figures show a rise of only 11,000 — from 41,000 in June 1932 to 52,000. *Statistisches Jahrbuch der SS der NSDAP, 1937*, p. 4. See the case of the double agent Cibulski, Himmler File, folder 332, Hoover Institution Library. Unruly SS in Franconia (Stegmann-Streicher case): T-580/roll 50/folder 278; T-580/roll 68/folder 319; T-580/roll 89/folder 449; Gebhardt and Rudhardt, p. 44. Unruly SS in Halle: Heiden, DF, p. 508. In Ansbach: *Das Freikorps* 1:1, February 1933, T-581/roll 17a/folder 1923. In Augsburg: BDC Biographical Records. In Hessen-Cassel: ibid.; and Heiden, DF, p. 516. SA and SS structure: *Nationalsozialistisches Jahrbuch 1933* (Munich, 1933), pp. 155–56, 158. Five Gruppenkommandos and eighteen Abschnitte: *SS-Befehlsblatt* 1:1, November 4, 1932, item 21, T-611/roll 4/folder 429. There were fifty-seven Standarten at this time. The early *Befehlsblätter* contain numerous provisions relating to rapid SS turnover, forbidding expulsions of SS men with seniority by lower echelons, permitting release of recruits by local units, etc.

60  The results of an inspection of SS units in the Greater Berlin area in December 1932 are reported by von Ulrich; the five *Stürme* he visited had an atten-

dance of thirty-one, sixty-three, sixty-six, seventy-three and ninety-seven, with Brandenburg the lowest and Pankow the highest. Attendance was 76 percent of strength; unemployment was 50 percent overall, and about half the SS were handworkers, a high figure for the SS. The battalion and regimental commanders, who were described as markedly above average, were all businessmen, supervisors, officials, and engineers or technicians. BDC Biographical Records. In the vitas which the SS officer-candidates submitted from 1932 on, the employment of parents and grandparents was often idealized, as was the work experience of the candidate himself. Only rarely does one find *Handarbeiter* (manual laborer), *Tagelöhner* (day laborer), *Dienstknecht* (hired man). The SS candidates seemed not so interested in boasting of their families' rise in the world (not uncommon) as in claiming status already earned by their fathers: BDC Biographical Records.

61 Himmler was present in preliminary negotiations as early as November 11, 1932. Keppler letter to Baron von Schroeder, November 13, 1932, U.S. Nuremberg doc. NI 209. An affidavit by the latter accounts for Himmler's and Hess's presence rather casually by their accompanying Hitler from Lippe: U.S. Nuremberg doc. NI 7990. Himmler was also involved in negotiations on January 10, and 18, 1933. Joachim von Ribbentrop, *Zwischen London und Moskau. Erinnerungen und letzte Aufzeichnungen* (Leoni am Starnberger See, 1953), pp. 37–39. See also Bracher, *Machtergreifung*, pp. 689–94, 707–8.

## Chapter 4: The Age of Opportunity

1 "The time of the great risks" — from a wartime letter in the biographical records of the Berlin Document Center.

2 Six thousand SS among 20,000: *Schriftgutverwaltung des Persönlichen Stabes, Reichsführer SS* (hereafter SGV), folder 263/photo 872K, BDC Biographical Records. Engelbrechten, p. 257.

3 Bracher, *Machtergreifung*, pp. 217, 414–15; Sauer, in Bracher, *Machtergreifung*, pp. 831, 901–2.

4 Schäfer, pp. 24–25, 32–34, 38–40, 48–49, 82–84.

5 Ibid., pp. 44, 49.

6 Kurt Lasch, SA-Gruppenführer in Thuringia, declared as late as the spring of 1934 that the goal of the national socialist revolution must be an SA-state. Deposition of General Weichs, *Institut für Zeitgeschichte*, cited by Sauer in Bracher, *Machtergreifung*, p. 925. *Jenseits von Partei und Staat* is the expression used by Hans Buchheim in his article, "Die SS in der Verfassung des Dritten Reiches," p. 139.

7 Bracher, *Machtergreifung*, p. 87; Schulz, in Bracher, *Machtergreifung*, p. 674; Sauer, in Bracher, *Machtergreifung*, p. 719; T. Vogelsang, "Neue Dokumente zur Geschichte der Reichswehr 1930–1933," VJHZ 2 (1954): 434.

8 Rauschning, *Men of Chaos*, p. 28.

9 *SA Akten*, folder 44, BDC.

10 On the SA as *eine totale Gewalt- und Zwangsorganisation*, "a complete sys-

tem of force and compulsion," see Sauer, in Bracher, *Machtergreifung*, pp. 830-31.

11 On the taming theory in general and Schleicher in particular, see Bracher, *Auflösung*, pp. 497-99. See also Franz von Papen, *Der Wahrheit eine Gasse* (Munich, 1952), pp. 269 ff., 289 ff. Both Blomberg and Reichenau (Sauer, in Bracher, *Machtergreifung*, p. 718) valued the *Menschenmaterial* (human material) of the SA (ibid., pp. 737-39). The SA was usually thought of as reinforcements for the border guard (*Grenzschutz*) units outside the Reichswehr. Gerhard Meinck, *Hitler und die deutsche Aufrüstung 1933-1937* (Wiesbaden, 1959), pp. 9-11, 16. Many young officers were swept along in the anticapitalistic *ressentiment* against *die gute Gesellschaft* ("polite society") which had accepted their more successful brethren in business and bureaucracy. Helmut Krausnick, "Der 30. Juni 1934," *Aus Politik und Zeitgeschichte. Beilage zu Das Parlament* 25 (1954): 318.

12 *Nebenregierung:* a term used as early as March 16, 1933 (Bracher, *Machtergreifung*, p. 437, note 240). The future *SS-Staat*—outside the party and the state proper—is foreshadowed in several SA institutions such as the *SA-Kommissare* (Schulz, in Bracher, *Machtergreifung*, pp. 463, 469) and the *SA-Verbindungsführer* (liaison officers) (Engelbrechten, p. 272).

13 Brawls: Bracher, *Machtergreifung*, p. 62; Schulz, in Bracher, *Machtergreifung*, p. 525; Engelbrechten, pp. 265 ff. *Anklage gegen O. Löblich, Ermittlungen. Schwurgericht Bremen, Institut für Zeitgeschichte*, 2544/60. "The police are not abject because they are threatened by Himmler; they are threatened by Himmler because they are abject": Edward Crankshaw, *The Gestapo, Instrument of Tyranny* (New York, 1956), p. 44.

14 *Sturm 33. Hans Maikowski. Schreiben von Kameraden des Toten* (Berlin-Schöneberg, 1933); Schulz, in Bracher, *Machtergreifung*, pp. 438-39, 468; Sauer, in Bracher, *Machtergreifung*, p. 866; Rudolf Diels, *Lucifer ante Portas* (Zurich, 1949), p. 131; *Streifendienst, Gutachten des Instituts für Zeitgeschichte* (Munich, 1958), p. 336. See also Engelbrechten, p. 268.

15 *Erlass des Kommissars des Reichs. Einberufung und Verwendung von Hilfspolizei*, T-175/roll 14/frames 2516670-88; Bracher, *Machtergreifung*, pp. 72-74; Schulz, in Bracher, *Machtergreifung*, pp. 438-40; Sauer, in Bracher, *Machtergreifung*, p. 709; *Gutachten*, pp. 336-37; Engelbrechten, pp. 267-69.

16 SS as auxiliary police in Brunswick, Thuringia, and Westphalia: BDC Biographical Records. Elsewhere: Diels, pp. 36, 49, 135. Wolfgang Sauer recounts the clumsy efforts at restraint and cover-up of twenty-eight-year-old SS-Gruppenführer Fritz Weitzel in Düsseldorf: Bracher, *Machtergreifung*, p. 439.

17 Fritz Tobias, *Der Reichstagsbrand, Legende und Wirklichkeit* (Rastatt, 1962), pp. 236-57. See also Hans Mommsen, "Der Reichstagsbrand und seine politischen Folgen," *VJHZ* 11 (1963): 351-413. On Daluege: *Der Gegenangriff* (Prague) No. 16, April 21, 1934, T-580/roll 85/folder 402.

18 *Reichsgesetzblatt* (RGB), 1933, part 1, p. 83; Bracher, *Machtergreifung*, pp. 82-83; Diels, pp. 150, 152, 158, 160, 163, 165-67. Discussions on the for-

mation of the SS auxiliary police in Köslin (Pomerania), February 28, 1933: BDC Biographical Records. Göring speech: 1856-PS, IMT, vol. 19, p. 27.

19   Bracher, *Machtergreifung*, pp. 93–95. See also von Salomon, p. 391. Concept of "controlled chaos" expressed by Papen: Rudolf Morsey, "Der Beginn der Gleichschaltung in Preussen," VJHZ 11 (1963): 85–97. By Schacht: Albert Wucher, *Die Fahne hoch. Das Ende der Republik und Hitlers Macht-übernahme. Ein Dokumentarbericht* (Munich, 1963), pp. 215–20. By Blomberg: Sauer, in Bracher, *Machtergreifung*, pp. 723–24. By Goebbels: "Der bolschewistische Revolutionsversuch muss erst einmal aufflammen. Im geeigneten Moment werden wir dann zuschlagen." "The bolshevik attempt at revolution must first break into flame. At the right moment then we'll strike." (January 31, 1933.) *Kaiserhof*, p. 254; *Secret Conversation*, pp. 402–3.

20   Flag raisings in Cologne, Hamburg, Stuttgart: Bracher, *Machtergreifung*, pp. 135, 142–43; Schulz, in Bracher, *Machtergreifung*, p. 434. Karlsruhe: *Hakenkreuzbanner* (Schweiningen), March 9, 1933. Goebbels, *Kaiserhof*, pp. 276–77. Rollkommandos: Diels, pp. 213–16, 221. Liegnitz: Bracher, *Machtergreifung*, p. 134, note 81. Alleged accomplices of van der Lubbe: Tobias, p. 197.

21   Coups d'etat: Bracher, *Machtergreifung*, p. 140; Schulz, in Bracher, *Machtergreifung*, pp. 433–34. Reich Police Commissars: Bracher, *Machtergreifung*, pp. 142–43; Schulz, in Bracher, *Machtergreifung*, pp. 433–35. Reich Commissars: ibid., pp. 461, 463. Reichsstatthalter: RGB, 1933, vol. 1, p. 173 (April 7, 1933); Schulz, in Bracher, *Machtergreifung*, 464–65.

22   SA vendettas: Diels, pp. 201, 204; Schulz, in Bracher, *Machtergreifung*, p. 447. As late as March 24, 1933, the Jülich SS reported a truncheon attack by police in front of the *SS-Heim:* T-175/roll 15/frame 2518747. Georges Castellan, *Le Réarmement clandestin du Reich 1930–1935* (Paris, 1954), pp. 369–75. Castellan has a wealth of detailed material on the SA and SS (pp. 348 ff.), but not all of it has been verified. *Bunker* and concentration camps: Schulz, in Bracher, *Machtergreifung*, p. 440; Sauer, in Bracher, *Machtergreifung*, pp. 872–73; Diels, pp. 183–90. SA and SS guards in official jails: Diels, pp. 185–86; Stefan Lorant, *I Was Hitler's Prisoner* (New York, 1935), pp. 132–33, 138–39, 299.

23   Diels, pp. 205–6; Bracher, *Machtergreifung*, pp. 206–8. See also Ernst August Roloff, *Bürgertum und Nationalsozialismus, 1930–1933* (Hannover, 1961), pp. 137, 140–42, 153, 156–57. Schulz, in Bracher, *Machtergreifung*, pp. 436–37. East Prussia and Silesia were areas where party, SA, and SS leaders were particularly independent. BDC Biographical Records.

24   T-580/rolls 85–86/folders 402–3. See Bracher, *Machtergreifung*, p. 91; Sauer, in Bracher, *Machtergreifung*, pp. 865–66. *Landespolizeigruppe z.b.v. (Wecke)*, T-354/roll 199/folder 26 (*Sonderkommando Berlin*)/frames 3859719–816. Auxiliary police serving with this unit may have been the nucleus of the *Standarte Adolf Hitler* (*Leibstandarte*). T-354/roll 199/folder 26/frames 3859783–84. On Rudolf Diels, see his *Lucifer ante Portas*, pp. 110–33. Cf. *Gutachten*, p. 299. Levetzow: *Das deutsche Führerlexikon* (Berlin, 1934); Diels, pp. 159–62. Grauert: Hans Bernd Gisevius, *To the*

*Bitter End* (Boston, 1947), pp. 37–38. Helldorf: Engelbrechten, p. 269. A rival of Diels and Daluege was Himmler's contact, *Kriminalrat* Artur Nebe, made chief of the Prussian *Landeskriminalpolizeiamt* (state criminal police) by Göring: Ermenhild Neusüss-Hunkel, *Die SS* (Hannover/Frankfurt am Main, 1956), p. 41. Cf. Gisevius, *To the Bitter End*, pp. 46 ff.; and Aronson, pp. 79–82.

25  Buchheim, "Die SS in der Verfassung des Dritten Reichs," p. 133. See also Lorant, pp. 141–42, 162–63. Himmler also accepted a Prussian civil service position as *Preussischer Staatsrat* from Göring in July 1933: T-175/roll 99/ frame 2621206. On Röhm, see Schulz, in Bracher, *Machtergreifung*, p. 509. On Daluege: ibid., p. 539.

26  Early "warnings" to SA (March 10, 12): Diels, pp. 198–99; Bracher, *Machtergreifung*, pp. 148–49. SA excesses: Schulz, in Bracher, *Machtergreifung*, p. 522; Sauer, in Bracher, *Machtergreifung*, p. 870. Evidence of SA confusion: Röhm orders 1233/33 of May 30, 1933, and 1499/33 of September 8, 1933, OSAF *Verfügungen*, T-354/roll 194/folder 8/frames 3852505–6 and 3852384.

27  Violence: William S. Allen, *The Nazi Seizure of Power. The Experience of a Single German Town, 1930–1935* (Chicago, 1965), pp. 173–88. See also Diels, pp. 136–38, 176–77. Hopes for order: ibid., pp. 57, 87, 180–82, 195. Hans Bernd Gisevius is another such case who is, incidentally, very critical of Diels: *To the Bitter End*, pp. 37 ff.; IMT, vol. 12, pp. 167 ff. *Gestapa* decree: 2371-PS, IMT, vol. 30, pp. 287 ff. Concentration camps: Eugen Kogon, *Der SS-Staat* (Munich, 1946), pp. 39–40; Wolfgang Langhoff, *Die Moorsoldaten* (Berlin, 1950), pp. 48–51, 69, 81–87.

28  Schulz, in Bracher, *Machtergreifung*, pp. 633–34, 636–37, 644–45; Sauer, in Bracher, *Machtergreifung*, p. 870; Diels, p. 200. SA copying of the FM technique was not forbidden until August. OSAF IV/1780/33, *Verfügungen*, T-354/roll 194/folder 8/frame 3852448. See also BDC Schumacher Collection, folder 427-S; and BDC Biographical Records. A phenomenon parallel to that of 1933, dating back to 1932, is the internal SA and SA-SS rivalry in the sale of cigarettes. Various units secured special rebates on *Sturm, Kameradschaft*, or *Reemtsma* brands and beat up persons selling or smoking one of the others: Diels, p. 217; Bennecke, *Hitler und die SA*, pp. 204–5; William S. Allen, "The State of the Nazi *Sturmabteilung*," an unpublished manuscript using SA morale reports from T-81/roll 1 and rolls 91–92.

29  For the link between the alleged "atrocity stories" and the boycott, see Goebbels, *Kaiserhof*, p. 288; also Bracher, *Machtergreifung*, p. 278. The *Adolf Hitler Spende* (Hitler fund), initiated June 1, 1933, by influential businessmen who would later become known as "the Circle of Friends of the *Reichsführer* SS," was designed to supply the SA with funds so that it and other organizations would stop their "shakedowns": U.S. Nuremberg doc. NI 1224F and NI 3799. *IG Farben*, nevertheless, thought fit to supply the SA with 200,000 RM worth of coats the next winter (U.S. Nuremberg doc. NI 4833).

30  Churches: Buchheim, *Glaubenskrise*, pp. 64 ff.; Bracher, *Machtergreifung*,

pp. 334, 340. See also VB, August 23, 1933. A Röhm order of August 2, 1933, provides for armed SA units to attend church on a voluntary basis! OSAF I/B2773/33, *Verfügungen*, T-354/roll 194/folder 8/frame 3852464. Potsdam: Bracher, *Machtergreifung*, p. 150. Passage of the Enabling Act: according to Wheeler-Bennett, the SA chanted, "Give us the bill or else fire and murder" (*Wooden Titan*, p. 447); Matthias and Morsey, *Ende der Parteien*, pp. 360, 363.

31  Engelbrechten has pictures for 1927 (pp. 326–27), 1928 (pp. 334–35), 1930 (p. 359), and 1932 (pp. 400, 407). For the later pictures see also Manfred von Killinger, *Die SA in Wort und Bild* (Leipzig, 1933).

32  April 1: Goebbels, *Kaiserhof*, pp. 288–93. May 2: Diels, pp. 206–7. Hans-Adolf Jacobsen and Werner Jochmann, *Ausgewählte Dokumente zur Geschichte des Nationalsozialismus 1933*–1945 (Bielefeld, 1961), vol. 2, *Rundschreiben* Nr. 6/33 of Robert Ley, April 21, 1933.

33  Use of *Kommissare* in *Gleichschaltung:* Schulz, in Bracher, *Machtergreifung*, pp. 463, 469, 510, 613; Sauer, in Bracher, *Machtergreifung*, pp. 689–90. The "resisters" on the right, nevertheless, aided the Nazis in establishing their control system. Diels, pp. 213–16, 223–29. Friedrich Hossbach's memoirs offer a candid view of an indecisive, middle-of-the-road Hitler between 1933 and 1935: *Zwischen Wehrmacht und Hitler 1934 – 1938* (Wolfenbüttel, 1949), esp. pp. 54–55. Intraparty struggles at the lower level are well illustrated in Allen, *Nazi Seizure of Power*, pp. 236–40, 299–303. The "left" had already been rather successfully cleared from the Prussian government by Papen and by other conservative regimes in Thuringia, Anhalt, Brunswick, Lippe, and Oldenburg: Bracher, *Auflösung*, pp. 582–91, and *Machtergreifung*, p. 136. The illegal left survived well into 1934 as disclosed by assassinations (VB, February 19, 1934, T-580/roll 85/folder 402), secret weapons caches and presses (Diels, pp. 176–77), and a brisk importation of literature. Bernhard Vollmer, *Volksopposition im Polizeistaat: Gestapo- und Regierungsberichte 1934 – 36* (Stuttgart, 1957), pp. 28–29, 82. The short-sighted right: Lutz Graf von Schwerin-Krosigk, *Es geschah in Deutschland: Menschenbilder unseres Jahrhunderts* (Tübingen, 1951), pp. 179–83.

34  Röhm's views are perhaps too colorfully described in Hermann Rauschning, *Germany's Revolution of Destruction* (London, 1939), pp. 171–72. Cf. John W. Wheeler-Bennett, *The Nemesis of Power* (New York, 1954), pp. 305–8. For evidence of paramilitary training *in the SS* in January 1934, see *Richtlinien für die Ausbildung der SS in dem ersten Vierteljahr 1934*, T-175/roll 501/frames 9364802–7.

35  One of Röhm's devices to keep the SA in trim and in the public eye was the large rallies (*Appelle* — rollcalls; and *Treffen* — "meets") such as those at Döberitz, Annaberg, and Kiel in May: VB, May 16 and 25, 1933; Rehm, "Geschichte der SA," T-580/roll 85/folder 403. Röhm took the Wehrwolf into the SA and put the *Brigade Ehrhardt* into the SS. OSAF B 2333/33 and 1456/33, August 25 and 10, 1933, T-354/roll 194/folder 8. Himmler, however, proceeded with extreme caution. *Führungsstab* Nr. 6088, August 30, 1933, ibid., frame 3852447. See also Salomon, pp. 432–37; and Sauer, in

Bracher, *Machtergreifung*, pp. 886–87, 892–93. On SA-*Polizeipräsidenten* (Police Presidents): *Gutachten*, pp. 307–8. By January 1934, the SA had supplied 891 officers to the Prussian police and 1,007 lower ranks, while the SS had supplied 200 officers and 886 lower ranks: Schulz, in Bracher, *Machtergreifung*, p. 504; Sauer, in Bracher, *Machtergreifung*, p. 865. The evolution of SA-Kommissare z.b.V. (Special Commissars) through *Kommissare der OSAF* (Commissars of the Supreme SA Commander) to *Sonderbevollmächtigten der OSAF* (special plenipotentiaries of the Supreme SA Commander) "beyond the party and the state" is deserving of further study: ibid., p. 930; Schulz, in Bracher, *Machtergreifung*, p. 613; Volz, p. 101; *OSAF-Verfügungen*, T-354/roll 194/frames 3852120–21, 3852152, 3852183, 3852204. Another promising new area of SA activity was recruitment and training of university students, begun under the *Nationalsozialistischer Deutscher Studentenbund*, March 23, 1933: T-580/roll 85/folder 403.

36  Thilo Vogelsang, *Der Chef der AW* (Institut für Zeitgeschichte: Munich, 1959); Bracher, *Machtergreifung*, pp. 206–8; Sauer, in Bracher, *Machtergreifung*, p. 726; Theodor Duesterberg, *Der Stahlhelm und Hitler* (Wolfenbüttel und Hannover, 1949), pp. 67–68; testimony of Theodor Gruss, IMT, vol. 21, pp. 106–23, and of Max Jüttner, ibid., pp. 123–28; "Am schwarzen Brett," October 1, 1933, T-580/roll 85/folder 402; memorandum of the British military attaché, Colonel Thorne, July 3, 1934, *Documents on British Foreign Policy* (hereafter DBFP), series 2, vol. 6, p. 799; *OSAF-Verfügungen* of August 25, September 12, September 13, September 26, and October 21, 1933, T-354/roll 194/folder 8/frames 3852417, 3852359, 3852351, 2852306, 3852243–44.

37  Heinrich Bennecke, in *Die Reichswehr und der "Röhm-Putsch"* (Munich/Vienna, 1964), pp. 26–34, links the AW to the mysterious Berlin *Gruppenstab z.b.V.* (division headquarters' staff for special purposes) of 1932. See Sauer, in Bracher, *Machtergreifung*, pp. 797, 888–96. Elements of the future *Leibstandarte* had army short courses at Zossen, Döberitz, and Jüterbog from May 1933 on: T-354/roll 199/folders 25–26 (*Sonderkommando Berlin*)/frames 3859273, 3859338, 3859347, 3859367–71, 3859424–26, 3859497, 3859556. Krüger file notes, 1850-PS, *IMT*, vol. 29, pp. 1–9. Hitler: Norman Baynes, ed., *The Speeches of Adolph Hitler* (London and New York, 1942), p. 554; VB, July 3, 1933, and August 22, 1933, as cited in Wheeler-Bennett, *Nemesis*, p. 307. According to BDC Biographical Records, the SS lured Jungstahlhelmer (Stahlhelm Youth) directly into their organization in July 1933. In 1935 a former SA officer who transferred to the SS wrote sadly to Krüger that their ideal in the SA had been to train boys of eighteen and under every Saturday in *Gelände- und Wehrsport* (field and military sport) so that the "inner soldier" would be already there when they entered the army (ibid.). SS subordination to SA rules was reaffirmed in the new service regulations for the General Inspector of the SA and SS (GISASS) of August 12, 1933, OSAF 1464/33, *Verfügungen*, T-354/roll 194/folder 8/frames 3852439–40.

38  Diels reports (p. 234) that "idealistic" anti-Communist students who had

been in the I-C (intelligence) department of the SA-Gruppe Berlin-Brandenburg withdrew, due to brutalities in the SA-Bunker. The SA regularly attacked *Stahlhelm* and the affiliated *Kampfring* personnel that summer: Bracher, *Machtergreifung*, p. 211, esp. note 191. On the other hand, there are numerous reports of beatings and incarcerations of SA men for indiscipline, theft, and violence: Werner Schäfer testimony, IMT, vol. 21, p. 74; Lorant, pp. 66, 111–12, 153–54, 225–28, 256, 265. Complaints: *Vossische Zeitung* and *Frankfurter Zeitung* of June 27, 1933, quoting the *Staatspressestelle der hessischen Regierung* (Hessian State Press Bureau). Expulsions and removals: OSAF II/1526/33, *Stellenbesetzungen*, T-354/roll 194/folder 8/frames 3852352, 3852356. Röhm had to forbid SA men to arrest SS men and vice versa except *in flagrante delicto*. OSAF II/1470/33, August 23, 1933, *OSAF Verfügungen*, T-354/roll 194/folder 8/frame 3852426. See also Bennecke, *Reichswehr und "Röhm-Putsch,"* pp. 36–40.

39  Volz, pp. 100–101; RGB, 1933, vol. 1, pp. 230, 921, 1016; Sauer, in Bracher, *Machtergreifung*, pp. 729–30, 879, 889, 929–30. Röhm's order OSAF 1415/33, T-580/roll 85/folder 403. Kerrl order of August 26, 1933: Schulz, in Bracher, *Machtergreifung*, pp. 512, 675. October decree: VB, January 12, 1934. For evidence of Röhm's larger ambitions for legal autonomy and his quarrels with Kerrl, see OSAF III/1449/33, of August 10, and II/1454/33, of August 11, 1933, *Verfügungen*, T-354/roll 194/folder 8/frames 3852442–43. On the other hand, Röhm felt constrained to order SA and SS cooperation in police matters with Frick's Reich Interior Ministry in response to a proposal of that office of August 7, 1933. (Frame 3852363.)

40  Sauer, in Bracher, *Machtergreifung*, p. 889; Heinrich Orb, *Nationalsozialismus, 13 Jahre Machtrausch* (Olten, 1945), pp. 110–11; *Gutachten*, p. 337–38; Gisevius, *To the Bitter End*, pp. 106–7. Engelbrechten's claim (p. 269) of a *Feldpolizei* in March 1933 is erroneous, but see pp. 278, 281. The Feldjäger were among the units financed privately by *IG Farben* in 1934. U.S. Nuremberg doc. NI 9200. See also a memorandum of the British attaché, Colonel Thorne, July 3, 1934, DBFP, series 2, vol. 6, pp. 792–93; and *OSAF Verfügungen*, 1547/33 and 1560/33, T-354/roll 194/folder 8/frames 3852273–83, 3852245. Efforts in March 1934 to make the Feldjäger subject to marriage approval on racial and eugenic grounds suggest a serious effort to compete with SS exclusivism. OSAF P 7100, ibid., frame 3852569. For the beginning of the Landespolizeitruppe Hermann Göring as a 500-man *SA-Stabswache Göring*, see T-354/roll 199/folder 26 (*Sonderkommando Berlin*)/frames 3859759, 3859817. For later developments, see roll 196/folder 16/frames 3855289–5301.

41  Reichswehr fears of SA: Bennecke, *Reichswehr und "Röhm-Putsch,"* pp. 45–46. For Himmler's measures see Himmler's speech to Wehrmacht officers in January 1937, 1992(A)-PS, IMT, vol. 29, pp. 209–10; on the SS oath, see pp. 89–91.

42  SS statistics: Some of the SS-*Standarten* in the "fifties" were founded in 1933, however. Most of the next fifty were founded in 1934. BDC Biographical Records. SA statistics: Hitler's claim of a 600,000 Eiserne Garde on

May 7 at Kiel would, of course, include the SS and may well be exaggerated. The SA-Gruppe Berlin-Brandenburg is said to have ordered a cessation of enlistments sometime in 1933 (May?) but unsuccessfully: Engelbrechten, p. 273. The BDC-*Sammellisten* for SA units are good evidence of steady enlistment throughout 1933. Paderborn grew from a Sturm of eighty on January 30, 1933, to Standarte (regimental) size in October! SA *Akten, Paderborn Vorfälle*, BDC. Von Killinger, in *Die SA in Wort und Bild*, p. 69, gives the following structure: five Obergruppen of 100,000 each; Gruppen of 25,000; Untergruppen of 6,000; Standarten of 2,000; Sturmbanne of 400; and Stürme of 100. Karl Ernst reported that the Gruppe Berlin-Brandenburg alone accounted for 107,000 men in September 1933. Hauptarchiv Berlin-Dahlem, Grauert Akten, *Rep.* 77/29. See also Bennecke, *Hitler und die SA*, pp. 215, 263–64, 277 ff. Röhm officially closed the SA on July 4, 1933, but, warned in August about disobedience to this order, announced in September a special reopening in November and exempted students from the order in October! *OSAF Verfügungen*, 1482/33, 1506/33, I/1586/33, T-354/roll 194/frames 3852413, 3852371, 3852259. The SS limited its "exceptions" to youths of age 17–23 and threatened to use screening commissions on top of that. T-354/roll 194/frame 3852371.

43  The 1943 *Organisationsbuch der NSDAP* (Munich, 1943), p. 427a, states that the Stabswache was ordered to be set up on March 17, 1933. Detailed documentation on the evolution of this Stabswache is to be found in T-354/rolls 194 and 199/folders 8–11, 25–26, *Leibstandarte Adolf Hitler (Sonderkommando Berlin)*. See also *SS Personalbefehle*, T-611/roll 3. Hitler admitted to Ambassador Phipps that he had 1,000 armed SS men as "a special guard of the government," December 8, 1933: DBFP, Series 2, vol. 6, p. 173. That they had reached this figure as early as August 1933 is shown in correspondence with Major Wecke, under whose control their billet (the old Lichterfelde *Kadettenanstalt*), training, pay, and weapons remained for several months. T-354/roll 199/folder 26/frames 3859271, 3859381, 3859756, 3859817, 3859841, 3859848.

44  *SS-Kommandos z.b.V.* (special details of the SS) existed for many types of guard duty in 1933 and 1934, and were attached to Standarten, Abschnitte, and Oberabschnitte: SS-*Personalbefehle* and *Verordnungsblätter*, T-611/roll 3/folder 429. By June 1, 1934, there were three Politische Bereitschaften: Standarte 1 at Dachau; Standarte 2 at Ellwangen; and Standarte 3 at Weimar. Each was composed of twelve companies, grouped four to a Sturmbann in the standard regimental structure. *Abzeichen*, T-611/roll 7/folder 434. Enlistments had to be for five or more years and the age twenty-three or less. *Aufnahmen*, SS-*Amt* II/9000, August 29, 1934, T-611/roll 7/folder 434.

45  Dachau in 1933 was run by SS men on special duty (*zur besonderen Verwendung*) from SS-Gruppe *Süd* — after November, known as *Oberabschnitt Süd: Personalbefehle*, T-611/roll 3/folder 429. In 1934 they became *Sturmbann "D"*: ibid. The term *Wachverbände* also dates from 1934, but Sonderkommando Sachsen, which ran several SS concentration camps in

Saxony, existed until the unification under Eicke as *Inspekteur der Konzentrationslager-Reichsführer SS*, December 24, 1934 (ibid.). In Hessen Werner Best sought to model his Wachkommandos and Sonderkommandos on the Standarte Adolf Hitler: Letter to Heydrich, September 7, 1933, T-354/roll 199/frames 3959630–31. On the other hand, Theodor Eicke, the future chief of the Wachverbände, confessed that when he took over the first guards in Dachau they were a terrible lot: BDC Biographical Records. Himmler's practice to assign as concentration camp guards *or commanders* men who had been transferred as punishment is illustrated in correspondence of November 1933, T-175/roll 99/frames 26209 ff.

46 Hoeppner testimony, IMT, vol. 21, pp. 188–89. In the course of 1933–34 about fifty men were made officers of the SD with SS numbers in the 36,000 range: *DAL 1934*. I-C personnel (sometimes "PI Referenten" — press and information specialists) were often listed "z.b.V." (special duty) in personnel records. Many of the SD with low SS numbers were in this category. BDC Biographical Records. Alwin Ramme thinks there were forty full-time SD and 250 unpaid (*Ehrenamtlichen*) personnel in the General SS, as well as SD branch offices at the SS-Abschnitt level: *Der Sicherheitsdienst der SS* (East Berlin, c. 1969), pp. 35–36. On Heydrich: Deschner, pp. 79–83. On the SD in 1933: Orb, pp. 85–86, 90–91; Diels, pp. 217–18. Aronson, pp. 139–64. When Werner Best speaks of "mutual interpenetration" of police and SS in 1933–1934, it does not appear that he has the SD exclusively in mind: *Die Deutsche Polizei* (Darmstadt, 1941), p. 99. Many SS officers went into the police in these years without going into the SD. BDC Biographical Records.

47 H. Reischle and W. Saure, *Der Reichsnährstand. Aufbau, Aufgaben und Bedeutung* (Berlin, 1940), pp. 24, 32, 36, 252. See also Bracher, *Machtergreifung*, pp. 187–89; Schulz, in Bracher, *Machtergreifung*, pp. 389–92. Agrarpolitischer Apparat: Schulz, in Bracher, *Machtergreifung*, p. 572; Reischle and Saure, *Der Reichsnährstand*, pp. 64–69. As an example of an older person, consider Darré's Reich Commissar for Milk Production, Freiherr Berndt von Kanne. An estate owner in Westphalia, he joined the party in 1930 to work with Darré, and was elected to the Prussian Landtag in 1932 and to the Reichstag in 1933. Unsuccessful as "Germany's milk czar," he joined the SS in 1934, and went into the Race and Settlement Office where he became chief of the genealogical section, 1935–1937: BDC Biographical Records.

48 Rasseamt: BDC Biographical Records. Procedures: Erich Spaarmann, "Meine Erfahrungen bei der rassischen Auslese," ibid. Alfred Eydt, "Der Sinn der Heiratsgenehmigung bei der SS," *Nationalsozialistische Monatshefte* 38 (May 1933).

## Chapter 5: The Betrayal

1 "The bullet came flying; is it for me or for you?" — from a very old folk song which was popular with the Nazis and was played on solemn occasions.

There is an implication of fate in the *es* (which does not refer to the bullet).
2 Contemporary observers: *Manchester Guardian*, July 21, 1933; Rauschning, *Voice of Destruction* (New York, 1940), pp. 154–59. Later evalua-
tions: Hermann Mau, "Die zweite Revolution," VJHZ 1 (1953): 119–20,
135–37; Krausnick, "Der 30. Juni, 1934," pp. 318 ff. For evidences of
Röhm's caution in dealing with the Reichswehr, see Seydel's warning of July
25, 1933, Z 1393/33 and Krüger's of July 19, 1933, V/R/360/33, *OSAF
Verfügungen*, T-354/roll 194/folder 8/frames 3852475, 3852481.
3 T-580/roll 86/folder 403; *Manchester Guardian*, July 21, 1933. See a pre-
mature (and partly erroneous) listing in the June 18, 1933, *Frankfurter Zeitung*. See also Krausnick, "Der 30. Juni," p. 318. Wehrkreis system: Jacques
Benoist-Mechin, *Histoire de l'Armée Allemande* (Paris, 1938), vol. 2, map
at rear. The tactical unit of the SA was the *Brigade* of three to five Standarten with supporting units "on the model of a German replacement division." There was nothing comparable in the SS. Memorandum of Colonel
Thorne, DBFP, series 2, vol. 6, pp. 792–93. See also *Erlass Nr. 2*, July 7,
1933, *OSAF Verfügungen*, T-354/roll 194/folder 8/frames 3852486–88. For
the brigade list, see OSAF 1525/33, September 8, 1933, T-354/roll 194/
folder 8/frames 3852375–77.
4 On the Tempelhof SA review of August 6, attended by deputations of Austrian, Russian, Danish, Dutch, Swedish, and Norwegian fascist groups:
"Rüdiger," *SA-und SS-Appell der Gruppe Berlin-Brandenburg und der
Gruppe Ost in Berlin* (Berlin-Schöneberg, 1933); and *Manchester Guardian*, August 7, 1933. AW courses: Vogelsang, *Chef der AW*, p. 7. Three-
week AW courses are mentioned as early as July 31, 1933, but by a non-SA
source: T-354/roll 194/frame 3852462. AW deputies in the SA-Gruppen and
Obergruppen were not named until September 15 (much later in the SS, if
at all). T-354/roll 194/frames 3852246–47, 3852370. Stahlhelm officers and
NCOs: Phipps despatch, February 7, 1934, and Thorne memorandum, July
3, 1934, DBFP, series 2, vol. 6, pp. 380, 789–90. Hochschulämter: T-580/
roll 85/folder 402; OSAF I/1586/33, *Verfügungen*, T-354/roll 194/folder 8/
frame 3852259. See Bennecke, *Reichswehr und "Röhm-Putsch,"* pp. 27–28.
Röhm also wooed artists and writers with a special art and literature section
in his Munich staff: *Gliederung des Stabes des Obersten SA-Führers*, BDC;
Willi Körbel, *In der SA wächst der kämpferische Künstler* (n.p., n.d.,
Wiener Library). The barracks tone is prominent in the summons to all Berlin SA-*Kulturreferenten* (culture specialists) to assemble February 7, 1934,
to report on their activities (the Leibstandarte refused). *OSAF Verfügungen*, T-354/roll 194/folder 11/frames 3853298–99.
5 Sports: OSAF 1507/33 and 1510/33, *OSAF Verfügungen*, September 9,
1933, T-354/roll 194/folder 8/frames 3852373, 3852369. Maneuvers: OSAF
I B 3516/33 (a warning not to disturb the deer!), September 30, 1933, T-354/
roll 194/frame 3852294. Press offices: Sauer, in Bracher, *Machtergreifung*,
pp. 879, 931; Engelbrechten, p. 273. Honorary SA officers: OSAF II/1509/
33, September 7, 1933, *OSAF Verfügungen*, T-354/roll 194/frames
3852392–94. Cf. U.S. Nuremberg doc. NI 8788. SA ranks: *Sturmmann*

(Pfc.), *Rottenführer* (Lance corporal), *Oberscharführer* (Senior corporal), *Obertruppenführer* (Staff sergeant), *Obersturmführer* (Lieutenant first class), *Sturmhauptführer* (Captain), *Obersturmbannführer* (Lieutenant Colonel), *Brigadeführer* (Brigadier General). *Frankfurter Zeitung*, July 22, 1933. Himmler: T-580/roll 37/folder 238 II. SA color: *Erlass Nr. 1*, May 26, 1933, *OSAF Verfügungen*, T-354/roll 194/frames 3852498–502. Röhm's speeches: Heiden, DF, pp. 723, 735; T-580/roll 85/folder 402.

6  Castellan, pp. 426–43. See also Bennecke, *Reichswehr und "Röhm-Putsch,"* who assigns the initiative to Reichenau (pp. 35, 54–58) and to F. W. Krüger (pp. 82–83).

7  Röhm's Dienstplan for September and October 1933 called for reorganizing *both* SA and SS. OSAF 1480/33, August 24, 1933, *OSAF Verfügungen*, T-354/roll 194/folder 8/frame 3852422. An order of January 6, 1934, limited SA regiments to 5,000 men, a figure far above the real strength in January 1933 (approximately 1,000). *Gruppenbefehl Nr. 1, Gruppe Hansa*, BDC. Proletarians in the SA: Diels, p. 157. SS admissions policy: T-611/roll 6/folder 432 (*Sachgebiete: Aufnahme*). Favored organizations were signals, cavalry, motor, engineers, naval, and flying units, all available in the SA as well. *Führungsstab* Nr. 1916, September 25, 1933, *OSAF Verfügungen*, T-354/roll 194/folder 8/frame 3852414.

8  Himmler speech at Frankfurt am Main, June 11, 1933: "We are the sword of the revolution": Albert Wucher, *Eichmanns gab es viele* (Munich, 1961), p. 115. The SS held its mass rally at Tempelhof a week after the SA: Rüdiger, *SA und SS Appell;* Daluege folders 57 and 62, "Korrespondenz," BDC; London *Times*, August 14, 1933. 1933 Nuremberg Rally: Engelbrechten (pictures), p. 421; *Manchester Guardian*, September 1, 1933. Newspaper article and protest: *Hamburger Illustrierte* 36 (1933): 14; BDC Biographical Records. On the differentiation, see Neusüss-Hunkel, pp. 15–17; Rauschning, *Men of Chaos*, p. 28. Efforts to maintain a common cooperative image by appealing to the Kampfzeit continued into December, however. See articles by Günther d'Alquen and Walter Hochmeister in *Der SA Mann* 2:52 (December 30, 1933).

9  See the list of honorary SA and SS officers appended to OSAF II 1134/34, January 27, 1934, T-580/roll 85/folder 403. Röhm had stipulated on October 14, 1933, that Himmler could only make honorary SS officers with his approval: *OSAF Verfügungen*, T-354/roll 194/folder 8/frame 3852265. The SA-SS rivalry for honorary members was still very intense in June 1934 and tied up with economic aid for their units. BDC Biographical Records. Goebbels and the SS: Schulz, in Bracher, *Machtergreifung*, p. 550; Mutschmann, *Akten des Obersten Parteigerichts*, BDC.

10  The SA advantage regarding the police, especially the police presidents, was lessened in the summer and fall as SS officers began to fill these posts in medium-sized towns like Wiesbaden, Bochum, and Nuremberg. BDC Biographical Records. Dietrich Klagges, the Minister President of Brunswick, helped the SS get control over the police there, in spite of SD intrigues against him and the local SS (which Himmler disavowed!): Aronson, pp.

164–67; BDC Biographical Records. Reich Interior Minister Frick's prohibition of *Verband* (SA, SS, Stahlhelm) membership to the police in May 1933 seems to have been ineffective. Sauer, in Bracher, *Machtergreifung*, p. 926. Weakness of Feldpolizei: Diels, pp. 255–56. Abolition of auxiliary police: London *Times* and *Manchester Guardian*, August 9, 1933. Hitler gave the number disbanded as 6,000: Phipps to Simon, December 8, 1933, DBFP, series 2, vol. 6, p. 173; Schulz, in Bracher, *Machtergreifung*, pp. 475–76; Sauer, in *Machtergreifung*, p. 880; Jüttner testimony, IMT, vol. 21, p. 219. An SS-Hilfspolizei Gruppe z.b.V. still existed in Düsseldorf on September 12, 1933, however: T-354/roll 199/folder 26/frame 3859659.

11 While alleged communist "ambushes" accounted for some of the shooting, cases of Nazi patrols shooting at one another also occurred: London *Times*, June 30, 1933; *Manchester Guardian*, August 11, 1933; VB, August 18, 1933. Feuding: Diels, pp. 231–34; Gisevius, *To the Bitter End*, pp. 106–8. For the case of a member of the Standarte Adolf Hitler arrested by the Feldpolizei at the Lichterfelde barracks, August 15, 1933, see the request for his release from the *General Pape-Strasse Kaserne*, T-354/roll 199/folder 25/frames 3859435, 3859437.

12 Himmler, who styled himself *Reichsführer SS und Politischer Polizeikommandeur Bayerns* (T-580/roll 37/folder 238 II), was as guilty as anyone of abridgements of justice, such as the arrest of the *Daily Telegraph* correspondent Noel Panter. *Deutsche Allgemeine Zeitung*, November 1, 3, 1933. See also 923-D, IMT, vol. 36, pp. 11–36, 41–58. On October 3, 1933, SS headquarters had to warn against raids by SS-Kommandos on the Prussian state forests: *OSAF Verfügungen*, T-354/roll 194/folder 8/frame 3852287.

13 Buchheim, "Die organisatorische Entwicklung der politischen Polizei in Deutschland in den Jahren 1933 und 1934," *Gutachten*, pp. 294–307. Neusüss-Hunkel (p. 9) cites a 1935 Hamburg dissertation by Lauer to the effect that the Neuaufbaugesetz of January 30, 1934, was instrumental in centralizing police authority under the aegis of Frick's Interior Ministry. Cf. Schulz, in Bracher, *Machtergreifung*, p. 602, who suggests the cooperation of Himmler and Heydrich with Frick. Phipps saw a three-way conflict among Göring, Himmler, and Frick, April 25, 1934: DBFP, series 2, vol. 6, pp. 649, 652. Cf. IMT, vol. 12, pp. 161–62; 779-PS, IMT, vol. 26, pp. 297–99. On Best, see Aronson, pp. 144–52.

14 As Leiter der Abteilung für Polizeifragen (Director of the Section for Police Matters) in the Reich Interior Ministry, Daluege had been given the task of centralizing the nonpolitical police of the Reich with special emphasis on the garrisoned police. They were to be concentrated near cities and industrial areas and brought into close liaison with regional SS commanders. Thorne memorandum, DBFP, series 2, vol. 6, pp. 792–73; Orb, pp. 107–12; Diels, pp. 321–31; Gisevius, *To the Bitter End*, pp. 51–53; Aronson, pp. 172–87; Schulz, in Bracher, *Machtergreifung*, p. 475. Symbolic of the revolutionary-conservative tone of the Gestapa was its official seal, a Hohenzollern eagle with a swastika on its breast, surmounted by the slogan *Gott mit uns!*: "An den Herrn Polizeigeneral Daluege," May 3, 1934, T-580/

roll 85/folder 402. Three of the chief areas of conflict between Göring and the SA were the concentration camps, the Sonderkommissare, and the patronage system of the Prussian State Council as well as the provincial and town councils: Gisevius, *To the Bitter End*, pp. 107–8; Schäfer testimony, IMT, vol. 21, pp. 78, 98; Diels, pp. 190–96; Schulz, in Bracher, *Machtergreifung*, pp. 513–14; Sauer, in Bracher, *Machtergreifung*, p. 877. In December 1933 Göring was forced to cut the patronage pie of the town councils three ways among party, SA, and SS: Schulz, in Bracher, *Machtergreifung*, p. 613. Röhm forced SA men on the Prussian payroll to contribute their fees to a special SA fund (*Sonderfond*): OSAF *Verfügungen* IV/3335/33 and IV/3335/33, T-354/roll 194/folder 8/frames 3852286, 3852602–6.

15  Schulz, in Bracher, *Machtergreifung*, pp. 537–40; Diels, pp. 255–58, 266–67, 273; Gisevius, *To the Bitter End*, pp. 146–48; IMT, vol. 12, p. 172. There were SS officers in the Gestapa as early as August 1933: T-354/roll 199/folder 25/frames 3859410, 3859425. Daluege wished to force Leibstandarte guards on the Gestapa as early as October 1933: T-354/roll 196/folder 15/frame 3855225.

16  *Nationalsozialistische Monatshefte* 5 (1934): 10, quoted by Sauer, in Bracher, *Machtergreifung*, p. 928. Eighteen-year-old members of the Hitler Youth were taken into either the SA or the SS during this ceremony, but only the SS used this oath. OSAF *Verfügungen*, T-354/roll 194/folder 8/frame 3852266. The annual reenactment of this swearing-in ceremony before the Feldherrnhalle at midnight became part of SS ritual: T-175/roll 32/frame 2540683. The official award of the title *Leibstandarte Adolf Hitler* on November 8, 1933, was also part of the SS's Führer-cult: T-175/roll 90/frame 2612641. In comparison, the new ADO (*Allgemeine Dienstordnung*, General Orders) of the SA of December 12, 1933, while it began with "The SA man is the political soldier of Adolf Hitler," stressed rights and duties toward the movement (*Bewegung*). 2820-PS, IMT, vol. 31, pp. 160–62 (in part). Articles 6 and 8 of the Law to Secure Unity of Party and State of December 1, 1933, placed the SA on a par with the party vis-à-vis Hitler and the public authorities. IMT, vol. 2, pp. 195–96.

17  On Hitler's purposes: Sauer, in Bracher, *Machtergreifung*, p. 932, citing inconclusive evidence, believes Hitler and Röhm clashed decisively as early as October 1933. It was in October that Röhm converted his Sonderkommissare into a system of *Sonderbevollmächtigten* (special plenipotentiaries) and *Sonderbeauftragten* (special commissioners) to constitute a "loyal opposition"! OSAF *Verfügungen*, 1560/33, T-354/roll 194/folder 8/frames 3852238–42. See also T-354/roll 194/frame 3852108. Röhm created a staff of twenty-three offices and even more sections (*Abteilungen*) of which the largest was the *Politisches Amt* under von Detten, comprising seven sections. *Gliederung des Stabes des Obersten SA-Führers*, BDC. Among von Detten's duties was supervision of the SA men on the Prussian town councils as well as the above-mentioned Sonderbevollmächtigten: Schulz, in Bracher, *Machtergreifung*, p. 613. There were also Sonderbevollmächtigten and Sonderbeauftragten in Bavaria as early as September 1933: OSAF I/

1490/33, *OSAF Verfügungen*, T-354/roll 194/frame 3852345. The deputy of the Sonderbevollmächtigter in Silesia was an SS colonel: T-354/roll 194/ frame 3852319. Hess was sworn in as a minister in an SS uniform, and he stressed before a party meeting that he and Röhm had purposely worn service uniforms. *Manchester Guardian*, December 9, 1933. The *Neue Zürcher Zeitung* recalled retrospectively on August 2, 1934, that Hess had worn the black uniform of the SS demonstratively as a gesture *against* the SA. In an article in the *Völkischer Beobachter* of January 22, 1934 (*SA und Partei*), Hess claimed that Himmler as a Reichsleiter did not receive his orders from the Stabschef but directly from Hitler, like himself.

18 *Verbindungsstab*: Schulz, in Bracher, *Machtergreifung*, p. 515, citing *Jahrbuch des öffentlichen Rechts der Gegenwart 1935* (Tübingen), p. 100. This installation was not dissolved when Hess began to attend cabinet meetings in May 1933 or even after December 1933. Some of its former members had to be forbidden to "hang around" in March 1934: T-580/roll 86/folder 418. Röhm created a still more elaborate system of SA ranks in January 1934 permitting various gradations of inactivity and affiliation (e.g., *Ehrenführer, Rangführer, zur Verfügung, zu besonderer Verwendung*, etc.): OSAF II/ 1134/34, T-580/roll 86/folder 403. Hitler named the high-ranking SA and SS leaders, and Himmler merely sent the latter a congratulatory letter! T-580/roll 85/folder 402. But on the other hand, Himmler vetoed the SS promotion of a conservative police official in no uncertain terms (November 1933) T-175/roll 99/frame 2621155.

19 Himmler spoke of 180,000 in a letter to an old friend in October 1933. T-175/roll 99/frame 2621089. SS officers: T-611/roll 6/folder 432, *Sachgebiete: Beförderung*. SS table of organization: June 20, 1934, T-611/roll 3/ folder 429. Headquarters structure: *Nationalsozialistisches Jahrbuch 1934* (Munich, 1934), p. 161. The Führungsstab was moved up to Berlin in May 1933, while the more purely administrative operations under SS-Amt aegis continued to be performed in the Arcis-Strasse headquarters in Munich. *Führungsstab* Nr. 1985/33, *OSAF Verfügungen*, T-354/roll 194/folder 8/ frame 3852504. In December 1933 Himmler envisioned an extensive reorganization in 1934, perhaps in connection with a big SA restructuring, when SS officers would be shifted about extensively. BDC Biographical Records. But in October 1934 some SS officers were still classified as *ortsgebunden* (immovable): ibid.

20 Although a thousand "old fighters" were made second lieutenants on Hitler's birthday, April 20, 1934, solely on the basis of their low SS numbers, the 1,800 officers commissioned before this date for better reasons were the real officer corps: *DAL 1934*; T-611/roll 6/folder 432 (*Sachgebiete: Beförderung*). SS special units: T-580/roll 87/folder 425. The creation of separate SS-Reserve units dates from December 1933, but the cavalry, motor, medical, and engineer units were not split. T-611/roll 7/folder 434 (*Sachgebiete: Reserve*). Social foundation of SS cavalry: Neusüss-Hunkel, pp. 16–17. See also Engelbrechten, pp. 271, 276. Röhm insisted on mixed SS and SA cavalry units, secretly under the AW, "unless special conditions war-

rant the formation of SS cavalry regiments." The SS cavalry were the only special unit under a joint SA and SS inspector: *OSAF Verfügungen*, T-354/roll 194/folder 8/frames 3892248, 3852361–62, 3852364–65. In June 1934 SS cavalry regiments existed in only four SS Main Sectors: East, Northeast, Southeast, and West. T-611/roll 3/folder 429.

21  The SS had 75,000 paid posts in all in 1934; the SA had 300,000. The Standarten ordinarily had two paid officers. The regional staffs were decidedly more fortunate, and the best positions were in the Munich and Berlin Oberstäbe. *Pariser Tageblatt*, March 27, 1934, citing *Der SA-Mann*; Neusüss-Hunkel, p. 25. The 1,000-man Leibstandarte was on the Reich payroll as of October 1, 1933: T-354/roll 194/folder 11/frame 3853318. On SA financing: Schulz, in Bracher, *Machtergreifung*, p. 509; *Pariser Tageblatt*, March 27, 1934, U.S. Nuremberg doc. NI 439, NI 1224, NI 3799, NI 4056, NI 4833, NI 8788, NI 9200. The SS seems to have had an early monopoly on the border police auxiliaries (*Hilfsgrenzangestellten*). *OSAF Verfügungen*, T-354/roll 194/folder 8/frame 3852324. *Frühlingskonzert* (spring concert): VB, April 19, 1934. The Leibstandarte band was also much sought after. *OSAF Verfügungen*, T-354/roll 194/folder 11/frames 3853305–12; *Auswärtiges Amt* to *Ministeramt*, June 9, 1934, T-580/roll 86/folder 418; SS report on *Wach- und Schliessgesellschaft*, May 2, 1934, ibid.

22  In spite of "revolutionary" slogans like "the battle of the boots" and SA generals shaking cups on street corners, the Winter Help campaign was rumored to be a slush fund for luxurious living in *SA-Heime*: VB, February 24, 1934; *Frankfurter Zeitung*, April 25, 1934; Wheeler-Bennett, *Wooden Titan*, p. 454. SA, SS, and Stahlhelm were to be favored in WPA-type employment by a June 1, 1933, law: RGB, 1933, part 1, p. 425; and on the Reichsbahn, *Deutsche Allgemeine Zeitung*, January 20, 1934. By a law of February 27, 1934, SA, SS, and Stahlhelm who had been wounded in the national cause before November 13, 1933, could draw benefits from the state as could the dependents of those killed before that date: RGB, 1934, part 1, pp. 133–36. The SA set up *Versorgungsstellen* (welfare offices) and *Versorgungsreferenten* (welfare specialists) to aid the unemployed: OSAF IV/3316/33, *OSAF Verfügungen*, T-354/roll 194/folder 8/frames 3852308–12; *Beilage Fürsorge zum Verordnungsblatt der Obersten SA-Führung*, vol. 1 (1934). Röhm complained in October 1933 that two million SA drew no state pay, and the over-organization of the SA that Hess complained about in his VB article of January 22, 1934, was surely the result of SA failure to place more of its men in the lucrative state bureaucracy: Heiden, DF, p. 731; Krausnick, "Der 30. Juni," p. 318. Ex-Communists in the SA: letter of Hess, September 16, 1933, T-580/roll 85/folder 402. See also a report by the British ambassador, November 21, 1933, DBFP, series 2, vol. 6, p. 86.

23  OSAF 80/34 and 1043/34, January 10 and February 1, 1934, *OSAF Verfügungen*, T-354/roll 194/folder 9/frames 3852775, 3852695–96; *Frankfurter Zeitung*, February 7, 1934; VB, February 21, 1934; *Frankfurter Zeitung*, March 4, 1934. T-580/roll 85/folder 402: clippings from VB, February 19, 1934; May 4, 1934; May 15, 1934; May 17, 1934; June 20, 1934. *OSAF Ver-*

*ordnungsblatt*, March 15, 1934, reprinted in *Deutsche Freiheit* (Saarbrücken), June 21, 1934. *Gruppe Berlin-Brandenburg: Geheimbefehl*, May 15, 1934, reprinted in *Pariser Tageblatt*, June 28, 1934. Ten thousand SA *Anwärter* expelled: *Frankfurter Zeitung*, June 20, 1934. See also *Deutsche Freiheit*, June 9, 1934; *Manchester Guardian*, March 3, 1934; and London *Times*, April 15, 1934.

24 Wheeler-Bennett, *Wooden Titan*, p. 454. Ribbentrop claimed that Röhm was trying to persuade Hitler of the desirability of effecting a rapprochement with France. Joachim von Ribbentrop, *The Ribbentrop Memoirs* (London, 1954), p. 52. Röhm's foreign connections, especially with France, go back to the twenties. See Bennecke, *Reichswehr und "Röhm-Putsch,"* p. 40. There was an effort to communicate with France in April 1931 through Dr. Bell: T-580/roll 85/folder 403. On Röhm's conferences: *Deutsche Allgemeine Zeitung*, October 5, 1933; VB, April 19, 1934; Sauer, in Bracher, *Machtergreifung*, pp. 884, 933. On French suspicions: *Manchester Guardian*, May 4, 1933; DBFP, series 2, vol. 6, p. 49 (November 11, 1933), 158–62, 233–43 (December–January 1934), 418 (February), 496 (March 1); *Manchester Guardian*, June 4, 1934. That Röhm was deeply interested in foreign affairs in December 1933 is shown by a sharp letter he addressed to Josias von Waldeck und Pyrmont, an SS-Gruppenführer on temporary duty in the Auswärtiges Amt, objecting to the officer's selection of personnel without his (Röhm's) approval and urging his resignation: BDC Biographical Records. Röhm was also dabbling in the Austrian sphere by urging young SA students in September to study at Austrian universities: *OSAF Verfügungen*, T-354/roll 194/folder 8/frame 3852380. On the other hand, SA-Standarten with the provocative place-names of *Strassburg* (169), *Graudenz* (129), and *Thorn* (167) were reassigned the names *Kehl*, *Cammin*, and *Stolp* as of July 31, 1933. *OSAF Verfügungen*, T-354/roll 194/folder 8/frame 3852327. Furthermore, when the Czech government protested the enrollment of one of its citizens in the SA, he was released, and SA units were warned to release other foreigners (February, 1934). T-580/roll 46/folder 418.

25 Hossbach, pp. 57–58; Diels, pp. 287–94, 298–301. Röhm-Himmler polarization: Sauer, in Bracher, *Machtergreifung*, p. 916; Diels, p. 378. An uncomfortable scolding in Himmler's presence was given SS-Standartenführer Arthur Greiser by Röhm in January 1934 for reporting SA excesses in Danzig "outside of channels." *OSAF Verfügungen*, T-354/roll 194/folder 9/frame 3852783. A Himmler order of April 18, 1934, which speaks of death sentences as "desirable" for SS men who mishandled persons in protective custody (T/611/roll 7/folder 432, *Sachgebiete: Ausstossung*) and the fact that three SS men *were* shot in Stettin for mishandling prisoners (Gürtner letter to Frick, May 14, 1935, 3751-PS, IMT, vol. 33, pp. 56–60) may have been a smokescreen to cover the lack of any real difference between SS and SA terror and to impress Göring and perhaps Frick. Aronson makes clear how little Himmler and Heydrich cooperated with efforts to rein in their own excesses: pp. 126–33, 183–85. The SS even succeeded in convincing

some of the British of a more systematic political comb-out operation than in the SA installations: Phipps to Simon, December 11, 1933, DBFP, series 2, vol. 6, p. 189. Göring's telephone listening center, disguised as a research center for the Air Ministry, provided Hitler with damning information at the time of the purge: Diels, pp. 170–72; Phipps's dispatch of July 11, 1934, DBFP, series 2, vol. 6, p. 969. For Göring's vain wooing of Fritsch against Heydrich, see Ulrich von Hassel, *Vom anderen Deutschland* (Zurich, 1946), p. 39.

26  Orb, pp. 139–48; Aronson, pp. 177–82, 226–32; Ramme, pp. 40–42. See Messersmith-Geist affidavit, 2386-PS, IMT, vol. 30, p. 317. Gestapo-Abwehr activities vis-à-vis Czechoslovakia in February 1934: T-580/roll 86/folder 418. A security plan for the Gestapa, May 4, 1934, refers to Himmler as the *Politischer Polizeikommandeur* (without reference to Bavaria) and lists as responsible office chiefs SS officers Patschowsky, Potzelt, Rattenhuber, Dunkern, Flesch, and Müller. T-354/roll 196/folder 15/frames 3855206–10. On Müller, see Kaltenbrunner testimony, IMT, vol. 11, p. 295. According to Ohlendorf, the Gestapa already began to function as a clearing house for Himmler's duties as Political Police Chief of the various Länder. IMT, vol. 4, p. 344.

27  Orb, pp. 63–80; *DAL 1934; DAL 1935; DAL 1936.*

28  The SD post for Silesia was occupied for the first time by an SS man without rank on March 20, 1934! *Anklage Osnabrück*, pp. 19, 34, cited by Sauer in Bracher, *Machtergreifung*, p. 949. A formal regional network, based on a simplified version of the new *SS-Oberabschnitte*, came into existence in 1934. Excluding Austria, there were six SD-Oberabschnitte: Berlin, Stettin, Dresden, Munich, Frankfurt, and Stuttgart. T-175/roll 239/frames 2728167, 2728197–99. See Orb, pp. 68–69. The *National-Sozialistisches Jahrbuch* for 1935 still gives a Munich address for the Sicherheitsamt SS: "Wittelsbacher Palais, Briennerstrasse, corner Türkenstrasse." This SD office was still regarded as part of the Reichsführung SS, since its members wore "RFSS" on their lower sleeves. BDC Biographical Records. Hess order (connected with the transfer of Rosenberg's *Inlandnachrichtenapparat des Aussenpolitischen Amtes*), *Parteikanzlei: Verfügungen*, vol. 1, pp. 598–99, Wiener Library. See Orb, p. 60. Hermann Foertsch, *Schuld und Verhängnis. Die Fritsch-Krise im Frühjahr 1938 als Wendepunkt in der Geschichte der nationalsozialistischen Zeit* (Stuttgart, 1951), pp. 48–49. Army intelligence: Krausnick, "Der 30. Juni," p. 321. See Bennecke, *Reichswehr und "Röhm-Putsch," pp.* 46-7, 50.

29  Letter of General Heinrici quoted in Foertsch, pp. 46–47. Erich von Manstein, *Aus einem Soldatenleben, 1887–1939* (Bonn, 1958), pp. 178–79. As late as February 1934, Fritsch and Blomberg believed that "valuable elements" in the SA required them to get along with Röhm. Sauer, in Bracher, *Machtergreifung*, p. 915. One of the July 20 martyrs, Mertz von Quirnheim, asked to be assigned to the SA from the Reichswehr in 1934: Hermann Teske, *Die silbernen Spiegel* (Heidelberg, 1952), pp. 31–32. Complaints against SA regional leaders for insubordination in January: Krausnick, "Der 30. Juni," p. 319. Conflicts with Reichenau, Blomberg, Obernitz, and Jagow: 1850-PS,

IMT, vol. 29, pp. 10–12. *Grenzschutz* issue: Sauer, in Bracher, *Machtergreifung*, pp. 939–40. Evidence of Reichswehr-AW cooperation in Geländesportschulenlehrplan: 1849-PS, IMT, vol. 28, pp. 585–603; *Standartensammellisten* Nos. 9 and 26 prepared for the Reichswehr (BDC); Reichenau memorandum of November 1933, 2822-PS, IMT, vol. 31, p. 164; and Jüttner testimony, IMT, vol. 21, pp. 174, 176.

30  Manstein, pp. 181–85. Weapons depots: Bennecke, *Reichswehr und "Röhm-Putsch,"* pp. 47–48, 76. AW-Stabschef: 2823-PS, IMT, vol. 31, pp. 165–67. Withdrawal of army training officers: Sauer, in Bracher, *Machtergreifung,* p. 805; and 2821-PS, IMT, vol. 31, pp. 162–63. An F. W. Krüger memorandum of February 23, 1934, showing the Reichswehr conception of the SA: 1849-PS, IMT, vol. 28, pp. 583–84. The inauguration of the SA-Sport insignia on November 28, 1933, also used by the SS, was part of the premilitary training. Bennecke, *Reichswehr und "Röhm-Putsch,"* p. 27; and Sauer, in Bracher, *Machtergreifung,* p. 895. The army was, however, completely uninterested in the SS as a military force: ibid., p. 889; and 2821-PS, IMT. Vogelsang, *Chef des AW.* On Fritsch, see Wheeler-Bennett, *Nemesis,* p. 309; and DBFP, series 2, vol. 4, pp. 265–66.

31  DBFP, series 2, vol. 6, pp. 24, 88, 127, 150, 196, 434, 449, 464, 657–58. See also *Morning Post,* April 27, 1934; *Neuer Vorwärts,* July 15, 1934; Meinck, pp. 89 ff.; Manstein, pp. 185–86; Anthony Eden, *Facing the Dictators* (Boston, 1962), pp. 70, 73–76. In December and again in February, Hitler threatened, perhaps half seriously, to turn the SA into military units if the British and French continued to regard them as such. DBFP, series 2, vol. 6, pp. 179–80, 460–61. "Hitler assured me that the SA and SS might be compared to the Salvation Army. (Here I regret to say I laughed.)" (Ibid., p. 173.) On the February cabinet episode and the abortive SA-Reichswehr "agreement": Wheeler-Bennett, *Nemesis,* p. 309; Sauer, in Bracher, *Machtergreifung,* pp. 749, 943–44. Hossbach (p. 56) emphasizes the *duality* of Hitler's views of political armies throughout his career.

32  Outbursts: Krausnick, "Der 30. Juni," p. 319; VB, January 21, 1934, April 10, 1934; *Frankfurter Zeitung,* May 4, 1934; T-580/roll 85/folder 402. Sauer, in Bracher, *Machtergreifung,* pp. 937–38, 942, 945. SA violence and loose talk by other SA and SS officers: memoranda of the Auswärtiges Amt, April 25 and May 4, 1934, T-580/roll 86/folder 418. Arming: 951-D, IMT, vol. 36, pp. 72–73; Phipps dispatch, March 24, 1934, DBFP, series 2, vol. 6, p. 584. Austrians: ibid., pp. 308, 388; Ulrich Eichstädt, *Von Dollfuss zu Hitler; Geschichte des Anschlusses Österreichs* (Wiesbaden, 1955), pp. 34–35. Contacts with the *Reichswehr:* Sauer, in Bracher, *Machtergreifung,* p. 957. Rumors of contacts with Schleicher: Wheeler-Bennett, *Nemesis,* pp. 315–16. André François-Poncet's story: *The Fateful Years* (New York, 1949), pp. 136, 139. Furlough: *Morning Post,* April 27, 1934; tied up with Hitler's Norwegian cruise on the *Deutschland* by the *Manchester Guardian,* June 29, 1934. Warning: T-580/roll 86/folder 403. This copy of the order arrived at the brigade level only on May 29. An I-C *(Abwehr)* system, however, was begun in some brigades in May. *Manchester Guardian,* July 3, 1934.

33  Röhm was not consistent. He oscillated between violent outbursts and con-

ciliatory moods. In December and again in March, he told foreign diplomats he would welcome foreign observers in the SA. DBFP, series 2, vol. 6, pp. 157, 532. On the other hand, he is said to have been angered by Hitler's *Uniform-Verbot* for the SA on their furlough. Phipp's dispatch, July 5, 1934, DBFP, series 2, vol. 6, p. 964; and *Morning Post*, July 3, 1934. Orb's theory that Hitler and Himmler were orginally part of Röhm's "putsch plans" is probably fantasy (pp. 260–68). Röhm's expectations and isolation: Bennecke, *Reichswehr und "Röhm-Putsch,"* pp. 40–44. Comparison of Röhm and Himmler: von Salomon, pp. 446–47, 454–55.

34 Army intelligence operations: Krausnick, "Der 30. Juni," p. 320; Manstein, pp. 186–87. Army liaison personnel with SA (*Organisations-Beauftragten*) are mentioned in a Göring memorandum to the Gestapo, May 16, 1934, T-175/roll 430/frame 2959932. While there was great tension among Hitler, the generals, and the rightist circles in April, no "deal" or "showdown" has been demonstrated. Phipps's dispatch, April 18, 1934, DBFP, series 2, vol. 6, p. 652. *Urteil Osnabrück*, pp. 17, 68, noted by Sauer in Bracher, *Machtergreifung*, p. 951. Himmler had other contacts in the Reichswehr, notably a high naval officer. Hossbach, p. 70 (quoting Fritsch).

35 See Himmler's notes for a report to Hitler of May 15, "Reorganization in East Prussia, Silesia, Pomerania," T-175/roll 94/frame 2615277. Staff meetings and inspections: Krausnick, "Der 30. Juni," p. 320. *Oberfranken* (May 7–13): T-580/roll 85/folder 402. SA-SS-Gruppenführer conference: *Frankfurter Zeitung*, May 4, 1934. Georges Castellan notes a Reichswehr-SA-SS conference on *Grenzsicherung West* at Bad Nauheim, May 4–7, 1934. See Wheeler-Bennett, *Nemesis*, p. 313. Harangues and intrigues: Sauer, in Bracher, *Machtergreifung*, pp. 906, 913; Heiden, DF, p. 742. One of the most suspicious of the SA was Karl Ernst in Berlin. Gisevius, *To the Bitter End*, pp. 129–30. SA in June: Sauer, in Bracher, *Machtergreifung*, p. 957. Efforts to cut down on SA "visibility": VB, June 13, 17, 1934, T-580/roll 85/ folder 402. Symptomatic of middle class confusion was the arrest in Nuremberg of an Oberscharführer of the SA reserve for "subversion" (*Zersetzung*); he had sought to recruit his comrades for the more conservative Frontkämpferbund. *Frankfurter Zeitung*, June 9, 1934. As late as May 1934, Röhm had had to warn the SA not to engage in punitive activity towards Stahlhelm units which refused to let their members join the SA. *News Chronicle*, May 15, 1934. See also Wilhelm Weiss, "SA und Frontsoldatentum," VB, May 17, 1934, T-580/roll 85/folder 402. On June 29, 1934, the *Manchester Guardian* concluded that *failure* to press an SA-Stahlhelm (Frontkämpferbund) quarrel in Pomerania was a sign of serious crisis in the Nazi movement. See also VB, June 26, 29, 1934, T-580/roll 85/folder 402.

36 *Staatsministerium des Inneren, Bayrische Politische Polizei* I/I W, I/I D, June 29–July 4, 1934, T-175/roll 240/frames 2730238–56; Sauer, in Bracher, *Machtergreifung*, p. 954, citing *Urteil Osnabrück*, p. 17, and *Anklage München*, pp. 49, 52; *Urteil München*, p. 84; Krausnick, "Der 30. Juni," p. 321. Wheeler-Bennett's theory of an earlier SS plan for a mid-June purge is unsupported: *Nemesis*, p. 317, and *Wooden Titan*, p. 457.

37  *Schulthess' europäischer Geschichtskalender, 1934* (Munich, 1935), p. 142. See Sauer, in Bracher, *Machtergreifung*, p. 952. SA press releases on Röhm furlough: VB, June 8, 9, 1934. See also *Daily Herald*, June 9, 1934; Foertsch, pp. 50–54. Papen's Marburg speech: Krausnick, "Der 30. Juni," p. 321. See also Papen, pp. 346–49. Important speeches by Goebbels and Hess, June 21 and 24: Sauer, in Bracher, *Machtergreifung*, p. 953.

38  Visit to Venice: DBFP, series 2, vol. 6, pp. 745–46; Hanfstaengl, *Unheard Witness* (Philadelphia and New York: J. B. Lippincott, 1957) pp. 247–57; Eichstädt, pp. 33–35, 45–46. Wheeler-Bennett believes the Neudeck visit involved conservative pressure through Hindenburg on Hitler to settle with the radicals: *Nemesis*, pp. 319–21. See also Sauer, in Bracher, *Machtergreifung*, p. 955.

39  Northern cruise: BDC Biographical Records. Alleged "ambush" of Himmler; Diels, p. 54; Frischauer, p. 64; Phipps's memorandum, July 5, 1934, DBFP, series 2, vol. 6, p. 968. Krausnick, "Der 30. Juni," p. 321. Mau, "Die 'Zweite Revolution,'" p. 131. Dresden: IMT, vol. 20, pp. 289, 312. Breslau, Kleist affidavit: Bennecke, *Reichswehr und "Röhm-Putsch,"* p. 85.

40  Bennecke, *Reichswehr und "Röhm-Putsch,"* pp. 51–53, citing Osnabrück SS trial. Mau, "Zweite Revolution," p. 133. See also Neusüss-Hunkel, pp. 11–13, citing Walter Hagen (pseudonym of Wilhelm Hoettl), *Die Geheime Front* (Stuttgart, 1952), p. 22; and Orb, pp. 73–75, 291–99 — both of dubious worth. See also Reitlinger, *SS: Alibi of a Nation. 1922–1945* (New York, 1957), pp. 59 ff.

41  Mau, "Zweite Revolution," p. 133; testimony of Paul Körner, IMT, vol. 11, p. 151; Krausnick, "Der 30. Juni," p. 322; Sauer, in Bracher, *Machtergreifung*, pp. 959–61. Extensive details on the Munich situation in *Der neue Vorwärts* (Karlsbad), July 15, 1934, T-580/roll 85/folder 402. See *London Observer*, July 1, 1934.

42  Mau, "Zweite Revolution," p. 134; Krausnick, "Der 30. Juni," pp. 322–23; Eberstein testimony, IMT, vol. 20, pp. 289–90; VB, July 8, 9, 10, 1934; *Frankfurter Zeitung*, July 10, 1934; letter of Regierungspräsident Bonsen, July 1, 1934, *Institut für Zeitgeschichte, Rep.* 77; London *Times*, July 2, 3, 1934; *Neuer Vorwärts*, July 15, 1934; *Manchester Guardian*, August 29, 1934; Gisevius, *To the Bitter End*, pp. 150–58; Papen, pp. 353–59; Schaumburg-Lippe, pp. 173, 176; Winfried Martini, "Zelle 474," *Der Monat* 9 (1957): 80–84; T-354/roll 196/folder 15/frame 3855136.

43  Two hundred figure: H. B. Gisevius, *Adolf Hitler* (Munich, 1963), p. 292. The *Morning Post* of September 26, 1934, claimed 218 persons had been admittedly killed, 100 in Munich, seventy in Berlin, thirty in Stuttgart, twelve in Breslau, six in Dresden. Rauschning's figure of 1,000 party members shot in *Voice of Destruction*, p. 166, reflects indefinite arrests and the consequent exaggerations of deaths. Fifty-five SA men appear on an *Institut für Zeitgeschichte* list of eighty-three killed. Bennecke, *Reichswehr und "Röhm-Putsch,"* pp. 86–88. Hitler admitted seventy-six executions: Baynes, *The Speeches of Adolf Hitler*, pp. 300–302. SS participation: *Anklage und Urteile, Schwurgerichte Osnabrück, Kassel, München, Berlin, Braun-*

*schweig, Hannover, Institut für Zeitgeschichte.* 135-L (affidavit of Willi Schmid's widow), IMT, vol. 37, pp. 581–87. Between 150 and 200 persons were called to Berlin and given daggers by Himmler inscribed "30. Juni, 1934." All SD men were promoted one grade. Krausnick, "Der 30. Juni," p. 322–23. One hundred forty-two SS officers were promoted July 1–6, 1934, among them eleven of the later Kommando des Reichsführers SS, z.b.V.: *DAL 1934; DAL 1935;* and Neusüss-Hunkel, p. 13. See von Salomon, pp. 444–49, citing the judgement of Walter Luetgebrune. Credit to SS: *Neuer Vorwärts,* July 15, 1934, T-580/roll 85/folder 402.

44  Intentional "excesses": Bennecke, *Reichswehr und "Röhm-Putsch,"* pp. 59–65. Report of Security Police at Stettin on Lutze's visit of August 17, 1935: ibid., pp. 89–90. SA vulnerability: Bennecke, *Hitler und die SA,* pp. 216–18.

45  Right-wing intimidated: Rauschning, *Voice of Destruction,* pp. 167–73. For a foreign view of the purge as a rightist victory, see *Manchester Guardian,* July 3, 1934. Reichswehr grudge: *Daily Telegraph,* July 9, 1934. SS armament: Foertsch, p. 57 (citing Blomberg). See Bennecke, *Reichswehr und "Röhm-Putsch,"* pp. 68–71. SS and police: T-175/rolls 70, 71/folders 240, 250.

46  The AW was exempted from the SA-*Uniform-Verbot* of July, 1934. *Frankfurter Zeitung,* July 4, 1934; Vogelsang, *Chef der AW,* pp. 11–14. AW personnel taken into the SS: BDC Biographical Records. SA house-cleaning by Daluege: T-580/roll 85/folder 403.

## Chapter 6: Years of Growth

1  "Thus we have assembled, and thus we march according to immutable laws, as a national socialist soldiers' order of Nordicly-determined men, and as a sworn community of their families, into a distant future — desiring and believing ourselves to be not merely the descendants who fought better, but even more, the grandsires of later generations essential for the life of the German-Germanic people." Heinrich Himmler at the annual National Farmers' Day Rally at Goslar, 1935. Quoted in Best, *Deutsche Polizei,* p. 101, but incorrectly dated (1936). See clipping of *Deutsche Allegemeine Zeitung,* November 23, 1935, T-580/roll 87/folder 425.

2  Foertsch, pp. 59, 63; Hossbach, p. 71. SS spying on Wehrmacht (via the Reichsarbeitsdienst), 1935: T-175/roll 32/frames 2539963–83. An additional factor was the bitter SA hatred for the SS, resulting even in a murder group known as "Röhm's Avengers" (*Rächer-Röhm Gruppe*): Kogon, p. 4; listed in SD subject file for 1936, T-175/roll 501/frame 9364620. According to a Gestapo report of August 13, 1934, some SS men "of good families" in Oldenburg refused to take the oath to the Führer. An order to send them to a concentration camp was canceled as too dangerous in view of the *Volksabstimmung* (plebiscite) on August 19. They were to be publicly degraded (*die Uniform ausgezogen*). T-175/roll 138/folder EAP 161-b-12/147.

3  *Gestapa Sonderbericht, Vergiftung des Verhältnisses der Nation und Träger*

*von Weltanschauung in Staat und Partei* (December 1934–January 1935), T-175/roll 432/frames 2962376–424; London *Times*, December 3, 28, 1934; *Manchester Guardian*, December, 4, 5, 1934, January 8, 1935; *Daily Mail*, December 7, 1934; *Daily Herald*, December 19, 27, 1934; *Morning Post*, January 11, 1935; *News Chronicle*, January 11, 1935. See also Hossbach, pp. 34–35; Wheeler-Bennett, *Nemesis*, pp. 341–42; Reitlinger, *SS*, pp. 73–74.

4  Paul Hausser, *Waffen-SS im Einsatz* (Pr. Oldendorf, 1953), p. 9; pp. 32, 47–48. A letter from a Leibstandarte officer to the Kanzlei des Führers of June 5, 1935, speaks of "the SS Division." T-354/roll 193/frame 3851556. Himmler excepted the Politische Bereitschaften in an order of September 27, 1934, canceling tactical military training in the SS: T-175/roll 501/frame 9364799. He was still pressing Hitler about funding *Führerschule Tölz* in December. T-175/roll 194/frame 2615268.

5  Führerbesprechung at Breslau growing out of SS crimes in Silesia, August 11–13, 1934: T-175/roll 138/folder EAP 161-b-12/147. See Krausnick, "Der 30. Juni," p. 317. Diels, pp. 305–6; Gisevius, *To the Bitter End*, pp. 179–96. The lawlessness of the concentration camps and the abuse of "protective custody" were particular objects of reform efforts from the right, especially from the newly merged Reich-and-Prussian Ministry of the Interior. 3751-PS, IMT, vol. 33, pp. 56–60. German conservatives were by no means unanimously interested in the "rowdy SS" as an alternative to the "rowdy SA" in the fall and winter of 1934. A series of Gestapo reports shows that they sought to reactivate the Stahlhelm (after March 1934 known as the National Socialist League of Front Soldiers): T-175/roll 430/frames 2960125–298. Only when this path was closed to them *and* when Himmler had modified the SS "image" could they proudly wear the black uniform. Hans Buchheim has a brilliant discussion of the process by which the SS image was "cleaned up": "Das Problem des Befehlsnotstandes bei den vom nationalsozialistischen Regime befohlenen Verbrechen in historischer Sicht. Gutachten von Dr. Hans Buchheim, June 5, 1964" (mimeographed), pp. 23–36. "Übernahme des Stahlhelms" (into SS, 1936–37), T-175/roll 131/folder EAP 161-b-12/241.

6  For extensive material on the prehistory of the Austrian SS, SA, and NSDAP, see T-580/rolls 61–63/folders 302–6. Graeschke was an SS-Altkämpfer (SS No. 14,470) from the Berlin free corps and SA, a lawyer to help the Illegalen, who also worked on the Linz *völkisch* newspaper *Deutschösterreich*. He quarreled with everybody, but maintained an espionage ring until December 1934. BDC Biographical Records.

7  The exact strength of the Austrian SS January 1, 1934, was supposed to be 4,980, of whom 949 were recognized by Munich. On July 14, 1934, their number had risen to 9,450 with only 1,752 recognized: BDC Biographical Records. One of the most famous Austrian refugee camps was *Lager Lechfeld*, run by the SS. *SS-Personalbefehl* Nr. 10, November 24, 1933, T-611/roll 3/folder 429.

8  Eichstädt, p. 33 and note 73; pp. 37–38. Margaret Ball, *Post-War German-Austrian Relations: the Anschluss Movement* (Stanford, 1937), pp. 200–201,

206; Kurt von Schuschnigg, *Driemal Österreich* (Vienna, 1937), pp. 242–45; DBFP, series 2, vol. 6, p. 389. Himmler negotiations with Starhemberg and Heimwehr: T-175/roll 58/folder 118; and BDC Biographical Records.

9   United States Department of State, *Documents on German Foreign Policy, 1918–1945*, series C (1933–1937) (Washington, D.C., 1949–1957) —hereafter DGFP(C) — 1:427, 2:188, 394, 3:116, 134. DBFP, Series 2, vol. 6, p. 996; 4013-PS, IMT, vol. 34, p. 56; *SS-Personalbefehl* Nr. 13, May 4, 1934, T-611/roll 3/folder 429; London *Times*, April 28, 1934.

10  BDC Schumacher Collection, folder 427, photos 634u–655u. The 89th SS-Standarte had ties with the Austrian army, from whom its members had recently been discharged for Nazi sympathies. See Höhne, pp. 248 ff. See also Alfred Vagts, *Hitler's Second Army* (Washington, D.C., 1943), p. 43, citing *Das Schwarze Korps*, May 12, 1938.

11  The BDC Biographical Records contain an order of July 24, 1934, canceling the assignment of a *Reichsdeutsch SS-Oberführer* (senior colonel) to the SS Main Sector Danube "in view of altered circumstances," and the *SS-Oberabschnitt VIII (Donau)* is reported dissolved as of November 1934. T-354/roll 194/frame 385987. See memoranda by one of the leading SS officers involved in the plot, with Himmler's note to him, June 9, 1938: "As you know, the whole inquiry into the matter of the July revolt has now been forbidden by the *Führer* and therefore quashed." T-175/roll 32/frames 2539538–53; 2539844; 2539850–64.

12  Vitas of SS martyrs: T-175/roll 26/folder 899. See 2968-PS, IMT, vol. 31, pp. 420–23. Troubles between German and Austrian SS in Munich, 1935: BDC Biographical Records.

13  Courts: T-354/roll 194/frames 3852977–78. See also *Frankfurter Zeitung*, July 25, 1934. For the internal system of SS "honor courts," see *SS-Dienstvorschrift Nr. 10: Schied- und Ehrengerichts-Ordnung der SS* (Miesbach, n.d. [1935?]). Reserves and discharges: T-354/roll 194/frames 3852983, 3852996, 3853004; RuSHa *Rundschreiben* 3/1934 of March 1, 1934, T-611/roll 19/folder 28; Neusüss-Hunkel, p. 18. See also *Frankfurter Zeitung*, August 30, 1934; and *Pariser Tageblatt*, September 1, 1934. Tightening: T-354/roll 194/frames 3852992, 3853013; BDC Schumacher Collection, folder 428. Himmler order forbidding SS uniforms in church, November 11, 1934: BDC Biographical Records. Removal of clergy: T-175/roll 97/frame 2617770. In 1940 Himmler wrote: "the mistake of 1934–35, of putting in officers without sufficient ability, must not be repeated." T-580/roll 87/folder 425. For a case study revealing the foibles and inadequacies of the General SS in the 1930s, see Robert John Shalka, "The General SS in Central Germany 1937–1939: A Social and Institutional Study of SS Main Sector Fulda-Werra" (Ph.D. dissertation, University of Wisconsin–Madison, 1972).

14  *Reichsführer SS. Chef des SS-Amtes (geheim). Einteilung der SS*, December 14, 1934, T-580/roll 87/folder 425. By the end of 1934 SS membership had sunk to 164,883, scattered in 1,777 *Stürme* or companies, representing considerably fewer communities, since many Stürme were in metropolitan

areas. Stürme composed of several village communities in a *Landkreis* (rural county) were exceptional. The typical Sturm outside metropolitan areas was identified with the county seat. Efforts to give the appearance of "blanketing" Germany with SS units resulted in the formation of 449 *Sturmbanne* (battalions) and 130 *Standarten* (regiments), a doubling of these units since 1932. In fact, like the twenty-nine *Abschnitte* (sectors), these exclusively urban staffs were still top-heavy with "honorary brass" even after the drastic reduction of the SS from its high of 250,000. *Nationalsozialistische Deutsche Arbeiterpartei. Hauptorganisationsamt. Parteistatistik* (Munich, 1935), vol. 3, pp. 89, 92.

15  Like their counterparts, the SA-Obergruppenführer, the *SS-Oberabschnittsführer* (Main Sector Commanders) had increased from seven to ten by the outset of 1935, all SS generals, and powerful figures. All were Altkämpfer. Four had titles of nobility, and six distinguished themselves subsequently in other SS positions. *DAL 1934, DAL 1935*, etc. See also Castellan, pp. 352–54. The inspectorate of concentration camps did not directly challenge their authority over the SS-Wachtruppe at first: *SS-Verordnungsblatt* 1:2, December 24, 1934, T-611/roll 31. See Neusüss-Hunkel, p. 53, citing Orb, pp. 154 ff. For the view that Hitler really was behind Eicke's appointment, see the testimony of Gottlob Berger, U.S. Military Tribunal Case Eleven, *Trials of War Criminals* (Washington, D.C., 1952) (hereafter TWC), vol. 13, p. 466. See also Plädoyer for Oswald Pohl, U.S. Military Tribunal Case Four, TWC. The term *aktiven Hundertschaften* as contrasted with Stürme of the General SS is under *Fahnen* (flags), an order of June 5, 1934, BDC Schumacher Collection, folder 428.

16  Testimony of Paul Hausser, IMT, vol. 20, pp. 357, 359–60. See also Neusüss-Hunkel, p. 23. Buchheim, "Die SS," VJHZ 3 (1955): 140. The SS officer candidate school at Bad Tölz came into existence in the spring of 1934 more or less as a parallel to the old *SA-Führerschule* in Munich, with a commander appointed June 1, 1934. *Personalbefehle* Nrs. 12, 14, T-611/roll 3/ folder 429. The second school, at Brunswick, organized in January 1935, was specifically designed as an OCS. *SS-Verordnungsblatt* 1:3, T-611/roll 3/ folder 429. See Castellan, pp. 360–61.

17  *Wehrmacht* decision of July 24, 1941, BDC Biographical Records; Hausser, *Waffen-SS*, pp. 9–10, 14; Horst Lehmann and Peter Wacker, "Die Waffen-SS," *Feldgrau* 1 (1954): 129. See also Buchheim, "Die SS," p. 141. Plädoyer for Pohl, U.S. Military Tribunal Case Four. See also Schulz, in Bracher, *Machtergreifung*, p. 676; Gisevius, *To the Bitter End*, p. 183.

18  Hans Buchheim has provided the fullest discussion of this problematical evolutionary process, with regard to both the police and the paramilitary units: *SS und Polizei im NS-Staat* (Duisdorf bei Bonn, 1964), esp. pp. 93–114. Neussüss-Hunkel, pp. 10–11, points out the early formulations of the quasi-state status by Alfred Schweder, *Die Politische Polizei* (Berlin, 1937). *SS-Dienstverträge*, BDC Biographical Records. While Sepp Dietrich tried to persuade the Gestapa as early as November 1933 that the Leibstandarte was independent of the SS-Gruppe Ost (T-354/roll 196/frame 3855216), an

order from the SS Main Office of February 22, 1935, reaffirmed that even
the Leibstandarte was subordinate to the regional SS headquarters (*Oberabschnitt Ost*). T-175/roll 96/frame 2615941. The chain of command from
the SS Main Office via the SS Main Sectors to the Politische Bereitschaften is
demonstrable in the BDC Biographical Records for 1935. Hausser recalled
that his contacts with the Main Sectors decreased in 1936 when the inspectorate was established, (IMT, vol. 20, p. 360). Casual discharges by local
Verfügungstruppe commanders and AWOLs (absences without leave),
1935: T-175/roll 97/frames 2617726 ff.

19  Orb, pp. 161 ff. The separate office of Inspector of Guard Units (*Wachverbände*) appeared November 1935: *SS-Verordnungsblatt* 1:11, T-611/roll 3/
folder 429. It became the office of Commander of Guard Units (later
Death's Head troops) April 1936: ibid., 2:2, T-611/roll 3/folder 429. Heydrich was issuing orders about the *state* concentration camps from January
1935 on (T-175/roll 422/frames 2949508, 2949524), but the Gestapo did not
gain the exclusive control over the camps in 1936 which Heydrich sought:
Buchheim, *SS und Polizei*, pp. 133–34. Concentration camp defiance of
Berlin *and* regional SS commanders still occurred in 1939. T-175/roll 40/
frames 2550870–76, 2550887.

20  T-354/roll 194/frames 3852948, 3853008; T-175/roll 96/frames 2616176,
2616185, 2616469–70, 2616479–83, 2616614–17; T-175/roll 97/frame
2617304; T-175/roll 414/frame 2939545.

21  *Stabsbefehl* Nr. 9/35, BDC Schumacher Collection, folder 427 (*Der Reichsführer SS. SS-Hauptamt*). See also T-175/roll 97/frames 2617419, 2617433,
orders of February and March 1935. The BDC Biographical Records reveal
not only the details of Himmler's personnel policies and the failings of so
many of his early selections, but also Himmler's sharp-tongued paternalism
toward them all.

22  T-354/roll 194/frames 3852993, 3853006. BDC Schumacher Collection,
folder 428 (*Der Reichsführer SS. SS-Hauptamt*). Change in Main Office
chiefs: T-175/roll 96/frame 2615910; and Höhne, p. 134.

23  BDC Schumacher Collection, folder 427 (*Verwaltung*); ibid., folder 428
(*Beschaffungsamt SS, Fördernde Mitglieder, Geldverwalter*). The Verwaltungsführer had their own Officers' Rank List (*Dienstaltersliste*) in 1934,
1935, and 1936 (copies in BDC). U.S. Nuremberg doc. NO 1574, letter of
Pohl to Himmler, October 1, 1935. Testimony of Pohl, TWC, vol. 5, pp.
319–25; *Richtlinien*, September 27, 1935, T-175/roll 96/frames 2616404–9.
By June 1936 the SS-Verwaltungschef had exclusive authority to enter into
business contracts for the SS: T-175/roll 96/frame 2616418. See Enno
Georg, *Die wirtschaftlichen Unternehmungen der SS* (Stuttgart, 1963), pp.
25–29. See also Buchheim, "Die SS," pp. 143–44. Creation of *Verwaltungs-
und Wirtschaftshauptamt*: NO 1451, TWC, vol. 5, p. 293. First VWHA order, April 20, 1939: U.S. Nuremberg doc. NO 1987.

24  Leadership Office chiefs: (1) The office manager: T-175/roll 96/frames
2615937, 2615954; T-354/roll 194/frame 3852989. (2) The police colonel:
T-354/roll 194/frame 3852995; T-175/roll 97/frames 2617290–91; his spe-

cial *Amt für Sicherungsaufgaben* replaced the Gruppenstab z.b.V. (T-175/ roll 96/frames 2615834, 2615837). (3) Consolidation with the position of the SS Main Office chief: T-175/roll 96/frames 2615880-84, 2615900. (4) Operation by Hausser and the ex-Reichswehr colonel: T-175/roll 97/frame 2617298; T-354/roll 194/frame 3852917.

25    T-175/roll 96/frames 2615836, 2615880-88, 2615954, 2616027-28, 2616036, 2616089-91, 2616222, 2616327, 2616565. BDC Schumacher Collection, folder 427 (*Ergänzung; SS-Hauptamt; Presse*). The place of the SS Hauptamt in the SS structure as of 1935 can be seen in the NSDAP *Parteistatistik*, vol. 3, p. 163. For the Main Office chief's interest in the *Nationalpolitische Erziehungsanstalten* (*Napolas*), see his vita (*Lebenslauf*), T-611/ roll 20/folder 82a. See also Horst Ueberhorst, ed., *Elite für die Diktatur. Die Nationalpolitischen Erziehungsanstalten 1933-1945. Ein Dokumentarbericht* (Düsseldorf, 1969), pp. 56-57, 60-62, 106 ff.

26    During 1935, the SS continued to experiment with several classes of reserves, at first distinguished from the "actives" as SS-Reserve I and II, and after May 1935 as SS II, SS-Reserve, and SS-Stamm-Abteilung. BDC Schumacher Collection/folder 427 (*SS-Reserve*). By 1936, this over-elaborated system was reduced to "actives" and Stamm-Abteilungen. See *DAL 1936. Neueinteilung des SS-Führerkorps*, January 23, 1936: T-175/roll 96/frames 2616303-7; T-354/roll 194/frame 3852830.

27    T-354/roll 194/frames 3852794-96, 3852801. A supplementary order of April 3, 1937 (BDC Schumacher Collection, folder 427 [*Recht*]), *Befehlsführung und Sachbearbeitung im Geschäftsbereich des Reichsführers SS*, clarifies the duties of the *Persönlicher Stab*.

28    Basic order creating Personal Staff, November 9, 1936, U.S. Nuremberg doc. NO 739 (T-175/roll 97/frame 2618342). Karl Wolff, the chief of this office, accompanied Himmler to Italy, and was one of three SS officers honored by the Italian monarch with a decoration; the other two were Daluege and Heydrich! VB, April 20, 1937. Again, in the 1941 issue of *Böhmen und Mähren*, an illustrated propaganda annual, his picture appears beside precisely these same gentlemen. Structure in October 1939 on distribution list, T-175/roll 40/frame 2550251.

29    The *Chef-Adjutantur* was housed in Berlin in the so-called *SS-Haus* at 9 *Prinz-Albrecht-Strasse*, next to the Gestapa. T-611/roll 20/folder 74. Letter-answering: T-175/roll 199/frames 2620633-35. Promotions: until December 1937 Himmler approved promotions of *all* NCOs; even, afterwards, of all officers: T-611/roll 6/folder 432 (*Sachgebiete: Beförderung*). He still approved NCO promotions in the Main Offices after 1937: BDC Schumacher Collection, folder 427 (*Sachgebiete: Personal Kanzlei*). Gifts: carved dish for bread and salt; Christmas (*Yule*) candle holder (*Julleuchter*), SS-*Kalender 1939* (printed by J. C. Huber, Diessen vor München). Eighty Julleuchter per SS regiment for Christmas 1937 to oldest SS families: T-175/roll 414/frame 2939504. Decorations (Death's Head rings, SS daggers, SS buttons for civilian clothing, runes for non-SS uniforms, medals): BDC Schumacher Collection, folder 428 (*Sachgebiete: Ehrensymbole*). Special tasks:

liaison in delicate matters with party offices (e.g. *Auslandsorganisation*), T-175/roll 80/frames 2600373-95; complaints about behavior at Junkerschulen: BDC Biographical Records. Focus of influence, e.g. contacts with *Deutscher Club*, 1937: T-175/roll 80/frames 2600422-24.

30  Georg, pp. 14-21. *Freundeskreis:* as early as 1933 SS vacations were paid for by *Hitler-Spende* – BDC Biographical Records; U.S. Nuremberg doc. NI 9200; Thyssen, p. 163; T-175/roll 15/frame 2518402. *SS Spargemeinschaft e.V.* (credit union): T-611/roll 9/folder 444 (*Sachgebiete: Pflichtsparen*). *Sonderkonto R:* T-175/roll 80/frame 2600457. *Representationszulagen* (entertainment allowance): T-175/roll 99/frame 2620406. Companies: T-175/ roll 414/frame 2939530; T-175/roll 97/folder 8b2. "Allach Ausstellung": *12-Uhr-Blatt*, May 4, 1937. "SS Porzellan Manufaktur": *Nationalsozialistische Landpost*, April 30, 1937. Houses: T-175/roll 80/frames 2599684, 2599692-93, 2599703, 2599889-90, 2599905. Job placement, Four Year Plan, and raw materials: ibid., frames 2600413-14, 2600485; T-175/roll 22/folder 123. Inventors and embezzlers: T-175/roll 32/frames 2540023-27; and Hitler, *Secret Conversations*, p. 486.

31  Georg, pp. 21-24; Hellmut Lehmann-Haupt, *Art under a Dictatorship* (New York, 1954), pp. 149-57; Samuel A. Goudsmit, *Alsos* (New York, 1947), pp. 201-10; Michael H. Kater, *Das Ahnenerbe der SS 1935-1945. Ein Beitrag zur Kulturpolitik des Dritten Reiches* (Stuttgart, 1974); T-580/roll 68; T-611/rolls 7, 22. Himmler used funds loaned to his cultural organizations for paying off debts of his deserving Altkämpfer and for business investments in concentration camps. T-580/roll 68/folder 329. On the other hand, Lebensborn and Ahnenerbe depended on income from the bicycle reflector company: Georg, p. 19, citing U.S. Nuremberg doc. NO 542 and NI 13423.

32  BDC Schumacher Collection, folder 427 (*Rasse- und Siedlungshauptamt*); T-354/roll 194/frames 3853000-3003. T-611/roll 19/folder 28; roll 21/folder 88. For a thorough treatment of RuSHa (and SS) "racial politics," see Manfred Wolfson, "The SS Leadership" (Ph.D. dissertation, University of California-Berkeley, 1965), pp. 82-101.

33  T-611/roll 19/folder 28; roll 20/folders 74, 83; roll 22/folder 88. See also doc. SS-1, IMT, vol. 42, p. 473; T-175/roll 96/frames 2615853, 2616441, 2616622, 2616884-85. Himmler himself continued to pass upon various borderline marriage cases and all marriages of career officers and even enlisted men of the Special Duty and Guard Troops. BDC Biographical Records. Many more marriage refusals were based on hereditary diseases (supposedly including diabetes) than on race. T-354/roll 194/frames 3852850-54, 3852982.

34  Whereas in January 1935 the party propagandists were trying to provide the Leibstandarte with "philosophical training" (T-354/roll 194/frames 3853263-64), by October 1936 they were using a popular SS lecturer from the RuSHa Schulungsamt for their programs. Ibid., frame 3853062. Changing RuSHa structure: T-611/roll 19/folder 26; roll 20/folders 74, 83; roll 21/folder 88. Himmler intervened personally to aid lagging promotions

in the Race and Settlement Office in September 1936. T-175/roll 96/frame 2616836.

35  T-175/roll 97/frame 2617166; T-354/roll 194/frame 3852941. T-611/roll 20/ folder 58; roll 21/folder 87. BDC Biographical Records.

36  2825-PS, IMT, vol. 31, p. 180; BDC Schumacher Collection, Folder 427 (*Sippenamt*); ibid., folder 428 (*Pflegestellen*); BDC Biographical Records. T-611/roll 19/folder 58; roll 20/folder 58; roll 21/folders 83, 88. U.S. Military Tribunal Case Eight, German transcript, p. 651. In 1937, the Office for Family Affairs was turned over to Dr. Arthur Gütt, the Nazi eugenics specialist, who brought with him an Office for Population Policy and Eugenics into the Sippenamt. Gütt was ineffectual, and the new Main Section on population and eugenics soon became a dead letter. *SS-Befehlsblatt*, November 25, 1937, T-175/roll 414/frame 2939524.

37  Several of the chief officers of the *Lebensborn* were tried by a U.S. Military Tribunal in Case Eight (all acquitted). See Prosecution Docs. NO 393, NO 2884, NO 3325, NO 4207; Ebner Defense Book I, Doc. 3. 2825-PS, IMT, vol. 31, pp. 177–78. T-354/roll 193/frames 3851416–30, 3851434–42, 3851450–52, 3851456–59. T-611/roll 20/folder 82a; roll 21/folder 83; roll 19/ folder 26. BDC Biographical Records.

38  As early as October 1935, Himmler forbade the SS to use Darré's ancient German month names (December = *Julmond*), which had previously headed RuSHa's stationery and the reports of some local units. T-354/roll 194/frame 3852931. But he himself pursued his runic studies and "archeological research": R. Koehl, "Heinrich the Great," *History Today* 7:3 (1957): 147–53. Training materials: T-611/roll 22/folder 88 (*Schulung*); the December 1935 issue of the *Leithefte* had to be withdrawn (roll 20/folder 74). Himmler's complaints about the Schulungsamt's "moralizing" (November 8, 1937): T-175/roll 94/frame 2615336; January 28, 1944, in retrospect — ibid., frames 2614803 ff.

39  Training Office issue: U.S. Nuremberg doc. NG 107 (Darré letter to Himmler, February 8, 1938); NG 1285 (Darré letter to former head of the Schulungsamt, April 18, 1939). Transfer to SS-Hauptamt, August 1, 1938: T-175/ roll 414/frame 2939638. Secret notice of Darré's resignation from RuSHa, September 10, 1938: BDC Schumacher Collection, folder 427 (*RuSHa*). Pohl, SS Chief of Administration, wanted to dissolve RuSHa entirely as early as March 1938 because of the cost, which the state was refusing to meet. He seems to have first proposed the transfer of the Training Office, but his real concern was the Sippenamt, which he wanted assigned to the Persönlicher Stab. Ibid. On the new RuSHa chief, see BDC Biographical Records. Himmler made seven regional Rasse- und Siedlungsführer attend the Sixth *Reichsbauerntag* at Goslar to keep up appearances with Darrë in November 1938 (T-611/roll 21/folder 84), a result of Himmler's continued backing of the RuSHa Settlement Office's recruitment program among farm elements inside and outside the SS. The Sippenamt was partially dismantled by transferring its medical section to the Chief SS Physician's Office. T-611/roll 20/folder 58. Himmler's directions for SS ideological train-

ing in 1938: T-580/roll 37/folder 428[I]. SS training material prepared in the SS-Hauptamt: U.S. Military Tribunal Case Eleven, prosecution doc. books 66-A and 66-B.

40  *Erste gemeinnützige Baugesellschaft für Kleinwohnungen, G.m.b.H. (Wien)*, BDC Biographical Records. Aryanization: T-175/roll 129/frame 2655405. Sudetenland: T-175/roll 58/folder 209; T-611/roll 20/folder 58; roll 22/folder 88. *Bodenamt Prag:* U.S. Military Tribunal Case Eight, English transcript. pp. 700–703, 720–21 (testimony of Günther Pancke). T-175/roll 23/folder 785. An article in the *Frankfurter Allgemeine Zeitung* of January 15, 1939, emphasized the SS tie with agricultural settlement by calling attention to items in the *Nationalsozialistische Parteikorrespondenz* about Hitler Youth in the Landdienst program as *recruits for the SS and future farmers* and officially describing Himmler as a leading member until 1928 of the mystical agrarians, the *Artamanen.*

41  U.S. Military Tribunal Case Eight, English transcript pp. 674–79; U.S. Nuremberg doc. NO 3162. T-611/roll 20/folder 58; roll 22/folder 88. T-175/roll 57/folders 51, 351. BDC Biographical Records.

42  Gisevius, *To the Bitter End*, pp. 181–94. Daluege himself put together folders EAP 172-b-05/11 and EAP 172-b-05/13 (T-175/rolls 3–4/frames 2503891–4166); documents, correspondence, an essay, and clippings illustrate his rise in the party and the police. See also T-580/roll 45/folder 258 (*Kommissar z.b.V.*). Daluege report on the Protectorate, September 1, 1942: NG 2068, TWC, vol. 12, pp, 899–901.

43  H.-J. Neufeldt in H.-J. Neufeldt, J. Huck, and G. Tessin, *Zur Geschichte der Ordnungspolizei 1936–1945*, Schriften des Bundesarchivs (Coblenz, 1957), Teil 1, pp. 8–10. A Bormann letter of May 12, 1936, calls Daluege *Befehlshaber der Deutschen Polizei:* T-175/roll 96/frame 2616757. See Kurt Daluege, *Nationalsozialistischer Kampf gegen das Verbrechertum* (Munich, 1936); BDC Biographical Records. As late as August 1935 uniformed policemen could not remain in the SS. T-175/roll 97/frames 2617631–32.

44  Neufeldt, pp. 11–27; 775-PS, IMT, vol. 26, pp. 289–91. See also Gisevius's testimony, IMT, vol. 12, p. 181, and his *To the Bitter End*, pp. 185, 193. *Reichsgesetzblatt*, 1936, vol. 1, pp. 487–88 (2073-PS); *Ministerialblatt des Reichs- und Preussischen Ministerium des Inneren* 1 (1936): 946–47. See Buchheim, "Die SS," p. 135. Buchheim points out the blend of intention and accident in this formulation and in much else involving the SS (p. 132). On usage of *Sicherheitsamt, Sicherheitshauptamt,* and *SD-Hauptamt,* see U.S. National Archives and Records Service, *Guides to German Records Microfilmed at Alexandria, Va.,* No. 39, Records of the Reich Leader of the SS and Chief of the German Police, part 3 (Washington, D.C., 1963), pp. v–vi, 107, 112.

45  Neufeldt, pp. 33 ff. See also Neusüss-Hunkel, p. 44. *Reichsgesetzblatt*, 1937, part 1, p. 325; 1940, part 1, p. 613. Himmler spoke of eighty to ninety thousand men in the uniformed police (ORPO) as of January 1937: 1992(A)-PS, IMT, vol. 29, p. 231. Recruiting of SS for ORPO: T-175/roll 414/frame 2939496. Runes: *Ministerialblatt*, 1937, p. 758. By 1938, SS membership

was open to Order Police in lower ranks who had been financial supporters of the SS (*Fördernde Mitglieder*) before January 30, 1933 (when direct SS membership was illegal for the police) or who, if they were not in the police, were in the SA, the party, or the Hitler Youth. *Ministerialblatt*, 1938, p. 390. This relatively selective process was abandoned piecemeal during the war, so that career policemen (e.g., rural gendarmerie!) became an important element in the wartime SS officers corps. See Buchheim, *SS und Polizei*, pp. 104–14.

46  Inspectors and General-Inspectors: Neussüss-Hunkel, p. 46–47; Neufeldt, pp. 39–40 and biographical data, pp. 106 ff. Crankshaw's statements (*The Gestapo*, p. 90) that both ORPO and SIPO Inspectors were appointed on September 20, 1936, in the *Wehrkreise* (army corps area), and that the commanders of the SS Main Sectors were made Chiefs of Police for their areas on that date, cannot be established. The latter is certainly incorrect. The *Ministerialblatt* (RMBliV) for 1936 contains only the decree creating the post of Inspector of the Security Police (not appointments), and specifically refers to provinces and Länder (pp. 1343–44). An SD memorandum of February 22, 1939, explains that the first SIPO Inspectors, appointed in 1937, followed this plan, but that appointment for army corps areas began in April 1938. T-175/roll 239/frame 2728189. While another memorandum of February 24, 1939, states that the Order Police made their inspectorships conform to the Wehrkreise, BDC Biographical Records show that the earliest appointments (1936–1937) of ORPO inspectors were made at provincial and *Land* capitals which were also corps area headquarters. See Neusüss-Hunkel, p. 47, citing *Das Recht der NSDAP* (Munich, 1937); also *Ministerialblatt*, 1936, p. 1614, an order of November 30, 1936, mentioning ORPO inspectors both inside and outside the regular table of organization. The length of the period of gestation of the important wartime institutions of both inspectorships was the result of disagreements and uncertainty in regard to other institutional developments in the SS-Police fusion, such as the Wehrkreis parallelism and the Superior SS and Police Leader's post (discussed in the two memoranda cited above). For the wartime role of the ORPO inspectorships, see Best, *Deutsche Polizei*, p. 68.

47  Neusüss-Hunkel, p. 36, has counted twenty-four Police Presidents in the 1938 *Dienstaltersliste*. Of these, ten were listed as SD. The SD field apparatus consisted of one or two low-ranking paid officers and NCOs in each SD Main Sector (*Leitabschnitt*) and each SD Sub-Sector (*Unterabschnitt*). SD Sectors were approximately the same as SS Main and Sub-Sectors except that some SS Main Sectors were consolidated to form one SD Main Sector. T-175/roll 239/frame 2728167; roll 240/frame 2729937. Himmler told Wehrmacht officers in January 1937 that the SD field apparatus would consist of 3,000 to 4,000 Referenten, many of them officers, "when it was complete." 1992(A)-PS. IMT, vol. 29, p. 223. Best made the specific parallel between the General SS officer or NCO, who held an unpaid SS position along with his regular employment, and the *ehrenamtliche Mitarbeiter des SD-Reichsführer SS* (p. 105). Neusüss-Hunkel points out two distinguishing

marks of the official SD in contradistinction to mere informants: the SD on the lower sleeve (left) of the uniform (1936), p. 30, and the subscription to an SD oath (1939), p. 32. Both paid and unpaid SD members would be so distinguished with the unpaid preponderating. Evidence that SD finances may have been a factor making for a large unpaid staff: Friedrich Zipfel, "Gestapo und SD in Berlin," *Jahrbuch für die Geschichte Mittel- und Ost-deutschlands* (hereafter *Jahrbuch*) 9–10 (1961): 272–73; and an SD memo-randum of 1939, T-175/roll 239/frames 2728099, 2728104.

48 Reinhard Heydrich, *Die Wandlungen unseres Kampfes* (Munich, 1935), re-printed from *Das Schwarze Korps;* Aronson, pp. 196–99; J. C. Fest, *Das Gesicht des Dritten Reiches* (Munich, 1963), pp. 139–55. See also Orb, pp. 136–38; Hoettl, pp. 15–16; Walter Schellenberg, *Memoiren* (Cologne, 1959), pp. 35–37. For the character of the SD personnel: Orb, pp. 59–60, 77–79, 80–83; Dr. François Bayle, *Psychologie et Éthique du National-Socialisme* (Paris, 1953), pp. 33–182; BDC Biographical Records. The pro-fessional SD can be distinguished from part-time "honorary" personnel in the *Dienstalterslisten* from 1934 on; the former are designated merely as "SD," while the latter are termed "SD-RFSS." A third distinct group, formed in October 1935 from the Begleitkommando des Führers and former SD personnel, was the *Reichssicherheitsdienst,* analogous to the American Secret Service for the protection of the President. T-175/roll 40/frames 2550984–85; roll 59/frames 2574464–67. See Neusüss-Hunkel, p. 29, citing *Zentraljustizblatt der britischen Besatzungszone* 4 (1948): 297.

49 Müller and Best: Orb, pp. 73–77, 143; Hoettl, pp. 71–75; Schellenberg, pp. 32, 34, 71 (note). See also Aronson, pp. 225–33, 238–42, 248–49. Within the Gestapa Best acquired the Main Departments I (Organization and Law) and III (*Abwehrpolizei* or counter-intelligence); in the new structure of June 26, 1936, Organization and Law was taken out of the Gestapa and made a separate office of the Security Police alongside the Gestapa and the criminal police headquarters. Buchheim, *SS und Polizei,* pp. 47–58. As *Ministerialdirigent,* a high bureaucratic official, Best headed this new of-fice as well as the Abwehrpolizei (III), while retaining personnel and ad-ministrative authority in the Gestapa. U.S. Nuremberg doc. NG 3366, cited by Raul Hilberg, *The Destruction of the European Jews* (Chicago, 1961), p. 119. See Best's testimony, IMT, vol. 20, p. 143. Müller had risen from sec-tion chief in charge of combating Marxism to become head of the Main De-partment II (Investigation and Prevention), later known as the Political Department. T-175/roll 432/frame 2962635. Creation of *Reichssicherheits-hauptamt,* September 27, 1939: 361-L, IMT, vol. 38, pp. 102–6. See also George Clark Browder, "SIPO and SD, 1931–1940. The Formation of an Instrument of Power" (Ph.D. dissertation, University of Wisconsin–Madison, 1968).

50 T-175/roll 240/frame 2729938; roll 432/frames 2962321–24, 2962540–41. See also Neusüss-Hunkel, pp. 40–41. The elaborate numerical subsectioning of the SS-Sichterheitshauptamt in the thirties was probably Best's, since it was changed when he left in 1940: *Amt* = I; *Zentralabteilung* = I/1; *Ab-*

*teilung* = I/11; *Referat* = I/111 (file system of 1936). Höppner testimony, IMT, vol. 20, p. 217; and T-175/roll 501/frames 9364554 ff. Amt II was Intelligence, Amt III was Counter-Intelligence, and Müller's SD personnel were conceived of as Amt Politische Polizei without numerical designation.

51 Testimony of Ohlendorf and Best, IMT, vol. 4, pp. 344–45, and vol. 20, p. 142. Zipfel, "Gestapo und SD in Berlin," pp. 282, 284–85. Zipfel has detailed statistics for the Gestapa and for the Berlin Stapostelle in June 1935: of 607 officials in the Gestapa system, 244 were SS members, half of whom had come in before April 1934; of 353 in the Stapostelle, only thirty-six were in the SS, but thirty-three had come in before April 1934! Gestapo unification decrees of August 28, 1936, and September 20, 1936: RMBliV, 1936, pp. 1343, 1344–46. Neusüss-Hunkel errs in asserting that the Stapo(leit)stellen were moved to conform with the SD and Wehrmacht boundary system in 1936. (Neusüss-Hunkel, p. 41–42, citing *Kalender für die Sicherheitspolizei*, 1943, pp. 227–29.) Insofar as this occurred, it took place considerably later, in wartime. Her point about the central budgeting of Gestapo offices after April 1, 1937, is accurate (RGB, 1937, part 1, p. 325), reflecting Himmler-Frick collaboration against the gauleiters, who retained some control over *criminal* police expenditures, even after their nationalization. On SD officers as a growing percentage of the whole SS-Führerkorps, see Ramme, pp. 83–84.

52 *Neuordnung der staatlichen Kriminalpolizei*, September 20, 1936; RMBliV, 1936, pp. 1341–43. The plan for a *Reichskriminalpolizeiamt* (National Criminal Investigation Office) went back to 1935. Gisevius, *To the Bitter End*, pp. 142, 197. Nebe: Hoettl, pp. 75–78; Schellenberg, p. 41; Crankshaw, pp. 227–28. R. Heydrich, "Aufgaben und Aufbau der Sicherheitspolizei im Dritten Reich," in Hans Pfundtner, ed., *Dr. Wilhelm Frick und sein Ministerium* (Munich, 1937), pp. 152–53. Extension of Heydrich's influence, October 26, 1936: RMBliV, 1936, p. 1441. See Neufeldt, pp. 22–23. The Wehrmacht Abwehr still considered the criminal police relatively immune to SD control in 1939. Paul Leverkuehn, *German Military Intelligence* (New York, 1954), p. 36.

53 An exaggerated form of this contention is given in Neusüss-Hunkel, p. 33, based on Orb, p. 93, and referring also to the views of the young SD officer Alfred Schwedler (*Die Politische Polizei*). See Zipfel, "Gestapo und SD in Berlin," *Jahrbuch* 9–10 (1961): note 37. For Himmler's own view of a *Staatsschutzkorps* combining the virtues of the Prussian official (*Beamter*) and Prussian soldier with the "unbureaucratic" (*unbeamtet*) and "nonmilitary" (*unsoldatenmässig*) SS, see Hans Frank, Heinrich Himmler, Werner Best, and Reinhard Höhn, *Grundfragen der deutschen Polizei. Bericht über die konstituierende Sitzung des Ausschusses für deutsches Recht am 11.10. 1936* (Hamburg, 1937). See also 1992(A)-PS, IMT, vol. 29, p. 228, his January 1937 talk to Wehrmacht officers ("a first-class police corps"). SIPO Inspectors: RMBliV, 1936, pp. 1343–44. Looser ties: affidavit of A. Bomhardt, SS-87, IMT, vol. 42. p. 658. See also Neusüss-Hunkel, p. 48; Best, *Deutsche Polizei*, pp. 72–73. Ultimately, the SIPO Inspectors were to take

the place of the SD Main Sector Chiefs. With an eleven-man staff, they were to compile the data which they acquired from the SD Sector Chiefs in their region. They were, of course, also armed with coordinative and executive authority over both state and SD agencies. The actual reorganization of the SD field system into Abschnitte and Leitabschnitte, modeled after the system of Stapostellen and Stapoleitstellen, was delayed until 1939: T-175/roll 239/frame 2728203. As was stated in note 46 (above), not all the SD Main Sector Chiefs were made SIPO Inspectors, and throughout the thirties there were more SS Main Sectors than SD Main Sectors, so that only a few of the best SD officers reached this post. See T-175/roll 239/frames 2728167, 2728197–99. Efforts to professionalize the SD intensified in 1939, and some of the oldest SD leaders, including several SIPO Inspectors, were removed. T-175/roll 239/frames 2728211–13; BDC Biographical Records.

54 Ohlendorf claimed that when he joined the SD headquarters in May 1936 there were only about twenty young people without a building of their own. U.S. Military Tribunal Case Nine, English transcript. p. 491; further testimony in IMT, vol. 4, pp. 352–53. Part of the change around 1936 was the shift away from the SD as a *party* intelligence bureau, under pressure from Bormann. *Parteikanzlei. Verfügungen*, vol. 1, pp. 602–4. Ohlendorf vita quoted in entirety in Bayle, pp. 37–41. Adolf Eichmann, "Papers relating to Adolph Eichmann compiled by the Wiener Library" (London, 1961). The evolution of the subsection II-112 in which Eichmann worked can be followed in some detail in T-175/roll 410/frames 2934811 ff. The so-called *Funktionsbefehl* (functional order) of July 1, 1937, provided that SD-*Inland* turn over surveillance of individuals to the Gestapa, receiving in turn the Gestapa's extensive files. T-175/roll 410/frame 2934968. See also SD-27, an affidavit cited in IMT, vol. 22, p. 15; and Buchheim, *SS und Polizei*, pp. 61–65. On Wewelsburg, see Schellenberg, pp. 39–40; and Aronson, p. 217. See also T-611/roll 7/folder 434 (*Sachgebiete: SS-Schule Haus Wewelsburg*).

55 Aronson, pp. 251–52; Schellenberg, pp. 32–33, 69–70. AMT II: T-175/roll 410/frames 2934905–26, 2934958. Six began as the SD press specialist in 1935: ibid., frames 2934854–59. See Reitlinger, *SS*, pp. 42–43.

56 Orb, pp. 64–66; Schellenberg, pp. 25 ff.; Leverkuehn, pp. 34–36; Wilhelm Hoettl, *Hitler's Paper Weapon* (London, 1955), pp. 19–21. There seems to have been a considerable amount of intrigue in Amt III dealing with the national socialist parties abroad as, for example, in Switzerland. T-175/roll 496/frames 9359406–62 (July–November 1935). Foreign contacts of the SD used for military espionage: T-175/roll 22/frames 2527123–44.

57 Again Neusüss-Hunkel's extreme views turn the whole retired system (*Stamm-Einheiten*) into agents of the SD and the parallelism of SS, SD, and Wehrmacht into a conspiracy (pp. 29–33). While the passage of individual officers from the Stamm to the SD can be demonstrated, and the "tapping" of general SS for SD recruits can also be shown (T-175/roll 96/frames 2616485–86), there is ample evidence of the genuine inactivity of Stamm members, and of actual objections in the SD to following the General SS's (and thus the Wehrmacht's) operational boundary structure: T-175/roll 239/

frames 2728158 ff. *DAL 1936, DAL 1937*, etc.; BDC Biographical Records. For evidence of SD and General SS boundary parallels, see T-175/roll 501/ frames 9364841–43. The SD Main Sectors were abandoned during the war (but later than September 1939). See Hoeppner testimony, IMT, vol. 20, pp. 223–24; and T-175/roll 431/frames 2961944–83. There is virtually no sign of movement from the Verfügungstruppen, Totenkopfverbände, and the officer candidate schools into the police, as Himmler had proposed. 1992(A)-PS, IMT, vol. 29, p. 228; and Best, *Deutsche Polizei*, p. 96. A 1937 provision that 50 percent of the higher administrative officers of the Security Police have passed through an SS-*Führerlager* (not the same as the officer candidate schools) cannot be verified; it is not clear what type of officers' training was intended. Neusüss-Hunkel, p. 43, citing *Kalender für die Sicherheitspolizei*, 1943, pp. 251 ff.

58 Affidavits of Adolf von Bomhard, SS-87, IMT, vol. 42, pp. 657–62; and U.S. Military Tribunal Case Eight, Otto Hofmann defense doc. 81. Best testimony, IMT, vol. 20, p. 132. As late as August 1937 Himmler had to complain to Daluege that an ORPO Inspector refused to work with an SS Main Sector Commander, and in the following May was importuning an Interior Ministry bureaucrat to speed up the naming of the same SS commander as Superior SS and Police Leader to strengthen his hand vis-à-vis the Order Police. BDC Biographical Records. SD fears were extensive enough to require special measures by Heydrich to combat "rumors" in April 1939: T-175/roll 239/frames 2728101–3. A memorandum of February 1939 originating with the SD treats the HSSPF's role as "undeveloped and unripe" — probably a criticism of its non-SD origins. The same writer pointed out acidly that, in Düsseldorf, the SIPO Inspector was legally bound to follow instructions from two separate Oberpräsidenten (and gauleiters): T-175/roll 239/frames 2728190–91.

59 There is probably a connection between Daluege's police system and the Superior SS and Police Leaders going back to Göring's "Superior Police Leaders — West and East" of the spring of 1933. Schulz, in Bracher, *Machtergreifung*, pp. 438–39, 468. In those days, neither Himmler nor Röhm was ready to place his revolutionary forces within the control of the state system, even under extraordinary authorities! For the earliest formulation of the HSSPF in an unpublished Interior Ministry decree of November 1937 and a detailed discussion of the problem, see Hans Buchheim, "Die Höheren SS- und Polizeiführer," VJHZ 11 (1963): 362–91. Neusüss-Hunkel's theory of a "staged" unwrapping of the connection, perhaps as a background to the coup against the generals Blomberg and Fritsch, fits here (pp. 29–33). Daluege and press release, BDC Biographical Records. When a lower police official made a public reference to the position in April 1938, he was charged by the Gestapo with giving away a Geheime Reichssache! BDC Biographical Records. *Ernennungsurkunden* (official appointments) were issued at different times in the summer of 1938 *after the coup*, and were not published in full. BDC Biographical Records. On the background of the party-state-SS rivalry in this regard, see Richard Hildebrandt testi-

mony, U.S. Military Tribunal Case Eight, English transcript, pp. 3884–87, 3918, 3920; affidavit of Gerbel, Hildebrandt Defense Doc. 122. Although Daluege still insisted in 1942 that the HSSPF was a *Beamtenstellung* (a government post) (BDC Biographical Records), Best states that it entailed control over the General SS through a new official, the *Stabsführer der Allgemeinen SS* (Executive Officer for the General SS): *Deutsche Polizei*, p. 51. Daluege was working with the gauleiters as late as July 1939 to strengthen their hands vis-à-vis the HSSPF's (BDC Biographical Records), but while Himmler constructed elaborate titles for the Superior SS and Police Leaders recognizing the authority of the Reich governors, he would not tolerate SS localism (*SS-Satrape mit kirchturmsmässigem Blick* — SS satraps with church-tower vision): T-580/roll 37/folder 238[II].

60 Kogon, p. 7; Langhoff, pp. 98 ff., esp. pp. 213–19; Benedikt Kautsky, *Teufel und Verdammte* (Zurich, 1946), pp. 17–25; Diels, pp. 57, 71, 189–97. Testimony of Wilhelm Schäfer, IMT, vol. 21, pp. 73–105; Paul Körner, IMT, vol. 9, p. 150; Erhard Milch, IMT, vol. 9, pp. 95–96. Low SS opinion of early guard personnel: BDC Biographical Records. The use of the camps for service punishments was investigated in March 1934. T-175/roll 240/frames 2730257–77. Use in Röhm purge: T-580/roll 69/folder 329. Gestapa section II-D, an order from Heydrich transferring some of its authority to Eicke, December 20, 1934: T-175/roll 422/frames 2949653–55. There was a Gestapo-operated concentration camp at Wittmoor, near Hamburg, as early as August 1933: T-580/roll 68/folder 329. Certain official concentration camps were run by the Criminal Police in Saxony in August 1933: Reimund Schnabel, *Macht ohne Moral* (Frankfurt am Main, 1957), pp. 105–7. Four camps are listed as official concentration camps for Prussia as of October 14, 1933: Papenburg, Sonnenburg, Lichtenburg, and Brandenburg. Ibid., p. 111. Eicke signed "Inspektion der Konzentrationslager RFSS" as early as August 1934: ibid., p. 138.

61 Martin Broszat, ed., *Kommandant in Auschwitz* (Stuttgart, 1958) (hereafter Hoess), notes 1, 3, pp. 53–54. Testimony of August Frank, U.S. Military Tribunal Case Four, TWC, vol. 5, p. 448. The forty or more camps of 1933 were reduced to fewer than a dozen in the course of 1934: IMT, vol. 21, p. 76; Orb, p. 161. Orb, whose work Neusüss-Hunkel uses uncritically (p. 53), is incorrect in including Buchenwald and Sachsenhausen, which were opened later. The number of camps in late 1934 depends on whether branch camps like Börgermoor and Neusüstrum (near Esterwegen-Papenburg), and camps staffed by SS but not run by Eicke (Fuhlsbüttel near Hamburg), are included. *Columbia Haus* and Lichtenburg were also at first operated by General SS-Standarten 42 and 26: T-580/roll 68/folder 329; Langhoff, 231. The numbering of the guard companies in 1935 probably indicates the order in which Eicke took over the camps: Dachau, Papenburg, Lichtenburg, Columbia-Oranienburg, and Sachsenburg. T-175/roll 40/frames 2550201–2. SS at concentration camps detached from their General SS units: *Personalbefehle* Nrs. 12–13, T-611/roll 2. Wachverbände: *SS-Verordnungsblatt* Nr. 1:1, T-611/roll 3/folder 429. "Aufbau der SS-Verwaltung," Septem-

ber 9, 1935: T-611/roll 2/folder 426-II. "Inspekteur der Wachverbände," *SS-Verordnungsblatt* Nr. 1:2, T-611/roll 3. The existence of the twenty-five Hundertschaften can be shown as early as March 1935 (T-580/roll 69/folder 329) and grouped under five regional names as of June 1935. SS-*Verordnungsblatt* Nr. 1:7, T-611, roll 3. Each regional Wachverband was assigned a roman numeral from one to five in an organizational chart of November 27, 1935: T-175/roll 219/frame 2756761. The Übungslager Dachau did not begin its independent existence until September 1935: T-354/roll 194/frame 3852938. Extensive descriptive material on the complex of Dachau camps may be found in BDC Schumacher Collection, folder 428, including a Party tour on May 8, 1936, and an issue of the *Münchener Neueste Nachrichten* for January 13, 1938. Ausrüstungslager, also called the *Kleidungslager* and the *Wirtschaftslager:* T-175/roll 97/frame 2617793.

62  Affidavits of Walter Gerlach, SS(A)-27, IMT, vol. 42, pp. 517–21. See also Hoess, p. 56; Kogon, pp. 28, 30–31. Eicke already designated himself (prematurely) as *Führer der Totenkopfverbände*, December 2, 1935: T-175/roll 96/frames 2616638–42. The official order authorized the terms as of March 29, 1936: ibid., frame 2616463. Reich budget and Ministry of the Interior: T-175/roll 40/frames 2550217, 2550224. See Lammers's testimony about state funding: IMT, vol. 11, p. 61. Personnel: *Statistik der Schutzstaffel 1936* (Berlin, 1937), p. 20. See also *Statistisches Jahrbuch der Schutzstaffel der NSDAP, 1937* (Berlin, 1938), T-175/roll 205/frames 4043266–67. Efforts of the SS Main Office to spur recruitment from the General SS in 1936 were hampered by the twelve-year enlistment and narrow age limits (various: 17–20 and 20–22!). T-175/roll 96/frame 2616370; T-580/roll 68/folder 329. Eicke was accepting "big" sixteen-years-olds (T-175/roll 40/frame 2550183). Hitler Youth resources: BDC Biographical Records. On the ambiguous position of the Politische Abteilung: Kautsky, pp. 67–68; Kogon, pp. 29–30. Continued control from Gestapa and Reichskriminalpolizeiamt in Hauptamt Sicherheitspolizei: T-175/roll 40/frame 2550218; T-175/roll 219/frames 2756764–65. Limitation to six concentration camps (Dachau, Esterwegen-Papenburg, Lichtenburg, Sachsenburg, Columbia, and Oranienburg-Sachsenhausen): letter from Reichssicherheitshauptamt, IV-C, of May 3, 1940, referring to 1936, T-175/roll 68/folder 329. New camps: Kautsky, pp. 25–28. Buchenwald: Kogon, pp. 23–27. Negotiations began as early as June 1936. Schnabel, pp. 121–25. The former SS concentration camp at Fuhlsbüttel was being run by the Gestapo, which sought guards from the SA in January 1937: T-580/roll 68/folder 329. On the other hand, an *SS-Schutzhaftlager* for women, begun in 1933, continued at Moringen near Göttingen until March 1938: T-175/roll 422/frame 2949801; Schnabel, p. 114. Some kind of "private SS" concentration camp was run by the SS Main Sector Southwest at Stuttgart in October 1936 and transferred to Eicke in 1937: *Sonderkommando Oberabschnitt Südwest*, T-175/roll 98/frame 2618392; *Sonderkommando Stuttgart*, T-611/roll 4/folder 430/I.

63  *Personalverfügung* 4, T-580/roll 69/folder 329; Himmler to Ministry of Jus-

tice, November 6, 1935, T-175/roll 40/frame 2550982. BDC Biographical Records, indicating perennial difficulties at Dachau; Best and Daluege were very critical, and Himmler seems to have toyed with the return of the camps to the regional SS commanders. Some of the old camp personnel were "too popular" with the inmates, according to the Gestapo. See Kautsky, pp. 71–101; Kogon, pp. 287–300; Orb, pp. 164–68. RuSHa training officer: T-611/roll 20/folder 74. Ideological indoctrination: T-175/roll 40/frame 2550175. See also Eicke's *Befehlsblatt der Totenkopfverbände-Inspekteur der Konzentrationslager*, beginning January 1937, esp. No. 4, April 1937: ibid., frame 2550196. Punishments: *Befehlsblatt SS-TV/KL*, April, May, 1937, ibid., frames 2550170–71, 2550181, 2550198. See also Hoess, *passim* in notes. The BDC Biographical Records show that some of the most corrupt and lazy of the SS-Altkämpfer in the concentration camp administrations were removed in this shake-up, and in some later ones even in the war years, but punishments were rare and re-employment in the SS not uncommon. *Konzentrationslager Sachsenhausen* is mentioned in the *SS-Verordnungsblatt* for the first time in November 1936 (2:7, November 9, 1936, T-611/roll 3/folder 429). Esterwegen: T-580/roll 68/folder 329; Reitlinger, *SS*, p. 257.

64    Oranienburg headquarters: Orb, p. 161; first mentioned in *SS-Verordnungsblatt* 1:9, September 5, 1935, T-611/roll 3/folder 429. The two branches had a common chancellery (*Zentralkanzlei*: T-175/roll 40/frame 2550181. Many of the economic personnel were defendants in U.S. Military Tribunal Case Four. A vita for each defendant was presented to the tribunal as a sworn affidavit, available at the Center for Research Libraries, Chicago, Ill., the Hoover Institution, and other deposit libraries. See also Georg, pp. 11–14, 124–32. For vitas of staff personnel for the Death's Head troops, see BDC Biographical Records. A medical service independent of the General SS was created in June 1936. *SS-Verordnungsblatt* 2:3, June 15, 1936, T-611/roll 3/folder 429.

65    Testimony of Pohl, TWC, vol. 5, pp. 332–33, 439. The view of the issue as one of predictability and control is essentially that of Neusüss-Hunkel, who recognizes the contradictions involved in the rational use of random and arbitrary terror (pp. 56–58). Cf. Aronson, pp. 233–43.

66    Workshops: testimony in Case Four, TWC, vol. 5, pp. 323–26, 329, 331, 336–37, 339–41. Georg, pp. 36–37 and note 86. See also Georg, p. 144. Round-ups for concentration camp labor: testimony of Helmut Bickel, U.S. Military Tribunal Case Four, English transcript, pp. 461–62. See also Kautsky, pp. 28–29; Kogon, pp. 14–18.

67    1992(A)-PS, IMT, vol. 29, pp. 221–22. See *Befehlsblatt TV/IKL Nr. 2*, T-175/roll 40/frame 2550208. The Totenkopfverbände increased from 3,500 to 4,833 by the end of 1937 and to 8,484 by December 31, 1938. *Statistisches Jahrbuch der Schutzstaffel der NSDAP, 1937* and *1938*, cited by Georg, p. 144, note 570. Both in 1937 and 1938 more than half were *Anwärter*, i.e. men with less than a year's service. Ibid., 1938, p. 79. Reorganization of July 6, 1937: *Befehlsblatt SS-TV/KL Nr. 6*, June 1937, T-175/roll

40/frames 2550159, 2550161, 2550174, 2550185. The recruits of 1938 continued to be very young men, without SS or army service: Himmler speech of November 8, 1938, T-175/roll 90/frame 2612395.

68  Common furlough regulations for VT und Wachverbände, December 1935: T-175/roll 97/frames 2617840 ff. Common treatment of AWOL (*Schutzhaft*): T-175/roll 414/frames 2940068–69. *Merkblatt für Einstellung bei der SS VT und TV (Ausgabe Dezember 1936)*: T-175/roll 96/frame 2616699. *Des Recht der NSDAP*, p. 74, cited in Neusüss-Hunkel, p. 38; *Reichsgesetzblatt*, 1937, vol. 1, p. 545. Sicherungsverbände: T-175/roll 98/frame 2618377 (an order making them available to Goebbels for propaganda activities!). Kasernierte SS (January 30, 1937): T-175/roll 97/frames 2618189–90. Bewaffnete SS (December 14, 1938): T-175/roll 39/frame 2548900. *Sonderkommandos zur besonderen Verfügung:* Buchheim, "Die SS," p. 140. The expressions *Allgemeine SS*, *Verfügungstruppe*, and *Wachverbände* date from a Himmler order of December 14, 1934, "Einteilung der SS" (T-580/roll 87/folder 425). Totenkopfverbände listed as General SS, June 1937, *Abzeichen der Allgemeinen SS:* T-175/roll 98/frames 2618387–93. Sonderkommando Sachsen: *SS-Personalbefehle* Nr. 13, and *SS-Verordnungsblatt* 1:3, T-611/roll 3/folder 429; and BDC Biographical Records. See Ernst-Günther Krätschmer, *Die Ritterkreuzträger der Waffen-SS* (Göttingen, 1957), p. 64.

69  Sepp Dietrich: T-354/roll 194/frames 3853318, 3353322; roll 199/frame 3859771. On the Leibstandarte, see the complete treatment of the unit by James J. Weingartner, *Hitler's Guard. The Story of the Leibstandarte SS Adolf Hitler, 1933–1945* (Carbondale-Edwardsville, Ill., 1974), pp. 2–19. *SS-Personalbefehle* Nrs. 10, 11, 14, T-611/roll 3/folder 429. See also Neusüss-Hunkel, p. 37. *Kasernierte Hundertschaften, Politische Bereitschaft Württemberg, Politische Bereitschaft Hamburg, Politische Bereitschaft München:* BDC Biographical Records. On March 25, 1935, Hitler told Sir John Simon that a few militarized sections of the SS formed substitutes for dissolved (!) police formations. U.S. Department of State, *Documents on German Foreign Policy, 1918–1945*, series C (1933–1937) (Washington, D.C., 1957) (hereafter DGFP[C]), vol. 3, pp. 1070–71. *Landespolizei:* Lothar Danner, *Ordnungspolizei Hamburg* (Hamburg, 1958), pp. 162 ff. Budgeting (LSAH): T-354/roll 196/frames 3854966, 3854972; roll 199/frames 3859771, 3859848. *Abzeichen der politischen Bereitschaften*, May 5, 1934, T-611/roll 7/folder 434 (*Sachgebiete: "P"*). See also *SS-Personalbefehle* Nrs. 13–14, T-611/roll 3. Formationsbezeichnungen: *SS-Befehlsblatt* 1:7, T-611/ roll 4/folder 430. Hundertschaften: Himmler speech, January 1937, 1992(A)-PS, IMT, vol. 29, p. 222. See also T-175/roll 97/frame 2617813.

70  *Gliederungen der SS im Gau München-Oberbayern*, November 4, 1937, T-611/roll 2/folder 426. *SS-Verordnungsblatt* 1:1, November 9, 1934, 1:2, December 24, 1934, 1:3, January 30, 1935, T-611/roll 3/folder 429. The separate quarters for I/SS 1 were begun at Dachau in October 1934 but not occupied until April 1936. Report of Party tour of Dachau, BDC Schumacher Collection, folder 428. Hilfswerklager Dachau: *SS-Personalbefehle*

Nr. 13, T-611/roll 3/folder 429. Treatment of Austrians: BDC Biographical Records.

71 III/SS 1: *SS-Verordnungsblatt* 1:1 and 1:3, T-611/roll 3/folder 429. See Orb, pp. 167–68. SS 2: *SS-Verordnungsblatt* 1:2, 1:3, and 1:6, T-611/roll 3/folder 429; *Verzeichnis anlässlich des Reichsparteitages 1935*, T-611/roll 2/folder 426. See also Hausser, *Waffen-SS*, pp. 9–12. Appointment of battalion and company commanders: *SS-Verordnungsblatt* 1:4 and 1:7, T-611/roll 3/folder 429. See also T-175/roll 97/frame 2617831. Leibstandarte training at Jüterbog and Zossen, 1933: T-354/roll 199/frames 3859218–30, 3859273–78, 3859338, 3859347–50, 3859424–26, 3859444, 3859471, 3859497, 3859556. On the other hand, the Leibstandarte sponsored a "war game" for other units (including Gruppenstab z.b.V.) in February 1935. *Richtlinien für die Heranziehung zur Ausbildung beim Heere*, T-175/roll 98/frame 2618489. See also T-175/roll 97/frames 2617831, 2617952. Specialized training and use of troop training areas: T-354/roll 194/frame 3852916; T-175/roll 97/frames 2617637, 2617760–63. Lack of training personnel and weapons: *Ausbildung der SS-VT in Übungsjahr 1936*, November 18 and December 3, 1935, T-175/roll 97/frames 2617894–902, 2617909–10.

72 *SS-Personalbefehle* Nrs. 12, 14, T-611/roll 3/folder 429; and *Gliederungen der SS im Gau München-Oberbayern*, November 4, 1937, T-611/roll 2/folder 426. *SS-Verordnungsblatt* 1:3, 1:6, 1:8, T-611/roll 3/folder 429. T-175/roll 96/frames 2616487–88; roll 97/frame 2617422. See also Hausser, pp. 12–13; Neusüss-Hunkel, p. 22; Orb, p. 213. Junkerschulen: *SS-Befehlsblatt* 5:8, T-611/roll 4/folder 430. "Stärkenachweisung der SS-Führerschulen" (February 5, 1935): T-78/roll 301/frames 6252294–300. Classes from *Dienstalterslisten*, 1935, 1936, 1937, 1938. The 1937–38 class at Brunswick sent its largest contingent to the *Ordnungspolizei* (fifty), the next largest to the Death's Head battalions (thirty-two). T-611/roll 7/folder 433 (*Sachgebiete: "J"*). In August 1938, when the Sudeten emergency required temporary withdrawal of some 70–80 new OCS graduates from administrative posts to the Verfügungstruppen and the Totenkopfverbände, thirty-nine were withdrawn from various Main District headquarters of the General SS. T-175/roll 32/frames 2540742–46. A speed-up of OCS classes to two per year with personnel largely drawn from Special Duty Troops is indicated in late 1938. T-175/roll 32/frames 2540618–22. Himmler told his assembled SS Generals in November 1938 that he had trained three or four times as many officers as had been authorized—presumably the four hundred reserve officers seconded elsewhere. T-175/roll 90/frame 2612563.

73 BDC Biographical Records; *SS-Statistik 1936*; and *Statistische Jahrbücher der SS, 1937* and *1938*. Other schools included: *SS-Reitschule Forst*, and *SS-Motorschule Berne*—T-175/roll 97/frames 2617808–9; *SS-Hauptreitschule München-Riem*—*SS-Verordnungsblatt* 2:7, T-175/roll 3/folder 429; *Führerschule Dachau*—*Das Schwarze Korps*, December 23, 1937, and VB, January 13, 1939. A critique of December 1939: T-611/roll 20/folder 58. Himmler stated that 40 percent of the SS officer candidates accepted before 1938 had had only an eighth-grade education; the biggest task was to bring

SS officers up to the Wehrmacht level in technical training. T-175/roll 90/ frames 2612393 ff.

74 *SS Statistik, 1936*, p. 17. *Der Ordensgedanke in der SS-Verfügungstruppe:* T-580/roll 87/folder 425. *DAL 1934, DAL 1935, DAL 1936.* There is a marked difference between the amateurism of the winter 1935–1936 training of the VT and the army service-manual type training schedule of the winter of 1936–1937: T-175/roll 97/frames 2617922–36, 2617987–93, 2617876–80. At the first course held for supply sergeants in September 1936, seventeen out of thirty-three had numbers below 50,000, twenty-six under 100,000. T-175/roll 97/frame 2617195. Recruitment in 1935: T-175/roll 97/ frames 2617787–88. In 1936: T-175/roll 96/frame 2616692; T-580/roll 87/ folder 436 (a memorandum of December 2, 1936, describes the procedures as no longer satisfactory). An order of July 18, 1937, speaks of ending "free recruiting" by VT and TV October 1, 1937; thereafter, their recruiters could go only to Labor Service Camps. T-175/roll 97/frames 2618332–33. In 1938 Himmler characterized all previous VT and TV recruitment as "suitable only for the Royal Prussian Army of yesteryear." T-175/roll 37/ frames 2546503–6. Cf. Hausser testimony, IMT, vol. 20, p. 360. The "independence" of the commanders of Leibstandarte, Verfügungstruppe, and Death's Head units was often noted, and both praised and blamed: Hausser, pp. 21–22, 237; Krätchmer, pp. 38–39; Felix Steiner, *Die Freiwilligen. Idee und Opfergang* (Göttingen, 1958), p. 67. As early as August 1935 Himmler had trouble with VT units which tried to put Wehrmacht cockades in their caps and made other unauthorized changes in uniform: T-175/roll 97/frame 2616698; T-354/roll 194/frame 3852944. In 1938 Hitler complained about their limp *Führergruss* (Hitler salute). T-175/roll 32/frame 2540483.

75 Separate promotion lists (for VT only): *SS-Verordnungsblatt* 1:12, T-611/ roll 3/folder 429. A clear-cut administrative reason for the VT-TV combination over and against the General SS was the separate budgeting which began in 1935 and was firmed up in 1936 (*Kassen- und Rechnungslegungsordnung für die VT und TV, SS-Dienstvorschrift 22*) (T-175/roll 97/frames 2617164, 2617199), and was most clearly expressed in the decision of the Verwaltungschef that the General SS budget would follow the Party Treasurer's decision to begin the party's fiscal year in January, while the VT-TV budget would continue to be based on the Reich budget beginning in April (frames 2617087–91). In November 1936 a VT regimental commander was refused General SS funds for travel to a meeting of the High Disciplinary Court (*Grosser Schiedshof*) of the General SS on the grounds that he was representing the VT. The decision was made by a lieutenant colonel who was both a long-time staff officer of the Verwaltungsamt and newly assigned to the Führungsstab der VT. BDC Biographical Records. Wehrmacht alarm: Hossbach (citing Fritsch), pp. 71–72; Siegfried Westphal, *Heer in Fesseln* (Bonn, 1950), p. 67. The General SS in shifting from the SA reserve system (Reserve I: ages 25–34; Reserve II: ages 35–44) to a twofold "active list" (SS I: ages 18–24; SS II: ages 25–34) on May 1, 1935, moved away from a combat-ready revolutionary troop: T-580/roll 87/folder 425.

In October 1936 they were still very cautious in removing those over forty-five and the inactive from the active SS. T-175/roll 97/frame 2618063. Meanwhile, Himmler courted the Wehrmacht by "adopting" a unit here and there and urging that young SS men serve their two years in these recommended units. The third battalion, 17th regiment at Goslar was recommended at the Reichsbauerntage there: T-175/roll 96/frame 2616756. Whereas in January 1935 Reichenau had stated that the VT would not possess mortars, anti-aircraft or anti-tank guns (Castellan, p. 360), in October 1936 a 13th company was designated in each regiment as *Infanterie-Geschütz (Minenwerfer-Sturm)*, i.e., regimental artillery—in fact, a mortar company which they hoped they could convert to light artillery; furthermore, a 14th company was designated (to be set up later) as an anti-tank company: T-175/roll 97/frame 2617812. Some 800 additional VT recruits were sought in a memorandum of June 27, 1936 (T-580/roll 87/folder 436); 500 were actually added in the last three months of 1936 (T-175/roll 96/frame 2616691; *SS-Statistik, 1936*, p. 17).

76  Wehrkreise in 1936: T-175/roll 496/frames 9359102, 9359109–10. 1937: ibid., frame 9359166. See maps in Benoist-Mechin, vol. 2. Changes in *Oberabschnitte* (Main Districts): SS — *SS-Statistik, 1936*, p. 14 (maps for 1934, 1936); *DAL 1937*, p. 400 (map). SD — illustrated for *Oberabschnitte Rhein* and *Fulda-Werra*, T-175/roll 501/frames 9364841–57. See also Neusüss-Hunkel, p. 34–35. Replacement districts: in September 1936, Himmler and the Wehrmacht agreed that only the Leibstandarte could recruit anywhere in Germany (T-175/roll 96/frame 2616690); the three regiments each had a recruiting office by February 1937 (T-175/roll 98/frame 2618460), but every General SS regiment and district (*Abschnitt*) was ordered to set up a recruiting office for VT and TV in November 1936 (T-580/roll 87/folder 436). Athough a failure (*Misserfolg*) was reported April 30, 1937, in the campaign to get each General SS regiment to recruit forty youths for VT and TV per year, 6,000 volunteers were reported from the General SS in 1937 (of which only 1,400 were taken). *Statistisches Jahrbuch der SS, 1937*, p. 44. The Hitler Youth was sought after by the SS for recruits from 1936 on: T-175/roll 96/frame 2616442; T-175/roll 97/frame 2618162; T-175/roll 98/frames 2619465–67. See Neusüss-Hunkel, p. 22. The travel discount was long fought over: T-354/roll 194/frame 3853009; T-175/roll 97/frame 2617238. Postal privileges: T-175/roll 97/frames 2617165, 2617206. Pensions: 1937 — T-175/roll 98/frames 2618462, 2618469–74; 1938 — *Reichsgesetzblatt*, 1938, vol. 1, pp. 1077–1124, 1607–8; *SS-Befehlsblatt* 6:2, T-611/roll 4/folder 430; 1939 — T-611/roll 7/folder 433 (*Sachgebiete: "J"*), letter of January 20, 1939. Use of weapons: *Reichsgesetzblatt*, 1937, vol. 1, p. 545. Efforts to get a separate *Gerichtsbarkeit* (court system) for the VT go back to 1935 (T-354/roll 194/frame 3852097), but were unsuccessful until November 1939. T-175/roll 40/frames 2550494–95.

77  Verfügungstruppe structure, March 30, 1936: T-175/roll 414/frame 2940013. Sturmbann IV, SS Deutschland: T-175/roll 96/frame 2616500. Standarte 3 (*SS Verordnungsblatt* 2:4, August 18, 1936, T-611/roll 3) can be

identified with Sturmbann N (Nürnberg), appearing in *SS-Verordnungs-blatt* 1:6 (April 20, 1935), *SS-Verordnungsblatt* 2:7 (November 9, 1936), and *SS-Befehlsblatt* 5:4 (April 28, 1937) (T-611/rolls 3–4), inasmuch as the same commander is named for both. BDC Biographical Records. SS VT Nürnberg, January 13, 1938: T-175/roll 98/frame 2619456. SS 1 was re-named "Deutschland" October 30, 1935: *SS-Verordnungsblatt* 1:10, T-611/roll 3/folder 429. SS 2 renamed "Germania": *SS-Befehlsblatt* 4:10, October 25, 1936, T-611/roll 4/folder 430. Creation of SS 3 for the third time as "Der Führer": Hausser, p. 10. The signal battalion was first mentioned at Adlers-hof September 21, 1936 (T-175/roll 97/frame 2617177); at Unna in 1937 (T-78/roll 301/frames 6252252–53). See "Vor 25 Jahren: Grundsteinlegung zur SS-Kaserne in Unna," *Der Freiwillige* 8 (1959): 23. Engineers battalion at Leisnig in 1936: Himmler speech, 1992(A)-PS, IMT, vol. 29, p. 231. At Dresden: *Anschriften-Verzeichnis*, October 1, 1937, T-611/roll 2/folder 426. Medical teams (July 15, 1936): T-175/roll 96/frames 2616913–17. Ärztliche Junkerschule (renamed *Ärztliche Akademie* in December 1938): T-175/roll 97/frame 2618238; BDC Schumacher Collection, folder 427.

78  Führungsstab der Verfügungstruppe: BDC Biographical Records; *DAL 1936*. First mentioned in *SS-Verordnungsblatt* 2:7, November 1936, T-611/roll 3/folder 429. Last appearance in April 1937: ibid., 3:3, T-611/roll 3/folder 429. Of the sixteen officer members of the Führungsstab in the 1936 *Dienstaltersliste*, ten reappear in the staff of the Inspector of the Special Duty Troops in the 1937 edition, four went to VT units, one went to an OCS, and one became the chief administrator of RuSHa. Creation of the inspectorate, with power to give orders directly to the units on organiza-tion, equipment and employment: T-175/roll 97/frames 2617889–92. See also Hausser, *Waffen-SS*, p. 10. In 1936, before the formation of the inspec-torate, promotions were authorized by the Oberabschnittsführer; in 1937, by the Inspector. BDC Biographical Records. On the other hand, Hausser had the power as head of the SS-Hauptamt's Führungsamt to sign orders for the chief of the Main Office itself, thus initiating aspects of policy toward the Main District Commanders. The SS colonel who countersigned an or-der of February 26, 1937, calling for semi-annual reports from the Oberab-schnittsführer, was to become a leading member of the wartime *Führungs-hauptamt*, the general staff of the Waffen-SS. T-175/roll 98/frame 2618456. For vicissitudes of the other personnel, see BDC Biographical Records. Himmler's order of July 1, 1938, restructuring the Recruitment Office, is very critical of inter-service rivalries between TV and VT, as well as between both and the "despised General SS": T-175/roll 37/frames 2546503–6. See also Neusüss-Hunkel, pp. 36–40.

79  BDC Biographical Records. See also Hellmuth Auerbach, "Eine nationalso-zialistische Stimme zum Wiener Putsch vom 25. Juli 1934," VJHZ 11 (1963): 201–18; Kaltenbrunner testimony, IMT, vol. 11, pp. 234–35. On HIGA and its successor, the *Grenz- und Wacheinheiten*, see T-175/rolls 96–97/frames 2615941, 2616830, 2617593; *DAL 1935, DAL 1936*, etc. On Border Police, see Buchheim, *SS und Polizei*, pp. 148–54.

80 Two reports and a speech by a participant, Friederich Rainer, form the chief sources for this narrative. 812-PS, IMT, vol. 26, pp. 344–59; 4004-PS, 4005-PS, IMT, vol. 34, pp. 1–39. See also Eichstädt, who checks the Rainer material against other evidence: pp. 72–80, 117–19, 124–29, 149–57, 170–207, 260–399. Additional documentation in U.S. Military Tribunal Case Eleven, partly reproduced in English in TWC, vol. 12, pp. 682–718. Extensive material on the SS in Austria can also be found in U.S. Department of State, *Documents on German Foreign Policy, 1918–1945*, series D (1937–1945) (Washington, D.C., 1949) (hereafter DGFP[D]), vol. 1, pp. 309–14; 471; items Nos. 170 and 262 deal with the SS-Hilfswerk system. For SS-Hilfswerk ties with the SS-Sammelstelle at Dachau, which survived through 1936, see T-354/rolls 194, 196/frames 3853117–19, 3855124; also *SS-Befehlsblatt* 4:1, 4:2, 5:5, T-611/roll 4/folder 430. A Himmler order of March 12, 1936, to prepare a card file of all SS members once in the Austrian SS: T-175/roll 96/frames 2616601–2. Possession of the "Austrian *Anschluss* medal," created May 1, 1938, is a good gauge of official participation by SS personnel in some phase of the operation. T-611/roll 20/folder 82a. Hitler on the illegal SS: *Secret Conversations*, p. 567. Cf. Frischauer, pp. 106–11.

81 Blomberg-Fritsch episode: Foertsch, pp. 85–155; Manstein, pp. 296–319, 322–26; Hans Hagen, *Zwischen Eid und Befehl* (Munich, 1958), pp. 49–54; Gisevius, *To the Bitter End*, p. 219–60; Heinz Guderian, *Erinnerungen eines Soldaten* (Heidelberg, 1951), pp. 42–49. Georg Tessin, "Die Stäbe und Truppeneinheiten der Ordnungspolizei," Teil 2 in Neufeldt, Huck, and Tessin, *Zur Geschichte der Ordnungspolizei*, pp. 9–11; Jodl diary, 1780-PS, IMT, vol. 28, pp. 356–72. On March 6, 1938, Himmler and Ribbentrop met to discuss a plan to exchange police officers with Austria, without the slightest reference to the imminent crisis: T-175/roll 32/frame 2540076. Operational orders: 102-C, 175-C, 182-C, IMT, vol. 34, pp. 335–37. 732–47, 774. See also testimony of Keitel, IMT, vol. 10, pp. 503–5; and Jodl, IMT, vol. 15, pp. 354–56. For Göring's role, telephone conversations: 2949-PS, IMT, vol. 31, pp. 354–84. Austrian SS at *Anschluss:* Kaltenbrunner testimony, IMT, vol. 11, p. 314. The "Austrian Legion" (SS): DGFP(D), vol. 1, pp. 495–97, 588 (Nos. 281 and 369).

82 Reorganization of Austrian SS: BDC Schumacher Collection, folder 428: *Statistisches Jahrbuch der SS, 1938*, p. 31. See also *SS-Übersichtskarten* 6 and 7 (1938), T-175/roll 196/frames 2736399–474; T-175/rolls 37, 39/frames 2546171, 2549239; Neusüss-Hunkel, p. 85. Gauleiters and Reich Commissar: Eichstädt, pp. 532–33 (note 88). See also 571-D, IMT, vol. 35, pp. 173–75; and T-175/roll 32/frames 2540079–80. Aryanization: Himmler order of March 3, 1939, T-611/roll 20/folder 58; report of the head of the SS-Gericht, October 1939, and a Himmler letter to Heydrich, September 1939, T-175/roll 32/frames 2539890–92. One of the reasons why the SS and police could seize properties right and left was the precedent-breaking Second Supplementary Order to the Reunification Law of March 18, 1938, whereby Himmler *as Reichsführer SS and Chief of the German Police* could

take measures "outside the legally established limits." *Reichsgesetzblatt,* 1939, vol. 1, p. 262. Formation of *Der Führer:* Otto Weidinger, *Kameraden bis zum Ende. Der Weg des SS-Panzergrenadier-Regiments 4 "Der Führer" 1939-1945* (Göttingen, 1962), pp. 15-18; SS *Verordnungsblatt* 4:4, T-611/roll 3/folder 429. Junkerschule Klagenfurt: Hausser, *Waffen-SS,* p. 29; and *Das Schwarze Korps,* November 26, 1942. Totenkopfstandarte Ostmark and Mauthausen concentration camp: T-175/roll 90/frame 2612536; testimony of Kaltenbrunner, IMT, vol. 11, pp. 329-335. Police reorganization: Tessin, in Neufeldt, Huck, and Tessin, *Zur Geschichte der Ordnungspolizei,* p. 20; Eichstädt, pp. 398, 428-29. The admission to the SS on March 12, 1938, of three of the Order Police commanders whose units entered Austria on that date not only betokened a broader assimilation of the police in the future but brought their units into better co-ordination with the SS for occupation purposes. Neusüss-Hunkel, p. 46.

83  U.S. Nuremberg doc. NG 5764; DGFP(D), 5:665, pp. 933-36; Hilberg, pp. 123, 259-60. Reitlinger, *SS,* p. 111; see also his *The Final Solution: The Attempt to Exterminate the Jews of Europe, 1939-1945* (London, 1953), pp. 25-26. Hannah Arendt, *Eichmann in Jerusalem* (New York, 1964), pp. 56-67. See also Adolf Eichmann, "Papers Relating to Adolph Eichmann Compiled by the Wiener Library" (London, 1961).

84  647-PS, IMT, vol. 26, pp. 190-98. This document appears in original form, minus the last page (with Hitler's signature), in the Schumacher Collection, T-580/roll 87/folder 425. Himmler's corrections are in his handwriting on the original. There is reference to this decree in later negotiations between the SS Main Office, the OKW, and the OKH. T-175/roll 104/frames 2626508 ff. See Kurt Kanis, compiler, *Waffen-SS im Bild* (Göttingen, 1957), pp. 217-18.

85  For discussions of this document, see Neusüss-Hunkel, pp. 61-64; and Buchheim, *SS und Polizei,* pp. 172-79. There appears to be a kind of commentary on this order (though it is not mentioned) in the *Frankfurter Zeitung* of February 16, 1939, reproducing an article by Werner Best in *Deutsches Recht* ("SS und Polizei als einheitliches Staatsschutzkorps").

86  Robert L. Koehl, *RKFDV: German Resettlement and Population Policy 1939-1945)* (Cambridge, Mass., 1957), pp. 37-40; testimony of Paul Schmidt, IMT, vol. 11, p. 219; Peter Kleist, *Zwischen Hitler und Stalin* (Bonn, 1950), pp. 10-15, 100-107. See also Neusüss-Hunkel, pp. 81-84; and Orb, pp. 360-73, 389-95 (both subject to the warning already noted). See also MacAlister Brown, "The Third Reich's Mobilization of the German Fifth Column in Eastern Europe," *Journal of Central European Affairs* (hereafter JCEA) 19:2 (1959): 130-34. In September 1937 there was close cooperation between the General Consuls in Torún and Poznań and the Gestapo to prevent ethnic Germans from leaving Poland. T-175/roll 15/frames 2517631-32. See also Ramme, pp. 87 ff.

87  VoMi trouble with ethnic Germans in Poland: Brown, p. 134; and Theodor Bierschenk, *Die deutsche Volksgruppe in Polen, 1934-1939* (Würzburg, 1954). For Austrian roots of the NSDAP, see Andrew Whiteside, *Austrian*

*National Socialism before 1918* (The Hague, 1962), pp. 105–6. The best treatment of the German-Czech relationship is in Ronald M. Smelser, *The Sudeten Problem, 1933–1938* (Middletown, Conn., 1975), esp. pp. 190–209. See also Radomír Luža, *The Transfer of the Sudeten Germans. A Study of Czech-German Relations 1933–1962* (New York, 1964), pp. 62–109; Helmuth K. G. Rönnefarth, *Die Sudetenkrise in der internationalen Politik. Entstehung, Verlauf, Auswirkung* (Wiesbaden, 1961), vol. 1, pp. 128–31; and Louis de Jong, *The German Fifth Column in the Second World War* (Chicago, 1956), pp. 282–94. Hoettl, *Geheime Front*, pp. 141 ff., 161 ff.; Bohuslav Bilek, *Fifth Column at Work* (London, 1945), pp. 89–90. Nazi-SS activities in Sudetenland dating before 1933: BDC Schumacher Collection, folder 313, T-580/rolls 66–67.

88 Martin Broszat, "Das Sudetendeutsche Freikorps," VJHZ 9 (1961): 30–36; Smelser, pp. 227–35. DGFP(D), vol. 1, pp. 65–66, 155; vol. 2, pp. 197–205, 228–29, 288; vol. 3, pp. 384–85, 556–63, 577. U.S. Nuremberg docs. NG 972, NG 4948. Brown, JCEA 19:2 (1961): 133–34; Neusüss-Hunkel, pp. 83–84; Bilek, pp. 137–39. Use of police to turn back or corral Sudeten refugees: T-175/roll 15/frames 2517738–40. Wehrmacht planning: 388-PS, IMT, vol. 25, pp. 414–75.

89 Report of Berger, the chief of the new Recruitment Office: T-175/roll 20/ frames 2524957 ff. Also *Gruppenführerbesprechung* of January 1939, "Allgemeine Erfahrungen bei Einziehung der Verstärkung der SS Totenkopfverbände im September 1938 sowie beim Gross-Einsatz der Allgemeinen-SS," T-175/roll 17/frames 2520626–43. Leibstandarte call-up of "reserves" in the form of drivers on temporary duty with the Gestapo: T-175/roll 240/ frame 2729962. Affidavits at Nuremberg trials: U.S. Nuremberg docs. NO 3029, NO 5715, NO 5812, 3036-PS. OKW records: 388-PS, IMT, vol. 25, pp. 475, 480–83. Broszat, "Sudetendeutsche Freikorps," pp. 36–41.

90 Karl Hermann Frank, "Freiwilliger Selbstschutz und SS," *Böhmen und Mähren* 3 (1941): 179; Luža, pp. 144–56; Broszat, "Sudetendeutsche Freikorps," pp. 44–49; Bilek, pp. 149–92; 388-PS, IMT, vol. 25, pp. 484–91; 366-EC, IMT, vol. 36, pp. 356–64; 1780-PS, vol. 28, pp. 381–89; T-175/roll 32/frame 2540701; DGFP(D), vol. 2, pp. 880, 968–69; testimony at Nuremberg, IMT, vol. 3, pp. 81–83, 96 ff., 152–53.

91 Military operations: 388-PS, IMT, vol. 25, pp. 491–527; T-78/roll 301/ frames 6251978–2005. SS officers with Wehrmacht: T-175/roll 90/frame 2612563. SS members who participated in the Sudeten-Aktion were eligible for the Sudeten-medal awarded October 1. T-611/roll 20/folder 82a. Einsatzstäbe, 509-USSR: IMT, vol. 39, pp. 536–51. Interior Ministry decree; RMBliV, 1938, p. 1906; and T-175/roll 414/frames 2939671–73. The team approach suggested itself for sabotage (de Jong, p. 287); resettlement (DGFP[D], vol. 2, pp. 267, 941–42); and intelligence (IMT, vol. 4, pp. 313–4; T-175/roll 32/frames 2540088–89; T-175/roll 432/frames 2962207–49).

92 Hoettl, *Hitler's Paper Weapon*, pp. 16–17. See also Martin Wight, "Eastern Europe," in *Survey of International Affairs, 1939–1946, 1: The World in March 1939*, ed. Arnold Toynbee and Veronica Toynbee (London, 1954),

pp. 270–93. Folk Group policy, including plans for resettlement and the manipulation of populations, is illustrated in DGFP(D), vol. 4, pp. 15, 20, 47–48, 53, 57, 59, 139, 152–53; vol. 5, pp. 81–93, 142–45, 161. See Joseph B. Schechtman, *European Population Transfers 1939–1945* (New York, 1946), p. 41; and Koehl, *RKFDV*, pp. 40–41. Gustav Föhler-Hauke, "Die Volksgruppe und Deutsche Arbeit in Böhmen, Mähren und der Slowakei," *Deutsche Volksforschung in Böhmen und Mähren* (Brünn), 1 (June 1939): 1–17; Luža, pp. 167–74; Josef Lettrich, *History of Modern Slovakia* (New York, 1955), pp. 103–9. Hitler's strategy of keeping all options open is illustrated in 136-C, 137-C, and 79-L, IMT, vol. 34, pp. 480, 482; vol. 37, pp. 548–49. Hitler's alleged remark to the SS in 1938 that he had been deprived of a triumphal entrance into Prague by Chamberlain (Schacht testimony, IMT, vol. 12, p. 531) may have been sincere *and* tailored to his audience.

93 DGFP(D), vol. 4, pp. 133–34, 140–42, 179–81, 183–85, 189, 195, 197; BDC Biographical Records. U.S. Nuremberg doc. 357-PS; NG 2937 and NG 3004 in TWC, XII, 878–80; 898. Karl Hermann Frank, "Freiwilliger Selbstschutz und SS," p. 179. Paul Seabury, *The Wilhelmstrasse. A Study of German Diplomats under the Nazi Regime* (Berkeley, 1954), pp. 50, 63–65, 70–72, 102, 106–9, 126–29.

94 DGFP(D), vol. 4, pp. 46–48, 209–13, 230–31; Lettrich, pp. 123–27; Luža, pp. 174–76; Frank, "Freiwilliger Selbstschutz und SS"; 2802-PS, IMT, vol. 31, pp. 150–53. Göring testimony: IMT, vol. 9, p. 304. Military actions from March 10: T-78/roll 301/frames 6252043–54; 6252074; 6252077–78; 6252082. See Schellenberg, pp. 57–59.

95 DGFP(D), vol. 4, pp. 185–86, 268; Lettrich, pp. 127–36; Luža, pp. 176–77; 2860-PS, 2861-PS, IMT, vol. 31, pp. 244–45. See also Erich Kordt, *Wahn und Wirklichkeit* (Stuttgart, 1948), p. 145.

96 DGFP(D), vol. 4, pp. 283–84; Luža, pp. 177–84; Lettrich, pp. 136–40. Military operations: T-78/roll 301/frames 6252117–18; 6252131; 6252152–53; 6252157–58; 6252162–63; 6252169–70; 6252183. See Kanis, p. 218. See also *Verordnungsblatt für Böhmen und Mähren* (Prague), beginning March 15, 1939 (1:1), pp. 7–10, 35, 43–45. General SS: T-175/roll 39/frame 2549229; T-580/rolls 63–64/folders 308–9. Death's Head units: T-580/roll 87/folder 425. Police: Schellenberg, pp. 58–59; and Lettrich, p. 145; Arendt, *Eichmann in Jerusalem*, pp. 66–67. Prague Land Office: U.S. Military Tribunal Case Eight, English transcript, pp. 700–703, 720–21, 729.

97 Both SA and SS played very important roles in preparing Memel for Nazi seizure. Brown, p. 140; Martin Broszat, "Die memeldeutschen Organisationen und der Nationalsozialismus 1933–1939," *Gutachten des Instituts für Zeitgeschichte*, pp. 395–400. Aldona Gaigalaité, "Klaipédos Krašto Užgrobimas 1939 Metais" (The Seizure of Memel Territory in 1939), *Lietuvos TSR Mokslu Akademijos Darbai*, Serija A, 2:7 (1959), pp. 105–30, esp. pp. 114–25 (translation supplied by Professor Alfred Senn, University of Wisconsin). VoMi and SD activity: DGFP(D), vol. 5, pp. 508, 512, 515–18, 520, 524. Historical perspective, based on German intelligence reporting as early as the Weimar era: Ernst Albrecht Plieg, *Das Memelland 1920–1939*.

*Deutsche Autonomiebestrebungen im litauischen Gesamtstaat* (Würzburg, 1962). Creation of 105th SS-Standarte and 20th Reiterstandarte: BDC Schumacher Collection, folder 428.

98 Danzig SS in 1926 are mentioned on page 24 of this book. Martin Broszat, "Die Anfänge der nationalsozialistischen Herrschaft in Danzig (1933–1936)," *Gutachten des Instituts für Zeitgeschichte*, pp. 392–94; Ludwig Denne, *Das Danzig-Problem in der deutschen Aussenpolitik, 1934–1939* (Bonn, 1959), pp. 75–76, 81–82, 87–88, 118–21, 211–13, 265–69; Brown, p. 144; de Jong, p. 155. See also Katherine Duff, "Danzig," in *Survey of International Affairs, 1939–1946, 10: The Eve of War, 1939*, ed. Arnold Toynbee and Veronica Toynbee (London, 1958), pp. 384–403.

99 Allgemeine SS reorganization and expansion: T-175/roll 39/frames 2548916–23, 2548989–92. A Dienstappell of one SS Main District (West) brought out 1,368 General SS officers in March 1939. Ibid., frame 2549072. Mobilization measures: ibid., frames 2548958, 2549112, 2549122; roll 6/frames 2506568, 2506573; roll 32/frames 2540665, 2540692, 2540707, 2540709; roll 197/frames 2737042–94; roll 229/frame 2767396; T-611/roll 19/folder 58; BDC Schumacher Collection, folder 427 (*Personalhauptamt*). Notdienstverpflichtung: Buchheim, *SS und Polizei*, pp. 180–82; Buchheim, *Das Problem des Befehlsnotstands*, pp. 62, 107.

100 Himmler had estimated that forty to fifty thousand General SS would be available as Death's Head Reinforcements: T-175/roll 90/frame 2612548. "Allgemeine Erfahrungen bei Einziehung der verstärkten SS Totenkopfstandarten": T-175/roll 17/frames 2520631, 2520637. Infanterie-Ersatz Sturmbann der Totenkopfstandarten Breslau: ibid., frame 2520870. Ergänzungsbataillone: T-175/roll 179/frames 2714837–39, 2714801–2, 2714805, 2714816. Discharges: ibid., frames 2714801–2, 2714837. Recruiting problems: T-175/roll 20/frames 2524958–60, 2524972–73, 2525015–16; T-611/roll 20/folder 58. See Brown, pp. 137–38. Recruitment at universities via General SS (*Mannschaftshäuser*): T-175/roll 39/frames 2548753–54. Twenty-five thousand armed SS: 1919-PS; and T-175/roll 91/frames 2613356 ff.

101 Einberufung Polizeiverstärkung, August 14, 1939: T-175/roll 40/frame 2550331. Special Duty troops: Walter Harzer, "Der Feldzug der 18 Tage," *Der Freiwillige* 10:8 (1964): 9 Cf. Robert W. Kennedy, *The German Campaign in Poland (1939)*, U.S. Department of the Army Pamphlet No. 20-255 (Washington, D.C., 1956), p. 62. Einsatzkommandos: Martin Broszat, *Nationalsozialistische Polenpolitik 1939–1945* (Stuttgart, 1961) (hereafter *Polenpolitik*), pp. 28, 58. Sabotage and provocation teams: IMT, vol. 2, pp. 449–51; vol. 3, pp. 10, 233–35; vol. 4, pp. 242–44. De Jong, pp. 150–56. Himmler: Schellenberg, pp. 70–75.

102 Albert Speer, *Infiltration* (New York, 1981).

## Chapter 7: Years of Tragic Fulfillment

1 ". . . the Movement must create a Germanic Reich of the German nation. Then the party can go to ruin"—Adolf Hitler in 1922. "Der völkische Ge-

danke und die Partei," in Jacobsen and Jochmann, *Ausgewählte Dokumente*, vol. 1 (looseleaf). ". . .We were told that it was a question of our security, and of people designated as security threats. . . ." — Otto Ohlendorf, under cross-examination concerning mass-murder. Robert M. W. Kempner, *SS im Kreuzverhör* (Munich, 1964), p. 112.

2 Hitler's remedy for a repetition of 1918 — a radical shake-up (*Durchgreifen*); all leaders of the opposition, including the Catholic clergy, arrested and executed. All occupants of concentration camps and criminals would be shot. *Secret Conversations* (1942), p. 388.

3 Extensive sample material on Nazi racial imperialism from the trial of the defendants from the RKFDV system in U.S. Military Tribunal Case Eight is available in translation in *Trials of War Criminals* (TWC), vols. 4–5, *United States* vs. *Ulrich Greifelt*.

4 The most thorough-going scholarly study of the Waffen-SS is George H. Stein, *The Waffen SS. Hitler's Elite Guard at War, 1939–1945* (Ithaca, 1966). The tangled question of the legal status of the "fourth arm of the Wehrmacht" has been the subject of two official German memoranda, the first by the Bundesarchiv in Coblenz (1955), cited by Felix Steiner, *Die Armee der Geächteten* (Göttingen, 1963), p. 118 (footnote); and the second by the Bundesministerium des Innerem (1961), cited in "Um Recht und Ehre," *Der Freiwillige. Kameradschaftsblatt der HIAG* 6:5 (1961): 4–8. See also in the same periodical: "Denkschrift. Die Waffen-SS und das Gesetz gemäss Artikel 131 GG," *Der Freiwillige* 4:4 (1959): 5–41; "Ein reines Soldatenrechtsproblem," 10:2 (1964): 6–7.

5 Himmler was extraordinarily frank about his fantasies concerning the future of Europe and the SS when he spoke to the higher SS officer corps — and, of course, surprisingly brutal. Besides the well-known lectures at Metz (U.S. Nuremberg doc. 1918-PS), and Posen (1919-PS), there are many fascinating and frightening details in the following Himmler speeches: Hegewald, near Zhitomir, September 16, 1942, in Jacobsen and Jochmann, *Ausgewählte Dokumente*, vol. 2 (looseleaf); Cracow, March 30, 1942, 910-PS, IMT, vol. 26, pp. 408–10; Ordensburg Sonthofen, May 5, 1944, T-175/roll 92/frames 2613448–545. (An extensive collection of Himmler's speeches exists in T-175/rolls 89–94.) See also Bradley F. Smith and Agnes F. Peterson, eds., *Heinrich Himmler, Geheimreden 1933 bis 1945, und andere Ansprachen* (Frankfurt/Main, 1974), e.g., "Verzeichnis der Reden Himmlers," pp. 268–77. Felix Kersten's *Totenkopf und Treue* (Hamburg, [1952] is probably quite reliable not only in regard to Himmler's naive *Wunschträume* (wishful thinking) and speculations, but also concerning the Reich Leader's lack of principle in bargaining during 1944 and 1945 (pp. 389–407). See also Randolf L. Braham, ed., *The Destruction of Hungarian Jewry. A Documentary Account* (New York, 1963), vol. 2, pp. 629–37, 833–928 (Brand-Kastner and Manfred Weiss deals).

6 There were 3,000 salaried SD personnel and 30,000 volunteers. Ohlendorf testimony, IMT, vol. 4, p. 329. Schellenberg's figures: Gestapo 40,000–45,000, Kripo 15,000–20,000, SD-*Inland* 2,000–2,500, SD-*Ausland* 400. Ibid., p. 380. Kaltenbrunner testified that only 5 percent of the whole

SIPO-SD system was SS. IMT, vol. 11, p. 316. See Hoettl testimony, ibid., p. 228; Schellenberg affidavit, 3033-PS, IMT, vol. 31, p. 498. Cf. Hilberg, p. 134. Tessin, in Neufeldt, Huck, and Tessin, *Zur Geschichte der Ordnungspolizei*, pp. 9, 13; Neufeldt, pp. 95–115. Zipfel, "Gestapo und SD in Berlin," pp. 277, 285. See Wolfgang Kraus and Gabriel A. Almond, "Resistance and Repression under the Nazis," in *The Struggle for Democracy in Germany*, ed. Gabriel A. Almond, (Chapel Hill, N.C., 1949), p. 41; Werner Best, *Die deutsche Polizei* pp. 95–96. The complexity of uniforms and insignia for Gestapo, SD, and SS during the war is illustrated in BDC Schumacher Collection, folder 428. For the inspectors of the Order Police, see Tessin, in Neufeldt, Huck, and Tessin, *Zur Geschichte der Ordnungspolizei*, pp. 19–23; for SIPO inspectors, see T-175/roll 430/frames 2959163–66.

7 See the two overlapping but not identical studies by Hans Buchheim: "Die Höheren SS- und Polizeiführer," VJHZ 11 (1963): 362–91; and *SS und Polizei*, pp. 114–48. Additional modifications in December based on Polish experience: T-175/roll 17/frames 2520811–13. A list of fifteen Superior SS and Police Leaders and their ORPO Inspectors as of December 15, 1939: T-175/roll 430/frames 2960095–102.

8 Testimony of Bach-Zelewski, U.S. Military Tribunal Case Eight transcript, p. 432; Best, *Deutsche Polizei*, pp. 107–10. SS and Police unity measures: T-175/roll 11/frames 2513105–6, 2513114–203, 2513243–80. Ideological training for SS and Police: Neufeldt, pp. 40, 91; T-175/roll 6/frames 2507471–588; 2507143, 2507270–72; 2507387–92. Evolution of SS and Police courts: Best, *Deutsche Polizei*, p. 102. *Reichsgesetzblatt*, 1939, vol. 1, pp. 2107, 2293–97; ibid., 1940, vol. 1, p. 659; T-175/roll 39/frames 2549100–102; T-175/roll 40/frames 2550494–95. See Hans Buchheim, "Die Organisation der Sondergerichtsbarkeit der SS und Polizei," *Gutachten des Instituts für Zeitgeschichte*, pp. 343–48.

9 Himmler address at 74 Unter den Linden (August 1938): T-175/roll 240/frame 2729960. Memoranda of February 24, 1939, T-175/roll 239/frames 2728157–86; April 25, 1939, ibid., frames 2728632–58; July 5, 1939, ibid., frames 2728620–28; September 2, 1939, and September 18, 1939, T-175/roll 432/frames 2962207–64. Order of September 27, 1939: 361-L, IMT, vol. 38, pp. 102–10.

10 Neufeldt, p. 21; 2346-PS, chart in rear pocket, IMT, vol. 30; testimony of Kuno Wirsich, U.S. Military Tribunal, Case Eight, German transcript, p. 300; testimony of Ohlendorf, IMT, vol. 4, pp. 327–28. Offices at 102 Wilhelmstrasse, April 1939: T-175/roll 239/frame 2728143.

11 Testimony of Höppner, IMT, vol. 20, pp. 186–87, 190–91, 199–200, 222–23; Zipfel, "Gestapo und SD in Berlin," pp. 271, 273–75, 279–81; Kraus and Almond, "Resistance and Repression," in Almond, *Struggle for Democracy in Germany*, pp. 36–40. SD-Ausland and cloak-and-dagger activity: Schellenberg, pp. 60–62, 76–95; Hoettl, *Hitler's Paper Weapon*, pp. 22–24, 31–33; Lahousen testimony, IMT, vol. 2, pp. 449–51, and vol. 3, pp. 10–11, 26; Karl Heinz Abshagen, *Canaris. Patriot und Weltbürger* (Stuttgart, 1950), pp. 196, 207. Cf. Edmund J. Osmańczyk, *Dowódy Prowokacji. Nieznane*

*archiwum Himmlera. Czytelnik* (Cracow, 1951), pp. 9–22, 35–48, and photographic reproductions, pp. 1–45. Organizational changes: Hoettl affidavit, IMT, vol. 11, p. 228; T-175/roll 414/frames 2940142–44; T-175/roll 240/frame 2730026; 185-L, IMT, vol. 38, pp. 1–24. Heydrich activity: Broszat, *Polenpolitik*, p. 61; EC-307-i, U.S. Military Tribunal Case Nine, TWC, vol. 4, pp. 119–23; T-175/roll 430/frame 2960070.

12 Einsatzkommando activity: Höppner testimony, IMT, vol. 20, pp. 198, 226; Lahousen testimony, vol. 2, pp. 446–47, and vol. 3, pp. 8–9. Keitel's allegation that these units were forbidden by the *Oberkommando des Heeres* (OKH) (IMT, vol. 40, p. 378) is not borne out by an SS statement from December 2, 1939, that all SS in Poland were subordinate to the Wehrmacht during the campaign: T-175/roll 40/frame 2550391. See also "Erschiessungen in Schwetz" in Karl Anders, *Im Nürnberger Irrgarten* (Nuremberg, 1948), pp. 209–13.

13 Broszat, *Polenpolitik*, pp. 60–62; "Selbstschutz—V Kolumna," *Biuletyn Głównej Komisji Badania Zbrodni Hitlerowskich w Polsce* (Warsaw, 1958), vol. 10, pp. 17–56 (with thirteen illustrations from SS sources); K. H. Frank, "Freiwilliger Selbstschutz und SS," p. 79, quoted in IMT, vol. 3, pp. 152–53; testimony of G. Berger, U.S. Military Tribunal Case Eight transcript, pp. 3837–39; U.S. Nuremberg doc. NO 2285; T-175/roll 19/frames 2523753–54, 2523757, 2523761–62; T-175/roll 20/frames 2524992–96; T-175/roll 40/frames 2550408, 2550430. Nazi-dominated Danzig was to be "occupied" by *Totenkopf Sturmbann Goetze*; at the last moment this unit was converted into *Heimwehr Danzig* and tactically subordinated to the army: T-175/roll 104/frame 2625579; and Himmler's Posen (Poznań) speech, "Die Rede Himmlers vor den Gauleitern am 3. August 1944," VJHZ 1 (1953): 368. Another "wild" SS Sturmbann, *Sturmbann Eimann* in Danzig even elicited Himmler's wrath: U.S. Nuremberg doc. NO 2275. See Hugo Landgraf, *Kampf um Danzig* (Dresden, 1940), pp. 9–10, 30, 34–36, 39, 42–43, 46–47.

14 Jerzy Sawicki, ed., *Vor dem polnischen Staatsanwalt* (Berlin, 1962), pp. 276–82. Memorandum of General Blaskowitz, U.S. Military Tribunal, Case Eight, prosecution doc. book V-A/exhibit 216/pp. 90–124; ibid., NO 4059, pp. 1–2; T-175/roll 414/frame 2939808. Halder Diary entries, September 19–20, 1939, U.S. Nuremberg doc. NO KW 3140. Himmler letter to Party treasurer F. X. Schwarz, September 13, 1939, and mimeographed order of September 26, 1939, "Selbstschutz im besetzten polnischen Gebiet": BDC Biographical Records. Minutes of Heydrich's SIPO-SD meetings of September 1939 regarding Poland: T-175/roll 239/frames 2728227–40. Alfred Schickel points out that SS and Police occupation forces were already freed from external military court-martials as early as October 1939: "Wehrmacht und SS: Eine Untersuchung über ihre Stellung und Rolle in den Planungen der nationalsozialistischen Führer," *Wehrwissenschaftliche Rundschau* 19:5 (1969): 251.

15 Telford Taylor, *Sword and Swastika* (New York, 1952), pp. 357–64; Kennedy, pp. 74, 119, 126–29; Broszat, *Polenpolitik*, pp. 58–60; Tessin, in Neu-

feldt, Huck, and Tessin, *Zur Geschichte der Ordnungspolizei*, pp. 27–34; testimony of Ernst Rode in Sawicki, pp. 70–71; *Verordnungsblatt des Generalgouvernements* (Cracow, 1939), Nos. 1–13; Hans Frank, *Im Angesicht des Galgens* (München-Gräfelfing, 1953), pp. 398–405.

16  Broszat, *Polenpolitik*, pp. 26–37; Hilberg, pp. 130–31, citing *Krakauer Zeitung*, January 28, 1941; BDC Biographical Records; T-175/roll 430/ frame 2959150; T-580/roll 68/folder 329. The Diary (*Tagebuch*) of Hans Frank for the whole period 1939–1945 is of the greatest importance as a resource for the study of the power struggle between Frank and the SS. U.S. National Archives Microfilm ML-382. Certain parts were presented at Nuremberg: 2233-PS. IMT, vol. 29, pp. 356–725. For a somewhat different selection, with commentary, see Stanisław Piotrowski, ed., *Sprawy polskie przed Miedzynarodowym Trybunalem Wojennym w Norymberdze*, Tom I, Dzennik Hansa Franka (Warsaw, 1956).

17  Broszat, *Polenpolitik*, pp. 37–57; *Reichsgesetzblatt*, 1939, vol. 1, pp. 2042, 2133. Hans Buchheim, "Rechtsstellung und Organisation des Reichskommissars für die Festigung deutschen Volkstums," *Gutachten des Institute für Zeitgeschichte*, pp. 239–49. Formation or transfer to the new territories of party and SS-Dienststellen: Clifton J. Child, "The Political Structure of Hitler's Europe: Administration," in *Survey of International Affairs, 1939–1946, 4: Hitler's Europe*, ed. Arnold Toynbee and Veronica Toynbee (London, 1954), pp. 106–8, 112–15. Cf. Zbigniew Janowicz, *Ustrój administracyjny ziem polskich wcielonych do Rzeszy Niemieckiej 1939–1945* (Poznan, 1951); T-175/roll 40/frames 2550409–10. Forster: U.S. Military Tribunal Case Eight transcript, pp. 1436–40, 3387–90, 3900–902.

18  Koehl, *RKFDV*, pp. 49–68; Buchheim, "Rechtsstellung und Organisation," *Gutachten des Instituts für Zeitgeschichte*, pp. 251–58; Janusz Deresiewicz, *Okupacja niemiecka na ziemiach polskich właczonych do Rzeszy (1939–1945)*. Badania nad Okupacja niemiecka w Polsce, vol. 4 (Poznan, 1950), pp. 1–108. Himmler speech at Metz: 1918-PS, IMT, vol. 29, pp. 104–5. Death's Head Reinforcements: Neusüss-Hunkel, pp. 62–66. BDC Schumacher Collection, folder 428 (*Totenkopf Standarten*); BDC Biographical Records. T-175/roll 20/frames 2524988–90, 2524998–99; T-175/roll 32/ frames 2539865–915; T-175/roll 40/frames 2550406–7, 2550432, 2550464, 2550467; T-175/roll 104/frames 2625574 ff., 2626023 ff., 2626349, 2626524 ff., 2626702; T-175/roll 219 frames 2756843–44, 2756972; T-175/roll 240/ frame 2730017. SS-28, IMT, vol. 42, p. 481. Franz Halder, *Kriegstagebuch* (Stuttgart, 1962), vol. 1, pp. 183–84. Reitlinger suggests an early tie between the units at Nisko in the General Government and Globocnik's later role at Lublin: *Final Solution*, pp. 43, 246, citing 3398-PS, IMT, vol. 32, pp. 255–57. "Wer den SS Rock anzog, verschrieb sich dem Verbrechen" (Whoever put on the SS coat signed up for crime): letter of a victim to the sister of an SS doctor, in Komitee der Antifaschistischen Widerstandskämpfer in der Deutschen Demokratischen Republik, *SS im Einsatz* (Berlin, 1957), pp. 293–96. See also Helmut Krausnick, "Hitler und die Morde in Polen," VJHZ 11 (1964): 196–209.

19 Hausser, *Waffen-SS*, p. 15; memorandum of *Zentraljustizamt für die Britische Zone*, Hamburg, April 21, 1947, p. 3, T-580/roll 87/folder 425; T-580/rolls 68–69/folder 329; T-175/roll 40/frames 2550305, 2550410, 2550462, 2550882; T-175/roll 104/frames 2626508 ff., 2626613 ff.; T-175/roll 107/frames 2629888 ff.; T-175/roll 430/frame 2959167; R-129, TWC, vol. 5, p. 298. The NSDAP-Ortsgruppe at concentration camp Buchenwald had to be liquidated April 5, 1940, due to the departure of the 3rd Totenkopf Standarte (BDC Biographical Records). Obviously the TK replacements were not party members!

20 A large selection of documents and testimony dealing with concentration camps and their economy during the war is contained in U.S. Military Tribunal Case Four, part of which have been reprinted in *Trials of War Criminals* (TWC), vol. 5, pp. 193–1273. A series of affidavits by concentration camp commanders, including Rudolf Hoess, 745-D, 746-D, 747-D, 748-D, 749-D, and the personnel officer of the concentration camp system, 750-D (IMT, vol. 35, pp. 483–94), reveals much of their psychology. See also an affidavit of Richard Hildebrandt, U.S. Military Tribunal Case Four, Volk defense doc. 42. Besides the Hoess memoirs, in Broszat, ed., *Kommandant in Auschwitz*, Hoess has left valuable sketches of many other personages of the SS and Police, which are still only available in Polish translation: Główna Komisja Badania Zbrodni Hitlerowskich w Polsce, *Wspomnienia Rudolfa Hoessa* (Warsaw, 1956), pp. 203–350.

21 NO 19-a, TWC, vol. 5, p. 294; T-580/rolls 68–69/folder 329; T-175/roll 40/frame 2550489; T-175/roll 94/frames 2615210–11; T-175/roll 214/frames 2752615 ff.; T-175/roll 218 frames 2755998 ff. Euthanasia: Reitlinger, *Final Solution*, pp. 123–39; Główna Komisja Badania Zbrodni niemieckich w Polsce, *German Crimes in Poland* (Warsaw, 1946), vol. 1, pp. 109–21.

22 569-D, IMT, vol. 35, pp. 163–68; T-580/rolls 68–69/folder 329; Leon Poliakov and Josef Wulf, *Das Dritte Reich und seine Diener* (Berlin-Grunewald, 1956), p. 486; Główna Komisja Badania Zbrodni Hitlerowskich w Polsce, *Oświecim-Brzezinka Concentration Camp* (Warsaw, 1961), pp. 12–25; Kempner, *SS im Kreuzverhör*, pp. 165–86; Kogon, pp. 215–24. See also "Regulamin obozow koncentracynych," Główna Komisja, in *Wspomnienia Rudolfa Hoessa*, pp. 280–90.

23 1063(a-b)-PS, IMT, vol. 26, pp. 695–98; U.S. Nuremberg docs. NO 1994, NO 4510, TWC, vol. 5, pp. 304–8; testimony of von Eberstein, IMT, vol. 20, pp. 306, 335–36. Rolls 211–19 of T-175 provide a thorough basis for a detailed study of concentration camp administration beyond that available in Case Four. (See descriptive analysis in U.S. National Archives *Guide No. 33 to German Records Microfilmed at Alexandria, Va.* [Washington, D.C., 1961], pp. 81–88.) T-580/rolls 68–70 deal with concentration camps (BDC Schumacher Collection folders).

24 3870-PS, IMT, vol. 32, p. 280; Leo Alexander, "War Crimes and Their Motivation: The Sociopsychological Structure of the SS and the Criminalization of the Society," *Journal of Criminal Law and Criminology* 39 (1949): 298–326; David Rousset, *The Other Kingdom* (New York, 1947), pp. 54–71,

100–116. Lack of experienced NCOs for Blockführer, May 1942: T-580/roll 69/folder 329. Tables of organization for the administration of concentration camps, July 1940: ibid. (Eighty-one officers). A list of sixty-six SS officers assigned to concentration camp administration as of July 1, 1944, included four colonels, six lieutenant colonels, fifteen majors, and forty-one captains. BDC Schumacher Collection, folder 427 (*Wirtschafts- und Verwaltungshauptamt*). The turnover from 1940 was about 50 percent.

25  Differentiated apparatuses: 1063 (a-b)-PS, IMT, vol. 26, pp. 699–700; Schnabel, pp. 506–7; Komitee, *SS im Einsatz*, pp. 464–69. Chaos and degradation: Schnabel, pp. 162–82; *SS im Einsatz*, pp. 167, 456–60. Efficiency of killing: Schnabel, pp. 346–59; *SS im Einsatz*, pp. 269, 390–401. Tatooing of blood-group in Waffen-SS: Główna Komisja, *Wspomnienia Rudolfa Hoessa*, p. 294.

26  Georg, pp. 42–69. Pictures in Komitee, *SS im Einsatz*, pp. 462–63. Affidavits of Fritz Goernnert, Otto Ambros, Walter Duerrfeld, Karl Wolff: ibid., pp. 435–44, 450–52.

27  Georg, pp. 27–41; "Der Weg in den SS Verwaltungsdienst," *Münchener Neueste Nachrichten*, October 2, 1940. "Verwaltungsschule Dachau," a report of September 3, 1941: BDC Biographical Records. In 1941 there were 1,330 administrative officers in the SS. Report of January 28, 1942, T-175/roll 19/frame 2523289. Some 480 of these with Waffen-SS commissions were serving in the Reich, in the occupied territories of the west and the General Government of May 16, 1942. BDC Biographical Records. Transfers of ten officers to set up new protective custody camp, October 7, 1941: Komitee, *SS im Einsatz*, pp. 196–97. Russian prisoners were sent to concentration camps as early as October 1941: T-580/roll 69/folder 329. Lists of camps for 1942 and 1943 showing increase: T-175/roll 219/frames 2756766, 2756788. The higher officers corps of the *Wirtschafts- und Verwaltungshauptamt* on July 1, 1944, included forty-five majors, twenty-three lieutenant colonels, fourteen colonels, nine brigadier generals, and three lieutenant generals, three major generals, and a colonel-general (*Oberst-Gruppenführer*). BDC Schumacher Collection, folder 427 (*Wirtschafts- und Verwaltungshauptamt*).

28  Testimony of Oswald Pohl, TWC, vol. 5, p. 331. "Inspektion der Konzentrationslager und SS Wachverbände," T-175/roll 219/frame 2756760. See a letter from Himmler to Eicke's successor, Richard Glücks, January 26, 1942, warning him of "new tasks to come" (economic exploitation of Jewish labor): T-580/roll 69/folder 329. The *Führungshauptamt* (FHA) listed twenty-nine companies in eight Totenkopf-Sturmbanne as Waffen-SS, April 22, 1941: T-175/roll 104/frame 2626950. Formal transfer of the inspectorate *from* the FHA to Wirtschafts- und Verwaltungshauptamt as *Amtsgruppe* D, March 3, 1942: 1063-f-PS, TWC, vol. 5, pp. 302–3. Vienna "aryanization" and Bodenamt Prag prosecutions: T-175/roll 60/frames 2576218–21, 2576235.

29  An interesting transitional phase of SS-sanctioned enrichment by individuals is the acquisition and remodeling of a 245,000 RM home for Heissmeier,

the retiring SS Main Office chief in 1940, involving financing through the SS firm *Gemeinnützige Wohnungs- und Heimstättengesellschaft.* "The work and materials came from Oranienburg," Himmler wrote to Speer March 6, 1943, when the latter threatened to prosecute. *Schriftgutverwaltung des Persönlichen Stabes, Reichsführer SS,* folder 204, photos 298–299w (BDC). Deutsche Wirtschaftsbetriebe: Georg, pp. 70–90. See also "Organizajcia Schmelt," in Główna Komisja, *Wspomnienia Rudolfa Hoessa,* pp. 203–4.

30 Best, *Deutsche Polizei,* Best, p. 102; Georg, pp. 107–32. "Organisation der Verwaltung," January 19, 1942: BDC Schumacher Collection, folder 427 (*Verwaltung*). "Aufgliederung des Hauptamt Verwaltung und Wirtschaft," September 17, 1941: ibid. See "Widersprüche und Wandel in der Zielsetzung," Neusüss-Hunkel, pp. 56–58. General report on the new regime in the concentration camps and order stressing economic goals, April 30, 1942: 129-R, IMT, vol. 38, pp. 362–67. Himmler's reply, May 29, 1942, warning his economic czar not to give the impression that preventive custody and re-education were mere subterfuges: NO 719, TWC, vol. 5, pp. 301–2.

31 Georg, pp. 101–6, 133–46. The super-killer Ohlendorf was precisely an "economic expert." Hilberg, p. 55. See the analysis of Dr. François Bayle in *Psychologie et ethique du national-socialisme,* pp. 70–90. See the testimony of another "economic expert" of the RSHA: IMT, vol. 13, pp. 205 ff., 211, 213. An I. G. Farben engineer pictured with Himmler at Auschwitz: Gerhard Schoenberner, *Der gelbe Stern. Die Judenverfolgung in Europa 1933 bis 1945. 2. Aufl.* (Hamburg, 1961), p. 157. See also Hilberg, pp. 586–600. Industry and SS: Speer, *Infiltration,* esp. pp. 23–25, 35, 62–68, 317–18; EC 453, IMT, vol. 35, pp. 532–33; 124-R, IMT, vol. 38, pp. 357, 360–61; 1584-(I)-PS, 1584-(III)-PS, IMT, vol. 27, pp. 351–64; T-175/roll 60/frames 2575785–805, 25757807–20, 25757834–37, 25757846–84. Prostitution of justice: 1063-(d)-PS, IMT, vol. 26, pp. 701–5; 654-PS, IMT, vol. 26, pp. 200–203. SS and F. X. Schwarz: U.S. Nuremberg doc. NO 29; T-175/roll 123/EAP folder 161-b-12/34; Schumacher Collection, folder 427 (*Verwaltung*).

32 Hilberg, pp. 18–39, 54–105, 609–18; Leon Poliakov and Josef Wulf, *Das Dritte Reich und die Juden* (Berlin-Grunewald, 1955), pp. 11–80; 4045-PS, IMT, vol. 34, pp. 110–13. Testimony of Walter Funk, IMT, vol. 13, pp. 170–79; and of two Reichsbank officials, ibid., pp. 565–90, 600–615. See also Kersten, pp. 35–40, 149–51, 200–202.

33 Arendt, *Eichmann in Jerusalem,* pp. 68–79; Poliakov and Wulf, *Dritte Reich und seine Diener,* pp. vii–xv *et passim;* Fest, pp. 139–55. See, for example, Christopher Browning, *The Final Solution and the German Foreign Office* (New York, 1978). See also Carl J. Burckhardt, *Meine Danziger Mission, 1937–1939* (Munich, 1960), pp. 54–57.

34 See the Wannsee protocol of January 20, 1942, NG 2586, in Poliakov and Wulf, *Dritte Reich und die Juden,* pp. 119–26. The best treatment here is Reitlinger, *Final Solution,* pp. 95–114; and Nora Levin, *The Holocaust* (New York, 1968), pp. 293–96, 469, 476.

35  569-D, IMT, vol. 35, p. 169; *Feldurteil des Obersten SS- und Polizeige-richts*, June 9, 1943, cited in Buchheim, "Problem des Befehlsnotstandes," pp. 60–61. Testimony of Bühler about passages in Frank Diary about AB-Aktion and SS: Sawicki, pp. 164–74. Order Police used to kill Jews in Poland: ibid., pp. 285–86. *Polizeiregiment Süd* (ORPO) used to kill Jews in Russia: *Ereignismeldung* Nr. 106, October 7, 1941, in Jacobsen and Jochmann, *Ausgewählte Dokumente*, vol. 2 (looseleaf). See Hilberg, pp. 177–224.

36  Schoenberner, pp. 48–75; Bühler testimony in Sawicki, pp. 191–200; Georg, pp. 90–99. Euthanasia order of Hitler, September 1, 1939: Jacobsen and Jochmann, *Ausgewählte Dokumente*, vol. 2 (looseleaf).

37  Hilberg, pp. 225–56, esp. 233. Case of Generalkommissar Wilhelm Kube and the SS: Alexander Dallin, *German Rule in Russia 1941–1945* (London–New York, 1957), pp. 203–9; and T-175/roll 59/folder 102 (*Vorgang 22*). See Helmut Heiber, "Aus den Akten des Gauleiters Kube," VJHZ 6 (1956): 67–92). Alexander Hohenstein, *Wartheländisches Tagebuch aus den Jahren 1941/2* (Stuttgart, 1961), pp. 45–52, 61–71, 88–94, 98–99. Testimony of Speer: IMT, vol. 16, pp. 518–20. Leon Weliczker, *Brygada Smierci (Sonderkommando 1005). Pamietnik* (Lódz, 1946).

38  Schoenberner, pp. 133–64; Hilberg, pp. 555–75, 624–29. Final report on Aktion-Reinhardt: 4024-PS, IMT, vol. 20, pp. 318–25.

39  Hilberg, pp. 575–80, 646–62; Fest, pp. 404–8; Buchheim, "Problem des Befehlsnotstandes," pp. 48–52; testimony of SS judge Reinecke, IMT, vol. 20, pp. 434–43, 475–82, 488–515.

40  Arendt, *Eichmann in Jerusalem*, pp. 151–205. Wisliceny report: Poliakov and Wulf, *Dritte Reich und die Juden*, pp. 87–98. For what appears to be a complete documentary account of the shipping off of one nation's Jews, see Randolph Braham, ed., *The Destruction of Hungarian Jewry. A Documentary Account* (New York, 1963), 2 vols. Schoenberner's pictures (pp. 44–47, 76–80, and 101–32) and Hilberg's gargantuan chapter 8 supply ample evidence of systematization. See also T-175/roll 432/frames 2962669, 2962674–75.

41  569-D, IMT, vol. 35, p. 168; testimony of Lahousen, IMT, vol. 2, pp. 458, 461, 471–73; testimony of Höppner, IMT, vol. 20, pp. 202, 205, 208–9; Testimony of Kaltenbrunner, IMT, vol. 11, pp. 252, 289. See also T-175/roll 432/frames 2962674–75. Details on Einsatzgruppen replacements, 1941–1942, and of a typical case of *Bewährung* (proving oneself): T-175/roll 240/frames 2730032–58. Cf. Reitlinger, *SS*, page 145, note 4. Schoenberner, pp. 39–41, 81–100.

42  Best, *Deutsche Polizei*, pp. 52–68, 101, and chart, p. 111; commentary of Höppner, IMT, vol. 20, p. 194. The mature police structure is shown on 219-L, rear pocket of IMT, vol. 18. Evolution of ORPO-Hauptamt: T-175/roll 60/folder 81/frame 2576140; T-175/roll 74/folder 253; T-175/roll 123/folder EAP 161-b-12/348. The Order Police were also responsible for the subordinate SS- und Polizeiführer and for the police strongpoints (*Polizeistützpunkte*) under their control: T-175/roll 40/frame 2550673; and BDC

Biographical Records. Role of Superior SS and Police Leaders in "final solution": Buchheim, SS und Polizei, pp. 128–31.

43 Daluege's ORPO-Hauptamt managed the creation of one of the new Superior SS and Police Leader posts too, e.g., Saar-Lothringen (Westland), July 9, 1940. BDC Biographical Records. In the case of Norway, an SS-Oberabschnittsführer Nord was appointed June 19, 1940, but he was not made Superior SS and Police Leader until April 9, 1941. BDC Biographical Records. On the other hand, Himmler personally appointed the Superior SS and Police Leader for the Netherlands (Nordwest) May 23, 1940. Ministerie van Onderwijs, Kunsten en Wetenschappen. Rijksinstituut voor Oorlogsdocumentatie. Bronnen-Publicaties. Processen. Nr. 5. Het Proces Rauter (Hague, 1952), p. 7. In April 1941, Himmler arranged for a blanket promotion (or appointment) of all Superior SS and Police Leaders to the rank of Generalmajor, Generalleutnant, or General der Polizei (dependent on their SS rank). They were to wear police epaulettes on a field gray uniform; they were not, however, taken into the Waffen-SS thereby — that occurred much later (after July 20, 1944). Newspaper publicity was forbidden. On the other hand, no budgetary provisions were ever made for the position of Superior SS and Police Leader as such; the personnel were carried first as General SS or as staff of the Reichsführer SS and Chief of the German Police on temporary duty, and only after 1942 in police Planstellen. BDC Biographical Records.

44 Buchheim, SS und Polizei, pp. 143–48. A list of Superior SS and Police Leaders as of October 1, 1941, provided for four in Russia (Ostland, Mitte, Süd, Kaukasien) with twenty-one subordinate SS and Police Leaders: U.S. Nuremberg doc. NO 5657. There were many modificiations in the location and personnel at the latter level. BDC Biographical Records. List of Superior SS and Police Leaders, August 4, 1942: T-175/roll 17/frame 2520592. "Aufbau der SS und Polizeidienststellen im Ostland (Zentralinstanzen)," Merkblatt für Polizeikräfte im Ostland, August 1, 1942, T-175/roll 11/frames 2512847–48. A detailed chart showing the relationship of SS and police to civil government in Russia: Mitteilungsblätter für die weltanschauliche Schulung der ORPO, August 10, 1942, T-175/roll 229/frame 2768153.

45 On Carl Schmitt, see Peter Schneider, Ausnahmezustand und Norm. Eine Studie zur Rechtslehre von Carl Schmitt (Stuttgart, 1957). The SD ordered the supression of a book which spelled out the logic of Landnahme in Poland. Hermann Schütze, Der Reichsgau Wartheland (Breslau, 1941); T-175/roll 467/frame 2987294. For the background of the Nazi power struggle over the Russian spoils, see Dallin, pp. 20–43.

46 Einsatzkommandos der SIPO und SD in Norway, April–October 1940: T-175/roll 9/frame 2511193. Wehrmacht efforts to weaken the SIPO-SD system via the draft were thwarted by Heydrich, June 1940: T-175/roll 430/frames 2960072–73.

47 MK, pp. 689–90, 739–43, 757; testimony of Bach-Zelewski, IMT, vol. 4, p. 482; Kersten, pp. 156–71 (Wehrbauern).

48 As late as November 1941 Harald Turner, the future Superior SS and Police

Leader for Serbia (named January 22, 1942), wrote: "As to the question of a Superior SS and Police Leader in the Balkans I am very skeptical, because we have a military government here. Under a civil government he would have some powers, but under a military government they would have all the power. That's a fantasy which I don't think will ever be realized — and the best proof is Paris and Brussels." (BDC Biographical Records.) Two months later Hitler as Commander in Chief had appointed the same man to be Himmler's deputy in Serbia, to set up a Serbian police, raise a Waffen-SS, and report to the Wehrmacht commander for Serbia. In January 1942 Himmler wrote Heydrich that Keitel had agreed to the creation of a Superior SS and Police Leader in Paris in exchange for cleaning out all communists and Jews from occupied France. T-580/roll 69/folder 329. Additional (later) appointments in the Balkans: T-175/roll 123/folder EAP 161-b-12/199. Channels of intelligence and emergency controls: T-175/roll 6/frames 2506528, 2506570-79. Armed SS units in their Main Sectors: T-175/roll 17/frame 2520810. See Buchheim, *SS und Polizei*, pp. 136–43.

49  There were eighteen Superior SS and Police Leaders within the Reich proper by 1942 (not counting the Protectorate and the General Government). Only Emil Mazuw in Stettin had held his post more than five years. Josias von Waldeck und Pyrmont, who managed to get his post moved to his ancestral residence, had been there five years. A third, with five years' service in the same spot, was about to be pensioned. Two or three had been transferred from one city to another, more or less as punishment. Several more were "proving themselves" as Superior SS and Police Leaders after less than distinguished tours in Berlin offices. Three or four were relatively "new men" to the SS from the police Laufbahn. Himmler's paternalistic correspondence with these, his henchmen and protegés, is the epitome of SS "byzantinism": abject dependence rather than loyalty, scolding pettifoggery in place of trust. BDC Biographical Records.

50  Determination to Germanize the Slovene marches led to the assignment as Superior SS and Police Leader of two of the most ruthless SS-Altkämpfer in Alpenland and Adriatisches Küstenland. While these borderlands were technically within the Reich, like Danzig-Westpreussen and Wartheland they demanded an outlook like that of the Kampfzeit: "Who is not with me is against me." Taking of hostages and *Sippenhaft* (imprisonment of relatives) were standard measures of repression by June 1942. BDC Biographical Records. Danzig-Westpreussen and Wartheland even had Superior SS and Police Leaders who had been known to "talk back" to Himmler as well as to party bosses. This was the case also of Himmler's men in Prague and Cracow. True enough, Himmler could tolerate very little back talk — he removed the "difficult man" in Danzig and the "impossible man" in Cracow — but he could not do without their iron nerves for long. BDC Biographical Records. On the other hand, Alsace and Lorraine were subjected to relatively soft, flexible Superior SS and Police Leaders, whose wickedness was mainly that of being tools of Himmler's and (especially) Hitler's ruthlessness. The gauleiters there took the lead in persecutions: U.S. Military Tribunal Case Eight, Creutz defense doc. 11; NO 5564, prosecution rebuttal book

A; opening statement of the prosecution, transcript, pp. 79–80; Brueckner defense doc. 2. Case Eleven, NG 3022, prosecution book 72-C; 114-R, IMT, vol. 38, pp. 330–36. See also Koehl, *RKFDV*, esp. pp. 166–68 and 206.

51 Hans Buchheim, "Die Aufnahme von Polizeiangehörigen in die SS und die Angleichung ihrer SS-Dienstgrade an ihre Beamtenränge (Dienstgradangleichung) in der Zeit des Dritten Reiches" (mimeographed) (Munich, 1960). Friedrich Zipfel, *Gestapo und Sicherheitsdienst* (Berlin-Grunewald, 1960), pp. 22–25. A fuller treatment by the same author: "Gestapo und SD in Berlin," *Jahrbuch* 9–10 (1961): 286–92. A masterlist of July 25, 1943, shows that forty-three of a total of seventy-three police presidencies and twenty-one of a total of forty-six directorships were in SS hands. About a third of these were truly SS-Altkämpfer; the rest were career policemen, the majority with service before 1933. T-175/roll 240/frames 2729800–811. While only seven of twenty-four Befehlshaber der Ordnungspolizei lacked SS rank in August 1944, none were career SS. Ibid., frames 2729796–98. All the inspectors (or commanders) of the security police and secret service in 1943 and 1944 were SS officers, but only seven were SA or SS-Altkämpfer from before the Machtergreifung. Twelve were young lawyers; half a dozen others had had police careers before 1933. Ibid., frames 2729812–19; BDC Biographical Records.

52 Nuremberg documents dealing with Himmler's struggle for an ever wider role in Barbarossa: 447-PS (March 13, 1941), IMT, vol. 26, pp. 53–58; 1316-PS (March 21, 1941); 1024-PS (April 29, 1941), pp. 560–66; NOKW-2079 (May 21, 1941); 1039-PS (June 28, 1941), pp. 584–92. See also affidavits by Keitel (Keitel-12) and Schellenberg (3710-PS): IMT, vol. 40, pp. 376–85; and IMT, vol. 32, pp. 471–75. See Helmuth Greiner, *Die oberste Wehrmachtführung 1939–1943* (Wiesbaden, 1951), pp. 369–71; Dallin, pp. 22–38; Gerald Reitlinger, *The House Built on Sand* (New York, 1960), pp. 66–85.

53 Joseph Goebbels, *The Goebbels Diaries, 1942–1943* (Garden City, N.Y., 1948), pp. 84–85, 182, 195, 201, 225, 261, 328, 438; Kleist, p. 132 ff; Dallin, pp. 664–73; Reitlinger, *House Built on Sand*, pp. 312–42. Heavy use of SS personnel to exploit Russian economic resources: by setting up concentration camps — 129-R, IMT, vol. 38, p. 364; by creating a network of SS *Wirtschafter* (managers) in the occupied areas subordinate to the Superior SS and Police Leaders but, like the concentration camp administrators, coordinated by the SS-Wirtschafts- und Verwaltungshauptamt — T-175/roll 54/folder 95. This sizeable officer-corps was scarcely smaller than that of the RSHA!

54 More Nuremberg documents showing Himmler's struggle on July 16–17, 1941: 221-L, IMT, vol. 38, pp. 86–94; 1056-PS, IMT, vol. 26, pp. 592–609; 1997-PS, IMT, vol. 29, pp. 234–37. Dallin, pp. 84–89, 99, 168–76, 209–13, 553–636; Reitlinger, *House Built on Sand*, pp. 86–97, 121–27. SS and Police in Yugoslavia: Hoettl, *Geheime Front*, pp. 216–17, 241–42, 248–50; Hilberg, pp. 433–42. (The *Staatsrat* in charge of civil administration in Serbia discussed by Hilberg was actually an SD-*Brigadeführer!*)

55 Waffen-SS casualties as a whole have been estimated between 300,000 and

400,000: Hausser, *Waffen-SS*, p. 16; *Der Freiwillige* 7:11 (1962): 9; Kaltenbrunner testimony, IMT, vol. 11, p. 315. Kaltenbrunner also testified that
about one-fifth of the 40,000 Gestapo people had executive authority; all
the rest were administrative and technical personnel. Ibid., p. 308. Of some
8,000 Gestapo executives, the great majority had posts in the Reich. BDC
Biographical Records. SIPO-SD officers with executive authority in Russia
probably did not exceed 1,000. See Ohlendorf testimony, IMT, vol. 4, p.
345. *Einsatzgruppe A* had 9.0 percent Gestapo, 4.1 percent KRIPO, and
3.5 percent SD personnel in October 1941: Stahlecker report, 180-L, enclo-
sure 1-A, IMT, vol. 4, p. 220. Top SIPO-SD personnel in the east in 1942 are
listed in appendices to similar reports: T-175/roll 16/frames 2519790 ff. See
also officer rosters of police and SD for 1944: T-175/roll 240/frames
2729796–98; roll 241/frames 2730304–85, 2730486–91. Executions: Kurt
Hirsch, *SS Gestern, heute und . . .* (Darmstadt, 1960), pp. 62–76; Schnabel, pp. 457–60, 472–95; 014-USSR, IMT, vol. 39, pp. 265–70. Kidnapping: 744-PS, IMT, vol. 26, pp. 284–87; 1786-PS, IMT, vol. 28, pp. 391–93.
Scorched earth: 119-USSR, vol. 39, pp. 372–75; BDC Biographical Records. Training and selection: Buchheim, "Problem des Befehlsnotstandes,"
pp. 22–41. Warfare conditions: *Minsker Zeitung*, December 23, 1943,
"Wehrdörfer- und Stützpunktennetz"; and BDC Biographical Records.

56  Günther Deschner, *Reinhard Heydrich. Statthalter der totalen Macht. Biographie* (Esslingen am Neckar, 1977), pp. 247 ff. Great Britain, Foreign
Office and Ministry of Economic Warfare, *Germany Basic Handbook*, vol.
1, part 3, "Occupied Europe" (London, 1944); United States, Office of Strategic Services, Research and Analysis Branch, *German Military Government over Europe*, vol. 2, part 1, "The SS and Police in Occupied Europe,"
R & A No. 2500/22 (Washington, D.C., 1945); Hitler, *Secret Conversations*, p. 188; Neusüss-Hunkel, p. 102. *Nacht und Nebel* decree: U.S. Nuremberg docs. NOKW-430 and NOKW-3064. A list of Nuremberg and
other captured German documents illustrating the evolution of SS occupation policy in specific countries would be valuable but enormous. See, for
example, IMT, vols. 23–24. Document series NO, NG, and NOKW used at
the U.S. Military Tribunal trials include thousands of individual items, still
not indexed. Also: *Befehlsblatt des Chefs der Sicherheitspolizei und SD,
1940–5*, T-611/rolls 12–14/folders 459–61. Selected countries on T-175
(largely *Schriftgutverwaltung des Persönlichen Stabes, SGV*): Belgium, roll
80/folder 56; Denmark, roll 59/folder 102, roll 17/folder 56; France, roll 9/
frames 2511132–316, roll 19/frame 2523231; Greece, rolls 7, 75, 123, 407–9,
474; Netherlands, roll 478/frames 9335583–916, roll 479/frames 9337252–
312, 9337716–900; Norway, roll 10/frames 2511529–680, roll 223/frames
2761706–43, roll 476/frames 2999270–767; Poland, roll 226/frames
2764651–5220, roll 474/frames 2996824–7193; Protectorate of Bohemia-
Moravia, roll 196/frames 2736753–56, roll 476/frames 2999220–69; Slovakia, roll 75/folder 6, rolls 539–63.

57  Vicious circle of retaliation with resistance: T-175/rolls 7–11. *Sonderauf-
träge* (special tasks): Hans Buchheim, "Höheren SS- und Polizeiführer,"

VJHZ 11 (1963): 371-78; Neusüss-Hunkel, pp. 101-3; Arendt, *Eichmann in Jerusalem*, pp. 165, 167-68; Braham, vol. 2, pp. xcv-ci, 539-627. Lists of Superior SS and Police Leaders — 1942: 3876-PS, IMT, vol. 33, p. 292. 1943: *Taschenbuch für Verwaltungsbeamte 1943*, pp. 84 ff. 1944: NO 973; T-175/roll 431/frames 2961984-86; T-175/roll 37/frames 2546773-75, 2546780-82, 2547041-43. The full complement of the staff of the Superior SS- and Police Leader in Hungary on March 31, 1944, consisted of a *Befehlshaber der Ordnungspolizei*, a *Befehlshaber der Sicherheitspolizei und SD*, a *Befehlshaber der Waffen-SS*, an *SS-Wirtschafter*, an *SS- und Polizeigericht*, and an *SS-Ergänzungsstelle*. BDC Biographical Records. On the other hand the Superior SS and Police Leader for Belgium and Northern France in July 1944 had, additionally: an adjutant, a personal *Referent*, a police adjutant, a *Stabsführer der Allgemeinen SS*, a medical officer, a communications officer, a Race and Settlement officer, an SS war correspondent and propagandist, a welfare officer, an Ethnic German liaison officer, three Waffen-SS administration officers, four Waffen-SS recruiting officers, four Waffen-SS training officers, and the manager of the *Lebensborn* lying-in home for unwed mothers. All were SS officers. BDC Biographical Records.

58 U.S. Nuremberg doc. NO 1115. Cf. Buchheim, "Höheren SS- und Polizeiführer," p. 371. Fritz von Siegler, *Die höheren Dienststellen der deutschen Wehrmacht 1933-1945* (Munich, 1953), p. 143. Both Buchheim and Neusüss-Hunkel call attention to the fact that toward the end of the war this institution (Höheren SS- und Polizeiführer) acquired more military features: (1) acquisition of control over Waffen-SS units via the Befehlshaber der Waffen-SS — Buchheim, p. 388; (2) control over prisoners of war — ibid., p. 386; (3) naming certain Supreme and Superior SS- and Police Leaders as Commanding Generals of the German Wehrmacht (*Bevollmächtigter General*) — Neusüss-Hunkel, pp. 102-3. See also T-175/roll 123/folder EAP 161-b-12/199.

59 Buchheim, "Höheren SS- und Polizeiführer," pp. 385, 387-88, 390-91; 3876-PS, IMT, vol. 33, p. 293; BDC Biographical Records; T-175/roll 37/frames 2547045-49. The latter SS and Police rosters from 1944 also include *politische Gebietsführer auf dem Balkan* (political territorial officers in the Balkans), another new variety of SS-Police institution. See also T-175/roll 81/folder 61 for the evolution of the other late innovation, *der Beauftragte des Reichsführer SS in Albanien* (the plenipotentiary of the Reich Leader SS in Albania). Gestapo, SD, SIPO, RSHA, Criminal Police, and Order Police rosters for 1940 and 1944: T-157/rolls 240, 430-32/frames 2729786, 2729812-19; 2729965; 2959170-72; 2959180-81; 2969859-983; 2962665-68. See Buchheim, "Die Aufnahme von Polizeiangehörigen . . ."; and 2786-PS, IMT, vol. 31, pp. 105-6.

60 Ihor Kamenetsky, *Secret Nazi Plans for Eastern Europe. A Study of Lebensraum Policies* (New York, 1961), p. 41. One instructive case among many of the General SS "leavening" may be traced in T-175/roll 240/frames 2730021-58, 2730064-95, 2730122-36, 2730185, 2730218-19. SS-Haupt-

amt, *Der Untermensch* (Berlin, 1942). Der Chef der SIPO und SD, *Der Rassegedanke und seine gesetzliche Gestaltung* (Schriften für politische und weltanschauliche Erziehung der Sicherheitspolizei und des SD; Ausgearbeitet von SS Hauptsturmführer Evert, Reichssicherheitshauptamt Gruppe I-B) (Berlin, n.d.). Himmler wrote to the Chief of SIPO and SD May 19, 1943: "I am sending you one hundred copies of *Die jüdischen Ritualmorde* by Helmuth Schramm, Theodor Fritsch Verlag, Berlin, for the men of the Einsatzkommandos and other SIPO-SD personnel assigned to the Jewish question . . ." BDC Biographical Records, *Schriftgutverwaltung* (SGV), folder 121, item 14. See Hilberg, p. 295; and 654-PS and 701-PS, IMT, vol. 26, pp. 200–203, 259–60, for one illustration of how the "system" worked. U.S. Nuremberg doc. NO 2524 is another one of thousands of RSHA orders signed by some SS lieutenant colonel with a Ph.D. which automatically transferred Jewish women from concentration camps to killing centers. The signer of the order was a nonentity without any significance in the SS. On the other hand, in March 1942 Frick urged Daluege to appoint a very vigorous SS-Altkämpfer as a Police General so that such a non-bureaucrat would not foul up the bureaucracy. That such an appointment would leave the bureaucracy in second place, as mere executors of SS policy, was beyond Frick. Daluege welcomed the recommendation. A few months later the same Daluege suggested that a police battalion withdrawn from Russia for furlough spend its furlough in France picking up Jews for deportation. BDC Biographical Records.

61 Buchheim, *SS und Polizei*, pp. 187–91; DGFP, vol. 8, pp. 184–89; L-70, IMT, vol. 37, pp. 506–19, 517, 522–23; Kersten, pp. 154–55; Der Reichsführer SS, SS-Hauptamt-Schulungsamt, *Sieg der Waffen — Sieg des Kindes* (Berlin, 1941). Plans for taking Czech children: T-175/roll 26/frames 2531939 ff. Promises of estates in the east to SS widows: T-175/roll 38/frames 2547558–675; Janusz Gumkowski and Kazimierz Leszczyński, *Poland under Nazi Occupation* (Warsaw, 1961), pp. 164–78. Corrupt practices in Slovenia: T-175/roll 19/frames 2523236, 2523245–49, 2523258–63; roll 20/frames 2524702–9; roll 72/folder 325.

62 Buchheim, "Rechtsstellung und Organisation des RKFDV," *Gutachten*, pp. 259–64; Hoettl, p. 303 (note); NO 4613, TWC, vol. 4, pp. 854–55; Heinrich Lohl affidavit, U.S. Military Tribunal Case Eight, Lorenz defense doc. book 1, pp. 33–34; Hans Hagen affidavit, ibid., pp. 26–31; testimony of Hagen, English transcript, pp. 4723–33; Fritz Fabritius affidavit, Case Eight, Lorenz defense doc. book 3, pp. 45–46; testimony of Hans Ehlich, Case Eight, English transcript, pp. 578–79; Case Eight Judgement, English transcript, pp. 5365–70; Records of the Office of the Reich Commissioner for the Strengthening of Germandom, U.S. National Archives Microcopy T-74/roll 10/frames 382576–627; "Verhandlungen mit den germanischenvölkischen Gruppen in den besetzten Gebieten," T-175/roll 26/folder 00087; "Überprüfung reichsdeutscher Rückkehrer im Rahmen des Um- und Ansiedlungsverfahrens," T-175/roll 49/folder 161.

63 Buchheim, "Rechtsstellung," *Gutachten des Instituts für Zeitgeschichte,*

pp. 265–67; Werner Gradmann, "Die Erfassung der Umsiedler," *Zeitschrift für Politik* 33 (1942): 346–51. Personnel: Bayle, pp. 115–16. Case Eight documents: NO 5322, TWC, vol. 4, pp. 855–59; NO 4674; NO 4237; NO 4640. EWZ Paris: orders of 1941, Case Eight, Lorenz defense doc. book 2/exhibit 25/42–45. Testimony of Hans Ehlich, Case Eight, English transcript, pp. 573–74, 583, 757, 617, 623–26; testimony of Lambert von Malsen-Ponickau, ibid., pp. 3530–56. T-611/rolls 29–38/folders 1, 3–5, 6a, 6b, 7–10, and 12–26 contain a full documentary record of this agency.

64 Koehl, *RFKDV*, pp. 78–81: Buchheim, "Rechtsstellung und Organisation," p. 267; Janowicz, pp. 154–56. U.S. Military Tribunal Case Eight documents: NO 5322, NO 5150. Testimony of Hans Ehlich, Case Eight, English transcript, p. 624; and testimony of Rudolf Hässler, ibid., pp. 3786–807. Cover letter of December 2, 1939, to *Denkschrift über die Neuordnung im ehemaligen polnischen Raum*, "Eindeutschung bzw. Vernichtung nicht eindeutschbarer Bevölkerung" ("Germanization or destruction of un-Germanizable population"): T-611/roll 20/folder 58. Some UWZ camps had been run as branches of Stutthof concentration camp in Danzig-West Prussia. T-580/roll 69/folder 329.

65 Buchheim, "Rechtsstellung und Organisation," pp. 267–68; U.S. Military Tribunal Case Eight doc. NO 2791 and NO 1393, TWC, vol. 4, pp. 735–36; testimony of Günther Pancke, Case Eight, English transcript, pp. 658–63; testimony of Rudolf Meyer and Emma Hoppe about Velpke home for children of eastern workers, ibid., pp. 1039–45; Case Eleven doc. NO 3600. Himmler correspondence with a gauleiter about treatment of children of eastern workers: T-175/roll 71/folder 316. As late as 1942–1943, even minor racial blemishes (borderline type—eighteenth-century Jewish ancestor) resulted in the removal of SS officers from their positions: T-175/roll 37/frames 2547376, 2548128–41. Regulations for SS racial examiners: T-175/roll 39/frames 2549189–91. For additional procedural rulings of RuSHa, see T-611/rolls 26–27/folder 168.

66 U.S. Military Tribunal Case Eight doc. NO 1402, NO 2576, NO 3224, NO 4098, NO 4100, NO 4104–9, NO 4111, NO 4113, NO 4116, NO 4119, NO 4121, NO 4184, and NO 5809; testimony of Wilhelm Radusch, German transcript, pp. 3298, 3309; testimony of Ernst Tesseraux, ibid., pp. 2938–79; testimony of Otto Hofmann, English transcript, pp. 277–81. SS-Wirtschafter: T-175/roll 67/folder 55. RuSHa files on settlement questions, e.g., *biologisch siedeln!* (Settle biologically!): T-611/roll 21/folder 87.

67 U.S. Military Tribunal Case Eight docs. NO 2578 and NO 4047; testimony of Ulrich Greifelt, English transcript, pp. 1450, 1684; testimony of Fritz Schwalm, ibid., pp. 3397–407; affidavits of Heinrich Sterzinger and Siegfried Golling, Greifelt defense doc. book 4; affidavit of Herbert Theilen, Hofmann defense doc. book 6. Pflegestellen: T-175/roll 40/frames 2550272–74, 2550537, 2550543–44. Financial support of SS widows: T-175/roll 55/folder 100. Rulings on SS-*Führsorge- und Versorgung* (Welfare and Maintenance): T-611/roll 8/folder 435.

68 Even so respectable a journal as the *Wiener Library Bulletin* published an

article by Richard Grunberger entitled "Lebensborn. Himmler's Selective Breeding Establishment": vol. 16 (1962): 52–53. See also *Der Freiwillige* 3:12 (1958), 4:1, 2, 3, 5 (January, February, March, May, 1959), and 6:3 (1961). U.S. Military Tribunal Case Eight docs. NO 1647, NO 3634, NO 4269, NO 4705, NO 4973, NO 5238. Unpublished Bormann memorandum on Hitler's views of January 29, 1944: Jacobsen and Jochmann, *Ausgewählte Dokumente*, vol. 2 (looseleaf). The famous appeal of the Reichsführer SS to procreate children, dated October 28, 1939, and the "correction" of January 30, 1940, are in T-611/roll 20/folder 82a. See also basic *Lebensborn* handbook and correspondence thereon: T-611/roll 7/folder 433 (*Lebensborn*). T-175 is very rich in Lebensborn material not utilized in Case Eight, but much of it is restricted. See, however, T-175/roll 17/frames 2520715–26; roll 19/frame 2523510; roll 20/folder 1156 (letter inquiring about breeding homes) and frame 2524517; roll 32/frame 2540945; roll 37/frames 2547405–7; roll 60/frames 2575665–78, 2575719–22; roll 94/frame 2615249.

69  *Nordland* (Oslo), vol. 1, December 21, 1940; Jean Henshaw, "Unaccompanied Children," *Background Material for the Official History of the UNRRA*, Archives Section, United Nations, 1948, pp. 29–60; S. M. Sawicka, "Zbrodnia niemiecka nad dzieckiem polskim," *Przegląd Zachodni* 3 (Poznań, 1947): 732; U.S. Military Tribunal Case Eight docs. NO 5813, NO 5819; testimony of Martha Heinze-Wisswede, English transcript, pp. 487–535. *Amt L:* T-175/roll 22/folder 108. Adoptions: T-175/roll 40/frames 2550553–800; BDC Biographical Records.

70  Lebensborn accounts and correspondence about its "dues": BDC Biographical Records. Interestingly enough, the Verein managed Himmler's income tax! U.S. Military Tribunal Case Eight docs. NO 3224, NO 4318, NO 4320, NO 5731, NO 5734, NO 5737–39. Testimony about Lidice orphans and other "valuable" children: English transcript, pp. 1337, 1372. See also T-175/roll 80/frames 2600233–46. Lebensborn annual reports: T-175/roll 25/folder 795; roll 35/folders 713, 732. Boarding schools (*Heimschulen*): T-175/roll 74/frames 2592001 ff. For Hitler's doubts about taking children, see *Secret Conversations*, pp. 325–26.

71  Buchheim, "Rechtsstellung und Organisation," pp. 275–79; U.S. Military Tribunal Case Eight docs. NO 2209, NO 2417, NO 3078 (the basic directive creating the *Dienststelle*); testimony of Rudolf Creutz, English transcript, p. 2155. Office lists for 1941–1944: T-74/roll 1/RDV 4, roll 3/RDV 11, roll 9/RDV 76. For a scheme to settle the much-debated South Tyrolese in the Crimea, see T-175/roll 53/frames 2567508–47. "The first German village in the Crimea," November 30, 1942: T-175/roll 40/frame 2550636. John Haag presents an interesting vignette of Stabshauptamt activity in "National Socialism in Action: The RKFDV and the Alvensleben-Schönborn Estate Case," *The Historian* 26 (February 1964): 244–66.

72  Wacław Jastrzębowski, *Gospodarka niemiecka w Polsce* (Warsaw, 1946), pp. 292–99; Deresiewicz, (Poznań, 1950). Badania nad okupacja niemiecka w Polsce, vol. 4, pp. xvi–xxiii, 1–29; Buchheim, "Rechtsstellung und Orga-

nisation," pp. 268–75. Buchheim, *SS und Polizei*, p. 193, citing U.S. Nuremberg doc. NO 5640 for *RuSHa teams* seizing property in Poland! Records of the *Deutsche Umsiedlungs-Treuhandgesellschaft, DUT* (German Resettlement Trusteeship Co.): T-611/rolls 40–42/folders 36, 37, 38a. Hegewald speech by Himmler, September 16, 1942, on settlement in the Ukraine: Jacobsen and Jochmann, *Ausgewählte Dokumente*, vol. 2; and T-74/roll 17/frames 389487–94. On the General Government, see U.S. Military Tribunal Case Eleven doc. NO 2202, TWC, vol. 13, pp. 620–24; and T-175/roll 74/folder 307. On Alsace-Lorraine, Case Eleven doc. NO 3022; and T-74/roll 15/frames 386690–732. The so-called *Generalplan Ost* referred to at Nuremberg and again in VJHZ 6 (1958): 281–325 was one of those grandiose Nazi terms referring to some RSHA scheme, now lost, and the schemes of Professor Konrad Meyer, dealt with in Koehl, *RKFDV*, pp. 150–51, 159. The documents following Helmut Hieber's commentary in the *Vierteljahrshefte* are *not* either of these plans, but commentaries.

73 Buchheim, "Rechtsstellung und Organisation," pp. 249–51. See also Koehl, *RKFDV*, pp. 89 ff. Case Eight documents illustrating improvisation: NO 3180, NO 4392, NO 5212. Testimony of Kuno Wirsich, English transcript, pp. 317, 325, 336, 342; testimony of Bach Zelewski, ibid., pp. 435, 755; testimony of Dr. Hans Ehlich, ibid., pp. 631–32. Affidavit of Wilhelm Stuckart, Meyer-Hetling defense doc. book 1. Ideological trimmings—"Der Eignungsprüfer," "Richtlinien für Rassenbestimmung," "Darf ich meine Base heiraten?" "Rassische Auslese und Volkstumspolitik": T-175/roll 496/frames 359465–84. Ulrich Greifelt, *Die Festigung deutschen Volkstums als zentrale Ostaufgabe* (Berlin, 1940): T-74/roll 10/frames 381802–15. *Planungsgrundlagen für den Aufbau der Ostgebiete* (Berlin, n.d.): T-74/roll 15/frames 386668–89. *Neues Bauerntum* 33: 12 (December 1941): T-74/roll 15/frames 387213–63. "Neuformung der angegliederten Ostgebiete," *Völkischer Beobachter*, April 8, 1943.

74 Bayle, p. 214. *SS-Hauptamt. Anschriftenverzeichnis der Amtschefs, Hauptabteilungsleiter, Abteilungsleiter und Sachbearbeiter*, September 23, 1943: Schumacher Collection, folder 427, BDC. *Mitteilungen des Chefs des SS-Hauptamts, I. Jahrgang, Nr.* 1, October 15, 1943, Reichsführer SS, Befehl 12: *Dienstgebäude des SS-Hauptamts:* Schumacher Collection, Folder 427, BDC. U.S. Nuremberg doc. NO 337, *Stellenbesetzung des SS-Hauptamts. Stand vom 1. 12. 1944.*

75 *Anschriftenverzeichnis der Schutzstaffel der NSDAP. Stand vom 1. 2. 1940:* T-611/roll 2/folder 426ᴵ. Letter of the chief recruiter to an immediate subordinate surveying his activities up to May 4, 1940: T-175/roll 70/folder 278. His appointment as head of the SS Main Office: T-175/roll 103/frame 2625795. More recuits: T-157/roll 110/frames 2634753 ff., 2634765–853. The range of the new Main Office chief's "demographic" interests is illustrated in T-175/roll 127/frames 2652221–414. Cf. NO 1825, Case Eleven prosecution doc. book 65.

76 Inspection of the Special Duty Troops at 9 *Prinz-Albrechtstrasse: Nationalsozialistisches Jahrbuch 1940* (Munich, 1940), p. 373. For illustration of

amateurish Kriegsspiele at the SS-Hauptamt in February 1939, see T-611/ roll 20/folder 58[II]. Assignments of SS military personnel and mobilization problems were also dealt with in the SS-Hauptamt (*Amt für Sicherungsaufgaben*) as late as October 1940: T-175/roll 40/frame 2550453. *Anschriftenverzeichnis der Schutzstaffel der NSDAP. Stand vom. 1. 2. 1940:* Schumacher Collection, folder 427, BDC. *Kommando der Waffen-SS, Verwaltungsmitteilungen für die Waffen-SS,* I *Jahrgang, Nr.* 16, June 12, 1940: ibid. *Führungshauptamt des Reichsführers SS. Reichsführer SS Tgb. Nr.* 1107/40 *geheim:* ibid. Change of name to *Kommandoamt der Waffen-SS* and transfer to Führungshauptamt: T-175/roll 103/frames 2625794-96.

77 Himmler's search for Rumanian ethnic Germans at German universities as recruits, March 10, 1937: T-175/roll 98/frame 2618453. Recruitment in newly independent Slovakia, April 19, 1939: T-175/roll 21/folder 169; T-175/roll 104/frame 2626192. Recruitment in North Schleswig and Estonia, April–May, 1939: DGFP(D), vol. 6, pp. 333–34, 515; T-175/roll 70/ folder 278. Robert Herzog, *Die Volksdeutschen in der Waffen-SS,* Studien des Instituts für Besatzungsfragen in Tübingen, Nr. 5 (Tübingen, 1955), pp. 3–4. Transylvania: BDC Biographical Records; Herzog, p. 14. See also T-580/roll 72/folder 341; T-175/roll 70/folder 278.

78 Waffen-SS Einstellungen: T-175/roll 20/frames 2524957-66; T-175/roll 104/ frames 2626592 ff., 2626657 ff. Early evidence of Führungshauptamt staff resistance to indiscriminate recruiting: T-175/roll 19/frames 2523349-57. VoMi resistance to recruiting ethnic Germans: U.S. Military Tribunal Case Eleven, prosecution doc. book 72-F, NO 1782, NO 2471, NO 3320, NO 3991.

79 Stein, p. 94. Stein dates the speech incorrectly as *October* 8, 1938. Himmler wrote to Seyss-Inquart, Hitler's plenipotentiary in the Netherlands, January 7, 1941: "We are certainly both absolutely clear about our historically vital mission of restoring nine million Germanic-Low German human beings, alienated for centuries from Germandom, to the German-Germanic community with a strong but gentle hand . . . that this task of creating a Germanic community of one hundred ten million is the only foundation for a truly great Germanic Reich . . ." Photographic copy 909o, SGV folder 274, BDC Biographical Records.

80 Stein, pp. 27–28, 32–33, 36–45, 107, citing extensively from T-175/rolls 104, 106. See also T-175/roll 70/folder 278. Buchheim, "Die SS," p. 141, and *SS und Polizei,* p. 181; "Führerlaufbahnen in der Waffen SS," *Deutsche Allgemeine Zeitung,* December 28, 1940; *Nationalsozialistisches Jahrbuch 1940* (Munich, 1940), pp. 367–70. Application forms and regulations: *Ergänzungsamt der Waffen-SS,* T-580/roll 69/folder 329; T-580/roll 87/folder 436. Schumacher Collection, folder 428, BDC.

81 Stein, pp. 32–35; Tessin, in Neufeldt, Huck, and Tessin, *Zur Geschichte der Ordnungspolizei,* pp. 12–15, 24–25. *Führer für weltanschauliche Erziehung in SS-Divisionen, Geheim,* September 2, 1939, listing a Verfügungs-, Totenkopf-, and Polizeidivision! — T-611/roll 20/folder 58[II]. Himmler may have given Hitler the notion that the Police Division was needed in Bohemia to keep order there in November 1939. T-175/roll 94/frame 2615045.

General SS recruited as reserves: BDC Biographical Records. *Gesamtstärke der Schutzstaffel, 1. Juli 1940,* in *SS-Hauptamt, Statistische Monatshefte,* November 1940, p. 1, T-74/roll 15/frame 386820. Much of the lawlessness and irregularity of the Death's Head Reinforcements' regime ("wild" deportations of Jews, wanton cruelty, killings, etc.) in the Poland of 1939–1940 was due to the informal connections between their personnel and the General SS at home in the Reich. The Viennese Globocnik's connections with Lublin probably started in this fashion with the Nisko deportation. IMT, vol. 16, pp. 101–2; vol. 33, pp. 256–57.

82 Memorandum of Meyer-Abich, April 27, 1947, *Der Generalinspektor, Zentraljustizamt der britischen Zone,* Hamburg, T-580/roll 87/folder 425. Twelve-year recruits for the Death's Head division, seventeen or eighteen years old, often signed up by subterfuges: BDC Biographical Records; see also Stein, p. 24. Seventy-five thousand armed SS: draft of Himmler letter to Walter Buch, November 13, 1939, BDC Biographical Records. The term *bewaffnete SS* (armed SS) seems to have been a transitional form, officially used as early as June 10, 1939. *Korpsarzt der bewaffneten SS:* T-611/roll 20/folder 58$^{II}$. Origins of the term *Waffen-SS:* Buchheim, *SS und Polizei,* p. 183. As early as February 1940, administratively autonomous Waffen-SS offices existed for (1) recruitment (*Ergänzungsamt der Waffen-SS*); (2) personnel (*Personalamt der Waffen-SS*); (3) welfare and supply (*Fürsorge- und Versorgungsamt der Waffen-SS*); (4) medical (*Sanitätsamt der Waffen-SS*); and (5) administration (*Verwaltungsamt der Waffen-SS*). T-175/roll 104/frames 2626508 ff. An OKW list of Waffen-SS units of March 8, 1940, also includes *Waffen- und Geräteamt der Waffen-SS* and *Amt Reichsverteidigung der Waffen-SS:* T-580/roll 87/folder 425. Military charisma: Neusüss-Hunkel, pp. 108, 110, 114–18. Buchheim, *Das Problem des Befehlsnotstands,* pp. 13–16. See Karl O. Paetel, "Die SS. Ein Beitrag zur Soziologie des Nationalsozialismus," VJHZ 2 (1954), footnote 80. See also Kanis, pp. 10, 13–14, 38.

83 Himmler wrote of "fifty percent casualties" in Poland to Brauchitsch in March 1940, which he certainly would not have admitted if he had not known that Brauchitsch knew it was true. T-580/roll 87/folder 425. Stein details the struggle with the army very well from T-175/roll 104, esp. pp. 43–48. See also Halder, vol. 1, pp. 186, 188, 198. Difficulties in recruiting party, SA, and Hitler Youth leaders: 3245-PS, IMT, vol. 32, pp. 55–56; T-175/roll 20/frames 2525117–31; T-175/roll 70/folder 278. François Duprat lists sixteen Totenkopfstandarten and seven other related units as of July 28, 1940, by garrison, commander, and troop strength: *Histoire des SS* (Paris, 1968), pp. 423–24.

84 Himmler-Brauchitsch correspondence, T-580/roll 87/folder 425; and T-175/roll 19/frames 2523345–46, 2523362 (not identical). Standarte Nordland: T-175/roll 59/frames 2574368 ff.; Photocopy 131-TI, BDC Miscellaneous Organizational Records (SS Hänge-Ordner 1719, B58). Standarte Westland: SGV folder 50/item 44, BDC Biographical Records. See also Stein, pp. 94–95.

85 Waffen-SS losses in the western campaigns: *SS-Hauptamt, Statistische Monatshefte*, November 1940, p. 3, T-74/roll 15/frame 386822; Stein, pp. 67–68, 73, 76–78, 82, 88. Weapons: T-175/roll 19/frames 2523352–58; photocopies 1199p–1200p, 1208–9p, BDC Biographical Records; Schumacher Collection, folder 427 (*Beschaffungsamt*); Stein, pp. 50–55, citing T-75/roll 104.

86 T-580/roll 88/folder 436 (*Ergänzung*); U.S. Military Tribunal Case Eleven, prosecution doc. book 65, NO 1825; Stein, pp. 96–98.

87 665-D, IMT, vol. 35, pp. 355–58; and Walter Warlimont, *Im Hauptquartier der deutschen Wehrmacht, 1939–1945* (Frankfurt am Main, 1962), pp. 119–20, footnote 1. Cf. Hitler, *Secret Conversations* (July 24–25, 1941), p. 12. The atmosphere of double-dealing in which the Waffen SS was conceived was certainly not permanently dispelled, as shown by Warlimont's disingenuous picture of the origins of what later became 665-D, which in turn may be a "doctored version" prepared for allied propaganda use. Himmler's plans for the General SS "after the war" (August 30, 1940) indicate a "freshening up" of its officer corps from the Waffen-SS, thorough pruning of "dead-wood," and conversion to pre- and post-military service training and drill like the SA — a course thoroughly consistent with the Staatstruppenpolizei conception: T-580/roll 87/folder 425

88 "Ansprache des Reichsführers SS an das Offizierskorps der Leibstandarte-SS 'Adolf Hitler' am Abend des Tages von Metz (Überreichung der Führerstandarte)": 1918-PS, IMT, vol. 29, pp. 99–105. See also Neusüss-Hunkel, p. 103. The Leibstandarte was stationed at Metz from July 1940 to February 1941. Kurt Meyer, *Grenadiere* (Munich, 1957), pp. 41–42.

89 Werner Best wrote in *Die Deutsche Polizei* (Darmstadt, 1941), a widely circulated survey: "Die Waffen SS . . . besteht aus der Verfügungstruppe, welche ausschliesslich dem Führer für besondere Aufgaben im Frieden und Kriege zur Verfügung steht, und aus den SS-Totenkopfstandarten, denen die Sonderaufgaben der Bewachung der Konzentrationslager und des Einsatzes für bestimmte Zwecke der Staatissicherung gestellt sind." (The Waffen-SS consists of the Special Duty Troops which are exclusively at the Führer's service for special tasks in peace and war, and the Death's Head regiments, which have been assigned the special duties of guarding the concentration camps and of specific purposes of state operations serving security.) Buchheim points out that the Waffen-SS *Soldbuch* (paybook) enabled its holder to enter the zone of operations without special permits, a valuable "cover" for execution commandos, intelligence personnel, and venal *Glücksritter* ("operators") from the General SS and the Main Offices: "Die SS," pp. 148–49. Waffen-SS were used in 191 executions in the Protectorate of Bohemia-Moravia as early as September 1941: T-175/roll 123/EAP 161/b/12/348. Ending VT-TV duality: Stein, pp. 104–5, 110.

90 Stein, pp. 143–44. Sennheim training camp: T-175/roll 20/frames 2524982–83, 2524968; T-611/roll 3/folder 429[II]. "Freiwillige für die SS Standarte Westland" (September 13, 1940): T-580/roll 90/folder 436. Increased flow from the southeast: T-175/roll 128/frames 2654201–399; T-175/roll 192/

frames 2655874–928. Branch recruiting offices (*Ergänzungsstellen*, later *Ersatzkommandos*): T-611/rolls 2–3/folders 426$^{II}$, 429$^{I}$; T-611/rolls 5–6/folders 431$^{I}$, 431$^{II}$; T-580/roll 89/folder 448; T-175/roll 5/frames 2544583–84; T-175/roll 28/frames 2534393–94. VoMi protests in U.S. Military Tribunal Case Eleven prosecution doc. book 72-F, discussed by former VoMi official Waldemar Rimann, in his Case Eight affidavit, Lorenz defense doc. book 1.

91 The foundation and evolution of the Germanic Guidance Office can be traced in BDC Schumacher Collection, folder 427, under "G", "H" (SS-*Hauptamt*), and "E" (*Ergänzung*), especially in *Stabsbefehle des Chefs des SS-Hauptamts*, 1/41, 5/41, 7/41, 19/41, and *Gliederungsplan des SS-Hauptamts*, February 28, 1941, T-175/roll 192/frames 2655313–16. The bypassing of the Auslands-Organisation is illustrated in Himmler's correspondence with Werner Best, the Reich Plenipotentiary in Denmark, 1941–1943: T-175/roll 59/folder 102. The older SS use of the AO can be seen in U.S. Department of State, Division of European Affairs, *National Socialism. Basic Principles. Their Application by the Nazi Party's Foreign Organization and the Use of Germans Abroad for Nazi Aims* (Washington, D.C., 1943), pp. 132–39; NG 2057, TWC, vol. 13, p. 1167; and T-175/roll 98/frame 2618397. The bastard organization known as the NSDAP *Hauptamt für Volkstumsfragen*, created on the basis of a Hess order of February 26, 1941, and staffed exclusively with SS personnel, though nominally a *party* installation, was also a device employed by the avid Main Office Chief to enter both the RKFDV sphere and the Brown House via a henchman of his who became executive director. There was no end to intrigue! Koehl, *RKFDV*, pp. 142–43; Buchheim, "Rechtsstellung und Organisation," pp. 268–70; T-175/roll 33/folder 230; T-175/roll 70/folder 284; *Mitteilungen des Chefs des SS-Hauptamts* 1:1 (October 15, 1943), item 8, BDC Schumacher Collection, folder 427, "H". One small indicator of the penetration by Himmler into Folk Group affairs (largely through the enterprise of Main Office boss Berger) is the picture of the Reichsführer SS in the 1944 yearbook of the *Deutsche Volksgruppe in Rumänien;* no other Reich German was so honored, except Hitler! *Deutsche Volksgruppe in Rumänien. Jahrbuch 1944* (Hermannstadt, 1944).

92 Stein, pp. 139, 148–56; Herzog, p. 6; U.S. Military Tribunal Case Eleven docs. NO 1087, NO 1479, NO 2015; correspondence with Heydrich, November 1941, T-175/roll 59/folder 4; correspondence with Schellenberg, October 2, 1942, T-580/roll 73/folder 341. A report on recruiting by the Main Office boss of approximately May–June 1942 (T-175/roll 20/frames 2524967–68, 2524981–82, 2524984–86) mentions a basic Himmler order of March 15, 1942, the probable draft text of which appears on frames 2524946–47, *Aufgaben in den germanischen Ländern.* Friction in the Waffen-SS over the volunteers and the desertion problem: Stein, pp. 158–62; and T-175/roll 22/frames 2527069–70, 2527077, 2527080–82.

93 K.-G. Klietmann, *Die Waffen-SS. Eine Dokumentation* (Osnabrück, 1965), pp. 307, 313–14, 354–55, 393–95, 501–2 (combat units); Stein, pp. 105–6,

120; A. Van Arendonck, *Vlamingen aan het Ostfront* (Antwerpen, 1973), pp. 49 ff.; SGV folder 84/EAP 161-b-12/150, T-175/roll 60. Inspekteur für Statistik beim Reichsführer SS: Stärkemeldungen der Schutzstaffel, 31. Dez. 1941. Owing to a library mishap, the original sources for this and all subsequent chapter notes were "trashed." Reconstruction in many cases has proved impossible, so that the notes provide only a part of the original evidence.

94  Smith and Peterson, pp. 146–47. SGV folder 00022/EAP 161-b-12/99, T-175/roll 41. *SS-Personalveränderungsblätter* and *SS-Verordnungsblätter*, 1938–1944. BDC records: Unclassified Foreign Service Despatch from Chief, Berlin Document Center, W. J. Mueller, No. 481, January 9, 1956. Twenty thousand SS officers: author's estimate. Bernd Wegner points out that the Waffen SS tables of organization actually called for high officer ratios (which could not be filled due to rapid expansion): "Das Führerkorps der Waffen SS im Kriege," in *Das deutsche Offizierkorps 1860–1960*, Hans Hubert Hofmann, ed. (Boppard am Rhein, 1981), p. 330, note 12.

95  Klietmann, pp. 43–44 (officer lists for SS-Hauptamt); SGV folder 219/EAP 161-b-12/132, T-175/roll 56. Folder of Obergruppenführer Hans Rauter (correspondence about high SS officers and Waffen-SS affairs). In a letter to Paul Hausser on August 8, 1941, Himmler described how Hitler praised *Das Reich* division but told him that he must be satisfied with only 1,500 officers and men as replacements "to fill the worst gaps": Himmler Files, SGV folder 66, Hoover Institution Library. Among the measures taken by Himmler, largely at the suggestion of Berger, were: (1) granting Dutch personnel the right to wear ribbons won in colonial service, January 25, 1941 (ibid.); (2) subsidies for marriages of SS men with nordic brides in 1942 (T-175/roll 17/frames 2523057, 2523063–67); (3) Himmler visits to nordic lands in 1943 (T-175/roll 22/frames 2526961 ff.); (4) publication of a special monthly magazine, *Aufbruch*, beginning July 1943 (BDC Biographical Records). The "ambitious pretensions" of the SS Main Office were really those of the Germanic Guidance Office. See *Der Soldatenfreund*, as cited by Karl O. Paetel in "Tipología de la orden negra," *Diógenes* 1 (1953): 109. The old SA officer had no use for incompetent, bureaucratic SS-Altkämpfer: T-175/roll 19/frame 2523691.

96  Buchheim, "Die Höheren SS-und Polizeiführer," pp. 381–89; Stein, p. 106. Revealing satire about the SS Recruitment Office and about Gottlob Berger: SGV folder 205/EAP 161-b-12/106, T-175/roll 47. Compare Steiner, *Freiwilligen*, pp. 67, 163–64, 217. For the quarrel between the SS Main Office and the Leadership Main Office (FHA) over training responsibilities, as well as the personnel make-up (showing SA and old army origins of *both* groups of officers), see BDC Schumacher Collection, folder 427, under "F", "H", and "V". See also Stein, pp. 197–200. Additional illustrations of the training issue, which spilled over into the recruitment area, for both FHA and SS-Hauptamt can be found in Himmler Files, SGV folder 274, Hoover Institution Library. By 1944 the Führungshauptamt was a huge agency just exactly like the SS-Hauptamt. The use of army ranks (rather than the SS grades, e.g. *Oberleutnant* instead of *Obersturmführer*) became increas-

ingly common, first in divisional orders (1941), later in FHA and Personalhauptamt orders too (1943–1945).

97  Klietmann, pp. 45–47 (organization of *Führungshauptamt*). SGV folder
    355/EAP 161-b-12/55, T-175/roll 30. *Vor- und Nachmilitärische Erziehung*
    (1938–1941). The BDC records of the Persönlicher Stab and the Personal-
    hauptamt are replete with the jealousy and self-serving "protests against in-
    justice" of military prima donnas: correspondence between the chief of
    Himmler's Personal Staff and the heads of FHA, the SS Main Office, and
    the Personnel Main Office, 1939–1944, SGV folder 1699, photos 626z–687z,
    SGV folder 1375, photo 694–700z, SGV folder 247, photo 407a–417a; cor-
    respondence with a prominent Obergruppenführer, January 8, 1942, and
    March 26, 1942, BDC Biographical Records; see Himmler's *Geheime Kom-
    mandosache* reproof to two Obergruppenführer for behaving like fighting
    cocks "with the enemy in the gates," July 14, 1944, ibid.; and Himmler's
    abolition of SS generals' striped pants as of September 1, 1944, SGV folder
    93, photostat 945o. Another Himmler reproof of a Waffen-SS Obergrup-
    penführer for warning in a divisional directive that it was a crime to give
    the Superior SS and Police Leader divisional information, January 13, 1943:
    SGV folder 239. The Personal Staff informed another prominent Superior
    SS and Police Leader as early as March 30, 1941, that he could *never* ap-
    point his General SS staff leader (*Stabsführer*) as his deputy (presumably
    because Waffen-SS and police channels did not wish to deal with General
    SS people): SGV folder 263, photos 821k. A General SS-*Standortappell*
    (garrison roll call) in Hamburg called by the Superior SS and Police Leader
    was virtually entirely devoted to Waffen-SS concerns: *Hamburger Frem-
    denblatt*, June 16, 1941. Creation of the *Kommandoamt der Allgemeinen
    SS* and tables of organization of the Leadership Main Office: BDC Schu-
    macher Collection, folder 427, "V". The new Superior SS and Police Lead-
    ers did create new General SS units: *Stabssturm der Allgemeinen SS im
    Oberabschnitt Nordwest* (Netherlands), July 7, 1941, BDC Biographical
    Records. FHA orders creating new General SS-Standarten (Alsace), No-
    vember 12, 1940: T-175/roll 129/frame 2656014. A skeleton structure was
    created by "temporary duty" assignments of able-bodied General SS offi-
    cers as early as 1940: BDC Biographical Records. Plans for a new
    "post-war" General SS devoted to military training (August 30, 1940,
    February 20, 1941): SGV folder 355, photostats 719–722a; T-580/roll
    37/folder 238[II]. A figure of 83,868 General SS *not* in military service (ex-
    cluding Reich Labor Service) on June 30, 1944, probably represents the
    older cadre of 1941–1942 also, out of a total General SS on December 31,
    1941, of 271,060: T-175/roll 60/frame 2576433; 878-D, IMT, vol. 35, p.
    627. Approval of a *larger* General SS budget in March 1942: T-175/roll 37/
    frames 2547076–77.

98  E. E. Knoebel, "Racial Illusion and Military Necessity: A Study of SS Politi-
    cal and Manpower Objectives in Occupied Belgium" (Ph.D. dissertation,
    University of Colorado, 1965), pp. 139 ff. *Germanische Leitstelle* growth:
    Denmark: T-175/roll 72 SGV/folder 299; correspondence of April 18 and

22, 1944, SGV folder 21, item 2, BDC Biographical Records. Norway (December 1943): *Goebbels Diaries*, p. 542. Belgium (publicity about Flemish SS volunteers): Wolfgang Schwarz, "Der Führer der Germanen," *Zeitschrift für Geopolitik* 18:9 (1941): 534–35. Netherlands: T-175/roll 74/SGV folder 261. Croatia: T-175/roll 73/SGV folder 270. On February 6, 1943, Lammers circulated a decree granting Himmler *exclusive* rights to negotiate with "Germanic" groups in occupied areas! U.S. Military Tribunal Case Eleven, prosecution doc. book 72-C, NG 2549. Delusions of grandeur are rampant in the table of organization of *Amtsgruppe D* (*Germanische Leitstelle*) of October 23, 1944, which listed seventy-eight *Referate* (specialists) including liaison posts for Great Britain, the Far East, and Arabia! U.S. Nuremberg doc. NO 143. Censorship bureau: 1941 — BDC Schumacher Collection, folder 427, "F" (SGV folder 55); 1942–1944 — T-175/roll 22/ frames 2527211–311 (SGV folder 125).

99  FHA orders of March 23, April 1, April 5, May 1, 1941, BDC Biographical Records. Appointments of Befehlshaber der Waffen-SS (1940–1945): Klietmann, pp. 435–39 (name-list of Befehlshaber der Waffen-SS); BDC Biographical Records; T-611/roll 2/folder 426. SS-Fürsorge- und Versorgungsamt within SS-Hauptamt, January 1941: BDC Schumacher Collection, folder 427, "Reichsführung SS." Welfare office reassigned to RuSHa: U.S. Military Tribunal Case Eight, prosecution doc. book II-C, NO 2577; and *Anschriftenverzeichnis der Schutzstaffel. Stand vom 20. April 1943*, T-611/ roll 2/folder 426. T-611/roll 8/folder 435: *SS-Fürsorge-und Versorgungsbestimmungen*, 1940–1944. Job training schools for wounded Waffen-SS men were operated by both the Leadership Main Office and the SS Main Office. The latter also ran a physical rehabilitation program in which Berger, a former physical education instructor, was extremely interested: BDC Schumacher Collection, folder 427, *Führungshauptamt* (SGV folder 56); *Mitteilungen des Chefs des SS-Hauptamts* 1:1 (October 15, 1943), items 4 and 15, BDC Schumacher Collection, folder 427, "H"; "Reichsschule für Leibeserziehung (Prag)," ibid., "R" (SGV folders 90, 92); Schumacher folder 428, "Inspekteur für Leibeserziehung beim Reichsführer SS und Chef der deutschen Polizei," October 7, 1943.

100  SS penetration into Rosenberg's top echelon: U.S. Military Tribunal Case Eleven, prosecution doc. book 72-C, Rosenberg to Lammers, May 6, 1942, NG 951; memorandum of Alfred Meyer, August 10, 1943, NO 349, TWC, vol. 13, pp. 317–18. Case Eight, Meyer-Hetling defense doc. book 4, affidavit of Hans Riecke, "Der Siedlungsausschuss beim Ostministerium." Memorandum of October 10, 1941, T-175/roll 22/frames 2527944–46; SGV folder 57, correspondence of 1942, T-175/roll 17/frames 2521056–58, 2521101–8, 2521145–46. Relations with Koch: SGV folder 113, correspondence of 1943, T-175/roll 22/frames 252791–95. U.S. Nuremberg docs. NO 4867, NO 4876, NO 4877, NO 4878, NO 4879, NO 4910, NO 4912. Case Eight, Meyer-Hetling defense doc. book 3, affidavit of Erhard Maeding, "Gut Krasne." Himmler Files, SGV folder 323, "Ukrainischer Werkdienst," Hoover Institution Library. The new RuSHa chief: Case Eight, prosecution

doc. book 2-C, NO 4716, NO 5122; 5-B, NO 4045; 6-C, NO 3224; 15, NO 2275, loose exhibits 844, 847, 849, 850, NO 5126, NO 4866, NO 1180, NO 5714; and BDC Biographical Records. RuSHa "training settlements" on collective farms: Reichsführer SS, Rasse- und Siedlungshauptamt, *Bestimmungen über die Erfassung, Auswahl und Zuführung der siedlungswilligen Angehörigen der Waffen-SS für die wiedergewonnenen Siedlungsräume* (Berlin, 1943). Case Eight, English transcript, pp. 85, 1284, 1297. Prosecution doc. book 2-C, NO 1402, NO 2576; 6-C, NO 3224; 14-C, exhibits 635–36; 638–52, NO 4122, NO 4121, NO 4100, NO 4119, NO 4105, NO 4109, NO 4880, NO 4099, NO 4104, NO 4103, NO 4111, NO 4113, NO 4107, NO 4108, NO 4115, NO 4116, NO 4098. Rebuttal book A, NO 5809; Huebner defense doc. book 3, exhibit 57, affidavit of Ernst Tesseraux. SS-*Wirtschafter* installed in July 1942: U.S. Nuremberg doc. NO 2128. "Erweiterung der Aufgaben der Wirtschaftsinspektionen der Waffen-SS und Truppenwirtschaftslager," March 16, 1942: T-175/roll 18/frames 2523316–17.

101 *Tagebuch des Herrn Generalgouverneurs für die besetzten polnischen Gebiete*, 25 Oktober 1939 bis 3 April 1945, U.S. National Archives Microcopy ML 382 (hereafter *Tagebuch*, ML382), roll A, vol. 3, pp. 79–81, 106–7, 136 (February 19, 21, 28, 1940); roll C, vol. 9, pp. 40–41 (April 23, 1940). Hans Buchheim et al., *Anatomie des SS-Staats* (Olten und Freiburg im Bresgau, 1965), vol. 1, pp. 156–7; vol. 2, pp. 219–20. Buchheim, *SS und Polizei*, pp. 135–36; Hausser, *Waffen-SS*, pp. 26–28; Neusüss-Hunkel, p. 109; von Siegler, p. 90; Stein, p. 111; Tessin, in Neufeldt, Huck, and Tessin, *Geschichte der Ordnungspolizei*, pp. 16–19, 27–36. NO 2455, TWC, vol. 13, pp. 514–15 (origin of infamous Dirlewanger *Sonderkommando* as police battalion).

102 Dallin, pp. 74–76, 96–99; Guderian, pp. 101–15; Edgar M. Howell, *The Soviet Partisan Movement* (Washington, D.C., 1956), pp. 117–18; Sawicki, pp. 17–83; Stein, pp. 273–77. Assignment of Chełmno (Kulmhof) SS killers to Prinz Eugen division (Sonderkommando SS-Hauptsturmführer Bothmann): SGV folder 81/EAP 161-b-12/150, T-175/roll 60/frames 2575972–88. U.S. Nuremberg doc. series NO 452–469 in folder EAP 172-c-11/24/1, T-175/roll 11/frames 2512674–700 shows the ruthless antipartisan methods used in Slovenia in 1942 by order of the Superior SS and Police Leader.

103 "Verluste im Kriege": T-611/roll 2/folder 426$^I$. Memorandum of Reichsführer SS, September 24, 1942: ibid., folder 426$^{II}$. "Bezeichnung der SS-Division (mot.)," December 1, 1942: *Verordnungsblatt der Waffen-SS* 3:23, T-611/roll 5/folder 431$^I$. Meyer, pp. 41–42; Steiner, *Die Armee der Geächteten*, p. 149; Stein, pp. 118, 120, 134–35, 201–2, citing T-175/rolls 105, 108. T-175/roll 56/SGV folder 77, draft letter of Himmler to Steiner, August 1942. The official description of the Waffen-SS for 1942 may be seen in pp. 427a–427b of the *Organisationsbuch der NSDAP* (Munich, 1943). See also Klietmann, pp. 55–56, 59, 71–85; and Weingartner, pp. 30–73.

104 The definite article *Das (Reich)* was not added until August 1942. *Verordnungsblatt der Waffen-SS* 3:16, T-611/roll 5/folder 431$^I$. Hausser, *Waffen-SS*, pp. 48–50, 52–57, 63–64; Klietmann, pp. 56, 87–105; Otto Weidinger,

*Division Das Reich. Der Weg der 2. SS-Panzer-Division Das Reich. Die Geschichte der Stammdivision der Waffen-SS*, 4 vols. (Osnabrück, 1967–1979), vol. 2 (1940–1941), pp. 351 ff. Stein tells an interesting story about the bad discipline of the 11th SS regiment: pp. 114–15. Commanders: BDC Biographical Records.

105  Hausser, *Waffen-SS*, pp. 66–68, 88, 103; Klietmann, pp. 56, 107–22. Lehmann and Wacker, "Waffen SS," pp. 31–32 ("Thule"); Stein, pp. 57–59; Steiner, *Freiwilligen*, pp. 136–37 ("Freikorps Danmark"); Charles W. Sydnor, Jr., *Soldiers of Destruction. The SS Death's Head Division, 1933–1945* (Princeton, 1977), pp. 152 ff. *Der Soldatenfreund. Sonderausgabe für die Männer der Totenkopfdivision der Waffen-SS*, Jahrgang II: Nr. 34 (July 1942). Eicke was shot down while in an observation plane: T-175/roll 22/ frames 2527031–40.

106  Hausser, *Waffen-SS*, p. 69; Friedrich Husemann, *Die guten Glaubens waren. Die Geschichte der SS-Polizei Division*, 2 vols. (Osnabrück, 1971–1973), vol. 1 (1939–1942), pp. 17 ff.; Klietmann, pp. 123–32; Steiner, *Freiwilligen*, pp. 200–201; Tessin, in Neufeldt, Huck, and Tessin, *Die Geschichte der Ordnungspolizei*, pp. 39–40.

107  Hausser, *Waffen-SS*, pp. 46, 103, 117: Klietmann, pp. 133–42; Stein, pp. 143, 149–50, 159; Steiner, *Freiwilligen*, p. 159; Peter Strassner, *Europäische Freiwillige. Die Geschichte der 5. SS Panzerdivision WIKING*, (Osnabrück, 1968), pp. 15–29, 97, 103, 106–12, 114–17, 127, 130; T-175/roll 56/ SGV folder 77, Himmler correspondence with Steiner from 1938 on; T-175/ roll 38/frames 2547831–35, evaluation of Wiking division, January 1942.

108  Hausser, *Waffen-SS*, pp. 41, 70–72, 75–76; Klietmann, pp. 56, 143–49; Franz Schreiber, *Kampf unter dem Nordlicht. Die Geschichte der 6. SS-Gebirgs-Division Nord* (Osnabrück, 1969), pp. 33–59, 70–71, 171, 193, 196–97; Stein, pp. 130–32.

109  Hausser, *Waffen-SS*, p. 106: Herzog, pp. 12–13; Klietmann, pp. 151–55; Stein, pp. 169–72, 274; Steiner, *Freiwilligen*, pp. 218–20; Holm Sundhaussen, "Zur Geschichte der Waffen SS in Kroatien 1941–45," *Südost-Forschungen* 30 (1971): 176–96; SGV folder 239/EAP 161-b-12/67, T-175/ roll 33 (folder of Obergruppenführer Arthur Phleps).

110  Hohenstein, *Wartheländisches Tagebuch*, p. 75; Klietmann, pp. 157–64; *SS-Kavallerie im Osten* (Braunschweig, 1942); Stein, pp. 109, 121, 172–74, 202; Herzog, pp. 4–5, 14.

111  Clifton J. Child, "The SS and the Germanic Ideal," in *Survey of International Affairs, 1939–1946, 4: Hitler's Europe*, ed. Arnold Toynbee and Veronica Toynbee (London, 1954), pp. 75–80; Albert de Jonghe, "L'Etablissement d'une administration civile en Belgique et dans le Nord de la France," *Cahiers d'histoire de la seconde guerre mondiale* 1 (August 1970): 67–129; Hitler, *Secret Conversations*, pp. 326–27; Klietmann, pp. 357–72; Stein, pp. 150, 152–57.

112  Hausser, *Waffen-SS*, p. 13; Hitler, *Secret Conversations*, pp. 177–78; Gerhard Rempel, "The Misguided Generation. Hitler Youth and SS: 1933–1945" (Ph.D. dissertation, University of Wisconsin-Madison, 1971), pp. 326–43; Stein, p. 203.

113 Hausser, *Waffen-SS*, pp. 46–48, 82–97; Stein, pp. 197–203; Steiner, *Freiwilligen*, pp. 199–200, 206; Alexander Werth, *Russia at War 1941–1945* (New York, 1964), pp. 441–55, 474.

114 Correspondence of Himmler with Gauleiter Eggeling regarding SS recruiting methods: SGV folder 83/EAP 161-b-12/135, T-175/roll 57. SGV folder 84/EAP 161-b-12/150, T-175/roll 60, Inspekteur für Statistik beim Reichsführer SS: Statistik des Ergänzungsamts der Waffen-SS, 1942.

115 *Organisationsbuch der NSDAP 1943*, pp. 419, 427.

116 Hausser, *Waffen-SS*, pp. 17, 69, 76–78; Husemann, p. 294; Klietmann, pp. 59–61; *Kriegstagebuch der Oberkommando der Wehrmacht (Wehrmachtführungsstab) 1940–1945 geführt von Helmuth Greiner und Percy Ernst Schramm*, 4 vols. (Frankfurt/M., 1961–1965), vol. 2, pp. 996, 1008, 1016, 1024, 1037, 1052, and in appendices, 1383, 1390, 1398, 1438; Stein, pp. 197–98, 202–3; Strassner, pp. 226, 276, 413–14.

117 Hausser, *Waffen-SS*, p. 104; *Hitlers Lagebesprechungen*, p. 335; Klietmann, pp. 165–73, 181–85; Meyer, pp. 204–8. Rempel, pp. 601–60; Stein, pp. 204–8; Steiner, *Freiwilligen*, p. 213; Wilhelm Tiecke, *Im Feuersturm letzter Kriegsjahre. II. SS-Panzerkorps mit 9. und 10. SS-Divisionen "Hohenstaufen" und "Frundsberg"* (Osnabrück, 1975), pp. 14–34.

118 Hausser, *Waffen-SS*, pp. 116–30; *Hitlers Lagebesprechungen* (Stuttgart, 1962), p. 207; Hitler, *Secret Conversations*, p. 138–39; Werner Klose, *Generation in Gleichschritt. Ein Dokumentarbericht)* (Hamburg-Oldenburg, 1964), pp. 256–58; Stein, pp. 209–10, 222; NO 031 and NO 2053, TWC, vol. 13, pp. 281–87; 1919-PS, IMT, vol. 29, pp. 110–73, esp. p. 140; Speer testimony, IMT, vol. 16, pp. 515, 517–18.

119 Hausser, *Waffen-SS*, pp. 104–6, 129–31, 184; Klietmann, pp. 61–64, 175–79, 203–7, 209–13; Stein, pp. 210–11; Steiner, *Freiwilligen*, pp. 214–16; H.-J. E. Stöber, *Die Eiserne Faust. Bildband und Chronik der 17. SS-Panzergrenadier-Division "Götz von Berlichingen"* (Neckargemünd, 1966). Bernd Wegner, "Auf dem Wege zur pangermanischen Armee. Dokumente zur Enstehungsgeschichte des III. ('Germanischen') SS-Panzerkorps," *Militärgeschichtliche Mitteilungen* 28:2 (1980): 101–36; 1919-PS, IMT, vol. 29, pp. 139–41.

120 Rempel, pp. 344–69; Stein, p. 204; BDC SS Officer list.

121 Josef Ackerman, *Heinrich Himmler als Ideologe* (Göttingen, 1970), pp. 228–29; "Reichsführer SS Himmler auf der Gauleitertagung am 3. August 1944 in Posen," VJHZ 1 (1953): 393–94; Speer, *Infiltration*, p. 295; 1919-PS, IMT, vol. 29, pp. 167, 171–72.

122 François Duprat, *Les Campagnes de la Waffen SS* (Paris, 1973), pp. 98–100; Hausser, *Waffen-SS*, pp. 104–6, 132, 184; Kersten, pp. 300–301, 317–23; Klietmann, pp. 187–91, 199–200; Paul Kluke, "Nationalsozialistische Europaideologie," VJHZ 3 (1955): 255–60, 264–68; 1919-PS, IMT, vol. 29, p. 141.

123 Helmut Heiber, ed., *Reichsführer! Briefe an und von Himmler* (Stuttgart, 1968), pp. 196–201 (Himmler-Berger correspondence, March 9–15, 1943); Sawicki, pp. 17–70; von Siegler, p. 143; BDC Biographical Records.

124 Bruce B. Campbell, "Waffen-SS voluntary military units in Estonia, Croa-

tia and the Polish Ukraine 1942–1945" (M.A. thesis, University of Wisconsin–Madison, 1978), pp. 48–93; Klietmann, pp. 383–92; Stein, pp. 174–79; Steiner, *Freiwilligen*, pp. 116–20, 124–30.

125  Child, "The Political Structure of Hitler's Europe: Administration," pp. 113–25; Larry V. Thompson, "Nazi Administrative Conflict: The Struggle for Executive Power in the General Government of Poland 1939–1943" (Ph.D. dissertation, University of Wisconsin-Madison, 1967), pp, 88–109, 207–16.

126  Dallin, p. 597, note 4; Seppo Myllyniemi, *Die Neuordnung der Baltischen Länder 1941–1944* (Helsinki, 1973), pp. 226–8. Stein, pp. 174–75; Steiner, *Freiwilligen*, pp. 77–78.

127  Dallin, pp. 596–97; Kersten, pp. 181–82, 267; Myllyniemi, pp. 228–38; Stein, pp. 152–53, 175–79; George H. Stein and Peter R. Krosby, "Das finnische Freiwilligen-Bataillon der Waffen-SS. Eine Studie zur SS-Diplomatie und zur ausländischen Freiwilligen-Bewegung," VJHZ 14 (1966): 413–53.

128  Campbell, pp. 104–42; Hausser, *Waffen-SS*, pp. 106–7; *Hitlers Lagebesprechungen*, pp. 200, note 2; Hoettl, *Geheime Front*, pp. 253–54; Kersten, pp. 259–60; Stein, pp. 180–85.

129  Dallin, pp. 597–99; Basil Dmytryshin, "The Nazis and the SS Volunteer Division 'Galicia,'" *American Slavic and East European Review* 15 (1956): 1–10. Wolf-Dietrich Heike, *Sie wollten die Freiheit. Die Geschichte der ukrainischen Division 1943–1945* (Dorheim, n.d.); *Hitlers Lagebesprechungen*, pp. 938–41; Klietmann, pp. 193–97, 275–77, 295–97; Stein, pp. 185–87.

130  Dallin, pp. 600–607, 611–12; *Hitlers Lagebesprechungen*, p. 536; Klietmann, pp. 379–82; Joseph B. Schechtman, *The Mufti and the Fuehrer* (New York, 1965), pp. 135–44; Stein, pp. 187–93; Steiner, *Freiwilligen*, pp. 85–86. "Quasi-SS" for *Ostvölker* (eastern peoples): "SS Helfer," *Der Freiwillige* 10:1 (1965): 15.

131  Höhne, pp. 425–26; folder EAP 161-b-12/381, T-175/roll 141. Statistisch-wissenschaftliches Institut des Reichsführers-SS, Stärke der SS am 31. December 1943. Author's estimates.

132  Bernd Wegner has analyzed the higher Waffen-SS officer corps of 1944 with great care. He finds four distinct elements, including Altkämpfer and young Nazis: "Das Führerkorps der Waffen-SS im Kriege," in *Das deutsche Offizierkorps*, ed. Hans Hubert Hofmann (Boppard am Rhein, 1981), pp. 331–50, esp. pp. 346–50. See also Hitler, *Secret Conversations*, pp. 138–39; and Stein, pp. 273, 275; SGV folder 84/EAP 161-b-12/150, T-175/roll 60, Inspekteur für Statistik beim Reichsführer SS: SS Führer 1943; SGV Folder 1260/EAP 161-b-12/147, T-175/roll 26. Recruitment in 1944: BDC Biographical Records. See also Der Reichsführer SS. SS-Hauptamt, *Dich ruft die SS* (Berlin, n.d.), pp. 41–66: "Führerlaufbahnen I-XVI."

133  Dallin, p. 614; *Hitlers Lagebesprechungen*, p. 69; Klietmann, pp. 299–302; "Die Brigade Kaminski," *Der Freiwillige* 9:8 (1964): 13–16; "Reichsführer SS Himmler auf der Gauleitertagung am 3. August 1944 in Posen," VJHZ 1

(1953): 377–78. "Die Männer mit dem Totenkopf sind über die Schlacht-felder Europas geschritten, stürmend und siegend. So wie jene ersten acht, wie jene kleine erste Schutzstaffel, die sich einst in finsteren Strassen und verqualmten Versammlungsaalen mit der roten oder schwarzen Unterwelt herumschlug." (The men with the Death's Head have strode across the bat-tlefields of Europe, storming and winning, like those eight of the first guard squadron, who once upon a time fought with the red and black underworld in dark streets and smoky meeting halls.) SS-Hauptamt, *Lehrplan für Sechsmonatige Schulung* (Berlin, n.d., c. 1942).

134  Höhne, p. 381; Stein, pp. 145–48; Steiner, *Freiwilligen*, pp. 184–85, 385–86. Affidavit of Herbert Dassler, Darré defense doc. book 2, U.S. Military Tribunal Case Eleven. SGV folder 77/EAP 161-b-12/129, T-175/rolls 51, 56: folder of Obergruppenführer Felix Steiner. SGV folder 85/EAP 161-b-12/135, T-175/roll 57: folder of Obergruppenführer Friedrich Wilhelm Krüger. SGV folder 22/item 24/EAP 161-b-12/136, T-175/roll 58: case of Untersturmführer Gustav Wilhaus, who requested front service. SGV folder 249/EAP 161-b-12/91, T-175/roll 38: case of Obersturmbannführer Ernst Fick. Two of the four categories in Bernd Wegner's typology of the wartime Waffen-SS officer corps fit the characterization of Nur-Soldaten: the higher ranks that came from the Reichswehr or Wehrmacht, and the majors and lieutenant colonels who had NCO or lieutenant ranks in World War I or the Reichswehr: "Das Führerkorps der Waffen SS im Kriege," in *Das deutsche Offizierkorps*, ed. Hans Hubert Hofmann, pp. 347–48.

135  Kempner, *SS im Kreuzverhör*, p. 281; "Reichsführer SS Himmler auf der Gauleitertagung am 3. August 1944 in Posen," VJHZ 1 (1953): 369–72; BDC Biographical Records. Survivors: Karl Wolff and Gottlob Berger lived to boast of (and misrepresent) their exploits. See Heinz Artzt, *Mörder in Uniform. Organisationen die zu Vollstreckern nationalsozialistischer Ver-brechen wurden* (Munich, 1979), pp. 113, 180.

136  SGV folder 80/EAP 161-b-12/129, T-175/rolls 51, 56: case of Gunter Pancke. Folder EAP 161-b-12/147, T−175/roll 138: case of Udo von Woyrsch. SGV folder 217/EAP 161-b-12/132, T-175/roll 56: case of Kurt Hintze. SGV folder 145/EAP 161-b-12/139, T-175/roll 58: case of Karl Zenner. See also Henry V. Dicks, *Licensed Mass Murder. A Socio-Psychological Study of Some SS Killers* (New York, 1972).

137  "Reichsführer SS Himmler auf der Gauleitertagung am 3. August 1944 in Posen," VJHZ 1 (1953): 390–92. SGV folder 142/item 13/EAP 161-b-12/139, T-175/roll 58: Himmler letter concerning Wehrmacht relations with Waffen-SS and ORPO (Order Police), January 19, 1943. SGV folder 142/items 17, 18/EAP 161-b-12/139, T-175/roll 58: Himmler correspondence re-garding state officials' relations with and attitudes toward the SS, January 1943. BDC Biographical Records.

138  Höhne, p. 403. NO 031, TWC, vol. 13, pp. 283–87: Berger letter to Himm-ler on SS officers, March 9, 1943. Folder EAP 161-b-12/147, T-175/roll 138: Berger letter to Himmler, September 26, 1944, an important general com-mentary on events and plans. BDC Biographical Records. The 1944 monthly

periodical series of the SS-Hauptamt, *Politischer Dienst für SS und Polizei* for SS officers, represents a notable exception to the low quality of SS "educational" materials, seeking to deal with fears of defeat, rumors, the nature of Soviet resistance, the treatment of the ethnic Germans and religious sects, and also containing book and film reviews. Who had time for this magazine? (Probably the university-educated newer generation in the SD and the honorary higher SS officer corps!)

139 878-D, IMT, vol. 25, pp. 626–28. Survey of SS strength, June 30, 1944: *Zahlenmässige Ubersicht der Waffen SS: Dienstaltersliste der Waffen SS. Stand vom 1. 7. 1944.* T-611/rolls 1–2. SGV folder 100/EAP 161-b-12/125, T-175/roll 55. financial support of widows of SS men (1942–1945): SGV folder 567/EAP 161-b-12/117, T-175/roll 52. request for front duty of an SS-Unterscharführer (1945): BDC Biographical Records.

140 SGV folder 365/EAP 161-b-12/138, T-175/roll 58: reorganization of SS-Oberabschnitte and jurisdictions of Superior SS and Police Leaders, 1944–1945. SGV folder 830/EAP 161-b-12/49, T-175/roll 29: solitary confinement as punishment for SS officers (1944). SGV Folder 845/EAP 161-b-12/49, T-175/roll 29: admission of ethnic Germans from Poland into the SS as officers (1944).

141 Hausser, *Waffen-SS*, pp. 24–25; Neusüss-Hunkel, p. 76; Steiner, *Freiwilligen*, pp. 368–70, 376; NO 4670, NO 4671, TWC, vol. 13, pp. 328, 379–82; 654-PS, IMT, vol. 16, pp. 200–203; Eberstein testimony, IMT, vol. 20, p. 306. SGV folder 353/EAP 161-b-12/54, T-175/roll 30: *Weltanschauliche Führung*, 1943–1945. SGV folder 702/EAP 161-b-12/74, T-175/roll 35: Gemeinschaftslager für germanische und europäische SS Freiwillige, organisiert von der SS-Panzer-Division "Das Reich" (1944).

142 André Brissaud, *Canaris. Le 'petit amiral' prince de l'espionage allemand (1887–1945)* (Paris, 1970), p. 657; Duprat, *Histoire des SS*, p. 425; Klietmann, pp. 303–6, 319–43; Neusüss-Hunkel, p. 46; Steiner, *Freiwilligen*, pp. 293–94; BDC Biographical Records.

143 Heiber, *Reichsführer!* pp. 181–82, 186–87, 207–9, 251 ff. "Des Teufels Adjutant?" *Der Freiwillige* 6:6 (1961): 10–13; "Noch einmal Des Teufels Adjutant?" *Der Freiwillige* 6:11 (1961): 27. For an overview of the whole SS-and-Police complex in 1944 see *Unterrichtsmappe SS- und Polizeiwesen, 1. Oktober 1944, herausgegeben vom SS-Hauptamt,* and *Einheitsaktenplan* of the *Schriftgutverwaltung,* both in record group 1010, U.S. National Archives (author's hand copies).

144 Ackermann, pp. 105–6; Steiner, *Die Freiwilligen*, pp. 257, 310–11, 324. Affidavits of Katherine von Pfeffer, Maria Margarete Lerch, and Erich Spaarmann regarding Richard Hildebrandt's plans for an SS *gremium:* U.S. Military Tribunal Case Eight, Hildebrandt defense doc. book 1, doc. 19, 21, 42.

145 Hausser, *Waffen-SS*, p. 24. Heiber, *Reichsführer!* p. 301: Himmler scolds Superior SS and Police Leader Mazuw, December 30, 1944. Klietmann, p. 465; Milton Shulman, *Defeat in the West* (New York, 1948), p. 315; BDC Biographical Records.

146 *Hitlers Lagebesprechungen*, pp. 625 ff.; Neufeldt, pp. 31–32, 35–37; West-

phal, pp. 285–89. 645-PS, IMT, vol. 26, pp. 200–203: Thierack notes. SGV Folder 344/EAP 161-b-12/124, T-175/roll 55: SS preoccupation with retreat of German troops and German population from eastern Germany (1944–1945). SGV Folder 351/EAP 161-b-12/55, T-175/roll 30: reports about circumstances of withdrawal of German forces from western occupied territories and from western Germany (1944–1945).

147 Allen Dulles, *Germany's Underground* (New York, 1947), pp. 162–64; Hoettl, *Geheime Front*, pp. 94–97; Schellenberg, pp. 294–97, 302, 332–37.

148 "SS Bericht über den 20, Juli aus den Papieren des Obersturmbannführers Dr. Georg Kiesel," *Kristall* 2:2 (1947): 5–34; Allen Dulles, *The Secret Surrender* (New York, 1966), pp. 55–58, 80–81; Gisevius, *To the Bitter End*, pp. 582–89; Hoettl, *Geheime Front*, p. 390.

149 Hausser, *Waffen-SS*, p. 130; Lothar Rendulic, *Soldat in stürzenden Reichen* (Munich, 1965), pp. 374–75; Schellenberg, pp. 349–55. For plans for an SS underground abroad, November 1944 – March 1945, see "Auslandskommandos" (Copenhagen, Oslo, Milan, Agram, Budapest, Triest), folder EAP 161-b-12/145, T-175/roll 123.

150 Arendt, *Eichmann in Jerusalem*, pp. 42, 137–47; Kersten, pp. 345 ff., 381 ff. Himmler-Musy negotiations regarding exchanges of equipment for Jews via Switzerland (1944–1945): EAP 161-b-12/141, T-175/roll 118. Report of Obersturmbannführer Becher, August 25, 1944: SGV folder 7/EAP 161-b-12/149, T-175/roll 59.

151 Albert de Jonghe, "La lutte Himmler-Reeder pour la nomination d'un HSSPF à Bruxelles (1942–44)," *Cahiers d'histoire de la seconde guerre mondiale* 3 (October 1974), 4 (December 1976), 5 (December 1978); Kersten, pp. 203–8, 321–24, 335–38; Hans-Dietrich Loock, "Zur grossgermanischen Politik des Dritten Reiches," *VJHZ* 8 (1960): 51–63. SGV folder 192/EAP 161-b-12/19, T-175/roll 54: SS discussions with Italian administrative authorities (1942). SGV folder 212/item 22/EAP 161-b-12/136, T-175/roll 58: arrangements for a conference between Himmler and Glaise-Horstenau about Croatian policy (July 1944). SGV folder 314/EAP 161-b-12/244, T-175/roll 71/frame 2588751; and SGV folder 7/EAP 161-b-12/149, T-175/roll 59/frames 2574538–43: quarrels with Foreign Office about Hungary (1944).

152 Heiber, *Reichsführer!* pp. 295–96: Himmler scolds Superior SS and Police Leader Otto Hofmann, November 29, 1944. SGV folder 117/EAP 161-b-12/89, T-175/roll 37/frames 2547036–62: list of Supreme, Superior, and SS and Police Leaders, 1944.

153 Höhne, pp. 502, 576; Schnabel, pp. 522–24.

154 "Die Eiserne Faust," *Der Freiwillige* 7:9 (1962): 23; Hausser, *Waffen-SS*, pp. 191–92, 205–6, 268. Klose, p. 259; Steiner, *Freiwilligen*, pp. 246–47. SGV folder 00023/EAP 161-b-12/99, T-175/roll 41: *SS-Personalveränderungsblatt* (1944–1945). SGV folder 105/EAP 161-b-12/113, T-175/roll 50: transfer of navy men to Waffen-SS (1945).

155 Hoettl, *Geheime Front*, pp. 382–83; Shulman, p. 317; Steiner, *Freiwilligen*, pp. 275–89. SGV folder 100/EAP 161-b-12/90, T-175/roll 36:

training of SS officers (1944–1945). SGV folder 1273/EAP 161-b-12/47, T-175/roll 28: training of SS officers and officer replacements in special courses at *Napolas*, Adolf Hitler schools, Reich Party School Feldafing, and selected state boarding schools (*Heimschulen*), 1944–1945.

156 Hausser, *Waffen-SS*, pp. 17, 112; Klietmann, pp. 55–57; Shulman, pp. 223–26, 229, 235–39; Stein, pp. 228–33; John Toland, *Battle. The Story of the Bulge* (New York, 1959), pp. 22–31; "Weihnachten 1944: Das Regiment Der Führer vom 22. bis 27.12.1944," *Der Freiwillige* 10:12 (1964): 13. See also "Die 1. SS Panzer Division Leibstandarte Adolf Hitler im Einsatz in der Ardennenoffensive 1944," *Der Freiwillige* 11:1, 2, 3, 4 (1965).

157 Hoettl, *Geheime Front*, pp. 455–67; Rodney G. Minott, *The Fortress That Never Was. Hitler's Bavarian Stronghold* (New York, 1964); Stein, pp. 238–39.

158 Dulles, *Secret Surrender*, pp. 96 ff.; Hoettl, *Geheime Front*, pp. 97–100; Schellenberg, pp. 356–63, 402–3, 406; Westphal, pp. 280–84; "Karl Wolffs Verdienst," *Der Freiwillige* 6:8 (1961): 7–11.

## Chapter 8: Conclusion

1 Speer, *Infiltration*, pp. 23–27, 35, 48–49.

2 Bernd Wegner, "The SS as a Military Force (1933–1945)" (unpublished paper kindly supplied by the author, November 1981).

3 Gunnar C. Boehnert, "The Third Reich and the Problem of 'Social Revolution': German Officers and the SS," in *Germany in the Age of Total War*, ed. V. Berghahn and M. Kitchen (London/Totowa, N.J., 1981), pp. 203–17.

4 Kersten, pp. 304, 306, 327–28.

5 Gunnar C. Boehnert, "An Analysis of the Age and Education of the SS Führerkorps 1925–1939," *Historical Social Research/Historische Sozialforschung*, No. 12 (October 1979): 4–17.

6 Robert Koehl, "Was there an SS Officer Corps?" *Proceedings of The Citadel Symposium on Hitler and the National Socialist Era, Charleston, South Carolina, April 24–25, 1980* (in press); and Robert Koehl, "SS Officer Profiles: The Altkämpfer" (unpublished paper delivered at Western German Studies Conference, Seattle, Wash., October 10, 1981).

7 Gunnar C. Boehnert, "The Jurists in the SS Führerkorps, 1925–1939," in *Der "Führerstaat": Mythos und Realität/The "Führer State": Myth and Reality*, ed. Gerhard Hirschfeld and Lothar Kettenacker (Stuttgart, 1981), pp. 361–74.

8 Stanley G. Payne, *Fascism. Comparison and Definition* (Madison, Wis., 1980), pp. 191–212; Hannah Arendt, *The Origins of Totalitarianism* (New York, 1951), pp. 376–434.

# Bibliography

Abshagen, Karl Heinz. *Canaris. Patriot und Weltbürger.* Stuttgart: Deutsche Verlagsgesellschaft, 1950.

Abshagen, Karl Heinz. *Schuld und Verhängnis. Ein Vierteljahrhundert deutscher Geschichte in Augenzeugenberichten.* Stuttgart: Union Verlagsanstalt, 1961.

Ackermann, Josef. *Heinrich Himmler als Ideologe.* Göttingen: Musterschmidt, 1970.

Alexander, Leo. "War Crimes and their Motivation: The Sociopsychological Structure of the SS and the Criminalization of the Society." *Journal of Criminal Law and Criminology* 39 (1949):298–326.

Allen, William S. *The Nazi Seizure of Power. The Experience of a Single German Town, 1930–1935.* Chicago: Quadrangle, 1965.

Allen, William S. "The State of the Nazi *Sturmabteilung.*" Unpublished manuscript.

Almond, Gabriel A., ed. *The Struggle for Democracy in Germany.* Chapel Hill: University of North Carolina Press, 1949.

d'Alquen, Günter. *Die SS, Geschichte, Aufgabe, Organisation. Bearbeitet im Auftrage des Reichsführer SS von SS-Standartenführer Günter d'Alquen.* Schriften der Hochschule für Politik. II. Der organisatorische Aufbau des Dritten Reiches, Heft 33. Berlin: Junker und Dünnhaupt, 1939.

Anders, Karl. *Im Nürnberger Irrgarten.* Nuremberg: Nest Verlag, 1948.

*Anschriften-Verzeichnis der Schutzstaffel der NSDAP.* Berlin-Wilmersdorf: SS Führungshauptamt, Kommandoamt der Allgemeinen SS, 1944.

Arendt, Hannah. *Eichmann in Jerusalem. A Report on the Banality of Evil.* New York: Viking, 1964.

Arendt, Hannah. *The Origins of Totalitarianism.* New York: Harcourt Brace, 1951.

Aronson, Shlomo. *Reinhard Heydrich und die Frühgeschichte von Gestapo und SD.* Stuttgart: Deutsche Verlagsanstalt, 1971.

Artzt, Heinz. *Mörder in Uniform. Organisationen, die zu Vollstreckern nationalsozialistischer Verbrechen wurden.* Munich: Kindler, 1979.

Auerbach, Hellmuth. "Eine nationalsozialistische Stimme zum Wiener Putsch vom 25. Juli 1934." *Vierteljahrshefte für Zeitgeschichte* 11 (1963):201–18.

Ayçoberry, Pierre. *The Nazi Question: An Essay on the Interpretations of National Socialism (1922–1975).* New York: Pantheon, 1981.

Ball, Margaret. *Post-War German-Austrian Relations: The Anschluss Movement, 1918–1936.* Stanford: Stanford University Press, 1937.

Bayle, François. *Psychologie et Éthique du national-socialisme. Étude anthro-pologique des Dirigeants S.S.* Paris: Presses universitaires, 1953.

Baynes, Norman, ed. *The Speeches of Adolf Hitler, April 1922–August 1939.* An English translation of representative passages arranged under subjects. Issued under the auspices of the Royal Institute of International Affairs. 2 vols. London and New York: Oxford University Press, 1942.

Beck, Friedrich Alfred. *Kampf und Sieg. Geschichte der NSDAP im Gau Westfalen-Süd.* Dortmund: Westfalen-Verlag, 1938.

*Beilage Fürsorge zum Verordnungsblatt der Obersten SA-Führung.* Vol. 1 (1934).

Bennecke, Heinrich. *Hitler und die SA.* Munich and Vienna: Günter Olzog Verlag, 1962.

Bennecke, Heinrich. *Die Reichswehr und der "Röhm-Putsch."* Beiheft 2 der Zweimonatsschrift *Politische Studien.* Munich and Vienna: Günter Olzog Verlag, 1964.

Bennecke, Heinrich. *Wirtschaftliche Depression und politischer Radikalismus 1918–1938.* Munich and Vienna: Günter Olzog, 1970.

Bennett, Edward W. *Germany and the Diplomacy of the Financial Crisis, 1931.* Cambridge: Harvard University Press, 1962.

Benoist-Mechin, Jacques. *Histoire de l'Armée Allemande.* 2 vols. Paris: Albin Michel, 1938.

Berchtold, Josef. "Koburg, Symbol unseres Sieges." *Der SA-Mann,* 1. *Jahrgang, Folge* 27 (October 15, 1932).

Best, Walter. *Mit der Leibstandarte im Westen. Berichte eines SS-Kriegsberichters.* Munich: Zentral Verlag der NSDAP, 1944.

Best, Werner. *Die deutsche Polizei.* Darmstadt: L. C. Wittich, 1941.

Bierschenk, Theodor. *Die deutsche Volksgruppe in Polen, 1934–1939.* Beiheft zum Jahrbuch der Albertus Universität. Königsbert/Pr., 10; Göttinger Arbeitskreis. Veröffentlichung Nr. 124. Würzburg: Holzner, 1954.

Bilek, Bohuslav. *Fifth Column at Work.* London: Trinity Press, 1945.

Biuletyn Głównej Komisji Badania Zbrodni Hitlerowskich w Polsce. (Bulletin of the Chief Commission for the Investigation of Hitlerite Crime in Poland.) Vols. 1– . Warsaw: Wydawnictwo Prawnicze, 1946– ).

Bloch, Charles. *Die SA und die Krise des NS-Regimes 1934.* Frankfurt am Main: Suhrkamp, 1970.

Boehnert, Gunnar C. "An Analysis of the Age and Education of the SS Führerkorps 1925–1939." *Historical Social Research/Historische Sozialforschung* 12 (October 1979):4–17.

Boehnert, Gunnar C. "The Jurists in the SS Führerkorps, 1925–1939." In *Der "Führerstaat": Mythos und Realität. Studien zur Struktur und Politik des Dritten Reiches/The "Führer State": Myth and Reality. Studies in the Structure and Politics of the Third Reich,* edited by Gerhard Hirschfeld and Lothar Kettenacker. Stuttgart: Klett-Cotta, 1981. Pp. 361–74.

Boehnert, Gunnar C. "The Third Reich and the Problem of 'Social Revolution': German Officers and the SS." In *Germany in the Age of Total War,* edited by V. Berghahn and M. Kitchen. London: Croom Helm; Totowa, N.J.: Barnes and Noble, 1981. Pp. 203–17.

Bollmus, Reinhard. *Das Amt Rosenberg und seine Gegner; Studien zum Macht-kampf im nationalsozialistischen Herrschaftssystem.* Stuttgart: Deutsche Ver-lagsanstalt, 1970.

Bracher, Karl Dietrich. *Die Auflösung der Weimarer Republik. Eine Studie zum Problem des Machtverfalls in der Demokratie.* Schriftenreihe des Insti-tuts für Politische Wissenschaft, 4. 3rd edition. Villingen/Schwarzwald: Ring Verlag, 1960.

Bracher, Karl Dietrich; Sauer, Wolfgang; and Schulz, Gerhard. *Die national-sozialistische Machtergreifung, Studien zur Errichtung des totalitären Herr-schaftssystems in Deutschland, 1933/34.* Cologne and Opladen: Westdeutscher Verlag, 1960.

Braham, Randolph L. *The Destruction of Hungarian Jewry. A Documentary Account.* 2 vols. New York: Pro Arte, 1963.

Bramsted, Ernest Kohn. *Dictatorship and Political Police. The Technique of Control by Fear.* International Library of Sociology and Social Reconstruc-tion. London: Kegan Paul, Trench Trubner, 1945.

"Die Brigade Kaminski." *Der Freiwillige* 9:8 (1964):13–16.

Brissaud, André. *Canaris. Le 'petit amiral' prince de l'espionage allemand (1887–1945).* Paris: Librairie academique Perrin, 1970.

Bronnen, Arnolt. *Rossbach.* Berlin: Rowohlt, 1930.

Broszat, Martin. "Die Anfänge der Berliner NSDAP 1926/27." *Vierteljahrshefte für Zeitgeschichte* 8 (1960):85–118.

Broszat, Martin, ed. *Kommandant in Auschwitz. Autobiographische Aufzeich-nungen von Rudolf Hoess.* Eingeleitet und kommentiert von Martin Broszat. Quellen und Darstellungen zur Zeitgeschichte, 5. Stuttgart: Deutsche Verlags-anstalt, 1958.

Broszat, Martin. *Nationalsozialistische Polenpolitik 1939–1945.* Schriftenreihe der Vierteljahrshefte für Zeitgeschichte, 2. Stuttgart: Deutsche Verlagsgesell-schaft, 1961.

Broszat, Martin. "Das Sudetendeutsche Freikorps." *Vierteljahrshefte für Zeitge-schichte* 9 (1961):30–49.

Browder, George Clark. "SIPO and SD, 1931–1940. The Formation of an Instru-ment of Power." Ph.D. dissertation, University of Wisconsin-Madison, 1968.

Brown, MacAlister. "The Third Reich's Mobilization of the German Fifth Col-umn in Eastern Europe." *Journal of Central European Affairs* 19 (1959):128–48.

Browning, Christopher R. *The Final Solution and the German Foreign Office.* New York: Holmes and Meier, 1978.

Buchheim, Hans. "Die Aufnahme von Polizeiangehörigen in die SS und die An-gleichung ihrer SS-Dienstgrade an ihre Beamtenränge (Dienstgradangleich-ung) in der Zeit des Dritten Reichs." Munich: Institut für Zeitgeschichte, 1960. Mimeographed.

Buchheim, Hans. *Glaubenskrise im Dritten Reich.* Stuttgart: Deutsche Verlags-anstalt, 1953.

Buchheim, Hans. "Die Höheren SS- und Polizeiführer." *Vierteljahrshefte für Zeitgeschichte* 11 (1963):362–91.

Buchheim, Hans. "Das Problem des Befehlsnotstandes bei den vom nationalso-zialistischen Regime befohlenen Verbrechen in historischer Sicht." Gutachten von Dr. Hans Buchheim, June 5, 1964. Mimeographed.

Buchheim, Hans. "Die Rolle der SS in der Entwicklung der NS-Herrschaft." *Colloquium. Eine Deutsche Studentenzeitschrift* 11:3 (1957):14–15; 11:4 (1957): 16–17.

Buchheim, Hans. "Die SS in der Verfassung des Dritten Reiches." *Vierteljahrshefte für Zeitgeschichte* 3 (1955):127–57.

Buchheim, Hans. *SS und Polizei im NS-Staat.* Staatspolitische Schriftenreihe. Duisdorf bei Bonn: Studiengesellschaft für Zeitprobleme, 1964.

Buchheim, Hans; Broszat, Martin; Jacobsen, Hans-Adolf; and Krausnick, Helmut. *Anatomie des SS-Staats.* 2 vols. Gutachten des Instituts für Zeitgeschichte. Olten and Freiburg im Breisgau: Walter-Verlag, 1965.

Bullock, Alan. *Hitler. A Study in Tyranny.* New York: Harpers, 1952.

Burckhardt, Carl J. *Meine Danziger Mission, 1937–1939.* Munich: Callway, 1960.

Campbell, Bruce B. "Waffen-SS Voluntary Military Units in Estonia, Croatia and the Polish Ukraine, 1942–1945." M.A. thesis, University of Wisconsin-Madison, 1978.

Cassel, E. J. "Geist, Kampf und Aufgabe der SS. Des Führers Schwarzes Korps. Bürge und Hüter der inneren Sicherheit des Reiches Adolf Hitlers." *NSK Wahlsonderdienst*, April 5, 1938, Folge 13, Blätter 4–7. T-580/roll 87/folder 425.

Castellan, Georges. *Le Réarmement clandestin du Reich 1930–1935.* Paris: Plon, 1954.

Der Chef der SIPO und SD. *Der Rassegedanke und seine gesetzliche Gestaltung.* Schriften für politische und weltanschauliche Erziehung der Sicherheitspolizei und des SD. Ausgearbeitet von SS-Hauptsturmführer Evert, RSHA, Gruppe I-B. Berlin: n.d.

Child, Clifton J. "The Political Structure of Hitler's Europe: Administration." In *Survey of International Affairs, 1939–1946*, vol. 4, *Hitler's Europe*, edited by Arnold Toynbee and Veronica M. Toynbee for the Royal Institute of International Affairs. London: Oxford University Press, 1954. Pp. 113–25.

Child, Clifton J. "The SS and the Germanic Ideal." In *Survey of International Affairs, 1939–1946* , vol. 4, *Hitler's Europe*, edited by Arnold Toynbee and Veronica M. Toynbee for the Royal Institute of International Affairs. London: Oxford University Press, 1954. Pp. 75–80.

Crankshaw, Edward. *The Gestapo, Instrument of Tyranny.* New York: Viking Press, 1956.

Cygański, Mirosław. *SS w polityce zagranicznej III. Rzeszy w latach 1934–1945.* (SS in the foreign policy of the Third Reich in the years 1935–1945.) Warsaw and Wrocław: Państwowe Wydawnictwo Naukowe, 1975.

Czech-Jochberg, Erich. *Hitler. Eine Deutsche Bewegung.* Oldenburg: Stalling Verlag, 1930.

*Daily Herald* (London). 1934.

*Daily Mail* (London). December 7, 1934.

*Daily Telegraph* (London). July 9, 1934.

Dallin, Alexander. *German Rule in Russia 1941–1945. A Study of Occupation Policies.* London and New York: St. Martin's Press, 1957.

Daluege, Kurt. *Nationalsozialistischer Kampf gegen das Verbrechertum.* Unter Mitarbeit von Regierungsdirektor Liebermann von Sonnenberg. Munich: Zentralverlag der NSDAP, 1936.

Danner, Lothar. *Ordnungspolizei Hamburg. Betrachtungen zu ihrer Geschichte 1918 bis 1933.* Hamburg: Verlag Deutsche Polizei, 1958.

Darré, Richard Walther. *Das Bauerntum als Lebensquelle der nordischen Rasse.* Munich: J. F. Lehmann, 1929.

Darré, Richard Walther. *Erkenntnisse und Werden. Aufsätze aus der Zeit vor der Machtergreifung.* Goslar: Verlag Blut und Boden, 1940.

Darré, Richard Walther. *Neuadel aus Blut und Boden.* Munich: J. F. Lehmann, 1930.

Darré, Richard Walther. *Ziel und Weg der Nationalsozialistischen Agrarpolitik. Rede vor dem diplomatischen Korps und der ausländischen Presse am 17. April 1934 bei einem Empfangsabend des Aussenpolitischen Amtes der NSDAP.* Hier spricht das Neue Deutschland, Heft 5. Munich: Eher, 1934.

Delarue, Jacques. *Histoire de la Gestapo.* Paris: Fayard, 1962.

Delmer, Sefton. *Trail Sinister.* London: Secker & Warburg, 1961.

"Denkschrift. Die Waffen-SS und das Gesetz gemäss Artikel 131 GG." *Der Freiwillige* 4:4 (1959):5–41.

Denne, Ludwig. *Das Danzig Problem in der deutschen Aussenpolitik, 1934–1939.* Bonn: Ludwig Röhrscheid, 1959.

Deresiewicz, Janusz. *Okupacja niemiecka na ziemiach polskich właczonych do Rzeszy (1939–1945).* (German occupation of Polish lands annexed to the Reich 1939–1945.) Badania nad okupacja niemiecką w Polsce, 4. Poznań: Instytut Zachodni, 1950.

Deschner, Günther. *Reinhard Heydrich. Statthalter der totalen Macht. Biographie.* Esslingen: Bechtle, 1977.

Deuerlein, Ernst, ed. *Der Hitlerputsch. Bayerische Dokumente zum 9. Nov. 1923.* Stuttgart: Deutsche Verlagsanstalt, 1962.

Deuerlein, Ernst. "Hitlers Eintritt in die Politik und die Reichswehr." (Dokumentation). *Vierteljahrshefte für Zeitgeschichte* 7 (1959):177–227.

*Deutsche Allgemeine Zeitung* (Berlin). 1933–1934; December 28, 1940.

*Deutsche Freiheit* (Saarbrücken). 1934.

*Das deutsche Führerlexikon.* Berlin: O. Stollberg, 1934. T-611/rolls 48–49.

*Deutsche Volksgruppe in Rumänien. Jahrbuch 1944.* Hermannstadt: Amt für Presse und Propaganda, 1944.

Dicks, Henry V. *Licensed Mass Murder. A Socio-Psychological Study of Some SS Killers.* New York: Basic Books, 1972.

Diehl-Thiede, Peter. *Partei und Staat im Dritten Reich; Untersuchungen zum Verhältnis von NSDAP und allgemeiner innerer Staatsverwaltung 1933–1945.* Munich: Beck, 1969.

Diels, Rudolf. *Lucifer ante Portas . . . es spricht der erste Chef der Gestapo . . .* Zurich: Interverlag, 1949.

*Dienstaltersliste der Schutzstaffel der NSDAP. Stand vom 1.Oktober 1934.* Bearbeitet von der Personalabteilung des Reichsführers-SS (München). T-175/roll 204/frames 2673853–95.

*Dienstaltersliste der Schutzstaffel der NSDAP. Stand vom 1.Juli 1935.* Bearbeitet von der Personalkanzlei des Reichsführers-SS (Berlin, 1935). T-175/roll 204/ frames 2673896–75.

*Dienstaltersliste der Schutzstaffel der NSDAP. Stand vom 1.Dezember 1936.* Bearbeitet von der Personalkanzlei des Reichsführers-SS (Berlin, 1936). T-175/ roll 204/frames 2673976–4125.

*Dienstaltersliste der Schutzstaffel der NSDAP. Stand vom 1.Dezember 1937.* Bearbeitet von der Personalkanzlei des Reichsführers-SS (Berlin, 1937). T-175/ roll 204/frames 2674126–327.

*Dienstalterliste der Schutzstaffel der NSDAP. Stand vom 1.Dezember 1938.* Bearbeitet von der Personalkanzlei des Reichsfjhrers-SS (Berlin, 1938). T-175/ roll 205/frames 2674328–35, 4041939–2198.

*Dienstaltersliste der Schutzstaffel der NSDAP. (SS-Oberstgruppenführer – SS-Standartenführer.) Stand vom 9.November 1944.* Herausgegeben vom SS-Personalhauptamt (Berlin: Reichsdruckerei, 1944). T-175/roll 205/frames 4042199–231.

*Dienstvorschrift für die SA der NSDAP (SADV).* Teil I. Diessen vor München: J. C. Huber, 30.Mai, 1931.

*Dienstvorschrift für die SA der NSDAP (SADV).* 2 vols. Diessen vor München: J. C. Huber, 1.Oktober, 1932.

Dmytryshin, Basil. "The Nazis and the SS Volunteer Division 'Galicia.'" *American Slavic and East European Review* 15 (1956):1–10.

Drage, Charles. *The Amiable Prussian.* London: Blond, 1958.

Duesterberg, Theodor. *Der Stahlhelm und Hitler.* Wolfenbüttel and Hannover: Wolfenbütteler Verlagsanstalt, 1949.

Duff, Katherine. "Danzig." In *Survey of International Affairs, 1939–1946,* vol. 10, *The Eve of War, 1939,* edited by Arnold Toynbee and Veronica M. Toynbee for the Royal Institute of International Affairs. London: Oxford University Press, 1958. Pp. 384–403.

Dulles, Allen Welsh. *Germany's Underground.* New York: Macmillan, 1947.

Dulles, Allen Welsh. *The Secret Surrender.* New York: Harper & Row, 1966.

Duprat, François. *Les Campagnes de la Waffen SS.* Paris: Les Sept Couleurs, 1973.

Duprat, François. *Histoire des SS.* Paris: Les Sept Couleurs, 1968.

Eichmann, Adolf. "Papers relating to Adolph Eichmann compiled by the Wiener Library." London: Micro-Methods, 1961.

Eichstädt, Ulrich. *Von Dollfuss zu Hitler; Geschichte des Anschlusses Österreichs, 1933–1938.* Wiesbaden: F. Steiner, 1955.

"Ein reines Soldatenrechtsproblem." *Der Freiwillige* 10:2 (1964):6–7.

"Die Eiserne Faust." *Der Freiwillige* 7:9 (1962):23.

Ellsworth, Faris. "Take-off Point for the National Socialist Party: The Landtag Election in Baden, 1929." *Central European History* 8 (June 1975):140–71.

Engelbrechten, J. K. von. *Eine braune Armee ensteht. Die Geschichte der Berlin-Brandenburger SA.* Munich: Zentralverlag der NSDAP, 1937.

Erb, Herbert, and von Grote, Hans-Henning. *Konstantin Hierl. Der Mann und sein Werk*. Munich: F. Eher Nachfolger, 1939.

Espe, Walter M. *Das Buch der NSDAP*. Berlin: Schönfelds, 1933.

Eyck, Erich. *Geschichte der Weimarer Republik*. 2 vols. Erlenbach-Zürich: Reutsch, 1954–56.

Eydt, Alfred. "Der Sinn der Heiratsgenehmigung bei der SS." *Nationalsozialistische Monatshefte* 38 (May 1933).

Fest, Joachim C. *Das Gesicht des Dritten Reiches. Profile einer totalitären Herrschaft*. Munich: Piper, 1963.

Fishman, Sterling. "The Rise of Hitler as a Beer Hall Orator." *The Review of Politics* 26 (1964): 244–56.

Foertsch, Hermann. *Schuld und Verhängnis. Die Fritsch-Krise im Frühjahr 1938 als Wendepunkt in der Geschichte der nationalsozialistischen Zeit*. Stuttgart: Deutsche Verlagsanstalt, 1951.

Föhler-Hauke, Gustav. "Die Volksgruppe und Deutsche Arbeit in Böhmen, Mähren und der Slowakei." *Deutsche Volksforschung in Böhmen und Mähren* (Brünn) 1 (Juni 1939):1–17.

François-Poncet, André. *The Fateful Years. Memoirs of a French Ambassador in Berlin, 1931–1938*. Translated by Jacques LeClercq. New York: Harcourt, Brace, 1949.

Frank, Hans. *Im Angesicht des Galgens. Deutung Hitlers und seiner Zeit auf Grund eigener Erlebnisse und Erkenntnisse*. München-Gräfelfing: F. A. Beck, 1953.

Frank, Hans; Himmler, Heinrich; Best, Werner; and Höhn, Reinhard. *Grundfragen der deutschen Polizei. Bericht über die konstituierende Sitzung des Ausschusses für deutsches Recht am 11.10.1936*. Hamburg: Akademie für Deutsches Recht, 1937.

Frank, Karl Hermann. "Freiwilliger Selbstschutz und SS." *Böhmen und Mähren* 2 (1941).

Frank, Robert Henry. "Hitler and the National-Socialist Coalition 1924–1932." Ph.D. dissertation, Johns Hopkins University, 1969.

*Frankfurter Allgemeine Zeitung*. June–July, 1934; January 15, 16, 1939.

Franz-Willing, Georg. *Ursprung der Hitlerbewegung. 1919–1922*. Preussisch Oldendorf: K. W. Schütz, 1974.

*Der Freiwillige für Einigkeit und Recht und Freiheit. Wikingruf – Kameradschaftsblatt der HIAG*, 3- (1958-). Organ of Hilfgemeinschaft ehemaliger Angehöriger der Waffen SS (HIAG).

Frischauer, Willi. *Himmler, the Evil Genius of the Third Reich*. London: Odhams Press, 1953.

Gaigalaité, Aldona. "Klaipédos Krašto Užgrobimas 1939 Metais" (The Seizure of the Memel Territory in 1939), *Lietuvos TSR Mokslu Akademijos Darbai*, Serija A, 2:7 (1959):105–30.

Gebhardt, [Standartenführer] Carl, and Rudhardt, [Obersturmführer] ——. "Die SA, ihre Entwicklung und Gliederung unter besonderer Berücksichtigung ihrer parteizweckmässigen und staatspolitischen Aufgabe als Glaubensträger" (Berlin, 1935). Mimeographed. T-580/roll 85/folder 402.

Georg, Enno. *Die wirtschaftlichen Unternehmungen der SS*. Schriftenreihe der

Vierteljahrshefte für Zeitgeschichte, 7. Stuttgart: Deutsche Verlagsanstalt, 1963.

Germany. *Ministerialblatt des Reichs- und Preussischen Ministerium des Innern.* Vols. 1–3 (1936–1938).

Germany. *Reichsgesetzblatt 1933* (Teil I); *1936* (Teil I); *1937* (Teil I); *1938* (Teil I); *1939* (Teil I); *1940* (Teil I).

Germany. Statistisches Reichsamt. *Statistisches Jahrbuch für das Deutsche Reich.* Teil II. 51.–52.Jahrgang, 1932–1933. Berlin, 1933.

Gisevius, Hans Bernd. *Adolf Hitler: Versuch einer Deutung.* Munich: Rütten und Loening, 1963.

Gisevius, Hans Bernd. *To the Bitter End.* Boston: Houghton Mifflin, 1947.

Główna Komisja Badania Zbrodni niemieckich w Polsce. *German Crimes in Poland,* 1–. Warsaw: Wydawnictwo prawnice, 1946–.

Główna Komisja Badania Zbrodni Hitlerowskitch w Polsce. *Oświeçim-Brzezinka Concentration Camp.* Warsaw: Wydawnictwo prawnice, 1961.

Główna Komisja Badania Zbrodni Hitlerowskich w Polsce. *Wspomnienia Rudolfa Hoessa. Komendanta obozu oswiecimskiego.* (Memoirs of Rudolf Hoess, Kommandant of Auschwitz [concentration] Camp.) Warsaw: Wydawnictwo prawnicze, 1956.

Goebbels, Joseph. *The Goebbels Diaries, 1942–1943.* Garden City, N.Y.: Doubleday, 1948.

Goebbels, Joseph. *Kampf um Berlin.* Munich: F. Eher, 1934.

Goebbels, Joseph. *Tagebuch von Joseph Goebbels 1925/26.* Mit weiteren Dokumenten hrsg. von Helmut Heiber. Schriftenreihe der Vierteljahrshefte für Zeitgeschichte, 1. Stuttgart: Deutsche Verlagsanstalt, 1960.

Goebbels, Joseph. *Vom Kaiserhof zur Reichskanzlei.* Munich: Eher, 1934.

Gordon, Harold J. *Hitler and the Beer Hall Putsch.* Princeton: Princeton University Press, 1972.

Gordon, Harold J. *The Reichswehr and the German Republic.* Princeton: Princeton University Press, 1957.

Görlitz, Walter, and Quint, Herbert A. *Adolf Hitler. Eine Biographie.* Stuttgart: Steingruben-Verlag, 1952.

Goudsmit, Samuel A. *Alsos.* New York: H. Schuman, 1947.

Gradmann, Werner. "Die Erfassung der Umsiedler." *Zeitschrift für Politik* 33 (1942):346–51.

Great Britain. Foreign Office. *Documents on British Foreign Policy, 1919–1939.* Edited by E. L. Woodward and Rohan Butler. Series 2. 18 vols. London: H.M. Stationery Office, 1946–.

Great Britain. Foreign Office and Ministry of Economic Welfare. *Germany Basic Handbook.* Vol. 1 (looseleaf), part 3, "Occupied Europe." London: H.M.S.O., 1944.

Greiner, Helmuth. *Die oberste Wehrmachtführung 1939–1943.* Wiesbaden: Limes, 1951.

*Der Grossdeutsche Reichstag 1938, IV. Wahlperiode.* Berlin: R. von Deckers Verlag G. Schenck, 1938. T-611/roll 48.

Grunberger, Richard. "Lebensborn. Himmler's Selective Breeding Establishment." *Wiener Library Bulletin* 16 (1962):52–53.

Guderian, Heinz. *Erinnerungen eines Soldaten*. Heidelberg: K. Vowinckel, 1951.

Gumbel, Emil Julius. *Verschwörer. Beiträge zur Geschichte und Soziologie der deutschen nationalistischen Geheimbünde seit 1918*. Vienna: Malik, 1924.

Gumkowski, Janusz, and Leszczyński, Kazimierz. *Poland under Nazi Occupation*. Warsaw: Polonia Publishing House, 1961.

Haag, John. "National Socialism in Action: The RKFDV and the Alvensleben-Schönborn Estate Case." *The Historian* 26 (February 1964):244–66.

Hagen, Hans Wilhelm. *Zwischen Eid und Befehl. Tatzeugenbericht von den Ereignissen am 20.Juli 1944 in Berlin und "Wolfsschanze."* Munich: Türmer Verlag, 1958.

Haidn, Carl, and Fischer, L., eds. *Das Recht der NSDAP. Vorschriften-Sammlung mit Anmerkungen, Verweisungen und Sachregister*. Munich: Zentralverlag der NSDAP, 1937.

*Hakenkreuzbanner* (Schweiningen). March 9, 1933.

*Halbmast. Das Heldenbuch der SA und SS*. Folge 1. Berlin: Braune Bücher, 1932.

Halder, Franz. *Kriegstagebuch. Tägliche Aufzeichnungen des Chefs des Generalstabs des Heeres 1939–1942*. 3 vols. Arbeitskreis für Wehrforschung, Stuttgart. Stuttgart: W. Kohlhammer, 1962–1964.

Hale, Oron. "Gottfried Feder Calls Hitler to Order." *Journal of Modern History* 30 (1958):358–62.

Hallgarten, George Wolfgang Felix. *Hitler, Reichswehr und Industrie; zur Geschichte der Jahre 1918–1933*. Frankfurt am Main: Europäische Verlagsanstalt, 1954.

Hambrecht, Rainer. *Der Aufstieg der NSDAP in Mittel- und Oberfranken (1925–1933)*. Nürnberger Werkstücke zur Stadt- und Landesgeschichte Schriftenreihe des Stadtarchivs Nürnberg, 17. Nuremberg: Stadtarchiv, 1976.

*Hamburger Fremdenblatt*. June 16, 1941.

*Hamburger Illustrierte*. 1933.

Hanfstaengl, Ernst F. S. *Hitler. The Missing Years*. London: Eyre and Spottiswood, 1957.

Harzer, Walter. "Der Feldzug der 18 Tage." *Der Freiwillige* 10:8 (1964):9–13.

Hassell, Ulrich von. *Vom anderen Deutschland*. Zurich: Atlantis, 1946.

*Haushaltsplanung der Schutzstaffel der NSDAP für das Rechnungsjahr 1937*. Berlin: 1936. T-175/roll 205/frames 4042363–92.

Hausser, Paul. *Soldaten wie andere auch. Der Weg der Waffen-SS*. Osnabrück: Munin, 1966.

Hausser, Paul. *Waffen-SS im Einsatz*. Göttingen: Plesse, 1953.

Heberle, Rudolf. *Landbevölkerung und Nationalsozialismus. Eine soziologische Untersuchung der politischen Willensbildung in Schleswig-Holstein 1918 bis 1932*. Schriftenriehe der Vierteljahrshefte für Zeitgeschichte, 6. Stuttgart: Deutsche Verlagsanstalt, 1963.

Heiber, Helmut. "Aus den Akten des Gauleiters Kube." *Vierteljahrshefte für Zeitgeschichte* 6 (1956):67–92.

Heiber, Helmut. "Der Generalplan Ost" (Dokumentation). *Vierteljahrshefte für Zeitgeschichte* 6 (1958):281–325.

Heiber, Helmut, ed. *Reichsführer! Briefe an und von Himmler*. Stuttgart: Deutsche Verlagsanstalt, 1968.

Heiden, Konrad. *Adolf Hitler. Eine Biographie*. 2 vols. Zurich: Europa, 1936–1937.

Heiden, Konrad. *A History of National Socialism*. New York: Knopf, 1935.

Heiden, Konrad. *Der Führer*. Boston: Houghton-Mifflin, 1944.

Heike, Wolf-Dietrich. *Sie wollten die Freiheit. Die Geschichte der ukrainischen Division 1943–1945*. Dorheim H.: Podzun Verlag, n.d.

Herzog, Robert. *Die Volksdeutschen in der Waffen-SS*. Studien des Instituts für Besatzungsfragen in Tübingen zu den deutschen Besetzungen im 2. Weltkrieg, Nr. 5. Tübingen: Institut für Besatzungsfragen, 1955.

Heydrich, Reinhard. *Die Wandlungen unseres Kampfes*. Aus dem Schwarzen Korps, Jahrgang 1, 1935. Munich: Eher, 1935.

Hilberg, Raul. *The Destruction of the European Jews*. Chicago: Quadrangle, 1961.

Hirsch, Kurt. *SS gestern, heute und . . .* Darmstadt: Progress, 1960.

Hitler, Adolf. *Mein Kampf*. Zentralverlag der NSDAP. Munich: Franz Eher Nachfolger, 1939.

Hitler, Adolf. *Secret Conversations. 1941–1944*. New York: Farrar, Straus and Young, 1953.

Hitler, Adolf. *Tischgespräche im Führerhauptquartier, 1941–42*. Im Auftrage des Deutschen Instituts für Geschichte der Nationalsozialistischen Zeit geordnet, eingeleitet und veröffentlicht von Gerhard Ritter. Edited by Henry Picker. Bonn: Athenäum, 1951.

*Hitlers Lagebesprechungen. Die Protokollfragmente seiner militärischen Konferenzen 1942–1945*. Edited by Helmut Hieber. Quellen und Darstellungen zur Zeitgeschichte, 10. Stuttgart: Deutsche Verlagsanstalt, 1962.

*The Hitler Trial before the People's Court in Munich*. Translated by H. Francis Freniere, Lucie Karcic, and Philip Fandek. 3 vols. Arlington, Va.: University Publications of America, 1976.

Hoegner, Wilhelm. *Der schwierige Aussenseiter*. Munich: Isar, 1959.

Hoegner, Wilhelm. *Die verratene Republik*. Munich: Isar, 1958.

Hoess, Rudolf. *Kommandant in Auschwitz*. Quellen und Darstellungen zur Zeitgeschichte, 5. Stuttgart: Deutsche Verlagsanstalt, 1958.

Hoettl, Wilhelm [Walter Hagen]. *Die geheime Front, Organisation, Personen und Aktionen des deutschen Geheimdienstes*. Linz and Vienna: Nibelungen, 1950.

Hoettl, Wilhelm. *Hitler's Paper Weapon*. London: Hart-Davis, 1955.

Hoffmann, Heinrich. *Das braune Heer. 100 Bilddokumente: Leben, Kampf, und Sieg der SA und SS*. Berlin: "Zeitgeschichte," 1933.

Hoffmann, Heinrich. *Hitler Was My Friend*. London: Burk, 1955.

Hofmann, Hanns Hubert. *Der Hitler-Putsch; Krisenjahre deutscher Geschichte, 1920–24*. Munich: Nymphenburger Verlagshandlung, 1961.

Hohenstein, Alexander [pseud.]. *Wartheländisches Tagebuch aus den Jahren 1941/42*. Quellen und Darstellungen zur Zeitgeschichte, 8. Stuttgart: Deutsche Verlagsanstalt, 1961.

Höhne, Heinz. *Der Orden unter dem Totenkopf. Die Geschichte der SS.* Gütersloh: Sigbert Mohn, 1967.

Höhne, Heinz. *The Order of the Death's Head. The Story of Hitler's SS.* London: Secker and Warburg, 1969.

Horn, Wolfgang. *Führerideologie und Parteiorganisation in der NSDAP (1919–1933). Geschichtliche Studien zu Politik und Gesellschaft, 3.* Düsseldorf: Droste, 1972.

Hossbach, Friedrich. *Zwischen Wehrmacht und Hitler 1934–1939.* Wolfenbüttel and Hannover: Wolfenbütteler Verlagsanstalt, 1949.

Howell, Edgar M. *The Soviet Partisan Movement 1941–1944.* Washington, D.C.: Government Printing Office, 1956.

Husemann, Friedrich. *Die guten Glaubens waren. Die Geschichte der SS-Polizei-Division.* 2 vols. Osnabrück: Munin, 1971–1973.

Hüttenberger, Peter. *Die Gauleiter. Studien zum Wandel des Machtgefüges in der NSDAP.* Schriften der Vierteljahrshefte für Zeitgeschichte, 19. Stuttgart: Deutsche Verlagsanstalt, 1969.

*Illustrierte Beobachter* (Munich). Nr. 21 (1936).

Institut für Zeitgeschichte. *Gutachten des Instituts für Zeitgeschichte.* Veröffentlichungen des Instituts für Zeitgeschichte. Munich: Selbstverlag des Instituts für Zeitgeschichte, 1958.

International Military Tribunal. *Trial of the Major War Criminals before the International Military Tribunal. Nuremberg 14 November 1945 – 1 October 1946.* 42 vols. Nuremberg, 1947–1948.

Jacobsen, Hans-Adolf, and Jochmann, Werner, eds. *Ausgewählte Dokumente zur Geschichte des Nationalsozialismus 1933–1945.* Arbeitsblätter für politische und soziale Bildung. 2 vols. Looseleaf. Bielefeld: Neue Gesellschaft, 1961.

Janowicz, Zbigniew. *Ustrój administracyjny ziem polskich wcielonych do Rzeszy Niemieckiej 1939–1945.* (Administrative structure of Polish lands annexed to the German Reich 1939–1945.) Badania nad okupacja niemiecka w Polsce, 5. Poznań: Instytut Zachódni, 1951.

Jastrzębowski, Wacław. *Gospodarka niemecka w Polsce. 1939–1944.* (German Rule in Poland.) Warsaw: Społdzielna wydawnicza "Czytelnik," 1946.

de Jong, Louis. *The German Fifth Column in the Second World War.* Chicago: University of Chicago Press, 1956.

de Jonghe, Albert. "L'Establissement d'une administration civile en Belgique et dans le Nord de la France." *Cahiers d'histoire de la seconde guerre mondiale* 1 (Août 1970):67–129.

de Jonghe, Albert. "La lutte Himmler-Reeder pour la nomination d'un HSSPF à Bruxelles (1942–44)." *Cahiers d'histoire de la seconde guerre mondiale* 3 (October 1974), 4 (December 1976), 5 (December 1978).

Jünger, Ernst. *Werke.* 10 vols. Stuttgart: Ernst Klett, 1960.

Kallenbach, Hans. *Mit Adolf Hitler auf Festung Landsberg.* Munich: Kress & Hornung, 1939.

Kamenetsky, Ihor. *Secret Nazi Plans for Eastern Europe. A Study of Lebensraum Policies.* New York: Bookman, 1961.

Kanis, Kurt, comp. *Waffen-SS im Bild.* Text und Gestaltung: Plesse Verlag. Kurt

Kanis und Angehörige der ehemaligen Waffen-SS. 2nd ed. Göttingen: Plesse, 1957.

Kanzler, Rudolf. *Bayerns Kampf gegen den Bolschewismus; Geschichte der Bayerischen Einwohnerwehr.* Munich: Parcus, 1931.

"Karl Wolffs Verdienst." *Der Freiwillige* 6:8 (1961):7–11.

Kater, Michael H. *Das Ahnenerbe der SS 1935–1945. Ein Beitrag zur Kulturpolitik des Dritten Reiches.* Stuttgart: Deutsche Verlagsanstalt, 1974.

Kater, Michael H. "Zur Soziographie der frühen NSDAP." *Vierteljahrshefte für Zeitgeschichte* 19 (April 1971):124–59.

Kater, Michael H. "Zum gegenseitigen Verhältnis von SA und SS in der Sozialgeschichte des Nationalsozialismus von 1925 bis 1939." *Vierteljahrschrift für Sozial- und Wirtschaftsgeschichte* 62:3 (1975):339–79.

Kaufmann, Walter. *Monarchism in the Weimar Republic.* New York: Bookman, 1953.

Kautsky, Benedikt. *Teufel und Verdammte. Erfahrungen und Erkenntnisse aus Sieben Jahren in deutschen Konzentrationslagern.* Zurich: Büchergilde Gutenberg, 1946.

Kempner, Robert Max Wasilii. *Blueprint for the Nazi Underground as Revealed in Confidential German Police Reports.* Lansdowne, Pa.: privately published, 1943.

Kempner, Robert Max Wasilii. *SS im Kreuzverhör.* Munich: Rütten & Loening, 1964.

Kennedy, Robert M. *The German Campaign in Poland (1939).* U.S. Department of the Army Pamphlet No. 20-255. Washington, D.C.: 1956.

Kersten, Felix. *Totenkopf und Treue. Heinrich Himmler ohne Uniform.* Aus den Tagebuchblättern des finnischen Medizinalrats. Hamburg: Robert Möhlich, [1952].

Killinger, Manfred von. *Die SA in Wort und Bild.* Leipzig: R. Kittler, 1933.

Kleist, Peter. *Zwischen Hitler und Stalin. Aufzeichnungen.* Bonn: Athenäum, 1950.

Klietmann, K.-G. *Die Waffen-SS. Eine Dokumentation.* Osnabrück: "Der Freiwillige," 1965.

Klose, Werner. *Generation im Gleichschritt. Ein Dokumentarbericht.* Hamburg and Oldenburg: Gerhard Stalling, 1964.

Kluke, Paul. "Nationalsozialistische Europaideologie." *Vierteljahrshefte für Zeitgeschichte* 3 (1955):240–75.

Knoebel, E. E. "Racial Illusion and Military Necessity: A Study of SS Political and Manpower Objectives in Occupied Belgium." Ph.D. dissertation, University of Colorado, 1965.

Koch, Karl. *Männer im Braunhemd.* Berlin: Herbert Stubenrauch Verlagsbuchhandlung, 1936.

Koehl, Robert L. "Heinrich the Great." *History Today* 7:3 (1957):147–53.

Koehl, Robert L. *RKFDY: German Resettlement and Population Policy 1939–1945.* Cambridge, Mass.: Harvard University Press, 1957.

Koehl, Robert L. "SS Officer Profiles: The Altkämpfer." Unpublished paper delivered at Western German Studies Conference, Seattle, Washington, October 10, 1981.

Koehl, Robert L. "Was there an SS Officer Corps?" *Proceedings of the Citadel Symposium on Hitler and the National Socialist Era, Charleston, South Carolina, April 24–25, 1980.*

Kogon, Eugen. *Der SS-Staat. Das System der deutschen Konzentrations-Lager.* Munich: Karl Alber, 1946.

Komitee der antifaschistischen Widerstandskämpfer in der Deutschen Demokratischen Republik. *SS im Einsatz. Eine Dokumentation über die Verbrechen der SS.* Berlin: Kongress, 1957.

Körbel, Willi. *In der SA wächst der kämpferische Künstler.* N.p.: n.d. Pamphlet deposited in Wiener Library, London.

Kordt, Erich. *Wahn und Wirklichkeit. Die Aussenpolitik des Dritten Reiches. Versuch einer Darstellung.* 2. Aufl. Stuttgart: Union Verlagsgesellschaft, 1948.

Krätschmer, Ernst-Günther. *Die Ritterkreuzträger der Waffen-SS.* Göttingen: Plesse, 1957.

Krausnick, Helmut. "Der 30. Juni. Bedeutung, Hintergründe, Verlauf." *Aus Politik und Zeitgeschichte. Beilage zu Das Parlament* 25 (June 30, 1954):318–22.

Krausnick, Helmut. "Hitler und die Morde in Polen. Ein Beitrag zum Konflikt zwischen Heer und SS um die Verwaltung der besetzten Gebiete." *Vierteljahrshefte für Zeitgeschichte* 11 (1964):196–209.

Krebs, Albert. *Tendenzen und Gestalten der NSDAP. Erinnerungen an die Frühzeit der Partei.* Quellen und Darstellungen zur Zeitgeschichte, 6. Stuttgart: Deutsche Verlagsanstalt, 1959.

*Kriegstagebuch des Oberkommandos der Wehrmacht (Wehrmacht Führungsstab) 1940–1945 geführt von Helmuth Greiner und Percy Ernst Schramm.* 4 vols. Im Auftrag des Arbeitskreises für Wehrforschung herausgegeben von P. E. Schramm. Frankfurt am Main: Bernard & Graefe Verlag für Wehrwesen, 1963.

Landgraf, Hugo. *Kampf um Danzig. Mit Mikrophon und Stahlhelm an der Danziger Front.* Dresden: Thienemann, 1940.

Langhoff, Wolfgang. *Die Moorsoldaten.* Berlin: Aufbau, 1950.

Lehmann, Horst, and Wacker, Peter. "Die Waffen-SS." *Feldgrau* 1 (1954):129; 2 (1955):31–32.

Lehmann-Haupt, Hellmut. *Art under a Dictatorship.* New York: Oxford, 1954.

Lerner, Daniel, with the collaboration of Ithiel de Sola Pool and George K. Schueller. *The Nazi Elite.* Hoover Institute Studies, series B, no. 3. Stanford: Stanford University Press, 1951.

Lettrich, Josef. *History of Modern Slovakia.* New York: Praeger, 1955.

Leverkuehn, Paul. *German Military Intelligence.* New York: Praeger, 1954.

Levin, Nora. *The Holocaust. The Destruction of European Jewry 1933–1945.* New York: Crowell, 1968.

Levine, Herbert S. *Hitler's Free City. A History of the Nazi Party in Danzig, 1925–1939.* Chicago: University of Chicago Press, 1973.

Levine, Herbert S. "Local Authority and the SS State. The Conflict over Population Policy in Danzig-West Prussia 1939–1945." *Central European History* 2 (December 1969):331–55.

Lippert, Julius. *Im Strom der Zeit. Erlebnisse und Eindrücke.* Berlin: Reimer, Andrews & Steiner, 1942.

Lohalm, Uwe. *Völkischer Radikalismus: die Geschichte des deutsch-völkischen Schutz- und Trutzbunds.* Hamburger Beiträge zur Zeitgeschichte, Nr. 6. Hamburg: Leibnitz, 1970.

Lohmann, Heinz. *SA räumt auf!* Hamburg: Hanseatische Verlagsanstalt, 1935.

*London Observer.* July 1, 1934.

Loock, Hans-Dietrich. "Zur grossgermanischen Politik des Dritten Reiches." *Vierteljahrshefte für Zeitgeschichte* 8 (1960):51–63.

Loomis, Charles P., and Beegle, J. Allen. "The Spread of German Nazism in Rural Areas." *American Sociological Review* 11 (1946):724–34.

Lorant, Stefan. *I Was Hitler's Prisoner. A Diary.* New York: G. P. Putnam's Sons, 1935.

Ludecke, Kurt. *I Knew Hitler.* New York: Scribner, 1938.

Ludendorff, Erich. *Vom Feldherrn zum Weltrevolutionär und Wegbereiter deutscher Volksschöpfung. Meine Lebenserinnerungen von 1919 bis 1925.* Munich: Ludendorff, 1940.

Luetgebrune, Walter. *Ein Kampf um Röhm.* Diessen vor München: J. C. Huber, 1933. T-580/roll 85/folder 403.

Luža, Radomír. *The Transfer of the Sudeten Germans. A Study of Czech-German Relations 1933–1962.* New York: New York University Press, 1964.

Majewski, Ryszard. *Waffen SS. Mity i rzeczywistość.* Wrocław: Zaklad narodowy imenia Ossolińskich wydawnictwo, 1977.

*Manchester Guardian.* 1933–1934.

Mann, Golo. *Deutsche Geschichte des 19. und 20. Jahrhunderts.* Frankfurt am Main: S. Fischer, 1958.

Manstein, Erich von. *Aus einem Soldatenleben, 1887–1939.* Bonn: Athenäum, 1958.

Manvell, Roger, and Fraenkel, Heinrich. *Heinrich Himmler.* London: Heinemann, 1965.

Martini, Winfried. "Zelle 474." *Der Monat* 9 (1957):80–84.

Maser, Werner. *Sturm auf die Republik. Frühgeschichte der NSDAP.* Stuttgart: Deutsche Verlagsanstalt, 1973.

Matthias, Erich, and Morsey, Rudolf, eds. *Das Ende der Parteien.* Düsseldorf: Droste, 1960.

Mau, Hermann. "Die 'Zweite Revolution' — Der 30.Juni 1934." *Vierteljahreshefte für Zeitgeschichte* 1 (1953):119–37.

Meinck, Gerhard. *Hitler und die deutsche Aufrüstung 1933–1937.* Wiesbaden: Steiner, 1959.

Merkl, Peter H. *The Making of a Storm Trooper.* Princeton: Princeton University Press, 1980.

Merkl, Peter H. *Political Violence under the Swastika: 581 Early Nazis.* Princeton: Princeton University Press, 1975.

Meyer, Kurt [Panzermeyer]. *Grenadiere. [Die 12. Panzer Grenadier-Division].* Munich and Lochhausen: Schild-Verlag, 1957.

*Meyers Orts- und Verkehrslexikon des Deutschen Reiches, der Freien Stadt Danzig und des Memelgebiets.* Leipzig: Bibliographisches Institut, 1935.

Minott, Rodney G. *The Fortress That Never Was. The Myth of Hitler's Bavarian Stronghold.* New York: Holt, Rinehart and Winston, 1964.

*Minsker Zeitung.* December 23, 1943.

*Mitteilungsblätter für die weltanschauliche Schulung der Ordnungspolizei.* Gruppe B, Folge 27. Berlin: February 2, 1943.

Mommsen, Hans. *Beamtentum im dritten Reich.* Stuttgart: Deutsche Verlagsanstalt, 1966.

Mommsen, Hans. "Der Reichstagsbrand und seine politischen Folgen." *Vierteljahrshefte für Zeitgeschichte* 11 (1963):351–413.

*Morning Post.* (London). 1934–1935.

Morsey, Rudolf. "Der Beginn der Gleichschaltung in Preussen." *Vierteljahrshefte für Zeitgeschichte* 11 (1963):85–97.

Müller-Claudius, Michael. *Der Antisemitismus und das deutsche Verhängnis.* Frankfurt am Main: J. Knecht, 1948.

*Münchener Neueste Nachrichten.* January 13, 1938; October 2, 1940.

Myllyniemi, Seppo. *Die Neuordnung der Baltischen Länder 1941–1944.* Zum nationalsozialistischen Inhalt der deutschen Besatzungspolitik. Dissertationes historicae, 2; Historiallisia tutkimuksia, 90. Helsinki, 1973.

Nationalsozialistische Deutsche Arbeiter-Partei. *Nationalsozialistisches Jahrbuch 1928.* Munich: Eher, 1928.

Nationalsozialistische Deutsche Arbeiter-Partei. *Nationalsozialistisches Jahrbuch 1932.* Munich: Eher, 1932.

Nationalsozialistische Deutsche Arbeiter-Partei. *Nationalsozialistisches Jahrbuch 1933.* Munich: Eher, 1933.

Nationalsozialistische Deutsche Arbeiter-Partei. *Nationalsozialistisches Jahrbuch 1934.* Munich: Eher, 1934.

Nationalsozialistische Deutsche Arbeiter-Partei. *Nationalsozialistisches Jahrbuch 1935.* Munich: Eher, 1935.

Nationalsozialistische Deutsche Arbeiter-Partei. *Organisationsbuch der NSDAP 1940.* Munich: Zentralverlag der NSDAP, 1940.

Nationalsozialistische Deutsche Arbeiter-Partei. *Organisationsbuch der NSDAP 1943.* Munich: Zentralverlag der NSDAP, 1943.

Nationalsozialistische Deutsche Arbeiter-Partei. *Sturm 33. Hans Maikowski. Schreiben von Kameraden des Toten.* Berlin-Schöneberg: Deutsche Kultur-Wacht, 1933.

Nationalsozialistische Deutsche Arbeiter-Partei. Hauptorganisationsamt. Amt für Statistik. *Parteistatistik.* 4 vols. Als Manuskript gedruckt. Munich: Der Reichsorganisationsleiter, 1935.

Nationalsozialistische Deutsche Arbeiter-Partei. Parteikanzlei. *Verfügen/Anordnungen/Bekanntgaben.* 4 vols. Munich: Zentralverlag der NSDAP, n.d.

Nationalsozialistische Deutsche Arbeiter-Partei Schutzstaffel. Chef des SS-Ergänzungsamtes. *Statistisches Jahrbuch. 3.Jahrgang, 1937.* Berlin, 1937.

*Nationalsozialistische Landpost* (Munich). April 30, 1937.

Netherlands. Ministerie van Onderwijs. Rijksinstituut voor Oorlogsdocumentatie. *Het Proces Rauter.* (The Rauter Trial.) Bronnen-publicaties: Processen, Nr. 5. Hague, 1952.

*Neuer Vorwärts* (Karlsbad), July 15, 1934. T-580/roll 85/folder 402.

*Neue Züricher Zeitung.* August 2, 1934.

Neufeldt, Hans-Joachim, et al. *Zur Geschichte der Ordnungspolizei 1936–1945.* Teil I: Hans-Joachim Neufeldt, "Entstehung und Organisation des Hauptamtes Ordnungspolizei"; Jürgen Huck, "Ausweichstellen und Aktenschicksal des Hauptamtes Ordnungspolizei im 2. Welktrieg." Teil II: Georg Tessin, "Die Stäbe und Truppeneinheiten der Ordnungspolizei." Schriften des Bundesarchivs, 3. Coblenz, 1957.

Neumann, Franz. *Behemoth. The Structure and Practice of National Socialism 1933–1944.* New York: Oxford University Press, 1944.

Neumann, Sigmund. *Die deutschen Parteien. Wesen und Wandel nach dem Krieg.* Berlin: Junker und Dünnhaupt, 1932.

Neusüss-Hunkel, Ermenhild. *Die SS.* Schriftenreihe des Instituts für wissenschaftliche Politik. Marburg/Lahn. Hannover and Frankfurt am Main: Norddeutsche Verlagsanstalt O. Goedel, 1956.

*News Chronicle* (London). 1934–1935.

Noakes, Jeremy. *The Nazi Party in Lower Saxony, 1921–1933.* New York: Oxford University Press, 1971.

"Noch einmal des Teufels Adjutant?" *Der Freiwillige* 6:11 (1961):27.

Nolte, Ernst, ed. *Theorien über den Faschismus.* Neue Wissenschaftliche Bibliothek, 21. Cologne and Berlin: Kiepenheuer & Witsch, 1967.

*Nordland (Nordlandir)* (Berlin). Vols. 1–5 (1940–1945).

Nyomarkay, Joseph. *Charisma and Factionalism in the Nazi Party.* Minneapolis: University of Minnesota Press, 1967.

O'Donnell, James P. "The Devil's Advocate." *New York Times Magazine,* October 26, 1969.

O'Lessker, Karl. "Who Voted for Hitler? A New Look at the Class Basis of Nazism." *American Journal of Sociology* 74:1 (July 1968).

Orb, Heinrich. *Nationalsozialismus, 13 Jahre Machtrausch.* Olten: O. Walter, 1945.

Orlow, Dietrich. *The History of the Nazi Party, 1919–1933.* Pittsburgh: University of Pittsburgh Press, 1969.

Orlow, Dietrich. *The History of the Nazi Party, 1933–1945.* Pittsburgh: University of Pittsburgh Press, 1973.

Orlow, Dietrich. *The Nazis in the Balkans. A Case Study of Totalitarian Politics.* Pittsburgh: University of Pittsburgh Press, 1968.

Osmańczyk, Edmund Jan. *Dowódy prowokacji. Nieznane Archiwum Himmlera.* Czytelnik. (Evidence of Provocation. An unknown Archive of Himmler. A Reader.) Cracow: Spółdzielnia Wydawniczo-Oświatowa, 1951.

Paetel, Karl O. "Die SS. Ein Beitrag zur Soziologie des Nationalsozialismus." *Vierteljahrshefte für Zeitgeschichte* 2 (1954):1–33.

Paetel, Karl O. "Tipología de la orden negra." *Diógenes* 1 (1953):93–113.

Papen, Franz von. *Der Wahrheit eine Gasse.* Munich: Paul List, 1952.

*Pariser Tageblatt.* 1934.

Payne, Stanley G. *Fascism. Comparison and Definition.* Madison, Wisconsin: University of Wisconsin Press, 1980.

Pfundtner, Hans, ed. *Dr. Wilhelm Frick und sein Ministerium.* Munich: Zentralverlag der NSDAP, 1937.

Phelps, Reginald H. "Anton Drexler, der Gründer der NSDAP." *Deutsche Rundschau* 87 (1962):1134–43.

Phelps, Reginald H. "Dokumente aus der Kampfzeit der NSDAP–1923." *Deutsche Rundschau* 84 (1958):459–68, 1034–44.

Phelps, Reginald H. "Hitler and the *Deutsche Arbeiter Partei.*" *American Historical Review* 68 (1963):974–86.

Piotrowski, Stanisław, ed. *Sprawy polskie przed Międzynarodowym Trybunałem Wojennym w Norymberdze.* (Polish Affairs before the International Military Tribunal at Nuremberg.) Tom I, Dzennik Hansa Franka. Warsaw: Wydawnictwo prawnicze, 1956.

Plieg, Ernst Albrecht. *Das Memelland 1920–1939. Deutsche Autonomiebestrebungen im litauischen Gesamtstaat.* Würzburg: Holzner, 1962.

Poliakov, Leon, and Wulf, Josef. *Das Dritte Reich und die Juden. Dokumente und Aufsätze.* Berlin-Grunewald: Arani, 1955.

Poliakov, Leon, and Wulf, Josef. *Das Dritte Reich und seine Diener (Auswärtiges Amt; Justiz; Wehrmacht).* Berlin and Grunewald: Arani, 1956.

Pridham, Geoffrey. *Hitler's Rise to Power. The Nazi Movement in Bavaria 1923–1933.* New York: Harper & Row, 1973.

Pünder, Hermann. *Politik in der Reichskanzlei.* Schriftenreihe der Vierteljahrshefte für Zeitgeschichte, 3. Stuttgart: Deutsche Verlagsanstalt, 1961.

Ramme, Alwin. *Der Sicherheitsdienst der SS. Zu seiner Funktion im faschistischen Machtapparat und im Besatzungsregime des sogenannten Generalgouvernements Polen.* Deutsche Akademie der Wissenschaften zu Berlin. Institut für Geschichte. Abteilung Militärgeschichte. Militärhistorische Studien, 12 (Neue Folge). Deutscher Militärverlag, c. 1969.

Rauschning, Hermann. *Germany's Revolution of Destruction.* London: W. Heinemann, 1939.

Rauschning, Hermann. *Men of Chaos.* New York: Putnam's, 1942.

Rauschning, Hermann. *Voice of Destruction.* New York: Putnam's, 1940.

Rehm, Hauptsturmführer ——. "Geschichte der SA." *Der SA-Mann, Sonderdruck* 4, June 1941. T-580/roll 85/folder 403.

"Reichsführer SS auf der Gauleitertagung am 3.August 1944 in Posen." Heading on first page of article: "Die Rede Himmlers vor den Gauleitern am 3.August 1944. Dokumentation." *Vierteljahrshefte für Zeitgeschichte* 1 (1953):357–94.

Der Reichsführer SS. Rasse- und Siedlungshauptamt. *Bestimmungen über die Erfassung, Auswahl und Zuführung der siedlungswilligen Angehörigen der Waffen-SS für die wiedergewonnenen Siedlungsräume.* Berlin, 1943.

Der Reichsführer SS. SS-Hauptamt. *Dich ruft die SS.* Berlin-Grunewald: Hermann Hilger K.-G., n.d.

Der Reichsführer SS. SS-Hauptamt. *Lehrplan für sechsmonatige Schulung.* Berlin, c. 1942.

Der Reichsführer SS. SS-Hauptamt. *Politischer Dienst für SS und Polizei.* (Monthly; 1:1 = January 1944?)

Der Reichsführer SS. SS-Hauptamt. *SS-Leithefte.* 11 vols. 1935–1945.

Der Reichsführer SS. SS-Hauptamt. *Der Untermensch.* Berlin: Nordland Verlag, 1942.

Der Reichsführer SS. SS-Hauptamt-Schulungsamt. *Sieg der Waffen — Sieg des Kindes.* Berlin: Nordland, 1941.

Reischle, Hermann. *Reichsbauernführer Darré. Der Kämpfer um Blut und Boden. Eine Lebensbeschreibung.* Berlin: "Zeitgeschichte," 1935.

Reischle, Hermann, and Saure, Wilhelm. *Der Reichsnährstand. Aufbau, Aufgaben und Bedeutung.* Berlin: Reichsnährstandverlag, 1940.

Reitlinger, Gerald. *The Final Solution: The Attempt to Exterminate the Jews of Europe, 1939–1945.* London: Vallentine, Mitchell, 1953.

Reitlinger, Gerald. *The House Built on Sand.* New York: Viking, 1960.

Reitlinger, Gerald. *SS: The Alibi of a Nation, 1922–1945.* New York: Viking, 1957.

Rempel, Gerhard. "The Misguided Generation. Hitler Youth and SS: 1933–1945." Ph.D. dissertation, University of Wisconsin-Madison, 1971.

Rendulic, Lothar. *Soldat in stürzenden Reichen.* Munich: Damm, 1965.

Reventlow, Ernst. *Der Weg zum neuen Deutschland. Der Wiederaufstieg des deutschen Volkes.* Essen: Zentralstelle für den deutschen Freiheitskampf, 1933.

Ribbentrop, Joachim von. *The Ribbentrop Memoirs.* Translated by Oliver Watson. London: Weidenfeld and Nicolson, 1954.

Ribbentrop, Joachim von. *Zwischen London und Moskau. Erinnerungen und letzte Aufzeichnungen.* Leoni am Starnberger See: Drüffel, 1953.

Rich, Norman. *Hitler's War Aims.* 2 vols. (Vol. 1: *Ideology, the Nazi State and the Course of Expansion.* Vol. 2: *The Establishment of the New Order.*) New York: Norton, 1974.

Röhm, Ernst. *Die Geschichte eines Hochverräters.* Munich: Eher, 1928.

Roloff, Ernst August. *Bürgertum und Nationalsozialismus 1930–1933.* Hannover: Verlag für Literatur und Zeitgeschehen, 1961.

Rönnefarth, Helmuth K. G. *Die Sudetenkrise in der internationalen Politik. Entstehung, Verlauf, Auswirkung.* Veröffentlichungen des Instituts für europäische Geschichte, Mainz, 21. 2 vols. Wiesbaden: F. Steiner, 1961.

Rossbach, Gerhard. *Mein Weg durch die Zeit. Erinnerungen und Bekenntnisse.* Weilburg and Lahn: Vereinigte Weilburger Buchdruckereien, 1950.

Rousset, David. *The Other Kingdom.* New York: Reynal & Hitchcock, 1947.

Royal Institute for International Affairs. *Survey of International Affairs, 1939–1946. The World in March 1939.* Edited by Arnold Toynbee and Veronica Toynbee. London: Oxford University Press, 1954.

Rüdiger [pseud.]. *SA- und SS-Appell der Gruppe Berlin-Brandenburg und der Gruppe Berlin Ost in Berlin.* Berlin-Schöneberg: NS Druck- und Verlagsanstalt, 1933.

Rühle, Gerd. *Das Dritte Reich: Dokumentarische Darstellung des Aufbaues der Nation,* vol. 1, *Die Kampfjahre 1918–1933.* Berlin: Hummelverlag, 1934.

Salomon, Ernst von. *Der Fragebogen.* Hamburg: Rowohlt, 1951.

*Der SA-Mann.* 1:27 (October 15, 1932); 2:52 (December 30, 1933).

Sawicka, S. M. "Zbrodnia niemiecka nad dzieckiem polskim." (German Crimes against Polish Children.) *Pregląd Zachodni* 3 (1947).

Sawicki, Jerzy, ed. *Vor dem polnischen Staatsanwalt.* Berlin: Deutscher Militärverlag, 1962.

Schäfer, Wolfgang, *NSDAP, Entwicklung und Struktur der Staatspartei des Dritten Reichs.* Hannover and Frankfurt am Main: Norddeutsche Verlagsanstalt, 1957.

Schaumburg-Lippe, Friederich Christian zu. *Zwischen Krone und Kerker.* Wiesbaden: Limes, 1952.

Schechtman, Joseph B. *European Population Transfers 1939–1945.* New York: Oxford University Press, 1946.

Schechtman, Joseph B. *The Mufti and the Fuehrer. The Rise and Fall of Haj Amin el Husseini.* New York: Thomas Yoseloff, 1965.

Schellenberg, Walter. *Memoiren.* Cologne: Verlag für Politik und Wirtschaft, 1959.

Scheringer, Richard. *Das grosse Los; Bauern und Rebellen.* Hamburg: Rowohlt, 1960.

Schickel, Alfred. "Wehrmacht und SS: Eine Untersuchung über ihre Stellung und Rolle in den Planungen der nationalsozialistischen Führer." *Wehrwissenschaftliche Rundschau* 19:5 (1969):241–64.

Schieder, Wolfgang, ed. *Faschismus als soziale Bewegung. Deutschland und Italien im Vergleich.* Historische Perspektiven, 3. Hamburg: Hoffmann und Campe, 1976.

Schnabel, Reimund. *Macht ohne Moral. Eine Dokumantation über die SS.* Frankfurt am Main: Röderbergverlag, 1957.

Schneider, Peter. *Ausnahmezustand und Norm. Eine Studie zur Rechtslehre von Carl Schmitt.* Stuttgart: Deutsche Verlagsanstalt, 1957.

Schoenbaum, David. *Hitler's Social Revolution: Class and Status in Nazi Germany, 1933–1939.* Garden City, N.Y.: Doubleday, 1966.

Schoenberner, Gerhard. *Der gelbe Stern. Die Judenverfolgung in Europa 1933 bis 1945.* 2nd ed. Hamburg: Rütten & Loening, 1961.

Schreiber, Franz. *Kampf unter dem Nordlicht. Die Geschichte der 6. SS-Gebirgs-Division Nord.* Osnabrück: Munin, 1969.

*Schulthess' europäischer Geschichtskalender, 1931.* Neue Serie, Band 47. Munich: C. H. Beck, 1932.

*Schulthess' europäischer Geschichtskalender, 1934.* Neue Serie, Band 50. Munich: C. H. Beck, 1935.

Schulz, Gerhard. *Aufstieg des Nationalsozialismus. Krise und Revolution in Deutschland.* Frankfurt am Main: Ullstein (Propyläen), 1975.

Schuschnigg, Kurt von. *Dreimal Österreich.* 2.Aufl. Vienna: Thomas-Verlag Jakob Hegner, 1937.

Schütze, Hermann. *Der Reichsgau Wartheland.* Breslau: F. Hirt, 1941.

*Die Schutzstaffel* 1:2 (December 1926). T-580/roll 87/folder 425.

Schwarz, Wolfgang. "Der Führer der Germanen." *Zeitschrift für Geopolitik* 18 (1941):534–35.

*Das Schwarze Korps. Zeitung der Schutzstaffel der NSDAP* 1–11 (1935–1945).

Schweder, Alfred. *Die Politische Polizei; Wesen und Begriff der politischen polizei im Metternichschen System, in der Weimarer Republik und im nationalsozialistischen Staate.* Berlin: C. Heymann, 1937.

Schweitzer, Arthur. *Big Business in the Third Reich.* Bloomington: University of Indiana Press, 1964.

Schwend, Karl. *Bayern zwischen Monarchie und Diktatur; Beiträge zur bayerischen Frage in der Zeit von 1918 bis 1933.* Munich: R. Pflaum, 1954.

Schwerin-Krosigk, Lutz Graf von. *Es geschah in Deutschland: Menschenbilder unseres Jahrhunderts.* Tübingen: H. Leins, 1951.

Schweyer, Franz. *Politische Geheimverbände. Blicke in die Vergangenheit und Gegenwart des Geheimbundwesens,* Freiburg im Breisgau: Herder, 1925.

Seabury, Paul. *The Wilhelmstrasse. A Study of German Diplomats under the Nazi Regime.* Berkeley: University of California Press, 1954.

Sebottendorf, Rudolf Glandeck, Freiherr von. *Bevor Hitler kam; Urkundliches aus der Frühzeit der nationalsozialistischen Bewegung.* Munich: Grassinger, 1933.

Shalka, Robert John. "The General SS in Central Germany 1937–1939: A Social and Institutional Study of SS Main Sector Fulda-Werra." Ph.D. dissertation, University of Wisconsin-Madison, 1972.

Shirer, William L. *The Rise and Fall of the Third Reich.* New York: Simon & Schuster, 1960.

Shulman, Milton. *Defeat in the West.* New York: E. P. Dutton, 1948.

Siegler, Fritz von. *Die höheren Dienststellen der deutschen Wehrmacht 1933–1945.* Munich: Institut für Zeitgeschichte, 1953.

Smelser, Ronald M. *The Sudeten Problem, 1933–1938. Volkstumspolitik and the Formulation of Nazi Foreign Policy.* Middletown, Conn.: Wesleyan University Press, 1975.

Smith, Bradley F. *Heinrich Himmler. A Nazi in the Making 1900–1926.* Stanford: Stanford University Press, 1971.

Smith, Bradley F., and Peterson, Agnes F., eds. *Heinrich Himmler, Geheimreden 1933 bis 1945, und andere Ansprachen.* Frankfurt am Main: Propyläen, 1974.

*Der Soldatenfreund. Sonderausgabe für die Männer der Totenkopfdivision der Waffen-SS.* 2.Jahrgang: Nr. 34 (July 1942).

Speer, Albert. *Infiltration.* New York: Macmillan, 1981.

Speer, Albert. *Inside the Third Reich: Memoirs.* New York: Macmillan, 1970.

"SS-Bericht über den 20.Juli aus den Papieren des Obersturmbannführers Dr. Georg Kiesel." *Kristall* 2:2 (1947):5–34.

*SS-Dienstvorschrift Nr. 10: Schied- und Ehrengerichts-Ordnung der SS.* Wilhelm Friedrich Mayr: Miesbach, n.d. [1935?]

"SS-Helfer." *Der Freiwillige* 10:1 (1965):15.

*SS-Kavallerie im Osten.* Herausgegeben von der SS-Kavallerie Brigade für ihre Führer und Männer. Braunschweig: G. Westermann, 1942.

"Die 1. SS-Panzer-Division Leibstandarte Adolf Hitler im Einsatz in der Ardennenoffensive 1944." *Der Freiwillige* 11:1–4 (1965).

*SS-Statistik, 1936.* Berlin, 1937. Photocopy in Library of Congress.

Stachura, Peter D., ed. *The Shaping of the Nazi State.* London: Croom Helm; New York: Barnes & Noble, 1978.

*Statistisches Jahrbuch der Schutzstaffel der NSDAP 1937.* (Berlin, 1938. T-175/ roll 205/frames 4042233–89.

*Statistisches Jahrbuch der Schutzstaffel der NSDAP 1938.* Berlin, 1939. T-175/ roll 205/frames 4042291–361.

Stein, George H. *The Waffen SS. Hitler's Elite Guard at War, 1939–1945.* Ithaca: Cornell University Press, 1966.

Stein, George H., and Krosby, Peter R. "Das finnische Freiwilligen-Bataillon der Waffen-SS. Eine Studie zur SS-Diplomatie und zur ausländischen Freiwilligen-Bewegung." *Vierteljahrshefte für Zeitgeschichte* 14 (1966):413–53.

Steiner, Felix. *Die Armee der Geächteten.* Göttingen: Plesse, 1963.

Steiner, Felix. *Die Freiwilligen. Idee und Opfergang.* Göttingen: Plesse, 1958.

Stelzner, Fritz. *Schicksal SA. Die Deutung eines grossen Geschehens von einem, der es selbst erlebte.* Munich: Eher, 1936.

Stephan, Werner. "Zur Soziologie der NSDAP." *Zeitschrift für Politik* 20 (1931): 793–800.

Stern, Michael, & Strasser, Otto. *Flight from Terror.* New York: McBride, 1943).

Stöber, Hans-J. E. *Die eiserne Faust. Bildband und Chronik der 17. SS-Panzergrenadier-Division "Götz von Berlichingen."* Neckargemünd: Vowinckel, 1966.

Strasser, Otto. *Hitler and I.* Boston: Houghton Mifflin, 1940.

Strassner, Peter. *Europäische Freiwillige. Die Geschichte der 5. SS-Panzerdivision WIKING.* Osnabrück: Munin, 1968.

Sundhaussen, Holm. "Zur Geschichte der Waffen-SS in Kroatien 1941–45." *Südost-Forschungen* 30 (1971):176–96.

Sydnor, Charles W., Jr. *Soldiers of Destruction. The SS Death's Head Division, 1933–1945* Princeton: Princeton University Press, 1977.

*Taschenbuch für Verwaltungsbeamte 1943.* Hrsg. von [Max] Warnack. Jahrgang 60. Berlin: C. Heymann, 1943.

Taylor, Telford. *Sword and Swastika. Generals and Nazis in the Third Reich.* New York: Simon & Schuster, 1952.

Teske, Hermann. *Die silbernen Spiegel. Generalstabsdienst unter der Lupe.* Heidelberg: K. Vowinckel, 1952.

"Des Teufels Adjutant?" *Der Freiwillige* 6:6 (1961):10–13.

Thompson, Larry V. "Nazi Administrative Conflict: The Struggle for Executive Power in the General Government of Poland 1939–1943." Ph.D. dissertation, University of Wisconsin–Madison, 1967.

Thyssen, Fritz. *I Paid Hitler.* New York: Farrar & Rinehart, 1941.

Tiecke, Wilhelm. *Im Feuersturm letzter Kriegsjahre. II. SS-Panzerkorps mit 9. und 10. SS-Divisionen "Hohenstaufen" und "Frundsberg."* Osnabrück: Munin, 1975.

*Times* (London). 1933–1934.

Tobias, Fritz. *Der Reichstagsbrand, Legende und Wirklichkeit.* Rastatt: Grote, 1962.

Toland, John. *Battle. The Story of the Bulge.* New York: Random House, 1959.

Toland, John. *The Last 100 Days.* New York: Random House, 1966.

Tracey, Donald R. "The Development of the National Socialist Party in Thuringia, 1924–30." *Central European History* 8 (March 1975):23–50.

Trevor-Roper, Hugh R. *The Last Days of Hitler.* New York: Macmillan, 1947.

*Trials of War Criminals before the Nuernberg Military Tribunals under Control*

*Council Law No. 10.* 15 vols. Washington, D.C.: Government Printing Office, 1949–1953.

Tyrell, Albrecht, ed. *Führer, befiehl. Selbstzeugnisse aus der Kampfzeit der NSDAP. Dokumentation und Analyse.* Düsseldorf: Droste, 1969.

Tyrell, Albrecht. *Vom Trommler zum Führer: der Wandel von Hitlers Selbstverständnis zwischen 1919 und 1924 und der Entwicklung der NSDAP* Munich: Fink, 1975.

Ueberhorst, Horst, ed. *Elite für die Diktatur. Die Nationalpolitischen Erziehungsanstalten 1933–1945. Ein Dokumentarbericht.* Düsseldorf: Droste, 1969.

*12-Uhr-Blatt* (Berlin). May 4, 1937.

Uhse, Bodo. *Söldner und Soldat. Roman.* Paris: Editions du Carrefour, 1935.

"Um Recht und Ehre." *Der Freiwillige* 6:5 (1961):4–8.

United States Department of State. *Documents on German Foreign Policy, 1918–1945.* Series C (1933–1937). 5 vols. Washington, D.C. Government Printing Office, 1957–1966.

United States Department of State. *Documents on German Foreign Policy, 1918–1945.* Series D (1937–1945). 13 vols. Washington, D.C.: Government Printing Office, 1949–1957.

United States. Department of State. Division of European Affairs. *National Socialism. Basic Principles. Their Application by the Nazi Party's Foreign Organization and the Use of Germans Abroad for Nazi Aims* (Publication 1864). Washington, D.C.: Government Printing Office, 1943.

United States National Archives. *Guides to German Records Microfilmed at Alexandria, Va.* No. 32. Records of the Reich Leader of the SS and Chief of the German Police (Part 1). Washington, D.C.: National Archives and Records Service, 1961.

United States National Archives. *Guides to German Records Microfilmed at Alexandria, Va.* No. 33. Records of the Reich Leader of the SS and Chief of the German Police (Part 2). Washington, D.C.: National Archives and Records Service, 1961.

United States National Archives. *Guides to German Records Microfilmed at Alexandria, Va.* No. 39. Records of the Reich Leader of the SS and Chief of the German Police (Part 3). Washington, D.C.: National Archives and Records Service, 1963.

United States. Office of Strategic Services. Research and Analysis Branch. "The SS and Police in Occupied Europe." In *German Military Government over Europe.* R & A No. 2500/22. Washington, D.C., 1945.

Usadel, Georg. *Zeitgeschichte in Wort und Bild.* 3 vols. 2nd ed. Oldenburg: Kultur und Aufbau, 1942.

Vagts, Alfred. *Hitler's Second Army.* Washington D.C.: Infantry Journal, 1943.

Van Arendonck, A. *Vlamingen aan het Ostfront.* (Flemings on the Eastern Front.) Het Vlams Legioen. Redactie: St. Maartensfonds, 1. Antwerpen: Etnika, 1973.

*Verordnungsblatt für Böhmen und Mähren* 1:1.

Vogelsang, Reinhard. *Der Freundeskreis Himmler.* Göttingen, Zurich, and Frankfurt: Musterschmidt, 1972.

Vogelsang, Thilo. *Der Chef der AW.* Munich: Institut für Zeitgeschichte, 1959.

Vogelsang, Thilo. "Neue Dokumente zur Geschichte der Reichswehr 1930–1933." *Vierteljahrshefte für Zeitgeschichte* 2 (1954):397–436.

Vogelsang, Thilo. "Die Reichswehr in Bayern und der Münchener Putsch 1923." *Vierteljahrshefte für Zeitgeschichte* 5 (1957):91–101.

Vogelsang, Thilo. *Reichswehr, Staat und NSDAP*. Stuttgart: Deutsche Verlagsanstalt, 1962.

Voggenreiter, Ludwig. *Der Hitler-Prozess. Das Fanal zum Erwachen Deutschlands*. Potsdam: L. Voggenreiter, 1934.

Vollmer, Bernhard. *Volksopposition im Polizeistaat: Gestapo- und Regierungsberichte 1934–36*. Stuttgart: Deutsche Verlagsanstalt, 1957.

*Vossische Zeitung* (Berlin). June 27, 1933.

Waite, Robert G. L. *Vanguard of Nazism. The Free Corps in Post War Germany, 1919–1923*. Cambridge, Mass.: Harvard University Press, 1952.

Warlimont, Walter. *Im Hauptquartier der deutschen Wehrmacht, 1939–1945. Grundlagen, Formen, Gestalten*. Frankfurt am Main: Bernard & Graefe Verlag für Wehrwesen, 1962.

Wegner, Bernd. "Auf dem Wege zur pangermanischen Armee. Dokumente zur Entstehungsgeschichte des III. ('Germanischen') SS-Panzerkorps." *Militärgeschichtliche Mitteilungen* 28:2 (1980):101–36.

Wegner, Bernd. "Das Führerkorps der Waffen-SS im Kriege." In *Das deutsche Offizierskorps 1860–1960*, edited by Hans Hubert Hofmann. Boppard am Rhein: Harald Boldt, 1981.

Wegner, Bernd. "The SS as a Military Force (1933–1945)." Unpublished paper kindly supplied by the author, November 1981.

Weidinger, Otto. *Division Das Reich. Der Weg der 2. SS-Panzer-Division Das Reich. Die Geschichte der Stammdivision der Waffen-SS*. 4 vols. Osnabrück: Munin, 1967–1979.

Weidinger, Otto. *Kameraden bis zum Ende. Der Weg des SS-Panzergrenadier-Regiments 4 "Der Führer," 1939–1945*. Göttingen: Plesse, 1962.

"Weihnachten 1944: Das Regiment Der Führer vom 22. bis 27.12.1944." *Der Freiwillige* 10:12 (1964):13.

Weingartner, James J. *Hitler's Guard. The Story of the Leibstandarte SS Adolf Hitler, 1933–1945*. Carbondale-Edwardsville, Ill.: Southern Illinois University Press, 1974.

Wells, Leon Weliczker. *Brigada Smierci (Sonderkommando 1005). Pamietnik.* (Brigade of Death — Special Detachment 1005. A Memoir) Wydawnictwa centralniej zydowskiej komisji historicznej przy Centralnym komitecie zydów polskich, 8. Lodz, 1946.

*Westdeutscher Beobachter* (Düsseldorf). 1936, 1938.

Westphal, Siegfried. *Heer in Fesseln. Aus den Papieren Rommel, Kesselring, von Rundstedt*. Bonn: Athenaeum, 1950.

Wheeler-Bennett, John W. *The Nemesis of Power. The German Army in Politics 1918–1945*. New York: St. Martin's Press, 1954.

Wheeler-Bennett, John W. *Wooden Titan: Hindenburg in Twenty Years of German History*. New York: William Morrow, 1936.

Whiteside, Andrew. *Austrian National Socialism before 1918*. The Hague: Nijhoff, 1962.

Wight, Martin. "Eastern Europe." In *Survey of International Affairs, 1939–1946*, vol. 1, The World in 1939, edited by Arnold Toynbee and Veronica M. Toynbee for the Royal Institute of International Affairs. London: Oxford University Press, 1954, Pp. 270–93.

Witzmann, Georg. *Thüringen von 1918–33. Erinnerungen eines Politikers.* Beiträge zur Mitteldeutschen Landes- und Volkskunde, 2. Meisenheim am Glan: A. Hain, 1958.

Wolfson, Manfred. "The SS Leadership." Ph.D. dissertation, University of California-Berkeley, 1965.

Wucher, Albert. *Eichmanns gab es viele. Ein Dokumentarbericht über die Endlösung der Judenfrage.* Munich: Droemersche Verlagsanstalt, 1961.

Wucher, Albert. *Die Fahne hoch. Das Ende der Republik und Hitlers Machtübernahme. Ein Dokumentarbericht.* Munich: Süddeutscher Verlag, 1963.

Zipfel, Friedrich. *Gestapo und Sicherheitsdienst.* Berlin: Arani, 1960.

Zipfel, Friedrich. "Gestapo und SD in Berlin." *Jahrbuch für die Geschichte Mittel- und Ostdeutschlands* 9–10 (1961):263–92.

## Archives and Microfilm

Berlin. Berlin Document Center. *Akten des Obersten Parteigerichts.*

Berlin. Berlin Document Center. Biographical Records of SS Officers with the rank of Oberführer and above.

Berlin. Berlin Document Center. Miscellaneous SS Records.

Berlin. Berlin Document Center. *SA-Akten.* Folder 44.

Berlin. Berlin Document Center. *SA-Sammellisten.*

Berlin. Berlin Document Center. Schriftgutverwaltung des Persönlichen Stabes, Reichsführer SS.

Berlin. Berlin Document Center. Schumacher Collection. SS folders.

Berlin. Berlin Document Center. SS-Hängeordner.

Berlin. Berlin Document Center. SS Officer Lists.

Berlin. Hauptarchiv Berlin-Dahlem. Grauert Akten. Rep. 77/29.

Chicago. Center for Research Libraries. U.S. Military Tribunal at Nuremberg. Cases Four, Eight, Nine, and Eleven.

Chicago. Center for Research Libraries. United States Nuremberg Documents.

Munich. Institut für Zeitgeschichte. Anklage and Urteile. Schwurgerichte Osnabrück, Kassel, München, Berlin, Braunschweig, Hannover.

Munich. Institut für Zeitgeschichte. Landgericht München I. Schwurgerichtsanklage gegen Joseph Dietrich et al. Ermittlungen.

Munich. Institut für Zeitgeschichte. Landgericht Osnabrück. Schwurgerichtsanklage gegen Udo von Woyrsch et al. Ermittlungen.

Munich. Institut für Zeitgeschichte. Letter of *Regierungspräsident* Bonsen, July 1, 1934. Rep. 77.

Munich. Institut für Zeitgeschichte. Schwurgericht Bremen. Anklage gegen O. Löblich. Ermittlungen.

New York. United Nations, Archives Section. Henshaw, Jean. "Unaccompanied Children." *Background Material for the Official History of the UNRRA.*

Stanford. Hoover Institution Library.
 Himmler Files:
  "Stennes Putsch";
  SGV folder 66;
  SGV folder 274;
  SGV folder 323;
  SGV folder 332.
Washington, D.C. National Archives. Heer. Oberkommando. Records of Head-
 quarters, German Army High Command, filmed at Alexandria, Virginia by
 the American Historical Association. National Archives Microcopy T-78.
Washington, D.C. National Archives. Nationalsozialistische Deutsche Arbeiter-
 Partei. Hauptarchiv. Filmed at the Berlin Document Center for the Hoover
 Institution Library. National Archives Microcopy T-581.
Washington, D.C. National Archives. Nationalsozialistische Deutsche Arbeiter-
 Partei. Records of the National Socialist German Workers Party filmed at
 Alexandria, Virginia by the American Historical Association. National Ar-
 chives Microcopy T-81.
Washington, D.C. National Archives. Nationalsozialistische Deutsche Arbeiter-
 Partei. World War II Collection of seized enemy records filmed at the Berlin
 Document Center for the University of Nebraska (1961). National Archives
 Microcopy T-611.
Washington, D.C. National Archives. Nationalsozialistische Deutsche Arbeiter-
 Partei. World War II Collection of seized enemy records filmed at the Berlin
 Document Center (Schumacher Material) by the American Historical Associa-
 tion. National Archives Microcopy T-580.
Washington, D.C. National Archives. Reichsführer SS und Chef der deutschen
 Polizei. Miscellaneous SS Records: Einwandererzentralstelle, Waffen-SS and
 SS-Oberabschnitte. World War II Collection of seized enemy records filmed at
 the Berlin Document Center by the American Historical Association. National
 Archives Microcopy T-354.
Washington, D.C. National Archives. Reichsführer SS und Chef der deutschen
 Polizei. World War II Collection of seized enemy records filmed at Alexan-
 dria, Virginia by the American Historical Association. National Archives Mi-
 crocopy T-175.
Washington, D.C. National Archives. Reichskommissar für die Festigung
 deutschen Volkstums. Records of the Office of the Reich Commissioner for the
 Strengthening of Germandom filmed at Alexandria, Virginia by the Ameri-
 can Historical Association. National Archives Microcopy T-74.
Washington D.C. National Archives. *Tagebuch des Herrn Generalgouverneurs
 für die besetzten polnischen Gebiete.* 25.Oktober 1939 bis 3.April 1945. 38
 vols. National Archives Microfilm ML-382.
Washington, D.C. National Archives. Record Group 1010. Reichsführer SS und
 Chef der deutschen Polizei Schriftgutverwaltung. Einheitsaktenplan. N.p.,
 n.d. Mimeographed.
Washington, D.C. National Archives. Record Group 1010. *Unterrichtsmappe SS
 und Polizeiwesen. 1.Oktober 1944.* Edited by SS-Hauptamt.

# Index

Aachen SS, 30

*Abschnitte* (sectors) of SS. *See also* Frontbann, organizational structure of
establishment of, in 1931, 44, 291n26
numbers of, 1932, 1934, 58, 321n14

Abwehr (Army Intelligence), 95, 220
acting in concert with SD, 155
activity in Sudetenland, 147, 148, 149, 150, 152
agents of, in AW, 97
relegation of SD to secondary place by, 162

Adolf Hitler Spende (Adolf Hitler's Fund), 301n29

Agrarpolitischer Apparat (Farm Policy Apparatus), 51, 81, 83

Agricultural advisers, 81, 116

Ahnenerbe (Ancestral Heritage) organization, 115, 231, 324n31

*Aktion Reinhardt* (concentration camp salvage operation), 176

Alarm footing, 56–57 and *n*

Albania, SS innovation in, 357n59

Albert, Wilhelm, 127

Alibi of a nation, SS as, 245

Allach Porcelain Works, 114

Allgemeine SS (General SS)
budget, 337n75
"captured" by FHA, 202
conversion of, to war footing, 154–55
Death's Head Reinforcements regiments of, 195–96
distinguished from armed SS, 135, 141
funding of, 110
headed for political oblivion, 219

in Wehrmacht, in Waffen-SS, 217, 218–19
members of, selected as police reinforcements, 185
organization ready for expansion in 1933, 97
personnel of, contrasted to "nominal SS" personnel, 211
reorganization of, in 1935, 112
source of term, 335n68
status and activity of, 1940–1945, 209, 211, 218–19, 367n97
structure parallel to SD until 1939, 128

Alpine redoubt, 222

Alquen, Günther d', 231

Alsace and Lorraine (Elsass-Lothringen), SS treatment of, 180, 354n50

*Altkämpfer* (old fighters), 57, 60, 138
as officers of Death's Head Police Reinforcements, 195–96
as SS generals, 179, 181, 241
as HSSPFs, 160, 182, 354n50
expansion of, into seized territories, 209
idealized in training materials, 372–73n133
in concentration camp SS, 166, 334n63
in killing operations, 176
in police, 128, 185, 355n51
in SD, 124, 160
promotion of, 311n20
rewarded by assignment abroad, 181
their view of SS, 239–42
vestiges of, in 1944–1945, 219

*Altreich* (German Reich of 1937), 187

Amann, Max, 18, 20, 283n21

JACKET DESIGNED BY BRUCE GORE
COMPOSED BY METRICOMP, GRUNDY CENTER, IOWA
MANUFACTURED BY MALLOY LITHOGRAPHING, INC., ANN ARBOR, MICHIGAN
TEXT AND DISPLAY LINES ARE SET IN CALEDONIA

Library of Congress Cataloging in Publication Data
Koehl, Robert Lewis, 1922–
The Black Corps.
Bibliography: pp. 377–401.
Includes index.
1. Nationalsozialistische Deutsche Arbeiter-Partei.
Schutzstaffel. I. Title.
DD253.6.K63 1983    943.08    81-69824
ISBN 0-299-09190-2